Ethics and Practical Reason

Edited by
GARRETT CULLITY
and
BERYS GAUT

CLARENDON PRESS · OXFORD

Oxford University Press, Great Clarendon Street, Oxford OX2 6DP

Oxford New York

Athens Auckland Bangkok Bogota Buenos Aires Calcutta
Cape Town Chennai Dar es Salaam Delhi Florence Hong Kong Istanbul
Karachi Kuala Lumpur Madrid Melbourne Mexico City Mumbai
Nairobi Paris São Paolo Singapore Taipei Tokyo Toronto Warsaw

and associated companies in
Berlin Ibadan

Oxford is a registered trade mark of Oxford University Press

Published in the United States by
Oxford University Press Inc., New York

First published in hardback and
paperback 1997
Reprinted in paperback 1998

British Library Cataloguing in Publication Data
Data available

Library of Congress Cataloging in Publication Data
Ethics and practical reason / edited by Garrett Cullity and Berys
Gaut.
"The majority of essays in this volume were presented in earlier
versions at the Ethics and Practical Reason Conference held by the
Department of Moral Philosophy at the University of St. Andrews from
23 to 26 March 1995"—Acknowledgements.
Includes bibliographical references and index.
1. Ethics—Congresses. 2. Reason—Congresses. I. Cullity,
Garrett. II. Gaut, Berys Nigel. III. Ethics and Practical Reason
Conference (1995 : Dept. of Moral Philosophy, University of St.
Andrews)
BJ1031.E83 1997 170—dc21[170] 97-15977
ISBN 0-19-823646-8
ISBN 0-19-823669-7 (Pbk.)

Printed in Great Britain
on acid-free paper by
Biddles Ltd., Guildford and King's Lynn

ACKNOWLEDGEMENTS

THE majority of essays in this volume were presented in earlier versions at the Ethics and Practical Reason Conference held by the Department of Moral Philosophy at the University of St Andrews from 23 to 26 March 1995. The conference was financially supported by the Analysis Committee, the Aristotelian Society, the British Academy, the Mind Association, the Royal Society of Edinburgh, the Scots Philosophical Club, and the University of St Andrews. We are grateful to all of these organizations.

We would also like to thank Christopher Bryant, the staff at Oxford University Press, and particularly Peter Momtchiloff and Robert Ritter, for their help in the preparation of this volume.

CONTENTS

Introduction

GARRETT CULLITY AND BERYS GAUT

1. Three Poles in Theorizing about Practical Reason

What ought I to do, how ought I to live? These are the central questions of moral thought; explaining the questions, and delimiting the range of acceptable answers, the tasks of moral philosophy. If so, the connection between morality and practical reason is already a close one: if one reads 'ought'-remarks, as many people do, as remarks about reasons, then our questions are questions about what one has reason to do, and call directly for a theory of practical reason. On this view, morality is a subdomain of practical reason. Maybe there is a way of reading these questions—as containing the moral 'ought', some will say—for which the relation is less close. There are some uses of 'ought'—in stating rules of etiquette, for example—which make it intelligible to ask 'Why should I do what I ought (in this sense) to do?' Maybe morality supplies such a sense.[1] On this view, moral answers to the opening questions will not always and for everyone supply reasons to act; but of course, it is precisely because of this that it will be important to specify the circumstances in which, and the agents for which, they do so. A developed moral outlook must at least be grounded in a satisfactory account of practical reasons, even if we do not hold that the former is contained in the latter.

The practical reasons that answer 'Why should I do that' are normative reasons—at least, they answer those root 'Why should I do that?' questions that contain a *should* for which 'Why do what I should do?' no longer makes sense. Normative reasons are those providing a justification of the actions for which they are reasons.

In saying this, though, there is a distinction to be made. Suppose your doctor tells you to take a certain medicine, but this happens to be a mistake, and it will harm you. What should you do? It is clear enough that given what you are justified in believing, you are justified in taking the medicine. There is a clear sense in which *that your doctor has told you to do so* is a

---

[1] See Philippa Foot, 'Morality as a System of Hypothetical Imperatives', repr. in her *Virtues and Vices* (Oxford: Blackwell, 1978), 157–73.

normative reason to take the medicine. However, there is an equally clear sense in which *that it will harm you* is a normative reason not to take it. We might call this the distinction between subjective and objective normative reasons, respectively. The relation between the two is clear enough: I have a subjective normative reason to ɸ whenever I am justified in believing that I have an objective normative reason to ɸ. It is also clear that in seeking an account of normative practical reasons, it is objective normative reasons that will be our primary concern: from this an account of subjective ones will follow. Notice, however, that an account of practical *rationality* must be given in terms of subjective reasons: one is practically rational to the extent to which one is guided by one's subjective normative reasons. In the example just described, doing what you have most objective reason to do would be irrational.

Normative reasons of both these kinds answer 'Why should I do that?' Talk of reasons for action can also apply to a further sort of consideration, the sort offered in response to the question, 'Why did she do that?' Reasons cited in answering this question are explanatory, but not necessarily normative; for the consideration that shows why she did what she did may not succeed in showing why she *should* have done it—we don't always do what we should. Normally, when we ask this explanatory question, we are asking what motivated the agent to act;[2] but there remain two ways in which this question can be taken, and accordingly, two kinds of entity that can be cited in response. A first kind of answer cites the consideration the agent regards as a normative reason for the action she has performed—what is sometimes called 'the agent's reason' for it.[3] As a response to the explanatory question, however, this style of answer will be elliptical. An 'agent's reason' is itself a consideration that someone recognizes; it can only be her *recognition* of that consideration that can contribute to an explanation of what she does. If what we are seeking is a non-elliptical motivational explanation of an action, what we will need to cite instead are those psychological states of an agent that constitute her being motivated to perform it. Citing these provides the second kind of answer to the question what motivated the agent to act as she did.[4]

Now although, as we have seen, explanatory practical reasons and normative ones are logically independent, there is widespread agreement on a certain conceptual connection between them. To begin with, on any credible view, it must be allowed that the explanation of an action may lie in the agent's awareness of the normative reasons he has for performing it. At

---

[2] That is, we are not normally looking for the sort of explanatory answer that cites e.g. his childhood deprivation as the explanation of why he did what he did.

[3] See e.g. Stephen L. Darwall, *Impartial Reason* (Ithaca, NY: Cornell Univ. Press, 1983), 32; Donald Davidson, 'Intending', in his *Essays on Actions and Events* (Oxford: Clarendon Press, 1980), 84.

[4] The phrase 'motivating reasons' has been prominently applied to both kinds of entity. Thomas Nagel first applied it to what we are calling agents' reasons—see *The Possibility of Altruism* (Princeton:

least sometimes, we are right about our reasons, and respond rationally to them; when this is the case, the explanation of our actions will take this form. More significantly, it seems that the explanation of an action can only ever fail to take this form in so far as an agent is either irrational or misinformed about his reasons. This follows from our earlier remarks about rationality. It seems to be analytic that a rational agent is guided by what he is justified in believing to be his normative reasons. Might an agent have normative reasons that he could never be justified in believing he had? Such a possibility is not worth considering, for 'reasons' of this sort would be considerations it would never make sense to act on. If not, it seems we must say this: a normative reason for me to φ must be a consideration my awareness of which would motivate me to φ if I were thinking about it fully rationally and with full knowledge.

This way of spelling out the 'internalism' requirement on normative practical reasons—the conceptual connection between normative reasons and motivation—is common ground to contemporary theorizing about practical reason.[5] As we shall see, however, it can be combined with widely diverging views about what full rationality consists in to yield widely diverging accounts of our reasons. What follows is a summary guide to the issues dividing contemporary theories of practical reason, within which to place the contributions to this volume. The history of moral philosophy invites us to think of that discussion as arranged around three prominent poles, the neo-Humean, the Aristotelian, and the Kantian. We can bring out the main points of contrast by considering three issues.

The first of these issues concerns the relation of the normative reasons an agent has to the motivational states he actually tends to have. The characteristically neo-Humean view is that all normative reasons are *hypothetical* —that they depend on the agent's actual motivational tendencies. This view is typically generated by combining the doctrine of internalism about normative practical reasons with a distinctive picture of the motivational explanation of action drawn from Hume. This picture characterizes all motivation, and hence all motivational explanation, as depending on the existence of motivational states which are themselves neither rational nor irrational. Desires are the most obvious examples of such states, and one

---

Univ. Press, 1970), 15—but it is now widely used to refer to motivational explanations in terms of psychological states—e.g. by Michael Smith, 'The Humean Theory of Motivation', *Mind*, 96 (1987), 36–61, and *The Moral Problem* (Oxford: Blackwell, 1994), ch. 4.

[5] The common ground is the conceptual connection itself—not the use of the words 'internal' and 'internalism' in relation to it. Thus for example the recent debate between John McDowell and Bernard Williams over whether all reasons are 'internal' is not a disagreement over the claim in the text, but over whether all reasons are *hypothetical*, in the sense we go on to identify. See John McDowell, 'Might there be External Reasons?', in J. E. J. Altham and Ross Harrison (eds.), *World, Mind and Ethics: Essays on the Ethical Philosophy of Bernard Williams* (Cambridge: Univ. Press, 1995), 68–85; Bernard Williams, 'Replies', in Altham and Harrison (eds.), *World, Mind and Ethics*, 186–94.

subject of much discussion is whether all such states must be at least partly constituted by an element properly describable as a desire.[6] At least on the linguistic face of it, it looks as though there is a great variety of states— aspirations, enthusiasms, attachments, thoughts about what one ought to do —which are states of motivation but which we ordinarily distinguish from desires. However that may be, if it is true that all motivational explanation relies on the presence of arational motivational states, then this will apply just as much to a motivational explanation that cites normative reasons as to any other. If my normative reasons must be capable of entering into motivational explanations of my actions, provided I am thinking about them fully rationally and knowledgeably, then a consideration can only be a norm-ative reason for me if I am the sort of person who would possess appropriate motivational states if he were thinking fully rationally and knowledgeably. And if, as it seems to Humeans, the motivational states I would be in if I were thinking fully rationally and knowledgeably depend on my actual motivational tendencies, then we must look to the nature of an agent's arational motivational tendencies to determine the character of his reasons. However, the Kantian and the Aristotelian, by contrast, hold that there are normative reasons that apply to us in virtue of the nature of free rational agency and of specifically human nature, respectively—independently of our contingent motivational natures. They believe in non-hypothetical, or *categorical*, reasons.

A second issue that a theory of practical reason must address is that of the relation between what an agent has a normative reason to do and what it would be good for her to do—between practical reason and value. A common view, and one that is common to the neo-Humean, Aristotelian, and Kantian poles, is that an agent has a normative reason to φ if and only if it would be good, all else equal, for her to φ. But notice the room this leaves for an important disagreement. Distinctive of Aristotelianism is its *recognitional* view of the relation between value and practical reason, according to which the role of the faculty of practical reason is to recognize whether an action is valuable, where the action's being valuable is consti-tuted independently of rational choice. On a *constructivist* view of the relation between value and practical reason, by contrast, an action's being valuable is held to be constituted by its being the object of rational choice (given full information). This conception is found in Kant in an especially pure form, but neo-Humeans are also naturally characterized as constructivists in this sense. For a generic conception of value shared by most Humeans characterizes the valuable for an agent as whatever that agent would value under conditions of rational reflection (with different versions adding their

---

[6] See e.g. G. F. Schueler, *Desire* (Cambridge, Mass.: MIT Press, 1995).

own further specification of those conditions). If the psychological state of valuing is elucidated by its connection with choice, the neo-Humean is a constructivist.

Our first two issues concerned the relation of my reasons to my motivation, and their relation to my values. The third concerns the relation of my reasons to everyone else's. Given that A has reason to φ in circumstances C, is it an a priori requirement that any rational agent has reason to φ in C (where the agent's circumstances are construed as including her psychological states)? While this has sometimes been denied,[7] we take it that all three poles endorse this *reasons universalist* view. The important point of difference is over the central Kantian doctrine that a further requirement —the requirement of *legislative universalism*—governs practical reason. Not only must a rational agent judge that any other rational agent in her circumstances has reason to φ, she must also be able to *will* as a universal law that every other rational agent in her circumstances φs. This, Kantians claim, goes beyond mere reasons-universalism in eliminating the possibility of a rational egoist, who judges that any agent has reasons to promote that agent's own interests, while preferring other agents not to act on those reasons.

This gives us a genuinely three-cornered relationship between the neo-Humean, Aristotelian, and Kantian poles, with each pair opposed to the central characteristic of the third. We arrive at the following simple picture:

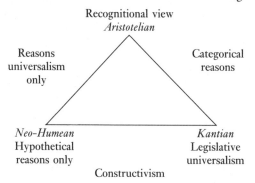

We have here three oppositions:

Recognitional view   vs Constructivism
Hypothetical reasons only vs Categorical reasons
Legislative universalism   vs Reasons universalism only.

The first element in each case is endorsed by one of the three poles, while its contrary is shared by the other two.

---

[7] For the view that there could be two rational agents in the same circumstances, one of whom has reason to φ while the other has no reason to φ, see David Wiggins, 'Truth, and Truth as Predicated of Moral Judgements', in *Needs, Values, Truth: Essays in the Philosophy of Value* (Oxford: Blackwell, 1987), 139–84 esp. sects. 14–16, and Peter Winch, 'The Universalizability of Moral Judgements', repr. in his *Ethics and Action* (Oxford: Blackwell, 1972), 151–70.

This is the background against which recent theorizing about practical reason has been conducted. In what follows, we articulate in greater detail the central issues of contention, outline the strategies to be pursued in addressing them, and introduce the present volume's contributions.

2. The Humean Challenge

We have characterized the neo-Humean pole in theorizing about practical reasons in terms of the thesis that an agent's normative reasons are relative to her actual motivational tendencies. And we have sketched the way in which proponents of this view typically draw on a characteristic claim concerning the desiderative ingredient in motivation. But while Hume himself certainly provides the inspiration for this view,[8] it contains some significant departures from his own position. First, it abandons Hume's claim that passions, which he conceives of as feelings, are an ingredient in all motivation, replacing it with a more defensible claim concerning desires, which one can have at a time without feeling them at that time. This is not a major revision, though. Neo-Humeans still take their cue in arguing for the desiderative claim from Hume's characterization of passions as 'original existences' (p. 415), reinterpreting this in terms of the characteristic 'world-to-mind direction of fit' of desires. They are goal-directed states rather than truth-directed states, and this is what fits them to play a role in motivation—indeed, makes motivation unintelligible without them.[9]

The more significant departure concerns Hume's scepticism about normative practical reasons. Given his understanding of reason as aiming at the truth, it is impossible for the non-truth-directed states essential to motivation to be contrary to reason (pp. 415–16). This is not to say that our being motivated to perform an action can never display irrationality, for it can be produced by irrational beliefs;[10] but according to the picture Hume himself offers us, criticisms of irrationality are only ever criticisms of theoretical irrationality: if the beliefs giving rise to my motivational states have themselves been formed rationally, there is no *further* criticism of irrationality that can be directed at my being motivated as I am. He puts the point as provocatively as he can:

'Tis not contrary to reason to prefer the destruction of the whole world to the scratching of my finger. 'Tis not contrary to reason for me to choose my total ruin, to prevent the least uneasiness of an *Indian* or person wholly unknown to me. 'Tis

---

[8] See David Hume, *A Treatise of Human Nature*, ed. L. A. Selby-Bigge, 2nd edn. (Oxford: Clarendon Press, 1978), II. iii. 3. Page references in the text are to this edition.

[9] See Smith, 'The Humean Theory of Motivation', and *The Moral Problem*, ch. 4. For criticism, see G. F. Schueler, 'Desires, Pro-Attitudes and Directions of Fit', *Mind*, 100 (1991), 277–81, and *Desire*.

[10] This involves another amendment to Hume, who talks of *false* beliefs in this connection (p. 416).

as little contrary to reason to prefer even my own acknowledged lesser good to my greater, and have a more ardent affection for the former than the latter.   (p. 416)

For Hume, then, although actions can be said to be irrational, in virtue of their being based on irrational beliefs, there is no content to give to the notion of a normative reason *for* action. Hume himself, therefore, cannot be located at our neo-Humean pole: on his view, there are no normative practical reasons, hypothetical or categorical.

But Hume's scepticism about normative practical reasons is uncompelling. For one thing, it is based on a premiss—the characterization of reason as confined to aiming at the truth—which simply assumes what is at issue. And beyond this, a non-sceptical view promises to make better sense of some of our considered judgements concerning rationality: first, that we can be assailed by impulses or urges that are themselves irrational, without having arrived at them as ways of satisfying further desires; and secondly, that there can be cases of what Christine Korsgaard calls 'true practical irrationality'.[11] The sort of aberration of instrumental reasoning that Hume covers is the derivation of a desire from a desire for an end in combination with an irrational belief about the means to its satisfaction; but what he cannot accommodate is the irrationality that might be involved in an agent's being motivated to achieve an end, rationally believing that performing a certain action is the best means to achieving it, but failing to be motivated by this to perform it.[12] The objection does not require that this is a common occurrence, or even that it has ever occurred. Rather, it seems obvious that it could be irrational if it did occur, but Hume's scepticism will not allow him to say so.

However, there is a recognizably neo-Humean yet non-sceptical position that commands a considerable measure of current support. Its variants standardly involve the combination we noted in Section 1, taking the internalist connection between normative practical reasons and motivation and adding a desiderative account of the latter. According to internalism, in order for a consideration to amount to a reason for me to φ, it must be the case that my awareness of it could belong to a motivating explanation of my φ-ing if I were deliberating rationally and knowledgeably. But in order for there to be a motivating explanation of my φ-ing, it must be the case (given the Humeanism about motivation) that I have an appropriate desire. And if we add a further characteristic assumption—that the desires I would have if I were deliberating in this way depend on my actual desiderative nature—then all normative reasons are conditional on the agent's possession of suitable desires.

---

[11] Christine M. Korsgaard, 'Skepticism about Practical Reason', *Journal of Philosophy*, 83 (1986), 12.
[12] This *might* be involved, but it needn't: discovering that *this* is what my end requires may make it rational to abandon it.

Perhaps the most frequent (though not the only)[13] ground on which neo-Humeans make this further assumption is through sharing Hume's own view that an agent's ultimate desires—those she possesses for no further reason—are not subject to rational criticism.[14] A neo-Humean who endorses this further claim possesses an *instrumental conception* of practical reason, according to which what one has a reason to do is what promotes the satisfaction of one's ultimate desires.[15]

In claiming that all normative reasons are hypothetical, neo-Humeans are not committed to holding that the content of an agent's reasons must always contain reference to her own desires. If they did, this would create difficulties. Surely, the consideration I *regard* as the normative reason for me to help someone will often seem to be that he needs it rather than that he needs it and that I want to help people who need it; we would be owed an explanation of the nature of this consistent mistake. But the neo-Humean does not need to allege any mistake here: the claim is that his needing it counts as a reason for me to help only *because* I have appropriate desires. There is no incompatibility. The claim is not that a reference to desires enters the *content* of one's reasons, but that desires are *conditions for the presence* of those reasons.

It is this latter claim, though, that is the subject of Thomas Nagel's influential and widely studied attack in *The Possibility of Altruism*, which targets the Humean account of motivation on which the claim draws. Some critics of the Humean account object that there are motivational states—deontic beliefs, beliefs about what one ought to do, being the usual candidates—that are not partly constituted by desires. Nagel, on the contrary, accepts the principle that such critics are attacking, that 'all motivation implies the presence of desire'.[16] However, he points out that this does not entail that the presence of an agent's reasons is conditional upon the antecedent presence of suitable desires.[17] After all, in all those frequent cases where a desire on which I act is itself a desire for which I regard myself as having a reason, my reason for that desire will be identical to my reason for the action. That is, there will be a single consideration, say R, my regarding which as a normative reason for φ-ing will be what explains *both* my φ-ing

---

[13] Williams, as we shall see, does not support the assumption in this way.

[14] See Hume, *An Enquiry Concerning the Principles of Morals*, ed. L. A. Selby-Bigge, 3rd edn. (Oxford: Clarendon Press, 1975), app. I, p. 293 (consideration V).

[15] Adding to this instrumental conception the further claim that all agents' ultimate desires are self-interested produces the 'economic conception' of practical reason.

[16] '[W]hatever may be the motivation for someone's intentional pursuit of a goal, it becomes in virtue of his pursuit *ipso facto* appropriate to ascribe to him a desire for that goal' (*The Possibility of Altruism*, 29).

[17] Ibid., ch. 5. A reminder: our use of the phrases 'agent's reason' and 'my reason' corresponds to Nagel's own use of 'motivating reason', to refer to the consideration the agent regards as a normative reason for an action or desire.

and my wanting to φ. And if so, R's occupying this status can hardly itself depend on my already wanting to φ. Therefore, in such cases, the desire to φ cannot itself be a condition on R's counting as my reason to φ. On Nagel's view, there is a sense in which the remark, 'All intentional action is motivated by desire' is true—the motivation of action is *constituted* by desire. His concern, though, is to point out that it does not follow from this that the remark is true when read as maintaining that desires must be invoked when *explaining* the motivation of action. Where my motivation can be explained by my regarding myself as having a reason, we have not yet seen why desires must be held to be components in the explanation.

The argument offered for the Humean account of motivation was that the motivational explanation of action is a species of teleological explanation; and that any teleological state of an agent must be conceived of desideratively. Nagel seemingly accepts this argument;[18] but is essentially observing that a Humean theory of the genesis of motivation doesn't follow from it. When a teleological explanation of action is given, what is *explained*—the motivation to act—is a desire; but the teleological character of such explanation does not show that desires must figure in the explanans.

Thus Nagel shows that the neo-Humean argument fails as an attempt to establish the conditionality of normative reasons upon the agent's desires. He can accept the internalist claim that a consideration can only be a reason for me if it can motivate me when I am deliberating rationally and knowledgeably about it. But if the neo-Humean has shown only that desires belong to the constitution of motivation and not to its explanation, then the possibility remains open that the recognition of reasons by someone who is deliberating appropriately is itself capable of giving rise to desideratively constituted motivation, independently of the agent's prior desires.

The neo-Humean has as yet supplied no obstacle to claiming that there are certain norms of practical reason in accordance with which any agent must be motivated, on pain of irrationality. Indeed, the norm of instrumental rationality already provides us with one kind of example of this. If I am motivated to achieve a certain end, then my failure either to be motivated to pursue what I reasonably believe to be an acceptable means to it or to abandon the end will be irrational, irrespective of my desires concerning either that means or the norm itself. So just as there are categorically binding norms of theoretical rationality—if I believe propositions instantiating the premises of the modus ponens schema, then my failure either to draw the appropriate conclusion or to abandon some of the premises is a failure of rationality, irrespective of the question of my

---

[18] Nagel does not give an argument for his claim that all motivation implies the presence of desire: if he rejects this one, though, it is hard to see why he should be attracted to the claim.

antecedent dispositions towards believing the proposition that instantiates the conclusion—so too there is at least one categorically binding norm of practical rationality. Concerning this instrumental norm, of course, the neo-Humean can still maintain that the reasons it supplies remain dependent upon the actual motivational states of the agent, since these are reflected in the ends to which the norm applies. But perhaps there are further norms of practical reason whose specification of reasons is not motivationally dependent in this way—norms that are not only themselves categorical, like the instrumental norm, but that go beyond it in delivering categorical *reasons*. Perhaps, for example, the fact that an action of mine would alleviate your pain is a reason for me to perform it, irrespective of my desires concerning it. Nagel famously argues just this, in the remaining chapters of *The Possibility of Altruism*. The avoidance of solipsism requires one to conceive of oneself as but one agent among others equally real, and this commits us, he argues, to accepting this and other 'objective' or categorical reason-generating norms as constraining what is to count as an acceptable normative practical reason.

It is fair to say that Nagel's defence of the categorical reason-giving force of morality has not attracted many adherents. His defence of this view turns on the claim that the avoidance of a solipsistic dissociation of personal and impersonal standpoints requires the attribution of the same motivational content to impersonal and personal judgements about what one has a reason to do.[19] I must be moved not only by the thought that I have a reason to φ, but by the thought that *this individual*, seen simply as one among many others, has a reason to φ. In reply, however, it may be conceded to Nagel that avoiding solipsism requires us to attribute the same *propositional* content to the two—I must agree that others' interests give them reasons in the same sense that mine give me reasons—but not the same motivational content.[20]

To object to Nagel in this way is not yet to show that there is no hope of defending this categorical status for morality. However, Bernard Williams is frequently read as presenting an argument with this ambition in 'Internal and External Reasons'.[21] His argument can be characterized as modifying in two fundamental respects the earlier neo-Humean argument, which combined a desiderative theory of motivation with a version of internalism to argue for the relativity of reasons to desires. The first of the modifications, however, is to drop the desiderative theory of motivation altogether. *However we decide*, on full consideration, to characterize those states of an agent

[19] Hume, *An Enquiry Concerning the Principles of Morals*, ch. 11.

[20] For this objection to Nagel, see Nicholas Sturgeon, 'Altruism, Solipsism and the Objectivity of Reasons', *Philosophical Review*, 83 (1974), 374–402, Stephen L. Darwall, 'Nagel's Argument for Altruism', *Philosophical Studies*, 25, (1974), 125–30, and Darwall, *Impartial Reason*, ch. 10.

[21] Bernard Williams, 'Internal and External Reasons', in his *Moral Luck* (Cambridge: Univ. Press, 1981), 101–13.

which are states of being motivated,[22] Williams argues that the normative practical reasons of any agent will be relative to those states. The second modification is to argue beyond the broad internalism of the earlier argument to a slightly narrower claim. According to internalism as spelt out so far, the potentially explanatory role of normative reasons shows that reasons must be capable of motivating rational agents for whom they are reasons. Williams's opponent—someone who believes that the status of a consideration as a reason can be independent of its relation to the agent's actual motivational states—must be claiming, as Nagel does, that the recognition of reasons can itself give rise to a new motivation, independently of the other motivational tendencies the agent may happen to have. However, simply for that recognition to give rise to motivation will not be enough to satisfy our requirement on the explanatory potential of the recognition of reasons. The new motivation must be produced by the agent's being rightly orientated in relation to his reasons, acting *for* them and not just *in accordance with* them: the motivation must be normatively guided and not just an eccentric causal consequence of the agent's state of normative awareness.[23] And if right orientation to reasons is a matter of rational deliberation and relevant knowledge, then internalism about normative practical reasons can be reformulated as follows:

> R is a normative reason for A to φ only if rational deliberation and relevant knowledge could rationally guide A to be motivated by R to φ.

If rational deliberation consists in the activities he mentions—instrumental and constitutive reasoning about the attainment of ends, the harmonization or ranking of competing ends, and an imaginative engagement with the prospect of their realization[24]—then it looks as though the motivational states that result from such deliberation will depend on those that are brought to it. A theory of normative practical reasons that characterizes some of them as categorical must then be saying that there is a kind of rational deliberation that will rationally guide the appropriate motivation whatever the agent's motivational dispositions may have been before he engaged in it. And as Williams puts it, 'I see no reason to suppose that these conditions could possibly be met.'[25]

Williams's argument should not, however, be read as an attempt to show the impossibility of categorical reasons. If this were the attempt, it would have failed; for neither an Aristotelian nor a Kantian response has been ruled out. The Aristotelian response is that what right orientation towards one's reasons involves, in addition to the deliberative activities Williams recognizes, is the further capacity to recognize what is truly valuable, for

---

[22] Such states he calls members of the agent's 'subjective motivational set'.
[23] 'Internal and External Reasons', 108–9.   [24] Ibid. 104.   [25] Ibid. 109.

which good upbringing is a precondition.[26] And the Kantian response is that Williams's argument cannot establish the non-existence of norms generating categorical reasons, for any such norms would themselves constitute additional constraints on the deliberation qualifying as *rational*.[27] Williams's own theory recognizes the categorical status of the instrumental norm, as any sensible theory must; in doing so, he incorporates it into his account of the conditions an agent must satisfy if he is to count as deliberating rationally. The issue between Williams and his opponents is whether there are further norms of practical reason which not only categorically apply to rational deliberation, but which also generate categorical reasons. But if there are, they will also have the status of constraints on what qualifies as rational deliberation. Williams's argument cannot demonstrate the non-existence of such norms: if this were the attempt, it would be employing a conception of rational deliberation that simply presupposes this conclusion.

But this is not the aim of Williams's argument. What it does successfully show is that the onus lies with the proponent of categorical reasons to argue for their existence.[28] Given the uncontroversial relevance of the activities he mentions to our judgements of the kinds of people who count as practically rational, a convincing argument must be mounted for placing further requirements on someone's counting as such.

A concern with this Humean challenge is at the heart of this volume. How can there be categorical reasons, and specifically, categorical *moral* reasons? In the broadest terms, the two main avenues of response to consider are these. First, one might advocate an account of value which makes what is good for an agent independent of that agent's motivational states, and derive from this an account of reasons which attributes to them a similar independence. Or, secondly, one might argue that the nature of rationality itself commits us to the recognition of categorical reasons. The two most fully developed and influential attempts to pursue these avenues are those of Aristotle and Kant, respectively. In the next two sections, we outline the main contours of those two attempts, explain why it should be thought that they stand to be improved on, and briefly describe some prominent current strategies for doing so.

3. The Aristotelian Response

For Aristotelians, as for neo-Humeans and Kantians, an action is the appropriate object of rational and fully informed choice for an agent if and

[26] See McDowell, 'Might there be External Reasons?'

[27] See Korsgaard, 'Skepticism about Practical Reason', 19–23.

[28] Cf. Williams, 'Internal Reasons and the Obscurity of Blame', in his *Making Sense of Humanity* (Cambridge: Univ. Press, 1995), 37 and n. 3; 44.

only if it would be good for that agent to perform it. But in its view of the relation of conceptual priority here, Aristotelianism as we construe it differs crucially from the other two poles. According to its recognitional view, what *makes* it rational to choose an action is that it is good—it is an appropriate object of rational choice *because* it is good—whereas for Kantian or neo-Humean constructivists, the converse relation holds. The distinctively Aristotelian approach to the theory of practical reason, then, is to begin with an independent account of the conditions under which actions are good, and to derive from this an account of practical rationality.

In Aristotle's account of good actions, the central role is played by the concept of the human *ergon*, a term translatable as 'function', 'characteristic activity', 'work', 'task', or 'job', though none of these is entirely satisfactory. The basic thought is this: just as a good knife is one that performs its *ergon* (cutting) well, so a good human is one that performs his or her *ergon* well. (Compare *NE* I. 7.)[29] This claim does not commit Aristotle, as is sometimes assumed, to a reduction of evaluative to non-evaluative facts. For even if we assume that the notion of *ergon* is non-evaluative, the claim is that a good human performs her function *well*: evaluative terms occur in both halves of the claim. The view is that the notion of the human *ergon*, and therefore of human nature, at least partially determines what kind of goodness a good human being—and hence, a good human action—possesses. Knives are good in virtue of their possession of certain properties (sharpness, rigidity, etc.), humans are good in virtue of their possession of a very different set of properties. Since those properties which allow a thing to perform its *ergon* well can be termed its virtues (we can speak of the virtues of a knife, for instance), Aristotle is not telling us anything substantive by saying that these properties of humans are virtues. He *does* say something substantive by holding that the human *ergon* is 'the soul's activity that expresses reason or requires reason' (*EN* I. 7, 1098a7–8). Hence the human virtues are those states the activation of which expresses reason (virtues of thought, such as theoretical and practical wisdom), or requires reason (virtues of character, ethical virtues, which concern whether we are well or badly off in relation to feelings). The human virtues we can broadly characterize, then, as 'reason-based excellences'.[30] And the good life for humans (which Aristotle follows Greek tradition in identifying with *eudaimonia*, happiness or flourishing) consists in activities that express these excellences (which activities also require sufficient external goods for their performance). The good life for humans, then, centrally involves activities

---

[29] i.e. *Nicomachean Ethics*, book I, ch. 7. The translation employed is by Terence Irwin (Indianapolis: Hackett, 1985).

[30] David Charles, 'Aristotle and Modern Realism', in Robert Heinaman (ed.), *Aristotle and Moral Realism* (London: UCL Press, 1995), 167.

according to reason: the exercise of reason *possesses* value, but this is not to hold with the constructivist that reason *confers* value.

The account of practical reason that Aristotle derives from this axiological theory is expressed in his picture of the *phronimos*, the man of practical wisdom. Practical wisdom, he tells us, is 'a state grasping the truth, involving reason, concerned with action about what is good or bad for a human being' (*EN* 6. 5, 1143b3–4). This statement is ambiguous: it might mean that practical wisdom is merely concerned with determining the means to given good ends, but has no role in determining whether an end is good; or it might mean that practical wisdom also has the role of determining whether an end is good. Some of what Aristotle says suggests the former reading: the distinctive *ergon* of the *phronimos* is to deliberate well, and 'We deliberate not about ends, but about what promotes ends' (*EN* 3. 3, 1112b11–12). Such an interpretation would ascribe to Aristotle the purely instrumental conception of practical reason mentioned earlier, and he has sometimes been understood to hold this view.[31] But the notion of what promotes an end is more plausibly construed to cover not just means–end reasoning, where the agent discovers the causes which would bring about the realization of his ends, but also to cover constitutive reasoning, by which he seeks to specify those ends. So, beginning from the most general description of the ultimate human end, as happiness, he seeks to specify in what his happiness here and now consists, and then performs instrumental reasoning to establish how this is best achieved.[32]

The task of the *phronimos* is thus to develop a conception of the good life, to determine what living the good life here and now consists in, and to act accordingly. Successful completion of this task involves a grasp of what it is best to do in a particular situation, which is a matter of experience and is akin to perception (6. 8, 1142a27–31): 'these people see correctly because experience has given them their eye' (6. 11, 1143b14). Further, the *phronimos* must actually act on his articulated and applied conception of the good life. This requires him not merely to have correct beliefs, but also to have desires that have the good as their object. Thus Aristotle agrees with the Humean theory of motivation, to the extent that a desire is required for motivation as well as a cognition, but he differs from it in so far as he holds that desires can be correct or incorrect, for they may or may not have what is really good as their object. Finally, these capacities can be possessed only if the *phronimos* possesses all the ethical virtues, for 'vice perverts us and produces false views about the origins of actions' (6. 12, 1144b34–5); conversely,

---

[31] For instance, Gilbert Harman talks of the 'Hume–Aristotle conception of practical reasoning', *The Nature of Morality* (New York: Oxford Univ. Press, 1977), 71.

[32] See David Wiggins, 'Deliberation and Practical Reason', in A. O. Rorty (ed.), *Essays on Aristotle's Ethics* (Berkeley: Univ. of California Press, 1980), 221–40.

possession of practical wisdom is sufficient for the possession of all the ethical virtues (6. 13, 1145a1–3). The capacities the *phronimos* possesses cannot be exhaustively specified in terms of a grasp of a set of principles linking evaluative to non-evaluative states of affairs: such capacities can only be completely specified by appeal to those paradigm people who exercise them, through their uncodifiable grasp of the particular features of a situation, possible only through the acquisition of appropriately absorbed experience and the development of appropriate habits of feeling. Aristotle often appeals[33] to health as an analogue of goodness, and to medical knowledge as an analogue of ethical knowledge, treating the *phronimos* as analogous to a good doctor, who needs to know some general medical principles (rules of thumb that admit of exceptions), but is chiefly distinguished by his diagnostic skills, his ability to detect the relevant features of a particular patient's condition.[34]

Given this outline of the Aristotelian view of practical reason, the way in which it addresses the Humean challenge is clear. An agent has a normative reason to perform an action if it is good, all else equal, and what makes the action good is independent of the contingencies of an individual's own motivational states. My actual motivational states may fail to have the good as their object, even after they have been subjected to the procedures of deliberative reflection that the Humean countenances. So on the Aristotelian view, there are categorical reasons—reasons for an agent that are independent of the agent's actual motivational tendencies.

A fundamental task for Aristotelians, though, is to give a compelling defence of the attribution of an *ergon* to human beings, on which the Aristotelian conception of practical reason depends. Perhaps the starkest objection to this attribution has been produced by Bernard Williams, who charges that it involves an outdated and false 'metaphysical teleology', and more generally an illegitimate attempt to derive evaluative claims from non-evaluative, scientific descriptions of human nature.[35] It is difficult to make the charges stick in this form, since the claim that humans have an *ergon* appears to be an empirical one (like the claim that knives do); and for reasons noted earlier it is a misconception to hold that Aristotle is engaged in any kind of reduction of evaluative to non-evaluative facts. However, to say this is to create the space for a defence of the Aristotelian claim, but not yet to produce it. The predominant strain in contemporary Aristotelian thought is the attempt to defend an 'internal' reading of Aristotle's

---

[33] For instance, at *EN* 2. 2, 1104a4, a16; and 3. 4, 1113b27–9.

[34] Note how the health analogy fits a recognitional construal of practical reason. Whether one is healthy or not is determined by how well one's bodily processes are functioning; health is not constituted as the object of a certain kind of rational choice, whether of people or doctors.

[35] Bernard Williams, *Ethics and the Limits of Philosophy* (London: Collins, 1985), ch. 3, esp. p. 44.

attribution of an *ergon* to human beings, where what is meant is that claims about the human *ergon* are already evaluative claims.

One of the most influential and seductively minimal of these positions is John McDowell's. McDowell holds that Aristotle's appeal to human nature does almost no work in his account, being 'a sort of rhetorical flourish, added to a conclusion already complete without it'.[36] Rather, Aristotle is trying to display and order the structure of our ethical intuitions without attempting to give them any external validation. Aristotle's hermeneutic task centres around the figure of the *phronimos*, for what we ought to do can only be determined by appeal to his ethical sensibility, the product of a particular social training, manifested not in a grasp of ethical principles, but in his uncodifiable sensitivities to particular aspects of his situation. As such, it may not be possible for someone who possesses only an external perspective (including a biological one) on his actions, who lacks his particular social training and sensitivities, to grasp the point of his ethical judgements. When Aristotle notes that the excellent person is 'a sort of standard and measure of what is fine and pleasant' (*EN* 3. 4, 1113a33–4), McDowell construes this in terms of a secondary-quality model—the good is a response-dependent property, just as much as blue is—and hence Aristotelian ethical realism is no more but no less robust than realism about colours. And just as the colour-blind person fails to make certain discriminations that are there to be made, so the amoralist, lacking appropriate ethical training, fails to see the ethical facts that are there to be grasped. So this picture still allows the grounding of categorical reasons, for one's subjective motivations may not be attuned to the ethical facts of the matter.[37]

Setting aside the question of the adequacy of this account as an interpretation of Aristotle, the main worry raised by this concerns the extent of its relativism. For it may be wondered whether the story about particularized sensitivities, torn free of their moorings in any substantial theory of human nature and thus subject only to internal criticism, can do justice to the objectivity of ethical discourse. Cannot many sensibilities, even those of a discriminating sadist, be subject to internal criticism and improvement by their own lights, yet be deeply wrong? And if there are no constraints on who counts as a *phronimos* other than internal ones, are we not merely spinning around in a tight, uninformative circle between good ethical judges and good ethical judgements?

[36] McDowell, 'The Role of *Eudaimonia* in Aristotle's Ethics', in Rorty, *Essays on Aristotle's Ethics*, 371; see also his 'Eudaimonism and Realism in Aristotle's Ethics', in Heinaman, *Aristotle and Moral Realism*.

[37] See McDowell, 'Are Moral Requirements Hypothetical Imperatives?', *Proceedings of the Aristotelian Society (Suppl.)*, 52 (1978), 13–29; and his 'Values and Secondary Qualities', in Ted Honderich (ed.), *Morality and Objectivity* (London: Routledge & Kegan Paul, 1985), 110–29.

A similar worry concerning relativism besets Alasdair MacIntyre's version of Aristotelianism, which gives greater prominence to questions of social and historical particularity. MacIntyre construes talk of the human *ergon* as talk of the point of human life, and holds that this is and has been a matter of social reflection throughout history.[38] Different societies have returned different answers to this question, answers that reflect the varying nature and demands of their social structures. Deliberation about fundamental values and about human nature and personal identity is thus radically contextual. The recurring challenge MacIntyre has faced is whether he can avoid the very relativism he criticizes in other accounts, given his stress on the historical variability of social deliberation.

A promising route to escaping these relativist worries, while retaining the 'internal' reading of *ergon*-attributes as themselves evaluative, has been developed by James Wallace. Wallace argues that Aristotle is entitled to appeal to biological facts, since such facts are themselves evaluative: biology is concerned with living organisms which have intrinsic goals, goals which form the basis for evaluations of success or failure.[39] If we construe *ergon* in terms of characteristic activity, then we must acknowledge the concept to be evaluative, since it is only the usual activity of a *healthy* organism in environmentally *favourable* conditions that counts as characteristic for it. But besides being evaluative, biological facts—facts about what an organism needs, or what is good for it, are prominent examples—are genuinely explanatory and objective, so that appeal to human nature places real constraints on accounts of the human good. Wallace also notes that the characteristic activity of humans is social, and that this explains why we hold certain dispositions to be virtues, for they play an important part in securing the maintenance and flourishing of social life. To these points we can add that 'biological' does not refer to the study of living bodies, but to the study of life, and that for Aristotle to possess a mind is to possess certain biological capacities. Since man is a rational animal, what it is to possess a mind must partly be a matter of receptiveness to rational demands, and therefore to certain values. So Aristotle's appeal to biology, including psychology, is an appeal to scientific facts, but *pace* William's initial objection, need not involve appeal to non-evaluative facts.

With this account, though, it is not relativism but a pair of different objections that must be addressed. The first worry concerns whether the evaluative yet explanatory biological claims to which Wallace appeals can survive the reductive ambitions of micro-biology: that is, whether their explanatory power is drawn from a level of micro-biological explanation at

---

[38] Alasdair MacIntyre, *After Virtue* (London: Duckworth, 1981).
[39] J. D. Wallace, *Virtues and Vices* (Ithaca, NY: Cornell Univ. Press, 1978), esp. ch. 1.

which the claim to detect an evaluative dimension becomes implausible. And the second, related worry concerns whether evolutionary biology, with its fundamental explanatory concept of the fitness of individuals (that is, the likelihood of their leaving offspring), rather than of their well-being, has the right explanatory shape to secure an Aristotelian view of value.[40]

The first task for contemporary Aristotelians concerning practical reason is to address worries of the kinds we have raised concerning their attribution of an *ergon* to human beings. However, notice that although relinquishing this attribution would be an important departure from Aristotle himself, it would not yet entail abandoning the Aristotelian pole in theorizing about practical reason, as we have characterized it. What is distinctive of that pole is a recognitional conception of the relation between reason and value that attributes goods to agents independently of their contingent motivational states, and infers the existence of categorical reasons. Perhaps the attribution of goods that are motivationally independent in this way can be defended without relying on claims about the human *ergon*: it is only if the broader claim is relinquished that the Aristotelian pole must be abandoned.

Even if the broader Aristotelian project cannot be sustained, we are still not entitled to conclude that all goods are motivationally dependent, and all reasons hypothetical. For maybe categorical reasons can be defended on a constructivist view of the relation between reason and value. For the most sustained attempt to argue that they can be, we need to turn to Kant.

4. The Kantian Response

Kant's concept of *a* categorical imperative is that of a principle expressible as an ought-statement, which represents 'an action as objectively necessary in itself, without reference to another end' (*G* 414).[41] That is, in particular, it represents an action as required by reason independently of its relation to the agent's contingent motivational nature. Kant holds that there is only one valid supreme principle that satisfies this concept, a principle which in one of its formulations reads, 'Act only according to that maxim whereby one can at the same time will that it should become a universal law' (*G* 421). It is this principle, given here in its Formula of Universal Law version, which he calls *the* categorical imperative (CI): according to Kant's legislative conception of practical reason, this is the supreme principle both of morality and rationality. A maxim is a subjective principle of action; that is, it specifies, in rule form, the description under which an agent wills his

---

[40] For the latter worry, see Williams, *Ethics and the Limits of Philosophy*, 44.

[41] *G* refers to Kant's *Grundlegung zur Metaphysik der Sitten*, the number following being the relevant page number in the Prussian Academy Edition (vol. iv). The translation used in this introduction is *Grounding for the Metaphysics of Morals* by James W. Ellington, 3rd edn. (Indianapolis: Hackett, 1993).

action. Since the will is 'the power to act according to his [the agent's] conception of laws, i.e., according to principles' (412) and all action is willed, all action is action on maxims. The CI is the test for whether these maxims are morally (and thereby rationally) permitted. If a maxim is not permitted, then its contrary is required. The test is one of legislative and not merely reasons-universalization: it requires of a normative reason for me not only that it applies to every similarly situated agent, but also that I can consistently *will* that everyone so act.

Kant's argument for categorical reasons, then, is an argument for *moral rationalism*—the view that moral requirements are requirements of reason —with the following broad structure: (*a*) moral requirements are categorical, since they are grounded in the CI; (*b*) the CI is a requirement of reason; therefore (*c*) there are categorical requirements of reason. He supports (*a*) in two ways: by a motivational argument, and by exemplification. The motivational argument, sometimes called the 'derivation' of the CI, runs in its main version through much of *G* section I, and culminates at 402. Roughly, it is the argument that only actions done from duty have true moral worth; that this moral worth is not derived from the purposes to be attained by the action; that acting from duty is action that is required by the supreme principle and is performed because of the agent's realization that it is so required; and that only the CI can satisfy the requirements that a supreme principle must satisfy for all these claims to be true. The route of exemplification is followed in *G* section II: there Kant tries to show that the CI in its three main formulations generates the duties that we generally think we have, including duties of promise-keeping and beneficence to others.[42]

There has been a large amount of recent discussion of the adequacy of these arguments. The derivation rests on the claim that only an action performed for the sake of duty has genuine moral worth: yet it has been objected that this is incompatible with much of our ordinary moral thought, including our views about the moral worth of motivation by feelings of sympathy and friendship.[43] Kantians have replied that such feelings strictly speaking lack moral content, which the thoughts that guide genuinely moral action must possess; and action for the sake of duty need only be understood as fixing a limiting condition on actions, rather than as producing a direct motivation in all cases of morally worthy action.[44] Defenders

---

[42] Note that Kant does not think that exemplification shows the validity of the CI: rather, he uses it to show that the CI generates specifically *moral* duties.

[43] e.g. Michael Stocker, 'The Schizophrenia of Modern Ethical Theories', *Journal of Philosophy*, 73 (1976), 453–66; Bernard Williams, 'Morality and the Emotions', in his *Problems of the Self* (Cambridge: Univ. Press, 1973), 207–29.

[44] See e.g. Barbara Herman, 'On the Value of Acting from the Motive of Duty', *Philosophical Review*, 90 (1981), 359–82, and 'Integrity and Impartiality', *Monist*, 66 (1983), 233–50.

of Kant have also aimed to clarify and defend or emend the rather mysterious derivation itself.[45] Another common objection against the CI is that of
empty formalism: the claim that no substantive duties can be derived from
the CI. Here again, Kantians have argued that when the notion of a maxim
is properly understood, the idea of contradiction in the will is carefully
explicated, and the interrelations between the different formulations of the
CI grasped, the CI can be shown to have substantive, and correct, implications about our duties.[46]

However, even if it is denied that morality is grounded in the CI, if the
CI is a requirement of reason then there are categorical requirements of
reason, and the Humean challenge has been answered. It is claim (*b*) that
is our chief concern here; and Kant's argument for it has its roots in the
rejection, in Kant's mature philosophy, of his own pre-critical foundation-
alism about reason.

How is one to justify treating something as a norm of reason? There
seem to be insuperable difficulties in a foundationalist conception of this
justificational task: it would involve relying on foundational claims concerning reason that were themselves unjustified. But dissatisfaction with a
dogmatism of this sort should not lead us into entertaining the idea that
scepticism concerning reason is a real alternative for us: for any creature for
whom the question arises, the attempt to reason is inescapable. What is the
alternative, then? According to the mature Kant, norms of reason can only
be grounded in the formal principle that reasons must be shareable by
other reasoning beings, and must not rely on the imposition of any authority external to that of reason itself. The latter requirement derives from the
attack on foundationalist dogmatism: for any such external imposition, the
question, '*Why* should I obey this authority?' will require an answer. A
non-dogmatic conception of reason, therefore, sees it as autonomous—as
governed by self-given laws. From this formal principle, norms of reason
can be derived provided it can be shown of them that their denial leads
either to unshareability or the reliance on external authority.[47]

This is a powerful line of thought, and the question Kant raises is one
that any non-sceptical view about practical reason has to address. The most

[45] Christine Korsgaard, 'Kant's Analysis of Obligation: The Argument of *Foundations* I', *The Monist*,
72 (1989), 311–40; and Henry Allison, 'On the Presumed Gap in the Derivation of the Categorical
Imperative', repr. in his *Idealism and Freedom* (Cambridge: Univ. Press, 1996), 143–54.

[46] See Christine Korsgaard, 'Kant's Formula of Universal Law', *Pacific Philosophical Quarterly*, 66
(1985), 24–7, and 'Kant's Formula of Humanity', *Kant-Studien*, 77 (1986), 183–202; Onora O'Neill,
'Consistency in Action' and 'Universal Laws and Ends-in-Themselves', both in her *Constructions of
Reason* (Cambridge: Univ. Press, 1989), 81–104, 126–44.

[47] For this line of thought, see Onora O'Neill, 'Vindicating Reason', in Paul Guyer (ed.), *The
Cambridge Companion to Kant* (Cambridge: Univ. Press, 1992), esp. sects. 1, 8–14; see also John Rawls,
'Themes in Kant's Moral Philosophy', esp. sect. 4, in Eckart Förster (ed.), *Kant's Transcendental
Deductions* (Stanford: Univ. Press, 1989), 81–113.

seemingly modest neo-Humeanism, advocating only the instrumental norm, faces the question of what justifies that advocacy. However, it is only the beginning of the argument that Kant needs to supply. How can he derive something as substantial as the CI out of these formal observations on the nature of rationality?

Humeans have sometimes objected that Kant's move at this point is simply a fallacious slide from reasons to legislative universalization.[48] However, as Henry Allison emphasizes, Kant in fact appeals to another feature of agents, beyond their mere rationality—their transcendental freedom—in grounding the claim that their maxims are subject to the CI.[49] Thus the argument that the CI is a requirement of reason, the 'deduction' of the CI, has in *G* section III two stages: first, that a rational being with a will must regard itself from the practical point of view (from the standpoint of agency) as transcendentally free, and secondly, that a transcendentally free agent is subject to the moral law (the CI).[50] The argument for the first stage rests on a parallel with theoretical reason, and a claim that 'we cannot possibly think of a reason that consciously lets itself be directed from outside as regards its judgments' (448). This first stage, and with it the deduction, is abandoned in the *Critique of Practical Reason* (*KpV* 47):[51] there Kant holds that the ground for holding ourselves to be free is our awareness of being subject to the moral law, which we know as 'a fact of reason' (*KpV* 30–1). But the second stage is still maintained, for it is entailed by a claim (which Allison has dubbed the *Reciprocity Thesis*) that Kant continues to hold, namely that 'a free will and a will subject to moral laws are one and the same' (*G* 447). The abandonment of the earlier stage of the argument in the *Critique* means that by Kant's earlier announced standards the rational requirement claim is not proven. But since plausibly our self-conception as free agents is rationally inescapable, the Reciprocity Thesis would still give strong support to the CI. Kant indeed continued to hold that his argument gives a 'credential' to the moral law (*KpV* 47).

What matters for Kant's argument, as we have reconstructed it, is a conditional entailed by the Reciprocity Thesis, a conditional which holds that if an agent is transcendentally free, then she is subject to the moral law (the CI). Kant argues for this conditional both in the *Groundwork* and in

---

[48] See Gilbert Harman, *The Nature of Morality*, 76.

[49] Henry E. Allison, *Kant's Theory of Freedom* (Cambridge: Univ. Press, 1990), part III. See also Thomas E. Hill, Jr., 'Kant's Argument for the Rationality of Moral Conduct', *Pacific Philosophical Quarterly*, 66 (1985), 3–23.

[50] Kant holds that as stated there is the danger of a circle in the deduction, and his attempt to avoid it introduces further complications, from which we prescind here.

[51] '*KpV*' refers to *Kritik der praktischen Vernunft*; the number following is the Prussian Academy Edition page number (vol. v); the translation used here is *Critique of Practical Reason* by Lewis White Beck (New York: Macmillan, 1956).

the *Critique*, the latter version being more compact and somewhat more explicit. It can be reconstructed as follows (*KpV* 29):

1. A free will must be independent of all empirical conditions. (That is, the free will must be transcendentally free. Empirical conditions include all inclinations, as well as all natural laws.)
2. A free will must also be determinable: that is, it must be subject to some law. (In *G* 446 this is grounded on the claim that the will is a causal power, and all causation requires laws.)
3. A law is comprised of a legislative form and a material.
4. The material of the law, that is the object (end) of the maxim, can only be given empirically. (That is, what we aim at is determined by our desires, impulses, natural character, etc., which are all empirically determined.)
5. Therefore, though a free will must have its determining ground in a law (by 2), it must be independent of the material of the law (by 1 and 4).
6. Therefore the determining ground of a free will must be purely the legislative form of the law (by 3 and 5).

Kant in section 7 simply identifies this legislative form with the CI, in the Formula of Universal Law version.

This argument, then, is of fundamental importance for Kant's attempt to ground categorical reasons. The biggest obstacle to its acceptance, though, is the view of transcendental freedom from which it argues in premiss 1, with its incompatibilism and its problematic picture of non-temporal action.[52] Although there are several characteristic Kantian claims that can be reformulated in compatibilist terms—most notably, the claim that the capacity for deliberative self-governance is a condition both of an agent's practical rationality and of the applicability of moral requirements to her—a compatibilist conception of freedom will not sustain this argument for the CI. The argument also faces further objections, the most serious of which is that it equivocates on key terms, particularly on 'legislative form'. In the minimal, uncontentious sense that makes premiss 3 true, the legislative form is simply the form of a *law*—its lawlike aspect, prescinding from the particular ends at which it aims—and Kant holds that this is a proposition's universality and necessity. So a practical law (a law of action) would have the form, 'All agents must ϕ', where ϕ is a variable ranging over action-types. But this notion of legislative form is weaker than that required to establish the *moral law*, which substitutes for this variable the action-type specified in, 'Act only on maxims that pass the CI test'.

[52] For a defence of a version of the latter view, see Korsgaard, 'Morality as Freedom', in Yirmiyahu Yovel (ed.), *Kant's Practical Philosophy Reconsidered* (Dordrecht: Kluwer, 1989), 23–48.

A number of Kantian moral philosophers are currently working to overcome these and other difficulties in seeking to reassemble a position close to Kant's own constructivist formalism, endorsing categorical moral reasons. Beyond this, there are several strategies employed by contemporary philosophers engaged in the more broadly Kantian project of defending categorical reasons on the basis of formal characteristics of practical reason. A first such strategy seeks to derive these characteristics from observations about the relationship of practical to theoretical reason. If we are to have a properly unified account of reason, it is argued, we must attribute to it, in its operation in both practical and theoretical spheres, characteristics such as universality, impersonality, impartiality, and coherence; and from features such as these categorical moral reasons can be derived.[53] A second strategy identifies the presuppositions of the acceptance of instrumental or prudential norms of practical reason, and argues that those presuppositions equally support categorical reasons of moral or other kinds. And a third seeks to infer them from claims about the constitutive aim of action.[54] The strongest version of each of these strategies involves claiming that the attempt to reject the attribution to practical reason of the characteristics from which categorical reasons are inferred is incoherent. A weaker claim is that a scepticism of this sort may not be incoherent, but its costs are insupportable.

All of these strategies are represented in the essays that follow, which we conclude by briefly introducing.

5. The Essays

We have been characterizing the dialectical situation as one in which the onus lies with the opponents of Humeanism to meet the Humean challenge of producing a compelling argument for categorical practical reasons. However, one effect of our discussion of Kant has been to call this characterization into question. Given any principle we recognize as a requirement of

---

[53] Cf. Korsgaard, 'Skepticism about Practical Reason', 17, and R. Jay Wallace, 'How to Argue about Practical Reason', *Mind*, 99 (1990), 383. For an argument that emphasizes the first three features, see Darwall, *Impartial Reason*; for an argument emphasizing the fourth, see Smith, *The Moral Problem*, ch. 5.

[54] David Velleman has argued that this third strategy reveals reasons that are both categorical and hypothetical. Anyone who has reasons for action has reasons determined by its constitutive aim, whatever the individual motivational tendencies that distinguish her from other agents—in this sense, they are categorical. But someone who lacked the motivational tendency constitutive of agency would have no reasons—so in this sense, all reasons are hypothetical. See Velleman, 'The Possibility of Practical Reason', *Ethics*, 106 (1996), 694–726.

Nagel's argument, discussed in Sect. 2, exemplifies a fourth strategy, of seeking to draw out the intolerable metaphysical consequences (in his argument, solipsism) of the rejection of categorical moral reasons.

practical reason, Kant's question arises: what justification do we have for treating it as such? And this question applies, it seems, to the non-sceptical neo-Humean's treatment of the instrumental norm as a categorical norm of reason, as much as to any other. How can neo-Humeans justify this? More generally, what kind of argument should be sought in order to vindicate fully a claim about a requirement of practical reason? This methodological question is the concern of the first two essays in this volume, by David Velleman and Peter Railton.

Velleman considers and rejects David Gauthier's view that our reasons for favouring a theory of practical reason can themselves be practical, on the grounds that an argument of this form could only draw on a conception of practical reason that is by its own admission arbitrary, and hence is incapable of conferring normative authority on any such conception by way of conclusion. The question of the best conception of practical rationality must be treated as a theoretical rather than a practical question—and one best pursued, Velleman argues, by identifying a constitutive aim of action. Any adequate account of the nature of action must allow that I can act now to influence my future actions without depriving my future self of autonomy; but from this observation, Velleman argues, we can derive moral constraints on genuine reasons for action. Could a view about the constitutive elements of deliberative agency supply a fully non-hypothetical defence of norms of practical reason? This is Railton's question. He distinguishes between the 'High Brow' claim that it is constitutive of being an agent that one aims at what one judges to be good, and the 'Low Brow' claim that it is constitutive of being an agent that one aims at what one wants. He shows how the Low Brow conception yields a kind of non-hypothetical grounding for instrumental reasoning: the attempt to challenge it by asking 'Why should I be interested in following the instrumental norm?' turns out to be self-undermining. Even so, however, the justifiability of the instrumental norm remains dependent on its being upheld as the outcome of the process of reaching reflective equilibrium; and this depends on the *hypothetical* elements we take into that process.

If the demand for a vindication of the instrumental norm can be met by an argument of this form—securing its rationally inescapable status by showing the unintelligibility of a demand for some further reason to observe it—does this support the neo-Humean position? James Dreier argues that it does. Following the instrumental norm is a condition of one's having practical reasons, in a way that other putative norms of practical reason are not. He argues that this makes it plausible to hold that the Humean challenge cannot be met, and in particular, that the existence of categorical moral reasons should be rejected. What, then, should neo-Humeans say about morality? They will want to allow that there are moral reasons, for agents with suitable motivational natures; but what kind of moral argument about those reasons will make sense, given their view? Garrett Cullity examines this question, looking at the way in which Bernard Williams's neo-Humeanism about practical reason grounds a powerful attack on revisionary ethical theorizing. However, Cullity argues that, although embracing a neo-Humean view of practical reason should affect one's conception of legitimate ethical theorizing, that view still contains resources for revisionary ethical argument that Williams overlooks.

Is it right, though, for neo-Humeans to think that they can make sense of moral reasons? Robert Audi argues that the instrumentalist conception of practical reason at the heart of neo-Humeanism is unable to do so. As we have seen, neo-Humeans standardly ground their challenge to categorical reasons in an internal connection they advocate between reason and motivation. Audi closely examines this connection in its various formulations, and argues that the sources of support commonly claimed for the stronger versions of internalism are inadequate.

The remainder of the volume is concerned with developing alternatives to the neo-Humean position. Berys Gaut and Terence Irwin write in defence of distinctively Aristotelian views. The principal point of distinction of the Aristotelian pole, as we have described it, is its recognitional conception of practical reason, and a defence of this conception, in particular against a Kantian form of the constructivist alternative, is the central concern of Gaut's essay. He argues that Kant's constructivism is undermined by its denial of the existence of a plurality of unconditional goods and by its failure to give an intuitively satisfactory account of which actions are rational. He also argues that Kant's regress argument for constructivism fails. In its place he defends the claim that value is a teleological—and specifically when applied to living beings a biological—category, and so cannot be thought of simply as the object of rational choice; and he defends the claim that this kind of recognitional conception is implicit in our everyday views of reason and agency.

Irwin presents the case for the Aristotelian outlook by arguing that a relationship of mutual support exists between two individually contentious theses: eudaemonism, and the reciprocity of virtue. Together, these two theses posit the existence of a single comprehensive end of human life, the correct conception of which is needed for the possession of any virtue; Irwin argues that the coherence of this combined view speaks in its favour. He approaches this Aristotelian picture via Aquinas's distinctive elaboration of it, and in doing so, introduces several notably Kantian themes, among them Aquinas's identification of doing good with achieving a rational structure in one's aims, and his emphasis on a virtuous agent's deliberating for himself about the point of his virtuous activity, rather than relying on any external authority. In their full Kantian manifestations, as moral rationalism and the identification of rationality and autonomy, these two themes are taken up in the following essays.

Christine Korsgaard approaches the defence of a Kantian position by reopening Railton and Dreier's question concerning the vindication of the instrumental norm, and arguing that demonstrating its rational inescapability does not support neo-Humeanism. First, she argues that a purely instrumental conception of rationality is incoherent, as the instrumental principle must be supplemented by a further principle telling us which ends are normative. But on the Kantian view, one's ends are what one wills; thus the instrumental principle can be normative provided my willing something makes it normative for me—that is, provided I possess autonomy, the capacity to give a law to myself. Like Korsgaard, David Brink objects against the neo-Humean conception of moral reasons that it renders them rationally arbitrary, seeking to derive them from rationally ungrounded motivational states. Kant is right, Brink argues, to suppose that a capacity for deliberative self-governance is a precondition of the intelligibility of moral requirements, but Brink maintains that our possession of that capacity can be interpreted naturalistically, without any commitment to the existence of transcendental freedom. And from here, he argues, there is a plausible Kantian argument from the inescapability of moral requirements—their applying to everyone—to their authority—their supplying everyone with reasons independently of our contingent motivational natures. Brink's second main question, given the existence of moral reasons that are categorical in this sense, concerns their relation to our other reasons. But here, he parts company from Korsgaard, and Kant: despite agreeing that Kant can plausibly uphold the harmonization of hypothetical and categorical imperatives, he resists the claim that moral reasons should be held to have overriding authority.

The next three essays share Brink's conviction that Kant is right that moral requirements apply to us in virtue of our possession of a capacity for deliberative self-governance, but wrong to think that this presupposes transcendental freedom. If so, the conditions for our possession of this capacity will supply a compatibilist account of moral responsibility—an account of the kind defended by Michael Smith. Smith shows that, given his own dispositional theory of value, this capacity should be thought of as comprising two components: a capacity to recognize and respond to the norms governing evaluative beliefs, and a capacity to have the desires one should have. But given the non-relativism of his theory, we should conceive of the capacity for deliberative self-control in which responsibility consists not as autonomy—control by self-generated laws—but as orthonomy—self-control in the light of the non-relative reasons that apply to everyone.

Jay Wallace's aim is to show the bearing that the conception of moral accountability in terms of the capacity for reflective self-control has upon a defensible view of the content of morality. Given this conception of it, he argues, moral accountability requires that one have reason to comply with moral demands. This requirement can certainly be satisfied if moral reasons can be held (despite Brink's opposition) to be overriding; and one's moral and non-moral reasons can be brought into convergence on ceding priority to morality, provided morality is not conceived of in a severely demanding way. Wallace then argues that this supplies an effective objection against severely demanding conceptions of moral requirements. In John Skorupski's essay, the claim that moral accountability requires that one have reason to comply with moral demands also occupies a central place. This puts him in broad agreement with Wallace, in holding that the content of what we accept as an agent's normative practical reasons will constrain what we can properly hold to be wrong actions of hers. But Skorupski is concerned to add that constraints on the content of morality are also exerted from a second, plainly anti-Kantian direction. Our reasons to blame someone, in holding that she acts wrongly, are themselves constrained by our affective natures—by what we are disposed to feel about the objects of our assessment under suitable conditions.

The volume closes with a sceptical perspective on its central issue. Joseph Raz's essay displays a recognitional conception of practical reason: he approaches the question of what a person has reason to do via the question of what has value for that person. However, his concern is not to develop an Aristotelian response to the Humean challenge; rather, it is to reject the challenge itself as ill-formed. Our efforts should not be directed towards identifying arguments for moral reasons in addition to our non-moral ones—in large part because the distinction itself is obscure. Rather, we should seek to display the interconnections between the various reasons we standardly have; and when we do, we find ourselves without a threat to which the attempt to defend categorical moral reasons could stand as an answer.[55]

---

[55] We are grateful to Samuel Kerstein for his comments on a draft of this Introduction.

I

Deciding How to Decide

J. DAVID VELLEMAN

By 'deciding how to decide', I mean using practical reasoning to regulate one's principles of practical reasoning. David Gauthier has suggested that deciding how to decide is something that every rational agent does.[1] Whether or not we agree with Gauthier about agents in general, we might think that his suggestion applies well enough to many of us moral philosophers. We assess rival principles of practical reasoning, which tell us how to choose among actions; and assessing how to choose among actions certainly sounds like deciding how to decide.

One of my goals in this essay is to argue, in opposition to Gauthier, that assessing rival principles of practical reasoning is a job for theoretical rather than practical reasoning. How to decide is something that we discover rather than decide.

The idea that our principles of practical reasoning can be regulated by practical reasoning is essential to Gauthier's defence of his own, somewhat unorthodox conception of those principles. And although I do not endorse the specifics of Gauthier's conception, I do endorse its spirit. There is a flaw in the orthodox conception of practical reasoning, and Gauthier has put his finger on it. Unfortunately, Gauthier's account of why it is a flaw, and how it should be fixed, ultimately rests on practical considerations, whose relevance is open to question if, as I believe, practical reasoning cannot regulate itself.

This essay therefore has a second goal, which complicates matters considerably. Although I want to reject Gauthier's notion that we decide how to decide, I also want to preserve what rests upon that notion, in Gauthier's view: I want to resettle Gauthier's critique of the orthodoxy on a new foundation. I shall try to carry out this delicate operation as follows. First I'll summarize Gauthier's critique of the orthodoxy about practical reasoning. Then I'll introduce Gauthier's alternative conception of practical reasoning

---

[1] Gauthier suggests that the capacity to choose one's conception of practical reason is essential to one's rational autonomy as an agent. See 'Reason and Maximization', in *Moral Dealing; Contract, Ethics, and Reason* (Ithaca, NY: Cornell Univ. Press, 1990), 209–33, at 231. See also *Morals By Agreement* (Oxford: Clarendon Press, 1986), 183–4.

and his practical argument for deciding upon it. After explaining why I think that practical reasoning cannot be self-regulated in this manner, I'll explain how I think that it must be regulated instead. Finally, I'll return to Gauthier's critique of the orthodox conception in order to reformulate it in theoretical terms.

1. Gauthier's Critique of Straightforward Maximization

The target of Gauthier's critique is what he calls the theory of straightforward maximization. The theory of straightforward maximization says that an agent should choose, from among the discrete actions currently available to him, the one that yields the greatest expectation of benefit for him.[2] Gauthier argues that the theory of straightforward maximization must be modified so as to enable rational agents to avoid falling into prisoner's dilemmas.

Prisoner's dilemmas get their name from a philosophical fiction in which two people—say, you and I—are arrested on suspicion of having committed a crime together. The police separate us for interrogation and offer us similar plea bargains: if either gives evidence against the other, his sentence (whatever it otherwise would have been) will be shortened by one year, and the other's sentence will be lengthened by two. In light of the expected benefits, maximizing rationality instructs each of us to give evidence against the other. The unfortunate result is that each sees his sentence shortened by one year in payment for his own testimony, but lengthened by two because of the other's testimony; and so we both spend one more year in jail than we would have if both had kept silent.

The moral of this story might appear to be, not just that crime doesn't pay, but that the pursuit of self-interest doesn't pay, either. But of course the individual pursuit of self-interest does pay in this story, since each of us does better by testifying than he would have by keeping silent, irrespective of what the other does. What fails to pay, in this story, is self-interested action on the part of two agents, when compared with self-sacrifice by both. Joint sacrifice would have yielded greater benefits for each of us than joint selfishness.

In order to illustrate Gauthier's complaint against the maximizing conception of practical reasoning, we must imagine that you and I have an opportunity

---

[2] Note that this theory does not spell out specific procedures for applying this principle of choice; it simply states the principle that ought to be implemented in one's deliberative procedures. All of the conceptions of rationality discussed below are articulated at the same level of generality, as principles of choice that will no doubt require more specific procedures for their implementation. To argue, as I do, that practical reasoning cannot regulate our principles of choice is not to argue that it cannot regulate the specific procedures in which those principles are implemented.

to confer before being separated for interrogation. Since we expect to be offered incentives to betray one another, we try to attain solidarity by means of an agreement. 'I'm willing to keep silent if you are,' I say, and you say, 'I am, too.'[3] We thus appear to have agreed on joint sacrifice, to our mutual advantage.

Yet once we are led into our separate interrogation rooms and offered our separate plea bargains, the expected benefits of the alternatives are unaffected by our attempt at collaboration.[4] Each still stands to gain by testifying against the other, irrespective of what the other does; and so the principle of maximization still instructs each of us to testify, in violation of our supposed agreement.

What's more, each of us could have predicted that the other would violate the agreement if only he had known that the other was a maximizer. And neither of us would have been willing to forgo his plea bargain in order to reach an agreement that the other was in any case going to violate. When I said 'I'm willing to keep silent if you are', I meant to express a willingness that would take effect in my behaviour, but only on the condition that you express a willingness that would be equally effective in yours. Had I known that any willingness you might express was likely to be overridden by maximizing calculations, I would have realized that your expressed willingness to keep silent would be of no value to me, and so I would never have offered mine. Hence if either party's allegiance to maximization had been known, no agreement would ever have been offered to him. Straightforward maximizers thus find themselves excluded from co-operative agreements.

Being excluded from co-operative agreements is a cost that counts against the maximizing conception of practical reasoning, in Gauthier's eyes. Who, he asks, would want to have deliberative principles that would exclude him from the co-operative agreements by which prisoner's dilemmas are avoided? In Gauthier's view, one is better off adopting deliberative principles that favour the fulfilment of mutually beneficial agreements, so that one will be offered an opportunity to enter them.

Gauthier therefore proposes an alternative to the maximizing conception of practical reasoning. The alternative conception instructs an agent to maximize except when he is deciding whether to fulfil a commitment, in which case it compares the benefits, not of fulfilling or violating the commitment, but rather of two overall courses of action, one being that of making and

---

[3] Note that I say, 'I'm willing to keep silent if you are,' not 'I'm willing to keep silent if you *do*.' For a discussion of how this commitment is formulated, see the Appendix to this essay.

[4] We can of course imagine mechanisms by which our agreement would have altered the expected benefits. For example, we might belong to a gang that exacts revenge on liars but not on stool-pigeons. But the argument depends on the assumption that no such mechanisms are in place.

fulfilling the commitment, the other being that of never having made the commitment at all.[5] The agent is instructed to fulfil his commitment if the package deal of making and fulfilling the commitment promises greater benefits than the package in which he never made it and so never had to consider fulfilling it.

But why should an agent base his decision on a comparison between these package deals? After all, an agent evaluates whether to fulfil a commitment at a juncture where never having made the commitment is no longer an option: the commitment has already been made. Why should he care whether, in fulfilling the commitment, he will complete a course of action whose consequences are better than those of an alternative that is no longer available? And why should his evaluation at this juncture ignore a course of action that still is available—namely, that of making the commitment and then violating it?[6]

Gauthier's answer to these questions is that the conception of practical reasoning that applies this comparison is superior to the straightforwardly maximizing conception, which compares all and only the discrete steps that are currently available.[7] What makes the alternative conception superior, Gauthier says, is that it enables the agent to make commitments that he can be counted on to fulfil, thus making him eligible as a partner in co-operative agreements. The benefits to be expected from co-operation give the agent reason for abandoning maximization and adopting Gauthier's alternative conception instead.

Here is where the notion of deciding how to decide first enters Gauthier's argument. His conception of practical reasoning is commended to the agent by practical considerations about the benefits of holding it. The deliberative principles that Gauthier favours are thus arrived at by deliberation.

The deliberations by which an agent arrives at these principles are articulated most fully in Gauthier's recent paper 'Assure and Threaten'.[8] There Gauthier explains that these deliberations are framed by an ultimate or overall goal of the agent's —say, the goal of having as good a life as possible. In furtherance of this master-goal, Gauthier argues, straightforward

---

[5] This proposal appears, in very different forms, in 'In the Neighborhood of the Newcomb-Predictor (Reflections on Rationality)', *Proceedings of the Aristotelian Society*, 89 (1988–9), 179–94, esp. 186–94; and 'Assure and Threaten', *Ethics*, 104 (1994), 690–721, esp. 704–7. I am glossing over differences in these two formulations of the proposal.

[6] As Michael Bratman puts it, Gauthier's conception of practical reasoning recommends 'ranking . . . courses of action that typically include elements no longer in the agent's causal control'. Bratman remarks, 'This seems to me not to do justice to the significance of temporal and causal location to our agency' ('Toxin, Temptation, and the Stability of Intention', in Jules Coleman and Christopher Morris (eds.), *Rational Commitment and Social Justice* (Cambridge: Univ. Press, forthcoming)).

[7] 'In the Neighborhood of the Newcomb-Predictor', 192; 'Assure and Threaten', 700–2.

[8] pp. 691–702.

maximization recommends its own replacement by the alternative conception, which will afford the agent a better life by affording him access to the benefits of co-operation.

At this point, however, we might suspect that an earlier problem has re-emerged. Suppose that an agent adopts Gauthier's conception of practical reasoning and is consequently offered a co-operative agreement, which he accepts. Holding Gauthier's conception will potentially have furthered the agent's master-goal by making the agreement available to him, since nobody would have offered to co-operate with a straightforward maximizer. But when the time for fulfilling the agreement arrives, Gauthier's conception of practical reasoning will no longer further the agent's goal, since his goal would be better served by reasoning that permitted him to violate the agreement.[9] If the agent's conception of practical reasoning were an object of choice in the sense that it was continually open to revision, then the agent would now find himself changing conceptions in midstream.

Of course, if the agent had been expected to change conceptions in midstream, then the co-operative agreement would never have been offered to him, in the first place, since his conception of practical reasoning, being thus revisable, would have offered no guarantee of his future co-operation. Hence Gauthier's conception of practical reasoning can create beneficial opportunities only if the agent appears unlikely to abandon that conception at a later date.

Gauthier has never explicitly addressed this problem, to my knowledge, but a solution to it is implicit in his discussions of the choice between conceptions of practical reasoning. The solution rests on the claim that Gauthier's conception, unlike straightforward maximization, is self-supporting.[10]

We have envisioned that an agent, having adopted Gauthier's conception of practical reasoning, might subsequently abandon it, at least temporarily, when he no longer benefits from holding it. But to abandon Gauthier's conception of practical reasoning on the grounds that it is no longer beneficial would be to apply the principle of straightforward maximization; whereas the agent, having adopted Gauthier's conception, is no longer a straightforward maximizer.

The question before the agent, at this juncture, is whether to retain a conception of practical reasoning, and this conception can be regarded as a commitment to deliberate according to particular principles on practical questions. The question before the agent therefore belongs to the very class of questions on which his current conception of practical reasoning differs

---

[9] For this point, see Derek Parfit, *Reasons and Persons* (Oxford: Clarendon Press, 1984), 505 n. 8.
[10] For a similar interpretation of Gauthier, see Stephen L. Darwall, *Impartial Reason* (Ithaca, NY: Cornell Univ. Press, 1983), 195–8.

from straightforward maximization—questions, that is, about whether to abide by a previously adopted commitment. The agent's current conception of practical reasoning recommends that he answer such a question in accordance with a comparison between the consequences of making and abiding by his commitment, on the one hand, and the consequences of never having made it, on the other, each considered as a package deal. Reasoning in this manner, the agent will find that the advantages of being offered a co-operative agreement outweigh the disadvantages of fulfilling it; and so he will decide to abide by his commitment, and hence to retain Gauthier's conception of practical reasoning.

Thus, Gauthier's conception is stable in a way that straightforward maximization is not. If a straightforward maximizer applies his deliberative principle to a comparison between itself and Gauthier's principle, it will lead him to adopt Gauthier's instead; but if he then applies his new deliberative principle to the same comparison again, it will lead him to stick with Gauthier's. Indeed, the benefits that attracted him to Gauthier's principle will have depended on the fact that it wouldn't lead to its own abandonment, since its stability in this respect is what made him eligible as a partner in co-operative agreements.

The notion of deciding how to decide has now entered Gauthier's argument at two distinct points. A straightforward maximizer will replace his conception of practical reasoning, according to the argument, because an alternative conception is more conducive to his master-goal and is thus recommended by practical reasoning as he now conceives it. And the alternative conception of practical reasoning will better serve the agent's master-goal only because, once adopted, it will be retained at the recommendation of practical reasoning as he *then* conceives it.

2. Gauthier's Argument for Deciding How to Decide

At both points the argument depends on the assumption that how to conceive of practical reasoning is a question to be settled by practical reason. Yet evaluating conceptions of practical reasoning need not be a practical matter.

What if there is an objectively correct way to deliberate—one principle, or set of principles, whose application constitutes valid practical reasoning?[11] In that case, the way to deliberate will be the correct way to deliberate, and the correct way to deliberate will not be up to us. Hence evaluating conceptions of practical reasoning will not be a practical matter that depends

---

[11] Of course, there may be more than one specific procedure by which these principles can be applied. But multiple procedures, in this sense, will all count as one way of deliberating, according to the scheme of individuation that was adopted in n. 2, above.

on the pragmatic advantages and disadvantages of holding various conceptions; it will rather be a theoretical matter, which depends on which conception is right.

Now, if evaluating conceptions of practical reasoning is not a practical but a theoretical inquiry, which aims to get the relevant principles right, then it won't be an inquiry of the sort to which a conception of practical reasoning would apply. And if it is not an inquiry to which such a conception would apply, then no conception of practical reasoning will militate either for or against itself as the conclusion of that inquiry. A conception of practical reasoning cannot lay down principles that would lead to its own adoption or rejection if its adoption or rejection doesn't depend on practical reasoning.[12]

In short, conceptions of practical reasoning cannot be self-supporting or self-defeating unless evaluating such conceptions is an instance of practical reasoning. And why should we think of it that way?

Gauthier answers this question by contrasting two pictures of how conceptions of practical reasoning should be evaluated. He first considers a picture in which actions are subject to an independent criterion of success, and deliberative principles can therefore be evaluated by their tendency to yield actions that meet this criterion. As Gauthier points out, this picture portrays the practical sphere as analogous to the theoretical, in which beliefs are subject to the independent standard of truth, and principles of theoretical reasoning can be evaluated by their tendency to yield true beliefs.

What Gauthier might have added is that this picture portrays the evaluation of deliberative principles as a theoretical matter, since the objective criterion of success for actions entails a criterion of correctness for deliberation. In this picture, the correct way to deliberate is whichever way best tracks the criterion of success for actions, just as the correct way to theorize is whichever way best tracks the truth. The criterion of success for actions isn't up to us, in this picture; the tendency of deliberative principles to track that criterion isn't up to us; and so the way to deliberate isn't up to us, either. Hence evaluating conceptions of practical reasoning isn't an instance of practical reasoning.

Gauthier considers a specific version of this picture, in which the independent criterion of success for actions is conduciveness to the agent's master-goal. According to this criterion of success, of course, Gauthier's deliberative principle takes second place to straightforward maximization, since it often recommends goal-defeating actions, such as the fulfilment of co-operative agreements. Not unsurprisingly, then, Gauthier prefers a

---

[12] The point made in this paragraph is made by Parfit on pp. 19–23 of *Reasons and Persons*.

different picture of how the agent's master-goal bears on his conception of practical reasoning.

In Gauthier's picture, the agent's master-goal sets a standard of success for deliberative principles, not for actions, and it bears on actions only indirectly: the rationality of actions depends on their issuing from the principles that best promote the goal. Deliberative principles can promote the master-goal not only through the actions that they recommend but also through collateral effects such as creating opportunities for action—for example, by making the agent eligible as a partner in co-operative agreements. On this standard, Gauthier's conception of practical reasoning surpasses straightforward maximization.

This picture favours Gauthier's conception of practical reasoning precisely because it portrays the evaluation of such conceptions as a practical matter. In this picture, there is nothing about actions that deliberative principles attempt to track in their recommendations, and so there is nothing to make them objectively correct or incorrect. Conceptions of practical reasoning must therefore be evaluated, not by whether they get the principles of deliberation right, but rather by the pragmatic pros and cons of holding them.

What reason does Gauthier offer for favouring the latter picture? He says that he favours it because it doesn't lead us to choose a conception of rationality that's self-defeating, as straightforward maximization appears to be. '[I]t is surely mistaken', he says, 'to treat rational deliberation as self-defeating, if a non-self-defeating account is available.'[13]

But now Gauthier has argued in a circle. He is currently comparing, not just rival conceptions of practical reasoning, but rival pictures of how conceptions of practical reasoning should be evaluated. In one picture, conceptions of practical reasoning are evaluated by whether their deliberative principles track actions that meet the relevant criterion of success, which (Gauthier envisions) is conduciveness to the agent's master-goal; and this evaluation militates against Gauthier's conception. In the other picture, conceptions of practical reasoning are evaluated by whether holding them is conducive to the agent's master-goal, and this evaluation militates in favour of Gauthier.

The question is which picture to adopt. Gauthier's answer is that we should adopt the latter picture, since the former recommends a self-defeating conception of practical reasoning. But as we have seen, a conception of practical reasoning cannot be self-defeating or self-supporting unless

---

[13] 'Assure and Threaten', 702.

it is self-applicable—that is, unless its own evaluation is an inquiry of the sort to which the conception itself applies. And in the picture that Gauthier rejects, evaluating conceptions of practical reasoning is not a practical but a theoretical inquiry, which seeks to ascertain which principles of deliberation are correct. How can Gauthier reject this picture on the grounds that it favours a self-defeating conception of practical reasoning? The picture itself portrays conceptions of practical reasoning as incapable of defeating themselves, because they do not apply to their own evaluation. Only in the picture adopted by Gauthier do conceptions of practical reasoning apply to their own evaluation and thereby qualify as self-supporting or -defeating.

We have to join Gauthier in adopting this picture, then, before we can see it as saving us from a self-defeating conception of practical reasoning. Gauthier's reasons for adopting the picture are therefore visible only after we have already adopted it.

What's worse, Gauthier's picture severely limits the normative force that's available to conceptions of practical reasoning. Of course, any conception of practical reasoning will be normative in content, simply by virtue of applying terms like 'reason' and 'rational': any conception of practical reasoning will tell us how to deliberate and, by extension, what to do. But precisely because any conception will tell us how to deliberate, and hence what to do, we need to find a conception whose injunctions are authoritative or valid or genuinely binding.

One problem is that Gauthier's picture seems to rule out the possibility of our recognizing a conception as authoritative in this sense. If how to conceive of practical reasoning is itself a practical question, as Gauthier claims, then we shall have no conception of how to answer it until we have a conception of practical reasoning; and so we shall have no conception of how to answer the question until we have already answered it. We shall therefore find ourselves either unable to answer the question at all or forced to answer it arbitrarily. Having chosen a conception arbitrarily, we shall be equipped to reconsider our choice, of course, but only in an arbitrarily chosen manner. The results of such a procedure are unlikely to inspire confidence.[14]

---

[14] Christine Korsgaard suggests that Kant's purely formal conception of practical reason is a solution to this problem. Imagine that an agent is free to choose his conception of a reason for acting. The current problem is that, in order to avoid adopting a conception arbitrarily, the agent would seem to need a reason for adopting one conception rather than another; and yet he has as yet no conception—or only an arbitrarily chosen conception—of what would count as a reason for doing so. But perhaps the agent can adopt, as his conception of a reason for acting, the mere *form* of a reason for acting. Or rather, he *already has* this much of a conception, in so far as he is already committed to adopting something that will qualify as a conception of a reason. Since nothing that failed to respect the form of a reason would qualify as a conception thereof, the agent who sets out to choose his conception of a reason already has this much of a conception, and he therefore needs no reason for choosing it. He can

This methodological problem may be tolerable by itself. Inquiry has to start somewhere, usually with received opinions, and it often relies on these opinions even in the process of criticizing and revising them. The principle of straightforward maximization may simply be the received opinion with which inquiry into practical reasoning is obliged to begin.

Yet Gauthier's picture portrays more than a methodology for answering the question how to conceive of practical reasoning; it portrays the very nature of that question, as one to which no one answer is better than another except in so far as it is favoured by practical reasoning. The picture consequently undermines, not just the possibility of our recognizing a conception as authoritative, but the very possibility of a conception's being authoritative, in the first place. The only authority available to a conception of practical reasoning, in Gauthier's picture, lies in the fact that the conception is supported by itself or by another conception that cannot boast even that much authority.[15] Why should we feel bound by principles whose only claim on us is that they are recommended by themselves or by other principles that have even less to recommend them?

For these reasons, I am inclined to prefer the picture that Gauthier rejects, in which conceptions of practical reasoning are evaluable in relation to an independent criterion of success for actions. The philosophy of rational choice must therefore begin by finding the criterion of success for actions, in relation to which conceptions of rationality can be evaluated.

One might think that this task will draw us into reasoning just as circular as that involved in Gauthier's picture. A criterion of success for actions would seem to embody a normative judgement about how one ought to act. Finding a criterion of success for actions would therefore seem to be a practical inquiry about how to act, an inquiry that requires us to deliberate and hence to have deliberative principles already in hand. How, then, can we expect our criterion of success for actions to guide us in choosing deliberative principles?

3. A Theoretical Foundation for Deliberative Principles

The answer to this question is provided, I think, by the analogy between theoretical and practical reasoning—the analogy that Gauthier declines to apply.[16] In the case of theoretical reasoning, our criterion of success for

---

end up with this purely formal conception of a reason without any circularity or arbitrariness. So, at least, says Korsgaard's version of Kant. ('Morality as Freedom', in Y. Yovel (ed.), *Kant's Practical Philosophy Reconsidered* (Dordrecht: Kluwer, 1989), 23–48, at 30–1.)

[15] This is the point that Parfit makes on pp. 19–20 of *Reasons and Persons*.

[16] This analogy is also being pursued by Peter Railton, with somewhat different results. See Essay 2 in the present volume, plus: 'What the Non-Cognitivist Helps us to See the Naturalist Must Help us

beliefs doesn't embody a normative judgement on our part; rather, the criterion of success for beliefs is determined by the internal goal of beliefs themselves.

As Gauthier observes, it is in the very nature of beliefs to aim at being true.[17] Propositional attitudes that do not aim at the truth simply don't constitute beliefs, whereas attitudes that constitute beliefs do so partly in virtue of having that aim. Hence being true is simply what would be required for beliefs to succeed in their own terms. That beliefs must be true in order to succeed is a fact about them, given their goal-directed nature; it's not a normative judgement at which we arrive by practical reasoning. What is to count as success for belief is not for us to decide, because it's determined by an aim that's internal to belief itself.

Similarly, we can avoid circularity in our account of practical reasoning by finding an internal aim in relation to which actions can be seen as succeeding or failing in their own terms. If actions have a constitutive aim, then they will be subject to a criterion of success that's determined by their nature rather than our practical reasoning; and so that criterion will be available in advance of deliberation, as a basis for evaluating deliberative principles.

Some deliberative principles will then bear objective authority as norms of practical reasoning. There will be an objective fact as to what makes action successful as action, just as there is a fact as to what makes belief successful as belief. And in so far as deliberative principles tend to issue in action that succeeds *as* action, they will qualify as objectively correct ways to regulate action; just as speculative principles qualify as correct ways to regulate belief in so far as they tend to issue in true belief, which succeeds *as* belief. The normative authority of deliberative principles will thus rest in the nature of action as constitutively directed at a particular aim.

Now, there are two possible views on the relation of aims to actions. One view is that there is no single aim that's constitutive of action in general, as aiming to be true is constitutive of belief. Actions are utterly heterogeneous as to their goals, according to this view: what's constitutive of action is simply having some goal or other.

---

to Explain', in John Haldane and Crispin Wright (eds.), *Reality, Representation, and Projection* (Oxford: Univ. Press, 1994), 292–4; and 'In Search of Nonsubjective Reasons', in J. B. Schneewind (ed.), *Reason, Ethics, and Society: Themes from Kurt Baier, with his Responses* (Chicago: Open Court, 1996), 117–43.

[17] 'Assure and Threaten', 699. Actually, what Gauthier says is that '[t]o believe is to believe true'. But this remark fails to pick out a distinctive feature of belief, since to desire is to desire true, to intend is to intend true, and so on, for all propositional attitudes. I assume, however, that Gauthier means to pick out the distinctive relation that belief bears to the truth, which is that to believe is to believe true *with the aim of thereby getting the truth right*. On this point, see my 'The Guise of the Good', *Noûs*, 26 (1992), 3–26, at 12–13; and 'The Possibility of Practical Reason', *Ethics*, 106 (1996), 694–726, n. 23.

This view yields a thoroughgoing instrumentalism about practical reason —an instrumentalism far more thorough, in fact, than that expressed in the norm of maximizing utility or value. For if the only goal internal to an action is the peculiar goal at which it is expressly directed by its agent, then each action will have to be judged a success or failure solely on the basis of its conduciveness to its peculiar goal. And very few actions are expressly directed by their agents at maximizing some overall measure of value. Most actions are directed at less ambitious aims, which would be the only aims in relation to which they could be said to succeed or fail in their own terms. A conception of practical reasoning would therefore have to be evaluated by its tendency to recommend actions that succeeded in promoting whatever they were severally intended to promote.

The alternative view is that there is a common goal that's constitutive of action—something at which behaviour must aim in order to qualify as an action, just as a propositional attitude must aim at being true in order to qualify as a belief. According to a tradition that stretches from Aristotle to Davidson, action has a constitutive aim of this sort—namely, the good.[18] Whatever an action aims at, according to this tradition, it aims at *sub specie boni*: in the guise of a good. In aiming at different things, actions are still aiming at things under the same description—as good—and so they share a constitutive aim.

This tradition might seem to offer a foundation for the maximizing conception of practical reasoning. If every action aims at something conceived as good, then conduciveness to the good would appear to be an internal criterion of success for actions—the criterion that actions must meet in order to succeed in their own terms. Since the most successful actions, by this criterion, are the ones that are most conducive to the good, the way to reach the truth about the success of actions will be to apply the method of maximization.

I believe that there are several errors in this foundational argument for the maximizing conception of practical reasoning. To begin with, aiming at things conceived individually as goods does not necessarily entail aiming to maximize a unified measure of goodness, since it doesn't necessarily entail regarding one's various ends as good in commensurable ways. More importantly, however, I doubt whether actions necessarily aim at things in the guise of goods.[19]

---

[18] See e.g. Davidson, 'How is Weakness of the Will Possible?', in *Essays on Actions and Events* (Oxford: Clarendon Press, 1980), 21–42, at 22: '[I]n so far as a person acts intentionally he acts, as Aquinas puts it, in the light of some imagined good.'

[19] This doubt is the theme of my paper 'The Guise of the Good'.

Yet the thesis that actions constitutively aim at the good is not the most plausible implementation of the view that they share a constitutive aim. This thesis assigns a constitutive aim to actions by claiming that they converge in their aims, in the sense that their various ends-in-view are all sought as means to, or components of, a single ulterior end. But the claim that actions converge in their aims is not necessary to the view that they share a constitutive aim.

The relation between the shared, constitutive aim of actions and their differing ends-in-view need not be that they aim to attain the former by attaining the latter; it may instead be that they aim to attain the former in the course of pursuing the latter. The constitutive aim of action, in other words, may be a goal with respect to the manner in which other goals are pursued, rather than a composite or expected consequence of those other goals.

Consider, for example, the goal of efficiency. You cannot pursue efficiency by itself, in a vacuum: you must have other goals in the pursuit of which you seek to be efficient. But then you can seek to be efficient at everything you do in the pursuit of those other goals. And in that case, efficiency is a goal of all your actions, not because you hope to attain it by attaining the various goals peculiar to those actions, but rather because you hope to attain it in the course of pursuing them.

I'm not claiming that efficiency is the constitutive goal of action: Lord, no. I'm just pointing out that actions can share a common aim even though their ends-in-view do not in any sense converge. Your actions can be aimed in as many different directions as you like and yet share the common aim of efficiency. My view is that there is a goal that is similar to efficiency in just this structural respect and that is shared by all your actions as such.

Identifying the relevant aim is not on my agenda for the present essay.[20] My reason for introducing the possibility of such an aim is simply to fill out the methodological picture that I am opposing to Gauthier's. In Gauthier's picture, how to decide between actions is a practical matter, which we decide by weighing the practical advantages and disadvantages of various deliberative principles. In my picture, the principles for deciding between actions are not for us to decide, because they are determined for us by the point of action itself.

Gauthier's picture suggests that we can hope for a pure theory of practical reasoning. Nothing underwrites our principles of practical reasoning,

---

[20] I defend the view that action has a constitutive aim in 'What Happens When Someone Acts?', *Mind*, 101 (1992), 461–81. I offer one account of this aim in *Practical Reflection* (Princeton: Univ. Press, 1989); and 'The Story of Rational Action', *Philosophical Topics*, 21 (1993), 229–53. I offer a different (though, I believe, compatible) account in 'The Possibility of Practical Reason'.

in his picture, other than the principles themselves. But my picture suggests that the philosophy of practical reasoning cannot be purified, in particular, of considerations from the philosophy of action. The correct principles of practical reasoning are determined by the constitutive aim of action—the thing at which behaviour must aim in order to qualify as action, in the way that propositional attitudes must aim at the truth in order to qualify as belief. What makes an action rational, then, must depend on what makes something an action, to begin with. The philosophy of action must provide a foundation for the philosophy of practical reasoning.

Of course, the order of logical dependence need not dictate the order of discovery. Rival conceptions of practical reasoning can be taken as proposals for what the underlying aim of action might be. In any deliberative principle, we can look for the implicit criterion of success that it tends to track, and we can ask whether satisfaction of that criterion might be the aim in virtue of which behaviour qualifies as action.

Indeed, I think that Gauthier's critique of straightforward maximization can be reformulated along these very lines. What the maximizer's approach to prisoner's dilemmas reveals is, not that his conception of practical reasoning is disadvantageous, but rather that the criterion of success that it tracks in actions—namely, maximizing value for the agent—doesn't express a shared aim in which their status as actions could possibly consist.

4. Gauthier's Critique Reformulated

In order to reformulate Gauthier's critique of maximization along these lines, I must return to our initial story, in which you and I expect to be offered incentives to testify against one another about a jointly committed crime. Gauthier's complaint against maximization is that it prevents us from reaching a mutually beneficial agreement to keep silent, since each of us would expect the other, as a maximizer, to violate such an agreement. Let me begin by re-examining this complaint.

The costs of being a maximizer are, in fact, less than obvious. Some philosophers have pointed out, for example, that the costs identified by Gauthier are primarily due, not to one's being a maximizer, but to one's being perceived as a maximizer; and they have argued against Gauthier's assumption that others can tell what one's conception of practical reasoning is.[21] But I want to grant Gauthier's assumption of translucency, as he calls it.[22] What is of greater interest for my purposes is that even translucent

---

[21] See e.g. Geoffrey Sayre-McCord, 'Deception and Reasons to be Moral', in Peter Vallentyne (ed.), *Contractarianism and Rational Choice: Essays on David Gauthier's Morals by Agreement* (Cambridge: Univ. Press, 1991), 181–95.   [22] *Morals By Agreement*, 174.

maximizers will not be excluded from co-operative agreements so long as they are capable of making commitments that are truly effective.

Suppose that when each of us says 'I'm willing to keep silent if you are', what he thereby makes translucent to the other agent is a disposition that will withstand any subsequent calculations—an irrevocable disposition to keep silent, under the specified conditions. In that case, forming and expressing a willingness to keep silent will be tantamount to making an effective commitment, which one's practical reasoning cannot overturn.[23] And the maximizing conception of practical reasoning will direct us to exchange such commitments, each conditional upon the other, since a conditional commitment will irrevocably dispose the issuer to keep silent only if the other agent has issued a reciprocal commitment, whose condition it will satisfy, so that the other will be irrevocably disposed to keep silent as well. Since each commitment will irrevocably lead to silence upon being reciprocated, silence will reign, and the harms of mutual betrayal will be avoided.

Rational maximizers seem to be capable of reaching co-operative agreements, then, provided that they can commit themselves effectively. So where are the costs of being a maximizer? And where is the need for a conception of practical reasoning that favours fulfilling co-operative agreements?

How, in fact, can there ever be a need for such a conception? The only commitment that either of us has an interest in making is one that is not only conditional on receipt of an effective commitment from the other but also sufficient to satisfy the condition on that reciprocal commitment, so that the other's silence will be ensured. And since each commitment will be conditional upon the efficacy of the other, each will have to be effective in order to satisfy the other's condition. Hence neither of us has any interest in making a commitment unless it is effective.[24]

So why do we need a conception of practical reasoning that will direct us to fulfil our commitments? The only commitments that we have any interest in making are effective commitments, sufficient to ensure their own fulfilment. A conception of practical reasoning that enjoined us to fulfil these commitments would thereby enjoin what is already guaranteed by the very existence of the commitments themselves. What would be the point?[25]

---

[23] Here I seem to imply that the disposition to keep silent is first formed and then expressed. I am inclined to believe, instead, that the disposition in question is formed precisely by being expressed. (See my 'How to Share an Intention', *Philosophy and Phenomenological Research*, 57 (1997), 29–50.)

[24] Here, as elsewhere, the argument relies on Gauthier's assumption of translucency.

[25] Versions of this point are considered by Derek Parfit, *Reasons and Persons*, 35–7; Holly Smith, 'Deriving Morality from Rationality', in Vallentyne (ed.), *Contractarianism and Rational Choice*, 229–53, n. 13; and Richmond Campbell, 'Gauthier's Theory of Morals by Agreement', *Philosophical Quarterly*, 38 (1988), 243–64, at 254, and 'Moral Justification and Freedom', *Journal of Philosophy*, 85 (1988), 192–213.

One might respond, on Gauthier's behalf, that commitments of such efficacy are beyond the capacity of human agents. But surely human agents are
capable of devising mechanisms for predetermining their future behaviour;
and in so far as they aren't, this lack of ingenuity cannot be held against the
maximizing conception of practical reasoning. A more plausible objection
is that human agents do not ordinarily commit themselves by the brute
predetermination of their behaviour. The exchange of such mechanistic
commitments wouldn't add up to a co-operative agreement in any ordinary
sense of the phrase.

Each of these commitments would be effective, we said, in the sense that
it would govern the agent's behaviour irrespective of his subsequent deliberations about whether to fulfil it. Its efficacy would therefore consist in the
fact that it left the agent no choice on that score. Yet if the agent would
have no choice whether to fulfil his commitment, then his fulfilling it
wouldn't qualify as an autonomous action on his part. And co-operative
agreements are ordinarily understood as leading, not just to co-ordinated
behaviour, but to co-operative action—that is, behaviour whose co-
ordination is wittingly and willingly sustained by the agents involved. The
envisioned commitments wouldn't enable rational maximizers to arrive
at anything that would deserve to be called co-operative agreements in
this sense.

Note that Gauthier's objection to maximizing rationality has now quietly
been transformed from the practical to the theoretical mode. The objection
is no longer that someone who holds the maximizing conception thereby
sacrifices the benefits of co-operative agreements. As we have seen, a
rational maximizer can obtain those benefits so long as he can determine
his future behaviour by means of an effective commitment. The objection
is now that although an effective commitment can help to produce the
benefits of a co-operative agreement, it can't help to constitute an agreement that would yield genuine co-operative action.

What's wrong with the maximizing conception, then, is that, in so far as
it can account for co-operation, it gets the nature of co-operative action
wrong. And getting the nature of co-operative action wrong is not a practical but a theoretical failing—in particular, a failing in the philosophy
of action.

Although Gauthier doesn't charge the maximizing conception with a theoretical flaw of this kind, it is the very flaw that his conception of practical
reasoning is suited to remedy. The need that's filled by a conception
favouring the fulfilment of co-operative agreements is the need to explain

how we can rationally exchange commitments that will leave us autonomous in carrying them out.[26]

The commitments envisioned thus far threaten the agent's autonomy because their efficacy depends on their power to withstand the agent's own deliberations about whether to fulfil them; and their efficacy depends on this power because the agent is assumed to be a maximizer, whose deliberations will direct him to violate his commitments. But suppose that the agent held Gauthier's alternative conception of rationality, which posits reasons for fulfilling mutually beneficial agreements. Then he could make commitments whose efficacy would consist precisely in the fact that he would subsequently be determined to fulfil them by his appreciation of reasons for doing so. And the agent's being determined to act by an appreciation of reasons wouldn't undermine his autonomy, since being determined by reasons is just what constitutes autonomy, according to compatibilism.[27] Rationally effective commitments wouldn't have to withstand the agent's subsequent deliberations about whether to fulfil them, thus leaving him no choice; rather, they would take effect through the agent's deliberations and consequently through his choice.

In sum, a theory like Gauthier's isn't needed to provide rational agents with the benefits of co-operation; it's needed to explain how rational agents can co-operate freely. The problem that Gauthier's theory solves, but the orthodox theory doesn't, is not the practical problem of how to achieve co-operation but the theoretical problem of how co-operating agents can be autonomous. This problem, I now suggest, is just an instance of a larger problem in characterizing the autonomy that rational agents enjoy over their future actions. The larger problem has nothing essentially to do with prisoner's dilemmas or co-operation or, for that matter, morality in general. It simply has to do with our nature as agents who exercise the power of choice over future actions.[28]

Our autonomy over future actions requires, on the one hand, that we have the power of making future-directed decisions that are effective, so that we can determine today what will get done by us tomorrow. On the other hand, our future-directed decisions must not simply cause future movements of our bodies. If they did, our later selves would lack autonomy

---

[26] Note the similarity to Rousseau's formulation of 'the fundamental problem' to be solved by the social contract: 'How to find a form of association which will defend the person and goods of each member with the collective force of all, and under which each individual, while uniting himself with the others, obeys no one but himself, and remains as free as before' (*The Social Contract*, trans. Maurice Cranston (Harmondsworth: Penguin, 1968), I. vi, p. 60).

[27] This point is made by Holly Smith, 'Deriving Morality from Rationality', n. 13.

[28] For a related discussion of this problem, see Elizabeth Anderson, 'Reasons, Attitudes, and Values: Replies to Sturgeon and Piper', *Ethics*, 106 (1996), 538–54, at 542.

of their own, since they would find their limbs being moved by the decisions of earlier selves, as if through remote volitional control. We must
exercise agential control over our own future behaviour, but in a way that
doesn't impair our own future agential control.

The only way to control our future behaviour without losing future
control, I believe, is by making decisions that our future selves will be
determined to execute of their own volition; and the only way to determine
our future selves to do something of their own volition is by giving them
reason to do it.[29] Hence future-directed intentions or commitments must
be capable of providing reasons to our future selves. Unless we can commit
ourselves today in a way that will generate reasons for us to act tomorrow,
we shall have to regard our day-older selves either as beyond the control of
today's decisions or as passive instruments of them.

Yet the maximizing conception of rationality does not guarantee, or even
make probable, that decisions made today will provide reasons tomorrow.
According to that conception, the reasons available to our day-older selves
will be generated by our day-older interests and day-older circumstances,
which may or may not militate in favour of carrying out decisions made
today. The maximizing conception of rationality therefore fails to account
for the diachronic autonomy that we exercise in our future-directed decisions.

One might wonder whether there is really a problem here. If an agent
forms an intention to do something in the future, and if he doesn't change
his mind, then the intention will remain in place and eventually come into

[29] This claim does not commit me to sharing Gauthier's view on the so-called toxin puzzle. In the
toxin puzzle, an agent is offered a large reward merely for forming a future-directed intention to do
something mildly harmful to himself, such as drinking a toxin. The puzzle was originally offered by
Gregory Kavka as a *reductio ad absurdum* of Gauthier's theory, which implies that after the agent has
collected the reward for intending to drink the toxin, he should follow through on his intention, even
though he has something to lose by doing so and nothing more to gain (see Kavka, 'The Toxin Puzzle',
Analysis, 43 (1983), 33–6). Gauthier has simply bitten the bullet in this case, arguing that the agent
should indeed drink the toxin ('Assure and Threaten', 707–9).

Yet I needn't endorse this course of action in order to hold that future-directed intentions provide
reasons for following through. For one thing, my view may not require that the reasons provided by
future-directed intentions outweigh all countervailing reasons; perhaps they should be required only to
carry some rational weight. On this version of the view, the agent in the toxin puzzle may form an
intention to drink the toxin, and thereby give his future self some reason to drink it, without giving him
sufficient reason.

Of course, an intention that doesn't provide sufficient reason for following through will be inefficacious, according to my view. The question therefore arises whether the reward is being offered only for
an efficacious intention, or whether an inefficacious intention would do. A reasonable answer might be
that an inefficacious intention wouldn't be much of an intention and, in fact, might not be an intention
at all. In that case, an agent's intending to drink the toxin would require giving his future self sufficient
reason for drinking it. Even so, I needn't conclude that a rational agent will find himself with sufficient
reason for drinking the toxin; I can conclude instead that a rational agent will be unable to muster an
intention to drink the toxin, precisely because he'll be unable to give his future self sufficient reason for
drinking it. (This treatment of the toxin puzzle corresponds to Dan Farrell's in 'Intention, Reason, and
Action', *American Philosophical Quarterly*, 26 (1989), 283–95.)

the hands of his future self. When the intention subsequently produces an action, the agent's future self will be acting of his own volition, since the intention producing the action will now be his.

Yet whether an agent acts of his own volition, when governed by an intention remaining from the past, depends on the manner in which it remains and governs. If the intention is simply a lit fuse leading to action by some self-sustaining causal mechanism that's insensitive or resistant to the agent's ongoing deliberations, then it is not really a volition of his current self; it's just a slow-acting volition from his past. In order for the volition to become his own, the agent must buy into—or, at least, not be shut out of—its governance over his behaviour.

Unfortunately, the practical reasoning of a straightforward maximizer will direct him to discard an intention whenever he stands to increase his expected benefits by doing so. An intention that doesn't continue to serve his interests can remain to govern his behaviour only by avoiding or resisting interference from his practical reasoning; and such an intention won't qualify as his own volition. The only intention whose fulfilment will be attributable to the maximizer himself, and not to some mechanism within him, is an intention whose fulfilment serves his interests.

A capacity for such fair-weather intentions simply isn't enough, in my opinion. Of course, we could circumvent the practical drawbacks of this capacity by adopting an axiology that guaranteed compatibility between the interests of our present and future selves.[30] In that case, commitments undertaken rationally would always be seconded by the rational deliberations of later selves, whose interests would necessarily harmonize with those which made the commitments rational to undertake. But this axiology wouldn't help to explain our actual capacity for future-directed commitments; it would merely wish away the real conflicts of interest in which the true nature of that capacity is revealed.

There are cases in which we have an interest in committing ourselves to future courses of action whose relation to our future interests is unknown, or even known to be adverse.[31] And experience tells us that we can often make rationally effective commitments in these cases. We can form resolutions that a future self will find rationally binding, whether or not they are seconded by his interests at the time.

Thus, our future-directed autonomy is not just a capacity to choose now what our future selves will in any case find reason for choosing then; nor is it a capacity to bind them to something else against their better judgement.

---

[30] This point was made in discussion at the St Andrews Conference by Joseph Raz and Michael Smith.

[31] Potential prisoner's dilemmas are not the only such cases. For additional examples, see Edward F. McClennan, *Rationality and Dynamic Choice: Foundational Explorations* (Cambridge: Univ. Press, 1990).

It's a capacity to make choices that our future selves will buy into but wouldn't otherwise have made. And the straightforwardly maximizing conception of rationality cannot accommodate rational efficacy of this sort.

To be sure, the maximizing conception of rationality doesn't rule out the possibility of giving our future selves reason to act. An agent may find or put in place arrangements whereby the interests that he will have tomorrow are somehow altered by the commitments he makes today. He can take out bets on his own constancy, for example, or he can train himself to feel costly pangs of self-reproach whenever he violates a past commitment. Making a commitment will then give his future self reason to follow through.

But these devices for conveying reasons to one's future selves would be external to rational agency, as the maximizing conception portrays it. One could be a fully-fledged and perfectly rational agent without having any of these devices in place, and hence without having autonomous control over one's future behaviour. What's more, employing these devices would entail treating one's future selves as one treats separate people, since it would entail influencing their behaviour indirectly, by modifying their incentives. If I offer you a large enough reward for following my directions, or threaten a large enough penalty for disregarding them, I put myself in a position to give you directions that will take effect without overriding your autonomy, but I do not thereby put myself in a position to decide what you are going to do. The ability to influence you by manipulating your expected pay-offs does not give me agential control over your behaviour. Yet the control I would enjoy over my own future behaviour via the devices under consideration would be no different.

Finally, some of these devices—indeed, the ones best able to resist being characterized as external manipulation—would depend on thoughts or feelings that the maximizing conception itself must regard as baseless. Training oneself to feel bad about violating commitments might enable one to undertake commitments that give one's future selves reasons to act; but it would entail training oneself to feel bad about something that one has no reason to feel bad about, according to the maximizing conception, since that conception treats violating commitments as a perfectly rational thing to do.

For all of these reasons, the devices at the disposal of the maximizing conception of rationality provide at most a simulation of diachronic autonomy. They enable an agent to induce his future selves to act, but not in a way that amounts to deciding on future actions.

I believe that in failing to accommodate this form of autonomy, the maximizing conception misrepresents what action is. The criterion of success that maximizing principles are designed to track doesn't express a constitutive aim for action, since behaviour oriented toward satisfying that criterion wouldn't amount to action, as we know it.

If an action were the sort of thing whose success or failure could be judged solely by utility-maximizing considerations, then it wouldn't be the sort of thing that we could decide on today in a way that would necessarily give us reason to perform it tomorrow, and so it wouldn't be behaviour over which rational agents had diachronic autonomy. But action *is* that sort of thing—it *is* behaviour over which rational agents have diachronic autonomy—and so it can't be the sort of thing whose success or failure can be judged solely by utility-maximizing considerations.

My view is that the constitutive aim of action—the aim in virtue of which behaviour becomes action, and against which it can be judged a success or failure as action—is autonomy itself.[32] How behaviour can aim at autonomy, and why it thereby qualifies as action, are questions beyond the scope of this paper.[33] Here I can merely point out that if autonomy is the constitutive goal of action, and hence the internal criterion of success for action, then reasons for acting will be considerations relevant to autonomy, rather than considerations relevant to utility or the good. And we can at least hope that reasons of this kind will be generated by future-directed decisions. An analysis of action as behaviour aimed at autonomy may therefore explain how future-directed decisions can govern future behaviour rationally; and so it may explain how the nature of action makes diachronic autonomy possible.

The notion of autonomy as the constitutive goal of action isn't essential to my present argument, however. Maybe other proposals for the constitutive goal of action would explain how considerations relevant to that goal forge an autonomy-preserving link between past decisions and future actions. My present argument invokes autonomy—specifically, diachronic autonomy—simply as a feature of action that cannot be explained by the orthodox conception of practical reason, because it gives no rational weight, and hence no autonomy-preserving influence, to past decisions.

There are of course those whose normative intuitions oppose giving rational weight to past decisions: they think that abiding by a commitment for its own sake is foolish. Then there are those whose normative intuitions demand rational weight for past decisions: they think that abandoning a commitment is fickle. But I am joining neither of these camps, since I cannot see how to settle the issue on normative grounds. What settles the issue, in my mind,

---

[32] Thanks to Christine Korsgaard for daring me to confess this view, in the discussion at St Andrews.
[33] But see my 'The Possibility of Practical Reason', 719 ff.

is not an intuition to the effect that we ought or ought not to give weight to past commitments. What settles the issue for me is that simply being rational agents enables us to exercise autonomy over our futures without impairing our future autonomy—something that we couldn't do unless past commitments had rational weight.

Gauthier's critique of straightforward maximization has now been removed from its foundation in practical reasoning and resettled on a new foundation in the philosophy of action. I believe that the philosophy of action can provide a foundation, not just for criticizing inadequate conceptions of practical reasoning, but also for constructing an adequate conception. What it will thereby provide, of course, is not a foundation for deciding how to decide. How to decide is something that we will discover, by discovering what it is to act.[34]

APPENDIX

Co-operative Agreements

Why do I formulate each commitment as making the agent's action conditional on the other agent's commitment rather than on the other agent's action? Consider.

A condition that an agent places on his action won't be enforceable unless he can test for its satisfaction before he has to act. Of course, Alphonse can refuse to act unless Gaston acts first; but then Gaston mustn't do likewise, or action will never get started. And Gaston cannot refuse to act unless Alphonse acts *afterwards*, since Gaston can't test for the satisfaction of this condition before he has to act. At best, Gaston can refuse to act unless something is present that will subsequently guarantee action from Alphonse. A transparently effective commitment on the part of Alphonse provides such an assurance.

Now, Alphonse shouldn't just commit himself to act on the condition that Gaston acts first. For suppose that Gaston would act first anyway, whether or not Alphonse was committed to reciprocate. In that case, Alphonse would unnecessarily have encumbered himself in advance with the costs of reciprocating, since he didn't have to do so in order to gain the benefits of Gaston's action. Alphonse should therefore commit himself to act on the condition that his being so committed is necessary to elicit action from Gaston.

But how can Alphonse test whether this condition is satisfied? If Gaston is to act first, what will make it the case that Alphonse's commitment was necessary to elicit his action? And how will Alphonse tell whether it was the case? The only way for

[34] I received valuable comments on this essay from Elizabeth Anderson, Jim Joyce, John Broome, and Stephen Darwall. It also had the benefit of an excellent commentary by Piers Rawling at the St Andrews conference, as well as comments from participants, including Christine Korsgaard, Peter Railton, Joseph Raz, Michael Smith, and the editors of this volume.

it to be the case that Alphonse's commitment was necessary, and for Alphonse to tell that it was, will be for Gaston to have previously framed a transparent commitment making his action (bi)conditional on Alphonse's commitment. If Alphonse wants to lay down an enforceable condition, then, he should commit himself to act on the condition that Gaston frame a commitment that's conditional on his, Alphonse's, being so committed.

Of course, if Gaston is to fulfil this condition, by framing a commitment, he will want to avoid thereby encumbering himself with the costs of acting unless his doing so is necessary in order to elicit action from Alphonse. So he will want to commit himself to act on the condition that Alphonse's commitment is conditional on his, Gaston's, being so committed. The agents will thus issue mirror-image commitments, each conditional upon the other.

Yet neither agent needs to spell out his commitment at such length. Each wants his commitment to be conditional on its being required to satisfy the condition on a commitment framed by other. And this condition can be imposed by a commitment to act simply on the condition that the other agent frame a similar commitment, since a similar commitment from the other agent will be one whose condition this commitment is required to satisfy.

A further problem arises, however, as to whether this commitment is sufficiently determinate in content. When Alphonse says 'I'll act if you frame a similar commitment', what he is undertaking depends on what would count as a similar commitment from Gaston; and yet what would count as a similar commitment depends on what exactly Alphonse is undertaking. Alphonse's commitment is thus self-referential in a way that leaves its content ungrounded.[a]

Some philosophers have proposed a syntactic solution to this problem.[b] According to this solution, Alphonse's commitment is conditional on Gaston's framing a commitment that is syntactically similar—that is, framed in the same words. But this solution is clearly unsatisfactory, since it interprets Alphonse's commitment as requiring him to co-operate so long as Gaston says 'I'll act if you undertake a similar commitment', even if Gaston is speaking an idiolect in which 'act' means 'refrain' or 'similar' means 'different'.

I think that the solution to the problem of ungroundedness, in this instance, is to recognize that a similar commitment can be defined as a commitment with the same determinate *or potentially indeterminate* content. Suppose that Alphonse frames

---

[a] Versions of this problem—or of a problem similar to it—are discussed by Holly Smith, 'Deriving Morality from Rationality', 240–2, esp. n. 18; Peter Danielson, 'Closing the Compliance Dilemma: How it's Rational to be Moral in a Lamarckian World', in Vallentyne (ed.), *Contractarianism and Rational Choice*, 307–15; and Richmond Campbell, 'Gauthier's Theory of Morals by Agreement', 250–1. Some of these authors formulate the relevant commitments as making each agent's action conditional on the other's action. For them, the problem is how Alphonse tells whether he should act, given that he has made his action conditional on Gaston's, which is in turn conditional on his, Alphonse's. This problem disappears if the agents make their actions conditional on one another's commitments. But the problem of each action's being conditional on the other action is then replaced by the problem of each commitment's being dependent for its content on the other's content.

[b] See Danielson, loc. cit., and J. V. Howard, 'Co-operation in the Prisoner's Dilemma', *Theory and Decision*, 24 (1988), 203–13.

the conditional commitment to act if and only if Gaston issues a particular commitment; but that he risks failing to specify the requisite commitment because he attempts to specify it as similar in content to his own. And suppose that Gaston frames the conditional commitment to act if and only if Alphonse issues a particular commitment; but that he risks failing to specify the requisite commitment because he attempts to specify it as similar in content to his own. In that case, Alphonse and Gaston have issued commitments that really are similar, precisely because they share the same potential indeterminacies of content in addition to the determinate aspects of content that they share. The upshot is that the risk of indeterminacy in their commitments has been avoided, after all, since it is perfectly determinate whether either person's commitment has the same potential indeterminacies as the other's.

2

On the Hypothetical and Non-Hypothetical in Reasoning about Belief and Action

PETER RAILTON

I am sure that I do not understand the idea of a reason for acting, and I wonder whether anyone else does either.

Philippa Foot

Perhaps it shouldn't be surprising when a central notion of common sense proves elusive on reflection—that's what makes the philosophical world go round. And some aspects of practical rationality seem obvious enough: rational agents form intentions, adjust means and ends, and so on. Yet even very elementary questions can excite not only controversy between conflicting, entrenched positions, but expert bafflement.

An indirect approach suggests itself: it might help us to understand reasons for action if we started with reasons for belief. First, action involves belief. Second, one of the most crucial and problematic notions in practical reason—the notion of *non-hypothetical* reasons or requirements (reasons or requirements not dependent upon contingent ends of the agent)—appears to be well domesticated within the literature on theoretical reasons.[1] On the usual view of things, two agents in the same epistemic situation (same evidence, same background beliefs) would have the same reasons for believing any given proposition, regardless of possible differences in their personal goals.[2]

I would like to dedicate this essay to the memory of Jean Hampton, who taught us much about practical rationality.

[1] This will function herein as something like a stipulation about the meaning of 'non-hypothetical'. Thus, reasons that depend upon ends *necessary* for agents as such would count as non-hypothetical for present purposes. One might distinguish *personal-goal* non-hypotheticalness (absence of dependence upon contingently held *ends* of the agent) from *personal-belief* non-hypotheticalness (absence of dependence upon contingently held *beliefs* of the agent). What I refer to in the text as 'well domesticated within the literature on theoretical reasons' is the idea that epistemic reasons are *personal-goal* non-hypothetical.

[2] I write 'personal goals' because there is a school within contemporary epistemology according to which theoretical reason is *end-oriented*. But the ends in question typically are assumed to belong to a special class of *epistemic* ends which are subject to at most limited variation across rational individuals.

Can the 'usual view of things' in the theoretical realm be given a principled basis? If so, can a similarly non-hypothetical basis be found in the practical realm? In what follows, we will be developing a sequence of arguments which purport to show just this. These arguments turn on considerations concerning belief and action of a kind David Velleman has called *constitutive*.[3] By way of conclusion, we will ask what the limitations of such arguments might be.

1. Reasoning about Belief

Let us begin with Gary, a student in our introductory course on the Theory of Knowledge one autumn term. He's confronting epistemology as a discipline for the first time, and he's been staring with silent but disarming intentness from the back of the room for several weeks. Now he's ready to speak: 'These philosophers we've been reading seem to agree that there are certain standards of belief, standards we should follow even when they lead us to conclusions we don't like. They spend all their time disagreeing about exactly what these standards are, but they just seem to assume that we'll want to follow them. Suppose I don't? What can they say to me?'

One can imagine our initial response: 'Well, you understand why you should eat your vegetables? You may not care about these epistemic standards as such, but you do care a lot about other things. And you're more likely to get what you want if you have warranted beliefs. Following epistemic norms won't guarantee reliability, but there isn't any better alternative short of magic or luck.'

Notice, though, that this line of response is *non-epistemic* and *hypothetical*. It advertises the existence of benefits accruing to an agent who follows epistemic norms, but the values or goals in question are not distinctively epistemic, nor do we assume that they carry distinctive epistemic presuppositions. To be sure, this hypothetical justification is, or purports to be, quite *robust*. Virtually any goal Gary might have would be well served by his following epistemic norms. Indeed, we might at this point refer Gary to the Dutch Book argument, to show that he is at risk of being a sure loser if he does not conform his degrees of belief to certain probabilistic principles.

Gary has obviously been preparing his case. He counters by asking the class to imagine an individual dying of an incurable disease, to whom little

---

[3] See David Velleman, 'The Guise of the Good', *Noûs*, 26 (1992), 3–26 and 'The Possibility of Practical Reason', *Ethics*, 106 (1996), 694–726. I am much indebted to Velleman's discussions and to his comments on earlier papers, though I do not mean to suggest that he would agree with my use of the notion. See also his contribution to the present volume.

or nothing matters besides peace of mind. Belief in the Hereafter would comfort him mightily and would come to him spontaneously if he could just relax his epistemic scruples. What makes us think that the balance of non-epistemic considerations will always favour keeping those scruples? Gary pushes his question: he wants to know whether there are any considerations that require or favour following epistemic standards that don't depend at all on our personal goals.

We can, of course, point out that although someone might find the thought of an afterlife reassuring, reassurance is not evidence and so does not yield *epistemic reasons for belief* in the Hereafter, only *practical reasons for being a believer-in* the Hereafter. Epistemic evaluation, then, appears to be quite untouched by Gary's death-bed example.

Gary, however, finds this serene lack of regard for whether agents are comforted or tormented by their beliefs off-putting. Moreover, he cannot see how appealing to 'epistemic reasons' could provide any sort of answer to his initial question. Isn't it circular to invoke epistemic reasons on behalf of epistemology? The fact that these epistemic reasons are themselves non-hypothetical is beside the point. After all, there are lots of norms which lay down standards that pay no attention to the agent's particular goals.

Gary asks us to consider 'anti-epistemology', which tells us to reduce our belief in proportion as evidence increases. This norm is just as non-hypothetical as orthodox epistemology, since it prescribes degrees of belief without making any allowance for the agent's personal goals. Why should we submit ourselves to the old-fashioned rigours of epistemology rather than take on the exciting new challenges of anti-epistemology?

It plainly will not do for us to say to him that epistemic norms recommend non-hypothetically against this, since anti-epistemic norms speak non-hypothetically for it. Of course, it is unlikely that Gary or anyone else would really be prepared to abide by anti-epistemic norms. Only a very singular set of personal goals and circumstances could make anti-epistemic thinking much of a boon. But we can see that this again affords no more than a very robust hypothetical and practical justification.

After all, we reflect, Gary might find himself in some pretty unusual circumstances. Perhaps it is he who lies on the death-bed, yearning for peace of mind. Or perhaps a powerful, mind-reading anti-epistemic demon is prepared to torment him mercilessly unless his beliefs fly in the face of evidence. We consider responding, 'Look. Belief isn't voluntary. You can't just decide what to believe.' But this threatens to show too much. There won't be much left of normative epistemology unless we recognize some forms of control over what we come to believe. However, there is something that might help explain the oft-repeated phrase that belief isn't voluntary, and that might also help with Gary.

Consider a form of 'Moore's paradox'—the extreme oddness of:

(1) h is true, but I don't believe it.

According to anti-epistemology, the more one takes the evidence to favour h, the weaker should be one's belief that h. In the limit, then, we find the anti-epistemologist saying:

(2) I recognize that the evidence for h has become conclusive, so I don't believe that h in the least.

But (2) seems (almost?) as odd as (1). Maybe anti-epistemology isn't a real alternative after all.

What makes (1)—and perhaps by extension (2) as well—so odd? Various explanations have been proposed. One might start by noting that belief is a propositional attitude partly characterized by its representation of its object as true. 'Belief is believing true', the saying goes.

But this is too quick. For even the propositional attitude of 'pretending that h' amounts to 'pretending that h is true'—such is the 'believe' in 'make-believe'. And there is nothing paradoxical about:

(3) h is true (or: I recognize that the evidence that h is true has become conclusive) but I'm pretending otherwise.

So we must go further. We might say this: a belief that h 'aims at' the truth of h.[4] A belief that h necessarily 'misses its target' when h is false, whereas a pretence that h does not. Beliefs are evaluable as true or false, and are false whenever their propositional objects are. To have mastered the distinction between belief and pretence is in part to understand this. That suggests:

(4) A believer that h holds that, necessarily, her belief that h is false if h itself is false.

This, however, is overloaded conceptually. Most of us think that school-age children have genuine beliefs and can distinguish belief from pretence quite well, even though we suspect that they do not explicitly hold the modal attitude expressed in (4). Rather, they manifest their awareness of the special tie between belief and truth implicitly, by showing sensitivity to the distinction between what is the case (as far as they can tell) and what they would like to be the case, and through their responses to evidence for or against h. Believers in effect hold their beliefs to be *accountable* to truth.[5]

To be sure, it is not false belief as such that is paradoxical. There is nothing odd about:

---

[4] Bernard Williams gives a seminal discussion of belief as 'aiming at' truth in 'Deciding to Believe', in his *Problems of the Self* (Cambridge: Univ. Press, 1973), 136–51.

[5] More precisely, a believer-that-h holds *this* attitude accountable to the truth of h. It cannot be essential to belief (in beings with finite minds, such as us) to hold that, for all p, if p is true then one should believe it.

(5) *h* is true, but I wrongly disbelieved it at the time.

Paradox emerges in (1)—or in (2)—not because the belief in question is false or incongruous with the world, but because the belief is incongruous with something else the agent already thinks.

What is the nature of this incongruity, and what sort of problem is it for the believer? There is, I am sure, often incongruity among my beliefs. To the extent that I remain unaware of incongruity, no Moore-like paradox arises. I can, for example, unthinkingly pick up the telephone to call the repair office to report that my phone is dead. This is a state manifesting incongruous beliefs, but not one that seems unattainable. By contrast, the state of mind that would be accurately expressed by (1)—or by (2)—seems not foolish but opaque. What *could* someone who confidently uttered (1)— or (2)—have in mind?[6]

The distinctive propositional attitude of belief is therefore one that not only represents its propositional contents as true, but also one that cannot represent itself as unresponsive to—unaccountable to—their truth. This is still an unacceptably crude formulation.[7] But fortunately for present purposes we need only a rough idea, since even the rough idea enables us to explain why anti-epistemology is untenable. In order for a propositional attitude to be an attitude of *belief*, it cannot represent itself as wholly unaccountable to truth or evidence.

We've been lost in thought for a bit, but now are in a position to respond to Gary with what looks like a non-hypothetical argument. For we can say why he must, at least in the limit, accord some deference to what he takes to be truth and evidence thereof in his belief-formation. It is part of the *price of admission* to belief as a propositional attitude that one not represent one's attitude as unaccountable to truth. Someone unwilling to pay this price—who, for example, insists that he will represent himself as accepting propositions just as it suits his fancy and without any commitment to their truth—would not succeed in *believing* these propositions at all. The special relation between belief and truth thus comes with the territory of belief, and is not hypothetical upon any contingent aim of the believer.

None of this argues against the possibility of belief that is in fact—even as the outcome of prior design—unresponsive to evidence or truth. One could, is seems, have some success in coming to believe certain convenient falsehoods through a suitable programme of self-imposed indoctrination. What the argument above purports to show is not the impossibility of such a programme but a *design constraint* upon it: if one is to succeed, one must

---

[6] See Sect. 3 below, for some further discussion.

[7] For some further discussion, see P. Railton, 'Truth, Reason, and the Regulation of Belief', *Philosophical Issues*, 5 (1994), 71–94.

somehow contrive to veil the programme's true nature from oneself. Transparent anti-epistemology, for example, is not an option.

Gary might, however, think that we have overstated what has been shown. He can say, 'Your answer to my challenge is still hypothetical, as far as I can see. It presupposes that I am in, or plan to enter, the belief business. But what if I opt out? Why can't I just do without belief, and manage my affairs instead with other propositional attitudes lacking its particular relation to truth?'

Here we might be tempted to reply, 'Well, why not do without automobiles and manage instead with boats? Beliefs, after all, play many roles in one's mental economy—in inference, deliberation, action, even emotion. They are evolutionarily "made for" these roles, and it is by no means obvious how many of these roles could be played by propositional attitudes other than belief.[8] Just ask whether a strong desire for self-defence, plus a *pretence* that a mortal enemy lurks behind the next hedge, would do the job in producing an action-guiding intention to engage in all-out self-defence.'

Gary is tenacious. 'Still hypothetical. You're telling me that people typically have goals that are better served by having some attitudes that play all the roles of belief—just as people typically have goals that are better served if they have vehicles that can play all the roles of cars, and don't have only bicycles and boats.' In atypical circumstances, he observes, things might be otherwise. He can remember one incident involving a broken guard-rail on the coastal highway south of Monterey when he quite suddenly found himself thinking just how much there is to be said for boats as opposed to cars.

'Very well,' we reply, 'you want a non-hypothetical argument and you will have it. But remember: To show that a norm or reason is non-hypothetical is not to show that it is utterly without condition. It is only to show that it would necessarily apply to any agent as such, regardless of her contingent personal ends.

'So. Consider how deeply implicated belief is in our notion of agency. An agent acts on intentions and plans, which constitutively involve beliefs and are formed deliberatively in part on the basis of beliefs. To replace *all* belief with (say) wishing would be to form no intentions at all. Moreover, our notion of ourselves as agents extended over time constitutively involves *memories* and *expectations*. These, too, involve beliefs. There is all the difference in the world between believing that one is the father of John, or believing that one will experience the pains of an unattended-to toothache,

---

[8] Those who think of *being a belief* as a purely functional property will presumably hold that any attitude playing all the roles of belief would simply *be* a belief. Here, however, we are supposing that the attitude would lack at least some of the central roles of belief, namely those involved in the 'internal relation' between what one believes and what one takes to be true or evidential.

and pretending or merely supposing these things. To delete all forms of belief from your mental repertoire would leave you with no recognizable notion of identity.

'Being "in the belief business" therefore isn't as optional as you imagine. It is a precondition of agency. So the argument is non-hypothetical in a familiar sense: as an agent you must possess beliefs; as a believer you must represent certain of your propositional attitudes as accountable to truth and as disciplined by truth-orientated norms (at least, in the limit); therefore, as an agent you must so represent at least some of your attitudes, irrespective of what other goals this might or might not serve.'

The argument is not dispositive. But it does place a certain burden on Gary. It seems that he would have to exhibit the compatibility of our notions of practical deliberation, agency, personal identity, etc. with a mental economy which contains no beliefs. The magnitude of this burden affords a prima-facie case for the following claim: paying the price of admission to belief is necessary to gain entry to agency. A self-representation of certain of one's attitudes as 'aiming at' truth is *partially constitutive* of belief, which in turn is *partially constitutive* of agency. Let us, then, call this sort of argument a *constitutive argument*.

Unlike our first, hypothetical, eat-your-vegetables defence of conforming to norms of theoretical reason, this constitutive argument concerns not an agent's actual conformity (or attempt to conform) to epistemic norms but her self-representation as such. Moreover, it concerns only a limiting case, the case of deeming certain evidence to be conclusive. Not very much normative epistemology can be wrung from that. Finally, Gary might surprise us and successfully discharge his burden of proof by showing that a genuinely alternative propositional attitude—or constellation of such attitudes—could play as many of the roles of belief as one would need to attain agency.

Rather than explore these issues further at this point, let us simply note that despite its limitations, the constitutive argument provides a prima-facie case for the non-hypothetical status of certain broad epistemic requirements.

2. *Reasoning about Action*

It is now the spring term. We find Gary, undaunted as ever, in our Introduction to the Theory of Action. This time he sits in the front row, and has his question ready earlier in the term. 'These philosophers,' he begins, 'each has his own view about what practical reasoning requires. But what makes any of these views something I have to pay attention to? How could any of them insist that I pay attention to their favourite norms if I didn't

care to? They might not be *my* favourite norms.' In particular, he concludes, he'd like to know how the practical case compares with the discussion of theoretical reasoning last term.

Let us see how much parallelism we can find. In the autumn we began
with a non-epistemic but robust hypothetical defence of familiar standards
of theoretical reason: Gary could expect to do better relative to almost any
of the goals he might have if he formed warranted beliefs. In effect, this
constituted a *practical* defence of theoretical reason. Would a parallel in the
present case be a practical defence of paying heed to norms of practical
reason? This time that would seem circular at the outset.

There is, however, at least one way of construing the question that would
avoid circularity—though this might not satisfy Gary. We can distinguish
two ways in which an agent's deliberations, decisions, and actions might be
said to follow a norm: objectively versus subjectively.

We will say that an agent's deliberations, decisions, and actions are *in
objective conformity with* a norm to the extent that he is actually succeeding
in complying with whatever the norm prescribes. Consider a norm that
directs one to act so as to maximize one's self-interest. An agent would be
in (full) objective conformity with this norm just in case his acts were
those, relative to available alternatives, that would maximally benefit him.

It would not follow, however, that this agent is acting exclusively for his
own sake, or even with his own benefit in mind. That is, it would not
follow that this agent's deliberation and actions are *subjectively patterned on*
a norm of maximizing self-interest.[9]

Using this distinction, we can interpret the question whether there might
be a practical defence for paying heed to norms of practical reasoning in the
following, non-circular way. Given any particular norm of practical reason,
one can ask whether in a particular instance—or in general—subjectively
patterning one's deliberation on this norm would constitute behaviour
in objective conformity with it. For many norms much of the time, the
most promising way of achieving objective conformity will indeed be subjectively to pattern one's deliberation on the norm. But not always. It
seems plausible, for example, that if one were to regulate one's conduct by
self-consciously and exclusively consulting one's self-interest one would be
incapable of the sorts of commitment to other individuals or to groups or
causes that are the source of some of life's deeper satisfactions.

If Gary wants to know whether, in his circumstances—or in general
—one would have good (objective) practical reason to be (subjectively)
practically rational, then he will be asking a genuine question to which the

---

[9] Subjective patterning on a norm *N* need not involve a second-order thought to the effect that 'I
do this in order to satisfy norm *N*'.

answer is not pre-ordained. For many theories of practical reason, it is a contingent matter.

But Gary is growing restless. He meant his question to be less internal to the domain of theories of practical reason. 'Objective or subjective,' he says, 'it matters little to me how you put it. I want to know whether you can give a good, non-circular defence of having anything to do with norms of practical reason. Why should I be bothered?'

This is starting to look like an impossible request. For either the defence presupposes a set of norms of practical reason, which would appear to be question-begging, or the defence makes no such presupposition, and there is nowhere to start.

However, something more might be said within the domain of practical reasoning. Philosophers often engage in a process that looks like a non-circular practical defence of practical norms—a process that sometimes leads them well away from their starting points.

The process begins with our many intuitive notions about which actions or principles of action make—or do not make—sense. These notions are much less coherent or articulate than a 'theory of practical reason'. Here, for example, is an appeal to intuition meant to raise doubts about whether maximizing one's expected utility really makes sense even as a basis for self-interested choice:

You are forced to play Russian roulette—but you can buy your way out. One bullet is placed in a six-cylinder revolver . . . What is the most you would pay to have the bullet removed?

Next . . . You are forced to play Russian roulette with four bullets in the revolver. Answer a new question: What is the most you would pay . . . to have *one* of the four bullets removed, leaving three? More? Or less?[10]

Most say 'Less'. Maximizing expected utility seems to say 'More'. This has the form of the 'Allais Paradox', though one might say that it is no paradox at all, but merely a counter-intuitive result. For our purposes what is most important is that the example does not appear to depend for its force upon people's acceptance of some alternative theory of practical rationality. Indeed, popular intuitions have proved exceedingly difficult to describe in any general, coherent way.

In consequence, one can also have the opposite response to the case: after being told that the choice 'More' would maximize expected utility, one might come to think that one *should* accept this answer as rational and

---

[10] The example itself is used by Daniel Kahneman and Amos Tversky, 'Prospect Theory: An Analysis of Decision under Risk', *Econometrica*, 47 (1979), 263–91, at 283, and attributed to Richard Zeckhauser. The version given here is quoted from Allan Gibbard, *Wise Choices, Apt Feelings* (Cambridge, Mass.: Harvard Univ. Press, 1990), 15.

simply ignore its intuitive oddness. Indeed, a considerable literature in cognitive psychology suggests that common-sense reasoning is prone to various errors and fallacies in assessing probabilities and risks.[11]

Such dialogue—an interplay of examples, intuitive responses, empirical theory, and proposed norms—is a form of *wide reflective equilibrium*. The critique and acceptance of norms of deliberation through such dialogue is surely a form of reasoning that deserves the name 'practical'. Yet reflective equilibrium arguments need not take a particular set of practical norms for granted. Inarticulate common-sense notions of practical rationality will figure in such a process and partially shape it, but they need not serve as a *constraint* on the process, or leave it intact.

A wide reflective equilibrium argument thus might answer to the demand for a non-circular practical justification, but would it be convincing to Gary? Convincing or not, he'd point out, the argument would none the less be *hypothetical*: which adjustments we are prepared to make in response to various intuitive tensions is sure to depend upon our particular goals and priorities.

Therefore Gary still wants to know whether there exists a non-hypothetical argument concerning fidelity to norms of practical reasoning, akin to the constitutive argument made in the case of theoretical reasoning. One established way of approaching this question is to ask whether there is anything in the realm of action which plays the role that truth plays in the realm of belief. We can think of ourselves as looking for a feature F such that one must represent oneself as 'aiming at' F in action in approximately the same sense in which one must represent oneself as 'aiming at' truth in belief.

Among philosophical accounts of the nature of intentional action which might be seen as offering a candidate for F, two have perhaps attracted the greatest interest historically. For each, I will argue, it is possible to construct a constitutive argument. Let us call the two philosophical accounts of agency we will be considering *High Brow* and *Low Brow*.

High Brow is a view with excellent pedigree, tracing its ancestry back to ancient Greece. According to High Brow, just as belief necessarily 'aims at' the True, action necessarily 'aims at' the Good. Deliberation seeks to identify the good, and action is guided by it. In choosing an action we place it (or find it to be) in a positive evaluative light, and deem it choiceworthy.

Note that the High Brow's claims concern action as such, not merely *rational* action. The constitutive argument for belief held that a self-presentation as 'aiming at' the truth is part of what makes a propositional

---

[11] See e.g. Daniel Kahneman, Paul Slovic, and Amos Tversky (eds.), *Judgment Under Uncertainty: Heuristics and Biases* (New York: Cambridge Univ. Press, 1982).

attitude be one of belief, rational or irrational alike. Similarly, the High Brow claims that action which is irrational—as distinct from arational or non-rational behaviour such as reflexes or kicking in one's sleep—is also in some sense 'aimed at' the good. Weakness of the will, as it is ordinarily understood, is a paradigm of practical irrationality which clearly manifests this. The akratic agent is said to be 'aiming at' the good but falling short due (say) to insufficient motivation or 'will-power'.

Of course, our description of High Brow is quite vague. Action requires representing one's choice in a positive evaluative light, but which? There are many varieties of goodness: good for oneself, good for one's kith and kin, morally good, aesthetically good, and so on. One might formulate High Brow by identifying one of these goods, or perhaps a *summum bonum*, as the true end of all action. This would, however, be needlessly ambitious for our purposes. We seek a constitutive feature of action as uncontroversial upon reflection as the connection between belief and truth, and a generic value claim is much less controversial. Action, our High Brow will say, involves representing the act chosen or the ends for which it is done as good *in some self-acknowledged sense*.

Despite its generic character, this claim is non-trivial. It implies, among other things, that individuals incapable of representing an end or a course of conduct as good—non-human animals, or (perhaps) human infants— would also be incapable of agency, properly so-called. Moreover, those among our fellow adults who have a latent capacity to represent a course of conduct as good, but who fail to develop or exercise it—that is, who fail or refuse to *acknowledge* any good—would also lack agency, properly so-called. Their lot might be a kind of motivation-driven behaviour that none the less remained in some profound sense aimless. Alternatively—and perhaps far more likely—individuals claiming not to acknowledge any good are actually kidding themselves. Their deliberation and action reveal their nihilism to be no more than a posture.

This suggests a High Brow response to Gary. Suppose that a visiting High Brow philosopher has just given a guest lecture in our class on practical reason. Gary's eager hand is up. Why, he asks, must he pay any attention to the good when deciding what to do? What magical force would stop him from simply ignoring questions of good and bad, or flying in their face, and acting as he pleases?

The High Brow philosopher can reply: 'I have claimed that deliberation and choice constitutively involve representing what you choose as in some sense good. You can no more decide to ignore questions of good and bad— of choiceworthiness—in your deliberation and action than you can decide to introspect someone else's thoughts rather than your own. No "magical force" is needed to police this constraint. Of course, you might lack the nerve, or will, or energy to follow through on your judgements of choice-worthiness. But to the extent that you are aware of this, you yourself will be sensible of it *as a lack*, a gap between what you value and what you do. You will be in no position to say "Well, that's nothing *to me*". If it weren't *something* to you, it wouldn't have been a choice in the first place.'[12]

Gary is being attributed paradoxical claims, which might be thought to echo—though in a practical setting—Moore:

(6) I believe I have reason to choose act *A*, but I can't see anything good about it.

(7) Act *A* would be good, but that's no reason for *me* to choose it.

One way of explaining the oddness of (6) and (7), according to the view under consideration, is that they seem to suggest the existence of a gap within practical deliberation that makes room for a purely *hypothetical* dependence of an agent's deliberation on judgements about the good. This gap presumably would need to be filled by the agent's possession of some independent, intermediating goal, such as that of 'doing what is good'. But such a view would be deeply confused, according to the High Brow. The deliberative role of judgements of goodness is indispensable and needs no mediation—it simply comes with the territory of acting. To use our earlier phrase, it is *partially constitutive* of agency that one perceive the landscape in an evaluative light, and steer toward the good as one sees it. Gary proposed to act in the face of, or indifferent to, questions of goodness. But anyone who managed to become a complete stranger to goodness would simply have dismantled his capacity for deliberate action and begun a life of merely behaving, of roaming at the behest of his appetites.

We thus have arrived at an argument in the practical realm that affords an interesting parallel to the argument made in the theoretical realm: both appeal to a constitutive condition to identify a non-hypothetical element in reasoning.

High Brow is, however, highbrow. Many philosophers, in my experience, are not. Gary, it seems, isn't either. He points to a long line of Low Brow thinkers, beginning perhaps with Hume, who have denied that an agent engaged in deliberate action necessarily 'aims at' the good.

If not the good, then what does action 'aim at'? To Hume is often ascribed the view that agency aims at no more than the satisfaction of current desires. But this might be wrong about Hume, and it in any event is not necessary for a Low Brow. Just as High Brow comes in both generic and brand-name forms—the latter identify a particular sort of good as 'the

---

[12] Sometimes, of course, we just *pick* rather than choosing. This can be seen, however, as a species of action in which it is decided simply to select an option rather than deliberate further.

aim' of action—so does Low Brow. We can see Hume as endorsing in the
first instance a generic Low Brow position: agents necessarily possess and
act on *ends*, and this involves both a *representational* and a *motivational*
component, though neither component need involve a judgement of, or an
'aiming at', what is good. The belief/desire view often attributed to Hume
is an example of this type. According to it, motivationally inert beliefs will
suffice for representation, and non-evaluative, intrinsic attractions and aver-
sions will suffice for motivation. Hume famously wrote:

Ask a man *why he uses exercise*; he will answer *because he desires to keep his health*.
If you then enquire *why he desires to keep his health*, he will readily reply *because
sickness is painful*. If you push your enquiries further and desire a reason *why he
hates pain*, it is impossible he can ever give any. This is an ultimate end, and is
never referred to any other object.[13]

Humean individuals engage in both theoretical and practical reasoning.
They inquire into causes and effects, form beliefs about the conduciveness
of means to ends, take into account the relative strength and independence
of desires, acquire habits, form intentions to act, formulate and respond to
rules and sanctions. Their conduct therefore can, it is claimed, be given
fully-fledged intentional, rational-agent explanations. Why-questions about
their conduct can often be answered correctly by citing *their reasons* for
behaving as they do, and these will include: how they represented the
situation, what their goals were, how they weighed their various ends, how
they adjusted means and ends, and so on.

Our interest in Humean individuals lies precisely with the claim that
they exemplify agency even though they do not by their nature 'aim at' the
good. We need not evaluate the stronger claim that reason-giving always
terminates in current intrinsic desires (or that belief must be motivationally inert).

The tenability of any Low Brow position therefore depends upon the
possibility of distinguishing *the possession of ends* from *the making of judgements that certain ends are good*. Desire appears at first to afford a clear case:
we often speak of acting on desire (so desire seems capable of playing the
necessary role in choice) and also of desiring something that we do not take
to be good (so desiring seems suitably distinct from evaluating).

But such claims might be challenged. To desire, it can be argued, is to
represent as desirable, and desirability is itself a species of good. When we
speak of desiring that which we take to be bad, this can be understood as
(say) reflecting the difference between a prima-facie and a conclusionary
judgement of value. This is, however, a very demanding position. It would

---

[13] David Hume, *An Enquiry concerning the Principles of Morals*, app. i, 'Concerning Moral Sentiment'.

force us to deny that young children, who (it seems) lack the evaluative concept of desirability, have desires. To reject the evaluative notion of desire need not be to treat desire as a mere animal appetite (whatever that might be). There is a great deal of psychic distance between a fish that swims to the surface 'because it is hungry' and a child who responds to our question 'Why did you come downstairs?' with the answer 'I'm hungry'. We can begin to account for this difference by pointing out that the child 'acted on a desire' in a way that the fish did not, and this despite our reluctance to suppose that the child has judged there to be something further that is good about having breakfast.[14]

Perhaps a more promising challenge to the Low Brow's distinction would be to argue that even if desires (say) are non-evaluative, they cannot function as *ends* until some suitable evaluative judgement has at least tacitly been made. This view is less severe. A young child can be spoken of as having desires in the familiar sense, but even when these 'mere desires' cause her behaviour, a child cannot be seen as *acting on reasons* or as *possessing an end that furnishes her rationale in acting* until she is capable of exercising a certain amount of judgement as to the appropriateness or worthwhileness of acting on her desires.

Perhaps the best Low Brow defence is to give illustrative examples. First, consider a case of a kind brought to our attention by Jean Hampton.[15] Our two children have been begging all week to go to the shore. Both, however, dislike long summer car rides. When the weekend comes one child absolutely refuses to get into the car. 'But we're going to the beach, which you love!' 'I don't care. I don't want to ride in this stuffy old car. I hate it! I won't do it.' He has to be carried bodily to the car and buckled in, thrashing. Once in the car, he still refuses to be jollied along. 'It's *your* fault I'm in this stuffy old car! I told you I hate it.' The second child confines her thrashing to loud complaints. 'Not another car ride! Last time I felt sick the whole time!' But when the time comes to leave she climbs into her seat of her own accord, waiting sulkily to be buckled in. On her face is a look that says 'OK, I'll ride in the car, but don't expect me to like it.'

The second child possesses a capacity for self-control (relative to her weightier desires) that the first child lacks, though, according to the Low Brow, we need not also impute to the second child a judgement that being at the beach is a good thing—beyond her strong desire for it. There is a sense in which the second child's thinking and conduct, but not the first's,

---

[14] We have been working throughout with generic High Brow views because of their greater plausibility. That complicates the present discussion, however, since open-endedness about the notion of the good can make it difficult to distinguish such views from Humean Low Brow views. Unless a certain amount of substance is built into the idea of goodness, it will be rather too easy (and uninformative) to think of any sort of desiring as 'deeming to be good'.

[15] I am grateful to Shelly Kagan for bringing this sort of example to my attention.

accord the strong desire to be at the beach the force of a *rationale* for the despised beach trip. The desire speaks on behalf of means toward its fulfilment, even unwanted means. By contrast, for the first child the desire to be at the beach does not yet function as end-setting, and his conduct is not rationalized even by his own desires.

Second, consider an example inspired by a case due to Michael Smith.[16] Two 'unwilling addicts'—individuals who strongly desire heroin but who also very much wish they did not[17]—are both beginning their day. Each has overslept—it is now too late even to consider going to work. 'I've got to quit this stuff. It's ruining my life. I won't even have a job by the end of the week—if I haven't been fired already.' This is no new resolve. Each has already judged his taking of heroin to be a bad thing on the whole. Though neither reconsiders this judgement, as the day grows longer the desire for heroin becomes fierce. By noon, each has set out to get a fix. One locates a needle and, trembling, injects himself. The other, who is just as aware as the first of how to use heroin, locates a needle and hungrily tries to eat it. He chokes to death.

We now ask why each has used the needle as he did. For the first, we are able to cite a reason, *his* reason: he strongly wanted to dose himself with heroin, and he knew that this is how to do it. For the second, we are at a loss. Without further information we must see his needle-eating conduct as inexplicable by any 'rational agent' explanation. Perhaps sheer craving somehow overcame him. The difference in intelligibility between the two cases is not attributable to the addicts' differing capacities to form and be guided by judgements of the good—they formed the same judgement on this score, and equally failed to be guided by it—but to their differing ability to adjust means to ends. Thus although we almost certainly regard the conduct of neither as truly *rational*, we do see the one's conduct as having a *rationale* in terms of what he believes and desires that the other's does not.

These two examples give us at least a prima-facie case for the Low Brow's distinguishing of the notion of an agent having and acting on ends from the High Brow notion of an agent aiming at the good.[18] We now must ask whether Low Brow conceptions of agency—which ordinarily are seen as allergic to anything non-hypothetical—can support a constitutive argument of their own. Perhaps so. Consider the Moore-like statement:

---

[16] Personal communication. He is obviously not to be held responsible either for the claims made about the example or for the interpretation offered of it.

[17] Psychologists would, I think, challenge the suggestion that the cravings of an addict can be understood as a subspecies of our familiar notion of desire. Let us, however, follow philosophical convention and set that concern aside.

[18] The Low Brow need not rule out the possibility of an agent also inquiring into or aiming at the good. His point is simply that this is at most an *option* for agents, and perhaps also that it presupposes the means/ends relationships that are the stuff of Low Brow agency.

(8) *E* is an end of mine, but that's nothing to me in my deliberation.[19]

Our original Moore-ism

(1) *h* is true, but I don't believe it

is a statement that could easily be true (there are many truths I do not believe) but which seemed deeply problematic for any agent to assert. Something similar holds for (8). It is hardly odd for someone to fail in a given case to take one of his ends into account. He might not even notice its relevance. But asserting (8) would be peculiar indeed, according to the Low Brow, since we have no clear idea what it could amount to for *E* to be acknowledged by me as an end of mine if it counted for nothing in my deliberation whether or not *E* is realized. Of course, we must make room for inattention, distraction, and depression. The connection suggested in (8) is non-hypothetical not in the sense that it has no conditions, but in the sense that it does not presuppose a further, contingent desire on my part 'that I realize my ends' or 'that I realize end *E*'.

It should be emphasized that (8)'s oddness manifests a *structural* connection, which, though non-hypothetical, is not a device for generating univalent, non-hypothetical imperatives. Thus, if an end *E* of mine would be advanced by act *A*, this can be taken as either counting in favour of performing *A* or counting against retaining *E*. If success in the army requires unquestioning obedience, for example, I might consider giving up my military ambitions.[20] The oddness of (8) points to the unavailability of a third option: genuinely retaining the end while in effect setting oneself to accord it no deliberative relevance. To see one's deliberation as guided (at least in part, in the limit, other things equal, in normal circumstances, etc.) by one's own ends thus comes along with the mere possession of ends.

Suppose, then, that a Low Brow philosopher visits our class. At the lecture's end, Gary raises his characteristic challenge. 'Maybe I can't have an end unless I take that to count in some way in thinking about how to act. Fair enough. But that's still hypothetical. You yourself admit that very young children might have desires or appetites but no ends as such. Maybe they know something you don't.'

The Low Brow philosopher can respond. 'You, like most of us, have ends, desires, appetites. Nothing prevents you from becoming a being with appetites and desires but no ends. There are lots of such beings around: infants, maybe animals. You could join their ranks. But then you would

---

[19] In this formula, *E* must be understood as occurrently taken by me as end of mine. As with belief, there is nothing odd about the diachronic case:

(8′) I once deemed *E* to be an end of mine, but that now counts for nothing in my deliberation.

[20] This is like the relevance of modus ponens to inference. If I already believe that (if *p* then *q*) and come to believe that *p*, should I conclude *q*? Perhaps, in light of *q*'s implausibility, I should question one or both of the premises.

cease *acting* on desire—you'd merely be behaving. If you are to remain an agent, you must have ends. And once you acknowledge ends—as you've conceded—you must (in the limit, under ordinary conditions, etc.) be to some degree engaged in the business of weighing courses of conduct in light of their tendency to contribute to the realization of your ends.' So, we reach a 'principled basis' for a Low Brow non-hypothetical response to Gary. An agent as such must in effect see herself as deliberating in a way that gives weight (in the limit, etc.) to the realization of what she takes to be her ends, independently of what these particular ends might be.[21] This is so even for agents who are acting *irrationally* relative to their ends.

3. Stocktaking

The High road and the Low road thus both lead to non-hypothetical requirements for practical reasoning. The path in each case proceeds via a constitutive argument that has much in common with the constitutive argument made for theoretical reasoning. In all three cases a linkage is made to the (alleged) nature of agency, thereby avoiding dependence upon contingent personal goals.

But have we found convincing answers to Gary's questions? Or convincing grounds for rejecting them? To simplify exposition, I will begin by narrowing the argumentative field, focusing largely on the case of theoretical reasoning and the Low Brow version of the practical case.[22]

Constitutive arguments have the strength that comes from purportedly necessary connections. And necessity is hard to argue with, even for Gary. But this strength can also be a weakness. If the necessity turns out to be linguistic, the argument may lack the power to sustain substantive conclusions. And if the necessity is of a more substantive kind, then the argument may have the unintended effect of pulling the claws of the very criticisms one wishes to make.[23] We now face both of these dangers. Let us look at them in turn.

First, the linguistic danger. Consider the Low Brow constitutive argument that connects taking oneself to have an end E with taking oneself to be responsive in deliberation to whether E is realized. Someone might see this as an analytic truth: 'That's just what it *means* for E to be an end

---

[21] It should perhaps be emphasized again that an agent's ends need not be self-orientated. They could include the well-being of others, moral or aesthetic causes, and so on.

[22] This might not be wholly unfair to High Brow theories. After all, High Brows can agree that means/ends reasoning is a central part of agency (even, of course, irrational agency).

[23] For a discussion of related concerns about the critical limitations of constitutive or linguistically necessary principles, though in connection with a conception of instrumental *rationality* rather than agency, see Christine Korsgaard's contribution to the current volume, Essay 8.

of yours—an end is something you see yourself as giving weight to in deliberation.' Gary, however, sought answers to seemingly substantive practical and epistemic questions: 'Why do things that way?', he wanted to know. It would be surprising if we could give an answer with nothing more than a few definitions. To be genuinely responsive to the concerns expressed, constitutive arguments must capture a substantive—not merely linguistic—necessity.

This brings us to the second danger, the danger of pulling the claws of criticism.[24] Assume, for example, that the connection between taking oneself to have an end and according that end deliberative weight is a substantively necessary, non-analytic connection of the same modality as the connection between being gold and having atomic number 79. What would we then be able to say by way of *criticism* of an agent who refused to give deliberative weight to his own acknowledged end *E*? Would he be 'necessarily deliberatively defective' or perhaps 'self-defeatingly irrational'?

If the constitutive argument is right, we cannot even raise the question! To fail to take oneself as according *E* deliberative weight is to fail to acknowledge *E* as an end. But then the agent cannot be 'self-defeating' or 'irrational' with respect to *E*. An analogy: to discover that the metal in the sample tray on one's laboratory bench has atomic number 82 is not to discover that it is 'defective gold', but rather that it is not gold at all.

A similar problem confronts all constitutive arguments. Suppose, for example, that someone has a propositional attitude toward *p* which involves, among other things, her representing *p* as true. Thus far, this attitude is a candidate for belief. But suppose further that she sees no relevance to this attitude of admitted evidence against *p*, even evidence she recognizes to be conclusive. When challenged, she is not defensive and produces no elaborate rationale, but simply points out that she is quite indifferent as to whether her attitude toward *p* is responsive to the truth of *p*.

According to the constitutive argument, she does not have an irrational or epistemically defective belief that *p*; she simply fails to *believe* that *p* at all. Perhaps she instead is *supposing* that *p*. What if she none the less claims that her attitude toward *p* is one of belief? It would seem that, on the strength of the constitutive argument, our only criticism could be that she has *mislabelled* her propositional attitude (like our mislabelling of the metal sample). Labelling errors are not, however, defects of rationality. Once she has found the right word for her propositional attitude, the criticism would vanish.

To be sure, we could at this point invoke a more general, higher-order constitutive argument. If we were to come across someone who failed quite

---

[24] I am indebted here to Shelly Kagan.

generally to deliberate in a way that he takes to be responsive to his ends, or who failed quite generally to form propositional attitudes that he takes to be responsive to evidence, we could argue that such an individual thereby would fail to possess ends or beliefs at all, and thus would fail to be an agent.

Indeed, we might raise the stakes still higher. Perhaps *speaking a natural language* itself presupposes the formation of beliefs and intentions, so that an individual without beliefs or intentions could not even offer an *argument* on behalf of his way of life—his vocalizations would not constitute speech. This is beginning to sound serious! Or is it? Now when he emits the sounds *bĭ-lēf'* or *ăk'-shən* we cannot even charge him with a linguistic mistake.

It seems that we are turning up the volume of criticism while simultaneously ensuring that the purported target of our criticism is ever more profoundly deaf. If we rely on these ascending constitutive arguments, we quickly reach a point in which the only thing left to say of someone is to dismiss him as not one of us. This is xenophobia, not criticism.

Eager for a secure justification, a knock-down answer to the likes of Gary, we sought a requirement—a 'must'—that applies non-hypothetically, arising from the very conditions of agency. That now looks unwise. For then there could be no such thing as failure to conform *on the part of an agent*. Perhaps we have asked too much, or the wrong thing, of our constitutive claims.

We may begin to regroup by recognizing that we have formulated the constitutive arguments too rigidly. Having beliefs and having ends are, even in the limit, complex phenomena to which we have not done justice. Beliefs, for example, come in degrees, and are not all or nothing. Moreover, having a belief involves possessing a large bundle of dispositions—not only to represent one's thinking in certain ways, but also to infer, to notice, to act, to avow, to assert, to claim a measure of authority, and so on. Psychological realism alone compels us to recognize that many of the attitudes in ourselves and others that we unhesitatingly call beliefs may from time to time lack one or another of the complex bundle of attitudes and dispositions paradigmatically associated with belief as an ideal type. Interpretative charity often demands that we be latitudinarian with respect to departures from the ideal type.

Now consider a person who has a propositional attitude toward p that he deems to be belief, but which he does not—or does not with any consistency —hold accountable to admitted evidence concerning the truth of p. If that person none the less allows this attitude to play all the other roles of belief —in assertion, in intention-formation, in expectation, etc.—then he will almost certainly find himself in a variety of difficulties, difficulties more serious than mislabelling, difficulties which mere relabelling could not remove. Given his attitude's extensive overlap with characteristic roles of belief, we would have some interpretative justification for calling it a 'belief'; but given its unresponsiveness to admitted evidence, we would also have some interpretative ground for calling it a 'belief *manqué*', or even a 'rationally defective' or 'irrational' belief.

Why 'rationally defective'? Consider an example. Suppose that I am a nervous flyer. I recognize there to be compelling statistical evidence that commercial aeroplane travel is very safe. Moreover, my frequency of electing to travel by air fits with what one would expect of an individual who deems it safe; for example, a small difference in travel time or cost will tip me toward air rather than rail or car. Yet I find that none the less, in the sense in which belief is connected with expectation and perception, I do not seem really to *believe* that air travel is relatively safe. This is not because my attitude is a mere supposition or pretence or the like—it has less in common with these attitudes than it does with belief, as my travel choices show. One might with some justice interpret me as partly believing that taking wing in a commercial airliner is safe, and partly disbelieving this.

But the division between belief and disbelief here is not a simple probability distribution, the way that I 'distribute' my belief over 'Clinton will win in November' and 'Clinton will not'. For in a suitably abstract context, I will sincerely and confidently assert the view or place a bet that flying on a commercial airliner is much safer than driving to work. In a different context, when I'm aboard a jet taxiing for take-off, I may find myself irresistibly believing that I am in a very precarious situation, wishing I were anywhere else, jumping to conclusions about the meaning of small sounds or little bumps and jiggles, and so on. By way of contrast, despite what I know of statistics, I have no such belief when speeding through traffic in my rattletrap of a car, clutching a cup of coffee between my knees, late for work (again!). How would I myself describe things? I would probably say that my beliefs on such subjects as the relative safety of air versus car travel, the safety of the particular flights or car trips on which I find myself, etc. are simply not wholly rational.[25]

We need to effect a similar relaxation of the Low Brow constitutive argument in the case of practical reasoning. When deliberating about what to do, a rational person takes her ends into account. But to have an end paradigmatically involves possession of a complex bundle of attitudes and dispositions, involving action, perception, sentiment, belief, and so on. As in the case of belief, interpretative charity will often license attributing an

---

[25] In cases like this, we might seem to be flirting with Moore's paradox. That is, I might be tempted to say: 'Yes, I grant that it is unquestionably true that commercial air travel is safer than car travel, but I don't really believe it.' Once we realize all that 'coming to believe' actually involves, this looks more like a needlessly paradoxical way of expressing a fairly familiar sort of imperfection in rational belief.

end to a person even though some of these elements are missing, or inconsistently present. An agent who arranges a considerable part of her life in order to promote a long-term goal will from time to time find herself in contexts in which she is attracted to other things, feels alternative pressures exclusively, or even lacks interest in her life. In such cases, even though she may see the bearing of her long-term goal, and even though she may remain disposed to avow it, she may none the less find herself giving it no weight in certain deliberations.[26] Do we say she no longer has the end? Or that she has the end but isn't at the moment being fully rational with respect to it? The agent herself—at least, if she is like me—will sometimes opt for the latter description.

Failures of rationality come in many shapes and sizes, and do not form a unified type. But it may be useful to think of some forms of theoretical or practical irrationality as instances of incomplete-yet-nearly-complete approximation of believing or having an end. How many of the elements in the bundle must one possess to be 'nearly complete'? There are limits, but vague limits, no doubt. And dynamic, holistic limits—they concern chunks of one's thought and stretches of time. Particular elements may come and go, but may do so in mutually compensating ways or so that, at any given time, enough hold.

We thus remove from the constitutive arguments an artificial rigidity. But are we any closer to an answer to Gary? We may have made matters worse. If having a belief or possessing an end is a complex phenomenon, with vague and holistic limits, then we have left behind the Manichaean world of the original argument. In that world there seemed to be only stark choices: to be an agent or . . . infantile, or a beast. Now it seems one could pass almost imperceptibly from belief to near-belief, and thus from agency to something else. And that something else therefore might not be so terribly alien.[27]

Gary asked why he should pay attention to epistemic norms. If we reply that this is necessary in order to be a believer and thus to be an agent, he can respond: 'But just how severe a cost does this threaten me with? Somewhere on the continuum between the ideal type of belief, on the one end, and clear non-belief on the other, there is a region which forms the borderland of genuine belief. I want to know why my attitudes should be

---

[26] This sort of case differs from classic cases of weakness of the will, in which the agent feels the positive deliberative force of an end, but is swayed to act otherwise. The case I am imagining is less psychologically conflictual.

[27] Bas van Fraassen recommends that the community of scientists take an attitude of *acceptance* rather than belief toward the truth of their theories, but should *also* behave as scientists in every other respect—inferential, experimental, etc.—as if they believed the theories to be true. If sustainable, this attitude would be a form of near-belief. Could it, perhaps, even spread beyond scientific theories? See *The Scientific Image* (Oxford: Clarendon, 1980).

on one side rather than the other of that borderland. The claim that I would cease to be an agent on one side of the region sounds dramatic. But if life on the believer side of the borderland has certain pluses and minuses, how do we know in advance that the balance must be worse on the other side? Mightn't it even be better, on the whole?'

Consider two possibilities. First, suppose that there is more that Gary would find enjoyable or valuable on the believer side of the borderland. Then we have a reply to Gary, but it once more looks hypothetical— whether Gary finds life sweet or sour seems unlikely to be independent of what he happens to desire. Second, suppose the opposite: there is more that Gary would find enjoyable or valuable on the other side. Then our reply to Gary can only be, 'The enjoyment, however great, would not be that of an agent. The value would not be the value of the life of an agent.'[28] This reply is indeed non-hypothetical, but Gary could be excused if he finds it unconvincing.

We might at this point be inclined to be dismissive. Surely once one has demonstrated that a condition is essential to agency one has justification enough. After all, we *are* agents and that seems to be a very deep fact about us. Justification has to start somewhere, and if it is to be justification *for us* it had better start where we are. Indeed, the mere fact of Gary's asking such a question, posed as matter for choice, seems to presuppose that he, too, is an agent. Yet all the same can be said for two much more difficult-to-dismiss questions.

Consider first a patient with a painful, incurable disease who wonders whether to elect to end his life by euthanasia rather than live out the disease's wretched course, destroying his family's finances and becoming every day less the sort of person he has aspired to be. He is an agent, and moreover his very posing of the matter as a question of choice presupposes his agency. To choose euthanasia would, however, be to put an end to his agency. Does this suffice to show that there can be no question of justified voluntary euthanasia? Can we say that, since life is a necessary condition of agency, 'choice of euthanasia' is ruled out as a practical contradiction? Most of us, I suspect, do not think so. The considerations on the side of ending his life, and thereby resigning agency, might be more compelling than the considerations on the side of continuing it. But then we can understand the idea of a rationally justified transition from agency to non-agency.

Second, imagine a Schellingesque case of a kind discussed by Derek Parfit.[29] You have been captured by mobsters. They seek revenge on members

---

[28] Note that we cannot uncontroversially say 'The value would not be *true* value.' We will see shortly some examples where ends of (what we agents deem) true value can be attained only at some cost to one's own agency.   [29] Derek Parfit, *Reasons and Persons* (Oxford: Clarendon, 1984), 12–13.

of your family who have testified against them and who now have new identities and locations thanks to the Federal Witness Protection Program. The mobsters will torture you to reveal your family members' whereabouts. You know that you will not be able to resist this torture. If you could abolish your agency by knocking yourself senseless—perhaps irrevocably— your captors could not extract from you the information they need. Does the fact that you would be crossing the borderland into non-agency show that such a choice could not be a genuine or appropriate option for you as an agent?

Dramas aside, non-agency need not be the end of life as we know it. We all pass from non-agency to agency sometime during the first years of life, and, arguably, we all commute daily back and forth to a state in which agency is at least temporarily disengaged when we sleep and awaken. Suppose we were to say to Gary: 'The pleasures (or other advantages) on the other side of the borderland couldn't possibly count *for you*. They wouldn't be *yours*. You're an agent—that's one of the deepest facts about you—and they'd be the pleasures of a non-agent.' This way of speaking is belied by our comfort with speaking of a life that stretches from birth to death as the life of a single person, despite its various transitions to and from non-agency, active versus suspended agency, and the like. We cannot simply refuse questions of partial or even complete border-crossing.

Earlier we spoke of the 'price of admission' to belief, action, or agency. Now we are discussing the 'exit price', temporary or permanent. Often that price will be high. Now is the time to remind ourselves, and Gary, that most of us most of the time will be in a much better position to figure out and accomplish what matters to us if we are agents. But a high-priced option is very different from an impossibility. High prices are sometimes worth paying, and circumstances (such as facing the end of one's life) can drive down the price. We arrive, then, at a somewhat unanticipated sense in which one might intelligibly ask for 'reasons for action'—reasons for agency versus non-agency as a way of being.

This very observation does show, however, that there is a sense in which Gary has not succeeded—even slightly—in suggesting anything like the possibility of an alternative to familiar forms of practical reasoning. When he asks, in effect, whether the exit price is worth paying, he is asking whether *being an agent* is the best or only way of getting what he most wants from life. This is itself a means/ends form of reasoning of the familiar, Low Brow sort. It therefore betrays Gary's deference to (at least) Low Brow notions of agency after all. When Gary contemplates a border-crossing and asks whether life on the other side might be an improvement, he is giving deliberative weight to the tendency of a means to promote an end.

Perhaps the grass really is greener on the other side. But then not only would Gary have good reason in the familiar sense for crossing over, he would also have good reason *to be* and *to stay* on the other side even after he ceased himself to be a fully-fledged agent. Indeed, unless Gary takes for granted means/ends reasoning, it is unclear what bearing the (possibly) high quality of life on the other side of the borderland would have upon what he should do.

We might be able to put this point more clearly by invoking another turn-of-the-century Englishman's paradox, not G. E. Moore's this time, but Lewis Carroll's.[30] Achilles entertains an argument:

(9) If p then q

(10) p

(C) So: q.

Carroll's Tortoise asks Achilles whether there isn't a gap in this argument, a missing premiss. Couldn't one grant both premisses but fail to be driven to the conclusion unless one also granted:

(11) If [(if p then q) & p] then q

to effect the connection between (9) and (10) and (C)?

This seems reasonable to Achilles, on whom it only slowly dawns that he has just launched a regress. For suppose our premisses now enlarged to be (9)–(11). Tortoise will cheerfully argue that we would need a new premiss to effect *their* relevance to the conclusion, namely:

(12) If { ([(if p then q) & p] then q) & (if p then q) & p } then q.

Were (12) added, Tortoise would notice the need for yet another premiss to link (9)–(12) with the conclusion (C). And so on.

The moral: one cannot treat rules of inference (such as modus ponens) as premisses, on pain of regress. Put another way (and using Carroll's own terminology): We cannot see rules of inference in logical argument as *hypotheticals*. This is not to say that we should see them as *necessary* or *non-hypothetical premisses*. Far from it. Taking premiss (12) to be a necessary truth—or as 'constitutive of logical inference'—would no more enable it to stop the regress than taking it to be simply true. Rules of inference differ essentially in *role* from premisses, not in modality.

Somewhat similarly, we should not be led by questions such as Gary's to think of the mutual bearing of ends upon means as itself hypothetical, or as something like a premiss in our deliberation about action, on pain of regress. For suppose we started with the practical argument:

[30] See Lewis Carroll, 'What the Tortoise said to Achilles', *Mind*, 4 (1895), 278–80. I have altered Carroll's example slightly.

(13) *E* is an end of mine

(14) Means *M* would secure *E*

(C*) So: There is that much to be said deliberatively in favour of my doing *M*, or against my having *E*.

And suppose Gary asked, 'Isn't this argument missing something?—Doesn't it suppose not only that I have end *E*, but that I also have the further aim, call it *F*, of choosing so as to bring about the realization of my ends? If I didn't have that further end, couldn't I reject any relevance of (13) and (14) to my deliberation?' It would seem that we need to add this premiss:

(15) *F* [= choosing so as to bring about the realization of my ends] is an end of mine.

But if one did not already recognize that having an end makes deliberatively relevant questions about the means that would advance it—if, that is, (14)–(15) were insufficient to support the conclusion (C*)—then adding the further premiss (15) could hardly help. And notice that the situation would not be improved by claiming that the end *F* is somehow necessary for agents as such. For if one cannot see the bearing of having an end upon the choice of actions, then knowing an end to be necessary would not enlighten one on that score.

So we arrive again at what we want to say to Gary. Not: 'Giving deliberative weight to one's ends is constitutive of agency, and you are, after all, an agent.' He might sensibly wonder whether *that* state of affairs should continue. Rather, we want to say: 'You already defer, in posing this question, to the very thing you seek to challenge. You must already see—and feel—the "practical logic" of what you claim to find arbitrary or problematic: the bearing of ends upon means. If you reply, "Well, so that's just another end of mine—I can change it" then we can answer "No, on pain of regress, it cannot be just another end of yours."'

Does this show that Gary cannot be raising a genuine issue about whether or not to be rational? Return to our earlier distinction between subjective and objective notions of conformity to norms.

Gary was dismissive of this distinction, since his ambition was to ask a question less 'internal' to the theory of practical reason in its orthodox form. 'Subjective or objective,' he said in effect, 'I want to know whether rationality's worth it.' It now appears that he succeeded instead in asking a more 'internal' question. Roughly: 'I want to know whether subjectively patterning my thinking along means/ends lines would really be in objective conformity with realizing my ends—especially, the end of living well.' This question, more internal than he imagined, is also more real than others have imagined. Constitutive arguments of the kind considered here can neither answer it nor set it aside. The Low Brow argument, if successful, would show that subjective patterning to means/ends reasoning—that is, representing oneself as deliberatively adjusting means and ends—is partially constitutive of agency. But whether a life of subjective patterning would be in objective accord with realizing one's most important ends is another question. Arguably, it is Gary's real question. Gary is asking, not 'Do ends bear on means?', but 'Why be the sort of creature who asks about ends and means?'

Lewis Carroll's paradox is sometimes used to argue that there cannot really be an 'alternative logic'—we cannot drop or pick up rules of inference like premisses. But this paradox cannot really establish that orthodox logic will be adequate to—or necessary for—the fullest possible development of our thought and experience. The paradox shows instead that a certain way of thinking about how an alternative logic might be introduced or argued for is absurd. We cannot say, for example, 'Just compare the implications of existing logical rules with those of my new rules . . .'. The very notion of *implication* presupposes that logical rules are already in place. Similarly, the present discussion cannot demonstrate that Low Brow means/ends reasoning will be adequate to—or necessary for—the fullest possible development of our thought and experience. We can at most show the absurdity of attempting to give a Low Brow rationale (in terms of objective conformity) for questioning whether Low Brow reasons (again, in the objective sense) are relevant for what to do or how to live. Gary seemed to be pursuing such a rationale, so his line of questioning can come to look a bit silly. One can't lift oneself by one's own bootstraps, but he seems to have managed to pull himself down thereby.

Yet Gary isn't without a 'less internal' response. He can, without absurdity, be seen as trying to find a way of keeping us aware that no one really knows where reflective equilibrium and our evolving experience might take us. Each step in a reflective equilibrium process is linked by intelligible forms of reasoning to the step before, but this does not mean that we could not take steps which would, in sum, yield the result that our conception of reasoning itself has changed. Experience has held some interesting surprises for those who thought certain principles—such as the Principle of Sufficient Reason—were constitutive of the entire possible domain of thought and action. Perhaps Gary just wants to remind us of this. Moreover, he could insist, it seems inevitable that wherever reflective equilibrium takes us, its route will depend upon facts about us and our contingent nature. As Gary never tires of pointing out, this shows our reasoning is never on a wholly non-hypothetical footing.

Where, then, are we left? We began with the question whether a non-hypothetical account could be given of why we must conform to certain forms of theoretical or practical reasoning. In that context, we developed several constitutive arguments that showed some prospect of returning an intelligible, positive answer. We now have also seen the limitations of such arguments. Especially, they cannot supply a self-sufficient non-hypothetical response.[31]

But we should not imagine that this means we are left with wholly hypothetical considerations. Another conclusion to be drawn from the Low Brow constitutive argument is that each element—hypothetical and non-hypothetical, end-setting and ends/means-adjusting—has its own distinctive role to play in reasoning about action. Neither can do the other's job. To ask, of a given piece of Low Brow reasoning, whether it owes its conclusion to hypothetical or non-hypothetical considerations is a bit like asking, of a deductive argument, whether we owe its conclusion to the premises or to the rules of inference. The answer, of course, is always both.[32]

---

[31] We have not, however, tried to demonstrate the impossibility of other types of argument which could provide the grounds for 'purely' non-hypothetical justifications.

[32] I am grateful to a number of people for helpful comments and conversation. In particular, I should mention Garrett Cullity, Stephen Darwall, Berys Gaut, Allan Gibbard, Shelly Kagan, Michael Smith, David Velleman, and an anonymous referee.

3

Humean Doubts about the Practical Justification of Morality

JAMES DREIER

Humeans[1] doubt that there is any categorical justification of morality, in that they doubt that practical reason demands compliance with morality. In this essay I examine the grounds for their scepticism. One kind of ground is dubious. After exposing its flaws, I explain why there is a plausible ground for scepticism anyway.

1. The Justification of Morality

Why is there a problem about the justification of morality? This question is, admittedly, too vague to have any good answer. Let me formulate it better.

Morality consists of rules. So saying, I certainly beg some questions, especially against virtue ethics. But the questions so begged are not going to be in question here, so I will beg them unabashedly. Morality consists of rules, in that it is constituted by some rules, rules that tell us what we are to do. Here I might be thought to be begging questions in favour of deontological conceptions of morality, and against teleological conceptions, since according to teleological conceptions of morality, it tells us which things are of value. But I don't think that the claim that morality consists of rules that tell us what to do does beg any questions against teleological conceptions. Teleologists, after they have told us what is of value, go on to tell us what to do: we are to maximize (or satisfice, or otherwise advance) the realization of value in the world.[2]

Now suppose a moral theorist has proposed a certain set of rules, as the set of moral rules, the set that constitutes morality. We are bound to have some questions. We might question whether these rules really do constitute morality. This challenge is a kind of request for justification: what is the

---

[1] 'Humean', as I use it, is the name of a kind of philosophical theory of practical reason. I do not address the historical question of whether Hume had a theory of this kind. Nor will I give any explicit definition of the kind.

[2] This point is spelled out nicely in William Kymlicka, 'Rawls on Teleology and Deontology', *Philosophy and Public Affairs*, 17 (1988), 173–90.

justification for the claim that these rules constitute morality? But we could also ask for another kind of justification. We could ask what reason we, or anyone, has to follow these rules. This would be a request for a practical justification.[3]

But why should we expect those rules to have any external justification? Why, for instance, could they not have a merely internal sort; they all hang together; or, perhaps they are simply very plausible, more so than any alternative; or they could just be *the rules of morality*, *by definition*, as the rules of chess are the rules of chess, by definition, with no justification necessary. Still, this last gambit would be a way of avoiding not the request for a practical justification, but the request for a theoretic justification. Presumably, if someone admitted that the rules of chess forbid castling when in check, but asked why this fact should have any grip on what he plans to do with the plastic pieces, we would either be prepared to give some reason or else to admit that the rules really don't have any justification.

We have strong feelings, and strong interests, that are served by the compliance of others with moral rules. So of course we do want others to follow moral rules, and we have that reason and other practical reasons to hope that we can give a justification.[4] This explains why we want there to be some justification for moral rules. And the model of the rules of games, and other various arbitrary collections of rules, explains the perfectly coherent worry that there might not be any such justification. I want to stress that such a worry is coherent. For sometimes it can seem as though the request for a justification of morality doesn't make sense at all. But we can see how an arbitrary set of rules might be justified. For example, if you want to play chess, then you must follow the game's rules. This is not exactly a practical justification, if all we mean is that these *are* the rules of chess, so that just by definition you can't play chess without following them. But consider instead some rules for playing chess well. For instance, you ought to try to control the centre of the board, you ought to castle early to get your king out of danger, and so on. There is a kind of practical justification for these rules, but it depends on your having a certain goal: to play chess well. That is typical of practical justifications of rules: their force for you depends on your having some relevant goal.

Now it looks as though an external justification of practical rules must have its ground in some other practical rules. At least this is ordinarily so.

---

[3] See David Copp, 'Moral Skepticism', *Philosophical Studies*, 62 (1991), 203–33. Whether it really is another kind, or whether in fact a justification for the claim that certain rules constitute morality is really the same thing as a justification for following them, I will leave open. Personally, I suspect that they do amount to the same sort of justification. But on their face they at least appear to be distinct.

[4] For example: it is very plausibly part of our ordinary moral view that we shouldn't coerce others unless we can justify our actions *to* them. If we can't justify morality to others who don't already accept our moral views, then we would often be unable to satisfy this ordinary moral requirement.

For example, a practical justification of laws would generally proceed by reference to moral considerations. It is a complication that there are also generally prudential reasons to follow laws. Independent of the prudential reasons, we often want some moral justification of legal obligations. And even if the justification offered were purely prudential, this would still be a justification by reference to other rules, namely, the rules of prudence. It is imprudent, extremely so, to take a significant chance of landing in prison.

We would not think of justifying morality by grounding it in just any old other system of rules. Of course, most systems of rules are obviously unable to provide anything like a justification for morality. For instance, when we want a justification for morality, it would be no help if we were shown that etiquette requires that we follow moral rules.[5] There are apparently only two systems of rules which look at all appropriate for providing some justificaton of morality, and they are the rules of prudence and the rules of rationality. And I think really, the rules of prudence have seemed appropriate *only* because they are sometimes taken to *be* rules of rationality, or to be derived from them.[6]

This is why the Kantian view of morality and its justification is so compelling. A justification of morality is a 'deduction' of its principles from the principles of rationality. Or perhaps even better, it is a demonstration that moral rules *are* rules of rationality. Such a justification would satisfy the demand, in a way that no other justification could. Why are the rules of rationality the ones that have to lie at the bottom of a satisfactory justification of morality? A request for justification is a request for reasons. So much seems obvious. Indeed, it is exactly why the request for justification can be of two different sorts. We can ask for reasons to believe that some philosopher's account of morality is correct, or we can ask for reasons to follow those moral rules.

Now, a certain set of rules will, in one sense, provide its own set of reasons. The reason we can't bring in Martinez to pitch, is that we pinch hit for him last inning. That reason comes from the rules of baseball. The reason for sending a cheque to the American Philosophical Association, even though they have lost their records and don't know whether or not you've already paid your dues, is that it would be unfair not to send it. That reason comes from the rules of morality. But we can also wonder whether there is any reason to follow those rules. In this sense, there being a rule does not in itself count as a reason. There is a more fundamental sense of 'having a reason', and it is in this sense that we can wonder whether we have any reason to follow moral rules. But even in this more

---

[5] Well, it might, but only under very special circumstances. It would not answer the philosopher's question, if someone did manage to show that it was rude to act wrongly.

[6] e.g. in Thomas Nagel, *The Possibility of Altruism* (Princeton: Princeton Univ. Press, 1970).

fundamental respect, I think, there is no sense at all to be made of the question whether we have a reason to follow the rules of rationality. To think that there might be reasons for following the rules of rationality, I would say, is to misunderstand what reasons are. Reasons are *in terms of* the rules of rationality. There is a reason to do something, just in case it is rational to do it. This is why there seems to be a pressing need for a justification of morality, but no similar need for a justification of rationality.[7] The contrast here seems to me to be important. I will argue below for my view that there is such a contrast, and try to explain why there is.

In what follows, I will examine the Humean attitude toward the issue of justifying morality. I would like to vindicate a central part of that attitude.

2. *Categorical Imperatives*

Humeans doubt that morality could be a set of categorical imperatives, and this doubt might even be thought of as a hallmark of Humeans. The question whether there are any categorical imperatives, and whether morality consists of categorical imperatives, is clearly related to the problem of the justification of morality. Before I explain what I think the relation between the questions is, I need to clarify what is meant by a categorical imperative. Following Foot,[8] we should really distinguish a couple of senses in which imperatives might be categorical. First, we might say that an imperative is categorical when our application of it to the behaviour (or deliberations) of someone does not depend on any aim, on any desire of that person. In this sense, the rule 'Practice your scales daily' is not categorical, since we should withdraw it upon learning that the addressee had no interest in learning to play the piano. There is little question that moral imperatives are categorical in this sense. Informing your critic that you aren't interested in according respect to other persons isn't going to make him withdraw the imperative to keep your promises. We are interested rather in a second sense of categoricity. A rough try at expressing this sense is to say that a categorical imperative is one that each person has reason to follow, no matter what her desires. This is only a *rough* try because whether it succeeds in explaining the sense of 'categorical' in which Humeans deny that morality could be categorical, depends on how we fill in an explanation of what it is to have a reason. But it will do for a start.

---

[7] So here I am disagreeing, I think, with some of Peter Railton's remarks in this volume. I am disagreeing more directly with his 'Some Questions about the Justification of Morality', in J. Tomberlin (ed.), *Philosophical Perspectives*, vi. *Ethics* (Atascadero, Calif.: Ridgeview, 1992), 27–53.

[8] Philippa Foot, 'Morality as a System of Hypothetical Imperatives', in her *Virtues and Vices* (Berkeley: Univ. of California Press, 1978), 157–73.

Humeans sometimes say that *no* imperatives are categorical. I think they are mistaken to say so, for reasons that will emerge. But let's focus first on the special case of moral imperatives. Why couldn't they be categorical, according to the Humean view?

Suppose we want to explain why someone acted the way he did. Suppose he walked to the corner shortly before noon, and we want to explain why. Since he does it intentionally, we typically cite some mental states of the agent that rationalize the action. We could cite mental states of his that merely cause the behaviour, but that is a different kind of explanation.[9] The classic form of explanation is the citing of a belief/desire pair. He walked to the corner shortly before noon, because he wanted to eat a sandwich at noon and believed that by walking to the corner shortly before noon he could bring it about that he would eat a sandwich at noon. In this explanation we cite the agent's reason. His reason is a belief/desire pair. For short, we might say that his reason was that he wanted a sandwich, or, that he thought that walking to the corner was the only way he could get a sandwich. Which is the sensible thing to say depends on context, of course. But it doesn't follow that what his reason really was depends on context. I am denying that it does depend on context. There are only pragmatic grounds, not deep ones, for describing the person's reason one way rather than another.

As I just admitted, in ordinary talk we can give reason-for-action explanations that do not make explicit reference to any desire. Maybe he walked to the corner shortly before noon because he believed that this was the only way to save his life. We would not ordinarily add, 'and he wanted to save his life'. But this is a shallow feature of ordinary talk. It is unusual but conceivable *not* to desire to save one's own life, and if indeed our agent does not, then citing his belief that walking to the corner shortly before noon was the only way to save his life provides no explanation of his walking, and so doesn't count as a reason in the explanatory sense of 'reason'. But it's also true that we sometimes seem to cite reasons for action without citing desires, when we aren't just failing to mention a desire that we assume must be present. Maybe the agent walked to the corner shortly before noon because he remembered his promise to meet his sister on the corner at noon. Do we need to add, 'and he wanted to keep his promise'? We might. But we might instead say, 'he believed that he had an obligation to keep the promise'. Then must we add, 'and he wanted to discharge his obligation'?

I think we *do* need to add *something*. For after all, some people recognize their obligations and do not act on them. What we need to add is

---

[9] Not to say that rationalizing explanations aren't also causal. I don't see how they could fail to be causal. I don't think this point matters to the main argument in the text.

something to the effect that this is a sort of person whom the thought of obligation normally moves to action. The question I want to examine now is how that sort of thing, that sort of fact about a person, can sensibly and illuminatingly be described. Once that is done, we'll be in position to understand why Humeans think that moral imperatives couldn't be categorical.

3. *Motivating Reasons*

A motivating reason is a reason that someone has to do something, where his doing it (if he does it) is explained by his having that reason. Following Michael Smith, among others, we can contrast this sort of reason with a normative reason. A normative reason is, to put it somewhat loosely, a reason that a person *ought* to do something. If she then does it, this is explained not by the fact that she had the reason, but by the fact that she recognized this reason and was motivated by it. For example, I had a normative reason to wear a suit to my brother's wedding. And I did wear one. That I did is explained not by the fact that I had this reason, but by the fact that I 'accepted' it, we might say, that I cared about that sort of reason and recognized that I had it.

Suppose a person has a belief, and that he performs some action, he ϕs. What must the belief be, and what do we need to add to the belief in order to explain the action by citing the agent's reason for performing it? The simplest Humean view would be that the belief must have a content of the form, By ϕ-ing I will ψ, and we must add that the agent has a desire to ψ. This is Michael Smith's account in *The Moral Problem*.[10] It requires a defence, a much longer one than I can give it here. But the main idea can be given fairly easily. The primary access that we have to the whole idea of a desire, is that it is a state of mind characterized by its output in behaviour. Let's allow ourselves a little weaselling: a desire to ϕ is a mental state that *normally* motivates its bearer to ϕ. 'Normally' clauses are very suspicious, but for now at least we'll take it in a loose and intuitive way; we aren't offering an analysis or placing any great weight on the claim.

Putting the weasel aside, then, we have very good grounds to say that a person has a motivating reason to ϕ only when she has a desire to ψ, and a belief that by ϕ-ing she will ψ. For suppose she believed that by ϕ-ing she would ψ, and that this explains why she ϕs—that's what's necessary for her to have a motivating reason to ϕ. What do we have to add? We have to add

---

[10] Michael Smith, *The Moral Problem* (Oxford: Blackwell, 1994).

that she had some motivation to do what she believed she would do by φ-ing. What state is that? A motivation to do what she believes she will do by φ-ing is a motivation to ψ (since that's what she believes she'll do by φ-ing). The state that explains this motivation is one which normally produces the motivation as its output. So it is a desire to ψ.

One might question whether this account of the desire to ψ is a correct analysis. I think this issue is probably a red herring. 'Desire' here is really a term of art. It covers what is covered in ordinary language by the notions of desire proper, wanting, valuing, having a goal, preferring, and probably many other things. What they have in common is precisely what the (weaselly) analysis says.

So much for the Humean view of motivating reasons. I intend it to convince only temporarily. With it in place, we return to the question of why Humeans say that moral imperatives couldn't be categorical.

A categorical imperative, I said, is one that each person has reason to follow, no matter what her desires. What kind of reason do we mean? Not a merely normative reason. Each person does have a normative reason to refrain from harming others, irrespective of what she wants. This is one sense of 'categorical', but not the one we want here. It seems that we want the sense of 'categorical' that results from plugging *motivating* reasons into the 'reason' slot of the formula. We can see now why anyone who accepts the Humean account of motivating reasons should think that what (motivating) reasons a person has is entirely dependent on what desires she has. For a person's having a motivating reason just is a matter of her having a belief and a desire. *That* reason, the one that she has, is a reason that she wouldn't have were she to lack *that* desire. This chunk of theory completes the simple Humean story. Let's recap.

Humeans doubt that morality could consist of categorical imperatives, because (i) a categorical imperative is one that you have reason to follow irrespective of your desires, and (ii) what you have motivating reason to do is not independent of your desires. Furthermore, morality can be justified only if someone can be given reasons to follow moral rules. If morality cannot consist of categorical imperatives, then a person can be given reasons to follow moral rules only if she has certain relevant desires. In particular, she must desire that she follow moral rules, or desire those things which the moral rules tell her to pursue, or the like. What desires we have is a contingent fact about us. So the justification of morality is a contingent matter. This is a disappointment, and falls short of the kind of justification we sometimes hope for. David Copp puts it this way: a justification for following moral rules that appeals to contingencies of the agent addressed is not a justification of morality *per se*, but only a justification of morality for someone.[11] Humeans think that it is a disappointment we will have to learn to live with.[12]

There is a major (glaring?) flaw in the reasoning of the last paragraph above. The conclusion, that the justification of morality is contingent, follows from the premiss (let's call it a 'lemma', since it was independently established), that morality does not consist of categorical imperatives, only if the kind of reason that fills out the content of the conclusion is the same as the kind of reason that gives content to the lemma. Are the kinds of reason the same? In the lemma, we are plugging motivating reasons into the slot. Is that the sort of reason we mean when we think about the justification of morality? This is still unsettled. We are thinking of reasons of rationality, which I argued are ultimate reasons in some sense. Motivating reasons are also ultimate, in a way. But it is not obvious that reasons of rationality and motivating reasons are the same thing. If they aren't, then it might be that morality can be justified to anyone, independent of her desires, because everyone has a reason of rationality to follow moral rules, even though whether a person has a motivating reason to follow moral rules is contingent.

Nearly all of the remainder of the essay is devoted to understanding the relation between motivating reasons and reasons of rationality. Only at the end will we return to the question of the justification of morality.

4. The Interpretation of Motivating Reasons

Are motivating reasons just the same as reasons of rationality? On the face of it, no. They do not seem to be the same *kind* of thing. Motivating reasons are psychologically real, since they are explanatory by nature. A

---

[11] 'Moral Skepticism'.

[12] There is a completely different sort of conclusion that one might draw, in fact, one which I have myself been inclined to draw. It is that the justification of morality is not contingent at all, but rather that the content of morality is relative to agents. The content of morality relative to an agent is always something that can be justified to that agent. In this essay I am ignoring this move, even though in fact I think it is very promising as a move in a different context. Here I am assuming that a proper justification, in the sense that's usually meant, must be a justification of the same content to each person, or more simply, a justification of a certain content of morality. In Kant's terms, I am interested in what must be the case 'if morality is to be something real' (Ak 445). The Humean view is that the necessary condition is not met, that morality is not 'something real', though we Humeans prefer not to put it in those terms.

My sense is that there is a lot of in-fighting among Humeans that is quite interesting to us Humeans. I include David Brink, a moral realist, who certainly would reject Kant's criteria for whether morality is something real; John Mackie, who accepts Kant's criteria and concludes straightforwardly that morality is nothing real at all; all expressivists, including quasi-realists who believe that morality is something quasi-real (and that quasi-real is good enough), but not R. M. Hare, whom I take to be a Kantian in the relevant sense. I find this in-fighting very interesting, but the present essay is about the grander dispute, in which all Humeans are on the same side.

motivating reason that you have is an empirical property that you bear, or how could it explain anything that you do? But a reason of rationality is something normative. For you to have a reason of rationality is for it to be the case that you *ought* to act in a certain way. As I said, citing a normative reason can be a kind of explanation, but it is only an explanation on the (tacit) assumption that the agent does, or at least is disposed to do, what she ought to do. As I have put it, citing a normative reason is explanatory only on the assumption that the agent *accepts* the norms in question. Here 'accepts' is really a term of art; there is a sense of 'accepting a reason', no doubt, according to which one may accept one and have not even the slightest tendency to act on it. But I am using 'accepts' for whatever it takes actually to be motivated by the kind of reason in question.

Since reasons of rationality are, after all, normative, they are not the same kind of thing as motivating reasons, so the Humean argument does not go through as sketched. I think this is an important fact, so let me support my claim. Someone might think that reasons of rationality are not really normative at all. Maybe standards of rationality are something like canons of interpretation, so that acting rationally is just a matter of being interpretable. To say that someone has a reason of rationality to ϕ, in that case, might just be to say that in case she does ϕ, her ϕ-ing is interpretable as intentional action. While I think there must be something to this idea, I also think it can't be correct as stated. For there is such a thing as irrational action. There is such a thing as fallacious reasoning. People do reason incorrectly, not merely from false premises, and when they do they are precisely reasoning as they *ought not* to reason. They have good reasons not to draw the conclusions they draw. What sorts of reasons could these be? Reasons of rationality. I will give examples below, but it seems to me that the point is clear enough in the abstract. Reasons of rationality are normative.

Here is a suggestion for why motivating reasons and normative reasons of rationality might be conflated. We are calling 'motivating reasons to ϕ' those belief–desire pairs of the following form: the desire to ψ, and the belief that by ϕ-ing I will ψ. So we have this claim:

> (MR) A has a motivating reason to ϕ iff there is some ψ such that A desires to ψ and believes that by ϕ-ing, she will ψ.

Now in fact, I think this claim can be understood in two different ways. According to one reading, it really is a normative claim. It says, in effect, that you ought to perform the necessary and sufficient means to your desired ends. You might not do this. You might, at least on occasion, find yourself lacking the motivation to perform the necessary and sufficient means to some end you desire. This would be a fault of yours, a failure of rationality. Glossing over some distinctions, we might say that your failure would be a failure of instrumental reason. So this reading of (MR) takes it to be a statement of the norm of instrumental reason.

Second, the claim could be understood in a different way. It might be a partial analysis of desire and belief; it might be a purported analytic truth. A motivating reason, according to this reading, would be something that actually does motivate you. The claim would be that unless you are in fact motivated to ϕ, there is no ψ such that you desire to ψ and believe that by ϕ-ing you will ψ. According to the analysis, a crude functionalist analysis, it is of the very essence of the desire to ψ that, when combined with the belief that by ϕ-ing you will ψ, it produces a desire in you to ϕ; and it is of the very essence of the belief that by ϕ-ing you will ψ that, when combined with the desire to ψ, it produces in you the desire to ϕ. Let's call this the 'constitutive' reading. According to it, belief and desire are partly constituted by the stated role in the production of motivation.

I object to the second reading, for reasons I have just given. It implies that it is impossible to desire to ψ, believe that by ϕ-ing you will ψ, and yet fail to desire to ϕ. But this does not seem to be impossible, it seems to be irrational. When I say how it 'seems', admittedly, I am reporting my intuitions, and the very existence of seriously held philosophical views to the contrary of mine demonstrates that these intuitions aren't universally shared. Mine are hardly unique, though. Kant says,

Whoever wills the end, wills (so far as reason has decisive influence on his actions) also the means that are indispensibly necessary and in his power. So far as willing is concerned, this proposition is analytic . . .   (Ak 417)

[I]t could alike be said 'Who wills the end, wills also (necessarily, if he accords with reason) the sole means which are in his power.'   (Ak 417–18)

The parenthetic condition, in each case, is crucial. The crude functionalist reading of (MR) would in effect leave out that condition, and say that willing the end *is* willing the means.[13]

Not to leave the point resting on my intuitions and the authority of Kant's, let me give some theoretic backing to my objection. The desire to ψ and belief that by ϕ-ing I will ψ do, I admit, have conceptual connections to the desire to ϕ. Can we imagine someone who under no circumstances would come to have the latter desire on the basis of the former plus the belief? Perhaps not. Maybe this would be a case of someone so wildly irrational that we could not think of her as an agent at all. But it is a long jump to conclude that there is a universal necessary connection between beliefs and desires of the sort postulated by (the second reading of) (MR). For desire has other conceptual facets. For instance, in us sophisticated

---

[13] Quite possibly the distinction between desiring and willing is important here.

linguistic creatures, beliefs and desires are normally available to introspection. So I ought to know whether I desire a French fry, and whether I believe that the one and only way to get one is by ordering some. So my sincere report that I so believe and so desire might be enough to ground the attribution to me, even if I don't order some French fries (or even want to order any). Good functionalist analyses ought to respect the plurality of links that mental states have to other states and to actions and linguistic behaviour, and to perceptual inputs, and the like. That is why I called the second reading of (MR) 'crude'.

But finally, even if my objection is not convincing, I want to insist on a weaker claim. We cannot have both readings of (MR) at once. They are exclusive. If (as I deny) (MR) can be read as a kind of functionalist analysis of belief and desire, then it cannot also be normative, it cannot be an expression of an instrumentalist conception of rationality. For norms are things which it is possible to violate. The idea of a norm which it is logically impossible to violate makes no sense. So reasons of rationality, which are normative, cannot be the same sorts of things as motivating reasons, which are explanatory of action. (MR) defines motivating reasons only on the second, functionalist reading, and it defines a normative means/ends principle only on the first reading.

To conclude this section, let's recall why this distinction, between motivating reasons and normative reasons of rationality, is important.

(1) Morality can be justified only if it consists of categorical imperatives.
(2) An imperative is categorical if and only if a person has reason to follow it independent of what she desires.
(3) A person's having reason to ϕ depends on there being some ψ such that she desires to ψ and believes that by ϕ-ing she will ψ.
(4) So any reason a person might have depends on a desire of hers.
(5) So there are no categorical imperatives.
(6) So morality cannot be justified.

This argument goes through just in case 'reason' can be understood univocally in the premises (1)–(3). (3) was offered and defended as a conception of motivating, explanatory reasons (though I cast some doubt on it even when construed that way). But (2) cannot be understood to be about motivating reasons, because if it is then the sense of 'categorical' it defines makes (1) terribly implausible. We don't deny that people sometimes behave immorally. If being able to justify morality meant being able to force people to behave morally by dint of argument, there would be no question of success.

The ground for scepticism about, and thus for scepticism about the justification of, morality, is very shaky. At least as I have presented it so far,

it relies on a dubious conflation of two kinds of reasons. We may doubt that
there are any motivating reasons to follow moral rules, that each person has
necessarily and independent of what she happens to desire, but that doesn't
in itself provide any ground for doubting that morality can be justified,
since justification is a matter of normative reasons.

I think that scepticism is called for none the less. I will argue that there
is something special about exactly the kind of norms of rationality that
Humeans accept.[14] This special status confers a kind of necessity on the
Humean norms which we may properly doubt can accrue to other sorts of
norms. The request for justification, I will argue, is intelligible as a demand
for reasons bearing just that kind of necessity. And we may properly doubt
that the demand for moral justification can be satisfied.

5. *Rules and Desires*

Suppose we tell Ann that she ought to ϕ. She asks why. We cite some rules,
R, that tell her to ϕ. She shrugs. These rules have no grip on her. She can
see that the rules do tell her to ϕ, but she doesn't accept the rules, they
don't motivate her. We might think, she is 'missing something'. What is
she missing? What must be true of her, that isn't, in order for her to be
motivated by our explanation? In so far as we think there is something
wrong with Ann for failing to be motivated by the belief that she is required by R to ϕ, we will think that her missing this something is exactly
what's wrong with her.

Schematic as this story is, there is an almost entirely general answer that
we can give. Ann is missing a desire. How can we know this? How do we
know that what she's missing isn't a capacity of some other sort, or a belief?
Couldn't what's wrong with Ann be that she believes something false, or
that she fails to believe some truth? We know that what's missing is a
desire, because we have enough characterization of the missing state to see
that it fits the bill to be a certain desire, a desire with a certain specifiable
content. Since she believes that were she to ϕ, she would comply with R,
and we want a state that gets her from that belief to the motivation to ϕ, we
know that the state is the desire to comply with R. That's what the desire
to comply with R *is*.

We have to be a bit careful here. We have already rejected the simple
functionalist definition of desire, so we can't say that S is a desire to ψ iff
S is a state producing a desire to ϕ upon input of a belief that by ϕ-ing one
will ψ. The means/end principle is a normative principle of rationality.

---

[14] See Elijah Millgram, 'Was Hume a Humean?', *Hume Studies*, 21 (1995), 75–93, on whether Hume
is a Humean in this sense.

Given that Ann is means/ends rational, all we need to give her in order to get her to φ, is the desire to comply with R.

I said that the missing desire answer is an *almost* entirely general answer to the question raised in the schematic story. Why only almost? We're taking it as a kind of methodological axiom that whatever is missing when someone has a belief and lacks a certain motivation is a desire of some sort or other. There doesn't seem to be any room for exceptions.

Suppose Ann's case is like this. We tell her that she ought to take a prep course for the Law School Admissions Test. She asks why. We point out that she wants to raise her chances of getting into a competitive law school, and she can raise her chances by taking the prep course. She admits as much, but still isn't motivated to take the prep course. So we cite a rule, the means/ends rule:

> M/E   If you desire to ψ, and believe that by φ-ing you will ψ, then you ought to φ.

Now suppose that Ann agrees that this rule does indeed instruct her to take the prep course, given what she believes and desires, but she shrugs at the rule. She doesn't accept it.

We must now conclude that there is something wrong with Ann. She *ought* to take the prep course, given what she believes and wants, but she doesn't, and she has no motivation to take the course.[15] The story is an instance of the schematic story. We can ask ourselves what exactly Ann is missing. What state is it that she lacks, the absence of which explains what's wrong with her? Isn't it a desire of some sort? For we thought that any state that bridges the gap between a belief and a motivation must be a desire. But not this one. What Ann is missing can't be any desire.

The desire that is supposed to bridge the gap between believing that a rule requires her to φ, and being motivated to φ, is the desire to comply with the rule. But suppose Ann's mental inventory were supplemented with a desire to comply with the rule, in this case to comply with M/E. Could this complete the picture? Were she to desire to comply with M/E, would she then be motivated to take the LSAT prep course? By hypothesis, Ann suffers from this failure of practical reason: she fails to be motivated by the acknowledged means to her desired ends. So adding a desired end does not in her bring about the motivation to perform the acknowledged means to that end. We cannot bring about in Ann the motivation to perform an action acknowledged by her to be a means to a certain end, by getting her to desire that end. That is a good way to motivate normal, rational agents, but in Ann's case it is futile. But this futile

---

[15] This point is made by Jean Hampton in her 'Hobbes and Ethical Naturalism', in Tomberlin (ed.), *Philosophical Perspectives*, vi. *Ethics*, 333–53.

attempt is exactly what we would be engaged in, if we were to try to bring
Ann to desire to take the LSAT prep course by giving her a desired end
(the end of complying with M/E) the means to which (she believes) is to
take the prep course. So what Ann is missing cannot be a desire. Call this
the Tortoise argument (for a reason I will explain shortly).

Maybe this argument looks too quick. We do agree that what's wrong
with Ann is that she is missing some sort of state. And that state takes the
input of belief (that taking the prep course is a necessary means to improving her chances of getting into a competitive law school) and desire (to get
into a competitive law school) to the output of motivation, or action. And
such states just *are* desires, one might say. After all, we are being broad in
our classification of desires. What prevents us from counting this state,
whatever its ordinary description, as a desire?[16] What prevents us is that
desires are typed by their content. When asked which desire Ann needs, we
have to be able to say something like, 'The desire that p', or 'The desire to
ϕ'. We can't just cite inputs and outputs. No doubt, what Ann is missing
is very much like a desire in certain respects, but if it isn't a desire to . . . or
a desire that . . . or even a desire for . . . , then it is no desire at all. But as
soon as some content is given to this purported desire, the one that is
supposed to be the missing state, then the Tortoise argument shows that it
could not be what Ann is missing.

Compare Lewis Carroll's Tortoise.[17] His problem, his irrationality, was
that he did not draw the logical conclusion of an argument whose premisses
he accepted and whose reasoning was valid and simple. What state was he
missing? He did not accept the inference rule, modus ponens. There is no
temptation here to suppose that what the Tortoise was missing was a desire
of any sort,[18] but there might be *some* temptation to think that his failure to
accept the rule was a matter of his lacking a certain belief. At least, Achilles
was so tempted. Achilles tried to get the Tortoise to believe that (an
instance of) modus ponens is valid. And he succeeded! But futilely. For
from this additional, otiose premiss, the Tortoise was still unable (or unwilling?) to draw the logically implied conclusion. I find this parallel striking.

Now we've singled out the means/ends rule as special. Once you have
(accept) the means/ends rule, what you need to get you to acceptance of
other rules is one or another desire. But no desire will get you to the
means/ends rule itself. (Compare modus ponens. Once you have modus
ponens, what you need to get you to acceptance of other rules is some

---

[16] Simon Blackburn put this objection to me.

[17] Lewis Carroll, 'What the Tortoise said to Achilles', *Mind*, 4 (1895), 278–80.

[18] But see Railton, 'Some Questions about the Justification of Morality'. Railton's use of the Tortoise
in the present volume is for a different end, though a related one. See also my 'Perspectives on the
Normativity of Ethics', *Noûs*, 28 (1994), 514–25, for the relevance of the Tortoise to the views
presented by Railton in 'Some Questions'.

conditional belief, the belief in some conditional. But a belief in a conditional won't get you modus ponens itself.) So means/ends rationality has a special status. But is this special status relevant to the question at hand?

When someone asks for a justification of practical rules, for example, morality, she is asking to be given a reason to follow them. The justification of morality is given by reasons, normative, practical reasons. Since they are normative reasons, they are grounded in some set of rules, some norms. When we give a justification we are either explicitly citing or adverting to some norms. But we can't just cite any old bunch of norms. Which norms count toward justification? The problem is that if we simply cite a bunch of rules, the agent may well ask, what are those rules to me? She may ask for a reason to follow them. And we can't just shrug this off. Suppose someone cited the laws of India in support of moral principles. We ourselves recognize that this sort of justification is useless. We have to say why the rules we cite are better.

If we cite the laws of India, and our subject asks what reason she has to follow them, we understand what she's asking. She's asking for reasons, again. She doesn't see any force in the rules we've cited. She's missing whatever it takes to be motivated by the belief we've instilled, namely, that the laws of India require her to abide by moral norms. That state is a desire. We can understand how someone might lack that desire. Asking for a reason, in this context, makes perfectly good sense.

If our subject were asking for some reason to follow M/E, the matter would be different. Suppose she isn't motivated to ϕ when she believes that by ϕ-ing she will ψ, and desires to ψ. So she asks what reason she has, and when we cite the M/E principle, she asks what reason she has to follow that. But now, I think, we are at a loss. Not merely at a loss to provide a compelling answer, but at a loss to know what to think of such a person. What would *count* as a reason, by her lights? As long as she accepts M/E, we know what would count as a reason: some belief that by following the rule to be justified she would achieve some end she desires.

Compare the theoretic case. Suppose someone asks for a theoretic justification of some proposition, q. We could try to get her to believe that p, and that if p then q. We know what's required; it's a matter of getting her to believe the right things, the propositions from which she can infer that q. But what about the Tortoise? We can't give him a justification to believe the conclusion, not one that he can see to be a justification. We can't give him a reason that he will see as a reason. That's because there doesn't seem to be anything that counts as a reason, for the Tortoise. Those conditionals we count on to give reasons have no affect on the Tortoise.

We give you reasons to believe something by finding things you believe and getting you to draw inferences. If you can't draw those inferences, then nothing counts as a reason for you. And similarly for practical reasons. We can give you practical reasons by finding things you want, and some things you believe, and getting you to draw practical inferences. If you can't draw the practical inference, not even the fundamental, M/E kind, then nothing counts as a reason for you. This is why M/E has a kind of ground-level normative status. I think it counts as a categorical imperative, too. Of course, the particular reasons that M/E generates are all hypothetical reasons. But M/E itself is not hypothetical. Its demands must be met by you, in so far as you are rational, no matter what desires you happen to have. That is why I said (in Section 2) that I think Humeans are mistaken to say that there are no categorical imperatives at all.

We would like to be able to give a justification for morality, in the sense of being able to give someone reasons for abiding by moral rules. Some people already want to abide by moral rules. Those people have reasons already. But their reasons seem to depend on their contingent wants. A satisfying justification of morality would give reasons that are independent of contingent wants. Humeans doubt that there is any such justification, because they doubt that there are any such reasons. For suppose someone cited a reason for complying with moral rules. Citing a reason is referring or adverting to some norm. If the reason cited is grounded in an arbitrary norm, say, in the laws of India, then it can't count as a justification, precisely because we may perfectly sensibly ask what reason there is to comply with *that* norm. Nor is this a facile tactic of demanding that reasons be given *ad infinitum*. The laws of India clearly do not count as a reason to comply with moral rules, even if they entail that we ought to comply with moral rules. Admitted: reasons must end somewhere. But they may not end just anywhere. Humeans may plausibly claim that instrumental reasons are ground-level reasons. But instrumental reasons are never independent of our contingent desires. This is the ground for Humean scepticism about the justification of morality.

In closing, here are some prospects for combating the scepticism.

I have claimed a kind of *sine qua non* status for M/E. Giving an M/E reason counts as giving a reason if anything does; if it doesn't count, then the request for reasons is empty. But no principle other than M/E has this status. So the only ultimate sort of reasons are instrumental reasons. And this means that moral rules are not categorical, they depend for their compelling force on contingent desires. So I claimed. I can see two ways that an anti-Humean could resist.

First, she might claim that there are other sorts of practical principles with the same status as M/E. Maybe these other principles could yield enough content, independent of contingent aims, to provide justification for moral rules. I think this is one way of seeing 'transcendental' Kantian arguments. One might think that something of this sort happens in the case of theoretic reason when we wonder about the justification of induction. On the one hand, the demand that we provide a reason to believe (that the future will resemble the past) does get some grip, since the sceptic is willing to count *deductive* reasons as reasons, and points out that all the deductive grounds for induction are question-begging. Inductive principles of reasoning are independent of deductive ones. On the other hand, arguably the willingness to infer future predications from past ones is as much embedded in the functional character of belief as modus ponens is embedded in the functional character of a conditional belief (by which I mean only, a belief whose content is a conditional). Are there practical principles apart from M/E that have a similar status?

Second, and to my mind more plausibly, she might claim that there are *alternatives* to M/E. Let me explain. The first line of resistance insists that M/E is only one of a set of principles, all of which must be accepted if the idea of a reason is to make sense at all. But instead it might be that M/E is only one of a set of principles, *one* of which must be accepted if the idea of a reason is to make sense at all. To illustrate, think again of the theoretic analogue. A person (or Tortoise) who doesn't accept modus ponens can't be brought to accept it by supplying him with some conditional premisses. But modus ponens is not unique in this respect. He might accept disjunctive syllogism, for example. Then we could get him to believe that q, when he believes already that p and that if p then q, by adding the premiss,

$$\neg(p \rightarrow q) \vee (\neg p \vee q)$$

which is, after all, a tautology.

He could then reach $(\neg p \vee q)$ from $(p \rightarrow q)$, which he has, plus the second premiss; and q from the p, which he has, plus the intermediary conclusion. The point is that you need some inference rule or other, in addition to your beliefs, to draw inferences, but there isn't any particular inference rule you need. It is not obvious what practical rules one might use as a general alternative to M/E.[19] This strategy *might* yield a principle, one having a status at least equal to M/E, which itself has substantial moral content.

It might, but I doubt it. When we first looked at M/E, we noted that it can be thought of in two ways. The way I chose, with some argument, was as a desire. According to this, the constitutive reading, someone who desires an end and believes that some action is a necessary means to that end, cannot fail to desire the means. It would count decisively against the

---

[19] But see Elijah Millgram and Paul Thagard, 'Inference to the Best Plan: A Coherence Theory of Decision', in D. Leake and A. Ram (eds.), *Goal-Driven Learning* (Cambridge, Mass.: MIT Press, 1996), 439–54.

attribution of the instrument-belief and the end-desire, that the agent did not desire the means. I argued that the constitutive reading is false—as stated, it is too strong a condition. I also said, though, that something like the constitutive reading seems right, something suitably weakened. The output of the means-desire is *partly* constitutive of the combined functions of the end-desire and the instrument-belief. Bringing about the means-desire when in the presence of the end-desire is a part of the concept of an instrument-belief, but the connection may fail and the state still be attributable, as long as there are some other conceptual connections in place, and as long as there is some story surrounding the failure that makes it understandable.

We might say, failure of M/E rationality cannot be 'global', an agent cannot be perfectly generally and always M/E irrational, or we could not see him as having those beliefs and those desires. It can be local, so long as the surrounding story gives us enough material to attribute the instrument-belief and the end-desire.

Other inferential principles do not seem to have this feature. If they don't, it's hard to see how an alternative to M/E could be established.

Let me forestall a possible misunderstanding of my argument. It is *not*: that you had better use M/E, or you will be unintelligible as having reasons. That, I think, is a dubious argument. It suggests that after all, everyone will want to be intelligible as having reasons, whatever else she wants.[20] Rather, the argument is that a request for reasons makes sense only if there is something that could count as a reason. Of course, in one sense the project of justifying morality straightforwardly fails if nothing counts as a reason at all. But, the reason there is a problem about the justification of morality is that there are (possible?) beings who can recognize reasons, who act on reasons, who are moved by reasons, but are not moved by moral considerations. A justification would show them what reason they have. So long as a person is M/E rational, there are reasons she can act on, that can motivate her, reasons that she accepts as reasons. If we cannot provide her with a reason to abide by moral rules, then we cannot justify morality. The problem of justifying morality stands in stark contrast to the problem of justifying the M/E principle itself. Someone who doesn't accept the M/E principle cannot be given reasons of any sort. That we cannot justify our principle to such a person is no more troubling than our inability to justify principles of deduction.

This argument has a transcendental feel about it quite alien to Humeanism. As a Humean myself, I think we should be up front about this. The special

---

[20] See Railton in this volume, Essay 2. Also relevant is Simon Blackburn, 'Practical Tortoise Raising', *Mind*, 104 (1995), 695–711.

status of instrumental reason is due to its being the *sine qua non* of having reasons at all. We shouldn't be embarrassed to take the insights of Kantian philosophizing to heart. Certain aspects of the Humean position deserve to be abandoned. We should abandon a hardline metaphysical position according to which the very idea of practical reason is mysterious. Our scepticism should consist in doubts that the content of practical reason is anything like the content of morality.[21] We should be contesting the normative ground, not contesting its very existence.

---

[21] The kind of scepticism mentioned and distinguished, but *not* discussed, in Christine Korsgaard, 'Skepticism about Practical Reason', *Journal of Philosophy*, 83 (1986), 5–25.

4

Practical Theory

GARRETT CULLITY

The critics of ethical theory concur in making the following claim: ethical theory seeks to impose on our ethical thinking a structure which there is no good reason for us to submit it to. But they hold this for different reasons. A first line of objection is that the onus lies on the theorist to show why our thinking should aspire to conform to any ethical theory, and that this onus remains undischarged.[1] A second goes further. It is not just that the onus lies on the theorist to show why our thinking should aspire to conform to his theory; rather, there are decisive reasons why it should not. One popular way of arguing this has been to maintain that holding our ethical thinking responsible for its justification to an ethical theory would itself be morally objectionable (perhaps because it would alienate us from the values to which that thinking is responsive).[2] Or, most fundamentally of all, one might say this: there is a decisive reason not to require our ethical thinking to conform to a theory, because it is of the nature of practical reason itself to preclude this.

---

[1] One objection of this form is that theory seeks to impose an inappropriate deductivist model upon our practical thought, whereby conclusions concerning individual actions are justified, if at all, in virtue of their entailment by the general principles contained in the theory. This, it is objected, yields a rule-bound, legalistic conception of moral thinking which is alien to much of it. (See Bernard Williams, *Ethics and the Limits of Philosophy* (London: Collins, 1985), ch. 10; Annette Baier, *Postures of the Mind* (Minneapolis: Univ. of Minnesota Press, 1985), 209–20, 234–6.) Similarly, it is complained that its ambition is to provide a precision in our practical judgements, and a unique determination of our practical conclusions, which our practice doesn't aspire to, but the reason for aspiring to which isn't clear. (See Stanley G. Clarke, 'Anti-Theory in Ethics', *American Philosophical Quarterly*, 24 (1987), 238–40; Baier, *Postures of the Mind*; and Stuart Hampshire, *Morality and Conflict* (Oxford: Blackwell, 1983).)

[2] In this spirit, it is argued that I cannot regard my friendships, for instance, as important only because they serve the demands of a theory: the non-theoretical stance is constitutive of participating in such values. (See Michael Stocker, 'The Schizophrenia of Modern Ethical Theories', *Journal of Philosophy*, 73 (1976), 453–66; Williams, 'Persons, Character and Morality', in *Moral Luck* (Cambridge: Univ. Press, 1981), 1–19.) Other objections are that the reductionist ambitions of theory stand in fundamental opposition to the variety of considerations that animate any one ethical outlook, and to the plurality of ethical outlooks which is itself of moral value. (For the first of these, see Baier, *Postures of the Mind*, and Hampshire, *Morality and Conflict*; for the second, Michael Walzer, *Spheres of Justice* (New York: Basic Books, 1983).) Friends of the moral virtues have objected that theory's preoccupation

Now of course, such claims are only evaluable given a clear understanding of what is to count as an ethical theory. Indeed, the standard form taken by theorists' rejoinders has been to maintain that once we gain such a clear understanding, we find that the objections are misdirected. A structure of moral thought can have features which make it sensible to think of it as *theoretical* without becoming an appropriate target of the objections.[3] The attacks simply misconceive the nature of ethical theory.

However, there is a version of the last, most fundamental, form of opposition to ethical theory—one that is central to Bernard Williams's attack on it—for which this style of rejoinder seems far more difficult to sustain. Substantiating this claim is my first aim in what follows. I shall trace Williams's objection to its roots in his conception of practical reason, and oppose T. M. Scanlon's recent attempt to meet it with a rejoinder of the standard form. The proper target of Williams's attack, I shall argue, is simply any account of what makes a normative reason ethical that claims to be able to provide us with practical reasons. Anyone who invokes an ethical theory to show us that we ought to revise our ethical practice is providing an account of that kind; therefore any ethical theorist needs a direct answer to Williams's objection. And any attempt to defend ethical theory against his attack without addressing the conception of practical reason is bound to fail.

The second aim is to give my own response to Williams. I shall argue that when we examine the character of the reasons possessed by morally virtuous agents, we can see that on any plausible theory of practical reason, there is a form of revisionary ethical theorizing that is acceptable, and that Williams's own theory of practical reason should be supplemented in a way that allows for it.

---

with act-evaluation finds it unable to accommodate them—see Clarke, 'Anti-Theory in Ethics', 240–1. And it is claimed that the epistemological pretensions of ethical theory commit it to a morally repugnant conception of ethical expertise. (This objection is tentatively attributed to Williams by T. M. Scanlon, 'The Aims and Authority of Moral Theory', *Oxford Journal of Legal Studies*, 12 (1992), 4. As I read him, though, Williams isn't seeking to convict all ethical theory of this. See also Allan Gibbard's reply to Scanlon, 'Why Theorize How to Live with Each Other?', *Philosophy and Phenomenological Research*, 55 (1995), 323–42.)

[3] See e.g. Robert B. Louden, *Morality and Moral Theory* (New York: Oxford Univ. Press, 1992); Scanlon, 'The Aims and Authority of Moral Theory'; Clarke, 'Anti-Theory in Ethics'. It has been less common to find theorists explicitly endorsing and defending conceptions of theory which do match the target identified by the anti-theorists, and arguing that the objections are misplaced, but some certainly have: Gibbard, 'Why Theorize How to Live with Each Other?', argues that the nature of our practical ethical thinking itself commits us to the aspiration to a theory which it is plausible to see as encouraging a notion of ethical expertise. And we are now seeing an interesting subsidiary debate opening up between the advocates of these incompatible defences of theory. (See the exchange between Gibbard, 'Why Theorize How to Live with Each Other?' and Scanlon, 'Moral Theory: Understanding and Disagreement', *Philosophy and Phenomenological Research*, 55 (1995), 343–56.)

1. Meta-Justification

Williams specifies the target of his attack as follows:

An ethical theory is a theoretical account of what ethical thought and practice are, which account either implies a general test for the correctness of basic ethical beliefs and principles or else implies that there cannot be such a test.[4]

Now questions are raised by the details of this definition—and in particular, the final disjunct—but they need not detain us. For Williams's further discussion makes it clear that it is the *revisionary* ambition of ethical theory that he is concerned to oppose: the ambition to give a general characterization of what correct ethical thinking consists in, deviations from which we ought—there is reason for us—to abandon. The central thrust of that opposition is contained in chapter 6 of *Ethics and the Limits of Philosophy*, where he also sets out his own conception of the alternative, non-theoretical form he thinks ethical reflection should take.

The kind of reflection on ethical life which, according to Williams, naturally encourages ethical theory is the kind 'that seeks *justificatory reasons*'.[5] Our ethical life, as it is, consists in a range of practices of reason-acceptance —practices of treating certain considerations as justifying certain actions and attitudes. (Williams's most prominent example of a consideration yielding such a practice is the distinction between a foetus and an infant.) Given such a practice, the thought that leads to theory is, 'What justifies that practice?' The demand that leads to theory, that is to say, is a demand for justificatory meta-reasons: justificatory reasons for engaging in the practice of treating considerations as first-order justifications for actions and attitudes.

What is Williams's objection to the making of the meta-justificational demand? With the example of the practically significant foetus/infant distinction in mind, he puts his complaint like this:

A practice may be so directly related to our experience that the reason it provides will simply count as stronger than any reason that might be advanced for it.[6]

Or, of course, against it. When I ask what I have most reason to do, the most decisive answers to the question will be provided by the simple practical considerations that simply *are* compelling for me. If a theorist then tries to offer me a justificatory meta-reason for or against my practice of treating those considerations as reasons, the question is how compelling the considerations which constitute those meta-reasons are; and if, as it usually will be, the answer is that they are less compelling for me than my

---

[4] *Ethics and the Limits of Philosophy*, 72. [5] Ibid. 112. [6] Ibid. 114.

first-order reasons, then the theorist's enterprise is otiose. He is offering me weaker reasons, either for or against what I am doing, than I already possess for doing it; his theory is without practical authority.

This reading of Williams has him objecting, given our practice of treating certain compelling considerations as providing strong practical reasons, to any attempt to hold that practice justificationally answerable to the provision of some further reason external to it. But this formulation of the objection would make it easy to dismiss, on two different grounds.

First, as T. M. Scanlon urges, this objection seems simply not to apply to any ethical theory whose construction is governed by a sensibly conceived coherentist methodology.[7] He distinguishes two kinds of ethical theory: Philosophical Enquiry aims 'to make clear in what sense, if any, moral judgements can be true or false, to explain what kind of truths they might be, how we can come to know them and what reasons we have for giving them the kind of importance they claim',[8] while Moral Enquiry aims to give us a clearer idea of which things fall into the most general of our moral categories (right and wrong, just and unjust, and so on) and why.[9] Moral Enquiry is best pursued by seeking a reflective equilibrium between our considered moral judgements and principles of some degree of generality that explain them.[10] Beyond this, we should seek to achieve a coherence between Philosophical and Moral Enquiry, which are interdependent.[11]

Thus theorizing of both the forms Scanlon wishes to defend, and which he maintains are what most theorists are engaged in, is governed by the need to cohere with and explain our ordinary considered understanding of the nature of our moral reasons. And if this is right, the response to Williams's attempt to attack ethical theory is straightforward: most ethical theory does not aspire to giving moral practice the external justification Williams is rejecting. Philosophical Enquiry is seeking 'to explain more clearly the kind of reasons those who accept morality have for doing so';[12]

---

[7] 'The Aims and Authority of Moral Theory', 17–21.

[8] Ibid. 14; see also p. 5. An instance is his own contractualist theory of wrong action as action whose 'performance under the circumstances would be disallowed by any system of rules for the general regulation of behaviour which no-one could reasonably reject as a basis for informed, unforced, general agreement'—Scanlon, 'Contractualism and Utilitarianism', in Amartya Sen and Bernard Williams (eds.), *Utilitarianism and Beyond* (Cambridge: Univ. Press, 1982), 110.
Scanlon is not operating with Williams's distinction between the ethical and the moral; nor am I.

[9] 'The Aims and Authority of Moral Theory', 8. This is illustrated by his own theory of promising, which seeks to explain the obligation of fidelity to one's promises as an instance of a more general obligation to give due weight to expectations one has knowingly created. See Scanlon, 'Promises and Practices', *Philosophy and Public Affairs*, 19 (1990), 199–226.

[10] 'The Aims and Authority of Moral Theory', 9. Scanlon's view is that the considered moral judgements to be brought into this equilibrium are more appropriately regarded as judgements about the relevance of a given consideration to a conclusion concerning the moral categorization of objects than as such conclusions themselves.

[11] Ibid. 13. I take it that Scanlon is thinking of this as one important part of the move from 'narrow' to 'wide' reflective equilibrium.   [12] Ibid. 14.

and in doing so, it should be treated 'not as an outside source from which particular conclusions must be derived but rather as a characterization of what it is that is appealing in these conclusions themselves'.[13] Likewise,

The aim of Moral Enquiry is not to justify our 'considered judgements' with reference to some new and independent standard, but to clarify the reasons that we already had for believing them to be correct and to determine whether, in the light of reflection, we still find them persuasive.[14]

In short, this first rejoinder to Williams's attack on ethical theory takes the standard form we met at the outset: most ethical theorizing is simply not an appropriate target of the objection.

But there is also a second, more straightforward rejoinder. No theorist need deny that there is a clear sense in which an agent's existing practical reasons may count as stronger, or more compelling, than any theoretical meta-reasons that may be advanced for or against them. But this is only the sense in which the agent *regards* these considerations as stronger reasons. The question the theorist is raising is whether he is right or wrong so to regard them.

However, both of these objections are premature. Williams's attack cannot be simply directed against anything that purports to be a practical justificatory meta-reason. For there are at least two varieties of such reasons he himself wants to endorse.

First, he allows that some of the considerations one counts as practical reasons may provide one with a justification for rejecting one's practice of counting others as reasons. His treatment of race and sex discrimination illustrates this.[15] A sexist who actually goes about treating *being a woman* as a reason for not hiring someone for a job will usually also have a good reason, in terms of his interests in hiring the best person for the job, for not treating the first consideration as a reason. His interests, which standardly function as first-order practical reasons, function also in this case as meta-reasons for not treating another consideration as a first-order practical reason.[16]

For a second kind of justificatory meta-reason that Williams endorses, we need to look elsewhere in his writings—to the paper 'Internal and External Reasons', in which he presents a theory of practical reason.[17] In endorsing that theory, he is maintaining that false claims are sometimes made concerning the first-order justifications people have for doing things,

---

[13] Ibid. 20.   [14] Ibid. 16.   [15] *Ethics and the Limits of Philosophy*, 115–16.

[16] Williams is concerned to emphasize that this style of argument won't always suffice to convict a sexist of irrationality, though.

[17] Bernard Williams, 'Internal and External Reasons', repr. in his *Moral Luck* (Cambridge: Univ. Press, 1981), 101–13.

and that his theory sorts the true from the false claims. In claiming that there are good reasons to accept his theory, he is claiming that there are good reasons to hold that first-order reasons are constituted as his theory says—in short, that there are justificatory meta-reasons. Those meta-reasons, moreover, will themselves be practical, since reasons to accept his theory of practical reason are reasons to act as it says. And in virtue of being a practical theory, it is potentially revisionary. If my practice of treating certain considerations as reasons is out of line with the theory, Williams's claim is that I have a reason to reform it.

This makes it clear that Williams's opposition to ethical theory cannot be an opposition to every demand for justificatory meta-reasons for our practices of treating considerations as first-order ethical reasons. There must be some special problem about doing this by appealing to an account of what makes a practical reason *ethical*. But if a theory of practical reason is itself practical, in virtue of telling us which considerations we can intelligibly treat as justificatory reasons for action, why can't an ethical theory be practical too? After all, it will tell us which considerations we can intelligibly treat as *ethical* reasons. And it seems that if there can be reasons to accept a theory of practical reason, there can be reasons of the same form to accept an ethical theory: namely, that the theory offers the clearest account of what is distinctive of the practice. If we can have a reason for accepting an ethical theory, then why isn't there an argument of the same form as we found a moment ago to show that such a theory can be practical? If we can have good meta-reasons to accept a theory of ethical reasons, then those meta-reasons are good reasons to think that we have ethical reasons to perform certain actions recommended by the theory; therefore we have good reasons to perform those actions.

2. Williams's Objection

To see Williams's case against a practical theory of ethics, we need to examine the details of his theory of practical reason. In briefest outline, his view is this. A crucial constraint on our notion of a normative reason for an action is that it should be capable of explaining that action, as performed by an agent who is rightly orientated towards the reason, in virtue of his being so orientated.[18] Williams derives from this a necessary condition on

[18] Compare Stephen L. Darwall, *Impartial Reason* (Ithaca, NY: Cornell Univ. Press, 1983), 20: 'a fact is a reason for a person to do something if he would be motivated to do it, other things equal, were he to consider that fact rationally'. The phrase 'other things equal' is presumably included to accommodate a view of motivational states according to which rational agents need not be motivated by those of their reasons that are outweighed by others. An advocate of this view will want to add a similar phrase to my formulation of Williams's account.

a consideration's being a normative reason for action, which I shall formulate as follows:[19]

> Consideration C is a normative reason for A to φ only if, if A deliberated rationally, and knew all the facts relevant to his deliberation, his recognition of C as recommending φ-ing would rationally guide him to be motivated to φ[20]

where rational deliberation consists principally in the five activities he mentions:[21]

— ascertaining causal means to the ends one is motivated to attain;[22]
— finding constitutive realizations of those ends;
— harmonizing ends by working out how to combine them;
— ranking ends, where harmonization proves impossible; and
— fully imagining the realization of ends.

The large question of the plausibility of Williams's derivation of this account from his explanatory constraint on practical reasons is one on which I shall have something to say below.[23] But let us first see how the account underpins his attack on ethical theory.

First, on Williams's view, it seems clear that one's reasons will be relative to the contingencies of one's motivational make-up; for it is plausible to hold that the kinds of objects one will be motivated to pursue after performing these five activities will be a function of those one was motivated

---

[19] There is clearly room for disagreement over the best interpretation of Williams's theory—even over a question as fundamental as whether he wants to say that an agent's actual reasons are those considerations by which he would be motivated after rational deliberation of this kind, or whether this process would produce new reasons. (I am adopting the former reading, as giving him a more plausible view; but for the latter, see Rachel Cohon, 'Internalism about Reasons for Action', *Pacific Philosophical Quarterly*, 74 (1993), 267.) However, the claim that my own formulation gives the best view to attribute to Williams is not one for which I shall argue here.

[20] A note on 'relevant facts'. This phrase only represents Williams's view if the relevance of a fact is a function not only of the influence it would have on A's deliberation if he knew it, but also of the proximity of the cognitive state he would be in to his actual cognitive state. See 'Internal and External Reasons', 103. A consequence of this is that there will be no sharp boundary between relevant and irrelevant facts.

[21] 'Internal and External Reasons', 104; see also 'Internal Reasons and the Obscurity of Blame', in Bernard Williams, *Making Sense of Humanity* (Cambridge: Univ. Press, 1995), 38. In the latter paper, Williams emphasizes that what counts as rational deliberation, and consequently what counts as a reason, will often be indeterminate on his view.

[22] This should not be read as itself an attempt to express the instrumental norm of practical reason: as Christine Korsgaard emphasizes in Essay 8 in this volume, taking the means to one's ends in *this* crude sense need not be something one has a reason to do. Rather, Williams's view is that the ends one would have after performing all five activities are normative for one—and that they have this status in virtue of their being the outcome of rational deliberation.

[23] For more, see the Introduction to this volume; also Christine Korsgaard, 'Skepticism about Practical Reason', *Journal of Philosophy*, 83 (1986), 5–25; John McDowell, 'Might there be External Reasons?', in J. E. J. Altham and Ross Harrison (eds.), *World, Mind and Ethics: Essays on the Ethical Philosophy of Bernard Williams* (Cambridge: Univ. Press, 1995), 68–85; and Williams, 'Internal Reasons and the Obscurity of Blame', and 'Replies', in *World, Mind and Ethics*, 186–94.

to pursue beforehand. If so, a first upshot of Williams's theory is that the question 'Why be moral?' cannot be guaranteed to be universally answerable.[24] There is nothing inconceivable in the idea of an agent whose amoral motivations survive deliberation of the five forms he identifies. But this point is mentioned in order to set it aside—Williams's case against ethical theory cannot rest on *this*. A theorist's concern need only be to maintain that those people who *do* have reason to act ethically have reason to act as her theory prescribes.

But it is this inference of the theorist's between claims about a person's practical reasons—if he has reason to act ethically, then he has reason to act as my ethical theory prescribes—that is blocked by Williams's theory of practical reason. On that theory, one can only be wrong in counting as a reason to φ a consideration on which one is motivated to φ if the motivation would not survive rational deliberation of the kinds he specifies, given knowledge of all the facts relevant to that deliberation. It does seem implausible to suppose that shortcomings of these kinds will be identified in relation to the various considerations that many people most confidently endorse as providing them with ethical reasons. But his central point is that, however that may be, the provision of an *ethical theory*, of either a coherentist or a foundational kind, won't to any extent help to do so. An ethical theory aspires to identify a systematic structure in relation to which a practical consideration can be identified as distinctively ethical; and on a coherentist conception of ethical theorizing, the claim will be that this is a structure which is implicit already in the practical thinking of anyone who is ethically motivated, and any divergences from which such an agent would be more rational to correct, bringing her thinking into line with the theory. But on Williams's conception of practical reason, susceptibility to systematization is not part of what makes considerations into practical reasons. If the considerations that would motivate me, after engaging in the kind of rational deliberation he allows for, and coming into possession of all the relevant facts, do not exhibit any kind of systematic unity—and it is hard to see anything that precludes this—then they are my reasons, irrespective of that fact. And if so, then I have no practical reason to revise my ethical practice to bring it into line with any further systematic structure.

This cannot quite be the whole of Williams's objection. For if I am rationally seeking to promote end E, I may well need a theory of E to tell me how to go about it. (If I am aiming to be healthy, the way I go about pursuing that aim will obviously depend crucially on what I conceive of good health as consisting in.) But if so, why doesn't this apply to the end

---

[24] *Ethics and the Limits of Philosophy*, ch. 2 gives Williams's views on what we ought to say in response to this question, as asked by the amoralist.

of doing what is ethically required? The case for this seems independent of the question whether my practical reasons, taken as a whole, must answer to some requirement of structural connectedness.

Williams's response to this, though, is in effect to ask why it should be thought that there is a single unified end referred to under the description 'doing what is ethically required'. There is a simple description that can be given to ethical considerations, from which no one need dissent: they are those considerations that support actions belonging to the life we ought to lead. But to many of us, according to Williams, those considerations present themselves as disparate—even conflicting.[25] For those agents for whom this is the case, Williams's theory of practical reason stands as a barrier to supposing that these disparate considerations must, if they are to provide us with genuine normative reasons, be capable of being brought into some systematic relationship to each other. For while it may be right to attribute to us the end of doing what is ethically required, it is those disparate considerations themselves that are our ethical reasons—provided only that they would continue to motivate us under the appropriate deliberative and informational conditions. Their motivating us under those conditions is not dependent on the further reason that acting on these considerations is ethically required: it is not *because it is ethically required* that other people's rights or interests matter to us. If ethical considerations do have their force for us individually in this way, then they individually supply the ends that generate our ethical reasons, without reference to the end of doing what is ethically required.

A simple extension of this point supplies Williams's general response to foundational ethical theories. Williams is no opponent of foundational reasons themselves: if I would be motivated to φ by consideration C under the appropriate deliberative and informational conditions, and C would motivate me to φ for no further reason, then C is indeed a foundational reason for me to φ. But indeed, this is precisely why he rejects the attempts of foundational ethical theorists to identify some subset of our ethical considerations to which the set as a whole is justificationally answerable. Our disparate ethical considerations themselves supply us with practical reasons, and their doing so is not conditioned on the availability of some further, more foundational reason that justifies this.

This, then, is Williams's case against ethical theories of either a foundational or a coherentist sort. A further putative meta-reason of either of these forms will simply be trumped by the compelling practical reasons one already has, if it is not a condition of their *being* compelling reasons that they meet

---

[25] See ibid. 17. A corollary of this is ch. 10's attack on the attempt of 'the morality system' to reduce all ethical considerations to moral obligations.

these theoretical conditions. If the structural or foundational theoretical demands are not ones that themselves determine what I would be motivated by if deliberating rationally and knowing all the relevant facts, then there is no place for them in revisionary argument about my practical reasons. It is in *this* sense that we should read his remark that an ethical practice may be 'so directly related to our experience' that its reasons will simply be stronger than any putative meta-reason.

But without an ethical theory, how can we make sense of ethical commitment as more than mere prejudice? Williams's answer is that what remains to us as a resource for critical reflection is the demand that we seek a full imaginative awareness of the nature of the practices in which we are participating, and of the motives with which we are participating in them.[26] The preceding discussion explains why. On Williams's view, the critical question to raise for any putatively ethical consideration is not whether it really qualifies as ethical, but whether it really supplies me with a reason for action. And to ask this is to ask whether I would be motivated by this consideration if adequately informed and deliberating rationally, where the latter requires of me, among other things, an imaginative engagement with the full nature of the actions which would result from my acting on the motivations I have. It is only if the things I am actually motivated to do would still motivate me were I fully to grasp their implications that they can be counted among the things I have a reason to do. Practical skill in the conducting of real ethical argument is a matter of finding the ways to bring one's interlocutor to such an understanding—where failing to find such ways means only that one has failed to show her that she is wrong to regard herself as having the reasons she does, and not that she is right. The ability of this sort of reflection to amount to revisionary criticism does depend on its ability to engage with those motivations to which the agent could be brought by a process of rational deliberation; however, the admission that there are no such points of engagement should not be regarded as any kind of threat to one's own ethical outlook. We should not underestimate the extent to which the reasons we have do embody a shared ethical outlook—the extent to which the ethical thoughts which engage us (whoever the 'us') can engage others—but if there is ultimately a failure of such engagement, this carries no implications for the unreasonableness of our own commitments.

3. *Practical Reason and Structure*

Given this account of Williams's attack on ethical theory, Scanlon's reply to it must fail. Williams's objection is not simply to the attempt to make

---

[26] *Ethics and the Limits of Philosophy*, 112.

ethical reasons answerable to the provision of an external justification; it is also to the attempt to make them answerable to a requirement of systematic unification such as is embodied in Scanlon's own coherentist approach to ethical theorizing.[27] As we have just seen, susceptibility to systematization is not part of what makes considerations into practical reasons on Williams's theory, and if not, no systematic ethical theory of this kind can claim to provide us with reasons for revising what we treat as practically compelling ethical considerations. When Scanlon emphasizes the modesty of his conception of normative moral inquiry, as aiming 'to clarify the reasons that we already had for believing [our considered moral judgements] to be correct and to determine whether, in the light of reflection, we still find them persuasive', Williams's reply should be that *this* is unexceptionable. His own conception of non-theoretical ethical reflection as full imaginative awareness would, after all, be well described in precisely these terms. However, Williams's challenge is to conceiving of that 'clarification' as consisting in the systematization of those considered judgements in reflective equilibrium with general principles.[28] That challenge is grounded in his theory of practical reason; without addressing that theory, Scanlon's reply fails.

Notice that this is not to say that Williams is committed to opposing all attempts to invoke a reflective equilibrium argument in justifying an ethical claim.[29] For recall the earlier point about seeking theories of the ends it is rational for me to pursue. Williams does need to resist the idea that *doing what is ethically* required presents me with a single unified end for which it would make sense to seek a theory of this kind. But this does not commit him to resisting the attempt to supply separate theories for our various disparate ethical ends. In particular, there is no obstacle to his agreeing that our concerns for justice and for others' well-being present themselves to us as focused on unified ends of which we should sensibly seek to supply general accounts.

My objection to Scanlon has been that he fails to address Williams's theory of practical reason, according to which systematizability is not part of what makes a consideration a practical reason. This would be a weak

---

[27] As I am understanding the terms, the degree to which a structure is *systematic* is the degree to which its members are linked by inferential chains. (A and B are linked by an inferential chain when they are the first and last members of a sequence each member of which bears a direct inferential relationship to the previous one—either being entailed by or entailing it.) A maximally systematic structure is one in which all members are linked by inferential chains to all other members. The degree to which a structure is *unified* is the degree to which its members have common inferential sources. A maximally unified structure is one in which one member is the single inferential source of all the others.

[28] See *Ethics and the Limits of Philosophy*, 99–102 for the strong assumptions that Williams thinks are required in order to supply a context in which the endeavour to bring one's considered judgements into reflective equilibrium with general principles makes sense.

[29] This is also the natural view to take of the methodology governing the production of his own theory of practical reason.

complaint, though, if Williams's theory were obviously flawed at just this point, as many ethical theorists would maintain. I do not think so—my own response to Williams takes a different form. But before presenting that response, I should explain why not.

Does Williams's account of what it is to deliberate rationally simply omit to mention a concern with integrating the ends towards which one is motivated to act into a unitary and cohesive structure? [30] This concern does seem to be distinctive of rational deliberation. If on a hot day I recognize that I have a reason to have a drink, but think I have no reason to get out of the sun, it looks as though a plausible complaint of irrationality can be brought against me. My getting a drink makes sense by subserving the more general end of making me comfortable, but that end would equally be subserved by getting out of the sun. Thus the irrationality of my attitudes, it can appear, lies in their structural incoherence. It would be more rational for me to adopt the more coherent structure. Likewise, it can seem attractive to explain the irrationality of pure impulsive action in the same way. If I succumb to the angry urge to kick my faulty bicycle, I do something paradigmatic of practical irrationality; but Williams seems to lack the resources to say this. If I am simply and suddenly motivated to act in this way, it seems quite possible that I will remain so after deliberating in the five ways Williams allows for. What we need to say, it can seem, is that the end towards which I am directed by this urge bears no structural relation to my other ends: it neither supports nor is supported by them.

However, examples of these kinds cannot succeed in showing that Williams's account is defective, when formulated as I have done above. In both cases, we need to ask what is the consideration that I see as recommending the action. In respect of cases of the second, impulsive kind, this will either turn out to be a consideration for which Williams will have no difficulty in maintaining that I would not see it as recommending the action if I were deliberating rationally (e.g. that my bicycle deserves to be kicked), or it will be the general consideration that it will make me feel better, *ceteris paribus*, for which there is no obstacle in Williams's maintaining that this is *a* normative reason for the action. And in respect of the first kind of case, if my reason for performing a given action is its promotion of some further end (making me comfortable), then the existence of reasons to perform the other actions promoting that end follows only from a requirement of instrumental rationality of the kind that Williams allows. This does not yet yield a further requirement that my individual ends must be assimilable into an overall structure in which they stand in relations of subordination to

---

[30] For this objection to Williams, see especially Michael Smith, *The Moral Problem* (Oxford: Blackwell, 1994), 158–61, and 'Internal Reasons', *Philosophy and Phenomenological Research*, 55 (1995), 113–16.

more ultimate ends. There is no uncontroversial observation about particular cases of irrationality that compels us to recognize this further requirement. Moreover, notice that Williams's aim need not be to establish his account of practical reason independently of his claims concerning the nature of moral reasoning. I take it that he would want to appeal to the nature of our *moral* thinking as one of his principal sources of support for excluding a concern with structuring from his account of rational deliberation. Our moral experience, he can plausibly claim, is an experience of the practical demands made by a variety of considerations of many different kinds, which strike us as reasons quite independently of our ability to integrate them into a single systematic structure with each other, let alone with reasons of other kinds.

From here, the argument concerning the structural requirement on rational deliberation will have to be pursued at a deeper level. An argument which is sometimes suggested runs as follows:[31] we need to be able to make sense of reason as a single faculty operating in both practical and theoretical spheres; but a rational structure of *beliefs* cannot be one in which they stand in isolation from one another, constrained only by a requirement of consistency; therefore we should conceive of reason as a structuring faculty.

However, Williams can resist this train of thought. What drives us towards characterizing theoretical reason as a structuring faculty is the requirement of preserving consistency in the face of vulnerability to new experience. A structure of merely mutually consistent beliefs, lacking explanatory interconnections, is unlikely to remain consistent with new experience. The issue of what makes a structurally coherent system of beliefs more likely to be true is of course a large one;[32] if it *is* more likely to be true, this makes it more rational to adopt it in preference to a merely consistent set. Thus the relevance of structural coherence to theoretical rationality is established via the requirement of responsiveness to the truth. And if so, the absence of this requirement in relation to practical reason seems to spoil the argument.[33]

This is hardly a conclusive defence of Williams's omission of a concern with structural coherence from the aims of rational deliberation. However, it does suffice to show that he is at least not obviously wrong, even if he is

---

[31] See e.g. Gilbert Harman, 'Practical Reasoning', *Review of Metaphysics*, 29 (1975–6), 431–63.

[32] Does the world just contingently happen to yield to interconnected explanations?

[33] This is not to say that Williams is committed to opposing the use of coherence methods to defend claims concerning norms of practical reason. For just as the status of certain principles as norms of theoretical reason is plausibly defended by arguing that they stand in reflective equilibrium with our considered judgements about our theoretical reasons, the same method (as Peter Railton emphasizes in this volume, Essay 2) offers an attractive way to defend claims about the status of principles such as the instrumental principle as norms of practical reason. Williams can accept this, while denying that it supports the attempt to impose a unitary structure on our practical reasons taken as a whole.

not obviously right. I shall take it as sufficient warrant for seeking a different response to Williams.

4. Underminers

I begin with a distinction between the content of a practical reason and the conditions for its presence. The content we ordinarily attribute to our practical reasons is quite straightforward. What we ordinarily cite as providing us with practical reasons—with varying degrees of completeness, depending on the pragmatics of our utterances in the circumstances in which they are made—are the respects in which we take our actions to contribute to our ends.[34] My reason for holding the party is that it will be fun; my reason for helping her is that this is in her interests. And unless it can be shown that we are universally mistaken about our reasons, it should be accepted that the content of the practical reasons we do have has the same simple form. Of course, one can combine this with a further theory setting out the conditions under which a consideration with this sort of content does qualify as a reason, as Williams does: according to him, consideration C is a normative reason for A to φ only if, if A deliberated rationally, and knew all the relevant facts, his recognition of C as recommending φ-ing would rationally guide him to be motivated to φ. But there is no obstacle to combining this set of conditions for the *presence* of a practical reason with the common-sense view of its *content*, as Williams indeed seems to be doing.

If this is right, then Williams is presenting us with a view according to which what we currently regard as reasons for actions will be so, provided we are indeed motivated to achieve the ends they specify, and provided our motivation would not be annihilated by further information and rational deliberation. And surely, it is reasonable to believe (even if possibly false) that the most commonplace and uncontroversial examples of considerations that we regard as practical reasons—considerations such as an action's being fun, or being in a beneficiary's interests—will indeed satisfy Williams's provisos. If so, then on Williams's account, we are justified in taking as our paradigm examples of practical reasons in what follows those simple considerations which we regard as such.

The question I wish to examine concerning these considerations—the ones we regard as reasons, and which a follower of Williams ought to

---

[34] Notice that this is not saying that *contributing to my ends* is always my reason for acting. Nor does it deny that it is a condition of any consideration's being a reason that the end it promotes is worth pursuing.

accept *are* our reasons—is their relation to the further considerations which can countervail against them. Suppose I hold the party, regarding its being fun as a decisive reason for doing so. Clearly, though, there are plenty of further considerations in the presence of which this would not have been counted by me as a decisive reason. The most obvious are those that would countervail by outweighing—considerations I would count as stronger reasons against the action than the one I have in its favour. However, there are also countervailing considerations of a second sort, on which we shall be concentrating in what follows. These considerations countervail by undermining—they show why I should cease to treat the consideration I have been treating as a reason elsewhere as one here. Suppose, for instance, that there has just been a grave public tragedy, in which many members of my community have been killed. I can intelligibly take myself under these circumstances as having reason not to have fun, while accepting that ordinarily, something's being fun would be a reason to do it. It is not as though there is one aspect of the party—its being fun—that is a reason for it, and another—its being disrespectful of the memory of the people who have been killed, perhaps—which is a stronger, outweighing reason against it. Rather, these circumstances show why it makes sense for me precisely to count something's being fun as a reason for avoiding it. Whereas before I needed to exercise my sensitivity to what was fun to see what to pursue, now I need to exercise that same sensitivity to see what to avoid. And since it is hard to see how a single feature of an action could give me reasons both for and against it, this suggests that the party's being fun is no longer a reason to hold it. The appropriateness of my being subdued in response to the tragedy in my community undermines the status of the consideration that an action is fun as a reason for performing it. I am presented, in short, with a meta-reason: a reason not to treat some further consideration as a reason for an action.[35]

But if this is right, then it is hard to see what grounds there could be for denying that our moral reasoning—on any recognizable demarcation of the moral from the non-moral—can have the same structure. For now, in the moral case, we find that the considerations that are regarded as providing such morally compelling reasons need be no more complicated or unusual than considerations of a non-moral kind.[36] In a thoroughly straightforward situation, the consideration I regard as a reason for performing some act of

[35] The examples of undermining discussed in this essay are also examples of polarity-reversal. Thus the recent tragedy is a reason not only not to take the party's being fun as a reason to hold it, but it is, more strongly, a reason to take it as a reason not to.

[36] How are we to distinguish 'moral' from 'non-moral' considerations? Williams's theory of practical reason will tend to undercut the idea that anything of importance could hang on answering this question. The important question is whether a putatively moral consideration provides me with a reason, and the issue of its classification as moral or non-moral does not bear on this.

assistance to another person need be no more complicated than that it
would be in his interests to be assisted. Of course, such a consideration will
not always be decisive. For instance, if the person's interests were themselves maliciously inspired, I would treat this as countervailing against the
fact that my assistance is in his interests as a reason for providing it. And
here again, we have a consideration that countervails not by outweighing
but by undermining—it shows why the other person's interests no longer
count in favour of the action. I am treating the fact that his interests are
malicious as a meta-reason—as a reason to regard his interest in being
assisted, which would normally give me a reason for acting, as not doing
so here.

Now let us pause over this claim, because it is the foundation for the rest
of my argument. Why not say that, in the straightforward circumstances, a
kind person's reason for helping someone else is that it is in his *morally
legitimate* interests, rather than saying that her reason is simply that it is in
his interests, but that their moral illegitimacy would undermine the status
of this consideration as a reason for her? After all, the claim is that she
would not regard herself as having a reason if she came to think those
interests were morally illegitimate. I have of course been agreeing that the
moral legitimacy of the interests is among the conditions for the presence
of the reason, but denying that it enters into the content of the reason in
the simple case. But the onus is on me to show what principled ground
there is for this distinction.

This can be shown given two plausible assumptions. First, unless we are
universally mistaken, the content of our normative practical reasons takes
the form we regard it as having. And secondly, it seems plausible to
agree with Williams that an agent's normative practical reasons are those
considerations her rational orientation towards which could explain her
performing the actions for which they are reasons. The kind of explanation
in question here is a motivational one: an explanation that may cite as a
component in the agent's motivation to perform an action her state of
recognizing a consideration as a normative reason for it. Thus if this second
assumption is right, the content of an agent's normative reasons will be the
content of the considerations it would be appropriate to cite in supplying
an explanation of this form of the actions for which they are reasons, if she
were rationally orientated towards them. But now notice that the content of
any explanation is relative to the background expectations of normality
governing the context in which the explanandum occurs. Whose expectations? Those of the audience to whom the explanation is addressed. And
who is the relevant audience to consider in the motivational explanation
of action? The answer to this is supplied by the first assumption. If
the normative reasons an agent has are standardly to be those she regards

herself as having, then the relevant audience to whom the motivational explanation is addressed is the agent herself. In regarding a consideration as one her rational orientation towards which explains her action, it is her own background expectations she brings to constrain the content of the relevant explanation. When an agent is right about her normative reasons, they will comprise those considerations her recognition of which as such contributes to the motivational explanation of her action, against the background of her own expectations of normality. While the presence of the relevant background will be a condition of a consideration's being a reason, it will not be part of the content of that reason.

But if this is right, it establishes the plausibility of my view about simple cases of kind action. It will only be against a background in which there is a real issue about the moral legitimacy of my beneficiary's interests that it will make sense for a self-explanation of my conferring the benefit to cite my recognizing that those interests are not morally illegitimate. In simple circumstances, where there is no such issue, it will not make sense to cite this. And if so, it cannot be part of what I regard as my reason; therefore, if I am right about my reason, it cannot be part of my reason.[37]

So the content of a moral agent's reasons, in ordinary, uncomplicated circumstances, will be simple. So far, we have been concentrating on the case of kindness: a kind person's distinctive reason for ϕ-ing, in the absence of countervailing considerations, will have the form, 'If I ϕ, then she will have G, and she will benefit from G.' It is not difficult to add to this a characterization of the core reason on which the possessors of other moral virtues act, in the absence of countervailing considerations. For honesty-as-veracity, it is, 'He wants to know whether or not P, and ϕ-ing tells him the truth about P.' For honesty-as-fidelity, it is, 'I have promised to ϕ.' For conscientiousness, it is 'I have a duty to ϕ.' And the core reasons of the just person include, 'If I ϕ, then distribution D of these goods will result, and D is the fair distribution'; 'If I ϕ, then she will have G, and she has a right to G'; and 'If I ϕ, then she will have G, and she deserves G.' A morally motivated agent, then, is a person who is motivated to act, in uncomplicated circumstances, on considerations such as the ones mentioned in this preliminary list.[38]

---

[37] These paragraphs might naturally be described as defending 'particularism' about practical reasons: treating a given feature of one action as a practical reason to perform it does not commit one to treating it as a reason to perform other actions of which it is a feature. It has become more usual, however, to associate 'particularism' with the corresponding claim concerning theoretical reasons for moral judgements—see e.g. Jonathan Dancy, *Moral Reasons* (Oxford: Blackwell, 1993), chs. 4–6.

Notice that both of these claims are consistent with the 'reasons universalism' described in sect. 1 of the Introduction to this volume.

[38] For a fuller discussion of the use of these core moral reasons to characterize the moral virtues, see my 'Aretaic Cognitivism', *American Philosophical Quarterly*, 32 (1995), 395–406.

Now for the next stage in my argument. I have been claiming that it is possible for a consideration C to be a reason for me to φ in ordinary circumstances, while failing to be a reason for me to φ in other circumstances, where an undermining consideration U is present. But why treat U as undermining the status of C as a reason to φ? This question, it is important to see, can have an answer. When it does make sense for an agent to treat U as undermining C, it is because the agent's possessing the core reasons she does explains how it makes sense. Unless this is the case, the underminer cannot sensibly be regarded as a reason for that agent to cease to treat C as a reason to φ.

Our examples illustrate this. In discussing the party example, which concerned a non-moral core reason—it would be fun—I did provide an explanation of this kind. In this case, the meta-reason—the reason for not treating the first-order consideration as a reason—was a reason not for an action but for an attitude: the public tragedy is a reason for me to be subdued. Given that I accept this attitudinal norm, that explains why under these circumstances I should be avoiding fun rather than pursuing it: the norm forbids it. But now consider this: I might treat *any* consideration whatever as an underminer. Suppose in July I do a lot of enjoyable things, because they're fun. In August I pass up a lot of similar opportunities, reasoning, 'It's August, so I shouldn't have fun.' This might of course be an elliptical way of introducing some longer explanation that makes sense; in itself, though, surely it doesn't. Unless I can supply a connection establishing the relevance of its being August to the status of something's being fun as a reason for doing it, the claim that this really could be a meta-reason for not regarding something's being fun as a reason isn't credible. Perhaps I *regard* it as a reason (although even this is hard to understand); but its *being* a reason is unintelligible.

The application of this point to moral reasons follows a strictly parallel course. In the example I gave, the consideration that someone else's interests will be furthered by an action is normally a reason for a kind person to perform it; but not if his interests are malicious. How do we explain why, for a kind agent, the maliciousness of another person's interests should undermine their status as a reason for acting in his favour?[39] This is easily done. A kind person is someone who accepts other people's interests (in uncomplicated circumstances) as normatively commanding. But if so, then it is easy to see why malicious interests are not the sort that someone with a kind person's concern should sensibly be advancing. Malicious interests are *constituted* by the repudiation of the normative command the acceptance

---

[39] Note that it is the maliciousness of the interests and not of the agent that is in question here. It could be kind to further the non-malicious interests of a malicious person.

of which is characteristic of kindness, and are therefore precisely the sort of interests that it is appropriate for a kind person to refuse to respect. Thus the explanation of why the maliciousness of the other person's interests intelligibly functions as an underminer for a morally motivated agent is straightforward, and has the same form as before. One's treating as normatively commanding the first-order considerations one does shows why one should not be motivated to pursue those objects that are themselves constituted by the repudiation of those normative commands.

In this case, we explain why the core moral reason is undermined by invoking the normative commandingness of that very reason. But this is a special case of a general phenomenon. In general, when a morally motivated agent can sensibly regard a core moral reason as being undermined, his doing so can be justified in terms of the first-order normative commands the acceptance of which is constitutive of moral motivation. That is to say, the justification may invoke a normative command whose acceptance is distinctive of a different moral virtue. For an illustration of this, consider the second sort of core moral reason I listed, for honesty-as-veracity. Suppose, as in the example Constant raised against Kant, I answer the door to a would-be murderer seeking the fugitive I have just concealed. Why does it make sense for a morally motivated agent not to tell the truth? Notice, first, that the core reason for φ-ing characteristic of veracity is not simply that φ-ing tells someone the truth; someone must at least strike me as *wanting* to know the truth about a subject before I have a reason to tell it to him. But if so, this creates scope for questions concerning the moral status of his wanting to know it. In Constant's example, the questioner's wanting to know the truth about the fugitive's whereabouts is itself part of an evilly orientated project. His wanting to know is part of a project that involves repudiating normative commands accepted by a morally motivated agent—at the very least, those distinctive of kindness and justice. So again, this explains why a morally motivated agent—someone who accepts, among others, the normative commands characteristic of kindness and justice—can sensibly think that the core reason characteristic of veracity is undermined in this case.

These are cases in which it does make sense for a morally motivated agent to regard a core moral reason as being undermined. But where there is no explanation of this form—where it cannot be shown that the core moral reason is directing me to pursue an object that is itself constituted by the repudiation of the normative commands constitutive of the moral point of view—then this does not make sense. And for an illustration of this, consider a racist or sexist attitude towards assisting other people. This sort of case is not covered by Williams's remarks about the way in which a discriminator may frustrate his own interests, but the account of moral motivation which has been sketched makes the statement of the moral objection to it straightforward. The claim that the race or sex of someone makes a difference to whether the advancing of her interests should be counted by a morally motivated agent as a reason for action is as unintelligible as the claim that its being August makes a difference to whether something's being fun should be counted as a reason for action. It is easy enough to come up with norms accepted by racists and sexists that would explain their treating the advancement of others' interests as undermined by considerations of race or sex. But if our question is how to explain this given the norms whose acceptance is constitutive of *moral* motivation, it cannot be done. And that is to say that a recognizably moral outlook cannot include that practice.

I am not claiming that Williams is somehow committed to refraining from judging that the racist or sexist attitude towards giving assistance is morally wrong. He can simply claim that treating the fact that it involves discrimination along these lines as a sufficient reason for avoidance and condemnation is part of a moral outlook that we share, while denying that this is demonstrable to someone outside that outlook. Moreover, I have not supplied anything more substantial than this in response to the prospect of someone who denies the claims concerning distinctively moral motivation on which my argument has been based: for instance, the contention that it is distinctive of moral agency that one takes the interests of other people as a reason to help them. I can, like Williams, take refuge in the thought that there is a widely shared outlook which recognizes the acceptance of such reasons as distinctively moral, and that the impossibility of finding reasons external to that outlook for compelling assent to it should not lead those of us who are within it to abandon it. But if so, it can look as though my case against the racist does not advance beyond Williams's.

However, my point is that, on the view I have defended, there is scope for *argument* to the conclusion that the discriminatory conduct is wrong. It is argument *from* an undefended claim, concerning the distinctive reasons that characterize moral concern—a claim that may have to be vindicated by making Williams's own Archimedean move. But its conclusion is not itself simply the object of such a move. Remember: my aim was not to answer 'Why be moral?', but to demonstrate the scope for revisionary ethical argument within the moral point of view. Delimiting the moral point of view where I do, with the treatment of considerations such as others' interests as practical reasons, is surely plausible.

More radically, consider what we should say concerning our relation to people starving in distant countries.[40] If kindness requires of us that we

---

[40] I develop this argument more fully in 'International Aid and the Scope of Kindness', *Ethics*, 105 (1994), 99–127.

make individually modest sacrifices to provide life-saving aid to people in our immediate vicinity, then it requires this of us equally in relation to distant people, unless there is some relevantly countervailing consideration. But it is hard to see how any of the differences that exist between these two cases is relevant to explaining why it would make sense for someone with the core concern distinctive of kindness to treat those differences as appropriately countervailing considerations. If this is right, then the resources for revisionary ethical argument extend well beyond those which Williams is prepared to countenance. Ethical criticism extends to demanding that the undermining of a first-order moral reason can itself be justified by showing that the object brought within its scope is constituted by the repudiation of the core normative commands whose acceptance is distinctive of moral motivation.

5. Rational Motivation

It may seem that Williams can meet this argument with a straightforward reply. His view is that a consideration is a reason for an agent to φ only if it would motivate her to φ if she were deliberating rationally and knew all the facts relevant to her deliberation. On this view, our first-order practical reasons can be said to stand in primitive relations of practical justification to the actions for which they are reasons. That is, the only sense to give to the question whether we have good reason to treat a given consideration as a first-order practical reason is as the question whether it would be so regarded by us under conditions of rational deliberation and knowledge of all the relevant facts. But this seems also to carry a clear corollary for the treatment of second-order underminers. The question whether a given first-order reason of mine is undermined by some consideration U simply amounts to the question whether I would continue to be motivated on it in the presence of U, if I were deliberating rationally and knew all the relevant facts. If not, that is what it is for my reason to be undermined by U. But this may seem to vitiate the argument that has just been presented. That argument relies on the demand for a justification of the practice of treating a consideration as a moral underminer, and claims that when the demand can be met, it will be in virtue of the relation of that practice to the normative commands characteristic of the moral point of view. However, we find that on Williams's view of practical reason, this demand itself should be rejected. Have I simply begged the question against Williams?

No—to press this reply would be to beg the question against me. My argument has drawn attention to a clear respect in which practical underminers must be held to be capable of justification. If respecting the normatively commanding status of one's own first-order reasons requires one to treat a consideration as a practical underminer, then this must be counted as a good justification for treating it as such. For obviously, what a justification of this form credits with justifying force—the normatively commanding status of one's own first-order reasons—must be accorded that force. Their having justifying force is what makes first-order reasons reasons, whether they possess it primitively, as on Williams's view, or not. And if so, then two things follow. First, practical underminers cannot be claimed to have a primitive justificational status—they are themselves susceptible of justification in this way. And secondly, when they cannot be given a justification of this form, they *lack* a justification of a kind for which it makes sense to ask. So although it does indeed seem to be a corollary of Williams's view of practical reason that the demand for a justification for our practice of treating considerations as underminers should be rejected, the conclusion we should draw, for the reasons I have given, is that his view is faulty in that respect.

This supplies us with a case for a limited reform to Williams's view, rather than its outright rejection. To see what we should say here, return to the grounding of his own theory of practical reason. His plausible internalist claim is that a normative practical reason for a given agent is a consideration for which that agent's being rightly orientated towards it could explain her acting on it. It is not enough simply that the agent be capable of being motivated to act on the consideration in question (any consideration could pass *that* test): it must be the case that the agent's *rationality* could explain her acting on it, if she were fully informed. What I have been arguing, though, is precisely that there is a rational orientation that one can bear or fail to bear towards a putative underminer: one can see why it should count as such for an agent possessing one's own first-order reasons. If so, *this* should be added to Williams's list of the forms of rational deliberation that one can be expected to perform in determining one's reasons.[41] Rational deliberation about practices includes seeking justification for them where it makes sense to do so, and we have just seen that there is a form of justification that our practices of treating considerations as practical underminers can either have or lack. This presents no obstacle to the claim that the only sense to give to the question whether we are justified in regarding certain considerations as practical underminers is as the question whether we would continue to regard them as such under conditions of rational deliberation and knowledge of all the relevant facts.

---

[41] What else should be added? If there are norms of practical reason that are not only themselves categorical, but deliver categorical reasons, then rational deliberation is constrained in ways that do compel the rejection of Williams's neo-Humean view altogether. See the Introduction to this volume, pp. 11–23.

But rational deliberation about our practical meta-reasons should be taken to include asking how our practice of first-order reason-acceptance justifies our treating as underminers the considerations we do so treat.

Notice, finally, the generality of the argument. First, my case for identifying the core reasons distinctive of the moral point of view with the simple considerations we regard as our reasons, and for denying that the absence of underminers is part of the content of those reasons, has not relied on any assumptions peculiarly favourable to Williams's view. And from here, the version of internalism I have attributed to Williams and from which I have been arguing is weak enough to be incontestable.[42] The issue of contention between Williams and plausible rival theories concerns what right orientation to reasons consists in, and not whether our reasons are considerations our being rightly orientated to which explains our acting on them. My argument has been that whatever the full account, it must include the form of deliberation about underminers I have described. Any other plausible theory of practical reason that countenances moral reasons should agree. But the acceptance of this, as we have seen, opens the way to a form of revisionary ethical theorizing.

6. *Ethical Theorizing*

This leaves us with the twofold conclusion I announced at the outset. First, Williams's attack on ethical theory cannot be met until his theory of practical reason is challenged. Moreover, it is not an obvious flaw in his conception of rational deliberation that it omits a concern to produce a systematic structure for the ends one is motivated to pursue. But we have found at least one respect in which that conception does need supplementation. Rational deliberation includes treating one's first-order reasons as undermined only by those considerations the treating of which as underminers makes sense in the light of one's possession of those first-order reasons. If the first-order reasons in question are moral ones, then they are only rationally undermined by considerations whose treatment as such can be justified in terms of the distinctive core concerns that characterize the various moral virtues. And from this, I have drawn my second conclusion: that there is a legitimate form of revisionary moral argument going beyond the kind of ethical reflection countenanced by Williams, and which should be endorsed, moreover, by any plausible theory of practical reason that countenances moral reasons.

---

[42] See the Introduction to this volume, pp. 11–12, and Korsgaard, 'Skepticism about Practical Reason', esp. 23.

Does this amount to the defence of an ethical *theory*? The sense of
'ethical theory' I identified as the target of Williams's argument was any
general characterization of what correct ethical thinking consists in that
grounds revisionary demands—that is, for which it is claimed that there is
reason for us to abandon deviations from it. And indeed, there is a clear
case for characterizing the position I have set out as offering something of
this sort. I have been relying on the claim that the treatment of certain core
considerations as first-order practical reasons is characteristically moral,
and have then added to this that good moral reasoning is also characterized
by the way in which a morally motivated agent's second-order reasons are
rendered intelligible by her possessing those first-order ones. The style of
revisionary argument drawn from these claims is thus clearly dependent on
the acceptance of assumptions concerning the characterization of certain
considerations as *moral* reasons.

However, it is also worth acknowledging the sense in which I have not
been advancing the sorts of claims which are naturally thought of as con-
stituting an ethical theory, even on the specialized definition adopted here.
For I have taken no view about what, if anything, can be said to explain
what unifies as moral reasons those considerations we treat as such—the
common characteristic in virtue of which they count as moral reasons—and
thus there is equally a sense in which, if an ethical theory requires an
account of what makes a normative reason ethical, I have offered no such
thing. I have said nothing here to vindicate the ambition of providing such
a unifying theory. Indeed, I have said nothing to mitigate the suggestion
that Williams has imposed an important obstacle in the way of any theory
of this kind. (Here, the central task for his opponents is the defence of a
structural constraint on practical reasons of the kind discussed in Section
3.) Rather, I have presented an independent argument for holding that,
whether or not this ambition can be vindicated, there is a further constraint
that must be satisfied by all good moral reasoning, and that consequently
grounds a style of effective revisionary moral argument. In advance of
defending a theory of the more ambitious sort, we know that revisionary
argument of this kind is available to us. There is at least one kind of
practical ethical theory.[43]

[43] This essay has been improved by the comments of audiences at the University of Stirling,
Australian National University, and Monash University—especially those of Antony Duff, Berys
Gaut, Richard Holton, Walter Sinnott-Armstrong, and Michael Smith.

5

Moral Judgement and Reasons for Action

ROBERT AUDI

The relation between intellect and will is a major concern of the theory of practical reason. In moral philosophy the central focus of this concern is the relation between reason and morality. Here the perennial question is often taken to be whether a rational person has reason to be moral. But there is really more than one question here, because there are at least two quite different though overlapping kinds of reasons: motivational reasons, roughly the kind that explain why an agent does a particular thing, and normative reasons, roughly the kind that indicate what an agent ought to do. The former are the kind an agent in some way responds to (else they could not explain); the latter are the kind that *rational* agents respond to and that can at least partially justify the action in question. There are also two directions of entailment to consider if we are to understand the relation between reason and morality: whether being rational entails being moral and whether being moral entails being rational.

Moral philosophers very commonly argue that there are overriding normative reasons to be moral, and hence that being (adequately) rational implies being moral; but as regards the converse implication, the preoccupying issue has been not the normative question whether a moral person is (*qua* moral) rational, or whether a moral person has normative reasons to act, but the motivational question whether the moral judgements such a person makes are by their very nature motivating—a question that on the face of it addresses the relation between intellect and will. It is here that I begin. Indeed, the question whether a rational person must be moral (or must at least intellectually accept moral standards) is not a direct concern of this essay. My main concern in the first three sections is whether an agent who makes a self-addressed moral judgement, such as 'I must resign' —an agent whose intellect is already in that sense moral at that place and time—must be motivated to act accordingly. Broadly stated, the issue is how, if at all, the behavioural will must respond to the moral intellect.

This last question concerns the relation between moral judgement and motivational reasons for action, a topic that has quite deservedly preoccupied philosophers, particularly in the past thirty years. The question is of interest both because it is closely connected with the relation between reason and morality and because it is pivotal for understanding the sense in which morality is 'practical', that is, bears on action. On some views, inspired by widely known arguments in Hume's *Treatise*, if morality is practical enough for its self-addressed judgements to be necessarily motivating, then it is not cognitive; and if it is cognitive enough for those judgements to be true (or false), then it is at best unclear how it can be practical.

The question of how moral judgement is related to motivation is complicated because motivational and normative reasons not only overlap, but are also discussed together (and sometimes conflated) in the literature; and it will soon be clear that the relation between moral judgement and motivating reasons cannot be adequately understood apart from some consideration of how each is related to normative reasons and how those in turn are connected with moral judgement.

My aim is to sharpen the issues and to offer the outline of an account of some major connections between moral judgement and reasons for action and of the varieties and grounds of such reasons. A subsidiary aim is to provide a taxonomy of some of the major positions concerning reason and morality and to introduce some terminology sufficiently intuitive and well defined to be of help to others examining or defending such positions. Section 1 will introduce the pivotal issues, lay out some essential distinctions between kinds of reason and types of judgement, and connect the former with specifically moral judgements. Sections 2 to 5 will appraise a form of what is often called *motivational internalism*. The main question here is the relation of moral judgement to motivation and hence of morality —as internally represented in judgement—to action. Moral judgements are supposed to be practical in providing motivational reasons for action. But do they necessarily do so, and can they do so apart from desire or some other independent motivational attitude?

Exploring the sense in which moral judgements may provide reasons for action brings us, in Section 6, to a related but quite different internalism, often called *reasons internalism*, a view concerning the basis of normative reasons for action. Different though they are, each of these internalisms is hard to understand adequately apart from a contrast with the other, and any systematic treatment of motivational internalism should distinguish it from the reasons variety liable to be confused with it. Both views, moreover, are found (if sometimes only implicitly) in Hume, and Sections 6 and 7 will bring the results of the examination of both internalisms to bear on the instrumentalist conception of rationality, of which Hume is often considered the historically most important source. The concluding section will sketch the wider implications of the essay for the general theory of reasons for action.

1. The Issues: Judgements, Motives, and Reasons

To see how motivation may be plausibly thought to be in some way internal to moral judgement, consider an example. Suppose that I judge, in response to a student's grade appeal sent to me after a course is over, that it would be (morally) unfair to raise the grade. Suppose further that my judgement is warranted relative to my evidence concerning the student's work and that of the rest of the class. Must I, by virtue of holding this judgement, have some degree of motivation to act accordingly, say to decline to raise the grade?[1] Many have thought so. In exploring this view I shall consider mainly moral judgements of this first-person sort, the self-addressed kind directly applicable to one's own future conduct. What we discover about these can be extended to other kinds of moral judgements.

Let us first focus on the judgement side of the issue: on what is implicit in moral judgements construed as held or sincerely made (I am taking a judgement one *holds*, as opposed to a judgement one simply entertains or makes merely for the sake of argument, to imply accepting the content judged, say that one must keep a promise). There are two questions here: whether, in *making* the judgement, I must *express* motivation, and whether, in *holding* the judgement, I must *have* motivation. Let us take these in turn.

It is natural to answer the first question, concerning the expressive content of moral judgement, affirmatively in so far as one takes 'expression' to have the sense it does when we say, for example, that a certain way of putting a complaint expresses anger: this is a linguistic, illocutionary, sense of 'express', not a causal sense, like that illustrated by 'His grief found expression in the intonation of his poems'. Expression in the linguistic sense does not entail having what one expresses. Since the main issue here is what actual motivation is essential to moral judgement, I leave this kind of expression aside and simply grant for the sake of argument that making a moral judgement expresses motivation in a sense implying that hearers are normally entitled to take it that one has some degree of motivation to act in accordance with the judgement.

The more important question for ethical theory is whether, in holding a judgement, one must *have* motivation to act accordingly, where holding such a judgement includes holding moral beliefs with the appropriate content even if they have not been formed through, or expressed in, *making* a judgement. If the answer is affirmative, then our moral judgements, whether we express them or not, are, by virtue of being intrinsically motivating, potentially predictive of our conduct, as, after all, we should like them to be.

---

[1] This is not the only way to act accordingly; I could e.g. also reassess the work of all the students and raise all the grades. For more complicated judgements there is an even greater variety of ways to act accordingly; that notion deserves analysis, but nothing I say will turn on the absence of one.

The main issue here can be put in terms of internality (a multifaceted notion shortly to be explicated). Is motivation in some way internal to moral judgement, as opposed to coming from something else, such as the fear of punishment? The view that it is internal—call it *generic motivational internalism*—is the position that holding a moral judgement (roughly, accepting its content) is necessarily motivating. Thus, if I hold a moral judgement, I must have some degree of motivation to act in accord with it. (Some of the several ways motivation may be conceived will be clarified shortly.)

The question whether some degree of motivation is internal to (holding) a moral judgement becomes even more complex when we try to understand motivation and reasons. Whatever we think it is that constitutes motivation, and whatever we take a reason to be, surely being motivated to do something implies having at least one kind of reason to do it. This is why locutions like 'He has no reason to oppose you' can be used to rebut the attribution of a motive. Thus, if motivation is internal to holding a moral judgement, then holding such a judgement, as I do in the grade appeals matter, entails having at least this kind of reason to act accordingly. It is often called a *motivational reason*[2] for the relevant actions, the kind of reason normally appealed to when a desire is invoked as a reason I have to do something or, if I do it, as a reason for which I did it.[3] This is not to say that desire exhausts motivation (it surely does not); desire is cited here because it is a paradigm case of motivation.[4]

A motivational reason may or may not lead to action. Having a motivational reason of the kind in question does not entail my performing an action my judgement motivates—for the motivational force of the reason may be outweighed by that of conflicting desires. But my holding the judgement does entail that, to some degree, and in some sense, I *want*, and thereby am disposed, to perform an action of the kind in question, and that I can adduce my judgement as a reason for an action of this kind, either retrospectively—say in explaining it—or prospectively, say in deliberating about whether to perform the action. The judgement is, then, at least a weak reason *for* performing it, since it expresses a consideration in favour of it, and is potentially a reason *why* I perform the action, since I could act for that reason.

---

[2] This term seems preferable to 'motivating reason' on at least one count: it does not suggest that any action motivated by the reason actually occurs.

[3] Two or more motivational reasons can jointly produce or jointly explain the same action. Such reasons are not merely potential causes of action but factors that can at least partially explain action as performed *for* them. An account of reasons distinguishing five main kinds of reasons for action is given in my 'Acting for Reasons', *Philosophical Review*, 95 (1986), 511–46.

[4] Arguably a desire is a case of motivation (to act), as opposed to a directionless energy source, only when the agent believes, or is at least disposed to believe, something to the effect that the agent's doing the deed in question would realize (or would contribute to realizing) the desired object.

The kind of wanting in question need not be desire, especially in a passional sense; wanting of the kind in question is the attitude whose content is expressed by the infinitive clause in explanations of the form of 'She did it in order to . . .'.[5] If one hesitates to take any notion of wanting to be broad enough for this role, the crucial point is that motivational attitudes, such as intentions and goals, are like wants and unlike beliefs both in not being true or false and in having a different 'direction of fit' to the world, roughly in the sense that whereas it is appropriate to beliefs to reflect the world, and in a sense they 'succeed' when they are true, it is appropriate to motivational attitudes, such as intentions and goals, to change the world, and they 'succeed' when one changes it (or at least it changes) in the wanted way.[6] The points made here about motivation do not, then, presuppose a Humean theory of motivation, which I shall here take to be in outline the view that wanting (as roughly equivalent to desiring) as well as believing figures in the explanation of every intentional action, and that beliefs as truth-valued attitudes do not entail wants.

Now consider normative reasons. Some who hold the non-sceptical view that there are such things—as opposed to motivational reasons conceived as mere tendencies to pursue what one wants—are none the less willing to dissociate them from motivation in various ways. Suppose, in contrast to the picture of moral judgement as entailing motivation, that no motivation is entailed by my holding the moral judgement that it would be unfair to raise the grade. Do I then still have a kind of reason for an action, such as a reason to decline (a reason why I should decline) to raise the grade? If so, it would surely be a kind of *normative* reason; for it would be the sort that can (to some extent) justify the relevant type of action. This is not to suggest that a normative reason cannot also be a motivational one. The point is that it seems intelligible to hold that a judgement could entail the former without entailing the latter, as it could entail the latter without entailing the former.

I want to consider mainly two positions on the relation between moral judgements and normative reasons for action. To keep the issue from becoming unmanageably broad I will focus only on normative reasons that are also moral.

First, on some views, simply in virtue of holding a moral judgement (at least assuming it is plausible) one has a (prima-facie) normative reason to

---

[5] Granted such explanations also indicate intending, but I have argued in 'Intending', *Journal of Philosophy*, 70 (1973), 387–403, that intending entails wanting in the relevant sense, and in 'The Concept of Wanting', *Philosophical Studies*, 21 (1973), 1–21, I have explicated the relevant kind of wanting. Both papers and supporting ones are in my *Action, Intention, and Reason* (Ithaca, NY, and London: Cornell Univ. Press, 1993).

[6] It has been held (e.g. by Donald Davidson) that intending *is* a kind of belief, but I cannot see that there is a compelling argument for this or even one with appropriate content or sufficient force to explain why (literal) talk of true and false intentions is simply not English.

act accordingly.[7] In favour of this view—taken as roughly equivalent to the thesis that holding such judgements constitutes (one case of) having reasons for acting—note that one can quite appropriately cite one's moral judgement, for instance that a deed is unfair, as a reason one has not to do it. This *judgements-as-reasons view*, as we might call it, does not entail motivational internalism. It is normative reason, and not motivational reason, that it takes to be internal to moral judgement.

There are two modifications of the judgements-as-reasons view that we should note, mainly to sharpen the issue and keep the modified versions distinct from the basic view. On the first, by virtue of holding a moral judgement, I would have not only a normative reason for acting, but also a motivational reason for acting.[8] One rationale for asserting this further consequence of holding a moral judgement is that only when a judgement is motivating would the reason it gives one be 'practical', and a genuine normative reason must be practical. The resulting position, which takes moral judgements as embodying *both* motivational and normative reasons, is simply the motivational internalist version of the judgements-as-reasons view. Call this the *motivational internalist judgements-as-reasons view*. On the second modification of the judgements-as-reasons view, a judgement provides a normative reason for action if and only if it entails motivation (as on the first modification), and beyond this, the motivation comes from some internal non-cognitive (hence non-truth-valued) practical state, such as desire. Call it the *non-cognitive-motivation-entailing judgements-as-reasons view*. If it is sound, then a moral judgement cannot provide a reason for action apart from embodying or implying some such state.

In short, the judgement-as-reasons view takes moral judgements to provide normative reasons; the internalist version of this view adds that those judgements also provide motivational reasons; and the non-cognitive version adds in turn that the motivation must come from a non-cognitive element—as one would hold if one maintained both motivational internalism and a Humean theory of motivation. The non-cognitive version does not, however, entail *non-cognitivism*: the point is that non-cognitive elements are crucial underpinnings of normative reasons, but it is not implied that a moral judgement cannot be cognitive, in the sense that their content is true or false ('cognizable' as opposed to, say, attitudinal). In terms of the widest

---

[7] Throughout, in speaking of normative reasons I shall mean prima-facie, as opposed to all-things-considered reasons. Nothing of importance in the essay turns on this restriction.

[8] At one point Thomas Nagel maintains this sort of view, at least in regard to the connection between a kind of judgement and being motivated to act accordingly: 'the first-person acknowledgement of a sufficient reason for doing something . . . is sufficient to explain one's doing it . . . There is no need to hold that "X acknowledges a reason to A" *entails* "X does A, or X wants to do A" . . .'. See *The Possibility of Altruism* (Oxford: Clarendon Press, 1970), 110–11. This is roughly equivalent to the view

issue that concerns us, the thrust of the non-cognitive version is not that the intellect cannot grasp morality, but that its doing so provides normative reasons for action only with the co-operation of some non-cognitive element —broadly, something in the will or having potential to move the will.

Suppose we now combine the twofold idea that moral judgements are necessarily motivating (motivational internalism) and that motivation is rooted in non-cognitive elements (as on the Humean theory of motivation) with another powerful idea prominent in the Humean tradition—the naturalistic position that reasons for action must be grounded in our psychology rather than in, say, a priori truths about the good. We can then see how the second major position we must examine comes in. This is *reasons internalism*. In a generic form, it is roughly the view that normative reasons for action must be grounded in some internal conative or at least non-cognitive motivational state, such as a want, desire, passion, or emotion: paradigmatically, the kind of attitude that can be in some way satisfied by actions in its service, but is not properly said to be true or false.[9] Perhaps the underlying idea is that normative reasons for doing something must represent it as fulfilling some kind of psychologically real goal, commonly the kind that produces a sense of need. Wanting food, for instance, yields a reason to get it.

For reasons internalism, to have a reason to do something is, in a simple and common kind of case, for that deed to be such that one can clearly see that it would best satisfy one's basic desires, say to relieve pain. As the view is usually developed, seeing that there are such reasons does not require either resorting to a priori truths or positing anything irreducibly normative. If we think moral judgements provide reasons for action, we must hold that they 'tap into' basic desires. But if, like Hume, we see humanity as having a suitable range of socially directed, sometimes even altruistic, desires, then we can explain both why there are (for normal people) reasons to be

that holding the kind of practical judgement we are speaking of is in itself motivationally sufficient for one's A-ing, thus an adequate *reason why* one As if one does. Nagel clarifies the claim (in a way that brings it close to another I shall later distinguish), by adding, 'All I wish to claim is that such an acknowledgement is by itself *capable* of providing a motivation in the appropriate direction—that there is no need to seek an alternative or supplementary explanation of action when that one is available . . .': ibid. 111. (The clause following the dash strengthens the preceding one, on the assumption that the reason why we need not seek more information is that sufficient motivation *is* present; but it is not clear how much weakening of the original claim, if any, is intended in the clarifying sentence.)

[9] Reasons internalism as thus characterized is close (but probably not equivalent) to the view Bernard Williams identifies as taking only internal reasons to be genuine reasons for action, in 'Internal and External Reasons', in his *Moral Luck* (Cambridge: Univ. Press, 1981), ch. 8. The judgements-as-reasons view could also be called a form of reasons internalism; for although it does not require that a reason be automatically motivating, it does allow an internal element like a moral judgement one holds, to constitute a reason; but this would be a weak internalism, since it neither makes internality a necessary condition for being a reason nor requires that a normative reason be (motivationally) practical. I mention the view simply to locate it in the spectrum and set it aside.

moral and how moral judgements imply both motivational and normative reasons to act accordingly.[10]

Reasons internalism is highly controversial. Many philosophers deny that reasons for action must be grounded in that way and maintain that the *truth* of moral judgement for or against one's possible future conduct, whether one holds the judgement or not, implies a normative reason for action, say a reason not to raise a grade, and can imply a normative reason for one to do something whether or not the action would satisfy any of one's non-cognitive motivational states. This position is a form of *reasons externalism*, which, generically, is simply the denial of reasons internalism. Positively conceived, it is roughly the view that one can have a normative reason for acting simply in virtue of the externally grounded truth of a judgement for or against some item of one's possible future conduct, where this kind of external grounding implies that one's normative reasons for action—the kind that would justify it—are not grounded in any of one's non-cognitive motivational states. Thus, if it would be plainly wrong to cheat someone, that fact could provide a reason not to do so, even if one had no non-cognitive motivational attitude also disfavouring the deed, such as a desire to have the person as a friend.

As this example indicates, there is an external sense of 'judgement' in which a judgement can be applicable to action without being *made*. Consider a case in which, after a mistake, one speaks of the judgement one should have made. A reason-giving judgement itself may thus be external at least in the sense that it may be a normative proposition that no one actually holds, hence is not internal to anyone's mind.[11] A stronger reasons externalism would maintain that some normative reasons for action *are* externally grounded in normative truths supporting the actions in question; a still stronger one would maintain that all of them are. A wide range of normative externalisms can be constructed not only by varying the kinds

---

[10] For reasons to doubt that this approach to normative reasons is adequate, see Christine Korsgaard's discussion (in this volume) of the problems a Humean faces in accounting for even the force of hypothetical imperatives. Related difficulties are brought out by Jean Hampton in 'On Instrumental Rationality', in J. B. Schneewind (ed.), *Reason, Ethics, and Society* (Chicago: Open Court, 1996).

[11] The relevant internality and externality are not easy to define and have not to my knowledge been sharply defined in the literature. In good part, the idea is that an external reason is in a certain way interpersonally and cross-culturally valid and does not depend for its normative force on what anyone believes or desires (except where the proposition is about beliefs or desires, as where a reason for doing something is that a person one loves wants more than anything else that one do it). As this suggests, some non-instrumental, non-cognitive grounding is allowable under externalism. For one thing, moral experience might be a ground; for another, where satisfying desire is taken as a prima-facie intrinsic good (as perhaps arguably in the case of loved ones), a desire might be at least part of the ground of an external reason. Neither of these elements would be considered a ground of a reason for action by paradigmatic reasons internalists; either of them could be so regarded by certain non-cognitivists, which shows that, given a non-cognitivist reading of 'truth' for moral judgements, externalism can be held by a non-cognitivist.

of normative reasons that must be externally grounded but also by changing such variables as the strength of the reasons provided by a judgement (conceived externally or otherwise), the kind or degree of their externality, and the kind of access the agent has to the grounds of the judgement.

One rationale for a fairly strong reasons externalism is apparent in our critical practices. Suppose I do not arrive at a morally sound conclusion in relation to the grade appeal and I mistakenly judge that I should change the grade. It now seems that *there is reason* for me not to change it, and to bring out that I am missing certain considerations, someone might say precisely this.[12] It appears that there is a sense in which this reason would have 'been there' even if no one had noticed it. On a strong externalism, normative reasons—reasons there *are* for an action—sometimes exist apart from what anyone actually believes or wants regarding the rightness or justifiability of that action.

This strong reasons externalist view concerning moral judgement should be associated with the external, non-psychological sense of 'judgement', taken to designate the content of a judgement someone does or might *hold* (this content is what one does or would judge to be the case). For instance, after being convinced that I was wrong in judging I should raise the grade, I might say that the right judgement was that I should leave it unchanged. This judgement (in the external sense) was not made by anyone, though it was, we might say, implicit in the facts, in that any proper assessment of them would yield it. Call it *judgement in the propositional sense*, or for short propositional judgement. It is of course not the kind of judgement plausibly thought to entail motivation. Propositional judgements are abstract elements that can be external even to the intellect; they may surely fail to be internal to the will. By contrast, judgements in the psychological sense are the holding or making of judgements in the propositional sense. The holding of a judgement is a dispositional state; the making of one is an occurrence, such as an assertion; the content of either is a judgement in the propositional sense.

A good understanding of the notions of judgement and, in particular, of holding a judgement, is crucial for exploring motivational internalism as well as for understanding the reasons variety. If (generic) motivational internalism is true, then holding a moral judgement implies having a motivational reason to act accordingly. Holding a moral judgement also implies having a normative reason for such action, given certain assumptions, chiefly that moral considerations *can* provide normative reasons—which seems plainly true—and that the moral judgement in question is not so ill-grounded

---

[12] There is also *a* reason, which seems a slightly weaker point. Normally, saying there is reason (to A) implies a significant degree of justification and a greater degree than is implied in saying there is a reason. Arguably, if there is a moral ground to A, there is always reason to A.

that the agent is foolish to hold it. If these assumptions are as plausible as they seem, then appraising motivational internalism leads us directly to the question of whether holding moral judgements is also essentially connected with normative reason—the notion for which reasons internalism provides a pivotal condition.

If the kind of motivation that goes with holding a moral judgement implies (at least in common circumstances) a normative reason for action, one may wonder about the converse relation, which is equally important in ethical theory. Motivational internalism does not claim, and at least some proponents of it would deny, that having a normative reason implies being motivated to act accordingly. Some version of this thesis is, however, central in any *reasons* internalism that roots one's normative reasons for action in one's desires: desires are paradigms of motivators. Both positions are crucial for understanding moral judgement and reasons for action. It will be best, I think, to take up motivational internalism first and then proceed to reasons internalism. But, as is perhaps apparent already, these two kinds of internalism are, though logically independent, so closely related and so integral to the theory of practical reason that it is difficult to discuss either one in any depth apart from the other.

2. *Motivational Reasons and Motivational Internalism*

Motivational internalism is of special interest not just because, at least in its generic form, it represents important common ground between Humeans and Kantians, but also because it is central to understanding the sense in which moral judgement is practical and, to that extent, the relation between reason and morality. To be sure, the Humean version in its main contemporary forms takes the internality of motivation to moral judgement to imply that such judgement is not cognitive (or at least does not 'come from reason'), whereas the Kantian version implies or at least permits the cognitivity of moral judgement and takes the internality of motivation to it to imply that morality is practical. But on both views moral judgement is motivating in a sense implying an action tendency. There is no adequate generally accepted definition of motivational internalism. Rather than argue for a single definition, I will indicate the crucial variables that any detailed account should reflect, and then propose a conception that can serve a number of purposes in moral theory.

It is important to characterize motivational internalism so that it is evident why it is so called and clear what is supposed to be internal to what, and in what way. Several aspects of the issue should be distinguished, and when they are we have the basis for identifying an entire family of motivational internalisms. There are at least five main dimensions of motivational internalism: (1) the *locus* of the motivation—what the motivation is internal *to*, for example, obligation, duty, or the sense of obligation or of duty, or a belief or judgement attributing an obligation or duty; (2) the kind of *internality* in question, for example, conceptual containment as opposed to mere necessary implication (a distinction shortly to be explained); (3) the *degree* of motivation implied, for example, only some degree versus enough to explain why an action was performed (but on most views not so much as to make weakness of will, conceived as implying uncompelled action against one's better judgement—say one's overall moral judgement— impossible);[13] (4) the *normative domain* of the obligation to which the motivation is supposed to be internal, for example, moral or also prudential (or perhaps religious or even aesthetic); and (5) the *modality* of the thesis asserting the connection, for instance its contingency or necessity (or analyticity).

Motivational internalisms representing nearly all of the combinations indicated here (and others) have been held or at least characterized as possible positions,[14] though to be sure the modality of the philosophical theses connecting judgement and motivation is most often taken to be necessity, since motivational internalists tend to regard their thesis as a kind of conceptual truth (one could, however, construe it as something weaker, say as a truth of 'human nature'). It should be clear that on the view I have been working with, it is to moral judgements, as held, that motivation is internal or external. The mere truth (or even the justifiability) of moral

---

[13] R. M. Hare may be an exception to this in apparently disallowing the kind of weakness of will here described. See e.g. ch. 5 of *The Language of Morals* (Oxford: Univ. Press, 1961).

[14] For a number of them, including many references to the literature on the topic, see W. D. Falk, '"Ought" and Motivation', *Proceedings of the Aristotelian Society*, 48 (1947–8), 111–38; William K. Frankena, 'Obligation and Motivation in Recent Moral Philosophy', in A. I. Melden (ed.), *Essays in Moral Philosophy* (Seattle: Univ. of Washington Press, 1958), 40–81; Nagel, *The Possibility of Altruism*; John McDowell, 'Are Moral Requirements Hypothetical Imperatives?', *Proceedings of the Aristotelian Society*, 13 (1978), 13–29; E. J. Bond, *Reason and Value* (Cambridge and New York: Cambridge Univ. Press, 1983); Stephen L. Darwall, *Impartial Reason* (Ithaca, NY: Cornell Univ. Press, 1983), esp. ch. 5; Christine M. Korsgaard, 'Skepticism about Practical Reason', *Journal of Philosophy*, 83 (1986), 5–25; Mark C. Timmons, 'Kant and the Possibility of Moral Motivation', *Southern Journal of Philosophy*, 23 (1985), 377–98; David Brink, *Moral Realism and the Foundations of Ethics* (Cambridge and New York: Cambridge Univ. Press, 1989); Onora O'Neill, *Constructions of Reason* (Cambridge and New York: Cambridge Univ. Press, 1989); my *Practical Reasoning* (London and New York: Routledge, 1989), esp. chs. 2 and 3; John Robertson, 'Hume on Practical Reason', *Proceedings of the Aristotelian Society*, 24 (1989), 267–82; Alfred R. Mele, 'Motivational Internalism: The Powers and Limits of Practical Reasoning', *Philosophia*, 19 (1989), 427–36; Michael Stocker, *Plural and Conflicting Values* (Oxford: Clarendon Press, 1990); James Dreier, 'Internalism and Speaker Relativism', *Ethics*, 101 (1990), 6–26; Jonathan Dancy, *Moral Reasons* (Oxford: Blackwell, 1993); Rachel Cohon, 'Internalism about Reasons for Action', *Pacific Philosophical Quarterly*, 74 (1993), 265–88; Michael Smith, *The Moral Problem* (Oxford: Blackwell, 1994); Kurt Baier, *The Rational and the Moral Order* (Chicago: Open Court, 1995); John Deigh, 'Empathy and Universalizability', *Ethics*, 105 (1995), 743–63; and Connie S. Rosati, 'Internalism and the Good for a Person', *Ethics*, 106 (1966), 247–73.

judgements in the propositional sense cannot be plausibly taken to imply that the relevant people are motivated accordingly. When we discover what we ought to have done, we commonly discover the truth of a moral judgement that was *not* accompanied by motivation on our part.[15]

I take *motivational internalism proper* to be the view that some degree of motivation is intrinsic (and in that sense internal) to the holding of a (self-addressed) moral judgement—especially the kind that is for or against some particular action or type of action clearly representing one's future possible conduct. This goes beyond generic motivational internalism in one way, whose significance will soon be evident: it requires that motivation be not only entailed by, but (conceptually) intrinsic to, holding a moral judgement. We should probably add, what is often intended by motivational internalists though not essential to the position, that the *degree* of motivation is sufficient to explain an action of the relevant kind: one that accords with the judgement. If any other variant of the view is needed, it can probably be constructed by specifying the position further on one of the five indicated dimensions.

What are the prospects for motivational internalism proper? The view seems most plausible when we imagine someone (sincerely) making a self-addressed moral judgement. We believe, for one thing, that actions speak louder than words, and we question the sincerity of people who express moral judgements but do not act accordingly when the occasion calls for it. Moreover, it is arguably deviant or even impermissible to say such things as 'It would be unfair for me to raise his grade, but I have no motivation whatever to resist doing it.'

These points in favour of motivational internalism are far from conclusive. For one thing, we could, on the basis of a strong statistical connection between moral judgement and motivation, doubt the sincerity of someone who exhibits a disparity between expressed moral judgements and the conduct they enjoin. Moreover, the oddity just noted could be merely pragmatic, like that of saying 'It is true that p, but I don't believe p.'

It must be remembered, however, that the most plausible internalisms will take only *some* degree of motivation to be implicit in holding a moral judgement. Critics thus have to imagine someone who genuinely holds such a judgement and has no motivation at all to act accordingly. Could one really judge that, for example, raising a grade would be unfair and, in a situation of forced choice, be content to flip a coin to decide whether to raise it? It may appear that one could not. But in so far as we take this

---

[15] This needs various qualifications; e.g. there is a non-cognitivist version, there is the possibility that one happened to be non-morally motivated to A before one discovered one ought to A, and there is of course the contention that general moral judgements (principles) could not be true unless there were some degree of motivation appropriate to them.

appearance to signify the internality of motivation to moral judgement, it may be because we are imagining a rational agent or a judgement made in 'normal' circumstances. One question we must therefore ask is how much apparent support for motivational internalism proper may come from assumptions about the kind of agent in question, or the circumstances of judgement, or both.

Suppose, then, that we restrict motivational internalism to rational agents. Moral persons, after all, are (most of the time, at least) rational agents. There is some reason to doubt that a *rational* person could judge that it would be unfair to raise a grade yet be content to flip a coin to decide whether to raise it, at least in a rational moment. For it seems implicit in the notion of such persons that they do not make moral judgements without taking them seriously at least to the extent of *tending* to act on them when nothing else is at stake. Arguably, then, rational agents are so constructed that they necessarily tend to act in accordance with their moral judgements.

The plausibility of this qualified internalism may, however, derive not from the internality of motivation to moral judgement but from whatever plausibility attaches to the view that *rational* agents must have desires that are in line with certain of their normative beliefs, above all their moral beliefs about what they should do (I am assuming that a judgement one *holds*, say that *p*, as opposed to a judgement that *p* which one merely states or supposes for argument's sake, implies the corresponding belief, here, that *p*). This view applies particularly to agents who are both rational and moral—the kind of agent most people writing on this issue in the literature have had in mind.

If, in rational agents, there is such an integration between moral judgement and motivation, then a kind of motivational internalism—call it *rational agent motivational internalism*—is true of them: they must have desires (or at least wants) that are in line with their moral beliefs about what they should do. This restricted internalism would not entail generic motivational internalism, but it would establish relationships whose obtaining is a good part of what motivational internalists want to affirm.[16]

If rational agent motivational internalism is true, it can, on one special assumption, explain even the thesis that it is *necessary* for anyone who holds a moral judgement to have some degree of motivation to act accordingly. The assumption, which is admittedly quite controversial, is that the kind

---

[16] Views that are at least similar receive sympathetic treatment in Korsgaard, 'Skepticism about Practical Reason', and in Smith, *The Moral Problem*, e.g. in ch. 3, where he considers the idea behind (motivational) internalism to be roughly that 'If an agent judges that it is right for her to φ in circumstances C, then either she is motivated to φ in C or she is practically irrational' (p. 61). For more recent statements see also Essays 8 and 10 in this volume.

and degree of rationality required to hold a moral judgement at all implies an integration between judgement and motivation adequate to produce the relevant degree of motivation to act in accord with the moral judgement. On this assumption, rational moral judges are, on pain of a kind of incoherence, always motivated to *some* degree in the direction of their moral judgements. Not only do actions speak louder than words; words unaccompanied by at least appropriate action tendencies are not fully intelligible.

3. *Practical Judgement and the Diversity of Internal Motivation*

The line of reasoning we have been exploring—connecting rational persons' moral judgements with their motivation—does not in the end support motivational internalism proper. For, from the indirect connection that the reasoning aims to establish between moral judgements and the actions they favour, it does not follow that these actions are motivated *by* the judgements, in the sense that this motivation is intrinsic to (holding) those judgements. The actions might be motivated by independent elements, for instance by moral experience or by a desire to do what is right. Thus, moral motivation might be entailed by the holding of a moral judgement— because of what holding it implies about the agent overall—yet not be internal to moral judgement. That, however, is what motivational internalism, as usually understood, requires.

We might put the point like this. Moral motivation may be entailed by, and so be *consequentially internal* to, moral judgement, even if it is not *constitutively internal*, and thereby an intrinsic element in, moral judgement. On one reading of Hume, he holds a consequential internalism; and on one reading of Kant, he holds a constitutive internalism. Both apparently hold generic motivational internalism. But for Hume, on this reading, a moral judgement that, say, an act one is considering is virtuous arises from a sense of pleasure felt upon the appropriate contemplation of the act, and this associated pleasure by its very nature provides positive motivation toward the act;[17] whereas for Kant, on one reading, the will *is* practical

---

[17] See e.g. the *Treatise*, III. i. 1, in which he says that 'when you pronounce any character or action to be vicious, you mean nothing, but that from the constitution of your nature you have a feeling or sentiment of blame from the contemplation of it' (p. 469 in the Selby-Bigge edn.), where such a feeling can be taken to be at once motivational and non-cognitive (at least in not being true or false), quite apart from whether it entails desire properly so called. This reading is neutral with respect to non-cognitivism; a judgement can arise from a sentiment of blame, e.g. whether it is propositional or, in a non-cognitive sense, expressive. Note, however, that in making a moral judgement one could express such a feeling only in the illocutionary sense and so not have it. Thus, if Hume holds a 'consequential internalism', it should be because there is something motivating he takes moral judgement itself to imply, as there is if it *must* arise from a feeling or sentiment construed as passional or otherwise motivational. Perhaps his considered view (and certainly another broadly Humean view) is that moral judgements are consequentially but contingently motivating.

reason, and therefore a genuine moral judgement, which represents a deliverance of practical reason—an imperative, in one sense—must be motivating.[18] In the first case, the judgement and motivation are more nearly common effects of the same causes than cause and effect; in the second case, the motivational and causal powers are intrinsic to holding (or at least to sincerely making) the judgement.

The motivational internalist wants to show a connection between moral judgement and motivation, not just one between a general—and doubtless controversial—notion of a rational person holding a moral judgement, that is, a rational moral judge, and motivation. Even a motivational externalist can grant rational agent motivational internalism, by arguing that the relevant motivation comes from the kinds of desires that rational persons, or at least rational moral judges, have (or from other non-judgemental motivational elements implied by the minimal rationality in question).[19]

In so far as rational agent motivational internalism is plausible, it provides an explanation of some of the data supporting generic motivational internalism. This explanation is potentially externalist, in the sense that in at least some cases it attributes an agent's motivation toward actions in accord with a moral judgement to factors not entailed just by the holding of that judgement. The availability of such an explanation is, of course, not a direct argument against generic motivational internalism, or even against motivational internalism proper; but it heightens the sense that the latter, in particular, needs further support if it is to survive as part of our account of the relation between reason and morality. A major segment of such support may come from a source quite different from the rationality of a moral judgement, namely, from one or another concept of moral judgement, a notion I now want to explore further.

I have already stressed the distinction between making and holding a moral judgement. There is a further distinction that bears on motivational internalism. It is between, on the one hand, making *or* holding a judgement as a matter of simple *propositional endorsement* and, on the other hand, making or holding it as a matter of *moral appraisal*. If there are moral propositions, then it may be possible to see their truth, even as applied to

---

[18] See e.g. the *Grundlegung*, 413, where he says that 'the will is a faculty of choosing only that which reason, independently of inclination, recognizes as practically necessary, i.e., as good.' See *Foundations of the Metaphysics of Morals*, trans. Lewis White Beck (New York: Liberal Arts Press, 1959). I discuss this kind of Kantian position, and explain how it may allow for weakness of will, in ch. 2 of *Practical Reasoning*, cited above. Korsgaard's essay in this volume is highly pertinent to this matter. Cf. John Deigh's discussion of Kant: 'if one holds, as Kant did, that an aversion to inconsistency is inherent in reason, then the motive would be internal to the cognitive operation and the account would therefore support taking the internalism of the categorical imperative to be true of our deeper knowledge of right and wrong' ('Empathy and Universalizability', 751).

[19] This paragraph and the preceding one derive in part from a section of my 'Autonomy, Reason, and Desire', *Pacific Philosophical Quarterly*, 72 (1992), 247–71.

one's own conduct, in a purely intellectual way. Indeed, even on the non-cognitivist view that there are no moral propositions and that moral utterances are in some way expressive (perhaps of a prescription), there could probably be a corresponding distinction between (i) expressing a mere classificatory moral assessment of an action—which bears on one's inferential tendencies but need not entail motivation regarding the action[20]—and (ii) expressing an attitude of action-guiding moral appraisal, which is the usual case. There is a vast difference between judgementally agreeing with someone on the proposition that publishing pornography is an immoral activity, where one cares little about the matter—this is simply expressing propositional endorsement—and morally judging (say as a concerned citizen advising the prosecuting attorney) that one should seek a life sentence for the ruthless kidnapper of a 5-year-old—this is making a moral appraisal. Perhaps, then, motivational internalism should be taken to concern only moral judgements held *as* moral appraisals.

This line is at least initially promising: if there is such a thing as simply making a cold judgement that it would be unfair to raise a grade, where one is just endorsing the proposition in question, this merely propositional judgement need not be motivational; but the normal appraising ('hot') judgement that a moral agent would make in such a case would typically be motivational. One might even go so far as to say that if there is no such motivation, then at least one of the following points holds: the agent (i) is not taking the moral point of view at all, (ii) is not judging morally (in a moral *way*), or, in the case where the judgement is made as well as held, (iii) is not making a move in moral discourse (in the moral game, if you like).

These distinctions seem important: there is a difference between, on the one hand, *holding* a moral proposition as a manifestation of arriving at it by taking the moral point of view on the matter and, on the other hand, simply *believing* that proposition; between judging a matter *morally*—in the engaged way characteristic of morality as applied to guiding daily conduct—and simply holding a detached judgement with *moral content*; and between *stating* a moral judgement simply as a truth and *making a move in moral discourse*, which has an entrenched action-guiding role in human life. But suppose we grant motivational internalism for the three rich cases.

---

[20] Here one might raise the question why we should not abandon the plausible view one might call *cognitive internalism*—roughly the thesis that beliefs motivate other beliefs when one judges the propositional object of the former to entail or strongly support that of the latter, independently of separate motivation, such as a desire to believe the consequences of what one believes. There is a great deal to say here. Two important points are, first, that we are here remaining in the cognitive domain as opposed to crossing from the cognitive realm to that of motivation, with a different direction of fit to the world; and second, a tendency to infer (though not necessarily to believe) consequences of what one believes is plainly in part constitutive of the notion of a rational person in a way instantiating motivational internalism is not plainly constitutive of that notion—a point to be argued in the next section.

What we get is another restricted form of motivational internalism: the thesis that some degree of motivation is internal to moral judgements held *from the moral point of view*, roughly, to making or holding a judgement from the moral perspective as opposed to merely believing a moral proposition (a propositional judgement) with the same content. Call this thesis (moral) *perspectival motivational internalism.*

Perspectival motivational internalism is certainly significant and is quite plausible. The moral judgements of the relevant kind, which we may call *morally anchored*, apparently are motivational. But the thesis we have arrived at still falls short of the unrestricted view, motivational internalism proper. For it is surely plausible to maintain that a central element in taking, or judging within, the moral point of view implies having some degree of motivation to act on the directives that emerge from one's moral reasoning and from one's assessments therein. Otherwise we have something like assuming the moral point of view for the sake of argument, simulating it, or merely mouthing it.

However plausible perspectival motivational internalism is, it still falls short of the unrestricted view, motivational internalism proper. If motivation to act on one's moral judgements, say in the form of a desire to live up to one's moral obligations, is what explains why holding those judgements implies motivation to act accordingly, there is no need, and probably no good reason, to take this motivation to be internal to holding them.[21] Motivation to act on one's moral judgements can be internal to taking the moral point of view without being internal to holding those judgements. Perhaps taking the moral point of view entails or at least causes the adoption of moral standards, or even leads to one's internalizing them in the will, so that one's moral judgements now operate on a foundation of awaiting volition. It does not follow that any such volition or any other motivational elements are intrinsic to moral judgements themselves.[22]

None of these considerations shows that motivational internalism proper cannot be sustained. But they do suggest that, at least from a cognitivist point of view, what gives it plausibility may be very largely considerations

---

[21] This position does not entail positing second-order desires or desires regarding one's judgements or moral standards, e.g. a desire to want to be moral or to act on one's moral judgements. There are many kinds of contents the appropriate desires could have, e.g. to be a certain kind of person, where that is understood in terms of doing the kinds of things in question, say grading students on their merits.

[22] It might be objected that there are moral judgements or moral beliefs, say that people are beings with dignity, that a person cannot hold *without* taking, or in some way partially internalizing, the moral point of view. If such taking and internalizing are distinguished from capacities and dispositions thereto, this claim would seem at best difficult to show. But even if it is true, motivational elements essential to taking or internalizing that point of view may still be the source of the motivational reasons for action that go with the belief or judgement that require such a taking or internalization; these reasons need not be internal to it.

better explained on the basis of related views that locate the crucial motivation elsewhere than in the moral judgement that was supposed to be its basis. Moreover, these views provide an important thing, perhaps the most important single thing, that motivational internalists (as such) want: a connection between reason and motivation, and, in so far as the moral judgements in question represent morality as a domain of practical reason and the motivation in question is directed toward moral conduct, between reason and morality.

What perspectival motivational internalism and similar views fail to provide that some motivational internalists have wanted is a strong connection between intellect and will. The desired connection is one whereby the will must respond to moral judgement—paradigmatically, by producing action or at least generating an intention or some other motivation to act in accord with the judgement—independently of any other source of motivation, even rational desire. I want to stress, however, that this goal is more ambitious than motivational internalism in any of its plausible forms. Failure to achieve it should be kept in perspective: the executive power that would be required of moral judgement to *guarantee* action is more than any plausible internalism can claim (and more than is claimed by the best theorists in this tradition, including Kant and leading Kantians). This is in part because such executive power would make it at best difficult to countenance the possibility of weakness of will. But quite apart from this point, even if generic motivational internalism is true, there is a gap between the potentially outweighed motivation that moral judgement entails and the actions it should produce. It would be one thing to show that holding a moral judgement entails motivation strong enough to explain action that accords with such judgement; it would be quite another to show that moral judgements imply motivation strong enough to put the will firmly under the power of moral reason wherever that is invoked by moral judgement.

4. Rational Agency and the Evidential Role of Moral Motivation

So far, I have spoken as if some form of rational agent motivational internalism may be provisionally taken as sound, so that at least the internalist idea that *in* rational persons, or at least in rational persons holding a prima-facie *rational* moral judgement, some degree of motivation is internal to moral judgement. I believe, however, that even this broadened internalist idea may be too strong.

To see the problem, consider a case in which a deontologically orientated father judges that he (morally) must punish his 16-year-old daughter for taking the car out without permission, something she had agreed not to do.

The judgement may come from a sense of good policy, a knowledge of his previous past practice with his older child, and consistency with his past pattern of discipline. We may think of the judgement as largely an inferential upshot of cool reflection based on these elements. Suppose now that his daughter gives an excuse in terms of a sudden need for some books, but he rejects the excuse as inadequate. The punishment he judges he should give her is to deny her a visit to a friend's home on the weekend. There is little reason to doubt that if he is *perfectly* rational he will have not only some degree of motivation to act on the judgement, but a degree appropriate to the context: sufficient, in the absence of obstacles or new evidence, to produce the punitive deed. But the issue is what holds for rational moral agents like you and me. If he is simply like most of us, and especially if he is even-tempered and unemotional about the matter, it is far from self-evident that he must, on pain of irrationality, be motivated to deny her the outing.

An important possibility is that despite his moral judgement's being both in character and at least minimally rational, it represents only a small segment of his overall structure of relevant beliefs and goals. Perhaps, deep down, he recognizes a young woman approaching adulthood, striving for autonomy, presuming on parental understanding, and duly penitent about breaking her word in so acting. He might, after careful reflection, recognize this and might, working from the largest perspective he is capable of, withdraw his moral judgement; but the fact that he *would* do this does not imply that either he or his moral judgement is irrational while he in fact holds it. Particularly in matters that are not earth-shaking for us, we quite normally make judgements rooted in the nearest region of the larger evidential field we could canvass if necessary. We usually succeed reasonably well and often arrive at rational judgements, though we sometimes revise our judgements in the light of a wider search.

My suggestion, then, is that the father may be motivationally influenced by the grounds for forgiveness that he senses but does not draw together into a counter-judgement. Their influence may in fact be one that he— and we—might rationally welcome as countermanding or even obliterating any motivation that would otherwise be carried by his punitive moral judgement. The case does not appeal to irrational influences: indeed, it recognizes some of the same kinds of connections between rational and motivational elements that motivational internalism seems to exaggerate or to posit with insufficient qualification. What we have, then, is not forces of reason overcoming irrational forces; his original judgement is not shown to be irrational by the more weighty considerations but only to be *less* rationally adequate than one he might form from a wider perspective.

In this special case, there seems to be no conceptual necessity, and probably no psychological necessity, that he be motivated at all to administer the punishment. Surely he may, when the moment of decision comes, have no motivation to deny his daughter the outing and may instead find himself seeking a compromise such as a rebuke.[23] Granted, his contrary motivation may lead him to reconsider and eventually abandon his judgement. The point is that even while he holds it, contrary motivation can be both rational and—possibly working together with other factors—strong enough to prevent his judgement from having its typical motivational effect.

If this is a possible case, it shows that even rational agent motivational internalism is too strong. The case suggests, however, something a proponent of that view would welcome: it is only where the *overall* weight of reason goes against a rational moral judgement that the judgement fails to motivate. This suggestion gains support from the breadth of relevant rational considerations: these are not only judgements and facts; the rational counterweight can apparently also come from either moral emotion, such as revulsion at punishing one's daughter, or from what is sometimes described as moral experience, say a sense that the deed would be wrong. This sense need not derive from a conflicting moral judgement and, in part because it is not true (or false), is not itself a judgement; it may instead be both a force that deprives the standing judgement of motivating power and a ground—both motivational and evidential—for forming a new judgement to replace the standing one.

It may well be, however, that even this restricted rational agent motivational internalism is too strong and that there are counter-instances to rational agent motivational internalism that do not depend on either the overall weight of reasons or on moral emotion or moral experience. The same father could be lacking motivation to act on his judgement even if love, or pity, or perhaps depression, rather than such things as a sense of why his daughter did what she did, is what blocks any motivational energy his moral judgement may have had or produced. It is at least not clear that this kind of motivational blockage implies any dramatic deficiency in rationality. In any case, once we can understand why motivational internalism is not a conceptual truth, the possibilities for explaining its empirical falsehood can be seen to be diverse.[24]

[23] This case bears important similarities to one I have offered to show that weak-willed action is not necessarily irrational on balance. For a description of that case and a theory of how it is possible that bears on the motivational counterpart presented here, see 'Weakness of Will and Rational Action', *Australasian Journal of Philosophy*, 68 (1990), 270–81, repr. in my *Action, Intention, and Reason*.

[24] For supporting data of the kind this paragraph notes, see Michael Stocker, 'Desiring the Bad', *Journal of Philosophy*, 79 (1979), 738–53. See also Alfred R. Mele, 'Motivation: Essentially Motivation-Constituting Attitudes', *Philosophical Review*, 104 (1995), 387–423, and 'Internalist Moral Cognitivism and Listlessness', *Ethics*, 106 (1966), 727–53. The former is also instructive concerning what constitutes motivation as opposed to cognition. One way to resist treating the connection between moral judgement and motivation as contingent is to argue that it is a conceptual and necessary truth that holding such a judgement *tends* to produce motivation. If this comes to saying that a full understanding of (holding

Granted, perspectival motivational internalism might still hold: we could say that in making the punitive judgement in question the father has not full-bloodedly taken the moral point of view. There is, however, an air of stipulation about this. Granted, too, that this man is perhaps not normal, or at any rate not highly rational, if his moral judgement has *no* motivational force. Still, that he is not highly rational is a weak thesis, and that he is not normal might follow from his violating a strong but merely contingent pattern.

The issue of normality is relevant in another way. Largely because, for our self-addressed moral judgements, we normally do have significantly strong motivation to act accordingly, citing such a judgement normally suffices to explain action of ours that we may be taken to have thought the judgement required of us.[25] This easily creates the impression that the judgement is itself automatically motivational. But that should not be inferred without further premises. Citing a lighted cigarette dropped in the leaves can explain how a fire started, but this does not in the least imply that the explanation does not depend on the additional factor of dryness, which is quite 'external' to the noted cause. Citing the contact of an open wound with poison ivy can explain a rash even if in a few cases such a rash does not occur after that kind of contact or can have another source. If we conclude, from the general success (in the relevant sense of rational acceptability) of explanations of actions by appeal to moral judgements, that such judgements are intrinsically motivational, we may be doing similarly defective reasoning.

The particular way in which I have argued that rational agent motivational internalism is too strong indicates something important both for the general issue of the relation between reason and morality and for understanding motivational internalism. Often our desires, moral emotions, moral experiences, and other non-truth-valued (and in that sense non-cognitive) states have evidential value. They may provide quite good grounds for a judgement, and indeed they are so commonly both the psychological and the normative basis for our moral judgements that it can be easy to think that moral judgements imply them. A common cause of something can look like an effect of it, or even a constituent in it, particularly when the causal relation can and often does run the other way. We do not need to be motivational internalists to see that one source of moral judgement is moral experience, say of revulsion or felt obligation, and that a common source of

a) moral judgement implies seeing its possible influence on motivation, there may be truth in it; but that (and I suspect the other plausible interpretations of the claim) is a quite weak thesis far short of motivational internalism.

[25] Nagel, among others, emphasizes this. See e.g. the quotation cited above from *The Possibility of Altruism*.

motivation to do a certain deed is a judgement—in some cases even one arrived at by intellectual intuition or cool reasoning—that one ought to do that deed.[26] But a close association need not derive from an entailment and may mislead us about which way the causal power runs.

A special feature of the association I am stressing between motivation and moral judgement is its non-causal aspect: the normative support that certain motivational states can provide to moral judgement. The suggested view—that certain motivational states can be evidence for normative judgements concerning their objects—might be called *motivational evidentialism*. The specifically moral version of it, on which such states as wants, attitudes, and emotions are evidence for moral judgements, would be moral motivational evidentialism. This view is interesting in its own right; but particularly since the evidential value of the relevant motivational states is greatest in rational agents, the view helps to explain why rational agent motivational internalism is plausible, even if the latter holds only for ideally rational agents. In rational agents, moral judgement may *derive* from motivational elements; it is then easily seen to be accompanied by them and can mistakenly be taken to be their source.

There are, then, many truths lying in the vicinity of rational agent motivational internalism; but it turns out, I believe, that one may have to choose between giving up even this quite plausible motivational internalism and maintaining it at the price of adopting a quite idealized notion of a rational agent. Much work must be done to show how far the relevant degree of idealization would take us beyond the usual capacities of ordinary moral agents.[27] Whatever that degree, one further conclusion seems warranted here: it seems doubtful that any motivational internalism, whether restricted to rational agents or not, is both defensible in the light of the distinctions and points suggested here and strong enough to provide a good premiss for non-cognitivism. If it is defensible in the light of those points, then it does not force a non-cognitive construal of moral judgement. Moral judgement, cognitively construed, can be allied with motivational factors that account for its apparently having the motivational power that is arguably incompatible with its being true or false and in that sense simply an intellectual attitude. An alliance of moral judgement with non-cognitive powers, rather than a lack of cognitivity in itself, can account for the appearance it sometimes has of intrinsic motivational power.

[26] For valuable discussions of how moral experience may evidence moral judgements see Michael William Tolhurst, 'On the Epistemic Value of Moral Experience', *Southern Journal of Philosophy*, Suppl. 29 (1990), 67–87; and Michael DePaul, *Balance and Refinement: Beyond Coherentism in Moral Inquiry* (London and New York: Routledge, 1993).

[27] It may be that, much of the time, Kant does work with an idealization. If so, I would stress that much of his overall position could be preserved even apart from the rational agent motivational internalism.

5. *Normative Reasons and Motivational Internalism*

Supposing that motivational internalism proper is mistaken, there may still be strong connections we have yet to discern between holding a moral judgement and having reasons for action. For one thing, the judgements-as-reasons view may still be true: holding a moral judgement may imply having a *normative* reason for action. This view is independent of motivational internalism, but the two have been closely associated, perhaps in part because each takes holding a moral judgement to entail having a kind of reason. The judgements-as-reasons view might be rationalized as follows. First, if a (self-addressed) moral judgement is true, the agent would arguably have a sound reason to act accordingly, since the agent holds a *correct judgement* of obligation; second, if the judgement is justified but not true —a *judgement correctly held*, we might say—the agent would also have a genuine though differently grounded normative (and so in a sense objective) reason for such action; and third, if it is neither justified nor true, the agent would presumably still have a kind of subjective reason for such action, one supporting the action from the agent's point of view. (I say 'presumably' because there may be judgements qualifying as moral that are so obviously false or unjustified that one cannot be said, in virtue of holding them, to have a reason for action at all, and in that case the judgements-as-reasons view would need qualification.)[28]

If, as the judgements-as-reasons view has it, moral judgements provide normative reasons for action, one might seek a route from this normative cousin of motivational internalism to a more moderate version of that view. Such an excursion is especially likely to seem promising on the plausible assumption that at least many of our most important normative and motivational reasons for action derive from common sources in 'human nature'. Some theorists attracted to motivational internalism might note that, between holding a moral judgement (or at least a justified one) and having motivation to act accordingly, there is a connection that can survive the rejection of motivational internalism in all the forms I have specified. For surely, it might be argued, one can have a normative reason to do something only if one *can* do it (intentionally); and if one cannot be motivated to do it, one cannot do it (intentionally). Hence, if holding a moral judgement entails having a moral reason to act accordingly, then holding a moral judgement also entails the capacity to act in accordance with it and thereby the capacity to be motivated to do it. Call this second entailment claim *capacity internalism* (*simpliciter*): it takes the capacity for motivation to be internal to holding a moral judgement.

---

[28] We must, however, account for the notion of a bad reason, one that is relevant but utterly lacking in cogency. This favours the liberal notion of a reason I use here.

Despite its modest appearance, capacity internalism of this sort is too strong. One could hold a moral judgement in ignorance of relevant incapacities to be motivated accordingly; these incapacities might be artificially induced (say, by brain manipulation) even if they never naturally occur. Moreover, unless just any moral judgement, however ill-considered, generates a normative reason, even the basis for this internalism is unsound.

Suppose, however, that we consider only moral judgements that are true or at least justified. It is quite plausible to hold that these judgements do entail a capacity to act accordingly and to be motivated to do so, since (for instance) the judgement that I should A would presumably not be justified if I could not A, which I apparently could not do (intentionally) if I could not be motivated to do it. More cautiously, it might be held that such a motivational capacity is entailed by one's holding such a judgement at least where holding it provides a normative reason for action—a view we might call *qualified capacity internalism*.[29]

Qualified capacity internalism is plausible; but it is quite weak. What sorts of things could one not even be capable of being motivated to do? Apart from the possibility that motivation is blocked by artificial manipulation of the brain, we might mention things one believes to be absolutely impossible. But are these candidates for things one could have reason to do? Perhaps they would be candidates if two conditions held: one had good reason to believe they are possible, and they in fact are. In any case, it is desirable to strengthen capacity internalism. In working toward a more plausible version it is natural to include a capacity for the moral judgement's playing a role *in* the motivation it implies one can have, since the point of the view is in part to connect moral judgement with the actions it should lead us to perform. But that also leaves us with a weak thesis; it would require only the capacity to want to act in accord with the moral judgement.[30] If, then, capacity for moral motivation can be derived from the notion of holding a justified moral judgement via such a judgement's implying that the judge has a normative reason, this does not come even close to deriving *actual* motivation from such judgements.

Suppose for the sake of argument that holding a true or justified moral judgement favouring an action is sufficient to give one a (moral) normative

---

[29] This kind of internalism is quite similar to a kind considered by Korsgaard, 'Skepticism about Practical Reason'. I bypass the point that what is entailed by holding the judgement is not necessarily *internal to it*, in which case the view under discussion is only a generic, as opposed to a constitutive, motivational internalism, since it is simply a thesis about what is implied by a person's holding a moral judgement. For discussion of a thesis related to capacity internalism see Cohon, 'Internalism about Reasons for Action'.

[30] This requirement is even weaker than it may look, for the reference is not to a desire whose *content* is: to act in accord with *J* (where *J* is the relevant judgement); the reference is to any of a range of action desires whose contents are appropriate to that judgement.

reason for that action. Is a moral judgement or something like it, such as a moral belief favouring the action in question, also *necessary* for one's having such a normative reason? It may seem so, since it may seem that the only way we can 'have' moral reasons for action is through some relevant consideration's entering our cognitive system, and this may be taken to require our holding an appropriate judgement or belief (perhaps on the assumption that moral reasons arise from practical reasoning whose concluding element is or implies such a judgement or belief). Call this cognitive representation requirement the *judgemental theory of moral reasons*. It is important in part because, if even generic motivational internalism is true, this view implies that having a (moral) normative reason for action entails motivation to act accordingly. That entailment, in turn, specifies an even stronger respect in which morality is practical than does motivational internalism itself: the mere having of a moral reason to do something would imply some degree of motivation to do it, since the only way to have it would require holding a moral judgement, and holding such a judgement is motivating.

The judgemental theory of moral reasons is surely too strong. For it plainly makes sense to ask whether an agent has a reason to do something even where the agent has made no judgement, and formed no belief, favouring it.[31] A colleague who knows me and my class might say that I have a good reason not to change the grade, even before I myself consider the matter and arrive at a moral judgement that explicitly states this reason not to do so. There are various ways to 'have' reasons—in moral as in other matters. The notion resists analysis, but part of the idea is this: where there are considerations, of a kind accessible to one by reflection, that favour an action sufficiently to count as reasons for it, one may be said to have those reasons.[32] The more readily accessible they are, for instance in terms of how much one would need to reflect to form the relevant beliefs—those expressing the reasons—the less implicitly the reasons are had.

This way of speaking may strike some philosophers as question-beggingly objectivist; for the suggestion is that there can *be* reasons for action which no one in any ordinary sense has, and that indeed one can discover reasons which, despite their relevance to one's conduct, one did not previously have. There can, for example, be reasons not to allow donors to a university to dictate the use of their gifts, whether we are aware of these reasons or not; and as this suggests, whether or not we have any motivation to act accordingly. Perhaps there cannot be reasons for any action of ours if we

---

[31] This claim is much less plausible if one assimilates dispositions to believe, e.g. tendencies to form beliefs upon reflecting on relevant data, to actual, dispositional beliefs. A case for rejecting the assimilation is given in my 'Dispositional Beliefs and Dispositions to Believe', *Noûs*, 28 (1994), 419–34.

[32] For an indication of the kinds and degrees of having see my 'Structural Justification', *Journal of Philosophical Research*, 16 (1991), 473–92, repr. in my *The Structure of Justification* (Cambridge and New York: Cambridge Univ. Press, 1993), 274–96.

could not become aware of them, but that may be true not because there are no objective reasons at all, but because any such reasons would not be reasons *for us* to do something unless we could become aware of them. These questions about the conditions for having reasons to act bring us to the second main kind of internalism to be considered in this essay: reasons internalism.

6. Reasons Internalism and Moral Motivation

There is perhaps less diversity concerning what constitutes reasons internalism than regarding what constitutes motivational internalism, but again I think the wisest course is to indicate what seems central and proceed to a working characterization. The basic thesis, in broad terms, is that a (normative) reason for action must be grounded in some internal conative or at least non-cognitive motivational state of the agent, for instance a desire, as opposed to deriving from an external requirement such as a categorical imperative or the intrinsic value of pleasure in the world.

Two philosophical motivations for reasons internalism are, first, a Humean conviction that moral and other normative considerations yielding reasons for action do not 'come from reason' (in a sense implying that these considerations are not true or false) and, second, a conviction that since morality is practical and can be so only if it supplies reasons for action that have the motivating power of conative states, it does supply such reasons. Commonly it is normative reasons, or at least subjective justificatory reasons —roughly the kind the agent would accept as justificatory—that are the primary concern of the view. Thus, if holding a moral judgement provides a normative reason for action, it provides an internal normative reason, just as, if holding such a judgement is intrinsically motivating, it provides an internal (motivational) reason for action.

There is a third philosophical motivation for reasons internalism, this time deriving from a positive Humean position. Reasons internalism seems most commonly to be inspired largely by the instrumentalist view of reasons for action, historically represented most powerfully by Hume and attractive even to non-Humeans for its apparent naturalism.[33] On this instrumentalist view (practical) reason functions to serve desire: it does not independently motivate desire, and the rationality of an action—roughly,

---

[33] Hume did not, however, use the terms employed here. For discussion of Hume on this question, with attention both to the *Treatise* and to selected secondary literature, see Elizabeth Radcliffe, 'How Does the Humean Sense of Duty Motivate', *Journal of the History of Philosophy*, 34 (1996), 47–70 and 'Hume on Passion, Pleasure, and the Reasonableness of Ends', *Southwest Philosophy Review*, 10 (1994), 1–11.

its being adequately supported by one or more appropriate kinds of reasons—is determined by how well it contributes to satisfying the agent's non-instrumental ('basic') desires—above all, desires for things as ends in themselves; and these desires are held not to admit of (substantive) appraisal as rational or irrational.[34] All reasons for action, then, are rooted in desire, broadly conceived.

It might be held that this version of Humean instrumentalism entails that there *is* no practical reason. This is a plausible interpretation because reason is neither normatively nor motivationally practical: it grounds neither judgements of what we should do nor motivation to do anything. Reason still has, however, a major directive role, above all in pointing the way to desire satisfaction. It may thus be considered *instrumentally practical*. It provides our map of the world; without that map no amount of desire would lead us to satisfaction, except by good fortune.[35] We may assume for the sake of argument that this role is sufficient to make such instrumentalism a candidate to account for (normative) reasons for action.

Where instrumentalism is the chief source of reasons internalism, we get a narrower reasons internalism than the version rooting normative reasons for action only in non-cognitive states: reasons for action must be grounded not only internally, as they might be in a sense of moral obligation, but in non-instrumental desire. Call this view *conative reasons internalism*. It allows a causal role for judgements as producers of desires and for desires or other conative states as producers of judgement; but judgements themselves, at least if construed as cognitive attitudes, do not ground reasons for action. One would not have a reason in virtue of holding a judgement, but at best in virtue of something produced by, or producing, that judgement, such as a desire to help a friend or pleasure at the thought of doing this.

Although reasons internalism is independent of motivational internalism, it helps us both to understand the appeal of that view and to see the implications of instrumentalist conceptions of normative reasons for action. I think it likely that one reason why motivational internalism is attractive to

---

[34] This is a rough characterization, in which 'substantive' is meant to allow instrumentalists to construe as irrational, desires for impossible states of affairs, especially those whose occurrence obviously entails a contradiction. Detailed treatments of the problem are given in my *Practical Reasoning*, esp. ch. 3, and 'Autonomy, Reason, and Desire', both cited above.

[35] This partial defence of instrumentalism is not meant to answer the kind of objection to it that Korsgaard's paper in this volume raises. More generally, it is arguable that if there are no non-instrumental reasons for action then instrumental reasons cannot render action rational, in part because it would seem that the reason for action provided by the prospect of bringing about only ends that are subservient to further ends is like the guarantee of a promised good expressed by an infinite series of conditional promises: to give one x if A gives one y, which A promises to give one provided B gives one z, which B promises to give one provided C . . . etc. An account of this issue is given in my 'Intrinsic Value and the Dignity of Persons', ch. 11 in *Moral Knowledge and Ethical Character* (Oxford and New York: Oxford Univ. Press, 1997).

some philosophers is that they hold an instrumentalist version of reasons internalism and want to accommodate our sense that (holding) moral judgement is full-bloodedly practical in providing both motivational and normative reason for action. If moral judgements do not motivate, at least in the broad sense of entailing that one has some want (suitably connected with the content of the judgement), then they obviously do not provide motivational reasons, and, by instrumentalist lights, they do not provide normative reasons either, since neither in themselves nor by what they entail do they appropriately serve desire (which implies wanting); hence, they are not practical in either of the main senses, the normative and the motivational. But notice two interconnected points that are easily overlooked or insufficiently emphasized. One concerns normative reasons, the other motivational reasons; and both indicate difficulties in the initially attractive project of combining an instrumentalist view of practical reason with motivational internalism, especially where the latter is conjoined with the usual and plausible view that moral judgements (at least when justified) provide normative reasons for action. Here are two major and closely related difficulties.

First, if, as motivational internalism proper implies, moral judgements by themselves provide normative reasons for action—independently of embodying or at least serving the agent's non-instrumental desires, for instance by indicating means to what one wants—then instrumentalism about practical rationality must be abandoned. For those judgements would provide normative reasons for action that are not necessarily rooted in the agent's desires (or in anything 'passional'). Judging that I ought to keep a promise, for example, may derive from beliefs about moral standards and may indicate nothing about how my doing so serves my basic desires. Instrumentalists might reply that their view can allow moral judgements to *cause* intrinsic desires to act accordingly, and they may still claim that only intrinsic desires ultimately are, or ground, reasons for action. Granted. Still, this way of saving motivational internalism—moving to a (contingent) consequential version—has a price: it greatly attenuates the sense in which moral judgements are in themselves practical. They imply motivation only conditionally, even if the relevant conditions are commonly satisfied in normal people. Thus, if it is a Humean instrumentalism about the status of (normative) reasons for action that leads one to a commitment to motivational internalism, it may in the end be at best difficult to reconcile the two positions.[36]

---

[36] Did Hume himself have a problem? He does say that morals influence action and reason by itself does not, but he does not seem committed to saying that moral judgements provide even motivational reasons for action independently of non-instrumental desires.

Second, supposing that instrumentalism is taken to hold that our basic desires are the ground not only of normative reasons but also of motivational reasons (and so of practical reasons in general), motivational internalism must be abandoned, at least given two assumptions: that it implies, as it does in the constitutive version, that holding a moral judgement provides in itself a motivating reason for action, and that moral judgement is cognitively construed, as it must be on the natural (if resistible) assumption that it is true or false. For a moral judgement, cognitively construed, does not by itself entail possession of any relevant desire, as opposed to some other kind of motivation. These points may help to explain why, for instrumentalists committed to motivational internalism, non-cognitivism is so attractive.

More generally, a common and important view—motivational internalism proper—which takes motivation to be internal to moral judgements as such, turns out to be (in its cognitive versions) incompatible with instrumentalism, and instrumentalists committed to motivational internalism must retreat to its weaker, consequential version, which is both consistent with reasons externalism—in part because lack of motivation to act on a moral judgement is perfectly consistent with having a normative reason to act on it—and too weak to be a good premiss for non-cognitivism. One response would be to argue that non-cognitivism can be shown independently of motivational internalism and then to adopt a non-cognitivist instrumentalism. But demonstrating that is no easy task; and if establishing non-cognitivism can be shown to rely on arguments independent of motivational internalism, that would be a significant step.

7. Reasons Externalism and Moral Motivation

By contrast with instrumentalists in the theory of practical reason, Kantians and other objectivists about practical reason, should not be construed as reasons internalists, and Kant, on one plausible reading, cannot be one. Much depends on what is required for a reason to count as internally grounded. If reasons depend on desires or on any non-cognitive elements that motivate action independently of practical judgement, then Kantians cannot be construed as reasons internalists.

There is, however, at least one kind of internalism—an epistemic version —that is consistent with objectivism about ethics and practical reason. It must be distinguished from other kinds of reasons internalism both for clarity about the grounds and accessibility of reasons for action and lest its plausibility be mistakenly taken to support those other views. This internalist position might be called *accessibility reasons internalism*: it says simply that a reason for action, normative or motivational, must be such that the agent can, in a suitable psychological sense, *have* it, for instance be appropriately aware of it. Thus, if I can see, by reflection, that a deed would advance my ideals, I have a reason to do it, whereas an esoteric argument for doing it that I cannot understand is not accessible to me and does not provide a reason for my doing it. Advancing my ideals, moreover, need not be just a matter of desire satisfaction. Hence this epistemic internalist requirement does not entail reasons internalism. Internalism about theoretical reason is compatible with the objectivity of reasons affirmed by externalism about practical reason.

In contrast with Kantians, a reasons internalist attracted to the epistemic internality requirement might, in the theory of practical reason, hold a stronger view than such a theorist typically affirms, one we might call *actual state reasons internalism*. It says that a reason for action must be or reside in an actual non-cognitive motivational state of the agent, such as a desire, and in that sense be a reason one *has*. Neither reasons internalist view rules out *non-occurrent* desires as sources of reasons, but the actual state view does exclude hypothetical desires and other hypothetical attitudes.[37] *Pure instrumentalist reasons internalism*, would be a special case of the actual state variety; for such an instrumentalism, hypothetical desires do not count as sources of reasons for action, and only non-instrumental actual desires count as reason-providing internal states. And whereas the conative version merely restricts the sources to conative states, actual or hypothetical, the pure instrumentalist version requires both a desire as the relevant kind of conative state and its actuality. Roughly, the idea is that our current reasons for action reside wholly in our current desires; these are taken to express our motivational nature conceived as the source of those reasons.[38]

It is essential to see that accessibility internalism—which represents an important and plausible range of positions in moral epistemology—lends no support to reasons internalism of any kind. It requires only that reasons for action be internally accessible, not that they must be expressed in an actual state of the agent such as a desire or belief, much less that their source be desire or only some non-cognitive state. Hence, there can be what are commonly considered *external*, objective reasons for action: such considerations as the unfairness of a certain assessment, the disrespectfulness of a certain editorial, and the beneficence of a certain policy. These can, at a given time, be reasons why we *should* do something, and can become reasons why we in fact *do* it, even if, at that time, we have no desires, and

---

[37] The relevant distinction between a non-occurrent desire and a disposition to form one (which some might call a kind of hypothetical desire) is not easy to draw; a detailed account of it is given in my 'Dispositional Beliefs and Dispositions to Believe'.

[38] These actual desires might, but need not, include a second-order desire to act on desires one now lacks but would form on certain kinds of reflection; if they do not, then it might be argued that taking hypothetical desires to supply reasons is like allowing a hypothetical nature one might or would have to dictate to the nature one does have.

hold no judgements, that favour the action. We need only be such that by suitable reflection, say by thinking, in the light of moral standards we accept or would accept on reflection, about the factual propositions we believe, we would hold the appropriate judgement and could have the motivation appropriate to it.[39]

Judgement and motivation emerge as important, then, but not as preconditions for the existence of reasons for action: instead, they are possibilities whose realization may constitute a necessary condition for reasons' playing a practical role. I might, for instance, have to judge that raising the grade would be unfair before I actually do anything in response to the request for reconsideration. This could be either because the judgement produces or enhances motivation I already have or because the judgement triggers action by behaviourally focusing my already sufficiently strong moral desires regarding my grading.

At this point an instrumentalist might maintain that the reasons externalist has simply replaced actual desire with hypothetical desire as the ground of so-called external reasons for action. The objection might be that the accessibility requirement on reasons is really intended to guarantee—or is in any case plausible only so far as it is seen as guaranteeing—that if we have a (normative) reason for action, then we would form a desire appropriate to ground that reason. Rational action, then, is still subservient to desire, but the desire may be hypothetical. There are at least two difficulties with this line of reply.

One difficulty is that it is only moral judgement that the relevant reasons externalism (the kind compatible with accessibility internalism) says we *would* hold under appropriate conditions of information and reflection; by contrast, the relevant desires are, for such externalism, only such that we *could* have them—a very weak requirement, as already explained. The requirement is certainly too weak to guarantee a conative basis for holding the relevant moral judgement (the kind of basis one must have, by pure instrumentalist lights, in order for the judgement to express a reason for action). It could be, for instance, that on reflection I would judge that I ought to prepare a resit exam, yet owing to how unpleasant doing it would seem to me to be, I would lack the desires necessary to get me to do it and would suffer weakness of will if brought to the test. Apart from an implausible motivational internalism so strong as to preclude weakness of will in such cases, this possibility cannot be ruled out.

Second, suppose the accessibility requirement, as embedded in a reasons externalism, did imply that we would have desires that motivate actions

---

[39] This is not an ordinary empirical 'could'; in any case, empirically one could be brain-manipulated to make some of the desires in fact impossible.

appropriate to our moral judgements. It would not follow that these hypothetical desires are the *ground* of the normative reasons in question. *Both*
those reasons and the desires might be grounded in the judgements or in
some other potentially rational source, as surely a plausible reasons externalism would require. Perhaps I would want to keep my promise because I
would judge that I must keep it, as opposed to judging I must because
of an antecedent empathic desire. Moreover, the normative grounds of my
judgement could be external. Again, accessibility reasons internalism can be
seen to be compatible with reasons externalism.

I conclude here that the most plausible reasons internalism is the
(epistemic) accessibility kind compatible with what is commonly called
reasons externalism, and that the most plausible versions of this epistemic
variety of reasons internalism are incompatible with the instrumentalist
conception of reasons for action. It appears that there can *be* reasons for us
to act, whether they reside in judgements or desires of ours or not, and that
we can *have* reasons for action residing in moral judgements we hold,
whether those judgements motivate us or not. These plausible theses are
among the qualified forms of reasons externalism and motivational
externalism that seem to be true.

8. Conclusion

Given the points that have emerged in this essay, we may draw a number
of broad conclusions about the four relationships that have been our central
concern: those between intellect and will, reason and morality, judgement
and motivation, and normative and motivational reasons. Let us start with
the status of normative reasons, which is probably the most important
preoccupation of the theory of practical reason.

If the qualified externalist—and internalist—positions I have proposed
as plausible views are true, then the instrumentalist conception of (normative) reasons for action is mistaken. This is a powerful conception which
I cannot directly criticize here.[40] It is important to see, however, that the
most significant opposition in the theory of practical reason is probably not
between motivational internalists and motivational externalists but between
instrumentalists, who are a kind of reasons internalist, and objectivists, who
are a kind of reasons externalist. Important as the motivational issue is,
those who, like Kantians and Rossian intuitionists, disagree about what
motivation, if any, is intrinsic to moral judgement can still agree that there

---

[40] For direct criticism see Thomas Nagel's *The View from Nowhere* (Oxford and New York: Oxford
Univ. Press, 1986). Some of my critical discussion is in 'Autonomy, Reason, and Desire', cited above,
and 'The Architecture of Reason', in *The Structure of Justification*, cited above.

are external reasons for action, and that accordingly reason *should* govern desire, whether, causally speaking, it does or not.

Motivational internalists and motivational externalists can also largely agree on what, overall, constitutes a rational person, for instance on what sort of motivation a rational person who holds certain moral judgements should have. They will differ on the sources of that motivation. Instrumentalists, by contrast, conceive both (normative) reasons for action and the rational agent quite differently from not only all reasons externalists, but also Kantian and many other motivational internalists. Even apart from a direct assessment of instrumentalism, we should ask how the instrumentalist can account for moral reasons.

Above all, for instrumentalism, moral reasons are at the mercy of what one's non-instrumental desires happen to be. If I have no non-instrumental desires to meet moral standards, and, perhaps because there is, in Hume's phrase, too little of the dove kneaded into my frame, I have no such desires to whose realization I do or would believe my meeting those standards contributes, then I have no reasons to be moral—and this is so even if I happen to make moral judgements. If motivational internalism (proper) were true, I *could* not make such judgements without thereby having some motivation. But if, for reasons suggested above, it is mistaken, then instrumentalists cannot appeal to moral judgement as automatically motivational and in that sense reason-giving, nor can non-cognitivists appeal to such a motivational constituent in moral judgement as a premiss undermining its cognitivity.

This is an important point. In addition to undermining an initially plausible and rather elegant Humean argument for non-cognitivism, it deprives instrumentalism of one of its major resources for accounting for moral reasons: all normal adults make moral judgements; these in turn normally imply motivation—typically non-instrumental motivation capable of grounding reasons for action; hence, morality is, if only because of the desires it arouses in us, a source of reasons for action. Hume would not have put it like this, because he wanted to dissociate 'morals' from reason; but that was above all to prevent moral judgement from being grounded *in reason*, which cannot by itself motivate and so cannot produce moral judgement conceived as motivating. He need not have denied (if he did) that holding moral judgements may, in a causal sense, provide one with reasons for action in the only sense in which, for Humeans, one can have such reasons: in virtue of one's having the appropriate non-instrumental desires, for moral judgements can certainly cause such desires.[41] To be sure, this makes the moral

---

[41] For a textually detailed account of Humean practical rationality and of how Hume provides for the possibility of moral judgements figuring in practical reasoning, see Elizabeth Radcliffe, 'Disentangling Hume's Instrumentalism from Kant's Hypothetical Imperative', *Canadian Journal of Philosophy* (forthcoming).

judgements we hold only causes of our having reasons and in themselves not expressions of actual reasons; but at least moral judgements have a practical role. They are not an autonomous voice of practical reason, but they can ultimately produce the same practical effects.

If this assessment of the relation between instrumentalism and motivational internalism is sound, then for pure instrumentalism, the only motivational or moral reasons there are either are constituted by or depend on desires with appropriate content. If I do not have these desires, I not only *have* no moral reasons, there also *are* none affecting me. It might be, then, that there is no moral reason why I should not raise a grade even if doing this is unfair. That seems paradoxical. How could its being unfair not provide a moral reason to abstain? The question to ask here is what there is for 'unfair' to mean that, for instrumentalism, allows for the existence of such a reason. The word can have a conventional meaning, in terms of how society normally views such matters. But morality is not merely convention. Morality can have a moral grip on others through their desires; but whether it does is a contingent matter, and the main point here is in any case to account not for others' having reason to prevent my being unfair, but for my self-addressed judgement of unfairness to provide me with a reason for action. Indeed, on some views it is a hallmark of moral reasons for action that they can be normative reasons to act *against* one's non-instrumental desires and need not themselves be rooted in desires.

These and similar considerations should lead one to wonder whether instrumentalism can adequately account for what appears to be the autonomy —or at least the autonomy relative to *actual* desire—of moral reasons. I leave open that moral reasons may depend on non-moral ones, as hedonists and others have maintained. This dependence would still leave *practical* reasons autonomous from actual non-instrumental *desires*. I have not tried to show that instrumentalism cannot in some way deal with this autonomy problem. Elements in Hume and his successors are certainly suggestive.[42] But the job will be more difficult without the aid of motivational internalism and in the light of some of the distinctions I have stressed.

If we give up motivational internalism in any of its forms strong enough to undermine the existence of objective, external reasons for action, we must grant that reason, as exercised in moral judgement, need not always

---

[42] One notable approach is taken by Richard Fumerton in *Reason and Morality* (Ithaca, NY: Cornell Univ. Press, 1990). There are also powerful Humean strains in Bernard Williams's work, e.g. in his *Ethics and the Limits of Philosophy* (Cambridge, Mass.: Harvard Univ. Press, 1985). Cf. Donald C. Hubin, 'Hypothetical Motivation', *Noûs*, 30 (1966), 31–54 and 'Irrational Desires', *Philosophical Studies*, 62 (1991), 23–44. John Rawls, in *A Theory of Justice* (Cambridge, Mass.: Harvard Univ. Press, 1971) does not endorse instrumentalism in general but does try to derive his principles of justice from an instrumentalist conception of rationality, apart from the special assumption that rational persons do not suffer from envy. The relevant references and some discussion of his approach are given in my 'Autonomy, Reason, and Desire', cited above. For a detailed examination of autonomy and the role of reasons therein see Alfred R. Mele, *Autonomous Agents* (Oxford and New York: Oxford Univ. Press, 1995).

be *motivationally practical*, since these judgements do not entail motivational reasons. This concession in turn implies that reason—simply as reflected in moral judgement—has limited sovereignty over the will. But it does not entail that reason, as exercised in moral judgement, is not always *normatively practical*, thereby providing normative reasons: this is precisely what moral judgement must be if, even apart from entailing motivational reasons for action, it can provide normative reasons for action. Nor need we give up motivational internalism in its perspectival form: the idea that for those really judging *from the moral point of view*, holding a moral judgement implies motivation to act accordingly. More generally, we might retain *some* version of rational agent motivational internalism, perhaps the idea that, in those having a *sufficiently* good integration between intellect and will, holding a moral judgement implies motivation to act accordingly. We might even plausibly hold that in these restricted—but surely not uncommon —cases the motivation is adequate to permit explaining actions based on the judgement as performed in the service of that judgement.

It would be good if the sheer grasp of moral truth produced an appropriately strong inclination to act accordingly. We could educate the intellect and thereby properly direct the will. But although desire is commonly influenced by moral and other practical judgements—and must be substantially so influenced in truly rational persons—the influence is far from automatic. A benefit of this position is that it frees us from commitment to the idea that weak or perverse will can automatically block the perception of truths relevant to one's conduct. Reason can light our way even if the will does not or even cannot follow.

A further implication, then, of rejecting the versions of motivational internalism I have criticized is that if we expect people to be moral, we must educate their desires, emotions, and sensibilities, not just their intellects. Once we do, however—and especially if we build upon the empathy in human nature—then desires, emotions, and experiences, like judgements, can provide normative reasons for action as well as motivation to perform them. To speak of genuine normative reasons for action is in one way to give a biased account of practical reason, since it tends to presuppose that there are some things, including moral ends, that it is reasonable to want for their own sake. That, in turn, implies that there are external reasons, a thesis that it is very difficult to show in the theory of practical reason. I believe, however, that its truth may well be a presupposition of morality.[43]

[43] This paper benefited much from discussion and comments at the St Andrews Conference on Ethics and Practical Reason in 1995. For helpful written comments on earlier versions I thank John Deigh, Hugh McCann, Alfred Mele, Joseph Mendola, Elizabeth Radcliffe, Sophia Reibetanz, John Robertson, Michael Stocker, Mark Timmons, Mark van Roojen, Nick Zangwill, an anonymous reader, and especially, Garrett Cullity and Berys Gaut. Though drafted for the conference, this paper was first published in my *Moral Knowledge and Ethical Character* (Oxford and New York: Oxford Univ. Press, 1997), and I thank the Press for permission to reprint it.

6

The Structure of Practical Reason

BERYS GAUT

1. Two Models of Practical Reason

The structure of practical reason needs to be specified in at least two fundamental respects. On the one hand, we need an account of the relation between reason and motivation. This is the *motivational aspect* of reason. Practical reasons, reasons to act, must be capable of motivating an agent, for reasons guide action, and therefore an agent must be capable of acting on them under suitable conditions. These conditions are specifiable in terms of rationality: plausibly it is analytic that reasons motivate an agent in so far as she is rational and aware of the reasons. For this truism about rational motivation to yield a more substantive truth requires a specification of the powers by virtue of which an agent is rational and is appropriately motivated. A further structural aspect of practical reason that needs to be specified is the relation of practical reason to the good. This is the *evaluative aspect* of practical reason. Again, there is a plausibly analytic truth here: an agent in so far as she is rational accepts that she has a reason to perform some action available to her only if she represents that action as good.[1] But again, to yield a more substantive truth we need to be told more about the relation between reason and value. It is this second, evaluative aspect of practical reason that will be addressed here. And as we shall see, the account given of the relation between reason and value also conditions one's account of the motivational aspect of reason.

In describing the relation between practical reason and the good, perhaps the most natural view is what we can call the *recognitional* model of practical reason. This model holds that the goodness of actions and of

---

[1] The truism needs to be understood so that 'good' covers both agent-relative (good for me) and agent-neutral (good *simpliciter*) senses.

It may be objected that the truism is incompatible with the existence of deliberate wrongdoers, i.e. agents who intentionally perform an act because they believe it is morally wicked. But this possibility can be handled in various ways, consistent with maintaining the truism, depending on how the situation is further specified and on one's theory of rationality. Thus, these agents might be held simply to be irrational; or it might be held that they believe it is good (all things considered) to be morally wicked; or that they believe the action is good for them, but not good *simpliciter*.

states of affairs in general is constituted independently of those actions and states of affairs being the objects of rational choice. The role of practical reason is then to recognize the obtaining of goodness, and to bring it about that the agent performs good actions and brings about good states of affairs. What makes it rational to do such things is that they are good. There are many examples of recognitional views: a simple hedonic model of practical reason would hold that a good action is one which produces a large amount of pleasure; it could then hold that the role of practical reason is to recognize which actions produce pleasure, and to bring it about that the agent performs such actions. A more complex account is due to G. E. Moore, who in *Principia Ethica* holds that certain organic unities, such as beauty and its contemplation, have intrinsic worth, and that the rational agent acts to bring into existence as many of these organic unities as she can.[2] Yet another version is due to Aristotle. For him *phronēsis*, practical wisdom, is 'a state grasping the truth, involving reason, concerned with action about what is good or bad for a human being' (*EN* 6. 5, 1140b4–6).[3] Practical wisdom for Aristotle is a rational state, which grasps what is good or bad for humans, and which motivates the *phronimos* accordingly (the possessor of practical wisdom cannot be akratic). What is good is defined with reference to the human function, so that the good is constituted independently of being the object of rational choice (though of course Aristotle also makes the *substantive* claim that the exercise of reason, including practical reason, is the fundamental human good).

The recognitional account of practical reason has not gone unopposed. In particular this account appears to make it mysterious how reason can motivate: for if the good is specified independently of what we have reason to choose, then it seems possible for an agent to recognize something as good, yet be indifferent to it. But that surely severs the tie between reason and motivation that we saw constitutes an essential aspect of practical reason. The other major model of the relation advertises itself as being capable of securing this motivational connection. The *value-conferral* or *constructivist* model of practical reason holds that the good simply is constituted as the object of rational choice — what *makes* something good is that it is the object of rational choice.[4] The notion of the good, then, is conceptually dependent on that of rational choice. This model of practical reason finds its greatest exponent in Kant. In the *Critique of Practical Reason*, he writes of what he describes as the 'paradox' of his method: 'The paradox is

---

[2] G. E. Moore, *Principia Ethica* (Cambridge: Univ. Press, 1903), esp. chs. 1 and 5.

[3] Aristotle, *Nicomachean Ethics*, trans. Terence Irwin (Indianapolis: Hackett, 1985).

[4] Note that the rational agent should be understood in specifications of the constructivist account as also having full information relevant to the making of her choice. (Full information does not include of course information about any independently constituted evaluative facts, since there are no such facts on the constructivist view.)

that the concept of good and evil is not defined prior to the moral law, to which, it would seem, the former would have to serve as foundation; rather the concept of good and evil must be defined after and by means of the law' (*KpV* 62–3).[5] Since for Kant the moral law is the deliverance of pure practical reason, this passage entails that the notion of good and evil can only be defined by means of practical reason, and hence that they are not specifiable independently of it. Kant was well aware how revolutionary his reconstrual of the relation between practical reason and value was, and its importance has been stressed by several contemporary Kantians. John Rawls has noted how Kant's moral theory begins from a description of a rational choice situation, specifies principles of the right as those which would be chosen in such a situation, and then in turn specifies the conception of the good as that which would be chosen in the rational choice situation, given the constraints imposed by the previously chosen principles of the right.[6] It is this procedure that Rawls terms *constructivism*. Christine Korsgaard calls the Kantian account the view that practical reason *confers* value on the world, or as she also puts it, that practical reason is the source of value. The good will, that is, the will completely determined by pure practical reason is, she writes, 'the source and condition of all the goodness in the world; goodness, as it were, flows into the world from the good will, and there would be none without it'.[7]

The constructivist model of the relation between reason and value imposes a constraint on the way we specify reason. To hold that the good simply is the object of rational choice, we must in the last analysis specify what it is to make such a choice independently of saying that it is a choice of actions because they are good, or else the conferral account would collapse back into the recognitional view. Hence this account of practical reason must specify practical reason in formal terms, that is, without recourse to ineliminable reference to evaluative content. And this, of course, is what Kant does: the notion of reason to which he appeals is characterized in terms of universalizability, autonomy, unconditionality, and sufficiency, and not in terms of being the sort of capacity that reveals what it is good

---

[5] The following abbreviations are used throughout: *KpV* for *Critique of Practical Reason*, trans. Lewis White Beck (New York: Macmillan, 1956); *G* for *Grounding for the Metaphysics of Morals*, trans. James W. Ellington, 3rd edn. (Indianapolis: Hackett, 1993); and *KU* for *Critique of Judgment*, trans. Werner S. Pluhar (Indianapolis: Hackett, 1987). Prussian Academy Edition page numbers of the appropriate volume are used throughout.

[6] John Rawls, 'Themes in Kant's Moral Philosophy', in Eckart Förster (ed.), *Kant's Transcendental Deductions* (Stanford: Univ. Press, 1989), esp. sect. III. See my 'Rawls and the Claims of Liberal Legitimacy', *Philosophical Papers*, 24 (1995), 1–22, for a critique of Rawls's attempt to support political liberalism by appeal to a notion of constructivism that is less metaphysically laden than Kant's.

[7] Christine Korsgaard, 'Two Distinctions in Goodness', *Philosophical Review*, 92 (1983), 169–95, at 181. The goodness to which she refers is 'the kind of goodness that marks a thing out as worthy of choice', p. 169.

to do. (As a formal account, the conferral model of practical reason in turn requires us to hold that reasons require the presence of principles. The recognitional account, on the other hand, need not hold that practical reason is a matter of a grasp of principles, for the good may be sufficiently complex and variegated in its distribution that only a sensitivity to particular features of a context allows one to grasp its presence. And this is the view of Aristotle, who holds that the *phronimos* has a sensibility conditioned by the virtues, which are exhibited in his knowledge of how to do the right things in the right way for the right reasons, and which require a grasp of particulars (cf. *EN* 2. 9, 1110a23–4). Thus constructivist models of practical reason have implications for the role of principles in practical reason, implications which recognitional models do not possess.)

With the rise of Kantian theories in moral and political philosophy over the last fifteen years or so, and the increasing attention that Kantian theories of practical reason have begun to attract, the issue of the correctness of Kant's constructivist model of practical reason has become of considerable importance. What I argue here is that two of his central arguments for constructivism fail, and that the constructivist account he gives is fundamentally flawed. In its place, I provide a brief sketch of a recognitional account of practical reason that is Aristotelian in spirit, though not always in letter, and show how this account can meet the kind of criticisms that are often levelled against recognitional theories. If the argument advanced here is correct, Kant's theory of practical reason and his moral and political philosophy in so far as it is derived from this theory should be rejected. There are of course other possible constructivist views besides Kantian ones. Views are constructivist just in case they hold that what makes something good is that it is the object of rational choice. But constructivists differ in how they further specify the norms of rationality. Kantianism holds a distinctive view of rationality which grounds its moral rationalism, that is, its claim that moral requirements are requirements of reason.[8] But other constructivists may adopt a different conception of rationality: for instance it is open to neo-Humeans (though not to Hume, given his scepticism about practical reason) to be constructivists, while denying the particular Kantian connection between rationality and morality. The argument in the present essay is directed specifically against Kant's version of constructivism both because of its greater current influence and because of the sophistication, power, and detailed elaboration of his version. However, though certain of the points advanced here (particularly some of those

---

[8] See the Introduction to this volume, especially sects. 1 and 4, for a discussion of Kant's view that reason is subject to a requirement of legislative universalism and how neo-Humeans and others embrace only a requirement of reasons universalism. Kant's moral rationalism is saliently displayed in his views about the good will, discussed in the next section.

concerning the good will) will challenge only the Kantian version, some objections will provide difficulties for any form of constructivism.

2. The Good Will

The *Grounding for the Metaphysics of Morals* famously begins with the claim 'There is no possibility of thinking of anything at all in the world, or even out of it, which can be regarded as good without qualification, except a *good will*' (G 393). This may seem far removed from an account of the relation between practical reason and the good, but it is in fact closely related to it. Kant will later argue that the good will is a will that is determined by pure reason. The will displays itself in acts of choice: a good willing involves the purely rational choice of some action. In saying that such a will is good without qualification, Kant means that it has 'intrinsic unconditional worth' (G 394), that is, its goodness is not dependent on some condition being fulfilled, and hence this will is good in all possible circumstances (and conversely anything that is good in all possible circumstances is unconditionally good, since it does not require any further condition to be fulfilled in order for it to be good). Now, holding that the only thing that is unconditionally good is the good will does not entail that the good will is the condition of all conditional goods. But Kant believes this stronger claim too, for he believes in the supremacy of moral values, holding that actions and all personal qualities have value only if the will that possesses them is good. The examples he gives, as we shall see shortly, illustrate the stronger claim; his key assertion here is that 'a good will seems to constitute the indispensable condition of being even worthy of happiness' (G 393), for happiness for Kant is the sum of inclinations, which include all desires other than morally grounded ones. Thus, putting these claims together, the condition for an agent's actions and qualities being good is that she makes purely rational choices: and hence the goodness of her actions is conditional on their being purely rationally chosen.

Thus Kant's views about the good will entail constructivism about practical reason. Conversely, constructivism holds that any object is valuable only if rationally chosen, so that there is at most one unconditional value that is the condition of all other values: namely, rational choice.[9] So, given Kant's identification of purely rational choice with the good will, his constructivism entails his claims about the good will.

Is Kant's claim that the good will is the only thing that is unconditionally good correct? He asserts it at the beginning of section I of the *Grounding*,

---

[9] I say 'at most one', since it is consistent with constructivism to hold that rational choice is not itself a value, though its exercise is the condition of its objects' possessing value (see Sect. 3).

which is entitled 'Transition from the Ordinary Rational Knowledge of Morality to the Philosophical'. So Kant intends the claim to be one that is endorsed by ordinary rational knowledge—what we might term reflective common sense. And indeed it is by appeal to our intuitions that he supports it. Talents such as intelligence and judgement, and features of temperament such as courage, perseverance, and the capacity for calm deliberation, can become 'extremely bad and harmful' if the will is not good. Gifts of fortune such as wealth, health, and happiness 'make for pride and often hereby even arrogance' without a good will, and 'The sight of a being who is not graced by any touch of a pure and good will but who yet enjoys an uninterrupted prosperity can never delight a rational and impartial spectator' (*G* 393). Elsewhere he discusses pain, which might seem unconditionally bad. But he argues it is not: 'Whoever submits to a surgical operation feels it without doubt as an ill [i.e. as painful], but by reason he and everyone else will describe it as good. When, however, someone who delights in annoying and vexing peace-loving folk receives at last a right good beating, it is certainly an ill, but everyone approves of it and considers it as good in itself even if nothing further results from it' (*KpV* 61). In contrast, the goodness of the good will is not conditional on anything else: even if the good will could accomplish nothing despite its greatest efforts, 'yet would it, like a jewel, still shine by its own light as something which has its full value in itself' (*G* 394).

Suppose that Francis as an act of beneficence, motivated by duty, gives some money to a beggar, who asks for it because he says he wants something to eat. The beggar looks sincere, and Francis does not have any reason to doubt that he will spend the money on food. But the beggar in fact spends it all on a large bottle of hard liquor, gulps it down in short order, and swiftly dies of alcohol poisoning. Was Francis's beneficent act good? It seems not: the world would have been a better place had that particular act of good will not been undertaken, since a person has needlessly died because of it. So it seems that the good will cannot be unconditionally good: its goodness depends on what it effects or accomplishes, and therefore it is not good in itself.

Kant has the resources to meet this kind of objection. In discussing coolness of deliberation, which in many contexts is a good thing (think of the coolness of a surgeon or of an airline pilot), he notes that 'the coolness of a villain makes him not only much more dangerous but also immediately more abominable in our eyes than he would have been regarded by us without it' (*G* 394). So distinguish between the good will and its effects: Kant's claim about the good will is that the exercise of the good will, disregarding its consequences, is good in all contexts. Thus its value is to be distinguished from that of, say, an act of cool deliberation, since in some contexts (that of the surgeon or airline pilot) cool deliberation is a good thing, whereas in other contexts (that of the villain) it is a bad thing. The claim, thus construed, is that an act of good will is the only thing that considered in itself is good in every context, and is therefore unconditionally good. All other qualities exhibit a *value reversal* in some contexts: in some contexts the exercise of that quality is good, in others it is bad.

The claim is now more plausible, and has been endorsed in something like this form by Paton.[10] Yet as thus construed, the problem is no longer that the good will is not unconditionally good, but that many other things are as well. Take courage, which Kant claims is only conditionally good. On the value-reversal test, we would have to hold that the courage of a terrorist makes him not only more dangerous (which is true), but also 'immediately more abominable in our eyes'. But is this so?[11] Consider a cowardly terrorist, who refuses to expose himself to any danger in carrying out his campaign. Suppose that over time he changes, and comes to exhibit courage: he is now willing to endanger himself for the good of the cause he espouses. Does he become 'immediately more abominable'? On the contrary, though he now is more dangerous, he becomes somewhat less abominable: at least now he is prepared to stand up for his beliefs. This is not to say that we admire him—he is after all a murderer—but we can see something redeeming in the courage he exhibits. One might deny this, holding that the courageous terrorist is worse, for he has, as it were, prostituted his courage in order to advance his evil ends, and therefore has fallen a greater moral distance than a terrorist who lacks the capacity to be courageous. But that this is uncompelling is demonstrated by the case under consideration: perhaps the terrorist far from prostituting his good quality only actually developed it because of the exposure to danger that his terrorist activities produced.

There are other qualities where similar considerations can be advanced against the value-reversal construal. Consider the intellectual virtues, cleverness, for instance. A confidence trickster manages, by an elaborate story, to extract a large sum of money from me: certainly, in some ways he is more dangerous than the brutish thief, who shoves me against a wall and demands my wallet, for the conman has greater capacities for successful thievery. Nevertheless, his cleverness does not make him immediately more abominable: on the contrary, the subtlety with which he played on my self-delusions and gullibility may mean that I can't help awarding him a grudging respect, an acknowledgement that I was rather brilliantly had.

[10] H. J. Paton, *The Categorical Imperative: A Study in Kant's Moral Philosophy* (London: Hutchinson, 1947), 38.

[11] I am assuming that a terrorist can exhibit courage: if this is denied, perhaps because of a strong version of the unity of the virtues thesis, then some other description of the quality he possesses should be given: it does not matter for present purposes whether this quality is courage, or something else, since it can be argued that whatever it is, it has unconditional value.

His cleverness may in a way be admirable, though I morally condemn his conduct. Or consider the computer hacker, who breaks into some high-security system, and criminally alters records: here again, one may admire his ingenuity and skill. (Indeed, hackers have in some quarters become folk heroes, modern counterparts of those nineteenth-century robbers in the American West who stole from banks and railway companies.) Besides cleverness, we can admire other qualities in contexts where they are used for immoral ends: for instance, those of the forger, who uses his consider-able artistic skills in order to defraud the purchasers of his pictures (and again, forgers such as Tom Keating, Eric Hebborn, and Van Meegeren, have been treated as heroes by some). Or consider the bank robbery which is done by deploying exquisite technical skills in blowing the safe and planning the get-away.

So executive virtues, such as courage, intellectual virtues, such as clev-erness, artistic abilities, such as painting skills, and practical and technical skills, such as those exhibited in the bank robbery, can all be admired, and do not make their possessor 'immediately more abominable in our eyes'. And there are other states that pass the value-reversal test. The growth of knowledge is surely a good thing. The reason for denying that it is uncon-ditionally good would be that it can be used for bad ends: knowledge of the structure of the atom was used, for instance, to build the atomic bomb. But since on the value-reversal test, we are supposed to distinguish between the quality itself and the effects it may have, we can judge that the possession of knowledge is a good thing, even though its possession may be used for morally bad ends. And consider too Kant's arguments against the view that pain is unconditionally bad. To his surgery case we can respond that the pain resulting from the surgery is bad in itself, but that it has good effects (or more strictly that the pain is produced by something—the surgery—which has good effects). And the claim that the pain of the person who receives a 'right good beating' is a good pain, independently of its effects, sounds alarmingly vindictive: if all that is achieved is that the person suffers, without any tendency to make him see the wrongness of his ways or to reform him, is it at all clear that his suffering pain is a good thing?

So what we are left with is not the view that there is only one intrinsic (unconditional) value, but that there are a plurality of such values, includ-ing the possession of knowledge, the absence of pain, the possession of certain executive virtues, intellectual skills, and artistic abilities. And if this is so, then it cannot be that the good will—pure rational choice—is the condition of all these other things possessing value. Hence Kant's version of constructivism is false.

The pluralism of intrinsic values has been argued, of course, simply by appeal to intuitions, that is, to our pre-theoretical evaluative commitments.

As such, the argument has only defeasible weight. But it should be remembered that Kant himself supports his view at this stage only by appeal to intuitions, so we have responded to him at the same level at which he has entered the debate. And we can add to our position a theory of error, a partial explanation of why Kant may have taken the considerations he gives to be decisive, though they are not. For when Kant talks of the good will, it is clear from his usage that it is the *morally good* will that he has in mind. And when he talks about the good will being the only thing that is unconditionally good and the condition of all other values, the claim needs to be stronger than simply that any other feature is morally good only if its possessor has a good will. For he wants to be a constructivist about the *value* of actions, not just about their *moral* value. Yet sometimes his claims plausibly support only the weaker position that some quality is morally good only if its possessor has a good will. For instance, he holds that no rational and impartial spectator can delight in the happiness of a being without any trace of a good will. This is true at best of what such a spectator would *morally* approve of;[12] but she might approve on other grounds of the happiness of such a being—because for instance it is the happiness of someone who has achieved great things (one can admire Picasso for his extraordinary artistic achievement, and so be pleased that his life was a happy one, whilst morally disapproving of much of his personal conduct). Thus one source of error in Kant's position stems from his elision in these passages of moral value with value in general.[13]

(In response to these objections, Kant might construe the unconditionality claim not as the view that the good will is the only thing that is always valuable in every context, but in the weaker sense that it is the only thing that does not vary in value in different contexts. The good will 'has its full value in itself. Its usefulness or fruitlessness can neither augment nor diminish this value' (*G* 394). Thus the claim would be that the courage of the arsonist may still have some value, but it does not have as great a value as the courage of the fire-fighter, whereas a good will has the same value, no matter what its context. But this weaker reading is not promising. On the one hand, it is not clear that the good will can itself pass the test: the tactless person may will just as strongly to comfort someone as the sensitive

---

[12] I say 'at best' because animals, not being rational, cannot possess a good will, yet a rational and impartial spectator could surely take delight in their happiness.

[13] A further worry is whether the good will itself is always unconditionally good, even construing the claim on the value-reversal test. Kant holds that the good will of a dependent being is manifested in acting from duty. Notoriously, acting from duty is sometimes the wrong thing to do: if Smith visits his friend in hospital out of a sense of duty, then his friend might legitimately feel disappointed. (See Michael Stocker, 'The Schizophrenia of Modern Ethical Theories', *Journal of Philosophy*, 68 (1976), 453–66.) I will not explore this objection here: for perhaps the best Kantian response, see Barbara Herman, 'On the Value of Acting from the Motive of Duty', *Philosophical Review*, 90 (1981), 359–82.

person does who is successful in her efforts at comfort. But is it so clear that the good will of the former is just as good as the good will displayed by the latter? Some intentions in order to have full moral worth require appropriate knowledge and skills to be exercised. Further, if for instance courage always has some positive value, which can vary, then we can take the minimal positive value that courage possesses, and hold that courage as manifested at this minimal level is what is unconditionally valuable. Hence this manœuvre would not save Kant's thesis.)

3. The Regress Argument

So far, we have seen that at the level of intuitions it is false that the good will is, as Korsgaard phrases it, 'the source and condition of all the goodness in the world'. There are a plurality of unconditional values in the world, of which the exercise of a good will—the exercise of purely rational choice—is at best one. The argument up to this point has been conducted by appeal to intuitions, yet Kant has a further argument for the constructivist view, which may appear to be independent of these intuitions, and to offer a deeper grounding for constructivism. This argument, because it regresses on the conditions for a choice to be good, can be entitled the *regress argument*, and has been identified by Korsgaard as occurring at *G* 428–9.[14] It is explicitly directed towards showing that the categorical imperative is expressible in terms of the Formula of Humanity, but incorporates a defence of constructivism as an essential part of the argument.

We need to consider first the context of the argument. Kant is arguing for the Formula of Humanity: 'Act in such a way that you treat humanity, whether in your own person or in the person of another, always at the same time as an end and never simply as a means' (*G* 429). Kant uses the term 'humanity' here to mean the same as 'rational nature', and the latter is the power to set ends (*G* 437), or as we might say, the power of rational choice. He says that the ground of the Formula of Humanity is that 'rational nature exists as an end in itself' (*G* 429). An end in itself is something that has absolute, that is, unconditional value. Hence he is claiming that the power of rational choice has unconditional value, and he believes again that it is the only thing that has unconditional value.

Kant's claim here may appear to be inconsistent with his earlier claim that the only thing that has unconditional value is the good will: for surely one can rationally choose something, yet make an immoral choice. So it

---

[14] Christine Korsgaard, 'Kant's Formula of Humanity', *Kant-Studien*, 77 (1986), 183–202.

seems that two things—the good will and rational choice—have unconditional value. But in fact this is not so: he says that 'morality and humanity,
insofar as it is capable of morality, alone have dignity', and dignity is what
has intrinsic, unconditional worth (*G* 435). So the view is that humanity
has worth because it has the *capacity* to be moral: humanity is the power of
rational choice, the good will is *fully* rational choice, so humanity when
perfected is the good will.[15] So the view is still that there is only one
thing—perfected rational choice—which has unconditional value.

The regress argument occurs in the context where Kant has just written
'let us suppose that there were something whose existence has in itself an
absolute worth, something which as an end in itself could be a ground of
determinate laws. In it, and in it alone, would there be the ground of a
possible categorical imperative, i.e., of a practical law' (*G* 428). So there
being something of unconditional value is both necessary and sufficient for
there to be a categorical imperative. The conditional to which Kant appeals
in the regress argument is that if there is a categorical imperative, there is
something which has unconditional value: 'if all value were conditioned
and hence contingent, then no supreme practical principle could be found
for reason at all' (*G* 428). Kant supports this claim by arguing that if all
ends were relative (had their worth only relative to the contingent desires
of rational beings) then there would be no practical laws, since such laws
hold for all rational beings, no matter what their contingent desires. Hence
the existence of a categorical imperative, a practical law, requires there to
be something of absolute, unconditional worth (*G* 427–8). We can also note
that a categorical imperative represents 'an action as objectively necessary
in itself, without reference to another end' (*G* 414). What holds objectively
holds 'on grounds valid for every rational being as such' (*G* 413); and the
good is the practically necessary (*G* 412). So if there is a categorical imperative, there are actions which are good in themselves, that is, unconditionally good, and since all actions have an end, there must be at least one
end that is good in itself.[16] However, Kant in *G* section II does not try to
argue that there is a categorical imperative.

The task of the regress argument is to show that this unconditionally
good end is the power of rational choice, and in so doing to show that the
good is the object of rational choice. The argument proceeds as a regress on
the conditions for some action being good, and shows that the unconditional condition for an action being good is that it is rationally chosen. In
an important and perceptive article, Korsgaard offers a reconstruction of
Kant's argument, which can be represented in outline as follows.

---

[15] Ibid. 197.   [16] For further discussion, see ibid. 186 and 190–2.

What is the condition of an action, F, being good?[17]

1. The condition of F being good is not that it possesses a real property of goodness, which it possesses independently of our inclinations. For 'All the objects of inclinations have only a conditioned value; for if there were not these inclinations and the needs founded on them, then their object would be without value' (*G* 428).

2. But it is not, either, that F is good simply because I am inclined to do it. (i) For 'the inclinations themselves, being sources of needs, are so far from having an absolute value such as to render them desirable for their own sake that the universal wish of every rational being must be, rather, to be wholly free from them' (*G* 428). (ii) Kant can also appeal to the fact that not every inclination grounds a reason to act: cravings do not, for instance.

3. Though Kant does not explicitly assert this in the passage under consideration, he also needs to show that the condition of F being good is not simply that it is consistent with one's happiness. And he has the resources to do this: (i) we have already seen from the earlier argument about the good will that happiness is good only on condition that it is the happiness of a being with a good will (*G* 393); and (ii) the agent can't rationally hold that F is good simply because it promotes her happiness, since what is so special about her? And the agent can't hold that F is good because it promotes each person's happiness and that this is always unconditionally good, since the conditions for making one person happy can conflict with those for making another person happy. Yet 'What we call good must be, in the judgement of every reasonable man, an object of the faculty of desire' (*KpV* 60–1).

4. The remaining option is that what makes F good is simply that it is chosen by a rational being; that is, it is the object of rational choice.

5. But if this is so, then, since something has to have unconditional value (assuming that there is a categorical imperative), then the power of rational choice must have it: that is, 'rational nature exists as an end in itself' (*G* 429). In support of the latter claim, Kant holds that (i) we do think of ourselves this way: 'In this way man necessarily thinks of his own existence; thus far is it a subjective principle of human actions';[18] and (ii), more strongly, it also grounds an objective principle, that is, one binding on all rational beings: 'in this way also

---

[17] For further discussion, see Korsgaard, 'Kant's Formula of Humanity', 186 and 190–2. 194–7. I have paraphrased and compressed her presentation of the argument.

[18] Ibid. 196, takes Kant to be saying by this that we view ourselves as having value-conferring status in virtue of our rational nature. As she correctly notes, this claim supports what I am labelling step 4. However, in addition Kant is claiming something stronger, since the notion of an end in itself is of something which has unconditional value, not just of something which is the condition of value. So I have moved the claims about the subjective and objective principles to stage 5.

does every other rational being think of his existence on the same rational ground that holds also for me' (*G* 429).

6. Finally, from the fact that rational nature exists as an end in itself, it follows that rational nature must always be treated as an end, not merely as a means. And that is what the Formula of Humanity asserts.

The upshot of the argument relevant for our purposes is 'that rational choice has what I will call a value-conferring status'.[19] Korsgaard makes out an excellent case that something like the above argument is available to Kant. Some of the steps are explicit at *G* 428–9, and with considerable ingenuity Korsgaard mobilizes resources to fill the argument out in the way described. However, we need to make two amendments to make it more true to Kant's text. First, there is a footnote, not mentioned by Korsgaard, attached to 5 (ii), the claim that every other rational being thinks of itself as an end in itself. The footnote says: 'This proposition I here put forward as a postulate. The grounds for it will be found in the last section' (*G* 429). Thus, whereas Korsgaard attempts to support 5 (ii) with an argument implicit in the passage (omitted here), it is clear that Kant thinks that the argument is given later, and depends on the deduction of the categorical imperative, a deduction that Kant famously later came to think of as defective.[20] And it is clear that Kant cannot be arguing here for the claim that any rational being must think of itself as an end in itself, since otherwise he would have shown that the categorical imperative is objectively valid (since as earlier noted he holds that if there is an unconditionally valuable end, then there is a categorical imperative). And that is something he several times says he is not arguing for in section II of the *Grounding*.

Secondly, Korsgaard talks of the power of purely rational choice as being *the* source of value for Kant. The good will is 'the source and condition of all the goodness in the world; goodness, as it were, flows into the world from the good will, and there would be none without it.'[21] If we take this strictly, then there is only one source of value: the good will, that is, purely rational choice. But that is too strong: provided I have a good will, it would mean that I had reason to do anything I chose to do (since by virtue of my choice it would be valuable), whether or not I wanted to. I would have reason to crawl along the floor now, if I so chose, even though I had not the slightest inclination to do so. This might be termed the *pure conferral view*, and it should be rejected. Instead, one should hold that informed desire is

[19] Ibid. 196.

[20] See *KpV* 47: 'the objective reality of the moral law can be proved through no deduction'. This is what Karl Ameriks has called Kant's 'great reversal', in his *Kant's Theory of Mind* (Oxford: Clarendon Press, 1982), ch. 6.

[21] Korsgaard, 'Two Distinctions in Goodness', 181. As noted earlier, the goodness to which she refers is 'the kind of goodness that marks a thing out as worthy of choice', 169.

also required for an action to be valuable, if the action is morally permitted but not required. I do not now desire to crawl along the floor, so I have no reason to do so, even if I choose to do so.[22] So Kant should hold, and I think does hold, the following view. The good is the object of rational choice (that is the basic constructivist claim); for the object of choice to be good, willing it must *either* be morally required (such that the good will must will it), *or* be morally permitted (such that the good will can will it) and be the object of informed desire. If either of the disjuncts is satisfied, a person has reason to perform the action.[23] It is this *complex conferral view* that I will discuss.

Is the regress argument, as thus construed, sound? First, note a limitation: since the argument is a regress on the condition of some action being valuable, all it shows on its own is that *if* an action has value, then it is because it is the object of rational choice. But that is compatible with no action having any value at all, that is, it is compatible with value nihilism, a position that any constructivist should seek to rule out.

Secondly, even if we agree that the unconditional condition of an action being good is that it is the object of rational choice, it does not follow that rational choice is itself valuable. For it isn't true that if something has the power to confer some property, then the thing must possess that property. Consider the president of a university, who has the power to confer degrees. It doesn't follow that he has to have a degree himself. Nor is it the case that the institution, which we might hold is what really has the power to confer degrees, must have a degree—indeed, institutions can't hold degrees. So the argument is at best incomplete: it needs to be shown that value is a property such that its conferrer must possess it.

Thirdly, the argument on its own doesn't show that men have to regard their own existence as an end in itself (that is, it doesn't even establish the subjective principle). For such an end is an *absolute* value. But why should I not think of my power of rational choice not as an agent-neutral, but as an agent-relative value? So I consider that I confer value in the sense that the action is made *good for me*. I do not have to judge that anyone else has reason to pursue it, or to help me to pursue it. Many of our actions seem

---

[22] Korsgaard, 'Two Distinctions in Goodness', 190, notes that desirability is an 'initial condition' of the goodness of many good things. So here Korsgaard acknowledges that being willed by the good will is not always a sufficient condition for an object possessing value: the complex value-conferral view is in effect what she adopts at this point.

[23] Note that constructivists do not deny that an action being good gives an agent a reason to perform it. This is a claim common to both recognitional and constructivist views. (The difference between them of course is that constructivists hold that the goodness of the action consists in it being rationally chosen, whilst recognitional theorists hold that its goodness is constituted independently of rational choice.) Thus I am not illicitly ascribing a recognitional view in noting the implications of the conferral claims for theories of reasons.

to have only agent-relative value: the fact that I value writing a paper on Kant's theory of practical reason does not in itself give you any reason to help me to do so. So even if one accepts the value-conferring role of rational choice, the value conferred need not be agent-neutral.

Kant may seem to be able to deny this, for as we have seen, he holds at step 3 that 'What we call good must be, in the judgement of every reasonable man, an object of the faculty of desire' (*KpV* 60–1). That is, the good is what all rational beings desire. But even if one accepted this, it does not follow that to say that something is *good for me* requires that every other reasonable person desires it for me. All that is required is that other rational beings hold that *were they in my position* they would desire what I desire (where being in my position includes having my basic mental constitution). So the notion of agent-relative value is untouched by Kant's claim about goodness and universal rational desire, even if the latter is correct.

However, Kant as we saw earlier holds to be true the conditional that if there is a categorical imperative, there is something that is unconditionally valuable. Since if something exists which is unconditionally valuable, then *a fortiori* it is valuable, and so value nihilism is false. And if something is unconditionally valuable, then the condition of value which the regress argument identifies with the power of rational choice must itself be unconditionally valuable.[24] And further, since unconditional value is agent-neutral, the power of rational choice must be agent-neutrally valuable. So the three objections can be met by appeal to the conditional just given and to Kant's argument that there is a categorical imperative. However, the latter argument is deeply problematic, though this is not the place to discuss it.[25] Suffice it to say that one cannot hope to run the regress argument on its own to yield Kantian constructivism, for without appeal to the categorical imperative and the conditional noted the argument would succumb to the three objections just noted. The threat of value-nihilism is one that can perhaps be met by appeal to the convergence of our evaluative judgements on many central issues, but the other two objections are not so easily answered.

Further, even if one thought that the existence of a categorical imperative could be established, by Kant's argument or by some other, the stages of the argument up to step 4 also need to be sound. And in addition a non-Kantian constructivist who denied the possibility of establishing the existence of a categorical imperative could note that though we have

---

[24] Suppose that something other than the power of rational choice were unconditionally valuable. Call this thing 'X'. Then since by the first four steps of the regress argument, X is valuable only if it is rationally chosen, X is not unconditionally valuable. So given the regress argument, if something is unconditionally valuable, it must be the power of rational choice.

[25] For a brief critical discussion, see the Introduction to the present volume, sect. 4.

questioned some important claims of Kant's version of constructivism—
that rational choice has value, and that it confers agent-neutral value—we
have said little against the minimal constructivist claim reached at step
4, a minimal claim that the non-Kantian constructivist would also endorse.
So we need to look at the first four steps of the regress argument, what we
might call the minimal regress argument: it too is vulnerable.

Consider step 3. Kant appeals there to the claim that happiness is not
unconditionally valuable because it is only the happiness of a being with a
good will that is unconditionally valuable. But as noted in Section 2, this is
plausible only if we interpret that as a statement about what is *morally*
valuable: that is, we judge the happiness of a villain as a morally bad state
of affairs. But the argument is supposed to be about the value in general of
actions, not merely about their moral value. For if it were the latter alone,
then we would not have shown that rational choice had value-conferring
power, but only that it had the power of conferring *moral* value. So this
step is insufficient to support the position in its full generality. Worse, one
could hold, consistently with Kant's point about conflicts of happiness, that
what has unconditional value is the happiness of all rational beings, provided that the happiness of each is consistent with that of the others. That
is, what is unconditionally valuable is the non-conflicting happiness of all
rational beings.[26] Nor has a utilitarian position yet been ruled out, which
holds that the unconditional value is the greatest overall happiness of
rational beings, where in cases of conflict the action that produces the
greater happiness is better. Thus there are several ways to block the regress
to rational choice at step 3.

The main objection I wish to urge, however, occurs at the very first step.
This step holds that an action cannot be good because of any property of
goodness it possesses, independently of the inclinations we have to pursue
it. As Korsgaard says, the view adopted at this step is that 'the things that
you want, if they are good at all, are good because you want them—rather
than your wanting them because they are good'.[27] However, this claim
simply begs the question against the recognitional model of practical
reason, which holds that we choose actions because they are good, where
their being good is not simply construed as their being the object of rational
choice. And in fact this way of thinking about our choices is intuitively
more correct. If a person is asked why she watched an opera rather than a
soap opera, her reply may be 'because the opera is better'. She wanted to
watch it because it was good: it wasn't good merely because she wanted to

---

[26] I owe this point to Samuel Kerstein. Note that this way of meeting Kant's argument not only
blocks the regress to rational choice, but also does not require that all rational beings be morally good,
since there are other ways of achieving consistent happiness than by restricting all rational beings to
morally good actions.   [27] Korsgaard, 'Kant's Formula of Humanity', 195.

watch it. Likewise, someone can answer as to why he stopped exercising that 'it became too painful'. Its painfulness gives him a reason to stop, independently of whether he wants to or not. And when a physicist is asked why he is interested in his research, he can reply that it may reveal fundamental truths about the universe. Thus, the pluralism of intrinsic values, for which we argued earlier—the values of aesthetics, freedom from pain, and cognition, etc.—here provide coherent grounds for why people want the things they do. So it is not just that the question is begged here, but also intuitively the Kantian claim is weaker than the recognitional view.[28]

(One Kantian response is to hold that when we say that we choose something because it is good, we mean that we choose it because of its virtues and what makes certain of its properties virtues is that we want the thing to possess them—'its virtues are still relative to our desires, or, more accurately, to the conditions that give rise to those desires'.[29] However, this response fails: in many cases, what the virtues of a thing are is dependent on the nature of the thing, not on what we want or need them to be. The fact that friendship exists in human society is in the end dependent on people needing and wanting friends. But given that there are friends, their virtues are fixed by what a friend is. A good friend could not be someone who betrayed you for the pure enjoyment of betrayal. If we all wanted our friends to betray us, and even if we needed them to do so for some reason, that would not make betrayal a virtue of friends. Rather, one would no longer be wanting friends to be friends: there would be a new category of desired betrayers. Similar remarks apply to functionally characterized objects. The existence of knives is explained by the fact that we want objects with which to cut. But even if we all wanted to use knives for drumsticks, that would not make the ability to be used in drumming a virtue of knives: rather one would now be assessing them as drumsticks, not as knives. So while the *existence* of certain objects is dependent on our needs and desires, it does not follow that what are the *virtues* of those objects is so dependent.)[30]

Besides the unsoundness of the argument, the conclusion has its own deep problems; for the idea of practical reason as value-conferring generates untenable results. As earlier noted, to avoid collapsing into the recognitional conception, the value-conferring view must specify practical

---

[28] When at step 5 Kant claims that man necessarily thinks of his own rational nature as an end in itself, part of what he means is that we necessarily think of ourselves as having this value-conferring status. The objection in the text shows that this incorrectly represents the phenomenology of choice—in choosing we think of ourselves as striving to recognize what is good to do and to act appropriately, rather than as conferring goodness on states of affairs by our choices.

[29] Korsgaard, 'Two Distinctions in Goodness', 189.

[30] Cf. Philippa Foot, 'Goodness and Choice', in her *Virtues and Vices* (Oxford: Blackwell, 1978), 132–47.

reason without ineliminable reference to evaluative content. Practical reason must then be specified in terms of a set of formal (non-evaluative) principles, and any choice governed by these principles (and on the complex conferral view, a choice which is also the object of informed desire) confers goodness on its object, and one has reason to pursue that object. More specifically, on Kant's view provided an action is consistent with the good will (i.e. a will governed by pure reason, specified by formal principles), and an agent has a (presumably informed) inclination to act on it, then the action is a valuable one, and thus the agent has reason to perform it, and others have reason to help her to do so. Suppose that what I most want to do, on reflection, is every two hours to push a block of wood across the floor of my living-room by exactly one inch. (Note that the action is universalizable, and can be adopted autonomously.) I organize my life around this goal, I turn down well-paid jobs that are interesting and satisfying, since they prevent me from getting back to my living-room floor every two hours to push that block by that one inch. I refuse to have children, since they might move the block from its proper position. And when I fail, as occasionally I must, to move the block on time, I am thrown into deep despondency. On the value-conferring view, for me to push the block of wood on time at the expense of all else is good, and I ought to do so. I am thus rational in my actions. Yet in fact my actions are completely crazy: I am sacrificing import-ant aspects of a good life for a course of action that has no significant value whatsoever. The proper criterion for being rational here is the ability to recognize what it is good to do: practical reason must have ineliminable evaluative content. But that is not something that the constructivist view of practical reason can acknowledge. Thus constructivism is flawed in its claims about value, reasons, and rationality.

A second fundamental problem with the conclusion is that goodness is not in general identical with being the object of rational choice. Some trees have good roots. But that does not mean that they are the sort of roots it is rational for a tree to choose (rational 'trees' are not trees).[31] Nor are they the sort of roots that it is necessarily rational for people to choose for trees, for people's interests may diverge from what is best for the tree: a landscape gardener may prefer trees to have shallow roots so that they are decorative, but this may stunt the trees. As the example makes clear, the notion of goodness is a broadly teleological, not a narrowly rational, category, and for living beings the teleology is biologically characterized, linked to what fulfils the needs or advances the interests of a living being—and not all living beings are rational.[32]

---

[31] See Foot, 'Goodness and Choice'.

[32] In the *Critique of Judgment*, Kant holds that 'the good always contains the concept of a purpose' (*KU* 207), which may seem to commit him to the broader teleological understanding of goodness. But in fact he still affirms that 'the good is the object of the will' (*KU* 209), so the connection to rationality

One reply open to the constructivist is to distinguish between goodness as it applies to things, plants, and animals, and goodness as a property of actions, practical goodness, that is, what is choiceworthy. So Kant, as we have seen, at one point equates the good with the practically necessary: that is, what is required in action (*G* 412).[33] Then he could claim that the constructivist account holds true only of the latter concept. However, now there are two radically distinct notions of goodness—one a rational concept, the other not—and we need some motivation for the distinction, other than simply as an *ad hoc* move to save the theory. Lacking such a motivation, we should accept that the broader and simpler teleological account of goodness is to be preferred to Kant's.

A different constructivist response is to preserve the univocity of 'goodness' and hold that plants and animals are to be regarded as having purely instrumental value, serving the purposes of mankind. On this view good roots would be those it would be rational for us to choose in a tree relative to what purposes we wanted the tree to serve, whether it be for decorative purposes, or alternatively for purposes that required the tree not be stunted. Kant seems to have embraced something like an instrumentalist view (*KU* 425–7), and he holds that man as possessor of the good will is the final purpose of nature 'to which all of nature is teleologically subordinated' (*KU* 436), so that 'without man all of creation would be a mere wasteland, gratuitous and without a final purpose' (*KU* 442). On such a view, the value of animals and plants is completely dependent on that of people. Now suppose I can bring it about either that all life on earth is destroyed, or that all human life is destroyed, but that animals and plants are spared. The instrumentalist should hold that these two scenarios are indifferent from the point of view of value, yet anyone who sincerely thought that would be complacent about an eco-terrorism of horrendous proportions. We properly do not regard animals and plants as having only instrumental value.[34]

4. A Recognitional Model of Practical Reason

Kant's method in the first two sections of the *Grounding* is what he describes as 'analytic'. That is, he is not concerned to give a deduction, a justification

is maintained. The explanation of this partly lies in his understanding of purpose, which as Pluhar puts it is 'an object or state of affairs insofar as it is, or is regarded as, the effect brought about by some cause through a concept that this cause has of it' (*Critique of Judgment*, trans. Pluhar, p. xxv). Since only rational beings can possess concepts strictly speaking, there is an essential connection between the concept of a purpose and that of a rational being.

[33] See also Korsgaard, 'Two Distinctions in Goodness', 169.

[34] Note that the two points directed against the conclusion are objections not just to Kantian but to *any* version of constructivism, and the objections to the regress argument, particularly to the first and third steps, also pose a problem for any constructivism which draws on this kind of argument for its support.

of morality, but is merely concerned to analyse our pre-reflective moral convictions, show their structure, and display their presuppositions. To use terminology that emerged later in the history of philosophy, his task is hermeneutic: he is concerned to interpret our evaluative practices, displaying their deep structure. I have argued that he gets this structure wrong, failing to capture the pluralism of intrinsic values, and giving a constructivist account of reason that makes certain actions rational that are not and gives us no reason to perform certain actions that there is reason to perform. I now give a diagnosis of why he goes wrong in his hermeneutic task, locating the source of his error in an account of human agency that is deeply problematic. Then I will try to perform Kant's hermeneutic task again, showing what account of reason and what account of human agency is presupposed in our evaluative commitments. I will argue that what is presupposed in our evaluative practices is a recognitional account of reason and a naturalistic account of human agency. These accounts will in turn ground the objections that I have made to Kant's account of reason and value.

Korsgaard in her construal of the regress argument provides Kant with several extra premises that are available to him, and the argument has been discussed in these terms. But it is striking that what Kant explicitly says would get him the same result more directly. Recall that he says that 'the inclinations themselves, being sources of needs, are so far from having an absolute value such as to render them desirable for their own sake that the universal wish of every rational being must be, rather, to be wholly free from them' (*G* 428).[35] Korsgaard does not comment on or endorse this claim, and it is not difficult to understand why: it involves two strikingly odd assertions. First, Kant claims that inclinations are the sources of needs, not that needs are the sources of inclinations. Yet it is the latter that is surely correct: hunger, my inclination to eat, has its source in my physiological need to eat, not vice versa. Even if I had no inclination to eat (perhaps because I had been slipped an appetite-suppressant), I would still need to eat, and that need would give me a reason to eat, even if I did not recognize it. Yet Kant is firm in his claim, talking again of 'inclinations and the needs founded on them' (*G* 428). Thus Kant at least in this passage simply dismisses as an independent class a whole set of reasons—those founded on needs.[36] We shall see the significance of this shortly. The second oddity is the main claim that a rational being wishes to be wholly free of inclinations and needs. This is not merely a passing remark, but is

---

[35] Since Kant holds that happiness is 'the sum of satisfaction of all inclinations' (*G* 399), it follows from the claim at 428 that a rational being wishes to be free of the demands of happiness too. (Note that this is compatible with the view that the greatest good for dependent beings is virtue and happiness in proportion to virtue, since the above wish is in effect not to be a dependent being.)

[36] A different way to read these passages is to hold that by 'needs' Kant means what one needs (what is required) in order to fulfil one's inclinations; then the objection is that Kant fails here to consider the distinct sense of 'needs' in which needs are the sources of desires and ground reasons on their own.

something that emerges from deep within Kant's theory of agency. At the core of transcendental idealism stands the distinction between things as they are in themselves which lie outside space and time, and their appearances which are within space and time. The will is what we really are, whereas all other mental phenomena, including inclinations, are alien, mere appearances to ourselves. Kant writes that man 'does not even hold himself responsible for such inclinations and impulses or ascribe them to his proper self, i.e., his will, although he does ascribe to his will any indulgence which he might extend to them if he allowed them any influence on his maxims to the detriment of the rational laws of his will' (*G* 458). Thus our proper self is our will, that is, practical reason. Inclinations are mental phenomena for which we are not responsible, presumably because Kant holds that we passively have them, whereas the will is active. Inclinations are thus a threat to the autonomy of the will, for the will on its own wills according to the moral law, and if it fails to do so, it is because of the influence of inclinations on it, which tempt it to make exceptions for itself to the moral law. Hence a rational being with a will wishes to be rid of its inclinations.

So according to Kant what a human agent really is is a will, and a will that is outside space and time. The body, our distinctively human needs, our emotions, and our desires, are all mere appearances. As we have seen, it is this picture of the human agent that explains the route that Kant explicitly takes in the regress argument. And it also helps explain why reason for him is specified in formal terms, such as universalizability, rather than in terms of the ability to recognize independently constituted evaluative states of affairs: for if reason were specified in the latter terms, then the will (which is practical reason) would be determined by something outside itself, by alien causes, and therefore would not be free.

This picture of human agency is deeply flawed. Indeed, if we trundle onto the stage the full apparatus of transcendental idealism, it is probably incoherent: for it makes no sense to talk of a will being outside time. Acts of will (decisions to act) are individuated by who makes them and by when they are made. Yet if we abstract away from all temporal information and from all that can separate one individual from another (spatio-temporal position and individual characteristics), then we cannot individuate acts of will. Nor, since causation is a spatio-temporal relation, does it make any sense to talk about acts of will causing actions. So the transcendental idealist picture of the will turns out to be incompatible with the presuppositions required for reference to acts of will.[37] And even if we prescind from this picture, problems remain. The motivation for the claim that the will is our

---

[37] Note this is just as true on the 'two aspects' interpretation of the doctrine as it is on the 'two worlds' interpretation of it, since the former requires us to view the will from a timeless perspective: but from such a perspective we cannot individuate acts of will. Nor can we individuate the individuals whose willings they are.

proper self is inadequate: we are passive with respect to a large class of our beliefs (those derived from perception especially), but they are still our own beliefs, and an indispensable part of our activity of theoretical reasoning. And one certainly can hold oneself responsible for one's inclinations and not just one's actions: I can feel guilty because of lust, or anger, or amusement I feel inappropriately. (Kant can allow that we are responsible for *trying* not to feel these things, for trying is an act of the will; but the point here is that we can also actually be responsible for what we feel.) And the claim that we are really our will, and all other psychological features are alien to us, is a priori false. The will, says Kant, is 'the power to act according to his [man's] conception of laws, i.e., according to principles' (*G* 412). But if I were offered survival merely as a will, I would lose all that is distinctive of me as an individual: my body, my personality traits, my memories, my attachments to particular causes and people, and so forth. Whatever remained once all these were stripped away would not be recognizable as me. So the will cannot be identical with my 'proper self'.[38]

Kant's particular interpretation of our evaluative commitments is, then, rooted in a theory of agency which should be rejected. But then what is the correct hermeneutics for these commitments, and what theory of agency is required by them? Consider some of the points we have made in criticism of Kant's position. We have seen that there is a pluralism of intrinsic values, and that the specification of value in terms of the object of rational choice leads to the claim that certain actions are valuable, the undertaking of which would be irrational. Recall the man who wants to move a block of wood an inch across the floor every two hours. The claim here is not that his action is unintelligible (which is the conclusion that Anscombe draws from her famous example of wanting a saucer of mud).[39] For the action *is* intelligible in the sense that we can explain it: the man wants very much to push the block of wood around, and that is why he does so. Rather, the point is that he is sacrificing major goods of friendship, having children, having a satisfying job, and so forth, in order to pursue a task that is all but worthless. But we could make his action rational if we fill out the story in various ways: perhaps it is part of some religious observance he is pledged to perform, or perhaps it is a scientific experiment, or perhaps he is even doing it for love ('I'd do anything for you', he says starry-eyed to his beloved: 'well, what about *this*?' she retorts). So the action can be rendered rational by changing the example so that the action is in pursuit of one or

---

[38] These kinds of considerations are similar to those which Michael Sandel urges against Rawls in his fully-fledged Kantian phase: see Michael J. Sandel, *Liberalism and the Limits of Justice* (Cambridge: Univ. Press, 1982).

[39] G. E. M. Anscombe, *Intention* (Oxford: Blackwell, 1957), sect. 37.

more recognizable values. And not just any putative value can feature here (for instance, the value of pushing blocks of wood around can't). So what we seem to be appealing to is, to use Parfit's phrase, an Objective List account of values;[40] and the attempt to achieve one or more of these values in an action makes that action rational. Such things as the possession of friendship and love, the pursuit of knowledge and practical skills, the appreciation and creation of art and beauty, the avoidance of pain, the maintenance and fostering of political communities, and so forth, are plausible candidates for the list. Some who support such Objective List accounts think that the mere satisfaction of desire has no value whatsoever, but this seems too strong a claim. For suppose that I have a desire—a whim—to move a book that is on my floor by precisely one inch in a north-west direction. Is acting on that desire irrational? It is difficult to see why it should be: if I don't act on it, I will likely have some felt dissatisfaction and the avoidance of that has some minimal value. But acting on that particular desire is not something that structures my life, requiring sacrifice of friends, meaningful work, and so on. So the point isn't that mere desire-satisfaction has no objective value at all; it is that it has very little: it cannot make action rational that undermines substantial objective values, it cannot be the structuring principle of a good life.

If this is so, we can construe practical reason as the capacity to recognize and be motivated by what has objective value, in the sense just indicated. Thus practical reason cannot be specified purely formally, that is, by principles that lack ineliminable reference to values, but must be specified in evaluative terms.

Now even if I am correct in thinking that something like this picture is implicit in our evaluative commitments and our judgements of what is rational, that picture seems to run into a host of clamouring objections. First, epistemic: how does one establish what is on the list? Endless disputes seem possible that undermine any claim to objectivity. Secondly, motivational: why should one be motivated to pursue such values? They obtain independently of the will, so why should we be motivated to bring them about? Thirdly, ontological: are we not committed by this view to mysterious properties of goodness, somehow written into the fabric of the universe?[41]

1. The epistemic question is answered by appeal to experience: we ask what knowledgeable, experienced people have found to make for a worthwhile life. We have the entire field of human experience, and its representation

---

[40] Derek Parfit, *Reasons and Persons* (Oxford: Clarendon Press, 1984), app. C.
[41] Recall Mackie's famous argument from queerness: J. L. Mackie, *Ethics: Inventing Right and Wrong* (Harmondsworth: Penguin, 1977), ch. 1.

within literature and the arts, as our epistemic ground here. And we can conduct thought-experiments of the kind already adduced to judge whether certain activities and states are valuable. There are certain to be disputes and indeterminacies at various points, but that does not entail that there is nothing to know. This simple thought is not new: Aristotle's *phronimos* is someone of practical wisdom, who has been brought up to be sensitive to the range of values achievable in a human life, who has wide experience (young people need not apply), and the capacities for rational reflection and behavioural control that allow him to use that experience well. In similar vein, J. S. Mill appeals for his standard of higher quality pleasures to the judgement of all those competent judges (or to the majority if they disagree) who have experience of the relevant pleasures and the capacity to reflect well thereon.[42]

2. The motivational objection can be put like this: if value is an objective property, independent of the will, why should one be motivated to pursue it? The answer is straightforward here as well. Recall the truism about rationality and motivation noted at the beginning of this essay: reasons to act motivate agents in so far as they are rational and are aware of the reasons. On the recognitional account of reason, reasons involve the recognition of some action or state of affairs as good. Since a rational agent is motivated to act on reasons, a rational agent, given the recognitional account, is motivated to act on what she judges to be good. So from the truism and the recognitional view that a rational agent is one who has the capacity to recognize value, it follows that it is also constitutive of such an agent that she is *motivated* to do what she recognizes as valuable.

3. These simple points may seem too simple. Consider the answer to the epistemic objection. One can experience something only if it is there to be experienced; but how can there exist objective values of the kind that the recognitional view claims? Rawls, for instance, sees as the only alternative to constructivism about reason what he terms 'rational intuitionism', which holds that what makes a moral judgement true is that it is 'true of a prior and independent order of moral values'.[43] This conjures up a picture of values as simple monadic properties, holding of objects in the world, which would continue to exist even if all life were wiped out. But it is important to see that there is another alternative on the recognitional account: the claim here is not that there are values that hold independently of living beings. As noted earlier, value is a teleological, biological category: trees

---

[42] *Utilitarianism*, ch. 2, in J. S. Mill, *On Liberty and Other Essays*, ed. John Gray (Oxford: Univ. Press, 1991).
[43] Rawls, 'Themes in Kant's Moral Philosophy', 100.

can have good roots because trees have goals, specified by their nature, and good roots are those which help achieve these goals. (Note we can apply teleological categories to plants: roots are sent out *in order to* extract nutrition from the soil and to support the tree.) What makes such things as artistic achievement, deep personal relationships, the pursuit of knowledge be values for us is that they are constitutive parts of good human lives (which is not, of course, to say that every good human life must possess them all). These values are not a rag-bag of different qualities: their unity is revealed in the unity of a good human life. And what is a good life for a human being is partly determined by her nature: by her capacities, tendencies, and needs. The good life for a tree is having plenty of sun and rain and nutrients, reproducing, and being firmly planted in the ground. Being firmly planted in the ground is not an aspect of the good life for a human being. A good life for a dog involves having plenty of exercise and food, participating in the collective life of the pack, investigating pungently smelly things, and so forth. Any human being who sincerely thought this was the good life for her would be barking mad. The good life for a human is then partly determined by her nature: by her capacities, tendencies, and needs, including the needs for meaningful work, close personal relationships, and the exercise and development of her rational powers, displayed not just in theoretical and practical reason, but also in her emotional life. The exercise of rationality is a good for an animal that possesses it and has the tendency to use it.

The property of goodness is thus not a mysterious ontological property, but a teleological one, and for living beings specifically a biological one, which has an explanatory role in the world.[44] To get a grip on this role, consider the concept of need. Appeal to what an organism needs helps explain why it behaved in a certain fashion. For instance, one can partly explain why a plant sent out a tendril towards an illuminated area by the fact that the plant needs light to survive. (One has also of course to appeal to the biological mechanisms which allow the plant to satisfy that need.) Now the notion of a need is not correctly represented by a two-place predicate: X needs Y, the plant needs light. It must be represented by a three-place predicate: X needs Y in order to Z. For instance, a car needs petrol in order to run. In the case of organisms, the third relatum is not simply *in order to live*. This might be called the subsistence notion of a need: a need is something that allows an organism simply to live. But it makes sense to say of a tree that is living, though it is weak and stunted,

---

[44] I mean by 'biological' what has to do with life, rather than the narrower concept of what has to do with the body.

that it does not have as much nutrition and shelter as it needs. The tree does not have enough to flourish, that is, it does not have enough nutrition to live a good life for a tree. Hence the notion of a need is correlative to that of flourishing, which is an evaluative concept.[45] But as we have seen, the notion of a need is an explanatory one, which therefore we can know about, so that the notion of value, which is implicated in it, is also explanatory, and therefore knowable.[46] And we noted earlier that to say that someone needs something is to offer a reason why they should have it, even if they do not desire to have it. Thus it is not surprising that Kant should have inverted the relation between inclinations and needs in the regress argument, for once one acknowledges the importance of needs and the fact that they are not grounded on inclinations, one can see that there is a notion of value that is not constituted simply as the object of rational choice.[47]

The picture of value and reason being offered here, then, is that there are objective values, constituted independently of our capacity for rational choice, which are partly fixed by facts about us as biological entities. We are embodied beings, with certain physical and psychological needs, and these needs are correlative to the notion of human flourishing. As rational animals, the exercise of reason is itself a prime value for us, as well as being the way that we establish what has value. But to say that the exercise of reason is the *object* of value and is the *discoverer* of value is not to say that it *confers* value. What is the good life for us is thus partly determined by

[45] See also David Wiggins, 'Claims of Need', in his *Needs, Values, Truths: Essays in the Philosophy of Value* (Oxford: Blackwell, 1987), 1–57, for a related discussion, though Wiggins makes direct use of the notion of harm in his analysis of 'need'.

[46] It may be objected that more scientifically advanced explanations, such as those proffered by microbiology and evolutionary theory, make no appeal to evaluative concepts, so that the explanatory role of value is illusory. But this is not so. Microbiological explanations are incomplete unless they include not merely how a biological process occurs, but also what the function of the process is (indeed, even the notion of a mechanism presupposes that of a function). The notion of a function possesses a certain kind of normativity (things can malfunction), and for familiar reasons has evaluative implications (if A has the function of ϕ-ing, we know what a good A is, and what is good for A). Further, a complete biological explanation needs to state why the parts or behaviour of an organism have the function of ϕ-ing, rather than ψ-ing, and such explanations have at some point to appeal to the fact that the organism *needs* to ϕ rather than to ψ in order to live a certain kind of life (the life characteristic of its kind). Similar remarks apply to evolutionary explanations, which are also incomplete without appeal to the function of the parts and behaviour of organisms.

[47] It may be objected that to the extent that we appeal to needs here, we have covertly returned to the story about the good being conditional—conditional on needs. However, even if this were so, it would still be distinct from Kant's claim in the regress argument, which, as we saw, gives needs no independent role in determining what we have reason to do. (Though Korsgaard in 'Two Distinctions in Goodness' in giving a broader Kantian account does talk about goodness being conditional on the conditions, including needs, that give rise to desires e.g. p. 189.) But in any case, because the notion of need is of what one requires in order to live a *good* life, goodness is not conditional on any other kind of thing (such as rational choice), and hence the constructivist view is not supported. Rather, the goodness of certain objects of choice is dependent on their contribution to the goodness of lives, so that the notion of goodness is still basic, good states of affairs being constituted independently of rational choice. Intrinsic values are on this view to be understood as those which are constituents of good lives.

facts about our nature, including our rational nature. We discover how to lead a good life by experiencing which lives go well and badly, drawing on individual experience and the accumulated wisdom of the past, and by deliberating individually and collectively in the light of this experience about what is the good life for us. Thus the picture of human agency required to make sense of our evaluative commitments is not Kant's picture of the transcendentally free agent, but rather of an embodied, naturally evolved, historically located animal, with certain needs, tendencies, and capacities, that possesses reason as part of its natural endowment, and whose inclinations are not something alien to it, but are to be assessed in terms of whether or not they help promote the good life for it. Because this agent can recognize as objective values such things as the absence of pain and the preservation of a flourishing life, it can recognize as values too the absence of pain in animals, and the value of a flourishing life in other species. It is because of the objective value of such things that the lives of other beings which possess the capacities to realize some of the values that we pursue possess value too. This model of human agency fits neatly with the structure of our evaluative commitments as I have represented it; it is also considered on its own a more plausible and coherent view than the Kantian picture of the transcendental agent, whose will confronts its empirical nature as an alien force. A naturalist picture of agency and a recognitional view of its practical reason fit smoothly together.[48]

The attempt to rerun the hermeneutical project of the first two sections of the *Grounding*, free of the demands imposed by the transcendental view of agency, has yielded a picture of the structure of practical reason that is strikingly different from Kant's. That hermeneutical project has revealed a recognitional model of reason that fits smoothly with the nature of our evaluative commitments, and with a naturalistic view of human agency. And since Kant's constructivist account of reason has proved to have deep problems, and the regress argument for it to be flawed, the value-recognitional model of reason should be granted to be superior to it. The argument has chiefly been directed against Kantian constructivism, but several of the problems raised have been generic to constructivism *per se*

---

[48] This recognitional model of practical reason would presumably be classified by Kant as a particularly egregious example of heteronomy, and so as incompatible with the freedom of the will. This accusation ought not to worry the friend of the recognitional view. Kant holds that a free agent is one who has the capacity to direct her conduct by reason. One can agree with this: the wanton (who has no capacity for rational reflection on her desires) is not free. (See Harry G. Frankfurt, 'Freedom of the Will and the Concept of a Person', in Gary Watson (ed.), *Free Will* (Oxford: Univ. Press, 1982), 81–95). Nor is the person free who has this reflective capacity, but whose capacity has no causal power over her conduct. Nothing in the recognitional model of practical reason prevents one from honouring both of these features. It is Kant's connection of freedom with autonomy, in the sense of the ability to give oneself the moral law, that the recognitional theorist would dispute, since the notion of giving oneself a law is closely connected to the idea of reason as value-conferring which she denies.

(for instance, the difficulties illustrated by the block of wood example, the biological role of value, and the problems of employing even the minimal version of the regress argument). I have, of course, delineated only the briefest sketch of the notion of value to which the recognitional model of reason can appeal, and what I have said on that subject is compatible with a wide range of ethical theories.[49] But my goal has been to show that the sense one can sometimes get from contemporary Kantians in particular—that one is either an adherent of constructivism, or a believer in mysterious non-natural properties of goodness—is not exhaustive of the field of possible views about value and reason. It should thus go some way to defusing the sense that there are no acceptable alternatives to constructivism. In the dispute over the structure of practical reason, the more traditional recognitional account has, then, shown itself to be superior to its constructivist challenger.[50]

[49] For my own view of which ethical theory is best, see my 'Moral Pluralism', *Philosophical Papers*, 22 (1993), 17–40.

[50] I would like to thank Garrett Cullity, and members of the Philosophy Department of the University of Maryland, College Park, with particular thanks to Samuel Kerstein, for their comments on earlier drafts of this essay.

7

Practical Reason Divided: Aquinas and his Critics

T. H. IRWIN

1. Aristotle and the Reciprocity of the Virtues

Early in his discussion of virtue of character, Aristotle takes it to be obvious that virtue is somehow connected with practical reason: 'First, then, actions should express correct reason. That is a common [belief], and let us assume it; later we will say what correct reason is and how it is related to the other virtues' (*Nicomachean Ethics* 1103b31–4).[1] When he argues that virtue lies in a mean, he adds that the mean is 'determined by reason, and by the reason by which the prudent person would determine it' (1106b36–1107a2). To make his account of virtue not only true but perspicuous, he seeks an account of prudence (1138b18–34).[2] At the end of his account of prudence, he claims to have answered the question about the nature of correct reason: 'it is not merely the state expressing correct reason, but the state involving correct reason, that is virtue. And it is prudence that is correct reason in this area' (1144b26–8).

Having argued for a connection between virtue and prudence, Aristotle infers that we cannot have any of the virtues without having all of them:

In this way we can also solve the dialectical argument that someone might use to show that the virtues are separated from each other. For [it is argued], since the same person is not naturally best suited for all the virtues, someone will already have one virtue before he has got another. This is indeed possible with the natural virtues. It is not possible, however, with the [full] virtues that someone must have to be called unconditionally good; for as soon as he has prudence, which is one,[3] he has all the virtues as well.   (1144b32–1145a2)

In rejecting the view that the virtues are separable, Aristotle does not argue directly that they require one another. He argues that since virtue requires prudence and prudence requires all the virtues, the virtues require one another.

---

[1] Hereinafter cited as *EN*.

[2] I use 'prudence' to translate both Aristotle's term *phronēsis* and the Latin *prudentia*, the standard rendering of *phronēsis*.

[3] In 1145a2 I am inclined to read *mia(i) ousē(i)*, rather than *mia(i) huparchousē(i)*.

Aristotle's belief in the 'reciprocity of the virtues' (RV) has often been found difficult to believe. Even moralists who are sympathetic to Aristotle and to an approach that emphasizes the centrality of the virtues have been unwilling to accept RV. In this essay I will not defend RV as a whole.[4] I will simply examine Aristotle's claims that (i) there is some one body of knowledge grasped by prudence, and that (ii) this one body of knowledge is necessary for any genuine virtue. Since Aristotle's conception of prudence is his conception of the correct use of practical reason, a clearer understanding of his claims about the nature of prudence and its role in virtue will give us a clearer understanding of his views about the role of practical reason in virtue.

Before I try to expound or defend Aristotle, I will set out some objections raised against RV; many of them are presented in some form by Scotus and Ockham in their critique of Aquinas's defence of RV. These objections will help us to ask the right questions when we consider possible defences of the Aristotelian position.

2. *Some Objections to the Reciprocity of Virtue*

Every defender of RV, from Socrates onwards, has had to face the fact that common sense stubbornly affirms the separability of the virtues; it seems perfectly obvious that the same person can be brave but intemperate, or generous but dishonest. As Aristotle himself recognizes, different virtues require different training, so that we can apparently acquire one virtue without the others.[5] Ockham notices that we may be in the circumstances relevant to temperance—if we find ourselves needing to control our desire for certain pleasures—without being in the circumstances relevant to bravery; for circumstances that tempt us to the wrong pleasures need not also involve danger that needs to be faced without fear. Hence, apparently, we can exercise temperance without having acquired bravery.[6]

---

[4] RV includes two conditionals: (1) If we have any virtue, we have prudence. (2) If we have prudence, we have all the virtues. I will be concerned mainly with (1). Certainly (2) raises several important questions about Aristotle's views on the nature of prudence and on the connection between its cognitive and affective elements, but I have no room to deal with these questions here. I discuss them briefly in 'Some Rational Aspects of Incontinence', *Southern Journal of Philosophy*, suppl. 27 (1988), 49–88, at 81–3. Medieval writers discuss RV under the head of the 'connection' of the virtues. In this essay I do not discuss the belief in the unity of the virtues, according to which the supposedly different virtues are in fact one and the same virtue.

[5] Some predecessors of Aquinas who discuss this issue are cited by O. Lottin, *Psychologie et Morale aux XIIe et XIIIe siècles* (Louvain: Gembloux, 1948), iii. 209–23.

[6] '[S]e exercere circa materiam illius virtutis, adquirendo temperantiam et non fortitudinem, per rationem suam', Ockham, *Opera Theologica* (St Bonaventure: Franciscan Institute, 1967–86), viii. 344 = *Quaest. var.* q7, a3.

Opponents of RV maintain that Aristotle's own account of virtue as a state in accordance with right reason does not support, but actually undermines, the belief in RV. Scotus argues:

The character of a virtuous act or state needs nothing except conformity to right reason, which is evident from the first chapter[7] of the second book of the Ethics: 'A virtue is a state that elects,[8] existing in a mean, determined[9] as a wise person will determine it.' But without any agreement of virtues concurring in the same agent, it is possible for there to be such conformity, of state no less than act, to right reason in accordance with which one elects. What is assumed is evident; for one does not elect rightly about the matter of temperance except by right reason preceding and prescribing about such-and-such an object of election; but it is possible for the correct prescription of one virtue to precede without any prescription of reason about the matter of a second virtue.[10]

Scotus rejects the argument we attributed to Aristotle, from the demand for right reason to the acceptance of RV. He suggests that the separability of the virtues is best understood if we take them to be analogous to different senses (388).

If we agree that each virtue requires the right motives, and that these must include the appropriately co-operative attitude towards the other virtues, we may still resist RV; for we may still maintain that the desires and aims characteristic of one virtue are independent of those characteristic of another (Ockham, *OT* viii. 330). Ockham, for instance, argues that even if we have some degree of intemperance, as long as it is not complete intemperance, we can still have the will (*velle*) to carry out the actions required by justice (*OT* viii. 346). If, for instance, we recognize that justice requires us to aim at the common good, we can have this aim while still having some tendency to intemperance.[11]

Aristotle maintains that the virtues are connected in so far as they all require prudence; but even if he is right about this, RV does not follow. Ockham argues that we can have prudence and right reason about the subject-matter of one virtue (for instance, temperance) and not about the

---

[7] Perhaps Scotus is thinking of 1103b31, though he actually quotes 1106b36.

[8] I use 'election' to render *electio* in Aquinas and *prohairesis* in Aristotle, in order to avoid the frequent but misleading English rendering 'choice'.

[9] Aristotle actually says 'determined by reason, and by the reason by which the prudent person would determine it'. Though Scotus omits the reference to determination by reason, his comment shows that he has it in mind.

[10] *John Duns Scotus on the Will and Morality*, trans. A. B. Wolter (Washington: Catholic University of America Press, 1986), 384. Other passages in Scotus are cited from Wolter. I have not always followed Wolter's translation. (Here it omits the first clause of the passage quoted, as well as the previous clause.)

[11] Presumably Ockham means that we are not so intemperate that we would be willing to damage the common good for the sake of our intemperate desires, but we are intemperate enough to indulge our intemperate desires when we do not seem to harm the common good.

subject-matter of another (for instance, generosity). Hence, Ockham agrees with Scotus in rejecting the unity of prudence (*OT* viii. 284–5 = *Quaest. var.* q6, a10). He admits that the virtues are connected in so far as they all accept certain universal principles such as 'everything honourable is to be done', 'everything good is to be loved', and 'everything prescribed by right reason is to be done'. But to reach a practical conclusion from these general principles we need the different types of prudence that are acquired by experience in the different areas of the different virtues.[12] Prudence in the proper sense has to be both about particulars and acquired by experience, and so there is a different prudence for each virtue (*OT* viii. 282 = *Quaest. var.* q6, a10).

Ockham sees that this division of prudence seems to conflict with Aristotle's view that there is one prudence for many virtues (*OT* vi. 406 = *Sent.* iii, q12, a4).[13] Ockham replies that there are different types of prudence for the general principles and for the particular conclusions. In fact he thinks that prudence is most properly about particular things that we can do (*OT* viii. 419). In his view, the unity that Aristotle attributes to prudence must be a purely generic unity that allows different and independent species of prudence to belong to different virtues. In this treatment of prudence Ockham agrees with Scotus, who argues that 'different things to be done require different prudences' (410), so that prudence is really a generic unity embracing the different specific types of prudence belonging to the different virtues.

Ockham concedes that when one virtue is sufficiently perfected, it inclines us towards the primary expression (*actus*) of another virtue (*OT* viii. 347–8; cf. vi. 426); he also allows that the virtues share their common principles (vi. 425–6). But this is as far as he goes in endorsing RV; he still insists that each virtue requires its own prudence derived from the experience that is necessary for that virtue and unnecessary for other virtues.

Common sense supports Scotus and Ockham in their rejection of RV. If they are right, then the rather general and plausible Aristotelian claim that virtue requires action in accordance with correct reason does not justify the apparently counter-intuitive conclusion that the virtues are inseparable.

3. Perfect Virtue

Defenders of RV appeal to a distinction between perfect and imperfect virtue. Aristotle insists that RV applies only to virtue in the 'full' or 'strict'

---

[12] '[N]otitiae (sc. of conclusions) sunt prudentiae directivae in diversis actibus virtuosis', *OT* viii. 285. Cf. vi. 425.

[13] The editors of *OT* suggest that Ockham is referring to *EN* 1140a25–7, but 1145a1–2 seems a more appropriate passage.

sense (*kuria aretē, virtus principalis*); this is the virtue that makes a person 'good without qualification' (*haplōs agathos, simpliciter bonus*). He freely admits that RV does not hold for the 'natural virtues', the natural tendencies towards the different virtues. These natural tendencies may conflict, and may actually be harmful for the agent. They need to be developed into states that necessarily include prudence:

> just as a heavy body moving around unable to see suffers a heavy fall because it has no sight, so it is with virtue. But if [someone] acquires understanding, he improves in his actions; and the state he now has, being similar, will now be virtue fully. (1144b10–14)

As Aquinas explains this passage, our natural tendency (to brave or generous actions, for instance) has to accept the guidance of understanding, so that it acts with 'discrimination' (*discretio*); when this has happened the resulting state is a perfect virtue, which is a genuine moral virtue.[14]

Defenders of RV exploit this distinction to counter the different objections we have considered. Aristotle's contrast between natural tendencies, which are separable and potentially conflicting, and genuine virtues, which are internally connected to prudence, suggests a broader contrast between imperfectly developed virtues and the complete virtues that require prudence. Defenders argue that separable virtues are imperfect virtues, and the perfect virtues of character do not show the same signs of separability. Hence, Aquinas exploits the distinction between perfect and imperfect virtues in order to defend RV (1–2, q65, a1). Henry of Ghent defends RV with the help of an elaborate list of degrees of virtue; he claims that the highest degree of any specific virtue—of temperance, for instance—requires the other virtues too.[15]

Defenders of RV, then, are free to concede some truth to the intuitive conviction that we can have one virtue without the others. In their view, we can appropriately attribute bravery to people who lack temperance and justice. They will insist, however, that this is not perfect bravery, and that perfect bravery requires the other virtues.

To see the point of this claim, we may contrast a perfectly virtuous person, as conceived by defenders of RV, with a perfect translator for (let us say) meetings of the European Community. The perfect translator is fluent in all the languages used in EC business, but her mastery of one of these languages does not involve mastery of all the others. She begins, say, as a fluent German-speaker, and she retains this very same fluency while

---

[14] Aquinas, *In decem libros Ethicorum Aristotelis ad Nicomachum Expositio*, ed. R. Spiazzi, 3rd edn. (Turin: Marietti, 1964), 1279. (Cited hereinafter as *in EN*.) He takes the subject of 'acquires understanding' to be the natural tendency, rather than (as I have translated) the person who has it.

[15] Henry of Ghent, *Quodlibet* 5, q16–17, discussed by Scotus 380 ff.

adding fluency in French, English, and so on; her fluency in German, however, does not change in such a way that it now requires fluency in English. We might say that the perfect translator has a purely conjunctive fluency in these different languages.

An analogous purely conjunctive claim about the virtues is endorsed by Scotus, in opposition to RV. He uses the analogy with the senses to explain the conjunctive claim:

One is not . . . a moral person without qualification unless one has all the virtues, just as one is not a perceiver (*sentiens*) without qualification unless one has all the senses. But one is none the less perfectly temperate, even if one is less perfectly moral, just as one is not less perfect as a seer or hearer even if one is less perfect as a perceiver. (388)

Scotus, then, takes a perfectly virtuous person to have a merely conjunctive state, composed of the different specific virtues; each of these would be no less complete if it were present without the others.

RV rejects this purely conjunctive view of the virtues of the perfectly virtuous person. It claims that the perfectly virtuous person's bravery is essentially qualified by temperance and the other virtues, and that the same is true for every other virtue. In this person, recognition of the demands of prudence and the other virtues is an internal feature of each virtue; it is not an external constraint imposed on one virtue by prudence or by the other virtues. We may say that in the perfectly virtuous person, according to RV, each virtue is internally connected to prudence and to the other virtues, whereas a purely conjunctive conception of the virtues would imply only an external connection.

The perfectly virtuous person described in this conception of the virtues may be regarded as the proper conclusion of moral training. Defenders of RV claim that moral training properly aims at a condition in which each virtue is internally connected to the other virtues. Whether or not most people reach this condition, the theorist ought to describe it, so that we can see the complete structure of virtue that makes our various demands on the virtues intelligible.

4. Defences of the Reciprocity of the Virtues

Relying on this conception of perfect virtue, Aristotle argues that the virtues cannot conflict, because they all rely on prudence:

Nor is virtue contrary to virtue. For it is by nature subject to reason, however it prescribes, so that wherever reason leads virtue inclines. For reason is what chooses the better. For neither do the other virtues arise without prudence nor is prudence complete without the other virtues, but they co-operate in some way with each other under the guidance of prudence. (*Magna Moralia* 1200a5–11)[16]

Aristotle assumes that each virtue is subject to the direction of prudence, because the point of each virtue is to achieve what is best, and each accepts the judgement of prudence about that.

The guidance of prudence does not eliminate the possibility of moral conflicts; for the prudent person must recognize conflicts if all available courses of action are costly (cf. *EN* 1110a29–30). Conflicts, however, do not result from competition between the claims of competing virtues, since the virtues do not compete. We have no reason to suppose that we have reached a full and complete virtue until we have directed ourselves to aim at what is best, and therefore we will always expect each virtue to include prudence; on this point there will be no conflict among the virtues themselves. Prudence is part of each virtue, and it has to be consulted before any virtue directs us towards a particular action.

This doctrine of internal connection between virtue and prudence is supported, in Aristotle's view, by other reasonable assumptions about the virtues. (1) Virtuous people are those who make the best use of the goods they have (*MM* 1200a24–7). If each virtue has this supervisory function, the virtues cannot conflict; for each of them relies on prudence to find the best use of the other goods, and accepts the judgement of prudence. (2) We reach the same result if we agree that the virtues are the sorts of goods that we cannot have too much of. This would not be true if they could conflict; for if each of them consists solely in the development of a psychological trait opposed to the trait developed in some other virtue, then apparently one virtue could be over-developed at the expense of others, and so we could have too much of it. In agreeing that we cannot have too much of the virtues, we must accept Aristotle's view that each of them is the optimal development, not an over-development, because it includes the regulative functions of prudence. (3) The doctrine of virtue as a mean already implies the co-operation of the virtues (*MM* 1200a31–4). A true conception of a particular virtue as a mean does not simply consider a specific range of actions or feelings to reach some balance internal to it, but also considers the co-operation of one state of character with the others, for the benefit of the appropriate people. That is why the mean in which a virtue lies must be determined by the sort of reason by which the prudent person would determine it (*EN* 1107a1–2). Only prudence takes the global point of view that is required for finding the appropriate mean that constitutes any of the virtues.

---

[16] I am assuming that the *Magna Moralia* is substantially genuine. It was not known to Aquinas.

Aristotle's belief that virtues must be regulated and formed by the demands of other virtues is the basis for one traditional defence of RV. Augustine, for instance, argues that genuine bravery must be regulated by prudence, and that therefore we cannot say that Bill and Ben are equally brave, but Bill is more prudent than Ben.[17] Agreeing with Aristotle, Augustine argues that prudence has a special role in making the virtues conform to one another so that each virtue respects the requirements of the other virtues.[18] In claiming that bravery itself must be prudent and just, Augustine makes it clear that the demands of prudence and the other virtues must be recognized as demands of bravery itself, not external demands that inhibit or reject the demands of bravery.[19]

5. Further Objections

If this is what defenders of RV mean by claiming that the perfect virtues are inseparable, their claim is not as violently paradoxical as it initially seems. Still, it is not beyond question. Further reflection suggests that even if it does not violate common sense, it rests on theoretical misconceptions about the virtues.

The very idea that there could be a perfectly virtuous agent with all the virtues may seem to rest on a misunderstanding of the character of the

---

[17] 'For if you say that these people are equal in bravery, but that one excels in prudence, it follows that this one's bravery is less prudent; but thereby they are not equal in bravery either, since that one's bravery is more prudent.' (Augustine, *De Trinitate* vi. 6. Cf. *Epistulae* 167. 5, 7. Aquinas discusses Augustine in *De virtutibus cardinalibus*, ad 12, quoting the passage from *Trin.*)

[18] 'But has he who has one virtue all virtues? And has he no virtues who lacks one? . . . As to the inseparable coexistence of the virtues, this is a doctrine as to which, if indeed I remember rightly what, indeed, I have almost forgotten (though perhaps I am mistaken), all philosophers who affirm that virtues are essential to the right conduct of life are agreed. . . . Those who maintain that he who has one virtue has all, and that he who lacks one lacks all, reason correctly from the fact that prudence cannot be cowardly, nor unjust, nor intemperate; for if it were any of these, it would no longer be prudence. Moreover, if it is prudence only when it is brave, and just, and temperate, then certainly wherever it exists it must have the other virtues along with it. Similarly, bravery cannot be imprudent or intemperate or unjust; temperance must necessarily be prudent, brave, and just; and justice does not exist unless it is prudent, brave, and temperate.' (Augustine, *Epp.* 167. 4–5. See Lottin, *Psychologie*, iii, ch. 13.)

[19] It is sometimes argued, on the strength of *Ep.* 167, that Augustine doubts RV. See J. Walsh, 'Buridan on the Connexion of the Virtues', *Journal of the History of Philosophy*, 24 (1986), 453–82, at 455. In fact, however, Augustine agrees with the unanimous view of the philosophers (as he describes it) about RV. He does not dispute RV, but disputes the claim that all vices are equal. In the passage I omitted from the quotation he says: 'If this [sc. RV] is true, the view of the apostles is confirmed. But what I want is to have the view explained, not confirmed, since of itself it stands firmer in our esteem than all the authority of philosophers could make it. And even if what has just been said concerning virtues and vices were true, it would not follow that all sins are thereby equal.' In sect. 10 he repeats that RV lacks divine authority, and therefore is not properly cited as a way of confirming Scripture. But his solution in sect. 14 accepts RV, rejects the equality of sins, and argues that different people have virtues in them to different degrees.

virtues.[20] If it is a perfectly general claim about virtues, how does it reckon with the obvious fact that different traits have been regarded as virtues at different times? It is difficult to see how the virtues of a Greek hoplite are supposed to coexist with those of a medieval monk and with those of a twentieth-century social worker. If RV is taken to apply only to the virtues recognized at a particular time, it still seems difficult to believe; how can we predict that every set of virtues in every society and culture will be linked in the way required by RV?

Even if we set aside these historical objections, RV seems to conflict with fairly obvious facts. The best people we can think of, from our own time or other times, do not seem to exemplify all the virtues; indeed, we might suppose they would have had less of the virtues they had if they had also developed other virtues. The idea that everyone should ideally display all the same 'required' virtues seems not only unrealistic, but positively unattractive; perhaps the varieties and imperfections of different people's moral characters actually add appealing diversity to human life.

These objections to RV will seem especially compelling if we accept a general conception of the virtues as essentially remedial conditions. According to this view, they are different ways to remedy different specific tendencies for things to go wrong. We suffer, for instance, from our damaging proclivity to excessive fear or excessive pleasure. We need bravery to counteract one proclivity and temperance to counteract another. We tend to be partial in our attitude to the claims of others; to remedy that, we need justice. We tend to be indifferent to the needs of others; to remedy that, we need benevolence.[21]

The distinctive feature of a remedial view of the virtues is that virtues seek to remove what we take to be clear evils, not to form our characters so as to realize the good. Admittedly, our belief that certain things are evils implies some belief about the sorts of things that are good, but it does not seem to imply any conception of the good; for we may be confident that some things are beneficial and other things are harmful even if we cannot formulate any conception of an overall good that provides a standard for making these judgements of benefit and harm. The judgements that shape our conception of the virtues are judgements about the different things that can go wrong.

This remedial conception of the virtues makes it reasonable to reject the conception of perfect virtue that is used to support RV. If different virtues

---

[20] See P. F. Strawson, 'Social Morality and Individual Ideal', in *Freedom and Resentment and Other Essays* (London: Methuen, 1974), ch. 2, at pp. 27–9; O. Flanagan, *Varieties of Moral Personality* (Cambridge, Mass.: Harvard Univ. Press, 1991), 10–11.

[21] This view is developed by G. J. Warnock, *The Object of Morality* (London: Methuen, 1971), ch. 6; he rejects RV, p. 87. It is also accepted by Philippa Foot, *Virtues and Vices* (Oxford: Blackwell, 1978), 10, who rejects RV, p. 17.

are designed to counteract different dangerous tendencies, they need not be inseparable or free from conflict. Different medicines prescribed for different diseases can easily have conflicting effects; and most people do not believe in the reciprocity of medicines. Aquinas himself remarks that 'a medicine that would be adapted to one disease would be harmful to the second . . . and what would be a suitable medicine for one sin might provide an incentive to the second' (*Summa Theologiae*,[22] suppl. q9, a2).[23] If the virtues are to be understood as piecemeal remedies for specific dangers and threats, we have no reason to suppose that the complete development of each virtue will result in the incorporation of the other virtues; on the contrary, further development of any one virtue may include the growth of a tendency that actually makes it more difficult to acquire further virtues.

From this point of view, we can see why, as Philippa Foot puts it, the acquisition of different virtues involves an 'inevitable loss' that results from the choice between conflicting goods:

so far from forming a unity in the sense that Aristotle and Aquinas believed they did, the virtues actually conflict with each other: which is to say that if someone has one of them he inevitably fails to have some other.[24]

This belief in actual conflict and inevitable loss goes beyond what we need to say in order to cast doubt on RV. But it gives us a clear reason for believing that RV is not merely false, but quite misleading about the character and function of a virtue.

If the virtues are really a set of remedial conditions, and they apply conflicting remedies to different flaws, then perhaps it would actually be undesirable for someone to aim at them all. Aristotle's assumption that we cannot have too much of a virtue conflicts with a remedial view. Even if we agree that it is possible or desirable for a person to cultivate all the virtues, we may not agree that in a perfectly virtuous person the virtues are internally related; perhaps it would be a mistake, for instance, to suppose that the demands of justice or honesty should themselves incorporate the demands of generosity or kindness.

To see whether these are well-founded objections to RV, we need to consider whether Aristotle and Aquinas have good reasons for insisting that each virtue must not only incorporate prudence, but must also incorporate prudence as they conceive it. As they conceive prudence, it grasps a set of principles that turn out to express the requirements of all the virtues. We can sum up this conception of prudence by saying that, according to

---

[22] Cited hereinafter as *ST*.

[23] The passage is quoted by J. Mahoney, *The Making of Moral Theology* (Oxford: Clarendon Press, 1987), 20 n.

[24] P. Foot, 'Moral Dilemmas and Moral Realism', *Journal of Philosophy*, 80 (1983), 379–98, at 397.

this defence of RV, prudence takes a global point of view. The most controversial aspect of the Aristotelian–Thomist view is the claim that each virtue must include the sort of prudence that takes this global point of view.

Aquinas recognizes that this is a crucial issue. He introduces it in his comment on Aristotle's claim that prudence is one:

> He says 'being one', because, if there were different prudences concerned with the matters of different moral virtues, just as there are different kinds[25] of artefacts, it would be quite possible for one moral virtue to exist without another, each of them having a prudence corresponding to it. But this cannot be the case, because the principles of prudence are the same for the whole matter of morals, so that everything is derived from the standard of reason. And that is why because of the unity of prudence all the moral virtues are connected with one another.   (*in EN* #1288)

Aquinas implicitly rejects the interpretation of Aristotle that is offered by Scotus and Ockham in support of their rejection of RV. They argue that the unity of prudence is a merely generic unity that allows the existence of mutually independent species of prudence. Aquinas argues that prudence has more than a mere generic unity; it is a single body of knowledge that is required of every prudent person and of every person with a perfect virtue.

To understand Aquinas's side of this dispute, then, we must understand why he believes prudence is strongly unified. In examining Aquinas's conception of prudence, and the Aristotelian material from which he constructs it, we raise some central and familiar questions about the scope and nature of practical reason. I will simply try to say enough about these questions to make the issues about RV intelligible.

6. *Virtue, Prudence, and Ultimate Ends*

As Aquinas understands Aristotle, the practical intellect operates through the intellectual virtue of prudence. Prudence is concerned with deliberation about means to ends, and with the election of means as a result of deliberation.[26] In saying that prudence deliberates about means to ends, Aquinas implies that it assumes some conception of its end as the starting-point of deliberation; this conception itself cannot, without a vicious infinite regress, always be established by deliberation. Hence Aquinas often argues that, because prudence deliberates about means to ends, it does not set those ends.

---

[25] The Leonine edn. reads 'genera'. The Marietti edn. prints 'genere', which appears to be a misprint.

[26] See 1a, q22, a1 ad 3; q23, a4; q113, a1 ad 2; 1–2, q57, a5; 2–2, q47, a6; q56, a1. I use 'means' with the broad scope of Aristotle's *ta pros to telos* and Aquinas's 'ea quae sunt ad finem'. We find that *x* is a 'means' to *y*, not only when we find that *x* is causally sufficient for *y*, but also when we find that e.g. doing *x* constitutes, or counts as, doing *y*.

While this outline of Aquinas's position is fairly clear, its particular application to the virtues needs careful exposition, so that we avoid confusing the different roles of prudence in relation to different ends. Once we see these different roles, we can understand his belief in the unity of prudence.

Sometimes Aquinas insists that prudence does not prescribe the ends for moral virtue. Prudence presupposes the moral virtues, which turn us towards the right ends (*ST* 1–2, q58, a5); that is why there can be no prudence without the moral virtues. Prudence is deliberative, and deliberation and election are concerned with means to ends.

The ends for the moral virtues are fixed (*determinati*, 2–2, q47, a15), and are the objects of our natural inclination (1–2, q51, a1; q63, a1). We reach them by reason, since 'reason, in so far as it grasps the end, precedes desire for the end,[27] but desire for the end precedes reason reasoning towards electing the things that are towards the end, which belongs to prudence' (1–2, q58, a5 ad 1). Here Aquinas distinguishes the practical reason that precedes and forms the desire for the end from the practical reason that follows the desire for the end and finds means to that end; he attributes the second function of practical reason, but not the first, to prudence.

Aquinas distinguishes these two functions of practical reason by connecting them with universal and particular principles. We are rightly disposed towards the universal principles 'through the natural understanding of principles, through which a human being knows that nothing bad is to be done, or also[28] through some practical science. But this is not enough for reasoning correctly about particulars' (1–2, q58, a5). The universal principle by itself is not enough, because it can be corrupted by passion. If it is corrupted, we do not draw the appropriate conclusion from the universal principles; instead, the object of appetite (*concupiscentia*), for instance, seems good, and we do not have the right ends to begin our deliberation.[29]

How, then, do we find the right ends? It is not easy to answer this question on Aquinas's behalf. We may begin by considering the parallel he develops between the first principles of theoretical sciences and the first

---

[27] Cf. q12, a1 ad 1, 3.

[28] 'Vel etiam' suggests that in addition to *intellectus* of ultimate principles, giving us *cognitio* of their content, we may have *scientia* deriving further principles from the ultimate principles.

[29] Aquinas has in mind the two passages in which Aristotle argues that prudence requires virtue because vice corrupts the principle (1140b11–20, 1144a29–b1). In the second of these passages Aristotle claims that only the virtuous person is aware of the right end. He does not draw Aquinas's distinction between universal and particular ends. At *in EN* #1132 Aquinas seems to introduce his distinction into *logos ho henaka tinos*, 1139a32. But it is not clear that Aristotle has this in mind; no specific Aristotelian support can be found for Aquinas's distinction between the two roles of practical reason. Still, Aquinas may be right to draw the distinction on Aristotle's behalf. For we need some account of how we can form the ends that are characteristic of the virtuous person, and Aquinas is right to ask whether this task can be plausibly attributed to practical reason.

principles of practical reason. He believes that in both cases non-inferential 'understanding' (*intellectus*) grasps ultimate principles. The practical principles that guide our natural inclination are naturally known, as the first principles of theoretical sciences are (1–2, q63, a1; 2–2, q47, a6); and the special faculty that knows practical principles is synderesis (1a, q79, a12).[30]

And thus it does not belong to prudence to fix the end for the moral virtues, but only to arrange about the means to the end. (2–2, q47, a6) . . . What fixes the end for the moral virtues is the natural reason which is called synderesis. (q47, a6, ad 1)

Practical intellect is prior to the desire for the end, in so far as the apprehension precedes the desire (1–2, q58, a5 ad 1). The desire for the end, however, precedes the election of the means, which is the special concern of prudence. Virtue is focused on the right end, not because of prudence, but because of a distinct non-deliberative intellectual state that grasps the right ends; and this is synderesis. The sorts of truths that concern synderesis are sharply contrasted with those that concern prudence; for the right ends of human life are 'fixed' or 'definite' (2–2, q47, a15), whereas the means to these ends are not fixed, and hence are subject to the deliberative virtue of prudence.

The ultimate principles grasped by synderesis are the most universal principles of natural law. The very first of these is the principle that good is to be done. Aquinas compares this principle to the Principle of Non-Contradiction, which is the ultimate principle underlying all theoretical reasoning:

Just as being is the first thing that falls under apprehension without qualification, so good is the first thing that falls under the apprehension of practical reason, which is directed towards action; for every agent acts for the sake of an end, which has the character of good. And thus the first principle in practical reason is the one founded on the character of good, which [sc. character] is that good is what all things pursue. This, then, is the first precept of the law, that good is to be done and pursued, and evil is to be avoided. And on this precept all the other precepts of natural law are founded, so that all those things that natural reason naturally apprehends to be goods [or evils] for human beings belong to the precepts of natural law as things to be done or avoided. (1–2, q94, a2)[31]

---

[30] I leave 'synderesis' untranslated. It might be rendered 'observance'. See *Patristic Greek Lexicon*, ed. G. W. H. Lampe (Oxford: Univ. Press, 1961), s.v. *suntērēsis*, 2; Lottin, *Psychologie*, ii. 103; T. C. Potts, *Conscience in Mediaeval Philosophy* (Cambridge: Univ. Press, 1980), 10; M. B. Crowe, *The Changing Profile of the Natural Law* (The Hague: Nijhoff, 1977), 123–7.

[31] I have mostly followed the Dominican translation (London, 1920), assuming that Aquinas's intended meaning is captured by the insertion of 'or evils' after 'goods'. One might also translate 'All the things to be done or avoided belong to the precepts of natural law, which [things to be done and avoided] natural reason apprehends to be goods [or evils] for human beings.' Or one might take 'praecepta' to be the antecedent of 'quae'. Neither of these translations fits the previous sentence as well

In this passage Aquinas refers back to his discussion of the final good (1–2, qq 1–5). Once we keep this discussion in mind, we can see that the connection he recognizes between good and aiming is not tautologous or trivially analytic. In claiming that every agent acts for the sake of some good, Aquinas is not defining 'good' by reference to desire; he is claiming that rational agents, in acting for the sake of good, seek to achieve a rational structure in their aims. This rational structure is the one that he tries to articulate in his account of happiness.

In saying that the pursuit of this sort of good is the ultimate first principle of natural law, Aquinas claims that the various subordinate principles must describe a system of ends that embodies the rational structure of the ultimate good. This is not simply the very weak claim that whatever is prescribed by the natural law is good in some respect. It is the stronger claim that all these prescriptions must be concerned with the final good of human beings with the nature that they have.

In Aquinas's view, everyone grasps this ultimate first principle and the common first principles, which are immediate and obvious consequences of the ultimate first principle, that (for instance) we should act in accordance with reason and we should not harm human beings. Not everyone, however, grasps the secondary principles of natural law, which are less immediate but still obvious consequences—for instance, the precepts that forbid murder and theft (q94, a4).

Aquinas uses this division between common principles and secondary principles to explain how vicious people lack the right ends, even though they must somehow grasp the right ends. He believes that the law of nature cannot be destroyed from human hearts, as far as concerns the first common principles, taken universally, though its operation in particular cases can be prevented by appetite or some other passion.[32] The secondary precepts, however, can be destroyed from human hearts by evil persuasions or by bad habits or natural constitutions (q94, a6; q99, a2 ad 2).

The vicious person, therefore, accepts some correct principles—those grasped by synderesis—and his error is the result of passion or bad habits. The error does not cause him simply to lapse in particular cases, but to

---

as the rendering in the text fits it. I do not understand exactly how R. J. Henle, *The Treatise on Law* (Notre Dame, Ind.: Univ. Press, 1993), 247, construes the passage. (He appears not to translate 'facienda vel vitanda'.)

[32] 'And thus it is impossible for the judgement of synderesis to be extinguished universally. In a particular thing to be done, however, it is extinguished whenever someone sins in electing. For the power of appetite or some other passion so submerges reason that in electing one does not apply the universal judgement of synderesis to a particular action. But this does not extinguish synderesis without qualification, but only in one respect' (*De Veritate* q16, a3). '[The vicious person] is indeed corrupted about the principles of things to be done, not indeed in the universal, but in the particular thing to be done—namely, in so far as reason is abased through the state of vice, so that he does not apply the universal judgement in electing its particular thing to be done' (*DV* q16, a3 ad 3).

form the wrong conception of good and evil.[33] At the level of particular ends, as Aquinas puts it, he has the wrong convictions, but these wrong convictions are not the result of a serious effort to reach a rational conception of the good from the ultimate practical principles grasped by synderesis; they are the result of ignoring these principles and their implications because some particular goods seem immediately attractive.

7. Synderesis and Prudence

So far, we have found that Aquinas recognizes two roles for practical reason: (1) Prudence finds means to the conception of the end that is accepted by the moral virtues. (2) Synderesis, not prudence, grasps the end aimed at by the moral virtues (see 2–2, q47, a6 ad 1, quoted above). These two roles of practical reason, however, do not allow us to answer all the questions that are raised by Aquinas's claims about virtue and practical reason. The end that is the starting-point for the prudent person's deliberations about what to do is the end that is characteristic of the virtuous person in contrast to the vicious person; let us call this 'the specifically virtuous end'. Synderesis, however, cannot grasp the specifically virtuous end, since synderesis is common to virtuous and vicious people; that is why Aquinas insists that it is not extinguished in the vicious person.

Aquinas recognizes that synderesis does not distinguish virtuous from vicious people. It prescribes that we act in accordance with reason, but it does not say what we must do if we are to act in accordance with reason.

This very thing that is being conformed to correct reason is the proper end of each moral virtue. For temperance aims at (*intendit*) this, namely that a human being should not deviate from reason because of appetites; and similarly <the aim of> bravery is that a human being should not deviate from the correct judgement of reason because of fear or rashness. And this end is fixed for a human being in accordance with natural reason; for natural reason instructs each person to act in accordance with reason. (2–2, q47, a7)

When we discover that acting in accordance with reason requires a considerable degree of control over appetite, we have formed the specific end that is characteristic of the temperate person. The end that is 'fixed for a human being in accordance with natural reason' is not the specifically virtuous end that is characteristic of the virtuous person; it is the universal end that is common to the virtuous and the vicious person.

---

[33] 'The law of nature in some people's hearts, as it concerns some matters, is corrupted to the extent that they regard as good things that are naturally bad' (q94, a5 ad 1).

What, then, is needed to take us from the common end of acting in accordance with reason to the more specifically virtuous end of controlling one's appetites to an appropriate degree? Our infallible grasp of natural law does not tell us what specific types of action conform to nature and reason. Human beings have to find these actions 'by rational inquiry' (*per rationis inquisitionem*, 1–2, q94, a3). The virtue that succeeds in this rational inquiry is prudence.

But in what way and through what things a human being in acting is to reach the mean of reason—this belongs to the arrangement[34] made by prudence. For, granted that reaching the mean is the end of moral virtue, still the mean is found by the right arrangement of the things that are towards the end.   (2–2, q47, a7)

If we find 'the things that are towards the end', we find the specific end that fulfils the requirement of the universal end of acting in accordance with reason. This specific end is the one that distinguishes the virtuous person from the vicious.

The deliberative task that Aquinas assigns to prudence here is different from the more immediately practical task that he assigns to it elsewhere. The more immediately practical task is to find the actions that, here and now, are required by the specifically virtuous end. This is the task that Aquinas has in mind when he says that prudence must presuppose the specifically virtuous end. Let us say that this is a task for 'micro-prudence'. The broader task of finding the specifically virtuous end is a task, we may say, for 'macro-prudence'.

Once we distinguish the two aspects of prudence, and the two different ends that they begin from, we can understand why Aquinas's emphatic claim that prudence is not concerned with ends has a narrower scope than we might at first think. In his view, neither virtue nor prudence presents (*praestituere*) the end:

The end does not belong to the moral virtues as themselves presenting the end, but because they tend towards the end that is presented by natural reason. They are helped to do this through prudence, which prepares the way for them, by arranging (*disponendo*) the things that are towards the end. Hence the remaining possibility is that prudence is nobler than the moral virtues and sets them in motion. But synderesis sets prudence in motion, just as understanding of principles sets science in motion.   (2–2, q47, a6 ad 3)

When Aquinas speaks of 'things that are towards the end', the end he refers to is not the specifically virtuous end, but the universal end presented by natural reason. When he insists that prudence does not present the end to

---

[34] Reading 'dispositionem' (v.l. 'rationem').

the moral virtues, he is right in so far as prudence does not present the universal end. Still, prudence presents the specifically virtuous end as a result of deliberation about how to realize the universal end presented by synderesis.

If, then, we consider the claim that 'prudence does not set the end', we must keep in mind the two ways we can speak both of prudence and of the end. It is true, in Aquinas's view, that micro-prudence does not set the specifically virtuous end, and that macro-prudence does not set the universal end. Virtue sets the specifically virtuous end for micro-prudence and synderesis sets the universal end for macro-prudence. Once we draw these distinctions, we see the important role that Aquinas assigns to prudence in discovering ends: macro-prudence discovers the specifically virtuous end by inquiring about how to achieve the universal end.

This role of prudence explains why Aquinas says that prudence directs all the moral virtues.[35] He insists that this directing does not extend simply to the choice of means to ends, but also includes the 'presenting' or 'determining' (*determinare*) of the end, in so far as prudence determines the mean that the virtue consists in (1–2, q66, a3 ad 3). The claim that prudence presents the end is consistent with the claim elsewhere that it does not present the end (2–2, q47, a6). In the first passage Aquinas is speaking of the specifically virtuous end, which is presented by macro-prudence; in the second passage he is speaking of the universal end, which is presented by natural reason and not by macro-prudence.

Some of the different tasks that Aquinas attributes to prudence are distinguished by his successors. Henry of Ghent discusses the formation of the specifically virtuous end; he distinguishes natural prudence from genuinely practical prudence, and identifies natural prudence with synderesis. The principles of natural virtue are sources of moral virtues ('quaedam seminaria moralium virtutum'), but are not themselves sufficient for virtue. When practical intellect applies the principles of natural prudence in particular choices, we generate moral virtues.[36] This is a task for practical prudence, as opposed to natural prudence, and it includes two further tasks implicitly distinguished by Aquinas. One form of prudence begins its deliberation from the ultimate end; the other focuses on concrete particular situations. Aquinas's successors call the first form of prudence 'universal' prudence, and the second form 'particular' prudence.[37] These two forms of prudence mark the distinction between macro-prudence and micro-prudence that we have found it necessary to draw in discussing Aquinas.

[35] See 1–2, q21, a2 ad 2; q58, a2 ad 4; 2–2, q119, a3 ad 3.

[36] Henry of Ghent, *Quodl.* 12, q14 = *Opera* xvi (Leuven: Leuven University Press, 1987), 80.

[37] See James of Viterbo in Lottin, *Psychologie*, iv. 561; Henry of Ghent, *Quodl.* 5. 17. Other sources are discussed by Lottin, pp. 561–626.

8. *Different Forms of Prudence in Aristotle and Aquinas*

If we are right to claim that Aquinas implicitly recognizes the division between macro-prudence and micro-prudence, have we also shown that this is an Aristotelian distinction? Or does Aquinas depart from Aristotle on this point? Readers of Aristotle are unlikely to doubt that micro-prudence is Aristotelian; they are more likely to doubt the claim that Aristotle recognizes the functions of macro-prudence as genuine tasks for prudence.

To see how Aristotle recognizes a task for macro-prudence, we ought to remind ourselves of three connected claims in the *Ethics*: (1) Political science and prudence are the very same cognitive state, though the two names refer to different aspects of it (1141b23–4). (2) Both general legislation and judgements about particular situations belong to political science (1141b24–9). (3) The *Ethics* itself is a work of political science (1094b10–11). These remarks imply that the sort of reflection that is contained in the *Ethics* is itself an example of prudential thinking.

This claim about the scope of prudence is consistent with Aristotle's view that prudence is deliberative and considers means to ends. For Aristotle begins the *Ethics* by introducing the ultimate end, and by inviting us to consider what this is; he encourages us to do this with the thought that it will make a great difference to the way we lead our lives (1094a20–7). The deliberative task we face is how to achieve the ultimate end, and more precisely (as Aristotle explains) what we must do to achieve happiness. The result of deliberation is the election of specifically virtuous ends. As Aquinas says, 'the ends proper to the virtues are directed towards happiness as the ultimate end; and in this way there can be election of them' (1–2, q13, a3 ad 1). There can be election of ends in so far as they are directed towards the ultimate end (q13, a3 ad 2); and for this reason it is appropriate to speak of deliberation and election of virtues.[38] Our natural focus on happiness directs us towards a complete end, and we acquire no merit simply by pursuing that: 'but what that completion consists in, whether in the virtues, or in knowledge, or in pleasures, or in other things of this sort, is not determined for one by nature' (*De Veritate* q22, a7), and so we can acquire merit by following one view of what happiness consists in rather than another. In order to form the right conception of happiness, we must rely on deliberation.

These passages on deliberation and happiness explain why Aquinas is entitled to claim that macro-prudence takes us from the universal end

---

[38] I have discussed this aspect of Aquinas's position in 'The Scope of Deliberation: A Conflict in Aquinas', *Review of Metaphysics*, 44 (1990), 21–42.

grasped by natural reason to the specifically virtuous end. He can assign this task to the deliberative virtue of macro-prudence because he has a sufficiently broad conception of deliberation. He describes prudence in general terms as considering 'those things by which one achieves happiness' (1–2, q66, a5 ad 2). If prudence considers this question in its full generality, then it must include macro-prudence, which deliberates about different possible conceptions of happiness.

Aristotle's claims are intelligible if he recognizes macro-prudence as well as micro-prudence. When he attends to the connection between prudence and judgement about particular situations, he seems to have micro-prudence in mind. When he connects prudence with political science, he seems to be thinking of macro-prudence. Aquinas is entitled to claim an Aristotelian basis for his view that prudence takes us from the universal end to the specifically virtuous end. This is a task for macro-prudence, whereas micro-prudence takes us from the specifically virtuous end to the right actions. Macro-prudence begins from the precept of acting in accordance with reason and reaches the conclusion that we should (for instance) modify our tendency to fear so that we are ready to face danger in the right causes. This deliberation reaches the conclusion that bravery is a virtue to be cultivated. Micro-prudence is not concerned with any of these questions. It assumes that bravery is a virtue, and considers what the brave course of action would be in these particular circumstances.

9. The Task of Macro-Prudence

If we understand how Aristotle and Aquinas conceive macro-prudence, we may still doubt whether there is really any such thing, or, at least, whether it could reach the results that they expect from it. Can we realistically expect to begin our deliberation from a rather thin conception of happiness as the ultimate end and reach a conception of the specifically virtuous end?

To answer this question, we need to consider whether Aquinas argues convincingly, or has the resources to argue convincingly, that reflection on the aims and nature of a rational human agent shows that we need the different virtues of character that he recognizes. Broadly speaking, bravery and temperance strengthen and support one's correct rational goals against impediments and distraction, while justice forms our will so that we see our good in pursuing the good of others, and not in treating them simply as instruments or rivals.

To fill in this outline, and to show that it is correctly filled in with arguments for the virtues, is a complicated task that both requires close attention to the details of Aquinas's discussion and requires some reflection on arguments that might be used to replace or supplement parts of his discussion. I will confine myself to the claim that Aquinas's general aim is reasonable enough to make it worth our while to see what would follow if he could carry it out.

Even if we are willing to concede this much to Aquinas, however, we may doubt whether he is right about the relation of prudence to the moral agent and to moral virtues. Macro-prudence and micro-prudence seem to be two distinct virtues, since it seems that someone could be good at one of these deliberative tasks and bad at the other. Indeed, we might wonder whether macro-prudence is really a virtue of a moral agent at all. It seems to belong to a moral theorist who is asking what states of character are virtues and how to produce them. Both Aristotle and Aquinas ask these questions, and they display macro-prudence in reaching the right answers. But the ability to find the right answers at this high level does not seem to guarantee the ability or the experience that is needed to find answers about what to do in particular situations. Equally, it seems quite possible for someone to be a virtuous person who has the right ends and knows what to do to act on them in particular situations, without the macro-prudence that would provide an answer to the theorist's question.

If macro-prudence and micro-prudence are really the same virtue, then the theorist who constructs the *Nicomachean Ethics* displays the same deliberative virtue (if its conclusions are true and reached by appropriate arguments) that the virtuous agent displays in deciding what to do here and now, and the virtue of the virtuous agent is not complete without the understanding of the theorist. This conclusion has seemed so implausible to many interpreters that they have refused to ascribe it to Aristotle, and so they have denied that he accepts all the premisses.[39] Aquinas makes this issue all the clearer; for he distinguishes the universal end from the specifically virtuous end, and so points out the difference between the two functions of prudence. It is easy to conclude that separable types of knowledge belong to the two forms of prudence, and that only micro-prudence is a genuine moral virtue.

10. The Unity of Prudence

To see whether Aquinas can show that macro-prudence is a virtue of a moral agent, we may turn to his defence of the claim that prudence is a

---

[39] See S. W. Broadie, *Ethics with Aristotle* (Oxford: Univ. Press, 1991), 199: 'The person of practical wisdom would have (on such a theory) to be a philosopher or to have absorbed the teachings of philosophers. How else would he or she come by that comprehensive vision? . . . But in *EN* VI he [sc. Aristotle] shows no sign of holding that practical virtue itself, which includes practical wisdom, necessarily presupposes a command of philosophical ethics.'

virtue that is necessary to a human being. If his defence is cogent, and if it is applies to macro-prudence as well as micro-prudence, then he is entitled to claim that we ought to expect macro-prudence from moral agents as well as from moral theorists.

Aquinas argues that virtue requires not simply doing good actions, but acting well (*bene operari*, 1–2, q57, a5). We do not act well if we simply rely on other people's deliberation, because in that case 'one's own action is not yet completely perfected as far as concerns reason that directs and desire that sets us in motion' (1–2, q57, a5 ad 2). Virtuous agents do not simply take it for granted that their actions are right; they can give some rational account of the rightness of their actions. Moreover, their motives cannot simply be those that are effective in producing the right actions; they must also include the right sort of desire for the right features of the right actions.

These general demands on a virtuous agent require macro-prudence as well as micro-prudence. For if we deliberate for ourselves about how to fulfil the specifically virtuous end, but we rely on other people's deliberation to form the specifically virtuous end, then (by the argument presented here) we still do not have our own reason completely perfected.[40] Nor do we have our own desire completely perfected if we lack macro-prudence; for we will not be concerned about the properties of actions that make them contribute to the ultimate end. If Aquinas is right in his demand for the perfection of desire and reason, then he must demand macro-prudence.

Aquinas's argument about the importance of one's own deliberation and the perfection of one's own reason may well seem to rest on an unreasonably demanding conception of perfect virtue. This reaction, however, may be too hasty. His demand expresses, even if it exaggerates, a reasonable claim about the virtues. If he is right, then we may sometimes justifiably regard people as having less than a complete virtue if they do not see the point of the virtue and the actions it requires, and do not see how it ought to co-operate with the other virtues. Aquinas provides many relevant examples in his discussion of such virtues as bravery, magnificence, and magnanimity in the *Secunda Secundae* (qq 123–35). Many of the objections that he answers are derived from a conception of these virtues that, in his view, needs to be corrected by reference to other moral beliefs. These other beliefs explain why, for instance, bravery can be displayed by a martyr as well as by a soldier (2–2, q124, a2), and why the virtue of magnanimity does not conflict with the virtue of humility (q129, a3 ad 4). In these cases we will not understand what a particular virtue requires unless we have

---

[40] In 2–2, q47, a14 Aquinas explains why this does not mean that everyone has to be able to work out everything for himself. We can exercise prudence in choosing good advisers and in discriminating good advice from bad.

some macro-prudence; and if we have too narrow a conception of what a particular virtue requires, we will have the virtue imperfectly.

It is fairly easy to give more modern examples of the kind of thing Aquinas has in mind. The sense of honour that leads some characters in nineteenth-century novels to suppose that insults need to be avenged by duelling, or that gambling debts have to be paid first, or that different standards of fidelity apply to husbands and wives, turns out to rest on misunderstandings of the nature and point of different virtues and of their relation to each other. More recently, the assumption that concern for fairness and justice requires exclusive attention to merits and qualifications, narrowly conceived, can be challenged in various ways; one reasonable challenge argues that the assumption rests on a misconception of the nature of the relevant virtues and of their connection to other virtues and principles.

No doubt these examples are more heterogeneous than I have made them appear, and they do not support any simple claim about what can reasonably be expected of a virtuous person. I appeal to them, however, in order to suggest that it is difficult to divide the concerns of micro-prudence from those of macro-prudence, or the concerns of the moral agent from those of the moral theorist. Aquinas's suggestion that virtuous agents need macro-prudence to carry out the correct deliberation does not betray any exaggeration, or any tendency to confuse the agent with the theorist. While it would be exaggerated to suggest that a virtuous agent must be able to construct the sort of theory that Aristotle or Aquinas constructs, it is not exaggerated to suggest that a virtuous agent must understand (perhaps without formulating) the sorts of considerations that concern the theorist. Aquinas's own discussion of the virtuous illustrates this role for macro-prudence in influencing the outlook of agents on their virtues.

11. *Macro-Prudence and the Reciprocity of the Virtues*

I have examined Aquinas's claims about prudence at some length, because they affect his argument for RV. The fact that each virtue requires prudence would not support RV if prudence had a merely generic unity; for it might turn out that each virtue requires nothing more than its own independent species of prudence. If, however, Aquinas is right about the function of macro-prudence and about the inseparability of micro-prudence and macro-prudence, and we agree that macro-prudence can reasonably be demanded of a completely virtuous agent, then he has a much stronger case for RV.

Macro-prudence, according to Aquinas, aims at achieving the ultimate good. The genuinely virtuous person has to have the right conception of the end for the sake of which she does her different virtuous actions; the correct conception of this end, as Aristotle insists, is prudence (*EN* 1142b31–3). In

Aquinas's view, following Aristotle, prudence is concerned with 'the whole of human life' (*in EN* #1163); in explaining this, he adds that the end grasped by prudence is 'the common end of all of human life' (*in EN* #1233). This common end must be grasped if one is to have the right conception of the end that is needed for practical reasoning (1144a31–6; cf. Aquinas, *in EN* #1273–4). Grasp of this common end distinguishes the prudence that is peculiar to the virtuous person from the imperfect prudence (finding means to an end regarded as good) that is present in virtuous and in vicious people alike (2–2, q47, a13).

This common end is needed for the unity of prudence. Aquinas sees that Aristotle must recognize a common end if he is to appeal to prudence in support of RV. To answer the objection that prudence has a merely generic unity, Aquinas argues that the virtues are connected in so far as they are all about passions and actions that are clearly connected to one another (1–2, q65, a1 ad 3; *Virt. card.* a2 ad 4). This does not seem enough to show that prudence is more than generically unified. Aquinas has to add that the virtues are connected through the common end of human life, and that the correct conception of this single common end is required for every virtue.[41] He describes the common end of human life when he describes the ulti-mate good and the argument that leads us from it to an account of the virtues; this is the process that he has in mind when he says that the proper ends of the virtues are directed towards happiness as their ultimate end, and therefore there can be election of them (1–2, q13, a3 ad 1).

Once Aquinas secures this point, he has a good reason to claim that each virtue is internally connected to the other virtues. For when prudence forms the point of view of each virtue in the light of deliberation about the ultimate good, it thereby brings to bear the point of view of the other virtues. This is not an accidental connection between prudence and the virtues; for a state of character is shown to be a genuine virtue in so far as it is shown to be needed in the light of the requirements of prudence. Each virtue, therefore, has to incorporate the points of view of the other virtues, in so far as it incorporates the requirements of prudence.[42]

[41] This claim about prudence and RV is made explicit by Godfrey of Fontaines. See Lottin, *Psychologie*, iv. 595 f. (lines 217–37).

[42] Two questions might be raised about this argument: (1) If virtues are identified as the states that are demanded by prudence, does it not become rather trivial to claim that each virtue includes the point of view of all the others? (2) Even if each virtue includes the point of view of the others to the extent of recognizing their demands, surely this does not imply that if we are disposed to act on the demands of one virtue, we are also disposed to act on the demands of the others, so that it does not yet imply RV? In answer to the first question, we may concede that it follows from the Aristotelian concepts of virtue and prudence that each virtue incorporates the demands of prudence; but it is by no means trivial that the virtues meeting this criterion coincide with the virtues we ordinarily recognize, and both Aristotle and Aquinas argue for the coincidence. In answer to the second question, we need to consider the connection between being disposed to act on the virtues and grasping the requirements of prudence; this is an aspect of RV that I cannot, or at least will not, discuss here.

Virtuous agents, therefore, see the ways in which different virtues affect one another, and the ways in which the virtues together promote the final good. The requirements of justice, for instance, determine which causes make it appropriate to face danger, and so they influence the brave person's conception of why it is worth facing this danger and not worth facing that one. Moreover, the requirements of justice preserve a human community with a specific form of social life that can be shown to contribute to the human good; that is why the requirements of justice can legitimately be allowed to influence the requirements of bravery.

If Aquinas is right about this, then he has an answer to the arguments of Scotus and Ockham. Though they point out that we can recognize some motivational and deliberative aspects of virtue without endorsing RV, the motivational and deliberative aspects that they recognize do not satisfy Aquinas's demand for perfected desire and reason. For agents who lack macro-prudence cannot explain why these actions are really brave, or why co-operation with other virtues requires these actions; since they cannot explain these things themselves, they must rely on the deliberation of others.

Aquinas's argument to show that virtue requires prudence presents an important objection to the position of Scotus and Ockham. While their position initially appears more plausible and realistic than RV, it fails to explain some requirements that we apply in thinking about virtues. We do not apply these requirements on every occasion; we can recognize everyday virtuous acts, and take the virtue of the agent for granted, without demanding everything that Aquinas demands of the virtuous agent. But it would be a mistake to confine our attention to easy and everyday cases; states of character are revealed by difficult and testing situations (as Aristotle remarks, following Bias, *EN* 1130a1–2), and in these situations we can see that Aquinas's requirements are relevant, and the opponents of RV demand too little.

If this is the right way to understand the demands of RV, then we can defend it against some of the objections that appeal to historical and psychological counter-evidence. To say that virtuous agents must grasp the relation of a particular virtue to other virtues, and must guide their actions by their grasp of those relations, is not to claim that they must display all the virtues to an equal degree, or that their situations will require the actions characteristic of all the virtues. We may reasonably think of people 'specializing' in different virtues; the social and psychological facts may make specialization mandatory or desirable. But we can be specialized in one virtue without ignoring the claims of other virtues; and the demand for virtuous agents to attend to the claims of the different virtues is the central demand that makes RV plausible. The demand imposed by RV is certainly exacting, and we cannot take it for granted that even the people conventionally regarded as exemplars of the virtues have actually met this demand. But while it is exacting, it is neither unrealistic nor unreasonable.

12. Eudaemonism and the Unity of Prudence

The defence of RV by appeal to the unity of prudence marks a central disagreement between Aquinas and Scotus. According to Scotus, there is no common end that is the aim of all of the virtues or of every branch of prudence. For, in his view, the will aims either at the advantageous, if it follows our natural inclination, or at the just, if it exercises its freedom.[43] Since some of the moral virtues aim at the agent's own advantage, and some aim at the advantage of others, some appeal to our affection for advantage, and others appeal to our affection for the just. Scotus recognizes no comprehensive end regulating our tendency to follow these two affections; for the will has no further reason for following the affection for the just in these cases and the affection for advantage in other cases. If Scotus were to admit the sort of 'common end of all of human life' that Aquinas recognizes for the virtues and prudence, he would deprive himself of one of his arguments against Aquinas's eudaemonism.

Since Scotus rejects eudaemonism, he loses the sorts of reasons that persuade Aquinas to insist on RV. For Aquinas believes that reference to some single comprehensive end is necessary for rational willing; and so, if the virtuous person's deliberations are to conform to the conditions for rational willing, they must also refer to some single comprehensive end. Since Scotus firmly rejects any such condition on rational willing, he has no reason to agree that there would be anything defective about the virtuous person's deliberation if they did not refer to a comprehensive end; and so he has no reason to insist on RV.

It may seem rather hasty to suggest that acceptance of the unity of macro-prudence is necessary and sufficient for the acceptance of eudaemonism. Clearly Aquinas believes he has settled the truth of eudaemonism long before he raises any questions about RV and about the unity of prudence; and the issues about RV may appear not to tell one way or the other about eudaemonism. Even if the arguments and examples I offered to support Aquinas's claim that virtue requires macro-prudence were at all plausible, they did not seem to depend on acceptance of eudaemonism. Those arguments suggested that a virtuous person needs to see the point of different virtues and the ways in which one virtue may modify our views of the actions required by another; and we might apparently be convinced by

---

[43] See Wolter, *John Duns Scotus*, 178, 194–6, 468–70.

such arguments even if we do not believe that the virtues are connected to each other because they are all connected to some ultimate end. Aquinas, therefore, seems to go too fast in moving from the unity of macro-prudence to belief in a common end of human life that is to be identified with happiness. Conversely, Scotus seems to go too fast in moving from the rejection of eudaemonism to the rejection of the unity of macro-prudence.

I agree with this criticism of both Aquinas and Scotus, but I believe their moves, though hasty, are defensible. If we agree with Aquinas on macro-prudence, and accept his suggestion that the aims of the different virtues are connected and mutually supportive, we are not very far from accepting the assumptions about practical reason that underlie his belief in an ulti-mate end; in fact his belief in an ultimate end simply extends this picture of the virtuous person's reasoning to rational action in general. To show that this claim is correct, I would need to discuss the nature and grounds of Aquinas's belief in an ultimate end. I will not try to do that here. I will simply end by suggesting that Aquinas's view of macro-prudence and his eudaemonism support each other. If this is true, then examination of issues about the reciprocity of the virtues helps us to see the rather impressive coherence of the Aristotelian account of practical reason and of the virtues. If it is right to suggest that RV is more plausible than it may initially appear, then its plausibility may reasonably lead us to look more favourably on the whole Aristotelian account of practical reason.[44]

[44] I am grateful for comments from audiences at the conference in St Andrews, at the Warburg Institute, University of London, and at the University of Illinois, Chicago; from the editors of this volume; and from Richard Kraut, David Brink, Marco Zingano, and Jennifer Whiting.

8

The Normativity of Instrumental Reason

CHRISTINE M. KORSGAARD

1. The Problem

Most philosophers think it is both uncontroversial and unproblematic that practical reason requires us to take the means to our ends. If doing a certain action is necessary for or even just promotes a person's aims, the person obviously has at least a prima-facie reason to do it. Just as obviously, this reason is what we nowadays call an 'internal' reason, one which is capable of motivating the person to whom it applies. So those who hold that practical reasons *must* be internal point to the instrumental principle as a clear case of a source of reasons which pass that test.[1] But philosophers have, for the most part, been silent on the question of the normative foundation of this requirement. The interesting question, almost everyone agrees, is whether practical reason requires anything *more* of us than this.

In fact, in the philosophical tradition, three kinds of principles have been proposed as requirements of practical reason. First, there is the instrumental principle itself. Kant, one of the few philosophers who does discuss its foundation, identifies the instrumental principle as a kind of hypothetical imperative, a technical (*technisch*) imperative. But the instrumental principle is nowadays widely taken to extend to ways of realizing ends that are not in the technical sense 'means', for instance to what is sometimes called 'constitutive' reasoning. Say that my end is outdoor exercise; here is an opportunity to go hiking, which is outdoor exercise; therefore I have reason to take this opportunity, not strictly speaking as a means to my end,

---

[1] See e.g. Bernard Williams in 'Internal and External Reasons', in Williams, *Moral Luck* (Cambridge: Univ. Press, 1981), ch. 8, pp. 101–13. For a thorough discussion of the varieties of internalism, see Robert Audi, Essay 5 in this volume. Audi's focus, however, is on the internalism of moral judgements, while I am talking about the internalism of reasons or reason judgements more generally. In recent years, the literature on internalism has become increasingly intricate, and the *point* of settling the question whether a given type of consideration is 'internal' or not has become somewhat obscure. In my own view, practical reasons *must* be internal in the sense given in the text, and therefore the point of settling the question whether moral considerations or judgements are internal is that they cannot be regarded as *reasons* unless they are. As I will argue in Sect. 3, however, showing that a consideration is internal, although necessary, is not sufficient to show that it is a reason.

but as a way of realizing it. This is a helpful suggestion, but it should be handled with care. Taken to extremes, it makes it seem as if any case in which your action is guided by the application of a name or a concept to a particular is an instance of instrumental reasoning. Compare, for example: I need a hammer; *this* is a hammer; therefore I shall take *this*, not as a means to my end but as a way of realizing it. In this way the instrumental principle may be extended to cover *any* case of action that is self-conscious, in the sense that the agent is guided by a conception of what she is doing.[2] Now I do think that this is a natural way to extend the instrumental principle, and later I will suggest that this fact throws light on its foundation. But there is also a danger that such extensions will conceal important differences among the distinctive forms of reasoning by which human beings can be motivated.[3]

Second, there is what I will call the principle of prudence, which is sometimes identified with self-interest.[4] This principle concerns the ways in which we harmonize the pursuit of our various ends. Its correct formulation or extension is a matter of controversy. Some philosophers think it requires us to maximize the sum total of our satisfactions or pleasures over the course of our whole lives; others, that it requires us merely to give some

---

[2] Kant also called the technical imperative an imperative of skill, so one might put the point I am making here this way: The instrumental principle is now seen as requiring us to exercise not merely skill, but also judgement, in the pursuit of our ends. But any self-conscious action must be guided by judgement. Some of Aristotle's examples of practical syllogisms are explicitly like the example in the text. Consider for example: 'I want to drink, says appetite; this is drink, says sense or imagination or thought: straightaway I drink.' (*The Movement of Animals* 701a33–4, trans. by A. S. L. Farquharson in Jonathan Barnes (ed.), *The Complete Works of Aristotle: The Revised Oxford Translation* (Oxford: Univ. Press, 1984)). Or consider the notorious 'dry food' syllogism of *Nicomachean Ethics* 7, in which Aristotle toys with the idea that weakness of will occurs in a man who believes that 'Dry food is good for any man' when he reasons that 'I am a man' and 'such and such food is dry' but then fails to exercise the knowledge that 'this food is such and such' (*Nicomachean Ethics* 7, 1147a1–10; trans. by W. D. Ross and rev. by J. O. Urmson in *The Complete Works of Aristotle*). In these cases, there is no question of using technical means, but simply of the application of a principle to a case or a concept to a particular. This fact throws light on what Aristotle meant when he said that practical reasoning is not about ends but about what contributes to them (*EN* 3, 1112b12): in particular, it suggests that this remark is not meant to imply *any* limitation in the scope of practical reasoning. See also my 'From Duty and for the Sake of the Noble: Kant and Aristotle on Morally Good Action', in Stephen Engstrom and Jennifer Whiting (eds.), *Aristotle, Kant, and the Stoics: Rethinking Happiness and Duty* (Cambridge: Univ. Press, 1996).

[3] This is a difficulty, I think, in the strategy Williams adopts in 'Internal and External Reasons'. His argument seems to show that only natural extensions of the instrumental principle can meet the internalism requirement, but he is prepared to extend the instrumental principle so far that this turns out to be no limitation at all. See my 'Skepticism about Practical Reason', ch. 11 in Korsgaard, *Creating the Kingdom of Ends* (Cambridge: Univ. Press, 1996). Interestingly, however, the view I defend in this essay also tends to break down the distinctions among the different principles of practical reason. See n. 73.

[4] As others have noticed, we use the term 'prudence' confusingly, to refer both to attention to self-interested reasons and to attention to one's future reasons, whether or not they are self-interested. (See Nagel, in *The Possibility of Altruism* (Princeton: Univ. Press, 1970), 36.) Since I am not taking a stand on the formulation of the principle of prudence here, I don't bother to sort through this issue in the text.

weight, possibly discounted, to the ends and reasons we will have in the future as well as the ones we have now. Derek Parfit's 'present aim' theory requires only that we try to satisfy our 'present' desires, projects, and aims to as great an extent as possible.[5] The common element in all of these formulations is that they serve to remind us that we characteristically have more than one aim, and that rationality requires us to take this into account when we deliberate. We should deliberate not only about how to realize the aim that occupies us right now, but also about how doing so will affect the possibility of realizing our other aims. The principle of prudence is often understood as a requirement that we should deliberate in light of what is best for us on the whole, or of what I will call our 'overall good', where that is conceived as a special sort of higher-order *end* to which more particular ends serve, in an extended sense, as means. Partly because he has something like this in mind, Kant supposes that the principle of prudence is also a hypothetical imperative.[6]

Finally, of course, many philosophers have claimed that moral principles, which Kant identifies as categorical imperatives, represent requirements of practical reason. If all of these claims are true, we exhibit practical irrationality in failing to take the means to our ends; in pursuing local satisfactions at the expense of our overall good; and in acting immorally.

In the *Groundwork*, Kant asks 'How are all these imperatives possible?' What he wants to know, he explains, is 'how the necessitation of the will expressed by the imperative in setting a task can be conceived'.[7] In other words, Kant seeks an explanation of the normative force of all *three* kinds of imperatives, of their ability to set us the 'task' of performing certain actions. But this approach has not usually been followed in the Anglo-American tradition. Empiricist moral philosophers, as well the social scientists who have followed in their footsteps, have characteristically assumed that hypothetical imperatives do not require any philosophical justification, while categorical imperatives are mysterious and apparently external constraints on our conduct. Moral requirements, they think, must therefore be given a foundation in one of two ways. Either we must show that they are based on the supposedly uncontroversial hypothetical imperatives—say,

---

[5] Parfit, *Reasons and Persons* (Oxford: Clarendon Press, 1984) esp. ch. 6, sect. 45.

[6] Kant's other (and I think better) reason for regarding the imperative of prudence as hypothetical is that it holds only conditionally—it may be overridden when duty demands that we do something contrary to our interest. As some of the things I will say later suggest, I think that there are problems about understanding the principle of prudence as a hypothetical imperative and that Kant's account of this principle is in need of revision. Unfortunately I cannot give full treatment to the complex question of the status of prudence here.

[7] Kant, *Groundwork of the Metaphysics of Morals*, 417 in the pagination of the Prussian Academy Edition (Berlin: de Gruyter, 1902–) found in the margins of most translations. The translation I have used is James Ellington, *Grounding for the Metaphysics of Morals* (Indianapolis: Hackett, 1981). Hereinafter cited as e.g. *G* 417.

218 *Christine M. Korsgaard*

by showing that moral conduct is in our interest and so is required by the principle of prudence—or we must give them some sort of ontological foundation, by positing the existence of certain normative facts or entities to which moral requirements somehow refer.[8] The first option is the empiricist's own preferred method; while the second, moral realist option, represents the road taken by the dogmatic rationalists of the eighteenth century, as well as by many contemporary philosophers. Some philosophers with sympathies to the rationalist tradition—most notably Butler in the eighteenth century and Nagel in the twentieth—have pointed out that prudence, no less than morality, needs a normative foundation, and have proposed to throw light on the foundation of morality by investigating that of prudence. Parallel accounts of these two forms of normativity, they suggest, may be constructed.[9] But the instrumental principle has received very little attention from anyone.

One of the things I wish to do in this essay is to offer a diagnosis of this situation. Part of the problem is that empiricist philosophers and their social scientific followers have obscured the difference between the instrumental principle and the principle of prudence by making the handy but unwarranted assumption that a person's overall good is what he 'really' wants. Prudent action is then just a matter of taking the means to your *true* end; and the instrumental principle is the only non-moral imperative we need. I will say more about this in Section 2. More importantly, both empiricists and rationalists have supposed that the instrumental principle itself either needs no justification or has an essentially trivial one. Specifically, they have thought that the 'necessitation of the will' to which Kant refers can be conceived either as a form of causal necessity or as a response to logical necessity. Empiricists who conceive it as a form of causal necessity suppose that the instrumental principle is either obviously normative or does not need to be normative because we are reliably motivated to take the means to our ends. Instrumental thoughts cause motives. Rationalists who conceive it as a response to logical necessity suppose that conformity to the instrumental principle is normative because 'whoever wills the end also wills the means' is an analytic or logical truth, to which a rational agent as such conforms his will.

Behind these two accounts of instrumental reason lie two implicitly held conceptions of what it means for a person to be practically rational in

---

[8] As suggested for instance by John Mackie in *Ethics: Inventing Right and Wrong* (Harmondsworth: Penguin, 1977).

[9] Butler, *Fifteen Sermons Preached at the Rolls Chapel*, esp. sermons 1–3; and Nagel, *The Possibility of Altruism*. A parallel between the two problems is also suggested by Sidgwick in *The Methods of Ethics*, 7th edn. (Indianapolis: Hackett, 1981), 418–19, and, following him, by Parfit in *Reasons and Persons*, 307 ff.

general. On an empiricist view, to be practically rational is to be caused to act in a certain way—specifically, to have motives which are caused by the recognition of certain truths which are made relevant to action by one's pre-existing motives.[10] On a rationalist view, by contrast, to be rational is to deliberately conform one's will to certain rational truths, or truths about reasons, which exist independently of the will. In this essay I will argue that neither of these general conceptions of practical rationality yields an adequate account of instrumental rationality. A practical reason must function both as a motive and as a guide, or a requirement. I will show that the empiricist account explains how instrumental reasons can motivate us, but at the price of making it impossible to see how they could function as requirements or guides. The rationalist account, on the other hand, allows instrumental reasons to function as guides, but at the price of making it impossible for us to see any special reason why we should be motivated to follow these guides.[11]

Kant is usually thought of as a rationalist, but the Kantian conception of practical rationality represents a third and distinct alternative. According to the Kantian conception, to be rational *just is* to be autonomous. That is: to be governed by reason, and to govern yourself, are one and the same thing. The principles of practical reason are *constitutive* of autonomous action: they do not represent external *restrictions* on our actions, whose power to motivate us is therefore inexplicable, but instead *describe* the procedures involved in autonomous willing. But they also function as normative or guiding principles, because in following these procedures we are guiding ourselves.

The course of my argument requires an explanation. In Section 2, I argue against the empiricist view, focusing on the Humean texts which are usually taken to be its *locus classicus*. In Section 3, I argue both *against* the dogmatic rationalist view, and *for* the Kantian view, through a discussion of Kant's own remarks about instrumental rationality in the second section of the *Groundwork*. This structure is dictated in part by a fact about Kant's own development.[12] At the time he wrote the *Groundwork*, Kant's views

---

[10] The clearest statement of this view is again that of Williams in 'Internal and External Reasons'. The cumbersome phrase in the text is an attempt to do justice to Williams's attempt to express this theory in a way that leaves it open what forms of practical reason there are.

[11] The rationalist may of course speculate or stipulate that in so far as we are rational we must be motivated by the (alleged) principles of reason, and in this way meet the internalism requirement, but this leaves their power to motivate us essentially inexplicable. I discuss the difficulties with this sort of stipulation in Sect. 3. I believe that in 'Skepticism about Practical Reason' I may give the impression that I think a stipulation of this kind sufficient to meet the worries of those who complain that moral principles do not meet the internalism requirement. I don't believe that, although I now think, as I will explain later, that the real worry behind the internalism requirement is inadequately expressed by that requirement. In fact this shows up in the fact that the internalism requirement may be met by such a stipulation, but that this does not resolve the real worry.

[12] It is also partly dictated by the unavailability (at least as far as I know) of detailed discussions of the instrumental principle by the dogmatic rationalists themselves.

were in a transitional stage, and traces of the dogmatic rationalist view can be found in what he says, especially in this part of the text. By seeing what goes wrong with his early presentation of the instrumental principle, we are led to the mature Kantian view, which traces both instrumental reason and moral reason to a common normative source: the autonomy or self-government of the rational agent.[13]

My arguments for these points have another implication which I will be concerned to bring out in the course of the essay, namely, that the instrumental principle cannot stand alone. Unless there are normative principles directing us to the adoption of certain ends, there can be no requirement to take the means to our ends. The familiar view that the instrumental principle is the *only* requirement of practical reason is incoherent.

2. *Hume and the Empiricist Account*

It is common among empiricists to equate the question whether pure reason can be practical with the question whether we are ever motivated by belief alone. The impetus for this view comes from the so-called 'belief/desire' model of rational action. When we act in accordance with hypothetical imperatives, it is alleged, motivation is provided by the combination of a belief and a desire: say, I desire to avert the toothache foreseen, I believe that a trip to the dentist will enable me to do so, so I am motivated to go to the dentist. Since categorical imperatives are by definition not based on the presupposition of an existing desire, we must in following them be motivated by belief alone: perhaps simply the belief that a certain action is right or wrong, or, in a more complicated story, a belief, say, that someone else is in need.[14] Since the idea of being motivated by belief alone seems mysterious, the suspicion arises that categorical imperatives cannot meet the internalism requirement, and they are therefore supposed to be especially problematic.

But as Nagel points out in *The Possibility of Altruism*, the specifically rational character of going to the dentist to avert an unwanted toothache depends on *how* the belief and the desire are 'combined'. It is certainly not enough to say that they jointly *cause* the action, or that their bare co-presence effects a motive, for a person might be conditioned so that he responds in totally crazy ways to the co-presence of certain beliefs and

---

[13] At the end of Sect. 2, I will argue that even within the confines of a reconstructed Humean account, the normativity of the instrumental principle must be traced to the agent's self-government, specifically to his capacity to be motivated to shape his character in accordance with an ideal of virtue. So this is actually not just a point about how a Kantian account of reason works.

[14] I have in mind Nagel's account, in *The Possibility of Altruism*, although his view more strictly speaking is that we can be directly motivated by beliefs about other people's *reasons*.

desires. In Nagel's own example, a person has been conditioned so that whenever he wants a drink and believes the object before him is a pencil sharpener, he wants to put a coin into the pencil sharpener.[15] Here the co-presence of belief and desire reliably lead to a certain action, but the action is a mad one. What is the difference between this person and one who, rationally, wants to put a coin in a soda machine when she wants a drink? One may be tempted to say that a soda machine, unlike a pencil sharpener, is the source of a drink, so that the right kind of conceptual connection between the desire and the belief obtains. But so far that is only to note a fact about the relationship between the belief and the desire themselves, and that says nothing about the rationality of the *person* who is influenced by them. If the belief and desire still operate on that person merely by having a certain causal efficacy when co-present, the rational action is only accidentally or externally different from the mad one. After all, a person may be conditioned to do the correct thing as well as the incorrect thing; but the correctness of what she is conditioned to do does not make *her* any more rational. So neither the joint causal efficacy of the belief and the desire, nor the existence of an appropriate conceptual connection between them, nor the bare conjunction of these two facts, enables us to judge that a person acts rationally. For the person to act rationally, she must be motivated by her own *recognition* of the appropriate conceptual connection between the belief and the desire. We may say that she *herself* must combine the belief and the desire in the right way. A person acts rationally, then, only when her action is the expression of her own mental activity, and not merely the result of the operation of beliefs and desires *in* her.[16]

As a preliminary formulation of this point, let us say that a rational agent is one who is motivated by what I will call the *rational necessity* of doing something, say, of taking the means to an end, and who acts accordingly. Such an agent is *guided* by reason, and in particular, guided by what reason presents as necessary.[17] A comparison will help to illustrate the point. If all women are mortal, and I am a woman, then it necessarily follows that I am mortal. That is logical necessity. But if I *believe* that all women are mortal, and I *believe* that I am a woman, then I *ought* to conclude that I am mortal. The necessity embodied in that use of 'ought' is rational necessity. If I am

---

[15] Ibid. *The Possibility of Altruism*, 33–4.

[16] This point is related to an idea which Michael Smith emphasizes in Essay 10 in this volume, namely, that part of what is involved in regarding and interacting with someone as a person who has and is responsible for his beliefs is attributing to him the capacity to recognize and respond appropriately to the norms that govern belief. See especially p. 296.

[17] I characterize this as a 'preliminary formulation' since I am ultimately going to argue that a rational agent is guided by herself, that is, that being governed by reason amounts to being self-governed.

guided by reason, then I will conclude that I am mortal.[18] But of course it is not logically necessary that I accept this conclusion, for if it were, it would be impossible for me to fail to accept it. And it is perfectly possible for someone to fail to accept the logical implications of her own beliefs, even when those are pointed out to her. A rational believer is *guided* by reason in the determination of her beliefs. A rational agent would be *guided* by reason in the choice of her actions.[19]

But reason, in turn, is often thought to be guided by the passions; indeed, according to Hume, to be the slave of the passions. And empiricists who endorse the view that reason plays only an instrumental role in action commonly claim Hume as the founding father of their view.[20] Hume's view, however, seems to have a much more radical implication than that. The rationality of an action, I have just suggested, depends upon the agent's being motivated by her own recognition of the rational necessity of doing the action. But Hume repeatedly asserts that there is only one co-herent sense to be given to the idea of necessity.[21] All necessity is causal necessity, in Hume's somewhat special sense: the necessity with which observers draw the conclusion that the effect will follow from the cause.[22] Accordingly, it looks as if all Hume can say is that the person is in fact caused to act by the recognition that an action will promote her end. And all that in turn means is that observers who know what the person's ends are may predict that certain conduct will follow. The person herself, the one whose behaviour is in this way predicted, is not *guided* by any dictate of reason. This suggests that Hume's view is that there is no such thing as practical reason at all.[23]

---

[18] I don't of course mean to imply that a rational agent in fact actively entertains all of the logical consequences of her beliefs, since not all such consequences are presented as necessary, or presented at all.

[19] Kant holds that a moral agent's actions are not merely in accordance with duty but done *from* it (*G* 397). One way to put the point of this paragraph is to say that a rational agent must act not merely in accordance with reason but *from* it. The rational agent has a conception of her actions as rational or at least required, called for. The debate between the rationalists and the empiricists about rationality could then be constructed as proceeding in the way their debate about the relative merits of acting in accord-ance with duty and acting from it actually did. For an account of that debate, see my 'Kant's Analysis of Obligation: The Argument of *Groundwork I*', ch. 2 of Korsgaard, *Creating the Kingdom of Ends*.

[20] Hume, *A Treatise of Human Nature*, ed. L. A. Selby-Bigge and rev. P. H. Nidditch (Oxford: Clarendon Press, 1978), 415. Hereinafter cited as e.g. *T* 415.   [21] *T* 171; *T* 400.

[22] *T* 171.

[23] Some readers may be tempted to think that Hume's special notion of causality is at fault here: Rationality must be something 'inside' of the rational agent; causal judgements, as Hume understands them, are in the eye of the beholder, and therefore rationality cannot be reduced to a certain way of being caused, on Hume's conception. But (one might think) this doesn't show that rationality cannot be a certain way of being caused on some other, more objective, conception of causality. Now I don't think that this is right. The main argument of this part of the essay, as the reader will see, does not depend in any way on Hume's special notion of causality. But something close to it is right: namely that causal judgements are essentially third-personal, and rational ones are essentially first-personal.

And in fact there is another problem with supposing that Hume could have believed in instrumental reason. The instrumental principle, because it tells us only to take the means to our ends, cannot by itself give us a reason to *do* anything. It can operate only in conjunction with some view about how our ends are determined, about what they are. It is routinely assumed, by empiricists who see themselves as followers of Hume, that absent any other contenders, our ends will be determined by what we desire. But if you hold that the instrumental principle is the *only* principle of practical rationality, you cannot also hold that desiring something is a *reason* for pursuing it. The principle: 'take as your end that which you desire' is neither the instrumental principle itself nor an application of it. If the instrumental principle is the only principle of practical reason, then to say that something is your end is not to say that you have a reason to pursue it, but at most to say that you are *going* to pursue it (perhaps inspired by desire). And this shows that the instrumental principle will be formulated in different ways, depending on whether our theory of practical reason includes principles which determine ends or not. If we allow reason a role in determining ends, then the instrumental principle will be formulated this way: 'if you have a *reason* to pursue an end then you have a reason to take the means to that end'. But if we do not allow reason a role in determining ends, then the instrumental principle has to go like this: 'if you are *going* to pursue an end, then you have a reason to take the means to that end'. Now that first formulation—if you have a *reason* to pursue an end then you have a reason to take the means to that end—derives a reason from a reason, something normative from something normative. But the second formulation—if you are *going* to pursue an end then you have a reason to take the means to that end—derives, or attempts to derive, a reason from a fact. Now if Hume believed in instrumental reason, he would have to accept the second formulation, since it is perfectly clear that he thinks that reason does not play a role in the determination of ends. He would have to believe that the instrumental principle instructs us to derive a reason from what we are *going* to do. But Hume, after all, is famous for arguing that you cannot derive an 'Ought' from an 'Is'. And in the argument

(For more on this point, see my *The Sources of Normativity* (Cambridge: Univ. Press, 1996), sect.1.2.2, pp. 16–18). This is what prevents the empiricist reduction of rationality to a form of causality. So what matters here is not, so to speak, where the cause operates, but the point of view from which we make the judgement that it operates.

It's worth noticing that a parallel argument could be constructed for theoretical reason, suggesting that Hume doesn't believe in that either. I don't take this to be a problem for my account, for I don't think that Hume believes in rational belief any more than he does in rational action. His view is that beliefs are sentiments which are caused in us by perceptions and habits. Reason doesn't really enter into it.

that follows, I will show why he is right. This seems to me to be grounds for doubting that Hume himself could have believed in instrumental reason.

Let's take as a point of comparison Hume's attitude towards the other (supposedly) hypothetical imperative, the principle of prudence. Hume clearly denies that prudence is a rational requirement. In a very famous passage, he says:

'Tis not contrary to reason for me to prefer the destruction of the whole world to the scratching of my finger. 'Tis not contrary to reason for me to chuse my total ruin, to prevent the least uneasiness of an *Indian* or person wholly unknown to me. 'Tis as little contrary to reason to prefer even *my own acknowledg'd lesser good* to my greater, and have a more ardent affection for the former than the latter.[24]

But Hume does not claim that we in fact live for the moment, like the grasshopper in the fable, and never take the future into account. He offers us an alternative explanation of what is going on when we take our future interests into account. Three passages are relevant.

First of all, there is a discussion in book I, in the section entitled: 'Of the Influence of Belief'. Flatly contradicting the belief/desire model of action, Hume argues here that beliefs operate on us in the same way that present impressions do. Hume offers this argument as evidence for his view that what distinguishes a belief from a mere idea is the fact that it is forceful and vivacious in nearly the same way that an impression is. When you are convinced, by causal reasoning, that a certain painful effect will occur, you recoil from the causes of that effect in much the same way that you would recoil from the effect itself, from present pain. You draw back from putting your hand *into* the flame with the same automatic character with which you would draw your hand *out of* the flame if it were already in. And if the painful effect would be caused by an action you propose to yourself, you recoil in just this way from performing the action. This is how the future consequences of our actions motivate us.[25] Hume describes this as a kind of middle way which nature has taken in the construction of animals. He points out that if we could be motivated only by present impressions, we would always be getting into trouble, and foresight could not help us to avoid it. On the other hand, if we were motivated indiscriminately by all of our ideas, we would never enjoy a moment's peace and tranquillity. The bare idea of fear would fill us with fear. Hume says:

Nature has, therefore, chosen a medium, and has neither bestow'd on every idea of good and evil the power of actuating the will, nor yet has entirely excluded this

---

[24] *T* 416 (second emphasis mine).

[25] In *The Possibility of Altruism* Nagel appeals to exactly this sort of belief—a belief about future desires/pleasures/reasons—to show how odd the belief/desire model is. His point is that it would be bizarre to think that we needed a special desire to give motivational or normative force to a belief about a reason we will have later. Although for different reasons, Hume would agree.

influence. Tho' an idle fiction has no efficacy, yet we find by experience, that the ideas of those objects, which we believe either are or will be existent, produce in a lesser degree the same effect with those impressions, which are immediately present to the senses and perception.[26]

What is most notable about this passage is what Hume does *not* say. He does not say that it is rational to be motivated by a belief, because you think that the object of a belief exists and therefore really is apt to affect you, while the object of a mere idea need not exist, and so there is no reason to think that it will affect you.[27] He merely says that we are in fact so constructed.

This thought is picked up later in the introduction to the discussion of the direct passions. Hume says:

The mind by an *original instinct* tends to unite itself with the good, and to avoid the evil, tho' they be conceived merely in idea, and be consider'd as to exist in any future period of time.[28]

An 'original instinct', in Hume's terminology, is a psychological tendency that admits of no further explanation. In both passages, then, Hume asserts that our tendency to act prudently is not the result of our rational nature but rather of the original instincts which nature has implanted in us.

The third passage is in the section 'On the Influencing Motives of the Will'. Here we learn that the most general form of this tendency to desire the good—'the general appetite to good, and aversion to evil, consider'd merely as such'—is a calm passion, that is, one we know more from its effects than from its emotional turbulence.[29] When we are under the influence of this calm passion we do prudent things, say, we pursue our overall good at the expense of present pleasure. Hume thinks that we tend to confuse the operation of the calm passions with the operations of reason because those are also calm. This is why we imagine that prudent conduct is a form of rational conduct: when we act under the influence of the general desire for good, our minds are calculating and cool. Nevertheless, when we are not under the influence of this calm passion, and pursue present pleasure at the expense of our overall good, there is no irrationality in the case.

From all of this it is clear that Hume thinks that it is not a requirement of reason that we should have concern for our future, but that it is natural

---

[26] *T* 119.

[27] This makes Hume sound perverse, but in fact, given his account of belief, it is a tautology. If you thought that the thing were going to affect you then you would believe in its existence; that is, that's more or less what believing it amounts to. Even apart from Hume's theory, this doesn't seem completely crazy. One plausible, if rather idealistic (in the philosophical sense) account of what is meant by claiming that something exists is that it could conceivably affect you.   [28] *T* 438, my emphasis.

[29] *T* 417.

to have such a concern. By the *original* arrangements of human nature, we have the capacity to be motivated, at least sometimes, by our beliefs about what will happen in the future. Of course a *rational* requirement of prudence, if it existed, would demand much more than this. A rational requirement of prudence would not demand merely that we give some weight, some of the time, to considerations of our overall good. It would demand that we *do* what conduces to our overall good.[30] By contrast, the calm passion which Hume calls 'the general appetite to good' is just one desire among others, which occasionally takes precedence.

But why does Hume believe this? A moment ago I quoted the famous passage in which Hume rejects the rational requirement of prudence. It continues this way:

'Tis not contrary to reason to prefer even my own acknowledg'd lesser good to my greater, and have a more ardent affection for the former than the latter. A trivial good may, from certain circumstances, produce a desire superior to what arises from the greatest and most valuable enjoyment; nor is there anything more extraordinary in this, than in mechanics to see one pound weight raise up a hundred by the advantage of its situation.[31]

Hume here appeals to the fact that a desire for present pleasure may get the better of prudence, having been rendered stronger by 'the advantage of its situation'. But how is that fact supposed to show us that prudence is not rationally required? We might take this passage to be an argument, based on the internalism requirement. Hume could be thinking that since prudence sometimes fails to motivate us, the principle of prudence fails to meet the internalism requirement, and so cannot count as a rational principle.[32] As I have argued elsewhere, however, such an argument would have to be based on a *misunderstanding* of the internalism requirement.[33] The internalism requirement can only specify that practical reasons must motivate us *in so far as* we are susceptible to the influence of reason. The requirement cannot be that a consideration must *in fact* motivate a person

---

[30] Unless, perhaps, a sacrifice of one's personal interests is required by some yet more stringent principle of reason, such as a moral principle. Hume, however, does not think that this possibility is likely to arise. See his *Enquiry concerning the Principles of Morals*, sect. IX, conclusion, part II.

[31] *T* 416.

[32] Later Hume will argue that moral considerations cannot be based on reason, because reason does not motivate and moral considerations do (*T* 457). This suggests that he accepts internalism about moral considerations. Of course, it also suggests that he thinks reason cannot motivate us, generally speaking, and that may make the interpretative proposal in the text look implausible: if Hume doesn't think reason motivates, why should he suppose that considerations of prudence must motivate in order to be reasons? The answer, I think, is that Hume is an internalist about requirements, and the argument quoted above is supposed to show that reason cannot make prudence a requirement, and, more generally, that reason does not yield requirements. As we'll see later, Hume does think prudence is a requirement of virtue. [33] 'Skepticism about Practical Reason', sect. 3, pp. 318–21.

in order to *count* as a reason, for in that case, we could never judge that a person has acted irrationally; if the person were not moved by the consideration, we would have to say that it was not a reason for him. In any case, whether we do judge that an instance of imprudent conduct is irrational *depends* upon our views about whether prudence is a rational requirement, and not the reverse.

To see this, consider the case of Howard. Howard, who is in his thirties, needs medical treatment: specifically, he must have a course of injections, now, if he is going to live past fifty. But Howard declines to have this treatment, because he has a horror of injections. Let me just stipulate that, were it not for his horror of injections, Howard would have the treatment. It's not that he really secretly wants to die young anyway, or anything fancy like that. Howard's horror of injections is really what is motivating him. Notice that there are three different ways in which we may explain his conduct.

First, we may suppose that Howard *is* governed by what Hume calls the general appetite to good (or by prudence), but that he is miscalculating. He thinks that having a course of injections will be so dreadful that it is worth dying young to avoid it, even though he believes that if he had the treatments, a long and happy life would await him at the other end. While it might be interesting to know how someone could make this particular mistake, the possibility of mistake is not in general very interesting. In any case, I want to leave this interpretation aside, so let's again stipulate that he has not miscalculated or made a mistake. He sees that, if he were governed by considerations of prudence, he would have the injections: he agrees that a long and happy life is a greater good than avoiding the injections. But he still declines to have them: he chooses 'his own acknowledg'd lesser good'.

What we say next depends on whether or not we think that the principle of prudence is a rational requirement. If we think that it is, we will regard Howard's dread of the injections as something that interferes with his rationality, as a source of weakness of the will. But if we reject the idea that prudence is rationally required, we may say simply that, because Howard so dreads the needle, avoiding the injections is what he wants most. His decision to decline the needed medical treatment is then not irrational. Absent a principle determining which ends we should prefer, such as the principle of prudence, a person will follow his stronger desire and will not be irrational for doing so. The point is not that it is *rational* for him to follow his stronger desire because it is stronger. The point is that he is rational in the only remaining sense—he is (apparently) following the instrumental principle. Refusing to take the injections is the means to his end, in the sense that it is the means to the end he is *going* to pursue: namely, a life free from injections.

So what we say about this case depends on our attitude about the principle of prudence. If we suppose prudence is a rational requirement, we will say: fear prevents Howard from pursuing the end he *ought* to prefer, his overall good, and therefore he is acting irrationally. But if we reject the claim that prudence is a rational requirement, we will say: fear determines what Howard's preferred end is, but there is no irrationality in the case, for reason has nothing to say about which ends we should prefer.

Does Hume think that the instrumental principle, unlike the principle of prudence, is a rational requirement? If he does, then as the argument above shows, there should be cases in which Hume would be prepared to identify someone's conduct as 'instrumentally irrational', that is, cases in which, without miscalculating or making a mistake, people fail or decline to take the means to their own 'acknowledg'd' ends. Now Hume does not discuss this kind of case, but he does explicitly allow that actions can be irrational in two *derivative* ways: we act 'irrationally' when our passions are provoked by non-existent objects, or when we act on the basis of false causal judgements.[34] Both of these are cases of mistake; the actions that result are not, strictly speaking, irrational. And after discussing them, Hume asserts:

The moment we perceive the falsehood of any supposition, or the insufficiency of any means our passions yield to our reason without any opposition.[35]

This suggests that Hume thinks no one is ever guilty of violating the instrumental principle. Making a mistake, after all, is not a way of being irrational, and Hume thinks we do take the means to our ends as soon as mistakes are out of the way. But this is worrisome. How can there be rational action, in any sense, if there is no irrational action? How can there be an imperative which no one ever actually violates?

The problem is exacerbated when we see that Hume's view is not just that people don't *in fact* ever violate the instrumental principle. He is actually committed to the view that people *cannot* violate it. To see this, we need only consider why Hume might be led to deny that people are ever instrumentally irrational. Offhand, that denial doesn't seem very plausible. People fail to take the means to what they *say* are their ends all the time. And this does not happen only when those ends are demanded by abstract or distant considerations of what will conduce to the person's overall good. It happens in the case of more local ends that are expressly and directly wanted or chosen for their own sakes. You want to ride on this immense roller-coaster but you are prevented by terror. Every night of the carnival you go and look at it, get in line for a ticket, and then lose your nerve and shuffle meekly away. You don't think riding the roller-coaster is essential

<hr />

[34] See *T* 416.   [35] *T* 416.

to your overall good. Maybe you even think it's risky and a little foolish. But you've made up your mind to do it. And all you have to do is buy a ticket and get on—only you can't bring yourself to. You want to see the movie but you are too idle to go into town; you want to go out with him but you are too shy to call and ask him for a date; you want to work but depression holds you in its smothering embrace.

If we believe that the instrumental principle is a rational requirement, we will say that these people's terror, idleness, shyness, or depression is making them irrational and weak-willed, and so that they are failing to do what is necessary to promote their own ends. We will see these things as forces that block their susceptibility to the influence of reason. Now in the case of prudence, the other option was to reject the principle and say that Howard simply prefers to avoid the injections at any cost, and that he is not irrational for doing so. In this case, what is the other option? Could we *reject* the instrumental principle and say that the people in these examples simply *prefer* to indulge their terror, idleness, shyness, or depression, and that they are not irrational for doing so?

Well, notice that if we do say that, then it turns out that these people are *not* after all violating the instrumental principle, at least as Hume would have to formulate it. They are taking the means to the ends they are *going* to pursue, so we would not have rejected the instrumental principle after all. Now one thing that this means is that Hume cannot talk about the instrumental principle in the same way he talks about the principle of prudence. That is, if he *did* want to deny that the instrumental principle is a rational requirement, he could not do it by dramatically announcing: 'It is not contrary to reason to refuse to take the means to my end . . .' because according to Hume *that cannot happen*. Whatever you do is the means to the end which you are *going* to pursue. But how then can we claim that the instrumental principle is a principle of reason? Hume's view seems to exclude the possibility that we could be *guided* by the instrumental principle. For how can you be guided by a principle when anything you do counts as following it? In fact, this argument shows that Hume's famous dictum is correct: you cannot derive an *ought* from an *is*. In this case, we cannot derive the *requirement* of taking the means from *facts* about which end an agent is actually going to pursue.[36]

[36] Readers of earlier drafts of this essay have alerted me to the importance of making it clear what I am saying about Hume at this point. My primary target in this part of the essay is actually empiricists who endorse the view that the instrumental principle is the only principle of practical reason and who claim Hume for the founding father of their view. I am arguing that Hume could not have held such a view. I do not mean, however, to suggest that Hume himself tried to hold this view and failed: I do not believe that he thought the instrumental principle was a principle of reason. In n. 39 below, however, I argue that Hume's arguments for the normativity of virtue may depend on the normativity of prudence, and I think that a parallel and related point can be made about the normativity of the

Now it is clear enough where the problem here is coming from. The problem is coming from the fact that Hume identifies a person's *end* as what he *wants most*, and the criterion of what the person wants most appears to be what he actually *does*. The person's ends are taken to be revealed in his conduct. If we don't make a distinction between what a person's end is and what he actually pursues, it will be impossible to find a case in which he violates the instrumental principle. So the problem would be solved if we could make a distinction between a person's ends and what he actually pursues. Two ways suggest themselves: we could make a distinction between actual desire and rational desire, and say that a person's ends are not merely what he wants, but what he has reason to want. Or, we could make a more psychological distinction between what a person thinks he wants or locally wants and what he 'really wants'. After all, it does seem odd to say of the people in my examples that what they 'really want' are ends which are shaped by their terror, idleness, shyness, or depression. We know that these people would wish these conditions away if only they could. So perhaps it is plausible to say that these people do not do what they really want to do, and that therefore they are irrational.

But in order to distinguish rational desire from actual desire, it looks as if we need to have some rational principles determining which ends are worthy of preference or pursuit. So the first option takes us beyond instrumental rationality. The instrumental principle then tells us to promote those ends we have reason to want. But really the second option—the claim that these people are irrational because they do not promote the ends which they 'really want'—also takes us beyond instrumental rationality, although this may not be immediately obvious. If we are going to appeal to 'real' desires as a basis for making claims about whether people are acting rationally or not, we will have to argue that a person *ought* to pursue what he *really* wants rather than what he is in fact *going* to pursue. That is, we will have to accord these 'real' desires some normative force. It must be something like a requirement of reason that you should do what you 'really want', even when you are tempted not to. And then, again, we will have gone beyond instrumental rationality after all.

Let me now pay off a promissory note. According to a theory very fashionable in the social scientific and economic literature, sometimes called the self-interest or economic theory of rationality, it is rational for each person to pursue his overall good: to act on some variant of the principle of prudence. Many people who believe the self-interest theory of rationality

instrumental principle. Of course some interpreters also deny that Hume is trying to establish the normativity of virtue, but this is not the line that I have taken. For my interpretation of Hume's account of the normativity of morality see *The Sources of Normativity*, lecture 2, pp. 51–66. I thank Annette Baier and Barbara Herman for prodding me to be clearer on this point.

think that they also believe the theory that all practical reasons are instrumental. This combination of ideas is incoherent. The instrumental principle says nothing about our ends, so it is completely unequipped to say either that we ought to desire our overall good or that we ought to prefer it to more immediate or local satisfactions. The self-interest theory of rationality, because it is committed to the principle of prudence, *has to* go beyond the instrumental theory. Now how could the purveyors of this theory make such an obvious error? I believe that the answer lies in what I have just said. People who hold this theory *assume* that what a person 'really wants' is her overall good, and therefore that her ends, her real ends, just *are* the things that are consistent with or part of her overall good. The standard move is to treat the possibility that someone might desire something inconsistent with her overall good as if it were an uninteresting little piece of theoretical untidiness like the possibility that she might miscalculate or make a mistake. We all know that we cannot even start a discussion of rationality until we have applied *a little* spit and polish to people's desires. (You know the sort of thing I mean: 'we won't say that his desire to eat the apple provides a reason for him to do so, if it is based on his ignorance that it is made of wax . . .' etc.) Self-interest theorists treat harmonizing someone's local ends with her overall good as if it were just a part of this preliminary cleaning-up process. Following Hume (and with just as little plausibility) they might say 'The moment we perceive that an end is inconsistent with our overall good our passions yield to our reason without any opposition.'[37] The fans of morality could just as well stipulate that what we 'really want' are things consistent with love and respect for everybody, and then they too could claim that we don't need to go beyond instrumental rationality. Nothing is gained by such devices.

But Hume, unlike his would-be followers, does not build consistency with one's overall good into his notion of an end. As we have seen, he thinks we neither ought-to-want nor really-want only those ends which are consistent with our overall good. And that apparently means that he must accept the claim that local desires determine our ends, and with it, the implication that we cannot violate the instrumental principle. If we cannot violate it, then it cannot guide us, and that means that it is not a normative principle. This suggests that for Hume the desire to take the means to our ends is just a calm passion, one we have by the original constitution of our

---

[37] As Plato points out in the *Protagoras*, one idea that drives this position is the idea that the objects of desire are commensurable. If the choice is between getting $5 or 5 units of pleasure now, and $12 or 12 units of pleasure next week, it is *a little* more plausible to say that passion will conform *automatically* to the dictate of prudence—although only a little. But if the choice is between six weeks of passion with a charming scapegrace now, and a lifetime of marriage to a man of sweet reason, the claim that passion will yield *automatically* to prudence seems absurd. Economists, of course, do tend to assume commensurability.

nature. Hume might say of it just what he said of the principle of prudence, that we mistake it for reason because when we are under its influence our minds are calculating and cool.

One way to rescue the normativity of the instrumental principle is open to Hume. We might argue that the principle that distinguishes 'my end' from 'whatever I actually pursue' does not have to be a principle of reason. It only has to be some *normative* principle, since it has to pick out something I ought to pursue even if I don't.[38] Perhaps virtue itself picks out the ends we ought to pursue, and then the instrumental principle requires us to take the means to those. It is instructive here, that although Hume denies that prudence is a rational requirement, he certainly does think it is a virtue. He says:

What we call strength of mind, implies the prevalence of the calm passions above the violent; tho' we may easily observe, there is no man so constantly possess'd of this virtue, as never on any occasion to yield to the sollicitations of passion and desire.[39]

The parallel claim, about the instrumental principle, would be that resoluteness in the pursuit of our ends is itself a virtue, and that this accounts for the normativity of the instrumental principle. We can be guided by it in so far as we can be motivated to pursue an ideal of virtue.[40] But it would have to be resoluteness in the pursuit of *virtuous* ends, for otherwise, there would be no way to distinguish cases of resoluteness from any other actions. We would not say, except as a kind of joke, that Howard exhibits the virtue of resoluteness in steadfastly rejecting the medical treatment that he needs, or that my other exemplar displays it in slinking timidly away from the roller-coaster she longs to ride. If the theory we are now constructing on

[38] I owe this suggestion to Erin Kelly; I would also like to thank Charlotte Brown and Andrews Reath for discussions of this point.

[39] *T* 418. But there is a deep incoherence here. In Hume's moral theory, prudence is supposed to be a virtue because we approve of it from the general point of view. From this point of view, we approve of those qualities which are useful or agreeable to an agent himself or his associates. Hume identifies prudence as one of the virtues that is supposed to be good (because useful) for the agent who has it. But if an agent himself has no reason to prefer his greater good to the satisfaction of his local desires, then I do not see why we should think it is good for him to prefer it, and therefore why we should count it as a virtue. The real trouble, I think, is that Hume uses the word 'good' to describe the sum of satisfactions or pleasures over the course of a person's whole life without explaining either what entitles him to that usage or what follows from it. If the word 'good' is supposed to import normativity, it may seem like a raw contradiction to say an agent has no reason to prefer his greater good. Or to make the same point in reverse, if we have no reason to care about future pleasures and satisfactions, then there is no content to the idea that adding them up makes a 'greater good'.

[40] Notice that if this reconstruction works, it traces normativity to self-government, and in that sense, anticipates the view I will argue for in Sect. 3. But there are problems about the extent to which Hume can give a satisfactory explanation of this kind of motivation. These problems are explored in Charlotte Brown, 'Is Hume an Internalist?', *Journal of the History of Philosophy*, 25 (1988), 69–87, and 'From Spectator to Agent: Hume's Theory of Obligation', *Hume Studies*, 20 (1994), 19–35.

Hume's behalf works, we will call somebody 'resolute' only when he pursues ends of which we approve. The normativity of taking the means can then be derived from the normativity which our moral approval attaches to the end.[41]

But if Hume took this option, it would begin to become unclear why it should matter whether we use the words 'reason' and 'rational' to signify that normativity or whether we use 'virtue' and 'virtuous' or some other words. We will have rescued the instrumental requirement for Hume, but only at the cost of showing that the word 'virtue' simply does the work in his account of action that the word 'reason' does in his supposed opponent's accounts. Hume will have been engaging in what he supposedly despises, a verbal dispute. And he would still have to grant the central point of this argument, which is that a *normative* principle of instrumental action cannot exist unless there are also normative principles directing the adoption of ends.

Earlier, I suggested that the instrumental principle cannot function as a requirement in Hume's theory because he has no resources for distinguishing a person's ends from what she actually pursues. Another way to put the same point, which in the end comes to the same thing, is to say that Hume has no resources for distinguishing the activity of the person *herself* from the operation of beliefs, desires, and other forces *in her*. Unless Hume endorses the kind of reconstruction I have just described, his model does not allow us to see a person as guided by normative principles in her actions and choices because it leaves no room for the *person* to act and choose at all. Desire, fear, indolence, and whim shape the Humean agent's ends, and, through them, her actions. When her passions change, her ends change, and when her ends change, so do her actions. We can explain everything that she does without any reference to *her* at all. To say that

---

[41] In ordinary discourse we move freely between characterizing ends as real and characterizing them in normative terms, for our practices of psychological attribution themselves are normatively loaded in a rather deep way. Suppose a graduate student comes to your office and says, in despair: 'I'm going to give it up and leave graduate school, I am getting nowhere, it is all hopeless and I'd better just bag it and go to law school.' You might reply 'You don't *really want* to do that.' You're only partly talking about psychic reality—you are also guiding, giving a pep talk, *trying to create* psychic reality, and you and your student *both* know that. You mean something like: 'Don't give up: you are still capable of being what you think it's best for you to be.' Or suppose a man asks 'What do I really want?' and someone replies 'To kill your father and make love to your mother.' At least outside of the psychoanalytic context, this answer is a kind of category mistake; the man is not asking about the actual condition of his id. It is important, I think, to recognize how pervasive this normative use of psychological language is. 'You can do it!' we cheer from the sidelines of one another's lives. 'You're a reasonable person' I begin my argument, looking steadily into my opponent's eyes. In one sense, this sort of thing may seem to be, to use Bernard Williams's term, bluff. But if it is, then we ought to have a lot of respect for bluff. It plays an essential role in our efforts to hold ourselves and each other together, to stay on track of our projects and relationships in the face of the buffeting winds of local temptation and desire. (See Williams, 'Internal and External Reasons', 111.)

reason is the slave of the passions, and to say that a person is the slave of her passions, turn out to be one and the same thing.

3. Kant and the Rationalist Account

I have suggested that the instrumental principle can be rescued only if we take 'my end' to be something other than 'what I actually, just now, desire'. One possibility is to distinguish desire from volition, and to say that your end is what you *will*, not merely what you want.[42] This distinction is at the heart of Kant's moral psychology. In Kant's view, an inclination is a kind of attraction to something, which is grounded in our sensuous nature, and in the face of which we are passive.[43] By themselves, inclinations have no normative force; they are not reasons. But they do serve as 'incentives'— which means that we are predisposed to treat them as reasons, and so to adopt maxims of acting on them. Of course Kant thinks that they are not the only incentives, for reason also generates an incentive of its own, respect for the moral law, which inclines us to act morally. Volition consists in adopting a maxim of acting on some incentive or other. When we decide to act on an inclination—to do a desired action or seek a desired end—then its object becomes an object of volition. The essential point here is that the adoption of an end is conceived as the person's own free act. Inclination proposes, but it is the person herself who disposes. Given all this, it is not surprising to find Kant's version of the instrumental principle formulated in terms of the will, not in terms of desire. In general or schematic form, the instrumental principle tells us that if we *will* an end, then we ought to will the means to that end.[44] And Kant's argument for the instrumental principle depends essentially on the fact that it is formulated that way. He says:

---

[42] This possibility wasn't canvassed in Sect. 2 because it is not open to Hume or other empiricists. Hume thinks the will is merely the impression that accompanies voluntary action (*T* 399); other empiricists think it is merely the last desire that emerges from deliberation. Either way, volition does not provide a distinctive account of what it means to be an end.

[43] There are of course objections to this view, which I have discussed in sect. 3 of my 'Reply' in *The Sources of Normativity*, 238–42.

[44] Kant talks about both 'the' categorical imperative and categorical imperatives plural; but he does not talk about 'the' hypothetical imperative. I do not think that anything important turns on this fact: in this, as in much else in this part of the essay, I am in agreement with Thomas Hill, Jr., in his 'The Hypothetical Imperative', in Hill, *Dignity and Practical Reason in Kant's Moral Theory* (Ithaca, NY: Cornell Univ. Press, 1992), essay 1. Yet there's a possible issue here, for we can imagine someone interpreting the asymmetry along these lines: 'Kant thinks that although we can violate particular hypothetical imperatives, we could not in general violate "the" hypothetical imperative and still count as beings with rational wills, and, that being so, "the" hypothetical imperative isn't really an imperative. We can, however, violate the categorical imperative in general and still count as beings with rational wills, so it really is an imperative.' According to this view, the hypothetical imperative is merely descriptive of a rational will, while the categorical imperative is normative for but not descriptive of it, and so in effect represents a restriction on the will. It will emerge in due course that I think this view is wrong, both in fact, and as an interpretation of Kant's more considered position; but also that I think Kant had some tendency to fall into it in the *Groundwork*. As I will explain later, I think that both

How an imperative of skill is possible requires no special discussion. Whoever wills the end, wills (so far as reason has decisive influence on his actions) also the means that are indispensably necessary to his actions and that lie in his power. This proposition, as far as willing is concerned, is analytic. For in willing an object as my effect there is already thought the causality of myself as an acting cause, i.e., the use of means. The imperative derives the concept of actions necessary to this end from the concept of willing the end.[45]

Kant then adds that we do need some synthetic propositions — some causal laws—to arrive at these imperatives, but not for grounding the act of the will, only for determining what the means to the end are.

In other words, the imperative derives the concept of willing the means from the concept of willing the end, with the aid of some synthetic proposition telling us what the means are. So we begin with some willed end, say, health, and a causal (and so synthetic) proposition, say, that exercise is a cause of health. From the combination of these we derive the necessity of a will to exercise. What makes the derivation possible is an 'analytic proposition', namely, that whoever wills the end wills the means to that end, in so far as reason has decisive influence on his actions. This proposition is analytic because to will an end, rather than just to wish for it or desire it, is to be committed to causing that end actually to exist.[46] 'In willing an end,' Kant explains, 'the causality of myself as an acting cause' is 'already thought.' And to cause an end is of course to take the means to it. It follows that if someone wills to be healthy, then in so far as reason has decisive control over his actions, he wills to exercise.

Now the reconstruction I just gave is vague, for I have not said exactly *how* the analytic proposition makes it possible to combine willing the end with knowledge of the means so as to arrive at the necessity of willing the means. And it turns out that there is a problem about how this is supposed to work. The problem is revealed by two glitches that infect the argument as it stands. First, the claim that 'whoever wills the ends wills the means that are indispensably necessary and that lie in his power' seems to leave something out: the person in question must *know* that these are the means.

requirements, strictly speaking, represent procedures for constructing maxims rather than restrictions applied to them, and as such they are both constitutive of and normative for the rational will. See n. 73 for more on this topic.

[45] G 417.

[46] I am using 'wish' here in an ordinary sense, to refer to a sort of idle desire. In *The Metaphysical Principles of Virtue*, Kant uses the term 'Wunsch', translated by both Mary Gregor (in her complete translation of *The Metaphysics of Morals* (Cambridge: Univ. Press, 1991)) and James Ellington (in his translation in *Ethical Philosophy*, cited in n. 7 above) as 'wish', to describe the state in which an end is rationally endorsed, as a morally good end, but in which the agent sees no way to pursue it. (Prussian Academy, p. 213.) In that sense of 'wish', a wish does involve a commitment to taking the means, should the occasion arise. There Kant says that willing includes both 'choice'—an immediate determination to try to bring the object about—and 'wish'. See n. 59.

It is not true that if someone wills to be healthy, then he necessarily wills to exercise. He must also *know* that exercise is a cause of health. This point is more important than it looks, because it suggests that the agent *himself* must combine willing the end with knowing the means to arrive at the necessity of willing the means. And this recalls a point I made earlier, namely, that the rationality of action depends on the way in which the person's own mental activity is involved in its production, not just on its accidental conformity to some external standard.

So the agent himself must combine willing the end and knowing the means to arrive at the necessity of willing the means. And the analytic proposition is supposed to make this possible for him somehow. But at this point we run into the second glitch in the argument. There is a recurring caveat: the analytic proposition is that whoever wills the end wills the means *in so far as reason has decisive influence on his actions*. This caveat, as I will explain below, turns out to give rise to a problem in Kant's argument. Before explaining that, it will be helpful to consider why Kant adds the caveat.

At the beginning of the discussion, Kant says that imperatives are expressed by an *ought* because they are addressed to wills that are not necessarily determined by the objective laws of reason. After identifying the good with the practically necessary, Kant says, 'Imperatives say that something would be good (practically necessary) to do or refrain from doing, but they say it to a will that does not always therefore do something simply because it has been represented to the will as something good to do.'[47] In other words, imperatives are addressed to beings who may follow them or not. And this is true of the instrumental principle as well as of the others.

Now if this is right, it must be possible for a rational being (one who is subject to the instrumental principle) to disobey, resist, or fail to follow that principle. It must be possible for someone to will an end, and yet to fail to will the means to that end. And this means, once again, that there will be different ways to explain what happens when someone *apparently* fails to take the means to her end, or to what she says is her end.

Suppose someone claims that she wills an end: she asserts that all things considered, she has decided to pursue this end. And yet, when a means to this end is at hand she always fails to take it, even when it is expressly pointed out to her that it would promote or realize the end she has chosen. Timid Prudence says she has resolved to lead a more adventurous life, but when the opportunity for adventure knocks, Prudence always says 'tomorrow'. How are we to explain her conduct? One possible explanation of

---

[47] G 412–13.

course is that she does not really will to lead a more adventurous life. When she says that she does, she is self-deceived or she is lying to the rest of us. We finally say to Prudence in disgust, 'You really mean to live on the safe side of the street, and you had better just admit it.' Notice that in this case we imply that she is guilty of insincerity rather than of instrumental irrationality. If she doesn't really will to have an adventurous life, it is not irrational of her to let these opportunities go by, although it is insincere for her to pretend she has resolved upon adventure.

A second possible explanation appeals to the fact that the instrumental principle is hypothetical, and says that *if* you will an end you must be prepared to take the means. The hypothetical character of the principle implies that you can actually conform to it in either of two ways: you may take the means, or you may cease to will the end. It matters here that willing, unlike desiring, is an act, one we can decide to refrain from, or to cease to do. Sometimes, when we see what taking the means to an end will involve, we cease to will the end, deciding that all things considered it is not worth the trouble or the price. There is no irrationality in this, and it may be what happens to Prudence. Perhaps she believes that the means to adventure which are pointed out to her will be so painful or terrifying that she decides that, all things considered, an adventurous life is not worth it after all. So she gives the idea up. Prudence says: 'Well, I had resolved on leading a more adventurous life, but if I take any of the ways open to me right now, I am likely to end up in prison. I'd like to have more adventure, but it isn't really worth going to prison for.' Again she is not guilty of any irrationality.

Both of those explanations say that Prudence doesn't really will to have adventures after all. This being so, she has not violated the instrumental principle, which only instructs her to take the means to those ends which she does will. The third explanation is that she does violate the instrumental principle, and fails to take the means to her end, because something is interfering with her susceptibility to reason. This might happen, for instance, because she has been rendered inert by depression, or paralysed by terror, or because the means are painful and, although she judges the end to be worth the pain, she is simply unable to face it. Now we can say that she is violating the instrumental principle, and is guilty of irrational willing.[48]

Although we may not be sure which of these explanations is the best, the third one must be possible if the instrumental principle is a rational requirement. And it is worth noticing that there are cases where this third

---

[48] Peter Railton also emphasizes the necessity of allowing for this kind of case in Essay 2 in this volume, pp. 72–3.

explanation seems to be the best in any case. Consider a standard scene of horror in Western or Civil War movies. The doctor must saw off Tex's leg in order to save his life, and there is no anaesthetic or even any whiskey left in the house. Tex screams 'No, no, don't'; he tries to escape from the men holding him down, he tries to push the doctor away. Yet if the doctor asks 'Tex, don't you want to live?' Tex will of course say 'yes'. It would be stupid to say that because Tex rejects the means he is being insincere and doesn't really want to live, or that as the saw approaches he reconsiders his situation and makes a decision that all things considered, living isn't worth it. The right thing to say is that fear is making Tex irrational. After all, the judgement that someone is irrational doesn't have to be a criticism. The government of reason, like any other, requires certain background conditions in order to maintain its authority. Faced with the prospect of having his leg sawed off, Tex's sensible nature is quite understandably in revolt.

Kant, unlike the followers of Hume, recognizes that we cannot be guided by an imperative unless we can also fail to be guided by it. The caveat is necessary, then, because it must be logically possible for someone to fail to follow the instrumental principle, that is, to will an end but fail to will the means. The proposition is supposed to be analytic, so if we don't put the caveat in, failure to take the means to one's end will be logically impossible. But that means that without the caveat, the proposition can't be true after all.

But this in turn gives rise to the glitch I mentioned earlier, for it creates a problem about *how* the analytic proposition is supposed to make it possible for the agent to combine willing the end with knowing the means to *arrive at* a rational requirement of willing the means. On the model suggested by Kant's account, the agent arrives at the requirement by plugging himself in, so to speak, to a syllogism, of which the analytic proposition is the first premiss:

> Whoever wills the end wills the means.
> I will the end.
> → I will the means.

The trouble with this suggestion is obvious. As we have just seen, the principle 'whoever wills the end wills the means' isn't true. This shows up in the fact that the syllogism puts the modal operator in the wrong place: its conclusion is not that I must will the means, but rather that it must be the case that I will the means, which is false. The only proposition which Kant can claim is an analytic truth is the one with the caveat in it: the proposition that 'whoever wills the end wills the means in so far as reason has decisive influence over his actions'. So it looks as if the first premiss of the syllogism must include the caveat. Then it goes like this:

Whoever wills the end wills the means in so far as he is rational.

I will the end.

→ Therefore I will the means in so far as I am rational.

→ Therefore I *ought* to will the means.

(Recall that imperatives are expressed by an *ought*, according to Kant, because they are addressed to wills that do not necessarily do what reason demands: that's how this last step is made.)

But we cannot in any non-trivial way invoke this second syllogism to explain *why* the agent finds it rationally necessary to take the means to his end, for this syllogism's first premiss trivially incorporates the claim that taking the means to one's ends is rationally required.

I believe that there is an historical explanation for what has gone wrong here. At the time he wrote the *Groundwork*, Kant apparently identified our capacity to resist the dictates of reason with the imperfection of the human will, for he asserts rather confusingly that a perfectly good will, although 'subject' to the laws of reason, would not be necessitated to follow them and so would not be addressed in imperative form and in an *ought*. The reason for this is supposed to be that human beings are subject to incentives of inclination as well as those generated by reason itself, while a perfectly good will is moved only by the incentives generated by reason. Kant says: 'Therefore no imperatives hold for the divine will, and in general for a holy will; the *ought* is here out of place, because the *would* is already of itself necessarily in agreement with the law.'[49] This idea is picked up again in the third section of the *Groundwork*, when Kant claims that if we had only an intelligible existence (and so were perfectly rational) the moral law would be a 'would' for us rather than an 'ought'.[50] The structure of argument suggested by these remarks is this: God *does* so-and-so (or, a perfectly rational being does so-and-so) and therefore I *ought* to do so-and-so. This structure of argument is indeed found in the writings of dogmatic rationalists such as Leibniz and Clarke.[51] And it seems to be the model evoked in the second syllogism above: a perfectly rational being *would* take the means to

---

[49] *G* 414.

[50] *G* 454. This remark gives rise to serious problems, for since our actions spring from our intelligible nature, it seems to make the existence of immoral actions a mystery. I take these problems up in 'Morality as Freedom', ch. 6 in Korsgaard, *Creating the Kingdom of Ends*. For a somewhat different resolution of the problem presented directly by the passage at hand—the seeming implication that the laws of reason are not normative for purely rational beings—see n. 28 of 'Creating the Kingdom of Ends: Reciprocity and Responsibility in Personal Relations', ch. 7 in *Creating the Kingdom of Ends*, 218–19. Despite what I say here, that note suggests that there are ways of reading almost all of Kant's remarks that makes them come out true on what I believe is his more considered view.

[51] See for instance the selections from Samuel Clarke's *A Discourse Concerning the Unchangeable Obligations of Natural Religion, and the Truth and Certainty of the Christian Revelation*, the Boyle Lectures 1705, in D. D. Raphael (ed.), *British Moralists 1650–1800* (Indianapolis: Hackett, 1991), vol. i, esp. p. 199; Raphael para. 231.

his ends, therefore I *ought* to take the means to my ends. The model suggests that the normativity of the *ought* expresses a demand that we should emulate more perfect rational beings (possibly including our own noumenal selves) whose own conduct is not guided by normative principles at all, but instead describable in a set of logical truths. And this in turn suggests that rationality is a matter of conforming the will to standards of reason that exist independently of the will, as a set of truths about what there is reason to do. That is, it implies an essentially realist theory of reasons, and, as I am about to argue, a realist theory cannot provide a coherent account of rationality.[52]

According to dogmatic rationalism, or realism more generally, there are facts, which exist independently of the person's mind, about what there is reason to do; rationality consists in conforming one's conduct to those reasons. According to *moral* realism, facts about the rightness or wrongness of actions support those reasons; according to what we might call *instrumental* realism, facts about the instrumentality of actions to our ends support those reasons. The difficulty with this account in a way exists right on its surface, for the account invites the question why it is necessary to act in accordance with those reasons, and so seems to leave us in need of a reason to be rational. I have an end, and out there in the universe is a law saying what I must do if I have an end (take the means), but the reason why I must obey this law has not yet been given. To put the point less tendentiously, we must still explain why the person finds it *necessary* to act on those normative facts, or what it is about *her* that makes them normative *for her*. We must explain how these reasons get a grip on the agent. The dogmatic

---

[52] In his later ethical works, in particular in the *Critique of Practical Reason* and *Religion Within the Limits of Reason Alone*, Kant rejects the claim that susceptibility to sensuous incentives is what makes the will imperfect. In the *Religion* he denies the claim that sensibility is a source of evil. (See *Religion Within the Limits of Reason Alone*, trans. Theodore M. Greene and Hoyt H. Hudson (New York: Harper Torchbooks, 1960), 30.) In the *Critique of Practical Reason*, he acknowledges the possibility of noumenal evil. (See *Critique of Practical Reason*, trans. Lewis White Beck (Indiamapolis: Library of Liberal Arts, 1956); Prussian Academy, pp. 96–100.) He does not explicitly give up the view that the will's imperfection is what makes us subject to an *ought*, but it seems to me that he should have, for imperfection is a red herring here. Even a perfectly rational will cannot be conceived as *guided* by reason unless it is conceived as capable of resisting reason. It may be true, as Kant insists, that a divine will is not subject to temptation and so just would do what reason requires, but it is not true, as he seems to infer, that no *ought* applies to the divine will. There are a number of places where Kant suggests that we should only use 'ought' or 'duty' when the agent is necessitated *and* that this can only happen when the agent might want to resist the claim, some of them in the later writings. For example, in the *Metaphysical Principles of Virtue* Kant says that we cannot have a duty to pursue our own happiness because we inevitably want it anyway (Prussian Academy, p. 386). Obviously, one of the central ideas of this essay is that we can be subject to normative principles only if we can resist them, because without that possibility they cannot function as guides. But I do not agree with Kant that the absence of any specific temptation to resist them removes the possibility of resistance in the sense needed for normativity. It is not imperfection which places us under rational norms, but rather freedom, which brings with it the needed possibility of resistance to as well as of compliance with those norms.

rationalist's inability to do that is illustrated by the impossibility of forming a syllogism that shows, in any illuminating way, how the agent manages to *arrive at* the rational necessity of taking the means to her ends.

Now the *moral* realist may be tempted to try to overcome this problem by appeal to the extended version of the instrumental principle which I mentioned earlier, the one that sees the application of a concept as a limiting case of the discovery of a means. We would first have to assume (or produce an argument to show) that doing what is right is a necessary end for a rational agent. (This parallels the social scientific strategy, which we looked at in Section 2, of assuming that pursuit of the overall good is a necessary end for a rational agent.) With such an argument in hand, it might seem that we could connect the alleged normative facts about what is right to the person's practical reason by way of the extended version of the instrumental principle. Consider: my end is to do what is right, in these circumstances *this* is the right action, therefore I shall do *this*. The extended instrumental principle in this way is supposed to lend *its* normative or motivational character to the independent facts about the rightness of certain actions.

But there are two problems with this strategy. The first and more obvious problem is that all the philosophical work has been transferred to the (missing, or anyway unspecified) argument which is supposed to show that doing what is right is a necessary end for a rational agent. (Just as, in the social scientific case, all the work is really done by the missing argument that shows that what we 'really want' must be consistent with our overall good.) The second problem concerns the instrumental principle itself. If it is to provide the needed connection between the rational agent and the independent facts about reasons, it cannot in turn be based on independent facts itself. Suppose it is just a fact, independently of a person's own will, that an action's tendency to promote one of her ends constitutes a reason for doing it. Why must she care about *that* fact? We cannot appeal to the instrumental principle to explain how *that* fact gets a grip on the agent, for that is the principle we are trying to ground. You can see this by considering how the argument would have to go: Doing whatever promotes your own ends is a necessary end for a rational being; this action promotes one of your ends; therefore it promotes your end of doing what promotes your ends; and therefore you have reason to do it. The circularity, or infinite regress, is obvious.[53] The instrumental principle cannot be an evaluative truth which we apply in practice, because it is essentially the *principle of application* itself: that is, it is the principle in accordance with which we are

---

[53] Peter Railton makes the same point in Essay 2 in this volume, pp. 76–7.

operating *when* we apply truths in practice. So if we are to use the extended instrumental principle to make the connection between the rational agent and the external facts about reasons, we cannot give the instrumental principle a realist foundation. But if we cannot give a realist account of the instrumental principle, it seems unlikely that we will end up giving realist accounts of the other principles of practical reason.

Another way to understand the argument I have just given goes like this: Moral realism (or for that matter, realism about reasons of prudence) may be criticized on the grounds that it fails to meet the internalism requirement. The moral realist I am imagining tries to overcome that problem by tapping into the supposedly incontrovertible internalism of instrumental reason. The problem is that, on a realist interpretation, astonishingly enough, the instrumental principle *itself* fails to meet the internalism requirement. For all we can see, an agent may be indifferent to the fact that an action's instrumentality to her end constitutes a reason for her to act.

Now while that way of understanding the argument has some advantages, I have come to think that there is a problem with thinking of these issues in terms of the internalism requirement. The internalism requirement is concerned only with whether a consideration that purports to be a reason is capable of motivating the person to whom it applies. And I think the real question is not only whether the consideration can motivate the person, but whether it can do so while also functioning as a requirement or a guide. This, after all, is what is wrong with the empiricist account treated in Section 2: the empiricist *can* explain how we can be motivated by instrumental thoughts, but at the price of not being able to explain how we could see such thoughts as embodying a requirement or a guide. The dogmatic rationalist account does show how the instrumental principle can guide us. But it does not show why we must be motivated to follow that guide. The theory I just examined tries to patch together an empiricist account of instrumental reason with a rationalist account of morality and prudence, in order to patch together the motivational force of the one with the guiding force of the other.[54] But it ends up with neither, and that is revealed in the fact that the first of the two problems with the proposed strategy still stands: the patchwork account makes no progress towards showing *why* a rational agent must care about doing what is right.

---

[54] Leaving aside the argument in the text, I am inclined to treat such eclectic proposals as prima-facie objectionable. But not everyone would agree that we should expect to give parallel accounts of the normativity of all of the principles of practical reason. To take one example, in *A Theory of Justice* (Cambridge, Mass.: Harvard Univ. Press, 1971) Rawls suggests that the principles of justice are chosen or (in Rawls's later terms) constructed, while the principles of goodness are not (sect. 68). In Rawls's later work he avoids or anyway can avoid taking a position on this; constructivism is adopted only for political purposes and we do not need to say anything about general theories of rationality or the good.

There is one way in which the realist strategy still might seem to work. We could simply *define* a rational agent as one who responds in the appropriate way to reasons, whatever they are, and we could then give realist accounts of all practical reasons, including instrumental ones. There are a set of normative facts, about which reasons there are, and a rational agent is *by definition* someone whose actions are motivated by these reasons. But this proposal falls prey to a problem we looked at before. If all we mean is that the person is reliably caused to act in accordance with reasons, we fail to capture what is rational about the person. His actions may be rationally appropriate, but not because he sees that they are so: it seems to be a sort of accident that his motivational wiring follows the pathways of reason. On the other hand, if what we mean when we say that the person's actions are motivated by reasons is that the person is caused to act by his *recognition* of certain considerations *as* reasons, then we must say *what it is* that he recognizes. And the argument I have just given shows that what it is that he recognizes cannot be that 'whoever wills the end wills the means' is an analytic proposition. Because, as I have just argued, it is not. We seem to be back where we started, with Kant's argument, interpreted in a dogmatic rationalist way, having achieved nothing.

The point here is that we need a reciprocal account of rationality—as some sort of human function or capacity—and of reasons. We need an account that shows what those two things have to do with each other. The dogmatic rationalist's strategy is to first identify reasons—by asserting them to be parts of reality—and then to define rationality in terms of reasons: a rational being is by definition one who responds to reasons in the right way. This strategy necessarily leads to a purely definitional account of rationality, and can tell us nothing substantive about what function or power of the human mind rationality is. The alternative and more truly Kantian strategy is to first give an account of rationality—as we will see, as the autonomy of the human mind—and then to define reasons in terms of rationality—say, as that which can be autonomously willed, or as those considerations which accord with the principles of autonomous willing.

In other words, the dogmatic rationalist is unable to explain how reasons get a grip on the agent, because he supposes that reasons exist independently of the rational will, and as a result he misconceives the relationship between rational principles and the will. The dogmatic rationalist pictures that relationship this way: the person is willing something, so to speak *anyway*, and, inspired by an ambition to be rational, consults the principles of practical reason to see what restrictions they impose on his willing. When we translate this picture into Kantian terms it looks like this: I make a maxim, and *then* I see whether it meets the three standards of reason by determining first whether my action is a means to my end, then whether the pursuit of my end is consistent with my overall good, and finally whether my maxim is moral, that is, universalizable. The model, as I said earlier, seems to invite the question: but suppose I don't care about being rational? What then? And in Kant's philosophy this question should be impossible to ask. Rationality, as Kant conceives it, is the human plight that gives rise to the necessity of making free choices—not one of the options which we might choose or reject.[55]

One of the benefits of focusing on the instrumental principle is that it reveals how odd the dogmatic rationalist conception of reason's relation to the will is. The idea that you could make a maxim and *then* apply the instrumental principle to it makes no sense. A maxim that does not already at least aspire to conform to the instrumental principle is no maxim at all. So the instrumental principle does not come in as a restriction that is applied *to* the maxim. Instead, the act of making a maxim—the basic act of will—conforms to the instrumental principle by its very nature. To will an end just is to will to cause or realize the end, hence to will to take the means to the end. This is the sense in which the principle is analytic. The instrumental principle is *constitutive* of an act of the will. If you do not follow it, you are not willing the end at all.

Now this sounds like one of the views I have already rejected, so care must be taken here. The act of will of which conformity to the instrumental principle is *constitutive* in the way I have just described is not the act of will third-personally conceived. If we took 'willing an end' to be equivalent to 'actually pursuing or trying to pursue the means to that end' then we would get the paradox I have been insisting on all along. No violation of the instrumental principle would be possible, and it therefore could not function as a requirement or guide. If willing an end just amounted to actually attempting to realize the end, then there would be, so to speak, not enough distance between willing the end and willing the means for the one to *require* the other.[56] The dogmatic rationalist view, in which one conforms to a principle independent of the mind, achieves that distance, and so allows the principle to function as a guide. But as we have seen it gives rise to a new problem. Essentially, dogmatic rationalism conceives willing an end as being in a peculiar mental state or performing a mental act which somehow logically necessitates you to be in another mental state or perform another mental act, namely, willing the means. But we've just seen that this does not work either, for no mental state or act can logically necessitate you to

---

[55] See my *The Sources of Normativity*, sects. 3.2.1–3.2.3, pp. 92–8, for more on this point.

[56] In other words, the rationalist who takes 'trying to get' as a criterion of volition runs into exactly the same problem as the empiricist who takes 'trying to get' as a criterion of the strongest desire. The problem might seem even more likely to arise for the rationalist, for 'trying to get' is a more tempting criterion for volition than for the strongest desire. But if we make it our criterion of volition we can give no account of rationality.

be in *another* mental state or perform another mental act.[57] So willing the end is neither *the same as* being actually disposed to take the means nor as being in a particular mental state or performing a mental act which is *distinct from* willing the means. What then can it be?[58]

The answer is that willing an end just is *committing* yourself to realizing the end. Willing an end, in other words, is an essentially first-personal and normative act.[59] To will an end is to give oneself a law, hence, to govern oneself. That law is not the instrumental principle; it is some law of the form: Realize this end. That of course is equivalent to 'Take the means to this end'. So willing an end is equivalent to committing yourself, first-personally, to taking the means to that end.[60] In willing an end, just as Kant says, your causality—the use of means—is already thought. What is constitutive of willing the end is not the outward act of actually taking the means but rather the inward, volitional act of prescribing the end along with the means it requires to yourself.

Let me make the same point in another way. In my discussion of Hume, I contrasted two formulations of the instrumental principle. The first was 'if you *have a reason to pursue* an end, then you have a reason to take the means to that end' and the second was 'if you are *going* to pursue an end, then you have a reason to take the means to that end'. I argued that the second of those two formulations is defective because it attempts to derive an *Ought* from an *Is* (a reason from what you are *going* to do) and any imperative that attempts to do that cannot be followed because it cannot be violated. What about Kant's own formula? If it is to be like my first formulation, the one that works, then we get this result: for the instrumental principle to provide you with a reason, you must think that the fact that you will an end *is a reason* for the end. It's not exactly that there has to be a *further* reason; it's just that you must take the act of your own will to be

<hr />

[57] This is just another way of saying that the analytic principle is false without the caveat.

[58] A large part of the inspiration for this essay came from an occasion when Warren Quinn pressed me very hard on this point, and I am grateful to him for making me see the difficulty.

Peter Railton takes on what is essentially the same problem that I am examining here in Essay 2. If we say that willing the means is *constitutive* of willing the end then irrationality is impossible, while if we say that willing the means is not constitutive of willing the end then there is room for a sceptic to ask why he must do it. Thus there seems to be no possibility of identifying a prescription which we must, but do not inevitably, follow. Obviously something has gone wrong.

[59] One of the advantages of this account is that it makes it possible to explain how 'wish' (*Wunsch*), as a species of rational willing, in the sense described in n. 46 above, is possible. If willing were just the third-personal or objective act of *trying to get*, we could not make sense of this idea.

[60] Willing an end is in this respect like making a promise, and, accordingly, the contortions Hume undergoes when he tries to discover what act of the mind 'making a promise' is are relevant here (*T* 516–17). Hume ends by deciding that there is no such act, and this is not surprising, given that only third-personal options are available to him. Nietzsche's characterization of a promise as requiring a 'memory of the will' is, by contrast, right on target. (See *On the Genealogy of Morals* in *On the Genealogy of Morals and Ecce Homo*, trans. Walter Kaufmann and R. J. Hollingdale (New York: Random House, 1967), 58.)

normative for you.[61] And of course this cannot mean merely that you are *going* to pursue the end. It means that your willing the end gives it a normative status for you, that your willing the end in a sense makes it good. The instrumental principle can only be normative if we take ourselves to be capable of giving laws to ourselves—or, in Kant's own phrase, if we take our own wills to be *legislative*.

For this, of course, is almost already the third formulation of the categorical imperative, which Kant associates with 'the concept of a rational being as one who must regard himself as legislating universal law by all his will's maxims'.[62] The only difference is that the conception of oneself as a lawmaker required for the instrumental principle does not yet (or not obviously) involve universalizing over every rational agent.

Then what does it mean to say I take the act of my own will to be normative? Who makes a law for whom? The answer in the case of the instrumental principle is that I make a law *for me*.[63] And this is a law which I am capable of obeying or disobeying. At this moment, now, I decide to work; at the next moment, at any moment, I will certainly want to stop. If I am to work I must *will* it—I must resolve to stay on its track. Timidity, idleness, and depression will exert their claims in turn, will attempt to control or overrule my will, to divert me from my work. Am I to let these forces determine my actions? At each moment I must say to them: 'I am

---

[61] This is the basis of my account of Kant's argument for the Formula of Humanity in *The Sources of Normativity*, sects. 3.4.7–3.5.0, pp. 120–5; and in my 'Kant's Formula of Humanity', ch. 4 in *Creating the Kingdom of Ends*. The argument begins from our commitment to the conception of our own ends as good, which is traced to the conception of ourselves as ends-in-ourselves, which is in turn traced to the view of our own wills as legislative.

[62] *G* 433. It's worth noticing that here and elsewhere, Kant doesn't formulate the categorical imperative as a standard that is to be applied to our maxims, but rather as a way of regarding one's maxims or even of constructing them. But of course Kant does sometimes speak, in the *Groundwork*, as if the categorical imperative were a test we applied to our maxims after formulating them. On my reading, what this test shows is whether we are actually succeeding in performing an act of free will. Obviously, this requires more argument, but it is implied by Kant's view that the moral law *just is* the law of a free will. For an explication of this point see my 'Morality as Freedom', ch. 6 in *Creating the Kingdom of Ends*, esp. pp. 162–7; and *The Sources of Normativity*, sect. 3.2.3, pp. 97–8.

[63] This remark may arouse Wittgensteinian worries, associated with the private language argument, about whether I can make a law (just) for me. As I understand it, Wittgenstein's argument does not show that I cannot make a language which only I in fact understand, but rather that I cannot make a language which only I can understand. Any language I make for myself must be in principle teachable to others. The parallel point here would be that I cannot bind myself to a hypothetical imperative which no one else could be bound by, and this does have ethical implications, for it means that I cannot make something my end whose value cannot be communicated to others. This provides one route to one of the conclusions of this essay, namely, that hypothetical imperatives cannot exist unless there are also principles of reason determining our ends, since it means that nothing can be my end unless I can explain the reasons why I value it to others, and to do this I must have some reasons for valuing it. I have explored these points, albeit tentatively, in lecture 4 of *The Sources of Normativity* and in 'The Reasons We Can Share: An Attack on the Distinction Between Agent-Relative and Agent-Neutral Values', ch. 10 in *Creating the Kingdom of Ends*. I am grateful to Tamar Schapiro for alerting me to the possible relevance of this issue here.

not you; my will is this work.' Desire and temptation will also take their turns. 'I am not a shameful thing like terror', desire will say, 'follow me and your life will be sweet'. But if I give in to each claim as it appears *I* will do nothing and I will not have a life. For to will an end is not just to cause it, or even to allow an impulse in me to operate as its cause, but, so to speak, to consciously pick up the reins, and make *myself* the cause of the end. And if I am to constitute *myself* as the cause of an end, then I must be able to distinguish between *my* causing the end and some desire or impulse that is 'in me' causing my body to act. I must be able to see *myself* as something that is distinct from any of my particular, first-order, impulses and motives. So the reason that I must conform to the instrumental principle is that if I don't conform to it, if I *always* allow myself to be derailed by timidity, idleness, or depression, then I never really *will* an end. The *desire* to pursue the end and the desires that draw me away from it each hold sway in their turn, but *my will* is never active.[64] The distinction between my will and the operation of the desires and impulses in me does not exist, and that means that I, considered as an agent, do not exist. Conformity to the instrumental principle is thus constitutive of having a will, in a sense it is even what gives you a will.[65]

Now I need to clarify these remarks in one important way. In the above argument I appealed to the possibility of being tempted away from the end on another, temporally later occasion. But the argument does not really require the possibility of a temporally later occasion. It only requires that there be two parts of me, one that is my governing self, my will, and one

---

[64] A story: Jeremy settles down at his desk one evening to study for an examination. Finding himself a little too restless to concentrate, he decides to take a walk in the fresh air. His walk takes him past a nearby bookstore, where the sight of an enticing title draws him in to look at a book. Before he finds it, however, he meets his friend Neil, who invites him to join some of the other kids at the bar next door for a beer. Jeremy decides he can afford to have just one, and goes with Neil to the bar. When he arrives there, however, he finds that the noise gives him a headache, and he decides to return home without having a beer. He is now, however, in too much pain to study. So Jeremy doesn't study for his examination, hardly gets a walk, doesn't buy a book, and doesn't drink a beer. If your reply is that Jeremy is a distractible adolescent, and following desire is not always like this, Kant's reply in turn will be that it is only an *accident* when it is not.

[65] This is not the place to spell this thought out, but I also take the view I have put forward here to be essentially the same as the view that Plato advances in the *Republic*: namely, that the normativity of the principles of practical reason springs from, or reflects the fact that, the soul that does not follow them ultimately disintegrates. See also my *The Sources of Normativity*, sect. 3.3.1, pp. 100–2. If one of the central arguments of this essay is also correct—that there can be no instrumental norms unless there are also unconditional norms—then this lends support to Plato's claim that a completely unjust soul would also be incapable of 'achieving anything as a unit' (Plato, *Republic*, trans. G. M. A. Grube and C. D. C. Reeve (Indianapolis: Hackett, 1992), bk. 1, l. 352, p. 28. David Velleman's remark that '[u]nless we can commit ourselves today in a way that will generate reasons for us to act tomorrow, we shall have to regard our day-older selves either as beyond the control of today's decisions or as passive instruments of them' makes a similar point to the one I am making in the text—that without the power of commitment implicit in conformity to the instrumental principle, the autonomous self shatters into a sequence of time slices. See Essay 1 in this volume, p. 46.

that must be governed, and is capable of resisting my will. The possibility of resistance exists even now, on this occasion. The possibility of self-government essentially involves the possibility of its failure; and the principles of reason are therefore ineluctably normative.[66]

It is worth pointing out that an exactly parallel argument could be made about believing. We are neither inevitably inclined nor logically necessitated to believe the logical implications of our beliefs. The rational necessity of believing the logical implications of our beliefs cannot be explained by our plugging ourselves into a syllogism, like this: 'No one who believes X also believes ~X. I believe X, therefore I do not believe ~X.' The first premiss of such a syllogism is false, and if we add the caveat—that no one who is rational believes both of these things—then the syllogism cannot provide a non-trivial explanation of why it is irrational to believe a contradiction. The rational necessity of believing the implications of our beliefs can only be explained if we regard believing itself as a normative act. To believe something is not to be in a certain mental state, but to make a certain commitment. It is, we might say, to be committed to constructing one's view of the world in one way rather than another.

And trying to persuade someone who actually doubted the instrumental principle that she should act on it would be like trying to persuade someone who actually doubted the principle of non-contradiction that he should believe it. It would be *exactly* like that. When Aristotle said that trying to persuade someone of the principle of non-contradiction is like trying to argue with a vegetable, he was not just being abusive.[67] A person who denies the principle of non-contradiction asserts that anything may follow from anything, and that therefore he is committed to nothing. And if he commits himself to nothing there is nothing he believes, and so no point from which to start the argument. This is why Aristotle says that if you can just get him to assert something, you have already won the argument. A person who rejects the principle of non-contradiction does not reject a particular restriction on his beliefs. Since he commits himself to nothing, he rejects the very project of having beliefs.[68] And parallel points can be made about someone who denies the instrumental principle. This is why it matters that, as I pointed out at the beginning, the instrumental principle can naturally be extended so that it seems to be the principle of self-conscious action quite generally. A rejection of the instrumental principle is a rejection of self-conscious action itself.[69]

---

[66] The last two paragraphs are lifted almost verbatim from sect. 1 of my 'Reply', in *The Sources of Normativity*, 219–33; see esp. pp. 230–1.   [67] *Metaphysics* 4. 4, 1006a15.

[68] Peter Railton makes a parallel point—that someone who rejects the requirement that his beliefs be true is rejecting the project of having beliefs—in Essay 2 in this volume, pp. 56–9.

[69] Recent work in the philosophy of mind and action has been hampered by the presupposition that 'belief' and 'desire' are analogous states, the one demanding that the mind match the world, the other

On reflection, it looks as if no other solution is possible. We are trying to justify a norm, a principle, which claims to govern a certain activity. Why must we conform to the instrumental principle? Here we come to an important distinction, between norms which are constitutive of, and so internal to, the activities which they claim to govern, and norms which are external to those activities. If I say 'bake a cake, and make it taste good' and you ask *why* you should make it taste good, we may think that you don't know what baking cakes is all about. But if I say 'bake a cake, and make it ten feet high' and you ask *why* you should make it ten feet high, your question is perfectly in order. External norms give rise to further questions, and space for sceptical doubt. But if we can identify something as an internal norm, the question why you should conform to the norm answers itself. And some norms, unlike the norm of making cakes taste good, come not from the desired product of the activity, but from the nature of the activity itself. 'Put one foot in front of the other' is a norm of walking, and 'a sentence must contain both a subject and a verb' is a norm of linguistic action.[70] And yet, you can try to walk, fail to put one foot in front of another, and trip; and as all of us who grade student papers know, you can try to take linguistic action, and yet founder for want of a verb. Although these norms are constitutive, they are still norms, and not *mere* descriptions of the activities in question. They are, as it were, instructions for performing the activities in question. And so there's no room to ask why you should follow them: if you don't put one foot in front of the other you will not be walking and you will get nowhere; if you don't have both a subject and a verb you will not be speaking and you will say nothing. The instrumental principle is, in this way, a constitutive norm of willing, of deliberate action. If you are going to act at all, then you must conform to it.[71] And being human, you have no choice but to act.

Although of course I cannot give the argument for it here, it is important now to recall that on Kant's view, the moral law *just is* the law of an autonomous will. To say that moral laws are the laws of autonomy is not to say that our autonomy somehow requires us to *restrict* ourselves in accordance with them, but rather to say that they are constitutive of autonomous action. Kant thinks that in so far as we are autonomous, we just *do* will our maxims as universal laws. What I have argued in this essay is that this is also true

demanding that the world match the mind. As the view in the text suggests, I think that the analogue of belief is volition or choice; desire is more properly construed as the analogue of perception. Of course, the view advanced in the text—that belief and choice must be understood as first-personal commitments if we are to make sense of rationality—has important implications for the philosophy of mind.

[70] I owe the linguistic example to Barbara Herman.

[71] I also discuss the idea of constitutive norms in *The Sources of Normativity*, Reply, sect. 2, pp. 234–7.

of the principle of instrumental reason.[72] Kant therefore has a *unified* account of practical rationality: to be guided by reason just is to be autonomous, to give laws to oneself.[73]

Now let me go back to my other point. I claimed before that what my argument showed was that hypothetical imperatives cannot exist without categorical ones, or anyway without principles which direct us to the pursuit of certain ends, or anyway without *something* which gives normative status to our ends. Does this account support that claim? The long answer to that question is another project, but the short answer will do for now. If I am to will an end, to be and to remain committed to it even in the face of desires that would distract and weaknesses that would dissuade me, it looks as if I must have something to *say to myself* about why I am doing that—something better, moreover, than the fact that this is what I wanted yesterday. It looks as if the end is one that has to be *good*, in some sense that

---

[72] If, contrary to the argument of this essay, the instrumental principle were the only norm constitutive of rational action, then rational action would essentially be production, and action that was good *qua* action would be action that achieved its end. Aristotle explicitly rejects that view in book 6 of the *Nicomachean Ethics*, and this is part of his reason for thinking that actions are subject to special standards—ethical standards—that mere productions as such are not. For a discussion of the similarity between Aristotle and Kant on this point, see my 'From Duty and for the Sake of the Noble: Kant and Aristotle on Morally Good Action' (n. 2 above).

[73] This remark will naturally evoke the question what then becomes of Kant's claim that the moral law is synthetic, while the instrumental principle is analytic. In fact, on my reading, it may seem unclear what distinction is marked by those terms. In one way, I make it sound as if both the moral principle and the instrumental principle are analytic, for both are, if Kant's arguments succeed, constitutive of rational agency. In another way, I make it sound as if both the moral principle and the instrumental principle are synthetic, for both depend on the freedom inherent in the deliberative standpoint, and this parallels the way that synthetic principles of the understanding depend on the spacio-temporal structure of intuition. Choices are presented to us *in* freedom, just as objects are presented to us *in* space and time. On the other hand, Kant's more mundane point still holds: the necessity of taking the means is analytically derivable from our commitment to the end, while our commitment to the end is not in that way analytically derivable from anything. On my reading, however, this difference throws little important light on the source of their normativity. I am not certain what to say on this point, but I am inclined to think that my argument shows the distinction to be less important than Kant thought. I am indebted here to a discussion with Sidney Morgenbesser.

I also want to thank Sidney Morgenbesser, Joseph Raz, and Michael Thompson for pointing out a related and in a way more radical implication of the argument here, which is that it tends to break down the distinction between the different principles of practical reason described at the outset of this essay. If the argument of this essay is correct, moral or unconditional principles and the instrumental principle are both expressions of the basic requirement of giving oneself a law, and bring out different implications of that requirement. This lends support to Onora O'Neill's claim, in 'Reason and Politics in the Kantian Enterprise', that the categorical imperative is the supreme principle of reason in general. (See O'Neill, *Constructions of Reason* (Cambridge: Univ. Press, 1989), ch. 1.) But it also raises issues about the distinguishability of different kinds of practical rationality and irrationality. I am inclined to think that the right thing to say about this parallels what I take to be the right thing to say about Aristotle's theory of the unity of the virtues. There is really only one virtue, but there are many different vices, different ways to fall away from virtue, and when we assign someone a particular virtue, what we really mean is that she does not have the corresponding vice. In a similar way, there is only one principle of practical reason, the categorical imperative viewed as the law of autonomy, but there are different ways to fall away from autonomy, and the different principles of practical reason really instruct us not to fall away from our autonomy in these different ways.

goes beyond the locally desirable. I have to be able to make sense to myself of effort and deprivation and frustration, and it is hard to see how the reflection that this *is* what I wanted yesterday can do that by itself, especially when I want something else today. I do not have an argument that shows that this is *impossible*. I suppose that through some heroic existentialist act, one might just take one's will at a certain moment to be normative, and commit oneself forever to the end selected at that moment, without thinking that the end is in any way good, and perhaps for no other reason than that some such commitment is essential if one is to have a *will* at all. But it is hard to see how a self-conscious being who must talk to herself about her actions could live with that solution. To that extent, the normative force of the instrumental principle does seem to depend on our having a way to say to ourselves of some ends that there are reasons for them, that they are good.[74] However that may be, even the heroic existentialist is committed to the view that an act of his own will is the source of a reason— and *that* reason cannot possibly be derived from the instrumental principle. So the conclusion in any case follows—the view that all practical reason is instrumental is incoherent, for the instrumental principle cannot stand alone.

EPILOGUE

I won't attempt to sum up the long and complex argument of this essay. But by way of conclusion, it may be useful to say something about where, if my argument is correct, it leaves us.[75] What do I suppose I've shown, and if I'm right, what is both still necessary and still possible in the theory of practical reason?

First, as I've just said, I think the argument shows that the instrumental principle cannot stand alone. Unless something attaches normativity to our ends, there can be no requirement to take the means to them. Of course, even if our ends lack such normativity, so long as they continue to be the

---

[74] In Essay 2 in this volume, pp. 62 ff. Peter Railton distinguishes between 'High Brow' accounts of practical reasoning, according to which rational agents necessarily aim at the good, and 'Low Brow' accounts, like Hume's, according to which rational agents may aim simply at the satisfaction of their desires or ends. Because I have argued that the instrumental principle cannot stand alone, my argument favours High Brow views. The case of the heroic existentialist, however, shows that the sense in which it does so is rather thin. The heroic existentialist's ends are not merely the objects of his desires, but rather of his will, so he is not merely given them by nature: he has endorsed them, and to that extent he does see them as things he has reason to pursue. But since he has not endorsed them for any further reason, it would be a bit of a stretch to say that he thinks they are good. The claim in the text—that the heroic existentialist's position is hard to live with—shows why I think that my argument also gives rise at least to pressure towards a more substantively High Brow view. I say a little more about this in the Epilogue below.

[75] I have been pressed on this point by quite a few people who read or heard drafts of this essay, but I would particularly like to thank Allan Gibbard.

ends we have in view, or the ones we effectively want most, we may certainly be inspired by instrumental thoughts to take the means to them: that is, instrumental thoughts may *cause* us to *want* to take those means. This is how it is with intelligent but non-rational animals, and, if Hume were right, this is how it would be with us. Indeed, this kind of instrumental *intelligence* seems pretty clearly to be a prerequisite for instrumental *rationality*, and, to that extent, this *is* how it is with us. But no account of a *requirement* of taking the means to our ends can be derived from the mere fact that we possess this kind of intelligence. If there is a principle of practical reason which *requires* us to take the means to our ends, then those ends must be, not merely ones that we happen to have in view, but ones that we have some reason to keep in view. There must be unconditional reasons for having certain ends, and, it seems, unconditional principles from which those reasons are derived. So now two further questions arise: have I done anything towards showing whether there are any such principles, or what they would have to be like?

In one sense, the answer to the first question, whether I have shown that there are unconditional principles, is no. The conclusion of this essay is hypothetical: the argument shows that *if* there are any instrumental requirements, then there must be unconditional requirements as well. Conversely, if there are unconditional requirements to adopt certain ends, then there are also requirements to take the means to those ends, since a commitment to taking the means is what makes a difference between willing an end and merely wishing for it or wanting it or thinking that it would be nice if it were realized. But these arguments show only that unconditional and conditional requirements are mutually dependent. Complete practical normative scepticism is still an option, although its price is high—a point I will come back to.[76]

The answer to the second question: 'does this argument show us anything substantive about the unconditional principles of practical reason— about what they would have to be like?' is also no. At least I have shown nothing so far about the *content* of those principles. As far as the argument of this essay goes, they could be principles of prudence, or moral principles, or something else. In fact, as the possibility of the 'heroic existentialist' I described at the end of Section 3 shows, the reason to pursue the end which is needed to support the reason to take the means can be as thin and insubstantial as the agent's arbitrary will, his raw and unmotivated decision that he will take a certain end to be normative for himself, for no other reason than that he wills it so.

Yet even my heroic existentialist is autonomous, and this leads me to the more positive side of the argument: for I think that the argument

[76] See also my *The Sources of Normativity*, sects. 4.4.1–4.4.2, pp. 160–4.

of Section 3 establishes not only that instrumental principles depend on unconditional ones, but also that particular instrumental requirements must be self-given laws, grounded in our autonomy. This raises the further question whether the unconditional reasons on which hypothetical reasons depend must also be, according to my argument, grounded in autonomy, or whether we could give, say, a dogmatic rationalist account of the unconditional reasons for having certain ends.[77] I believe that the argument does show that unconditional reasons, as well as hypothetical ones, must be grounded in autonomy. This is because the arguments of Section 3, both those against dogmatic rationalism, and those in favour of the view that the principles of practical reason are constitutive norms of autonomy, are not specific to the principle of instrumental reason. They are concerned with the question how we can account for the normativity of practical reasons generally. The point of focusing on the instrumental principle is really just that this conclusion is, in its case, more unexpected and striking.

But if the argument shows that our unconditional principles must be laws of autonomy, then it brings us back home to the old Hegelian question: can any substantive requirements be derived from the mere fact of our autonomy? How much determinate content do the constitutive norms of autonomy have? And does this content coincide with, or include, morality? For this is the real question behind the familiar worry whether Kant's Formula of Universal Law has content. As I see it, then, only three positions are possible: either (i) the Kantian argument that autonomy commits us to certain substantive principles can be made to work; or (ii) we are left in the position of the heroic existentialist, who must ultimately define his will through acts of unconditional commitment that have no further ground; or (iii) complete practical normative scepticism is in order.

My own view is that the Kantian argument can be made to succeed, but that of course is another story—if I am right, it is *the* other story, where practical reason is concerned.[78] But it's worth saying something here about what's left to choose between existentialism and complete practical normative scepticism, if the Kantian project does not work out. And this brings us back to the question of the price of complete practical normative scepticism.

The argument of this essay makes a strong connection between having a will, and being bound by the principles of practical reason—or at least, by the principle of instrumental reason. Conformity to the principle of instrumental reason—prescribing to oneself in accordance with this

---

[77] Here again I would especially like to thank Allan Gibbard.

[78] The question whether there are substantive, constitutive norms of autonomy, and whether those coincide with moral norms, is a complex question which may be divided into a number of different parts, responsive to different ways in which the claim can be challenged. For an account of these different challenges, and of my own attempts to respond to them, see my *The Sources of Normativity*, sect. 1 of the Reply, pp. 220–2.

principle—is constitutive of having a will. And having a will, I believe, is constitutive of being a person. As I have argued in both Section 2 and Section 3, a person who does not conform to the instrumental principle becomes a mere location for the play of desires and impulses, the field of their battle for dominance over the body through which they seek satisfaction.[79] The price of complete practical normative scepticism, then, is nothing short of the loss of personal identity. The existentialist, however arbitrarily, does preserve his will and so his identity. It's important to see that the practical form in which I'm putting these claims—the sceptic *loses* his identity; the existentialist *preserves* his will—is not a mistake or a literary conceit. With realism denied, the question becomes a practical one. It is not the question whether we really have such wills as are constituted by these principles, but whether we are to conduct ourselves so as to have such wills, by acting in accordance with these principles. The final answer, then, to the question—what gives the instrumental principle its normativity?— is this: conformity to the instrumental principle is an essential part of what makes you a person. There is no position from which you can reject the government of instrumental reason: for if you reject it, there is no you.[80]

---

[79] See Sect. 2, pp. 233–4, and Sect. 3, pp. 246–7. This is part of the reason why Plato thinks that the soul completely ungoverned by reason ultimately becomes 'tyrannical'. See n. 65 above and *Republic*, bk. 9.

[80] This essay leaves me with many debts. Final revisions were made while I was a Fellow at the University Center for Human Values in Princeton, for whose support I am deeply grateful. I discussed the essay or parts of the essay with audiences at the Twenty-First Annual Meeting of the Hume Society, with commentary by Charlotte Brown; at the St Andrews Conference on Ethics and Practical Reason, with commentary by Ralph Wedgwood; at the American Philosophical Association, with commentary by Allan Gibbard; at the Fellows Seminar at the Center for Human Values in Princeton, with commentary by Michael Thompson; at the Philosophy Departments at Bowling Green University, the University of California at Irvine, the University of California at Los Angeles, the University of Michigan, and the University of Reading; at the Columbia Legal Theory Workshop; and at the New York University Colloquium in Law, Philosophy, and Political Theory. I am grateful to all of these audiences, and my commentators especially. I also received generous and extremely helpful written comments from Annette Baier, Kurt Baier, Alyssa Bernstein, Barbara Herman, Brad Hooker, Peter Hylton, Arthur Kuflik, Andrews Reath, Tamar Schapiro, Allen Wood, and the editors of this volume, and excellent written comments in addition to their presented commentaries from Charlotte Brown and Allan Gibbard. I would also like to thank John Broome, Erin Kelly, Edward McClennan, Sidney Morgenbesser, John Rawls, Joseph Raz, and Michael Robins for useful remarks made in discussion, and Barbara Herman for extensive discussion in addition to her written comments. I thank all of these people for their incisive criticisms, many of which I have not been able to answer, and for their interest and support. Finally, I would like to reiterate my gratitude to the late Warren Quinn for pressing me to clarify Kant's account of the hypothetical imperative.

9

Kantian Rationalism: Inescapability, Authority, and Supremacy

DAVID O. BRINK

Kant appears to be the ultimate rationalist about moral psychology.[1] In claiming that moral requirements express categorical imperatives, he defends the existence of objective moral requirements that are part of practical reason and are supposed to have overriding authority. I want to examine and assess different strands in Kant's rationalism. In particular, I believe that in claiming that moral requirements are categorical imperatives Kant commits himself to three distinguishable claims. (*a*) If moral requirements are categorical imperatives, they are objective or inescapable; their application to an agent does not depend on the agent's own contingent inclinations or interests. Let us call this the *inescapability* thesis. (*b*) If moral requirements are categorical imperatives, they are requirements of reason; moral requirements have rational authority such that it is *pro tanto* irrational to fail to act in accordance with them, and this authority is independent of the agent's own aims or interests. Let us call this the *authority* thesis. (*c*) Kant also believes that the categorical character of moral requirements implies that their authority is always overriding. Let us call this the *supremacy* thesis.

Once we distinguish these three aspects of Kantian rationalism, we may not find them equally plausible. In her interesting and provocative article 'Morality as a System of Hypothetical Imperatives' Philippa Foot distinguishes, in effect, between the inescapability and authority theses and argues that only the inescapability thesis is defensible.[2] Though I take

---

[1] References to Kant are to the Prussian Academy pagination in the following works: *Kritik der reinen Vernunft* (cited as *KrV*) and trans. as *Immanuel Kant's Critique of Pure Reason*, by Norman Kemp Smith (New York: St Martin's, 1963); *Grundlegung der Metaphysik der Sitten* (cited as *G*) and trans. as *Grounding for the Metaphysics of Morals*, by J. Ellington (Indianapolis: Hackett, 1981); *Kritik der praktischen Vernunft* (cited as *KpV*) and trans. as *Critique of Practical Reason*, by L. W. Beck (Indianapolis: Library of Liberal Arts, 1956); *Metaphysik der Sitten* (cited as *M*) and trans. as *The Metaphysics of Morals* in *Kant's Ethical Philosophy*, by J. Ellington (Indianapolis: Hackett, 1983); *Kritik der Urteilskraft* (cited as *KU*) and trans. as *Critique of Judgment* by W. Pluhar (Indianapolis: Hackett, 1987).

[2] *Philosophical Review*, 81 (1972), 305–16; repr. with postscript in Philippa Foot, *Virtues and Vices* (Los Angeles: Univ. of California Press, 1978), 157–73.

Foot's claims seriously, I argue, by contrast, that Kant has a plausible argument from the inescapability of moral requirements to their authority. However, I express scepticism about Kant's arguments for the supremacy thesis. In fact, I believe that Kant may have to recognize a kind of dualism of practical reason between agent-centred and impartial imperatives. Unless this dualism can be resolved, the supremacy thesis must remain doubtful.

1. The Rational Authority of Morality

My interest in Kantian rationalism grows out of my attempt to understand and assess different conceptions of the rational authority of morality. It is common to think of morality as both impartial and objective, in particular, as containing various other-regarding duties of co-operation, forbearance, and aid that apply to agents independently of their own aims and interests. Most of us also regard moral obligations as authoritative practical considerations. But heeding these obligations appears sometimes to constrain the agent's pursuit of his own interest or aims. If we associate rationality with the agent's own point of view, we may wonder whether moral conduct is always rationally justifiable. We can capture this tension in common views in terms of a puzzle about the authority of morality.[3]

1. Moral requirements include impartial other-regarding obligations that do not apply to agents in virtue of their own aims or interests.
2. Moral requirements provide agents with overriding reasons for action; necessarily, it is on balance irrational to act contrary to moral requirements.
3. Rational action is action that achieves the agent's aims or promotes her interests.
4. Fulfilling other-regarding obligations need not advance the agent's aims or interests.

(1) articulates one conception of ethical objectivity, according to which moral requirements appear as impartial constraints on conduct that do not apply in virtue of the agent's own aims or interests. For instance, I do not defeat an ascription of obligation to me to help another by pointing out that doing so will serve no aim or interest that I have. (2) implies the weak rationalist thesis that there is always reason to be moral such that contra-moral behaviour is *pro tanto* irrational; but it also expresses the strong rationalist thesis that contra-moral behaviour is always on balance irrational.

---

[3] I have discussed the puzzle and various solutions elsewhere; see my 'A Puzzle about the Rational Authority of Morality', *Philosophical Perspectives*, 6 (1992), 1–26 and 'Objectivity, Motivation, and Authority in Ethics' (unpublished).

It is one way of attempting to understand the special authority moral considerations seem to have in practical deliberation. (3) expresses a common view of practical rationality, according to which it is instrumental or prudential. Though prudential and instrumental conceptions of rationality are different in significant ways, both represent the rationality of other-regarding conduct as *derivative*. Though no labels seem entirely satisfactory, we might describe this common assumption as the assumption that practical reason is *agent-centred*; by contrast, practical reason is *impartial* if it implies that there is non-derivative reason to engage in other-regarding conduct.[4] Finally, (4) reflects a common assumption about the independence of different people's interests and attitudes, which we might call the *independence assumption*. Though agents often do care about the welfare of others and there are often connections between an agent's own interests and those of others, neither connection holds either universally or necessarily. My aims could be largely self-confined, and my own good can be specified in terms that make no essential reference to the good of others, say, in terms of my own pleasure or the satisfaction of my desires.

Though each element of the puzzle might seem appealing and has appealed to some, not all four claims can be true. In fact, a number of

---

[4] (a) My contrast between agent-centred and impartial conceptions of rationality is different from the contrast, some have drawn, between agent-relative and agent-neutral reasons. Cf. Thomas Nagel, *The View from Nowhere* (New York: Oxford Univ. Press, 1986), 152–3. According to the latter distinction, reasons are agent-relative if their general form involves essential reference to the agent who has them; otherwise, reasons are agent-neutral. Agent-neutral theories are typically understood to be consequentialist, whereas agent-relative theories are quite varied. Prudential and instrumental conceptions of rationality are both agent-relative, though in different ways. A crucial issue as regards the authority of ethics is whether the justification of other-regarding moral conduct is derivative, as both prudential and instrumental conceptions of rationality must claim it is, or whether it is non-derivative. The distinction between agent-centred and impartial conceptions of rationality gets at this issue, whereas the distinction between agent-relative and agent-neutral conceptions of rationality does not. This can be illustrated by considering the view Broad called *self-referential altruism*, according to which an agent has non-derivative reason to benefit others, as well as herself, but the weight or strength of her reasons is a function of the nature of the relationship in which she stands to potential beneficiaries. Cf. C. D. Broad, 'Self and Others', repr. in *Broad's Critical Essays in Moral Psychology*, ed. D. Cheney (London: George Allen & Unwin, 1971), 279–80. Though self-referential altruism is agent-relative, its altruistic or impartial component makes its justification of other-regarding conduct non-derivative in a way that is alien to prudential and instrumental conceptions of rationality. I am here interested in the contrast between the way in which prudential and instrumental conceptions of rationality make the justification of other-regarding conduct derivative and the way in which agent-neutral theories and some agent-relative theories (e.g. self-referential altruism) do not. Though no labels seem entirely satisfactory, I refer to these two approaches as agent-centred and impartial conceptions, respectively. Notice that in so doing we leave it open whether impartiality should take an agent-neutral or agent-relative form. (b) We should also note that impartiality, in this sense, need not preclude some forms of partiality; it need not preclude greater concern for oneself and others to whom one stands in special relationships than to comparative strangers. Even agent-neutral interpretations of impartiality try to accommodate some kinds of partiality. And, as self-referential altruism makes plain, some theories that are impartial, in my sense, can recognize partiality at a fairly fundamental level. So the fact that Kant recognizes some kinds of partiality (*M* 451–2) is consistent with my claim that he accepts an impartial conception of practical reason.

influential historical and contemporary views can be seen as responses, perhaps tacit, to this puzzle that reject at least one element of the puzzle on the strength of others. Some *moral relativists* and *minimalists* appeal to (2)–(4) and reject the existence of impartial and objective moral norms asserted in (1); they claim that genuine moral requirements must be relativized to and further the agent's interests or aims in some way.[5] A weak rationalist might resist the strong rationalist thesis in (2). But those who appeal to (1), (3), and (4) to reject (2) typically reject even the weak rationalist claim; *anti-rationalists* deny (2) and claim that failure to act on moral requirements is not necessarily irrational. Others reject the agent-centred assumptions about practical rationality in (3) and defend the existence of *impartial practical reason*.[6] Finally, *metaphysical egoists* reject the independence assumption in (4) and resolve the puzzle by arguing that, properly understood, people's interests are interdependent such that acting on other-regarding moral requirements is a counterfactually reliable way of promoting the agent's own interests.[7]

Kant accepts (1), (2), and (4) and denies (3); he claims that practical reason can be impartial. Foot also accepts (1), but because she accepts (3) and (4), she rejects (2). She is an anti-rationalist; immoral action need not be irrational.[8]

My aim is to understand and assess the Kantian solution to the puzzle about the rational authority of morality. I am interested in a careful and sympathetic interpretation of Kant's texts, especially the *Groundwork*. But because my main interest in Kant derives from my systematic concerns with the authority of morality, I am more interested in the themes and resources of Kantian rationalism than in scholarship, especially those themes and resources that do not presuppose transcendental idealism, in particular, transcendental freedom.

[5] This view is represented by Callicles' claims about natural justice in Plato's *Gorgias* and by that strand of social contract theory—including Epicurus, Hobbes, and Gauthier—that understands the scope, content, and authority of morality in terms of rational agreement. See *Gorgias* 482de, 483ab, 488b–490a; Epicurus, *Kuriai Doxa* 31–8; Thomas Hobbes, *Leviathan*, esp. chs. xiii–xv; and David Gauthier, *Morals by Agreement* (Oxford: Clarendon Press, 1986). A more clearly relativistic version of the view is Gilbert Harman, 'Moral Relativism Defended', *Philosophical Review*, 85 (1975), 3–22.

[6] An important contemporary defence of impartial practical reason is Thomas Nagel, *The Possibility of Altruism* (Princeton: Univ. Press, 1970).

[7] For one such view and a discussion of its classical roots, see my 'Self-Love and Altruism', *Social Philosophy and Policy*, 14 (1997), 122–57.

[8] This is a fair characterization of Foot's view in 'Morality as a System of Hypothetical Imperatives'. However, recently she has changed her view; see Philippa Foot, 'Does Moral Subjectivism Rest on a Mistake?', *Oxford Journal of Legal Studies*, 15 (1995), 1–14. There, in direct opposition to her view in 'Morality as a System of Hypothetical Imperatives', Foot understands moral requirements as requirements of practical reason and rejects agent-centred assumptions about practical reason. She attempts to explain why familiar other-regarding demands are requirements of practical reason by representing them as 'Aristotelian necessities', without the general observance of which social life and its benefits would be difficult if not impossible. I won't explore this suggestion or its adequacy here.

2. *Inescapability without Authority*

Kant, of course, distinguishes between hypothetical and categorical imperatives. He writes

Now all imperatives command either hypothetically or categorically. The former represent the practical necessity of a possible action as a means of attaining something else that one wants (*will*) (or may possibly want) (*wolle*). The categorical imperative would be one which represented an action as objectively necessary in itself, without reference to another end. (*G* 414)

Here and elsewhere (*KpV* 20–1) Kant claims that hypothetical imperatives are conditional on what an agent wants (or wills).[9] If so, instrumental imperatives are hypothetical imperatives. But he must also think that prudential imperatives are hypothetical.[10] For prudential imperatives presumably represent action as necessary to achieve a distinct end, namely, the agent's happiness or interest. And Kant clearly regards Greek eudaemonist theories as heteronomous and, hence, as containing only hypothetical imperatives (*KpV* 24, 64–5, 109, 111–13). If so, we can understand hypothetical imperatives to be conditional on whether the conduct enjoined promotes the agent's antecedent aims or interests, whereas categorical imperatives are not.

Following Foot, we might identify two distinguishable senses in which imperatives might be categorical. In one sense, imperatives are categorical just in case they *apply* to people independently of their aims or interests; if so, we might say they express *categorical norms*. Imperatives are categorical in another sense just in case they provide those to whom they apply with *reasons for action* independently of their aims or interests; if so, we might say they generate *categorical reasons*.

Famously, Kant claims that moral requirements express categorical, rather than hypothetical, imperatives (*G* 416, 425). Presumably, he thinks moral requirements are categorical imperatives in both senses; they express categorical norms that generate categorical reasons. But once we distinguish clearly between inescapability and authority, we might accept inescapability without authority; we might agree that moral requirements express categorical norms but deny that they generate categorical reasons.

Various systems of norms appear to express categorical norms whose authority, however, is not (obviously) categorical. For instance, it is natural,

---

[9] *Wollen* can be translated as 'to want' or as 'to will'. Kant does not think that every object of one's desire is an object of one's will; to will something is to have one's choice in some way determined by practical reason (*G* 412, 427, 446). If so, it is possible to read this passage (*G* 414) as saying that hypothetical imperatives represent as practically necessary actions that secure means or necessary conditions to what the agent wills, and not merely to what she wants. I will discuss the significance of this interpretation of Kant's remarks about hypothetical imperatives later (sect. 10).

[10] Indeed, Kant appears to equate all empirical motivation with self-love (*KpV* 22, 34).

and I think plausible, to view legal and occupational requirements this way. But legal and occupational requirements are often morally or prudentially important. It is, I think, because she wants to examine morality's relation to something agreed to be fairly unimportant that Foot explains her assessment of Kant with an analogy between morality and etiquette. Indeed, rules of etiquette often overlap with requirements of morality or prudence. The focus on etiquette must be on those rules of etiquette that seem especially unimportant morally or prudentially, for instance, rules requiring that invitations addressed in the third person be answered in the third person. She invites us to compare morality and *mere* etiquette.

According to Foot, both rules of (mere) etiquette and moral requirements are inescapable; they express categorical norms. The moral duty to help others in distress, when you can do so at little cost to yourself, does not fail to apply to you—we do not withdraw our ascription of obligation to you—just because you are indifferent to your neighbour's suffering and in a hurry to read your mail, as would be the case if it was a hypothetical norm. In the same way, rules against replying to a third-person invitation in the first person don't fail to apply to you—we don't take back our ascriptions of duties of etiquette to you—just because you think etiquette is silly or you have a desire to annoy your host, as would be the case if rules of etiquette stated hypothetical norms.

But rules of etiquette seem to lack *authority*; they appear to generate hypothetical, not categorical reasons. On this view, rules of etiquette may state categorical norms, but failure to observe these norms does not seem irrational unless this in some way undermines the agent's interests or aims. Here too moral requirements may seem on a par with requirements of etiquette. If the independence assumption is correct, obligations of forbearance, mutual aid, and justice need further no aims or interests of the agent. Though we do not need to withdraw the ascription of obligation in such cases, perhaps we should allow that immoral conduct in such a case is not irrational. This is Foot's view.

[I]t is supposed [by Kant and others] that moral considerations necessarily give reasons for acting to any man. The difficulty is, of course, to defend this proposition which is more often repeated than explained. . . . The fact is that the man who rejects morality because he sees no reason to obey its rules can be convicted of villainy but not of inconsistency. Nor will his action necessarily be irrational. Irrational actions are those in which a man in some way defeats his own purposes, doing what is calculated to be disadvantageous or to frustrate his ends. Immorality does not *necessarily* involve any such thing.[11]

---

[11] 'Morality as a System of Hypothetical Imperatives', 161–2.

So Foot accepts the inescapability thesis but rejects the authority thesis. Because she assumes that practical reason is agent-centred, she finds the authority thesis mysterious. In fact, she thinks that Kantians mistakenly appeal to the inescapability thesis to support the authority thesis.[12]

We can now see the sense in which Foot thinks morality is a system of hypothetical imperatives. For whereas she does think that moral requirements, like requirements of etiquette, express categorical norms, she thinks that they, also like requirements of etiquette, generate hypothetical, rather than categorical reasons. Because Kant would not want to regard requirements of etiquette as categorical imperatives, this shows that the basic sense of categoricity is that in which, on her view, moral requirements are not categorical imperatives.

3. Authority

On Foot's version of anti-rationalism, the authority, but not the scope or content, of morality depends on the aims or interests of agents. But the analogy between morals and manners as yet provides no explanation of the common belief that morality has a special authority. On one reading of her claims, Foot seems to say that the special authority of morality is just an illusion—an artefact of moral education. But she also claims that the authority of morality does not require categorical imperatives. The part of morality most obviously threatened by agent-centred rationality is other-regarding morality, for it is obligations of forbearance, mutual aid, and justice that are most likely to frustrate the agent's own interests and desires. But Foot thinks that people can be and are committed to the interests of other people and common causes, as morality requires, and that these social interests and sentiments ensure that they do act as morality requires and that they have (hypothetical) reason to do so.

This conclusion may, as I said, appear dangerous and subversive of morality. We are apt to panic at the thought that we ourselves, or other people, might stop caring about the things we do care about, and we feel that the categorical imperative gives us some control over the situation. But it is interesting that the people of Leningrad were not struck by the thought that only the *contingent* fact that other citizens shared their loyalty and devotion to the city stood between them and the Germans during the terrible years of the siege. Perhaps we should be less troubled than we are by fear of defection from the moral cause . . .[13]

If we rely on purely instrumental assumptions about rationality, we can establish the authority of other-regarding moral requirements to those who

[12] Ibid. 162.   [13] Ibid. 167.

have suitable other-regarding attitudes. Especially if such attitudes are strong and widespread, this may seem an adequate account of the authority of other-regarding morality.

But the instrumental justification of morality appeals to other-regarding attitudes without grounding them; as a result, it seems unable to explain why those who lack these attitudes should cultivate them or why those who do have them should maintain them. This is presumably part of what Kant has in mind when he objects to accounts of moral motivation that make it dependent on contingent and variable inclination; he concludes that the authority of morality must depend on features of rational agents as such (*G* 389–90, 397–400, 427, 442–3; *KpV* 21, 24–6, 36).

A more traditional defence of morality is to argue that the demands of morality and enlightened self-interest coincide. The main lines of this story are familiar enough. Much of impartial other-regarding morality involves norms of co-operation (e.g. fidelity and fair play), forbearance, and aid. Each individual has an interest in the fruits of interaction conducted according to these norms. Though it might be desirable to reap the benefits of other people's compliance with norms of forbearance and co-operation without incurring the burdens of one's own, the opportunities to do this are infrequent. Non-compliance is generally detectable, and others won't be forbearing and co-operative toward those who are known to be non-compliant. For this reason, compliance is typically necessary to enjoy the benefits of others' continued compliance. Moreover, because each has an interest in others' co-operation and restraint, communities will tend to reinforce compliant behaviour and discourage non-compliant behaviour. If so, compliance is often necessary to avoid such social sanctions. Whereas non-compliance secures short-term benefits that compliance does not, compliance typically secures greater long-term benefits than non-compliance. In this way, compliance with other-regarding norms of co-operation, forbearance, and aid might be claimed to further the agent's interests. In so far as this is true, the rational egoist can ground other-regarding sentiments and explain why those who do not have them should cultivate them and those who do have them should maintain them.

However, as long as we rely on pre-theoretical understandings of self-interest, the coincidence between other-regarding morality and enlightened self-interest, on this view, must remain imperfect. Sometimes non-compliance would go undetected; and even where non-compliance is detected, the benefits of non-compliance sometimes outweigh the costs of being excluded from future co-operative interaction. Moreover, even if the coincidence between morality and self-interest were extensionally adequate, it would be counterfactually fragile. On this justification of compliance with other-regarding norms, compliance involves costs, as well as benefits; it must remain a second-best option, behind undetected non-compliance, in which one enjoys the benefits of others' compliance without the costs of one's own. But then if one had some way of ensuring that one's own non-compliance would go undetected—for instance, one had sole access to the ring of Gyges—one could enjoy the benefits of the compliance of others without the burdens of one's own, and one would have no reason to be compliant. The imperfect coincidence of morality and self-interest, which the independence assumption ensures, implies that immorality need not always be irrational. And this is presumably part of what troubles Kant about accounts of moral motivation that make it dependent on the agent's own happiness (*G* 425–7, 442–3; *KpV* 20–1, 24, 64–5, 109, 111–13).

None the less, anti-rationalists may find this acceptable. It allows us to explain why everyone has some stake in morality, and why people generally have reason to behave morally, but it insists that immoral action is not always irrational. As long as we have not tied the scope and content of morality to its rationality, we can reproach the immoralist with immorality. What is lost if we cannot also reproach him with irrationality?

Anti-rationalism would be more satisfactory if morality and rationality were two independent but co-ordinate perspectives. For then it might seem to be an open question whether an agent should side with morality or rationality when they conflict. But in the present context, practical rationality is not just one standard or perspective among others, with no obviously privileged position; it should be understood to concern whatever fundamentally matters in practical deliberation or whatever it is ultimately reasonable to do. So, for example, if I have doubts about whether I have reason to act on a particular norm, I should be interpreted as having doubts about whether that is a norm of practical rationality, rather than as having doubts about rationality. But then anti-rationalism has the potentially unsettling consequence that morality need not always have authority in our deliberations.

We might ask why Foot and other anti-rationalists assume that practical reason must be agent-centred. One reason appeals to apparent connections between practical rationality and motivation. It seems plausible that judgements of practical rationality normally give rise to motivation. If recognition of reasons for action normally motivates, this may seem to require that reasons for actions be grounded in antecedently motivational facts or states of the agent, such as her interests or desires.[14] But we can respect this link between practical judgement and motivation without supposing that

---

[14] Cf. Bernard Williams, 'Internal and External Reasons', repr. in his *Moral Luck* (Cambridge: Univ. Press, 1981). Williams argues from a somewhat stronger assumption about the link between recognizing the truth of practical judgements and motivations to a kind of instrumental conception of rationality that grounds reasons for action in the agent's antecedent pro-attitudes.

rationality is constrained by what is antecedently motivational or that
motivation might be produced by cognitive states alone. We can accept the
common view that motivation requires a desire or pro-attitude. On this
view, intentional action is the product of representational states, such as
belief, which aim to conform to the world, and practical states or pro-
attitudes, such as desires, which aim to make the world conform to them.
As such, normative motivation, like all motivation, requires pro-attitudes.
But, other things being equal, our motivational states track our beliefs
about what we have reason to do. Given that practical reason concerns
whatever fundamentally matters in practical reasoning, we should expect
results of practical deliberation normally to affect one's motivational set.[15]
Believing it is best that things be a certain way normally produces a desire
or pro-attitude to make things be that way.[16] If so, motivation can be
consequential on practical rationality, not the other way around (G 460-1).
So if there are good arguments for thinking that practical rationality can be
impartial, the connection between rationality and motivation is no obstacle
to rationalism.[17]

4. Kantian Inescapability

Foot complains that Kantians appeal to the inescapability thesis to support
the authority thesis. If these are independent theses, this is a mistake. But
even if they are distinct theses, they need not be independent. In fact, Kant
believes that the way in which moral requirements are inescapable explains
their authority. To explain Kant's argument from inescapability to authority, we will need to examine his views about the Categorical Imperative at
some length.

Kant often claims that common-sense morality presupposes that moral
requirements, or at least their foundations, must be justifiable a priori and
not on the basis of experience (G 388-9, 410). There are at least two
different claims here.

---

[15] Action based on *moral* feeling is not heteronomous; moral feelings are consequential on recognizing the authority of pure practical reason (G 401 n.; KpV 24-5, 75-82).

[16] I defend this as a systematic claim at greater length in 'Objectivity, Motivation, and Authority in
Ethics', sects. 1-4. Allison says that Kant explicitly dismisses a similar claim about how practical reason
might motivate; see Henry Allison, *Kant's Theory of Freedom* (New York: Cambridge Univ. Press,
1990), 122-3. Allison does not say enough about the view he thinks Kant dismisses or his grounds for
dismissing it for me to evaluate his (Allison's) claim. I do not think Kant needs to or even does reject
the picture I have sketched of the relation between judgements of practical reason and motivation.

[17] My answer to this motivational challenge to the possibility of impartial practical reason is similar
to some claims made by Christine Korsgaard in 'Skepticism about Practical Reason', *Journal of Philosophy*, 83 (1986), esp. 21-3. But, whereas she seems to think that the motivational capacity of judgements
of practical reason requires a prior desire to be rational, I think that such a desire need play no role in
the production of motivation.

One claim concerns particular duties (e.g. Sam's duty to fulfil his contractual obligation to sell his widgets to Ben). Though an agent's particular duties do depend upon certain contingent circumstances, such as his past actions (e.g. the fact that Sam signed a contract to sell his widgets to Ben), they do not depend upon contingent facts about the agent's interests and desires at the time of action. In particular, an agent cannot defeat a claim that he has a duty simply by pleading disinclination or disinterest. If so, we can know an agent's particular duties independently of knowing these empirical facts about him. We have already accepted this idea in accepting the inescapability thesis.

But this does not yet establish the strong claim that morality is justifiable a priori; for this to be true, morality must in some way be independent of all contingent empirical facts about agents. Kant supposes that particular, concrete duties are established by the application of quite general moral principles, such as the requirement to treat others as ends and not merely as means, to contingent empirical circumstances (e.g. the circumstances of Sam's promise to Ben) (*M* 217). Moreover, he believes that these more abstract principles must be independent not only of the agent's particular interests and desires at the time of acting but independent of all contingent facts about the agent and his circumstances; they must depend upon general features of moral agents (*G* 408). Indeed, this is presumably the difference between the Categorical Imperative, in its various formulations, and particular categorical imperatives. Whereas the Categorical Imperative is supposed to be justified independently of empirical facts, particular categorical imperatives result from the application of the Categorical Imperative to particular circumstances. If these abstract principles are treated as the *ground* of the more concrete, particular duties, then we can understand why Kant would believe that there is a sense in which even these more particular duties apply to agents independently of contingent facts about themselves and their circumstances; their ground is so independent and is, therefore, knowable independently of knowledge of these contingent facts (*G* 389).[18]

But what would it be for moral duties to apply to agents in virtue of general features of moral agents? To be a moral agent is presumably to be *responsible*; only responsible agents are properly praised and blamed, because only they can be held accountable for their actions. Non-responsible agents, such as brutes and small children, appear to act on their strongest desires or, if they deliberate, to deliberate only about the instrumental means to the satisfaction of their desires. By contrast, responsible agents, we assume,

---

[18] Cf. Allen Buchanan, 'Categorical Imperatives and Moral Principles', *Philosophical Studies*, 31 (1977), 249–60.

can distinguish between the *intensity* and *authority* of their desires and deliberate about the appropriateness of their desires and aims (*G* 396, 437, 448, 452; *KrV* A534/B562, A553–4/B581–2, A802/B830; *KpV* 61–2, 87; *M* 213, 391–2; *KU* 442–3).[19] Whether consciously or merely implicitly, a responsible agent can and does assess the desirability of her impulses, and her choices reflect these deliberations about her desires. If so, capacities for practical deliberation—formulating, assessing, revising, choosing, and implementing projects and goals—are essential to being an agent. Because moral agents are essentially reasoning and deliberative creatures, moral requirements must apply to rational agents as such if they are to apply to moral agents as such (*G* 408, 412, 423, 425–7; *KpV* 20–1, 29–30).[20] As Kant writes in the *Metaphysics of Morals*, 'They [requirements of morality] command everyone without regard to his inclinations, solely because and insofar as he is free and has practical reason' (*M* 216). If moral requirements apply to people in so far as they are rational beings and not in so far as they have contingent inclinations and interests, then we can see why they must be expressed by categorical, rather than hypothetical, imperatives. For hypothetical imperatives do, and categorical imperatives do not, apply to us in virtue of our contingent interests and inclinations.

Of course, Kant thinks we cannot know whether there are, in fact, any moral requirements until we can show that moral agents are free and responsible, a task he attempts to complete, among other places, in Section 3 of the *Groundwork*. There he argues that (*a*) freedom requires the capacity for determination by reasons, not one's kinaesthetically strongest desires (*G* 446–8, 457, 459–60; cf. *KrV* A534/B562, A553–4/B581–2, A802/B830; *G* 396, 437; *KpV* 61–2, 72, 87; *M* 213, 216, 391–2; *KU* 442–3), that (*b*) this capacity requires transcendental freedom (*G* 450–3, 455–7; cf. *KrV* A534/ B562; *KpV* 3–4, 43, 46, 94–106), and that (*c*) transcendental freedom is compatible with what we can and do know (*G* 450–3, 455–7; cf. *KrV* A538–58/B566–86; *KpV* 3–6, 47–9, 54, 95–106, 114, 133). These claims raise complex issues that I cannot address properly here. But my belief is that whereas (*a*) is plausible, (*b*) is not; responsibility requires deliberative self-government, but deliberative self-government does not require

---

[19] Cf. the use Irwin makes of self-consciousness in order to reconstruct Kant's views of rational agency; see Terence Irwin, 'Morality and Personality: Kant and Green', in A. Wood (ed.), *Self and Nature in Kant's Philosophy* (Ithaca, NY: Cornell Univ. Press, 1984), 31–56. Of course, the importance of such capacities of practical deliberation to agency is not peculiar to Kant. Cf. Plato, *Republic* 437e–442c; Aristotle, *De Anima* 2. 2 and *Nicomachean Ethics* 1102b13–1103a3, 1111b5–1113a14; Cicero, *De Officiis* 1. 11; Bishop Butler, *Fifteen Sermons*, ii. 13; Thomas Reid, *Essays on the Active Powers of the Human Mind*, ii. 2; T. H. Green, *Prolegomena to Ethics*, sects. 85–158.

[20] Morality applies to rational beings as such, that is, to beings in so far as they are rational. So moral duties apply to agents who have only a rational nature (e.g. gods) and to rational agents who also have an empirical nature (e.g. humans); but Kant thinks that moral duties appear *as imperatives* only to the latter class of agents (*G* 414, 455 and *KpV* 20, 32, 82; but see *KpV* 81).

transcendental freedom.[21] Transcendental freedom seems neither necessary nor sufficient for responsibility. It seems unnecessary, because responsible actions do not require choices that lie outside a causal nexus; they require only that choices not be determined by the agent's inclinations, independently of his deliberations. It seems insufficient, because an action's determination by aspects of an agent that are in principle unknowable (an agent *qua noumenon*) cannot explain why the agent is responsible for the action. If so, a defence of Kantian rationalism requires an account of our capacities for deliberative self-government that does not presuppose libertarianism or noumenal determination of the will. Any such account must explain our ability to recognize and respond to practical reasons in naturalistic terms. Certainly, such an account is required if we are to develop a Kantian moral psychology that does not presuppose transcendental idealism, in particular, transcendental freedom. In what follows I will assume that some naturalistic account of deliberative self-governance is possible.[22]

5. *The Categorical Imperative*

This understanding of why moral requirements must be represented by categorical imperatives leads Kant to the first of his three main formulations of the Categorical Imperative—the formula of Universality. If moral requirements are not to be based on empirical conditions, it seems they must be universal or universalizable. For an agent's action to be morally permissible, Kant argues, it must be possible for her to will that her maxims, or the subjective principles of her action (*G* 401 n., 421 n.), become a universal law of nature.

> F1 Act only on those maxims that you can at the same time will to be a universal law (*G* 421; *KpV* 30, 69; *M* 225–6).

This may sound like a hopelessly abstract claim, as Foot and others seem to think. But Kant offers two kinds of help in understanding F1. First, he offers examples of moral issues to which he then applies F1. He also links F1 with two other main formulations of the Categorical Imperative.[23]

---

[21] Contrast Allison, *Kant's Theory of Freedom*, esp. 35–41.

[22] It is instructive to see the role that capacities for deliberative self-government play in interesting versions of compatibilism; see e.g. Harry Frankfurt, 'Freedom of the Will and the Concept of a Person', *Journal of Philosophy*, 68 (1971), 5–20 and Gary Watson, 'Free Agency', *Journal of Philosophy*, 82 (1975), 205–20.

[23] In recognizing three main formulations of the Categorical Imperative, I do not distinguish as many formulations as others have. See e.g. the commentary by Paton in Immanuel Kant, *Groundwork for the Metaphysics of Morals*, trans. H. J. Paton (New York: Harper & Row, 1956) and Bruce Aune, *Kant's Theory of Morals* (Princeton: Univ. Press, 1979), 111–20. My more coarse-grained division is not unfamiliar and seems adequate for present purposes.

He claims that F1 implies a second formulation—the formula of Humanity (*G* 437).

F2 Treat humanity, whether yourself or any other rational agent, always as an end in itself and never merely as a means (*G* 429; *KpV* 87, 131; *M* 462).

And F2 is supposed to imply a third formulation—the formula of Autonomy (*G* 438).

F3 Every rational being should be regarded as an autonomous legislator in a kingdom of ends (*G* 431–3, 438).

Of course, F2 and F3 themselves require interpretation, but the fact that Kant identifies F1, F2, and F3 (*G* 436) may help in interpreting any one of them.

6. *The Formula of Universality*

What does it mean to say that an agent must be able to will his maxim to become a universal law?[24] What sort of universality or universalizability does F1 require? Kant claims that actions can violate F1 in one of two ways:

Some actions are so constituted that their maxims cannot without contradiction even be thought as a universal law of nature, much less be willed as what should become one. In the case of others this internal impossibility is indeed not found, but there is still no possibility of willing that their maxims should be raised to the universality of a law of nature, because such a will would contradict itself. (*G* 424)

Thus, an action violates F1 if its maxim is such that (*a*) it is impossible or inconceivable for everyone to act on it, or (*b*) its universalization, though conceivable, would reveal some contradiction in the agent's will.

Kant thinks that the case of false promises involves maxims whose universalization is inconceivable (*G* 403, 422; cf. *KpV* 27). I cannot will that my maxim of keeping promises only when it suits my interests be universal, because if everyone acted on this maxim, promises would often not be kept and the general level of trust necessary to sustain the practice of promising would not obtain. Thus, a general practice of false promising would prove self-defeating.

---

[24] Though quite different, my own reading of F1 has benefited from the discussions by Onora Nell (now O'Neill), *Acting on Principle: An Essay in Kantian Ethics* (New York: Columbia Univ. Press, 1975); Onora O'Neill, 'Consistency in Action', repr. in her *Constructions of Reason* (New York: Cambridge Univ. Press, 1989), 81–104; and Christine Korsgaard, 'Kant's Formula of Universal Law', repr. in her *Creating the Kingdom of Ends* (Cambridge: Univ. Press, 1996), 77–105.

However, this seems not to show that the universalization of a maxim of false promising is inconceivable. What it shows is that the practice of promising could not be sustained if everyone were to make false promises. But this just shows a certain consequence of universal false promising; there is nothing inconceivable about the resulting state of affairs. Moreover, this is a consequence not of universal false promising but of universal false promising *only if* each recognizes the promises of others as false. But then there seems nothing *self*-contradictory about universal false promising.

Moreover, this kind of inconceivability, if that is what it is, had better not be a sufficient condition of violating F1, because there appear to be many perfectly innocent activities that are not universalizable in this sense. No one could will to perform any activity that is part of some larger division of labour—for instance, practising philosophy or selling but not producing widgets—because, if everyone performed that one activity, no one would perform the other activities in the division of labour necessary to produce the products that sustain the division of labour.[25]

Fortunately, the conceivability interpretation of F1 appears not to be basic.[26] Some maxims whose universalization is conceivable (and presumably some Kant thinks are not) cannot be *willed* to be a universal law.

---

[25] Nell seems to think that this worry does not apply to Kant's conception test (*Acting on Principle*, 78–9). It may be that I am assuming, as she is not at this point, that the activity is part of a larger division of labour that must be sustained if the agent is to act on her maxim (cf. ibid. 68, 79). Kant might avoid this problem if he were to claim that the universalization of maxims could only be assessed *jointly*. But I'm not quite sure how this would go, and Kant appears to think the universalization of maxims can be assessed individually.

[26] This conclusion would have revisionary implications if we accepted, as many commentators do, Kant's suggestion that maxims whose universalization is inconceivable violate *perfect* duties whereas those whose universalization involves a contradiction in the will violate only *imperfect* duties (*G* 424). However, this suggestion had better not be Kant's considered view. Violation of the conceivability test is neither necessary nor sufficient for breach of a perfect duty. As I've claimed, some perfectly innocent activities that are components of larger divisions of labour—that violate neither perfect nor imperfect duties—are such that the universalization of their maxims appears to be, in Kant's sense, inconceivable. Moreover, many maxims whose universalization is conceivable but would, on Kant's view, involve a contradiction in the agent's will do violate perfect duties. For example, duties of mutual aid can only be established by the contradiction in the will test; universalization of the kind of resolute self-reliance that denies duties of mutual aid is perfectly conceivable (*G* 423). But, even if some duties of mutual aid, such as giving to charity, involve imperfect duties, others involve perfect duties, such as the duty to rescue a drowning child when this can be done with little cost or risk to the agent. Similar remarks could be made about perfect duties of forbearance, such as duties not to torture the infirm. The difference between perfect and imperfect duties, therefore, had better be picked out by something other than these two interpretations of F1. Fortunately, there appears to be a more straightforward way to distinguish between perfect and imperfect duties. We should locate this distinction not in different kinds or grounds of duty but rather in the *content* of one's duties and maxims. On the contradiction in the will test, the question is whether maxims can be willed to be a universal law. If not, it is impermissible to act on the maxim ($\sim$U(M) $\rightarrow$ $\sim$P(M)); if so, it is permissible to act on the maxim (U(M) $\rightarrow$ P(M)). As long as we accept a common correlativity principle, according to which a course of action is impermissible just in case it is obligatory not to do it ($\sim$P(a) $\equiv$ O($\sim a$)), it follows that if the contradictory of one's maxim cannot be universalized, then acting on it is obligatory ($\sim$U($\sim$M) $\rightarrow$ O(M)). Here O(M) specifies an obligation or duty to act on one's maxim. When M specifies that a

On one interpretation, a contradiction in the will would involve willing both P and ~P; this would make F1 a kind of practical analogue of the principle of non-contradiction. But this isn't involved, even in the case of false promises. In that case the agent wills that he take advantage of others' good faith. It's true that his ability to realize the object of his will presupposes others' good faith, and this presupposes that promises are in general kept. If, as Kant claims, he who wills the end, in so far as he is rational, also wills means and necessary conditions to the attainment of his end (*G* 417), then the agent also wills that the practice of promise-keeping continue. And this aim is undermined if everyone acts on his maxim and each recognizes that others are breaking their promises.[27] But the universalization is not part of his will; it's a constraint on acceptable willings that Kant introduces. So we don't have any formal contradiction in his will. He does not will both P and ~P. He wills P (that the practice of promise-keeping continue so that he may take advantage of it) and it's true that *if everyone observes his maxim and recognizes that others do . . . then ~P* (if everyone observes his maxim . . . then the practice of promise-keeping discontinues). For there to be a contradiction in his will of this sort, he would have to will the consequent of this conditional. Whereas he may believe that the conditional is true, I don't see any reason to suppose that he wills the consequent or, for that matter, the conditional or its antecedent.

A more common interpretation of F1 and consistency in one's will results if we ask if we can consistently accept the consequences of everyone acting with our motives. Kant suggests this reading of F1 in a preliminary discussion of false promising.

The most direct and infallible way, however, to answer the question as to whether a lying promise accords with duty is to ask myself whether I would really be *content* if my maxim (of extricating myself from difficulty by means of a false promise) were to hold as a universal law for myself as well as for others . . . (*G* 403; emphasis added)

certain sort of action always be done, O(M) expresses a perfect obligation or duty, and when M specifies of a certain sort of action that it need not always be done but that it must sometimes be done (when being at the discretion of the agent), then O(M) expresses an imperfect obligation. This suggestion about how Kant can and should draw the distinction between perfect and imperfect duties is compatible, I believe, with his suggestion in *The Metaphysics of Morals* that we understand the distinction as one between required actions and required ends (*M* 390). At another point in *The Metaphysics of Morals*, Kant suggests that we understand the distinction as one between duties that can or should be enforced by external sanction and those that cannot (*M* 383). This last account of the distinction between perfect and imperfect duties appears to be orthogonal to the others.

[27] This is somewhat similar to Korsgaard's favoured interpretation of the contradiction in conception test, which she calls 'the practical contradiction interpretation'; see Korsgaard, 'Kant's Formula of Universal Law'. But in addition to (other) problems it faces, which I discuss in the text, it seems clearly to involve a contradiction in the will. If so, it's hard to see how this could be a good interpretation of the contradiction in conception test, if only because it would make it unclear how Kant draws the distinction between contradictions in conception and contradictions in the will.

And, later, in discussing the fourth example involving the duty of mutual aid, Kant writes

A fourth man finds things going well for himself but sees others (whom he could help) struggling with great hardships; and he thinks: what does it matter to me? Let everyone be as happy as Heaven wills or as he can make himself; I shall take nothing from him nor even envy him; but I have no desire to contribute anything to his well-being or to his assistance when in need. . . . [E]ven though it is possible that a universal law of nature could subsist in accordance with that maxim, still it is impossible to will that such a principle should hold everywhere as a law of nature. For a will that resolved in this way would contradict itself, inasmuch as cases might often arise in which one would have *need* of the love and sympathy of others and in which he would deprive himself, by such a law of nature springing from his own will, of all hope of the aid he *wants* for himself.   (423; emphasis added)

These passages suggest an understanding of the universalization required by F1 that makes it out to be very much like the golden rule. Can you accept the consequences of everyone acting on your principles? If so, you may act on them; if not, you may not; and if the contradictory of your maxim cannot be universalized, acting on it is obligatory.

There are stronger and weaker interpretations of F1 depending on the range of consequences one must consider in universalizing. On one reading, which we might call *empirical* universalization, I must ask whether I can accept what would be the actual or probable consequences of everyone's acting on my maxim. Whereas on the other, stronger reading, which we might call *counterfactual* universalization, I must ask whether I can accept the consequences of everyone's acting on my maxim in all (epistemically) possible circumstances or worlds.[28] The difference between the two readings is easily brought out in connection with Kant's example involving mutual aid. If my own talents and resources are secure (e.g. I have a large and diversified investment portfolio), then I may have no difficulty accepting the consequences of the empirical universalization of my individualist maxim, because it may well be safe to assume that I will never be in need of help from others. However, it's much harder for me to accept the consequences of the counterfactual universalization of my individualist maxim, for there surely are possible worlds in which I lose my talents and resources or never

---

[28] Just as the weaker reading asks me to consider the probable consequences of everyone's acting on my maxim, the stronger reading should perhaps ask me to consider the consequences of everyone's acting on my maxim in all epistemically possible worlds. Certain features (e.g. my gender or my race) may be essential to me—if I have that feature, I have it in all (metaphysically) possible worlds in which I exist—yet I can conceive of not having that feature—for instance, I can conceive of discovering that, despite appearances, I do not in fact have that feature. A stronger version of universalization would require me to assess the consequences of everyone's acting on my maxim even in (epistemically possible) worlds in which I exist without these essential features.

had them in the first place. In these worlds I may well want assistance; if so, I cannot accept the counterfactual consequences of the universalization of my individualist maxim.[29]

The fact that Kant thinks the individualist maxim cannot be universalized is some evidence that he is concerned with counterfactual, and not merely empirical, universalization. Moreover, counterfactual universalization better makes duty independent of empirical conditions than does empirical universalization. But even counterfactual universalization is too weak. For counterfactual universalization, like empirical universalization, requires only consistency in one's attitudes, even if it requires consistency across a larger range of possible worlds. Like the golden rule, counterfactual universalization asks what consequences one can accept, and this must ultimately be a contingent psychological matter. Perhaps few of us could accept the consequences of everyone's acting on our individualist maxim in those (perhaps merely possible) circumstances in which we are destitute. But surely it's possible for someone—the *resolute* individualist—to accept even these consequences.[30] If so, and if we interpret Fi as requiring only counterfactual universalization, then the resolute individualist has no duty of mutual aid.

It is, I think, for this sort of reason that many readers have found Kant's discussion of the fourth example unsatisfactory and have concluded that the Universality formula is a formal test of consistency that has no determinate content. This is Hegel's 'empty formalism' charge.[31] But we have good reason to wonder whether counterfactual universalization is the best interpretation of the Universality formula. Kant wants moral duty or its ground to be independent of *all* desires and interests; moral duty is supposed to depend only upon features of rational beings as such. In fact, this is why he contrasts Fi with the golden rule (430 n.). The golden rule says 'Do unto others as you would have them do unto you.' The most natural interpretation of this claim is that it requires only the sort of role reversal test that we saw counterfactual universalization represents ('How would you like it if someone did that to you?'). But then the golden rule, like

[29] There are interesting and difficult issues here about how to weigh and combine one's preferences among possible worlds similar to issues about how to weigh and combine the claims of different persons within a possible world. Should I act as if each world were equiprobable and maximize expected average value over worlds, should I restrict myself to pair-wise comparisons of worlds, or should I employ some other method?

[30] Wolff notes this objection to his interpretation of the universal law formula but appears to conclude that this is a problem for Kant, not reason to look for a better interpretation. See Robert Paul Wolff, *The Autonomy of Reason* (New York: Harper & Row, 1973), 170–1. Cf. Hare's discussion of the 'fanatic' in R. M. Hare, *Freedom and Reason* (New York: Oxford Univ. Press, 1963), ch. 9.

[31] G. W. F. Hegel, *The Philosophy of Right*, trans. T. M. Knox (Oxford: Clarendon Press, 1952), sect. 135; cf. J. S. Mill, *Utilitarianism* (Indianapolis: Hackett, 1979), i. 4; Henry Sidgwick, *The Methods of Ethics*, 7th edn. (Indianapolis: Hackett, 1981), 389 n.; and C. D. Broad, *Five Types of Ethical Theory* (London: Routledge & Kegan Paul, 1930), 130.

counterfactual universalization, makes one's moral duties hostage to one's antecedent desires in a way Kant clearly wants to avoid.

How then should we interpret F1? Kant thinks that our duties must be determined by features of us as moral and, hence, rational agents (*G* 408, 412, 425–7, 432, 442; *KpV* 32). So we should interpret F1 as asking what rational beings can consistently will. But this claim is ambiguous. It might be interpreted as asking what *rational beings*—that is, *someone who is rational*—can consistently will. This test can depend on the contingent interests and desires possessed by rational beings, and so counterfactual universalization is one way of articulating it. Alternatively, F1 might be interpreted as asking the different question about what *rational beings as such*—that is, *someone in so far as she is rational*—can will. On this interpretation, F1 asks what we can will, not in so far as we have particular, contingent wants and interests, but what we can will in so far as we are rational beings (*KpV* 29–32, 43). If we distinguish between the will of an *impurely* rational agent—an agent in so far as she has contingent interests and desires—and the will of a *purely* rational agent—an agent solely in so far as she is rational—we might say that this test appeals to the will of a purely rational agent.[32] This seems to be the correct way to interpret the idea that our duties should depend only on features of us as moral and, hence, rational agents (*G* 426–7).

This interpretation has some interesting implications. On this interpretation, I ask whether—in so far as I am a rational being—I can consistently will that my maxim be a universal law. Rational beings are different from one another in countless ways, but not just in so far as they are rational. Different maxims will survive counterfactual universalization depending on the contingent interests and desires of the rational agent who tries to universalize. Not so under this interpretation. Because all agents are alike in so far as they are rational, the results of this sort of test do not depend on who performs it (*G* 427; *KpV* 20–1). Nor is it clear that universalization, as distinct from universality, is essential to F1. Universalizability is a way of counteracting the influence of certain contingent factors in the determination of moral requirements (*G* 424). Our worries about counterfactual universalization suggest that it is an inadequate remedy; our interpretation

---

[32] This distinction between purely and impurely rational beings should not be confused with Kant's own distinction between infinitely and finitely rational beings; finitely rational beings are rational beings with an empirical nature, whereas infinitely rational beings (e.g. gods) do not have an empirical nature (*KpV* 32, 82). Whereas Kant's distinction separates rational beings into disjoint classes, my distinction does not; it views rational beings under two different aspects: in so far as they have an empirical nature and solely in so far as they are rational. Infinitely rational beings necessarily will things as purely rational beings, and only finitely rational beings can will things as impurely rational beings. But finitely rational beings, as well as infinitely rational beings, can will things as purely rational beings, because this is to will something in so far as one is rational. Indeed, much of my discussion focuses on finitely rational beings *qua* purely rational beings.

of F1 shows that it is unnecessary. Kant secures the independence of duty from the relevant contingent factors by focusing on the will of a purely rational being. We need only ask what a rational being would will, *qua* rational being; it shouldn't matter whether you or I ask the question, and we shouldn't need to ask what if everyone did that.[33]

But we may wonder whether there *is* anything that a purely rational being would will. I can understand what it is for a rational being to will or choose various actions and outcomes on the basis of her interests and preferences. But what would an agent stripped of all such interests and preferences will or choose? It may seem that there is no basis left on which to will or choose. This may be another ground for the 'empty formalism' charge.

7. Connecting the Formulas

Kant does not agree. Among other things, he thinks that we can get from the idea of what someone would want or will in so far as she was rational (F1) to F2 and F3 (*G* 429, 432–3, 436). Kant thinks that the one thing that a purely rational being would will or choose for its own sake is *rational agency* (*G* 427–9). It seems reasonable that in so far as one is a rational agent one will value the exercise of rational agency. To be a rational agent is to deliberate about what is best to do. But then in so far as one is a rational agent, one must want one's choices and actions, whatever they are, to be regulated by the exercise of one's deliberative or rational capacities. This is to value the realization of rational agency or to regard rational agency as good in itself. And Kant might argue that a purely rational agent has no basis for finding anything else intrinsically valuable. Moreover, if I choose rational agency solely in so far as I am a rational being—solely in virtue of properties common to all rational agents as such—then I choose to develop rational agency as such, and not the rational agency of this or that being—in particular, not just my rational agency (*G* 427; *KpV* 20–1). If so, then F1 directs me to be concerned about other rational agents, as rational agents, for their own sakes.[34] Kant concludes that in so far as we

---

[33] This removes worries about whether the universalization of maxims to pursue innocent components of larger divisions of labour (that are themselves innocent) is conceivable, in Kant's sense. Because universalization is not really essential to F1, the apparent non-universalizability of these innocent activities does not imply that these activities are impermissible. Moreover, the way in which universalizability plays no real role in the favoured interpretation of F1 might usefully be compared with the way in which justice as fairness represents a problem in individual decision theory under special circumstances, rather than a contract among several parties with conflicting interests. For the thickness of the veil of ignorance in the original position aims to abstract from those features of individuals that set them at odds and would otherwise require a contract among them to be represented as a bargaining problem. See John Rawls, *A Theory of Justice* (Cambridge, Mass.: Harvard Univ. Press, 1971) (cited as *TJ*), 17, 119, 121, 138, 139.

[34] Cf. Christine Korsgaard, 'Kant's Formula of Humanity', *Kant-Studien*, 77 (1986), esp. 190–7.

are rational beings we would will that all rational agents be treated as ends in themselves and never merely as means (G 429). This is how he gets from F1 to F2.

The transition from F1 and F2 to F3 is more straightforward. If F1 represents a test for the permissibility of our maxims that we interpret in terms of the choice of a purely rational agent and, so interpreted, F1 equals or implies F2, then we get the following picture. We are free to act on maxims that we, as rational beings, can will to be universal and that treat other people as ends in themselves and never merely as means. This sounds very much like F3; every rational being should be regarded as an autonomous legislator in a kingdom of ends (G 432–3).

8. The Content of the Categorical Imperative

However, these claims about the relation among the three main formulations of the Categorical Imperative do not yet answer the 'empty formalism' charge. Moreover, if Kantian claims about the Categorical Imperative are to have a bearing on our puzzle about the rational authority of other-regarding morality, then we need some assurance that the Categorical Imperative will enjoin some familiar other-regarding duties. I'll briefly sketch two ways of articulating the content of the Categorical Imperative, though I regard them as complementary, rather than competing, strategies.

First, we might begin with F2. We get moral content by figuring out what it would be to treat someone as an end, and not merely as a means. To use something as a means is to treat it as an instrument or resource for one's own aims; to treat it merely as a means is to treat it only this way, in particular, not as something with interests or value of its own. Of course, this is acceptable where, as with tools, the means have no value of their own but only instrumental value. But with people and rational agents in general this is not true. To respect people as ends is, for Kant, to value them and recognize their worth as rational agents (KpV 87). If, as we've claimed, what it is to be a rational agent is to be able to distinguish between the intensity and authority of one's desires and to have capacities for deliberative self-governance, then F2 requires that we value rational agents as deliberative beings and not treat them as mere means to the satisfaction of our own aims.

F2 prohibits treating rational agents as mere means. This requires treating them as ends, whose deliberation and agency are valuable. This requires not simply that we refrain from doing things that would harm the agency of others but also that we do things to promote their rational agency. And this will involve a concern to promote or assist, where possible, the opportunities of others for deliberation and agency, the effectiveness of their deliberations, and the execution of their choices and commitments (*M* 450, 452). Kant makes this clear in his discussion of the application of F2 to the example involving mutual aid.

Now humanity might indeed subsist if nobody contributed anything to the happiness of others, provided he did not intentionally impair their happiness. But this, after all, would harmonize only negatively and not positively with humanity as an end in itself, if everyone does not strive, as much as he can, to further the ends of others. For the ends of any subject who is an end in himself must as far as possible be my ends also, if that conception of an end in itself is to have its full effect in me. (*G* 430)

Indeed, given the concern each must have for rational agents, it is reasonably clear how a maxim of complete indifference to the needs of others would represent a contradiction in the will of a purely rational being. For Kant believes that it is analytic that in so far as I will the end, I must, in so far as I am rational, will means and necessary conditions to that end (*G* 417). If this is analytic in Kant's sense (*KrV* A6–7/B10–11), then willing the means is part of willing the end. But various human needs are means or necessary conditions to the pursuit of rational agency. In so far as I am rational, I do will the pursuit of rational agency; but then I cannot in consistency fail to will that rational agents be supplied those things they need as means or necessary conditions to the exercise of their rational agency.

There appear to be two main limitations on one's duties to promote the rational agency of others. First, I am constrained in the ways I can promote the agency of others, in much the way that I am constrained in the ways that I can help you win a competitive race. I can help you train for the race, but I cannot run and win the race for you. It's like this with rational agency. The exercise of one's rational agency involves making one's fate dependent, so far as possible, on one's actions and making one's actions dependent, so far as possible, on one's deliberations. I can provide intellectual and material resources for your deliberations and the execution of your plans, but I cannot deliberate for you (*M* 386). I can promote your agency only in ways that engage your deliberative capacities.[35] Second, if we are to respect the constraint that F2 imposes, the agent's obligations to help

---

[35] Kant thinks that whereas each has a duty to promote her own perfection, each has a duty to promote the happiness, rather than the perfection, of others (*M* 385–8). In so far as this self/other asymmetry rests on this claim that I am constrained in the ways that I can promote the rational agency of another, it need not reflect a fundamental asymmetry. For I can promote the rational agency of others, by providing them with various intellectual and material resources for their practical deliberations, just not in ways that do not engage their own deliberative capacities. In other words, the issue is not so much about whether as about *how* to promote the rational agency of another. If so, such self/other asymmetry as there is is compatible with and, in fact, seems to depend upon a prior and deeper symmetrical concern for the rational agency of self and others. Indeed, some such deep symmetry seems to be needed if we are to square this asymmetry in *The Metaphysics of Morals* with the apparently symmetrical concern for self and others contained in F2.

others realize their agency cannot be so encompassing that she becomes a mere means to the realization of their ends; she must also treat herself as an end and recognize duties to herself (*G* 429–30).

The interesting and difficult issues concern what, if any, distributional constraints F2 imposes on concern for rational agency. What does F2 require when rational agents make competing claims on me? It is sometimes thought that F2 imposes a side-constraint on action, roughly, that I can and should act to promote rational agency only on the condition that I never harm or impede anyone's rational agency.[36] Suppose that only by causing harm to B's rational agency can A prevent individually comparable harms to the agency of C, D, and E. On this view, F2 forbids harming B's agency, even though so acting might better promote rational agency or at least minimize harms to rational agency. But it is not obvious that F2 requires such a side-constraint. F2 requires that one treat rational agents as ends and not merely as means. If A harms B's agency only in order to protect the agency of C, D, and E, perhaps A treats B as a means, but he does not treat her as a mere means. To do that would require viewing her as a mere instrument or tool, not as someone whose own agency is valuable. But A does not view her that way; A has taken her agency into account. A proceeds, but with great reluctance that derives from a concern with her agency; if A could have protected the agency of C, D, and E without harming her agency, he certainly would have. If A acts impermissibly in acting so as to minimize harm to rational agency, it is not because in so acting he must be treating those whose agency he harms as mere means.

It is natural to think that to treat every agent as an end is precisely to be impartial in a way that takes the agency of each affected party into account equally. I think that this is right and frames further reflection in a useful way. But it does not yet settle much, because there are alternative conceptions of impartiality and equality. On an *aggregative* interpretation of impartiality, we consider the interests of each affected party, *qua* rational agent, and balance benefits to some against harm to others, where necessary, so as to achieve that outcome that is on balance *best* from the perspective of rational agency. On this view, the claims of individual rational agents might be outvoted by a majority. By contrast, we might interpret impartiality to require *unanimity*. On this view, we require that benefits and harms be distributed in a way that is acceptable in a suitable sense to *each* affected agent. There is some reason to think that Kant favours the second interpretation of impartiality (*KpV* 87).[37] In discussing the application of

---

[36] Cf. Thomas E. Hill, Jr., 'Humanity as an End in Itself', repr. in his *Dignity and Practical Reason in Kant's Moral Theory* (Ithaca, NY: Cornell Univ. Press, 1992), 48–9, 52, 56.

[37] In so far as Kant endorses this interpretation of impartiality, partiality seems unlikely to enter into his moral theory at the most fundamental level (cf. n. 4 above).

F2 to the example of false promising, he writes 'For the man whom I want to use for my own purposes by such a promise cannot possibly concur with my way of acting toward him and hence cannot himself hold the end of this action' (G 429). But F2 cannot require the agreement of impurely rational agents. That interpretation of unanimity would impose an intolerable distributional constraint; for each could exercise a veto based on his contingent interests and inclinations. Moreover, this interpretation would make moral requirements depend on the contingent interests and inclinations of agents in a way Kant clearly eschews. Rather, Kant must mean that I am constrained to treat others in ways they could accept were their agreement to reflect only their rational nature. It is not entirely clear what distributional constraint this interpretation of unanimity imposes; in particular, it is not clear that it rules out interpersonal aggregation.[38] Moreover, this brings our interpretation of F2 back to our interpretation of F1.

We might try to determine the content of the Categorical Imperative by focusing on F1. On our interpretation, F1 asks what a rational being as such, independently of her contingent interests and inclinations, would will. We might model this as the problem of what terms of conduct one would choose—in so far as one was rational and valued rational agency— to govern a world of rational beings who have different, sometimes conflicting, contingent interests and desires in which resources are scarce. We might call these conditions the *circumstances of humanity*. These are not the circumstances of rational agency as such, and so, on Kant's view, they are not the circumstances of morality. But they are pervasive features of the human condition that help shape and characterize the kind of moral problems that we face. And we might get an idea of what moral requirements the Categorical Imperative generates for us by trying to model the choice that a purely rational being would make about the terms of social interaction for such circumstances. The natural way to do this is to represent the choice of the terms of conduct for the circumstances of humanity as one that must be made by someone subject to important motivational and informational constraints (G 427; KpV 21).

Our task might profitably be compared with Rawls's method for modelling the choice of principles of social justice in *A Theory of Justice*.[39] Our

---

[38] I explore some of these issues, though not especially with Kant in mind, in 'The Separateness of Persons, Distributive Norms, and Moral Theory', in R. Frey and C. Morris (eds.), *Value, Welfare, and Morality* (New York: Cambridge Univ. Press, 1993), 254–89.

[39] Rawls discusses the Kantian interpretation of justice as fairness in *TJ*, sect. 40 and in 'Kantian Constructivism in Moral Theory', *Journal of Philosophy*, 77 (1980), 515–72. He discusses various aspects of Kant's moral philosophy in 'Themes in Kant's Moral Philosophy', in E. Förster (ed.), *Kant's Transcendental Deductions* (Stanford: Univ. Press, 1989), 81–113. Whereas Rawls's explicit motivation for the conditions in the original position is an appeal to considerations of fairness in an agreement to terms of institutional design, the Kantian motivation for the special conditions from which the terms of interaction in the circumstances of humanity are chosen is an appeal to the idea of a rational agent

chooser knows that she will live with others in the contingent circumstances of humanity—that she will have particular characteristics, information, and preferences—but her choice of rules governing conduct in the circumstances of humanity is to be based on her concern for rational agency as such. So we place her behind a *veil of ignorance* that deprives her of knowledge about her various personal and social characteristics, such as her sex, talents, preferences, conception of the good, social position in society, society, and generation. In depriving her of this information, we make her choice independent not only of contingent facts about her interests and desires but also of knowledge as to which rational being she is. This is important if her choice is to reflect the will of a rational being as such and not a parochial concern for rational agency manifested here or there. Her positive motivation, of course, will be to choose principles that will most realize rational agency in the circumstances of humanity. Here she will be concerned with conditions that favour the development and exercise of deliberative capacities, where these include the capacities for forming, revising, assessing, choosing, and implementing structured plans and projects. It's plausible to suppose a rational being as such would favour certain principles of institutional design. Given her ignorance as to which projects and plans, talents, and resources she will have when the veil is lifted, this kind of motivation will obviously lead her to give priority to those goods and resources that serve as necessary conditions to exercising these deliberative capacities and as maximally flexible resources in pursuing her conception of the good once this is known. Following Rawls, we might call such goods and resources *primary goods* (*TJ*, sect. 15). They will include such things as the conditions of physical and mental well-being, education, personal and civic liberties, and economic resources. Her interest in rational agency suggests that above a certain minimum level of material resources, she will assign some kind of priority to personal and civic liberties necessary to exercise her capacities for practical deliberation.[40] And because of her ignorance as to which impurely rational agent she will be, when the veil is lifted, she will presumably assign some kind of presumption to principles that ensure the equal distribution of these conditions for pursuing rational agency.

Whatever principles of just institutional design emerge from this sort of *ex ante* choice will frame and constrain principles of interpersonal morality.

as such. However, it is reasonable to think that these two different motivations converge on a common description of the initial circumstances of choice (*TJ* 251–5). Also, whereas Rawls's focus is on defending principles of justice for the basic structure of society (*TJ* 7, 17, 54), the Kantian has the more comprehensive aim of ascertaining principles of right conduct as well as institutional design. Whereas Rawls calls his project *justice as fairness*, we might call the Kantian project *rightness as rational agency*.

[40] However, I doubt the priority of personal and civic liberties over other primary goods should be lexical, as Rawls claims.

One possibility is that principles of interpersonal morality might be generated by a sequence of choices, the successive stages of which gradually lift the veil of ignorance (cf. *TJ*, sect. 31). At the first stage a choice is made, as we have described, behind a very thick veil of ignorance; at the next stage the veil is lifted so as to reveal what sort of society, with what sort of natural and social resources, the chooser will occupy; at the third stage, the veil is lifted so as to reveal everything about the society and its occupants except which person the chooser is. The idea would be that principles chosen at any stage would be constrained by principles accepted at earlier stages. It is reasonable to think that it is an open question whether someone choosing out of a concern for rational agency but in ignorance of whether he will be A, B, C, D, or E will choose to avoid harming rational agency or will choose instead to minimize harms to rational agency.

A natural worry about this strategy for interpreting F1 is that it may seem to reintroduce contingent facts into the determination of moral requirements in just the way we spent so much time weeding out. For it asks what a rational being as such would will for the circumstances of humanity, and these circumstances include contingent conditions of human need, interest, and desire. But this objection to modelling F1 in this way confuses the conditions or circumstances under which a choice is *made* and the conditions or circumstances that a choice is *for*. It is the former, not the latter, that must be free of contingent factors on the Kantian view. F1 requires that the choice be made by rational beings in so far as they are rational; but the choices certainly apply in circumstances in which agents have particular, contingent desires and needs. Indeed, Kant thinks that the choices of purely rational agents appear as imperatives *only* to impurely rational agents (*G* 414, 455; *KpV* 20, 32, 82). But then there should be no objection to modelling F1 as a choice made by purely rational beings for the circumstances of humanity.

These remarks about the interpretation of F1 and F2 merely outline strategies for developing a substantive moral theory. But this may be enough for present purposes. The fact that both strategies ground moral requirements in an impartial concern for rational agents in the circumstances of humanity makes the 'empty formalism' charge less compelling. It also assures us that Kant can recognize categorical imperatives that enjoin other-regarding action about whose rational authority we can inquire.

9. *From Inescapability to Authority*

We should now have some grip on the way Kant thinks that moral requirements express categorical norms. Does this account of morality and its inescapability help explain its authority? In claiming that moral requirements express categorical imperatives, Kant claims that they apply to us in virtue simply of our being moral agents, not in virtue of our contingent circumstances and attributes. What makes us responsible agents is our ability to distinguish the intensity and authority of our desires, to deliberate about our actions, and to regulate our actions in accordance with these deliberations. These capacities for deliberative self-governance are the features that make us rational agents, and this is why moral requirements apply to us in so far as we are rational agents. But if some requirements apply to me in virtue of those very features that make me a responsible agent, capable of practical deliberation and subject to reasons for action, then these requirements presumably give me reason to act, such that failure to fulfil those requirements is *pro tanto* irrational. Because, according to Kant, moral requirements do apply to me in virtue of my being a rational agent and not in virtue of my contingent interests and aims, they must give me reason for action, independently of my interests and aims; they give me categorical reasons.

Notice that this route from inescapability to authority is not available for all categorical norms. Legal requirements and requirements of etiquette are categorical norms; they do not apply to someone, to whom they apply, in virtue of her aims or interests. We would not withdraw ascriptions of legal duties or duties of etiquette upon learning that performing her duties would further no aim or interest the agent has. In virtue of what features these requirements do apply is not entirely clear. Particular legal duties presumably apply to one in virtue of one's being a member of or falling within the jurisdiction of a certain kind of social system, defined perhaps by a set of first-order rules and second-order rules specifying the ways in which the first-order rules can be recognized, adjudicated, and changed.[41] Particular duties of etiquette presumably apply to one in virtue of one's belonging to a group in which certain social conventions and rituals, designed to grease the wheels of social interaction, are operative. Though requirements of law and etiquette are in one sense inescapable, they lack authority, because, unlike moral requirements, their inescapability is not grounded in facts about rational agents as such. It is not a condition of being a rational agent that one live by any particular standards of law or etiquette, and perhaps a rational agent need not live under the rule of law or etiquette at all. But moral requirements, according to Kant, apply to any rational agent in virtue of those very deliberative capacities that make her a responsible agent, capable of having reasons for action. If so, it is the way in which moral requirements are categorical norms that explains why they have special authority, not enjoyed by etiquette or law.

---

[41] See H. L. A. Hart, *The Concept of Law* (Oxford: Clarendon Press, 1961).

Hence, to say that moral requirements express categorical norms and that they provide categorical reasons is to say two distinct things. Though distinct, the two claims are not independent. For it is precisely the way in which moral requirements are categorical norms—they apply to anyone in so far as she is a rational agent—that explains why they provide reasons for action, independently of the agent's interests and aims. If so, Kant does not confuse morality's inescapability and authority, as Foot suggests; he argues from its inescapability to its authority.

Because the Categorical Imperative applies to rational agents as such, it enjoins impartial concern for any rational agent as such. If so, Kant can claim that practical reason can be impartial; I have non-derivative reason to be concerned about any rational agent as such. If practical reason can be impartial, then it is clear how Kant can defend the rational authority of impartial morality against an anti-rationalist threat.

10. Authority without Supremacy?

If this is right, Kant can defend a rationalist thesis about the authority of morality; necessarily, there is reason to fulfil other-regarding moral requirements, such that failure to do so is prima-facie or *pro tanto* irrational. Important as this (weak) rationalist thesis is, however, it does not deliver the strong rationalist thesis that contra-moral behaviour is always on balance irrational. A prima-facie or *pro tanto* reason to do something may be overridden or defeated by countervailing reasons. But Kant presumably accepts this stronger rationalist thesis, as well. For instance, he claims that a morally good will—a will that conforms to duty for the sake of duty (*G* 390, 397–8; *KpV* 71–2, 81, 151)—is incomparably good (*G* 434–6).

This estimation, therefore, lets the worth of such a disposition [i.e. the morally good disposition] be recognized as dignity and puts it infinitely beyond all price, without which it cannot in the least be brought into competition or comparison without, as it were, violating its sanctity. (*G* 435)

But Kant's claim that a good will is incomparably better than other things is only a statement of the stronger rationalist thesis, not an argument for it. Is the stronger thesis plausible? The answer depends on whether there are competing reasons for action.

In the *Critique of Practical Reason* Kant identifies the highest good with the combination of virtue and happiness (*KpV* 110). If virtue and happiness were independent parts of the highest good, then there would appear to be room for a conflict between virtue and the agent's own happiness. But Kant does not understand virtue and happiness as independent elements of

the highest good. For Kant, happiness must always be *conditioned* by virtue; happiness or the satisfaction of desire (*KpV* 22, 34) has value only in
a life lived in accordance with the moral law (*KpV* 110–11, 119).[42] Kant's
claims about the highest good show that he does not recognize a conflict
between moral requirements and agent-centred demands, but they do not
themselves constitute an argument against the possibility of such conflicts.

One source of possible conflict is hypothetical imperatives. Unlike categorical imperatives, the necessity of hypothetical imperatives is conditional; they enjoin means necessary to furthering our empirical interests
and aims (*G* 414; *KpV* 20–1). On one interpretation, where this condition
is met—where the agent has the relevant empirical interest or aim—the
hypothetical imperative applies. If the independence assumption of the puzzle
about the authority of morality is true, then impartial moral requirements
need not further the agent's interests or aims. If hypothetical imperatives
generate (hypothetical) reasons, then it appears that there must be possible
conflicts between hypothetical reasons and categorical reasons. Unless there
is some reason to believe that hypothetical reasons are inferior reasons, the
supremacy thesis must seem doubtful.

This doubt about supremacy depends on two assumptions about hypothetical imperatives—that they are conditional only on the agent having the
relevant empirical interest or desire and that they supply reasons for action
when this condition is met. These assumptions fit some things Kant says
about hypothetical imperatives. The German allows us to read that on
which hypothetical imperatives are conditional—*wollen* and its cognates—
as what one wants or desires (*G* 414, 417; *KpV* 20–1). Moreover, in criticizing other moral systems that ground moral demands in human happiness
or sentiment as resting on inclination and, hence, as heteronomous, Kant
believes that they rest morality on a hypothetical imperative (*G* 432–3,
443–4; *KpV* 20–8, 35–6). In so far as Kant argues this way, he seems to
assume that hypothetical imperatives are conditional on the agent's interests or desires.[43] He may also seem to assume that hypothetical imperatives
provide reasons for action when the agent has the associated interest or
desire. For in describing the justification for the Hypothetical Imperative,
Kant claims that whoever wants or wills (*will*) the end must also, in so far
as he is rational, want or will (*will*) the means to that end (*G* 417). If we
read *will* in this passage as want or desire, then Kant seems to be saying
something like this:

---

[42] Cf. the useful discussion in Stephen Engstrom, 'Happiness and the Highest Good in Aristotle and
Kant', in S. Engstrom and J. Whiting (eds.), *Aristotle, Kant, and the Stoics: Rethinking Happiness and
Duty* (New York: Cambridge Univ. Press, 1996), 102–38.

[43] Moreover, this is a common way of interpreting these and other remarks Kant makes about
hypothetical imperatives. See e.g. Lewis White Beck, *A Commentary on Kant's Critique of Practical
Reason* (Chicago: Univ. Press, 1960), 85 and Allison, *Kant's Theory of Freedom*, 89.

(*a*) If one wants to φ, then one has reason to produce means and necessary conditions to φ-ing.

With these two assumptions in place, supremacy is jeopardized, because
wants or desires that would ground hypothetical imperatives and reasons
can and do conflict with categorical reasons.

But we need not accept the interpretation of hypothetical imperatives on
which this doubt about supremacy rests. It's not just that Kant thinks there
is more to practical reason than prudential or instrumental reason; he
denies, I think, that interests or desires automatically supply reasons to act,
as this interpretation of the Hypothetical Imperative implies. It is not at all
obvious that (*a*) is true. Why should one have reason to promote the
satisfaction of one's desires regardless of the content of those desires? In so
far as Kant regards hypothetical imperatives as conditional only on the
agent's wants or desires, it's not clear that he supposes that having the
relevant wants or desires automatically provides reason to act. In criticizing
other moral theories that ground morality in happiness or sentiment as
resting morality on hypothetical imperatives, Kant clearly thinks that they
are incapable of representing their demands as duties. Nor is it clear that he
thinks these theories even show that we have reason to act, so as to promote
these interests or inclinations. Moreover, Kant's claims about the highest
good should make us doubt that he accepts both assumptions about hypothetical imperatives. For, as we have seen, Kant claims there that happiness, which he understands to consist in the satisfaction of (empirical)
desire (K*p*V 22, 34), has value only when it is conditioned by virtue, that
is, when it occurs in a life lived in accord with the moral law (K*p*V 110–11,
119). But then he must think hypothetical imperatives are conditional on
more than simple possession of an interest or desire; he must deny that
hypothetical imperatives automatically provide reasons when the condition
of their application is met; or both.

Indeed, many of Kant's claims about hypothetical imperatives can be
interpreted as insisting that hypothetical imperatives are conditional on
something more than the agent's (empirical) interest or desires. Though
the German does allow us to read that on which hypothetical imperatives
are conditional—*wollen* and its cognates—as what one wants or desires, it
also allows us to represent hypothetical imperatives as conditional on what
one *wills*. On this interpretation, hypothetical imperatives are conditional
on what one wills (*G* 414; K*p*V 20), and the rationale for the Hypothetical
Imperative is that whoever wills the end must also, in so far as he is
rational, will the means to that end (*G* 417). To will something is, for Kant,
not simply to desire it or have an interest in it; the will (*Wille*) is a faculty
of choice in so far as the agent is rational (*G* 412, 427, 446). There are

different ways of trying to understand the significance of Kant's claim that hypothetical imperatives are conditional on what the agent wills.

A second interpretation holds that hypothetical imperatives are just conditional claims of practical reason; hypothetical imperatives instruct one to do those things that are means to or necessary conditions of doing those things that one already has reason to do. If so, we might interpret Kant's rationale for the Hypothetical Imperative as saying something more like this:

(*b*) If one has reason to φ, then one has reason to produce means and necessary conditions to φ-ing.

This claim grounds one reason in another reason, without grounding the first; as such, it does not fully ground hypothetical imperatives. This purely relational or conditional claim is quite plausible and, if true, arguably analytic. Though it clearly provides one way of understanding Kant's claims that hypothetical imperatives supply only conditional or relative reasons (*G* 420), it fails to identify any sense in which hypothetical imperatives depend on interest or desire. So this interpretation does not explain well why Kant thinks that moral systems grounded in happiness or sentiment reduce morality to a hypothetical imperative.[44] Nor does it explain well Kant's more general insistence that the requirements of happiness, at least when conditioned by the moral law, are hypothetical imperatives (*G* 389, 415–16, 433, 442–4; *KpV* 21, 24–6, 35–6, 64–5, 109).

This second interpretation does not really exploit Kant's idea that the will is a faculty of choice in so far as the agent is rational. This suggests we interpret the condition of a hypothetical imperative not simply as another reason but as something one has reason to pursue just in so far as one is rational. This also serves to ground the antecedent and, hence, the consequent reason in (*b*).

(*c*) If one would choose to φ just in so far as one was rational, then one has reason to produce means and necessary conditions to φ-ing.

But this third interpretation still fails to identify any sense in which hypothetical imperatives depend on interest or desire and so fails to explain his criticism of other moral systems as resting on hypothetical imperatives or his view that requirements of happiness are hypothetical imperatives. Indeed, on this interpretation it is hard to see how to distinguish hypothetical and categorical imperatives. For if hypothetical imperatives are simply

---

[44] A friend of the purely conditional reading might claim that moral theories grounded in happiness or sentiment are defective precisely because they represent as duties requirements of happiness or sentiment without establishing that these ends are reasonable (cf. *G* 444). This criticism does explain Kant's critical interest in moral theories that are conditioned, but is does not explain his evident critical interest in moral theories that are conditioned on happiness or sentiment (cf. *G* 425; *KpV* 20–8, 34–5, 41, 64–5).

requirements to secure means or necessary conditions to the ends of a purely rational being, and these conditions are part of the will of a purely rational being, then hypothetical imperatives appear to be just a special case of categorical imperatives. Recall that we must distinguish categorical imperatives and the Categorical Imperative and that the former are, at least in part, what the latter requires in particular circumstances and conditions (Section 4). But then hypothetical imperatives, on this purely conditional reading, must apparently be categorical imperatives.

A more attractive interpretation of Kant's considered view about hypothetical imperatives tries to preserve the insights and avoid the problems of the other interpretations. Unlike the first, it insists that hypothetical imperatives are conditional on the agent's will, and not simply her interests or desires; unlike the second and third, it insists that the agent's interests or desires are among the conditions of hypothetical imperatives. Recall Kant's claims about the role of happiness in the highest good: he thinks that happiness, which he understands to consist in the satisfaction of (empirical) desire (KpV 22, 34), has value only when it is conditioned by virtue, that is, when it occurs in a life lived in accord with the moral law (KpV 110–11, 119). This suggests another interpretation of many of Kant's claims about hypothetical imperatives. On this view, to say that hypothetical imperatives are conditional on what one wills is to say that they depend upon interests or desires that are conditioned by what one would choose just in so far as one is rational. In other words, hypothetical imperatives, on this view, are conditional on interests or desires that one has that are not ruled out or screened off by the moral law. Similarly, when Kant explains the Hypothetical Imperative by claiming that whoever wills the end, also, in so far as he is rational, wills the means to or necessary conditions of his ends (G 417), what he is claiming is analytic is not (a), (b), or (c) but something more like this:

(*d*) If one wants to φ and φ-ing is consistent with the demands of (pure) practical reason, then one has reason to produce means and necessary conditions to φ-ing.

I doubt that (*d*) is analytic, but it is more plausible than (*a*), and it secures dependence on interest or desire that (*b*) and (*c*) do not. To will the end, at least in these contexts, just is, I believe, to choose something based on one's desires in a way consistent with and regulated by those ends that a rational agent, as such, would endorse.[45] I don't know if we can understand

---

[45] Kant's later writings distinguish between *Wille* and *Willkür*, though the two are not distinguished in the *Groundwork* and the *Critique of Practical Reason*. *Wille* in a narrow sense refers to a capacity of practical reason, whereas *Willkür* refers to a capacity for choice on the basis of desire or inclination (*Triebfeder*); *Wille* is also used in a broad sense to refer to a will (*Willkür*) determined by *Wille* in the narrow sense. (Cf. *M* 213–14; Beck, *A Commentary on Kant's Critique of Practical Reason*, 176–81; and

all of Kant's remarks about hypothetical imperatives as premissed on this interpretation of the way in which hypothetical imperatives are conditional on the agent's will. But it does provide an attractive view of hypothetical imperatives and reasons that is consistent with many things he says and that affords him a plausible reply to this doubt about morality's supremacy. For one cannot will, in this sense, ends excluded by the Categorical Imperative. If so, it's hard to see how there might be hypothetical reasons that conflict with the impartial demands of the Categorical Imperative.[46]

11. A Dualism of Practical Reason

However, another threat to the supremacy of impartial moral requirements is harder to dismiss. Moral requirements generate categorical reasons, because they apply to rational agents as such—that is, to an agent in so far as he has those capacities that are essential to responsibility and the possession of reasons for action. These categorical reasons are impartial, because they apply to the agent just in so far as he is one rational agent among others, and not because he is a particular rational being (*G* 427; *KpV* 20–1). But I am essentially not just a rational agent but also a *particular* rational agent, numerically distinct from other agents. The claim that I am a particular rational agent is *not* the claim that I am a finite rational being with an idiosyncratic set of empirical needs and desires; this may secure some kind of particularity, but it is not the particularity I am concerned with here. I am interested, instead, in the particularity of purely rational beings. Purely rational agents are still particular beings, as is clear from the fact that even gods (infinitely rational beings) who have no empirical natures would still be numerically distinct from one another.

One view about what distinguishes rational agents as such that seems promising and has some Kantian credentials is that the identity of rational

Allison, *Kant's Theory of Freedom*, 129–36.) Whereas some of Kant's central claims in the *Groundwork* about the will are concerned with *Wille* in the narrow sense (*G* 412, 427, 446), I suppose that it is something like this broad sense of *Wille* on which, I think, Kant here makes hypothetical imperatives conditional. Indeed, it might not be too far wrong to think that the (*a*)-reading makes hypothetical imperatives conditional on *Wilkür*, the (*b*)-reading and (*c*)-reading make them conditional on *Wille* in the narrow sense, and the (*d*)-reading makes them conditional on *Wille* in the broad sense. We might also note a parallel between the (*a*)-reading and the (*d*)-reading and Kant's distinction between self-conceit and self-love (*KpV* 73–7). Like the (*a*)-reading, self-conceit treats any desire as giving reason for its satisfaction; by contrast, rational self-love, like the (*d*)-reading, conditions the rationality of pursuing one's desires on their conformity with the moral law.

[46] For some different but related claims about the Hypothetical Imperative and its relation to the Categorical Imperative, see Stephen Darwall, *Impartial Reason* (Ithaca, NY: Cornell Univ. Press, 1983), 16, 79; Thomas E. Hill, Jr., 'The Hypothetical Imperative', repr. in *Dignity and Practical Reason in Kant's Moral Theory*, 24, 32; and Christine Korsgaard, 'The Normativity of Instrumental Reason' (Essay 8 in this volume).

agents over time consists in a kind of continuous deliberative control of intentional states and actions. Deliberative control exists when intentional states—such as beliefs, desires, and intentions—are formed, maintained, and modified as the result of deliberation and when actions are regulated by prior deliberations. What makes lines of deliberative control distinct—even when the intentional states, deliberative processes, and actions in each line are qualitatively similar—is lack of functional integration. Intentional states, deliberations, and actions can be ascribed to the same agent just in case they are part of the same psychic economy; intentional states must be able to interact with each other so as to modify each other and produce action. For example, A's pain will directly tend to produce B's avoidance behaviour just in case A and B are the same agent. The same is true with A's intention to vote and B's plan about how to get to the polling booth, A's belief that it is raining and B's desire to get an umbrella from the closet, etc. On this view, intentional states and actions are correctly ascribed to a single agent just in case they are parts and products of a functionally integrated deliberative system. If so, what makes someone a rational agent is that he is capable of deliberating about his desires, in light of his other intentional states, and of taking actions that reflect those deliberations. For Kant, self-consciousness requires an ability to distinguish oneself from particular impulses and desires (*KrV* B132–5); so he must think that agency requires a capacity for self-consciousness precisely because agency requires a conception of oneself and what one should do that is distinct from the various particular impulses one has and what they incline one to do.[47] It is the functional integration of this deliberative control over time that makes someone a numerically distinct and temporally extended agent. For Kant, this requires a unified consciousness, one that is sufficiently unified to support self-consciousness (*KrV* A97, A107–8, A110, A117, B132–4, A212/B258–9, A352).

Given that there are a plurality of purely rational agents, there must be requirements concerned with my own agency that apply to me just in so far as I am a particular rational agent, independently of my contingent interests and desires, just as Kant believes there are requirements of impartial concern that apply to me simply in so far as I am a rational agent. We might call the former requirements of *categorical prudence*.[48] This is not simply the claim that I have reason to be concerned about my own rational agency, as well as that of others. For this kind of self-concern would

---

[47] Cf. Green, *Prolegomena to Ethics*, bk. ii, esp. sects. 85–8, 100, 120–9 and Irwin, 'Morality and Personality: Kant and Green'.

[48] So the demands of a certain kind of prudence constitute categorical or external reasons. Cf. Terence Irwin, 'Kant's Criticisms of Eudaimonism', in Engstrom and Whiting (eds.), *Aristotle, Kant, and the Stoics*, 63–101.

already be included in an impartial concern for all rational agents, as in F2. Rather, the idea is that I ought to have concern for my own rational agency that is grounded in my being a particular rational agent and not simply one rational agent among others. Categorical prudence is no more included in categorical impartiality than the claims of ethical egoism are included within the claims of utilitarianism. Whereas being a responsible agent capable of having reasons for action depends upon one having the same deliberative capacities that would make anyone else a responsible agent, responsibility is ascribed to particular rational agents on the basis of the way they exercise their deliberative capacities. If so, it seems I ought to possess reasons for action in virtue of facts about my own agency as well as in virtue of rational agency as such. But then I will have reason to promote my own rational agency, as well as to promote agency impartially.

It's worth distinguishing the imperatives of categorical prudence from the assertoric imperatives of conventional prudence. Kant understands the imperatives of prudence to be imperatives to pursue one's own happiness; he understands happiness to consist in the satisfaction of one's (empirical) desires (*G* 399; *KpV* 22, 34), and he conceives desires to be aimed at pleasure (*KpV* 21). It follows that the principle of prudence, according to Kant, is 'empirical and can furnish no practical laws' (*KpV* 21). Thus, even if everyone desires her own happiness, prudential imperatives are (at most) hypothetical and prudential motivation is heteronomous (*G* 389, 415–16, 433, 442–4; *KpV* 21, 24–6, 35–6, 64–5, 109).[49] But the imperatives of categorical prudence are categorical and not merely assertoric. They are imperatives to agents to promote their own rational agency; they apply to each agent in so far as she is a particular rational agent, not in virtue of contingent aims or feelings that are extraneous to her agency. If so, the imperatives of categorical prudence express categorical norms and generate categorical reasons.

But then an argument parallel to Kant's own argument for the claim that impartial moral requirements generate categorical reasons demonstrates that self-regarding requirements of categorical prudence also generate categorical reasons. In so far as the argument is parallel, I do not see how Kant can argue that the reasons of categorical prudence are inferior to those of morality. More generally, I see no reason to suppose that the imperatives of categorical impartiality will systematically override those of categorical

---

[49] This is how we should understand Kant's claim that such imperatives have only 'natural necessity' (*G* 415; *KpV* 25). Imperatives of conventional prudence do not apply to agents in virtue of their rational agency, because happiness or even the capacity for happiness, as Kant understands it, is not essential to my being an agent or even a particular agent. Unfortunately, he goes on to say that such assertoric imperatives apply to me in virtue of purposes that 'belong to my essence' (*G* 416). This cannot be his considered view; if it were, he would be committed to the claim that imperatives of conventional prudence stand on a footing with moral requirements and so are categorical imperatives.

prudence. If so, Kantian moral psychology must recognize a *dualism of practical reason* that threatens the supremacy of impartial moral requirements.[50]

It's not clear whether this dualism represents a conflict within morality or a conflict between morality and some practical perspective external to morality. The answer depends upon whether the demands of categorical prudence are themselves moral demands or are extra-moral demands. Because Kant does not recognize the demands of categorical prudence, it's hard to know what he would think. On the one hand, he thinks that moral requirements are expressions of the perspective of a rational agent as such (*G* 408, 412, 423, 425–7; *KpV* 20–1, 29–30; *M* 216). We can understand these requirements as applying in virtue of properties common to all rational agents. We can model the way in which these requirements are generated in terms of a choice behind a veil of ignorance that abstracts from various identifying features of the chooser (*G* 427; *KpV* 21). This reasoning naturally leads to F2's impartial concern for rational agents. In so far as Kant argues this way, he seems committed to regarding agent-centred requirements of categorical prudence as extra-moral demands. On this view, recognition of categorical prudence threatens the supreme authority of morality.

On the other hand, Kant appears sometimes to equate categorical imperatives and requirements of morality (*G* 416, 420). Because the demands of categorical prudence are categorical norms that generate categorical reasons, this may give us reason to regard them as moral demands. Moreover, Kant thinks of moral requirements as depending upon features common to all rational agents as such. Whereas each has the capacities for deliberative self-government that all the others have and that would make anyone a moral agent, each also is a particular rational agent. So particularity is also a feature common to all rational agents as such. But if what is true of rational agents as such grounds moral requirements, then the requirements of categorical prudence are moral requirements. On this view, recognition of categorical prudence threatens morality's impartiality.

But this obscures what the two interpretations of the dualism of practical reason have in common; both challenge the supremacy of impartial moral requirements. One accepts morality's impartiality and challenges its supremacy; the other accepts its supremacy and challenges its impartiality.

---

[50] This dualism of practical reason might be profitably compared with Sidgwick's dualism between egoism and utilitarianism; see *The Methods of Ethics*, esp. 496–509. However, the comparison is imperfect. Categorical prudence is not the same as hedonistic egoism; categorical prudence takes the rational agency, rather than the pleasure, of the agent to be the thing to be promoted. Similarly, categorical impartiality is not the same as hedonistic utilitarianism. It too is concerned with rational agency, rather than pleasure. Moreover, it is not clear that categorical impartiality should be understood in consequentialist terms; however, unlike many, I do not think it clear that it should not be understood in such terms (cf. Sect. 8 above).

Either way, the most serious challenge to Kantian rationalism is not the move from the inescapability of impartial moral demands to their authority but the one from their authority to their supremacy.

This leaves two responses to our puzzle about the rational authority of morality. The first response would be to abandon the supremacy of impartial morality. This would provide a weak form of rationalism without Kant's stronger rationalist aspirations. On this view, though we reject the agent-centred assumptions about practical reason in premiss (3) and maintain that necessarily there is reason to act on impartial moral requirements such that failure to do so is *pro tanto* irrational, we must also reject the strong rationalist premiss (2) that failure to act on impartial moral requirements is necessarily on balance irrational. Impartial moral requirements would necessarily enjoy authority, but would not necessarily enjoy supremacy. The other response would be to seek a *practical* resolution of the dualism by showing that the interests of distinct rational agents, when properly understood, are interdependent in such a way that acting on an impartial concern for rational agents is a counterfactually reliable way of promoting the agent's own rational agency (and vice versa). On this view, despite a dualism between agent-centred and impartial practical reason, we can try to maintain the strong rationalist thesis (2) by rejecting the independence assumption in premiss (4). To develop this response, however, we would need to look outside Kantian ethics to the eudaemonist tradition in Greek ethics, which Kant rejected, or to the ethics of self-realization found later in British idealism.[51]

---

[51] I have discussed this alternative in 'Self-Love and Altruism'. Of course, even if we can reduce the conflict between impartial and agent-centred concern with rational agency, we may not be able to eliminate it completely. If so, rejecting premisses (3) and (4) in the puzzle about the authority of morality may not be sufficient to deliver the strong rationalist commitment to the supreme authority of impartial morality, expressed in (2). See 'Self-Love and Altruism', sect. 12.

I would like to thank Henry Allison, Richard Arneson, Anne Margaret Baxley, Richard Boyd, Joshua Cohen, Garrett Cullity, Stephen Engstrom, Berys Gaut, Michael Hardimon, Paul Hoffman, Brad Hooker, Terence Irwin, Patricia Kitcher, Christine Korsgaard, Wayne Martin, Paul Pietroski, Geoffrey Sayre-McCord, Alan Sidelle, John Skorupski, Michael Smith, Jennifer Whiting, a UCSD graduate seminar, participants in the Ethics and Practical Reason Conference at the University of St Andrews, and an audience at the University of California, Davis for helpful discussion.

10

A Theory of Freedom and Responsibility

MICHAEL SMITH

Once we equip ourselves with a suitable version of the dispositional theory of value we can solve the various metaphysical, epistemological, and motivational puzzles that standardly arise in meta-ethics. So, at any rate, I have argued.[1]

Even if I am right about this, however, it might be thought that another set of problems in meta-ethics remains, problems which the dispositional theory of value goes no way towards solving. These are problems about the nature of freedom and the conditions of moral responsibility. A solution to these problems, it might be said, requires some super-added theory about the nature of the moral agent, something about which the dispositional theory of value remains silent. My task in the present essay is to address this concern and to show that it is unfounded. The dispositional theory delivers an intuitive and compelling conception of freedom. It delivers, more or less in and of itself, a plausible conception of the responsible moral agent.

I begin by drawing out some assumptions we make about the belief-forming capacities of those we are prepared to engage in conversation about what is the case: people whose beliefs we are willing to use as a reality check on our own. Since it seems undeniable that at least some people do have these belief-forming capacities, and that we are therefore right to make them answer for their beliefs, it is irresistible to ask whether these sorts of capacities, and the responsibility for our beliefs that they engender, could serve as the basis for an account of freedom and responsibility in the arena of action. The answer argued for in the remainder of the essay is that they can, and that the dispositional theory of value is what enables them to.

The essay divides into four main sections. In the first I outline the assumptions we make about people's belief-forming capacities when we take them to be answerable for their beliefs. In the second section I briefly

---

[1] See Michael Smith, 'Dispositional Theories of Value', *Proceedings of the Aristotelian Society*, suppl. 63 (1989), 89–111; 'Realism', in Peter Singer (ed.), *A Companion to Ethics* (Oxford: Blackwell, 1991), 399–410; 'Valuing, Desiring or Believing?', in David Charles and Kathleen Lennon (eds.), *Reduction, Explanation, Realism* (Oxford: Univ. Press, 1992), 323–60; *The Moral Problem* (Oxford: Blackwell, 1994); 'Internal Reasons', *Philosophy and Phenomenological Research*, 55 (1995), 109–31; 'Internalism's Wheel', *Ratio*, 8 (1995), 277–302.

rehearse the main features of the version of the dispositional theory of value I favour—the theory is non-relativist, rationalist, cognitivist, and internalist— and I explain why, because the theory has these features, it enables us to conceive of agents as responsible for their desires and actions in much the same way as they are responsible for their beliefs. Moreover, I explain why the capacities we take agents to enjoy, in so far as we take them to be responsible—capacities to form evaluative beliefs and desire accordingly— amount to nothing less than a capacity to be free in the arena of action. In the third section I consider some standard puzzle cases in the free-will literature, and I explain how the conceptions of freedom and responsibility that emerged in the previous section enable us to handle them. And then in the fourth and final section I compare the conception of freedom and responsibility that we get from the dispositional theory of value with its main competitor, the theory defended by Harry Frankfurt.[2]

1. Responsibility for Belief[3]

When we engage people in conversation about some matter of fact we oftentimes find ourselves in disagreement with them. Such disagreements can sometimes be resolved. Perhaps those with opposing views can learn from us, as we are better placed to have knowledge of the relevant part of reality than they are, something about which we can convince them, or we can learn from them, as they are better placed to have knowledge of the relevant part of reality than we are, something about which they can convince us. The picture we have, then, is of conversation as an arena in which people can talk through their reasons for and against their beliefs with others who may or may not have taken such reasons into account in forming their own contrary beliefs, thereby attempting to come to a resolution of their differences. Through conversation they work their way towards a common view as to how things are.

   Conversations of this sort seem to involve some rather specific assumptions about the norms to which the believers who are our conversational partners are subject, and about the capacities which they enjoy.[4] First, we assume that there are various norms governing what people ought to believe and ought not to believe—these 'ought's are, of course, all merely

---

[2] See Harry Frankfurt, 'Freedom of the Will and the Concept of a Person', repr. in Gary Watson (ed.), *Free Will* (Oxford: Univ. Press, 1982), 81–95 and 'Identification and Wholeheartedness', repr. in Frankfurt, *The Importance of What We Care About: Philosophical Essays* (Cambridge: Univ. Press, 1988), 159–76.

[3] In this section I repeat a line of argument that first appeared in the second section of Philip Pettit and Michael Smith, 'Freedom in Belief and Desire', *Journal of Philosophy*, 93 (1996), 429–49.

[4] See also Philip Pettit, *The Common Mind* (Oxford: Univ. Press, 1993).

prima-facie—norms that we assume to be inescapable. Thus, for example, if we are discussing whether Mt Kosciuszko is the tallest mountain in Australia then we assume that we should have this belief just in case Mt Kosciuszko is the tallest mountain in Australia, and that we should not have the belief just in case it is not. If we take the geographical maps of Australia that are found in atlases to be one possible source of evidence as to whether Mt Kosciuszko is the tallest mountain in Australia, then we assume that we should have the belief that Mt Kosciuszko is the tallest mountain in Australia just in case the maps show it to be, and that we should not have the belief just in case they do not. And if we take it that we already have beliefs which bear on whether Mt Kosciuszko is the tallest mountain in Australia— as we might if, for instance, we already have beliefs both about where, in Australia, the tallest mountain is to be found, and what the tallest mountain in that region of Australia is—then we assume that we should have the belief that Mt Kosciuszko is the tallest mountain in Australia just in case that is implied by what we already believe—provided, of course, we aren't prepared to revise our antecedent beliefs instead (I will omit this qualification from here on)—and that we should not believe that it is the tallest mountain in Australia just in case it is not. And so on and so forth.

I said we assume that these norms are inescapable. What I meant is that we assume that such norms apply to us simply in virtue of the fact that we are believers: they do not apply to us only because we are believers with a certain cultural background, say, or because we are believers with certain tastes or preferences. Thus, for example, the norm 'You ought to believe p just in case p' is not one that applies to us just in case we happen to come from a Western culture, or an analytic philosophy department, or a certain socio-economic background, or just in case we happen to have a taste for the true rather than the false. No psychological state could so much as count as a belief if it did not have representing things to be the way that they are as part of its proper function. It is in this sense that the norm is inescapable. The same goes for the other norms governing our beliefs.

This is not to say that our present views about the norms that govern belief are infallible. Indeed, quite the opposite is the case. Our beliefs about the norms that govern beliefs—our views about the nature of logic, say, or about the nature of evidence—can themselves vary from person to person, and so are as subject to the norm 'You ought to believe that p just in case p' as any other belief. The norms that govern our beliefs may therefore become the topic of a conversation whose aim is to figure out what the norms really are. The point is simply that—notwithstanding their contestable status—the norms that govern belief enter directly into the definition of the concept of belief itself by defining its proper function, and so enter directly into the definition of the concept of a believer as well. It therefore follows that we cannot separate out our views about which norms govern beliefs from our views about who the class of believers is. To think of someone as a believer at all is to think of them as falling under the norms that we think govern beliefs.

A second assumption we make concerns the capacities of believers. We assume not just that there are norms that govern belief, but that believers are capable of recognizing these norms. Thus, for example, if we have a disagreement with someone about which is the tallest mountain in Australia then we assume that they are capable of recognizing norms like 'You ought to believe that Mt Kosciuszko is the tallest mountain in Australia just in case it is the tallest mountain in Australia', and 'You ought to believe that Mt Kosciuszko is the tallest mountain in Australia if that is implied by other things you believe'. Someone who didn't have the capacity to recognize such norms—someone who, say, refused to believe that Mt Kosciuszko is the tallest mountain in Australia but who didn't acknowledge that they ought to believe that it is, given that that is implied by other things they believe—would not be someone with whom you could even begin to engage in a conversation as to whether or not Mt Kosciuszko is the tallest mountain in Australia. Their beliefs would not constitute a challenge of any sort to your contrary belief.

A third assumption we make also concerns the capacities of believers. We assume not just that they are capable of recognizing the norms that govern their beliefs, but that they are capable of responding appropriately to their recognition of such norms. Thus, to stick with our example, if we have a disagreement with someone over which is the tallest mountain in Australia—let's suppose that we believe it to be Mt Kosciuszko whereas they disbelieve this—then we assume not just that they are capable of recognizing that they ought to believe that it is Mt Kosciuszko, if their other beliefs imply that it is, but also that they are capable of responding appropriately. We assume, that is, that they are capable of actually coming to believe that Mt Kosciuszko is the tallest mountain in Australia because of their recognition of the reasons available to them for so believing. Someone who didn't have the capacity to respond would, once again, not be someone with whom you could even begin to engage in a conversation as to whether or not Mt Kosciuszko is the tallest mountain in Australia. Their beliefs would not constitute a challenge of any sort to your contrary belief.

The talk of capacities here is important because people can retain their capacity to recognize and respond to the norms that govern their beliefs even when they fail to recognize and respond to those norms on some particular occasion. Thus, for example, though there is a norm telling people to believe what is implied by the rest of their beliefs, they can still have beliefs that are inconsistent with the rest of their beliefs from time to time, despite retaining their capacity to recognize and respond to this norm. Indeed, the fact that they can retain their capacity even while failing to exercise it is what makes conversation about matters of fact appropriate. Through conversation we try to get people, ourselves included, to believe in the ways that they should, something that would hardly be appropriate if they were unable to do so.

Suppose someone fails to believe that Mt Kosciuszko is the tallest mountain in Australia, and yet believes both that the tallest mountain in Australia is near Canberra, and that the tallest mountain near Canberra is Mt Kosciuszko. If we did not think that this person had the capacity to recognize the gap in his beliefs, and then to respond appropriately by, say, acquiring the belief the Mt Kosciuszko is the tallest mountain in Australia, then we would not bother conversing with him. Note, moreover, that the capacity that we imagine him to have is entirely *his*. Our role in raising the gap in his beliefs with him in conversation is not essential. He has the capacity to recognize the gap not just when it is pointed out to him by someone else, but when he scrutinizes his own beliefs and updates them, something we assume to be a more or less permanent possibility in a believer.

Of course, there are various conditions believers can be in that remove— whether temporarily or permanently, locally or globally—their capacity either to recognize the norms that govern their beliefs, or their capacity to adjust their beliefs in response to their recognition of such norms, or both. Unconsciousness, illness, stubbornness, arrogance, self-deception, and drunkenness are some among them. We all know what it is like to talk with someone who has a belief which they cannot support in any way, but which they none the less find themselves totally committed to, just as we all know what it is like to talk with people who are not like this. It is in people of the latter sort that belief revision is assumed to be a more or less permanent possibility. Think again of some relatively normal person who believes both that the tallest mountain in Australia is near Canberra, and that the tallest mountain near Canberra is Mt Kosciuszko. He should indeed believe that Mt Kosciuszko is the tallest mountain in Australia because he could, right here and now, recognize the gap in his beliefs and respond appropriately. Or so we assume.

So far I have described only interpersonal conversations. But, of course, thinking itself is a kind of intrapersonal conversation. Suppose I find myself believing that Mt Kosciuszko is the tallest mountain in Australia when I remember that my earlier self believed otherwise. I then have to engage in a kind of conversation with my past self. I have to make sure that my reasons for now believing that Mt Kosciuszko is the tallest mountain in Australia are sufficient, in the light of my earlier self's reasons for having a contrary belief. I have to be able to tell myself a story either about why my earlier self made a mistake or error, or, failing that, why I have made a mistake or error now. In engaging in this sort of intrapersonal conversation I thus make various assumptions about the capacities of my present self and my earlier self to recognize and respond to the norms that govern my beliefs, assumptions which are exactly the same as those we make about each other in the context of interpersonal conversations.

This means that the conversational assumptions—the assumptions we make about the existence of norms and the capacities of believers to recognize and respond to their recognition of such norms—form the backdrop not just of all conversations we have with other people about what is the case, but of all our own thoughts about what is the case as well. To call into question the propriety of making these assumptions is thus to call into question the propriety not just of conversing with others, but of all thought. Even so, the fact that we enjoy these sorts of capacity can be made to seem more problematic than it ordinarily appears. An argument of Peter van Inwagen's has just this effect.[5]

Consider a philosophical discussion in which you reply in a certain way to a question, but realize later that another response would have been much better. There are at least two ways of fleshing out this case. You might think that the response you gave at the time was the best you could have given. Perhaps the later response only occurs to you after a good deal of subsequent discussion and further thought, or only after you read even more books and articles. Or, alternatively, you might think that the response you gave at the time isn't the best you could have given. You reprimand yourself for having failed to think of a better response at the time, a response you are convinced you could have thought of. Perhaps it was the obvious thing to say, and you'd even thought of working it into your answer before you began to speak, but it slipped from your mind as you went on.

Enter van Inwagen. Suppose that the actual world is deterministic, and consider the total state of the actual world at some time prior to you birth. That state of the world in conjunction with the laws of nature entail that, during the time of the discussion, you were not going to think of that response while you spoke. In order to have thought of that response you would therefore either have to have changed the past or violated a law of nature. But you have the ability to do neither of these things. In a perfectly straightforward sense, then, you did not have the ability to think of the better response, and so you could not have given the better response because

---

[5] Peter van Inwagen, 'The Incompatibility of Free Will and Determinism', repr. in Watson (ed.), *Free Will*, 46–58.

you could not have thought of it. If the actual world is deterministic, then van Inwagen's argument shows that the second possibility collapses into the first. Or does it?

Suppose you were able to think of the better response, and that if you had thought of it, then you would have given the better response. In fact, however, you did not think of it. Since all counterfactuals purport to tell us what would have happened had things been otherwise in some respect, in order to give an interpretation of this counterfactual we need to say where in the space of possibilities we are to find the possible worlds that differ from the actual world in history only in so far as you think of that better response. And since, if the actual world is deterministic, the actual history together with the actual laws of nature entail that you did not think of the better response, it follows that the possible worlds at issue will have to differ from the actual world in either or both history and laws. So much is clear.[6] But even though the possible worlds at issue must differ from the actual world in history or laws, it doesn't follow that we have to suppose ourselves to have the ability to change history or violate laws.

David Lewis points out that the possible worlds in which we are interested are those which, despite their differences, are yet maximally similar to the actual world—this is because similarity relations between possible worlds, relative to some interest we have, give us our fix on what could and could not have happened—and this in turn means that the possible worlds in which we are interested are those whose history and laws differ minimally from the history and laws of the actual world.[7] Lewis suggests that the smallest difference is one in which a local miracle occurs just prior to the time at which we suppose that you could have thought of the better response, a miracle which in turn causes you to think of that better response. This is because it is a very important fact about the actual world, in gauging its similarity to other worlds, that it has the history it actually has. And Lewis also suggests that the miracle should only be a miracle relative to the actual world, because possible worlds which have ever so slightly different laws to the laws of the actual world—laws whose differences suffice to ensure that the local miracle, relative to the actual world, is not a miracle at all relative to the laws of those worlds—are more similar to the actual world than are those possible worlds in which there are violations of their own laws. This is because it is a very important fact about the actual world, in gauging similarities, that there are no violations of law.

When we interpret the counterfactual in Lewis's way it thus emerges that, in the possible world in which you exercise your ability to think of the

---

[6] See esp. David Lewis, 'Counterfactual Dependence and Time's Arrow', repr. in his *Philosophical Papers*, ii (Oxford: Univ. Press, 1986), 32–52.

[7] David Lewis, 'Are We Free to Break the Laws?', repr. in his *Philosophical Papers*, ii, 291–8.

better response, we do not have to suppose that you exercise an ability to change history or violate a law at all. The local miracle that we have to imagine, in order to fix on the possible worlds which are maximally similar to the actual world in history, save for the fact that you think of the better response, is the cause of your action, not vice versa. Since you do not even cause the miraculous event, in the possible worlds we imagine, it follows that we do not have to suppose you to have the ability to cause it. Thus, though in giving an interpretation of the counterfactuals—as with any counterfactuals—we have to imagine possible worlds in which there is an ever so slightly different history, and ever so slightly different laws, we do not have to imagine that you have the ability to make the history or laws different. The van Inwagen style argument that if the world is deterministic then you do not have common-sense abilities—abilities like the ability to think of a better response to an argument than the one you in fact thought of—thus collapses.

This is all well and good. But what exactly does it mean to say that you were able to think of a better response to an argument than the one you in fact thought of? Does your possession of that ability require anything weird or transcendental of you? No it does not. Indeed, the discussion of Lewis shows that we can spell out the meaning of this claim in terms of possible worlds. To say that you were able to think of a better response to an argument than the one that you in fact thought of means, *inter alia*, that the possible worlds in which you think of the better response are near by, or very similar to, the actual world in which you don't. More commonsensically, the crucial point is that we do not need to imagine a massive transformation of your nature in order to imagine you thinking of a better response. We need simply to imagine you, pretty much as you actually are, but giving a better response. This will, of course, be the obvious thing for us to imagine if your failure to think of a better response to the argument on that occasion is atypical. If it is what happens in the actual world that we find hard to comprehend, not what we imagine happening in the possible world in which you give the better response instead, it will hardly be difficult to imagine the possibility in which you give the better response without imagining a massive transformation of your nature!

By contrast, when we say that you thought of the very best response that you could, and so weren't able to think of a better response, what we mean is *inter alia* that the possible worlds in which you think of a better response are remote from, or rather dissimilar to, the actual world. That is, in more common-sense terms, we do need to imagine a massive transformation of your nature in order to imagine you thinking of a better response because we first of all need to imagine you having read more books, or having had more discussions that impact on your background knowledge, or whatever.

This will, of course, be the obvious thing for us to imagine if you typically fail to give better responses to arguments, and if those who manage to give better responses differ from you in so far as they have read more books, or had more discussions.

Let me sum up the argument of this section. When we engage each other in conversation about what is the case—and, indeed, when we think about what is the case—we make various assumptions about both the norms that govern our beliefs and the capacities we possess as believers. We assume that there are norms governing what people ought to believe, and we assume that at least some people have the capacity to recognize these norms and respond to their recognition of them. These assumptions we make about people's capacities are in no way called into question by the possibility of determinism. Possession of such abilities requires nothing weird or transcendental of believers. Our reasons for believing that people have such abilities are more or less commonsensical.

2. *Responsibility for Evaluative Beliefs and Desires*

What does all of this have to do with giving an account of freedom in the arena of action and moral responsibility? As I see things, it has everything to do with it.[8]

The assumptions we make about the norms governing our beliefs, and about the capacities of believers, give us a picture of what it is to be a responsible believer, where responsibility presupposes certain abilities, abilities much like those traditionally associated with freedom. People ought to have certain beliefs, and because they have the capacity to recognize this fact and respond accordingly, we rightly hold them responsible for what they believe. We demand that such people believe what they should, and so rightly think well of them and praise them when they succeed—they might have failed, but to their credit they did not—and think less well of them and blame them when they fail—they could and should have believed otherwise: namely, rightly. If you accept the version of the dispositional theory of value I favour, then this story about responsibility for our beliefs is easily parlayed into a story about responsibility for our desires and actions as well.

According to the version of the dispositional theory I favour, facts about desirability are facts about the desires of our fully rational selves. More precisely, there is an analytic connection between the desirability of an agent's acting in a certain way in certain circumstances, and her desiring

---

[8] Pettit and Smith, 'Freedom in Belief and Desire', 440–9.

that she acts in that way in those circumstances if she were fully rational: that is, if she had the set of desires all agents would converge upon if, under the impact of increasing information, they came up with a maximally coherent and unified desire set. This theory has several important features.

First, the theory is non-relativist and rationalist. It is non-relativist and rationalist because facts about the desirability of our actions are facts about the reasons or justifications we have for performing them, where these reasons or justifications are reasons or justifications for all. The desirability of Bloggs's keeping his promise in certain circumstances C, for example, is a function of the fact that Bloggs would desire that he keeps his promise in C if he had the set of desires we would all converge upon if, under the impact of increasing information, we each came up with a maximally coherent and unified desire set. But if we would all converge upon the same set of desires, then the desirability of Bloggs's keeping his promise in C is not simply a fact about the desirability of his doing so relative to him. We too would desire that we keep our promise in circumstances C, so keeping our promise in C is the desirable thing for us to do in C as well. Reasons for one are thus reasons for all.

Note that the dispositional theory does not tell us anything yet about the content of our reasons. Thus it is so far consistent with the dispositional theory that if we had the set of desires we would all converge upon if we attempted to come up with a maximally coherent and unified desire set under the impact of increasing information, then we would all want ourselves to act on the same agent-neutral principles in all possible circumstances: maximize happiness and minimize suffering, say. But it is also consistent with the dispositional theory that we would all want ourselves to act on the same agent-relative principles: perhaps each of us would want ourselves to maximize our own happiness and minimize our own suffering, or, more radically and more implausibly, perhaps each of us would want ourselves to act on whichever beliefs and desires we happen to have in the circumstances of action that we face.[9] The substance of our reasons is thus a matter of discovery, according to the dispositional theory, a matter of finding out what we would all want if we had the set of...

[9] Why do I say that this is implausible? Because if I were caused by a drug pusher to desire heroin, or by an evil scientist to desire to eat dirt, or by someone else to perform some other activity that I deem utterly worthless and as having no rational justification at all, then, according to the suggestion just made in the text, the very fact that I come to have such a desire makes it desirable to act upon it. The acquisition of the desire provides the rational justification. I cannot imagine why anyone would believe this to be so. The mere fact that I have a desire, particularly one caused in the manner described, does not seem to me to have any normative significance at all. The important point, however, is that its being so is not ruled out, so far, by the dispositional theory of value. The dispositional theory tells us that whether it is or isn't so depends on whether, if we were fully rational, we would want ourselves to act on whatever beliefs and desires we happen to have. This is a matter that can be decided in a decisive way only after critical reflection and argument.

A second important feature of the dispositional theory follows on as a consequence. If facts about desirability are facts about the desires of our fully rational selves then, since there are *facts* about desirability, evaluative claims turn out to be truth-assessable—that is, they purport to represent these facts—and so a proper object of belief. Thus an agent who, say, believes that her φ-ing in certain circumstances C is desirable has a belief which is true just in case she would desire that she φs in C if she had the set of desires all agents would converge upon if, under the impact of increasing information, they came up with a maximally coherent and unified desire set, and which is false otherwise.

This is not, of course, to say that any of our evaluative beliefs are true. Perhaps there is some argument which decisively demonstrates that there are no desires that all agents would converge upon under conditions of full rationality, and so all such claims are false. I will return to this possibility towards the end. But that is neither here nor there with regard to the present point, which is that since evaluative claims are the proper object of belief, we therefore know what would be required for our evaluative beliefs to be true if any of them were true. The theory is thus a form of cognitivism.

A third feature of the theory is a consequence of the fact that it is cognitivist, non-relativist, and rationalist. The dispositional theory is internalist. Since so many people deny that this is so, and since it is so important to establish that it is so in order to see how the dispositional theory enables us to conceive of agents as both responsible and free in the arena of action, the point is worth dwelling on.

In her contribution to this volume Christine Korsgaard considers the idea that facts about the desirability of our actions are facts about the desires of our fully rational selves, but rejects it on the grounds that it violates the internalism requirement.[10] She argues that, properly interpreted, it amounts to the idea that the desirable actions, those we ought to perform, are the actions that our fully rational selves would perform. 'The model suggests that the normativity of the *ought* expresses a demand that we should emulate more perfect rational beings (possibly including our own noumenal selves).'[11] She then goes on to argue, convincingly, that evaluative beliefs, so interpreted, do not satisfy the internalism requirement. 'The model . . . seems to invite the question: but suppose I don't care about being rational? What then?' However the question is invited only because Korsgaard gives the idea that desirability is a matter of what our fully rational selves would want such an implausible interpretation. Let me first say why that interpretation is so implausible, and then say how the idea should be interpreted instead.

---

[10] Essay 8, pp. 239–46.   [11] Ibid. 240.

Suppose I suffer from an irrational fear of spiders, but there is a spider on the wall of my 8-year-old son's bedroom, a spider he is desperate for me to remove. I am frozen solid, utterly averse to the prospect of removing it. My feelings for him simply do not translate into a desire to do what he is desperate for me to do. Perhaps my fear causes me to be means–end irrational.[12] Now imagine I am told that my fully rational self, who doesn't suffer from an irrational fear of spiders at all and is thoroughly means–end rational, would simply pick up the spider in a tissue and remove it. Korsgaard's point—the point behind the question 'But suppose I don't care about being rational? What then?'—is that this information might well quite rightly leave me completely cold. Though there are no grounds for faulting my fully rational self's desire about what he is to do in his circumstances—he is, after all, fully rational, and so perfectly placed to form desires that are beyond reproach—there is a real question as to the relevance of what he would do in his circumstances for what I am to do in mine. I am in circumstances in which I have to deal with my completely irrational fear. I have to deal with a breakdown of my means–end rationality. Aren't these relevant considerations in deciding what I should do? If so, then the actions of my fully rational self are irrelevant.

For this reason I agree with Korsgaard that we go wrong if we interpret the idea that facts about desirability are facts about the desires of our fully rational selves in the way that she suggests. There is an alternative and more plausible interpretation of the idea, however. On this more plausible interpretation the desirable thing for me to do in my circumstances is whatever my fully rational self would desire, not himself to do in his circumstances, but me to do in my actual circumstances. As I have put it elsewhere, the model is not one in which we are supposed to emulate the behaviour of our fully rational selves, or to treat their behaviour as an example we are to follow, but rather one in which we are supposed to think of our fully rational selves as perched above us, in a superior position to give us advice about what we are to do in our less than fully rational circumstances.[13]

This interpretation of the idea that facts about desirability are facts about the desires of our fully rational selves—the advice model rather than the example model—seems to me to be the natural one given the processes in which we engage when we try to figure out what we have a rational

---

[12] For an explanation and discussion of this idea see Philip Pettit and Michael Smith, 'Brandt on Self-Control', in Brad Hooker (ed.), *Rationality, Rules and Utility* (Boulder, Colo.: Westview Press, 1993), 33–50; Jeanette Kennett and Michael Smith, 'Frog and Toad Lose Control', *Analysis*, 56 (1996), 63–73.

[13] See also Smith, 'Internal Reasons', sect. 1; 'Normative Reasons and Full Rationality, Reply to Swanton', *Analysis*, 56 (1996), 160–8. A similar distinction is made by Peter Railton when he attempts to analyse the concept of an individual's good in his 'Moral Realism', *Philosophical Review*, 95 (1986), 163–207.

justification for doing. Imagine me wondering what I should do. I have a dread fear of spiders, but there I see my son, hysterical, and anxiously waiting for me to remove the cause of his panic. He is relying on me. I am being put to the test. What am I to do?

If an answer to this question doesn't spring to mind immediately then one thing that might well is an image of myself reflecting on this situation on some later occasion, an occasion on which I am able to get some distance from my fear and to reflect, in a cool, calm state of mind, on all that happened. What will I then wish myself to have done here and now? This kind of thought has at least prima-facie normative force. The idea behind the dispositional theory, interpreted in the way I have suggested, is simply to extend this standard way of answering the question 'What should I do?' into a full-blown analysis. I should ask myself what I would want myself to do, here and now, with all my fears and foibles, not just on some later occasion on which I am able to get some distance from my fear, but in the possible world in which I have a maximally informed and coherent and unified set of desires. Presumably the answer will be that I would want myself to get the spider away from my son by one of the means available to me. Perhaps I should call for help, or if I am alone then perhaps I should just remove my son from the room and then try to chase the spider away, or perhaps I should do something else along these lines.[14]

Much as with the earlier interpretation, because the person whose desires I imagine is beyond rational reproach—he knows everything that is relevant, his desires have been arrived at by integrating mine into a systematic whole, and so on—I cannot fault his desires about what I am to do here and now in my actual circumstances. But because his desires concern my actual circumstances, and not his circumstances, I cannot rationally ignore his desires either.

In order to see this, compare two psychologies. One pairs the belief that acting in a certain way is what I would want myself to do in certain circumstances, if I had a maximally informed and coherent and unified set of desires, with a desire to act in that way. The other pairs that belief with indifference to acting in that way, or perhaps with an aversion to doing so. The former psychology seems clearly to exhibit more in the way of coherence or equilibrium than the latter. In the latter situation my indifference or aversion indicates a failure to have a desire that is clearly rationally better, in my own terms, than the desire I have, and this failure constitutes, in and of itself, a sort of disequilibrium or incoherence in my psychology.

---

[14] Now we can see why my fully rational self's actions are irrelevant as regards what I should do in my circumstances. Whereas I am in circumstances in which the options that are available to me are determined by my irrationality, my fully rational self is evidently never in such circumstances. For further discussion of this point see Pettit and Smith, 'Brandt on Self-Control'.

This means, in turn, that we can explain why rational people acquire desires that match those they believe their fully rational selves would have in terms of their disposition towards coherence. They do not just so happen to care about being coherent—something an equally rational creature may just so happen not to care about—rather, being rational is, *inter alia*, a matter of being disposed to restore coherence: the disposition towards coherence is partially constitutive of being rational, like the disposition to infer according to modus ponens.

The upshot is thus that when we interpret the idea that facts about desirability are facts about what our fully rational selves would want in the most natural way—that is, in terms of an advice model rather than an example model—evaluative beliefs do indeed satisfy the internalism requirement. Someone who believes that she would want that she φs in C if she had the desires all agents would converge upon if they had a maximally informed and coherent and unified set of desires either desires that she φs in C or else suffers from a sort of disequilibrium or incoherence in her psychology: agents thus desire what they believe desirable, in so far as they are rational.

We are now in a position to see how the dispositional theory enables us to conceive of agents as both free and responsible. Because the theory is cognitivist it follows that those with the capacity to recognize and respond to the norms that govern their evaluative beliefs are rightly thought well of for having evaluative beliefs that conform to these norms—they might have failed to have such beliefs but, to their credit, they succeeded—and they are rightly thought badly of for having beliefs that do not conform to these norms—they could and should have had beliefs that did. Moreover because the dispositional theory is rationalist and non-relativist, and because, as a result, it is also internalist, it follows that those with the capacity to restore and retain coherence in their overall psychology when they recognize the potential for incoherence or disequilibrium, even if perhaps only via stratagems of self-control, are rightly thought well of for desiring and acting in accordance with their evaluative beliefs—they could have failed but, to their credit, they succeeded—and they are rightly thought badly of for failing to desire and act in this way—they could and should have had such desires, and so performed such actions.[15]

It follows that people who satisfy two conditions are free and responsible in the arena of action. First, they must have the capacity to have the evaluative beliefs that they should have: that is, they must have the capacity to recognize and respond to the norms that govern evaluative beliefs, which

---

[15] Various techniques of self-control are discussed in Philip Pettit and Michael Smith, 'Practical Unreason', *Mind*, 102 (1993), 53–79; Pettit and Smith, 'Brandt on Self-Control'; and Kennett and Smith, 'Frog and Toad Lose Control'.

are beliefs about the reasons or justifications that there are for acting. And second, they must have the capacity to have the desires that they should have: that is, they must have the capacity to restore and retain coherence in their overall psychology by acquiring desires that match their evaluative beliefs—that is, their beliefs about these reasons or justifications—when they notice the potential for disequilibrium or incoherence. Those whose actions are the product of these dual rational capacities act freely because it is up to them whether the beliefs and desires that cause their actions are the right beliefs and the right desires, and they are responsible for their actions because, equipped as they are with these dual capacities, they can therefore rightly be made to answer for their successes and for their failures.

3. Some Puzzle Cases

Equipped with this conception of freedom and responsibility we are in a position to make plausible judgements about freedom and responsibility in various otherwise puzzling cases. In order to illustrate this fact consider four such cases, all of them familiar from the free-will literature.

(i) Brainwashed

Brainwashed has been kidnapped by a group of political activists who brainwash her into believing that the most desirable thing she could do is kill the president. She emerges from the brainwashing procedure utterly convinced, but squeamish. Because she possesses incredible powers of self-control, however, she manages to acquire a desire to kill the president, and subsequently acts. Intuitively, it seems that we would not think that Brainwashed acts freely. We would not hold her responsible. But why not?

Cases of brainwashing provide a problem for those accounts of freedom and responsibility according to which agents act freely, and so are responsible for what they do, if their first-order desires and actions accord with their values, or if their first-order desires and actions accord with their desires about which of their first-order desires are to be effective in action.[16] They provide a problem because we may suppose that Brainwashed's first-order desires and actions do accord with her values, and we may suppose that they also accord with her desires about which of her first-order desires are to be effective in action. The effect of brainwashing is, after all, precisely to change, and render immune from revision, an agent's values; or, alternatively, brainwashing can be thought of as changing an agent's desires

---

[16] Gary Watson makes a suggestion of the first kind in 'Free Agency', repr. in Watson (ed.), *Free Will*, 96–110; Harry Frankfurt makes a suggestion of the second kind in 'Freedom of the Will and the Concept of a Person'.

about which of her first-order desires are to be effective in action.[17] Cases of brainwashing provide no problem at all for the account of freedom and responsibility made available by the dispositional theory of value, however, because brainwashing evidently diminishes the capacity an agent has rationally to evaluate alternative hypotheses.

When Brainwashed acquires evidence that counts against the truth of the claim that killing the president is the most desirable thing to do, her having been brainwashed either causes her to ignore that evidence or to reinterpret it, or in some other way prevents the evidence from playing its proper cognitive role. We thus rightly deny that Brainwashed is free and responsible because we rightly deny that she could have believed otherwise than that it is most desirable to kill the president. In other words, Brainwashed's defect lies in the first of the two elements of a capacity for rational agency that we were forced to distinguish: her capacity to recognize and respond to the norms that govern belief.

Note that the political activists who kidnapped Brainwashed, and who are therefore like her in that they too believe that the most desirable thing for her to do is to kill the president, might well be quite unlike her in having arrived at their belief via the exercise of the capacity to form evaluative beliefs in the light of the norms that govern them. They might therefore be responsible for believing that the most desirable thing for Brainwashed to do is kill the president, and they might be responsible for the actions they perform because of the fact that they hold this belief. Thus, in kidnapping and brainwashing Brainwashed they might well do something for which they are properly held responsible. But if their belief is false, and if they should have realized this to be so—possessing as they do the capacity to evaluate beliefs in light of the norms that govern them— then they would properly be held responsible for getting their beliefs so badly wrong. We would blame them, and rightly so.

(ii) Kleptomaniac

Kleptomaniac has a compulsive desire to steal groceries. Whenever he goes to the supermarket he therefore finds himself concealing items and bringing them home without paying for them. He does not believe that this is in any sense a desirable thing to do. Indeed, he thinks that it is completely irrational behaviour. He believes that the desirable thing for him to do in his circumstances is to avoid the supermarket altogether and get someone else to buy his groceries on his behalf. None the less he regularly finds himself at the supermarket, stealing groceries. Intuitively, we would not

[17] Gary Watson, 'Introduction', in Watson (ed.), *Free Will*, 7 n. 9; Susan Wolf, *Freedom Within Reason* (Oxford: Univ. Press, 1990), 23–45.

think that Kleptomaniac steals groceries freely. We would not hold him responsible. But why not?

Cases of compulsion provide a problem for those accounts of freedom and responsibility according to which agents act freely, and so are responsible for what they do, if they would have done otherwise if they had so chosen or desired.[18] Perhaps Kleptomaniac would not have stolen if he had chosen or desired not to do so. But this is evidently quite irrelevant. The problem with Kleptomaniac is precisely that he could not have chosen or desired to do otherwise.[19] Cases of compulsion provide no problem at all for the account of freedom and responsibility made available by the dispositional theory of value, however.

What is the effect of Kleptomaniac's compulsion? His compulsion ensures that his belief that it is not desirable to steal plays no role at all in the genesis of his actions because it ensures that no technique of self-control available to him enables him to resist his desire. We are thus led to deny that Kleptomaniac could have desired or done otherwise than steal, and so quite properly deny that he is either free or responsible. In other words, Kleptomaniac's defect lies in the second of the two elements of a capacity for rational agency that we were forced to distinguish: his capacity to restore coherence in his overall psychology by acquiring desires that match his evaluative beliefs when he notices the potential for disequilibrium or incoherence. In more everyday terms, Kleptomaniac has no self-control, and so could not have done otherwise.

(iii) Pre-emptive Agent

Black wants Pre-emptive Agent to move his hand, but he doesn't want to interfere unnecessarily.[20] He therefore waits until Pre-emptive Agent is about to decide whether or not to move his hand and then, if he judges that Pre-emptive Agent is going to move his hand—Black is an excellent judge of such things—he does nothing. If he judges that Pre-emptive Agent is not going to move his hand, however, he has things so arranged that Pre-emptive Agent will decide, and do, just that. This is because Black, a mad scientist, has implanted an appropriate device in Pre-emptive Agent's brain, a device that is under his control and which will trigger the required decision in Pre-emptive Agent if needs be. As it happens, Pre-emptive Agent decides to move his hand and does so. Intuitively, we would think that Pre-emptive

[18] A. J. Ayer, 'Freedom and Necessity', repr. in Watson (ed.), *Free Will*, 15–23; Bruce Aune, 'Hypotheticals and "Can", Another Look', repr. in Watson (ed.), *Free Will*, 36–41.

[19] Roderick Chisholm, 'Human Freedom and the Self', repr. in Watson (ed.), *Free Will*, 24–35; Keith Lehrer, 'Cans Without Ifs', repr. in Watson (ed.), *Free Will*, 41–5.

[20] This example comes from Frankfurt, 'Alternate Possibilities and Moral Responsibility', repr. in Frankfurt, *The Importance of What We Care About, Philosophical Essays*, 1–10.

Agent moves his hand freely. We would hold him responsible for moving his hand. But why?

Cases in which agents act, thereby pre-empting a standby causal process that would have caused them to do just what they did if they hadn't already decided to do so for themselves, provide a problem for all accounts of freedom and responsibility according to which agents act freely, and so are responsible for what they do, just in case they could have done otherwise than what they in fact did.[21] If Black had foreseen that Pre-emptive Agent was going to decide to leave his hand at rest then he would have set in train the causal process that would have caused the device to cause him to decide to move his hand. In a relatively straightforward sense, then, Pre-emptive Agent could not have done otherwise than move his hand.[22] Cases of pre-emptive causation provide no problem at all for the account of freedom and responsibility that emerges if we accept a dispositional theory of value, however.

In order to see why this is so it will help if we first consider a rather different sort of case. Mark Johnston describes a shy but powerfully intuitive chameleon.[23] This is a chameleon that is green in the dark but which, when it intuits that it is about to be put into a viewing condition, instantaneously blushes bright red. Though it is green in the dark, if it were to be viewed it would thus look red. Does the case of the shy but powerfully intuitive chameleon show that there is something wrong in principle with the idea that something is a certain colour just in case it has a disposition to look that colour in standard viewing conditions?

The answer is that it does not. Rather, as Johnston points out, it simply shows that a dispositionalist about colour needs to remember two things. First, the dispositions of an object that interest us are constituted dispositions: in each case there is an intrinsic property the objects possess which causes the manifestation of the disposition in the appropriate viewing condition. And second, because the dispositions that interest us are constituted dispositions, it follows that they may therefore be 'masked', as Johnston puts it, either by other properties that the object possesses, or by properties possessed by other objects in its environment.

How can the dispositionalist characterize the dispositions that interest us? The dispositionalist can characterize them in terms of conditionals that abstract away from the effects of masking. He thus needs to distinguish those cases in which an object has no intrinsic property sufficient to underwrite

[21] G. E. Moore, *Ethics* (Oxford: Univ. Press, 1966); Ayer, 'Freedom and Necessity'; van Inwagen, 'The Incompatibility of Free Will and Determinism'.

[22] This is the main point Frankfurt makes in 'Alternate Possibilities and Moral Responsibility'. My aim here is, *inter alia*, to say why Frankfurt is wrong.

[23] Mark Johnston, 'Objectivity Refigured, Pragmatism Without Verificationism', in John Haldane and Crispin Wright (eds.), *Reality, Representation and Projection* (Oxford: Univ. Press, 1994), 85–130.

the conditionals that interest us, from those in which it does have such an intrinsic property, but there is also some other property possessed by the object, or by another object in its environment, and this pair of properties underwrites a conditional that doesn't interest us. Because a disposition to look green is constituted by intrinsic properties of the surface of the chameleon, and because its shyness and intuitiveness are not constituted by intrinsic properties of its surface, it follows that we can abstract away from the latter in considering the former. The chameleon is then green because, roughly, it has an intrinsic property, and this intrinsic property is sufficient to underwrite its looking green if viewed, at least in worlds in which it doesn't have the intrinsic properties that underwrite its being shy and intuitive as regards the presence of a viewer.

Let's now return to the case of Pre-emptive Agent. I have suggested that people whose actions are the product of two rational capacities act freely and responsibly. First, their actions must be the product of their capacity to have the evaluative beliefs that they should have—such people must therefore have the capacity to recognize and respond to the norms that govern beliefs—and second, their actions must be the product of their capacity to have the desires that they should have—such people must therefore have the capacity to restore and retain coherence in their overall psychology by acquiring desires that match their evaluative beliefs when they notice the potential for disequilibrium or incoherence. In determining whether or not people's actions are the product of these dual capacities we will certainly be interested in the various counterfactuals that are true of them. But as the case of the shy but powerfully intuitive chameleon reminds us, in constructing such counterfactuals we must be careful to weed out the effects of masking.

When we weed out the effects of masking it seems quite clear that Pre-emptive Agent's moving his hand is the product of these dual rational capacities. His action is the product of these dual rational capacities because, abstracting away from the presence of Black, he instantiates the right pattern of counterfactuals. Holding fixed his belief that it is desirable to move his arm, he would have exercised self-control if he had desired to act otherwise, and if he had believed it desirable to perform a different act, he would have desired and acted differently. Of course, in evaluating the truth of this last counterfactual we abstract away from the presence of Black, but we are entitled to do so in figuring out whether Pre-emptive Agent's moving his hand is the product of his dual rational capacities. We are entitled to do so because Black's presence does not, as such, undermine Pre-emptive Agent's possession of these capacities. Pre-emptive Agent does not stop being a rational agent in virtue of Black's presence. His intrinsic properties, those that ground his dual rational capacities, are in no way affected by Black's presence. Black's presence simply ensures that if certain actions are not the product of Pre-emptive Agent's dual capacities for rational agency, then they will happen anyway, despite Pre-emptive Agent's possession of these dual rational capacities. In this respect Black's presence is much like Johnston's chameleon's intuitiveness and shyness. Pre-emptive Agent is thus free and responsible because, abstracting away from Black's presence, he could have done otherwise.

(iv) Willingly Addicted

Willingly Addicted has a desire for heroin so strong that no technique of self-control would enable him to resist. Willingly Addicted knows this, but doesn't care less. He has thought things through and decided, quite independently of his addiction, that the most desirable thing for him to do is to inject himself with heroin. Does Willingly Addicted take heroin freely? Is he responsible for what he does?

The answer is that he does take heroin freely and that he is responsible. This is because Willingly Addicted's addiction is just like Black's disposition to interfere with Pre-emptive Agent should he not do what he wants him to.[24] Just as the mere fact of Black's presence, with his disposition to interfere with Pre-emptive Agent, does not cause any relevant change in Pre-emptive Agent's intrinsic nature, and so does nothing to change the fact that in Black's presence—provided, of course, that Black does not cause any change in Pre-emptive Agent's desires—Pre-emptive Agent manifests the same dual rational capacities required for free and responsible action that he manifests in Black's absence, so Willingly Addicted's addiction need not itself be thought of as causing any change in the relevant aspects of Willingly Addicted's intrinsic nature, and so need not be thought of as changing the fact that when addicted—provided the addiction does not cause any change in Willingly Addicted's desires—Willingly Addicted manifests the same dual rational capacities required for free and responsible action that he manifests in the absence of his addiction.

Now this might seem wrong, on the face of it. Willingly Addicted is, after all, *addicted*. While we can go along with the stipulation that his addiction has no effect on his capacity to reflect critically on the relative merits of alternative courses of action, surely we cannot suppose that it has no effect on his capacity to desire what he believes desirable. We cannot seriously suppose that Willingly Addicted retains the same capacity to

---

[24] See e.g. Frankfurt, 'Freedom of the Will and the Concept of a Person'. I am grateful to Jay Wallace and David Aman for conversations about the argument in this section.

desire what is desirable that he had in the absence of his addiction, because the fact that he will desire to take herion no matter what he believes desirable shows that he is out of control, in this respect. But if Willingly Addicted is out of control, then doesn't it follow that he lacks one of the capacities required for free and responsible action: namely, the capacity for self-control?

The answer is that Willingly Addicted needn't be thought of as being out of control because, despite his addiction, his psychology can retain aspects of the tendency towards overall coherence that it had in the absence of his addiction. Suppose, then, that Willingly Addicted acquires the desire to take heroin because, once he acquires the belief that it is desirable to take heroin, the desire to take heroin is produced in him by the tendency of his psychology towards overall coherence. We can then think of his taking heroin as pre-emptively caused by the desire to take heroin that is caused in him by his rational tendency, not by a desire that is caused in him by his addiction. His taking heroin manifests a rational tendency, not an addictive desire.

When we think of Willingly Addicted in this way his addiction looks, for all the world, just like Black's disposition to interfere with Pre-emptive Agent. It is a standby cause, a cause which has no effects of its own in the circumstances. Thus, just as in evaluating whether Pre-emptive Agent possessed the requisite capacity for self-control required for free and responsible agency we needed to establish the truth of various counterfactuals which abstracted away from Black's presence, so in evaluating whether Willingly Addicted possesses the requisite capacity for self-control required for free and responsible agency we need to establish the truth of various counterfactuals which abstract away from the fact that he is addicted. We need to ask whether Willingly Addicted would have desired not to take heroin, if he had believed it desirable not to do so, and in evaluating this counterfactual we must abstract away from the fact that Willingly Addicted is addicted. If the answer is 'yes' then Willingly Addicted acts freely and responsibly when he takes heroin.

The lesson to draw from our discussion of these four examples is clear enough. The dispositional theory of value makes the possession of the dual capacities to have the right evaluative beliefs and the right desires crucially relevant to the assessment of agents as free and responsible. As our discussion of the four examples makes plain, these dual capacities are indeed crucially relevant to the assessment of agents as free and responsible in just the way the dispositional theory insists they are. The dispositional theory's elegant handling of these otherwise puzzling cases thus provides an indirect argument for the theory.

4. A Comparison

In this final section I want to compare the account of freedom and responsibility made available by the dispositional theory of value with perhaps its main competitor, the account of freedom and responsibility developed by Harry Frankfurt.[25] In drawing out the similarities and the differences between the two accounts we will see not just how compelling the account of freedom and responsibility sketched here really is, but also how radical it is as well.

According to Frankfurt, to be capable of willing a creature needs only to be able to act on its first-order desires. All sorts of creatures are therefore capable of willing, including many non-human animals. Willing as such is thus not a phenomenon about which interesting questions of freedom can arise because the first-order desires a creature has may simply be the product of its environment. There may be no further feature such desires have that picks them out as desires which are such that, when a creature acts upon them, it is free in the special sense in which we suppose ourselves to be free.

Because we humans are capable of reflection, however, Frankfurt thinks that some of our first-order desires can have such a feature. We can act on first-order desires that answer, in an important way, to our reflective nature. We can step back and reflect on our wills and ask ourselves whether we have the wills we want, where such reflection is supposed to result in our having higher-order desires about which of our first-order desires are to be effective in action. When the effective first-order desires an agent has are those he wants, at the higher-order level, Frankfurt tells us that the agent identifies with his will, and when an agent acts on the basis of a desire with which he identifies, Frankfurt tells us that he can be said to act freely. He acts freely because he acts on the basis of the will he wants. This is the special sense in which we suppose ourselves to be free.

As Frankfurt points out, his theory is a version of compatibilism. It is a version of compatibilism because an agent may have the will he has because of causal forces beyond his control: the effects of his socialization and enculturation, say. But even if he does he may none the less act freely, according to Frankfurt, because he can make that will his own by identifying himself with it. This will be the case if, when he reflects, the agent comes up with a higher-order desire to have just those desires effective in action, and if in addition no further reflection would lead him to revise his higher-order desire. Agents who act freely are therefore responsible for what they do. They are responsible because in making their wills their

---

[25] 'Freedom of the Will and the Concept of a Person' and 'Identification and Wholeheartedness'.

own, they have made the actions that are the product of their wills their own as well.

There are many similarities between Frankfurt's view of freedom and responsibility in terms of higher-order identification and the idea of freedom and responsibility sketched here. According to both theories, the mere fact that an agent is able to act on the basis of her first-order desires tells us nothing about whether or not she acts freely or is responsible. According to both theories, whether or not an agent is free and responsible when she acts depends on whether her first-order desires answer, in a certain way, to her reflective nature.

There is, however, at least one crucial difference between Frankfurt's view of freedom and responsibility in terms of higher-order identification and the idea of freedom and responsibility sketched here. Whereas Frankfurt thinks that when an agent reflects, what that pattern of reflection causes in her is simply a further, higher-order, desire about which first-order desire is to be effective in the circumstances of action that she faces, according to the view of freedom and responsibility sketched here when an agent reflects what that pattern of reflection causes in her is an evaluative belief: that is, a belief about what she would want herself to do in the circumstances of action she faces if she had the set of desires all agents would converge upon if, under the impact of increasing information, they came to have a maximally coherent and unified desire set.

So much for the similarities and differences. Which theory of freedom and responsibility is more plausible? Popular though it is, it seems to me that Frankfurt's theory faces a formidable problem, and that the problem it faces can only be solved if we reject it and adopt instead the conception of freedom and responsibility made available by the dispositional theory. On the one hand, Frankfurt concedes that an agent who has a first-order desire to ϕ, and who acts on the basis of that desire, may or may not be acting freely. Merely desiring to ϕ, then, and acting on the basis of that desire, is insufficient to make that action the agent's own because the desire on which the agent acts may be one that he was caused to have by forces beyond his control, by the forces of socialization and enculturation or whatever. First-order desires thus stand in need of vindication in order for an agent to act freely when he acts on their basis. But, on the other hand, he then goes on to claim that what does the vindicating is simply another desire, a desire whose special status that equips it for its role as vindicator is that it is *higher order* and *formed on the basis of reflection*. But, as I will now argue, a desire's being higher order is irrelevant, and unless we give reflection the gloss suggested by the dispositional theory of value—a gloss Frankfurt evidently didn't intend—a desire's being formed on the basis of reflection is irrelevant as well. Neither of Frankfurt's conditions, neither severally nor jointly, is sufficient to equip a desire for its role as a vindicator of our first-order desires.

Consider a desire's being higher order first. Might it be this feature of a desire that enables it to vindicate a lower-order desire? Gary Watson points out that merely being higher order doesn't confer any special status on a desire that would make it an appropriate vehicle of vindication.[26] An agent who desires to φ, and who also desires not to desire to φ, is indeed someone who has at least one desire from which she will be alienated in some way. However it isn't obvious why the desire from which she should be alienated is the first-order rather than the second-order. It therefore isn't obvious why the second-order desire is the appropriate vehicle of vindication. Merely being higher order, then, is nothing special about a desire.

In that case, might it be the fact that a desire, even a first-order desire, has been formed on the basis of reflection that confers its special status upon it? Reflection can confer a special status on a desire only if the desire so formed is special relative to that reflective process. But the only way in which desires could be special relative to a reflective process is if, on the basis of such reflection, agents would all converge on the very same desires, or so it seems to me. Reflection thus confers a special status on desires only if 'reflection' is given a rationalistic gloss, a gloss Frankfurt evidently did not intend.

In order to see that being formed on the basis of reflection confers a special status on a desire only if 'reflection' is given a rationalistic gloss, suppose for a moment that we don't give 'reflection' this gloss. We will then need to invoke something other than reflection in order to explain why agents end up with the different desires they end up with when they reflect. If we are anti-rationalists, what we will invoke is, of course, our non-rational nature.[27] According to anti-rationalists, the desires agents end up with after reflection are a function of the desires they actually have to begin with, the desires they were caused to have by the forces of socialization and enculturation that made them what they are. Once we see that this is so, however, the difficulty involved in supposing that the desires we form on the basis of reflection could vindicate our first-order desires becomes manifest.

First-order desires stand in need of vindication, you will recall, because they may simply be caused in us by forces that are beyond our control. We are thus trying to find a special feature of our first-order desires, a feature *other than* having been caused by forces beyond our control, that will vindicate

---

[26] Watson, 'Free Agency', 107–9.

[27] This seems to be Bernard Williams's view in 'Internal and External Reasons', repr. in Williams, *Moral Luck* (Cambride: Univ. Press, 1981), 101–13. Contrast this with the view in Smith, *The Moral Problem*, 164–74.

them. But on the anti-rationalist's picture the desires we form on the basis of reflection themselves contain traces of just these sorts of causal forces. The desires one agent ends up with after reflection differ from those another agent ends up with because of the different causal forces to which they were subject in their pre-reflective state, the differences in their socialization and enculturation. If we give 'reflection' an anti-rationalistic gloss, then, having been formed on the basis of reflection is not a special feature of our desires, because it is not a feature that picks out desires that are *different enough* from those that have been caused in us by forces beyond our control.

Not so if we give 'reflection' a rationalistic gloss, however. The idea is then that reflection would lead us all to converge on the very same desires —or at any rate, that is what we suppose—because when we reflect we try to form beliefs about which acts it is desirable to perform in various circumstances, and what we believe when we believe that it is desirable to perform a certain act in certain circumstances is that we would all converge upon a desire that we act in that way in those circumstances if we attempted to come up with a maximally coherent and unified desire set under the impact of increasing information, and, when we form such a belief, provided we are rational, the belief we form will cause in us a corresponding desire.

It is therefore possible for the desires we form on the basis of reflection to be maximally different from those formed in us by the forces of socialization and enculturation because nothing but our natures as rational creatures is required to explain why we have them. At the limit, rational agents, provided they form their evaluative beliefs in the light of their capacity to have the beliefs they should have, and provided they form desires in the light of their capacity to have the desires they should have, will all end up with the same desires, provided they face the very same circumstances. It is irrelevant which desires we were caused to have by the forces of socialization and enculturation because these are transcended by our powers of rational reflection. Or so we suppose.

The failure of Frankfurt's theory of freedom thus leads us naturally to embrace the view of freedom and responsibility sketched here, the theory that emerges naturally once we accept a version of the dispositional theory of value that is non-relativist, rationalist, cognitivist, and internalist. Importantly, however, note that though the theory tells us that desires that are formed by the forces of socialization and enculturation are inappropriate vehicles of vindication, it may well be the case that, if we attempted to come up with a maximally coherent and unified desire set under the impact of increasing information, we would all converge upon a desire that we act in accordance with the desires that have been formed in us by the cultural or social practices in whose midst we find ourselves. The rationalistic conception of the self forced upon us by the dispositional theory is consistent with the idea that these culturally and socially formed desires do have rational significance.[28] It simply insists that what makes them have such significance is the fact that we would all converge upon a desire that we act in accordance with them if we were to...

5. *Conclusion*

If what I have said here is along the right lines then it seems to me that there needs to be a crucial shift in our thinking about freedom and responsibility. Let me conclude by saying a little about this shift.

The standard view, following Kant, has been that freedom is a kind of *autonomy*: that is, in Kant's words, freedom is 'the property which will has of being a law to itself'.[29] But, if I am right, freedom is not a matter of autonomy, not a matter of being a law unto oneself, but rather of *orthonomy*, a matter of having the capacity to be ruled by the right as opposed to the wrong.[30] This is because we are free and responsible to the extent that our actions are the product of our capacity for rational agency, and that in turn requires first, that we are able to have the right as opposed to the wrong beliefs about what it is desirable to do, and second, that we are able to have the right as opposed to the wrong desires.

This shift in our thinking about freedom and responsibility should be welcomed, I think, because it forces us to face up to the difficult questions we ought to be facing up to in deciding questions of moral responsibility. If people act in ways we deem wrong because they have very different evaluative beliefs from those that we have then we have to ask whether they could reasonably have been expected to believe otherwise, and if people act in ways we deem wrong because, despite the fact that they share our evaluative beliefs, they have desires that fail to match these evaluative beliefs, then we have to ask whether they could reasonably have been expected to exercise the requisite powers of rational self-control. In many cases it will be difficult to answer these questions.[31] But, if I am right, it is only by

---

[28] Here I echo the point I made in n. 9. Much as I said then, note that it would be implausible to suppose that we would all converge upon a desire to act in accordance with whatever desires happened to be caused in us by whatever cultural and social practices in the midst of which we find ourselves. It is easy enough to imagine cultural and social practices that cause us to desire to do things which are utterly worthless, so having no redeeming features whatsoever. Though consistent with assigning rational significance to the desires formed in us by social and cultural practices, the rationalistic conception of the self thus offers a critical perspective on the products of these practices as well.

[29] H. J. Paton, *The Moral Law* (London: Hutchinson, 1948), 101.

[30] The idea of orthonomy was first introduced in Philip Pettit and Michael Smith, 'Backgrounding Desire', *Philosophical Review*, 99 (1990), 565–92. The idea is elaborated in Pettit and Smith, 'Practical Unreason' and 'Freedom in Belief and Desire'.

[31] See e.g. Gary Watson's illuminating discussion of thrill-killer Robert Harris in his 'Responsibility and the Limits of Evil', in Ferdinand Schoeman (ed.), *Responsibility, Character and the Emotions: New*

answering these questions that we will know whether or not the people involved are really free and responsible.

It should be noted, however, that this shift in our thinking about freedom and moral responsibility comes at a price. For though I have argued that our concept of freedom presupposes a rationalistic conception of ourselves, I have not argued that that self-conception will survive critical scrutiny in the light of the empirical facts. Thus, for example, for all I have said here it may well be the case that if normative ethics progresses but without making any significant impact on the deep-seated disagreements that exist in the community on evaluative matters, then we will, for good reasons, come to lose our conviction that we would all converge on a single set of desires if we attempted to come up with a maximally coherent and unified desire set under the impact of increasing information. If what I have said here is right then coming to this conclusion may be tantamount to coming to believe that there are no values, and coming to that conclusion would be tantamount to coming to believe that we have no capacity to form the right evaluative beliefs. It would be tantamount to coming to believe that freedom and responsibility are an *illusion*.

Having said that I should add that I do not myself believe that we should draw this conclusion, but I well recognize that nothing I have said here tells against doing so.[32] Nor should this be thought a flaw in my argument, for my interests in this essay have been wholly conceptual. I have been concerned to spell out what our concepts of freedom and responsibility are. Whether or not we are in fact free and responsible, and the extent to which we are free and responsible if we are, is another question, one which needs to be addressed in its own terms. As these final remarks perhaps make clear, however, it seems to me that the answer to this question will be decided by engaging in substantive debate on normative matters and seeing whether such debates leave our commitment to non-relative evaluative facts, and the rationalistic conception of the self with its dual rational capacities, intact. Whether our concepts of freedom, responsibility, and value stand or fall, they do so together.[33]

Essays in Moral Psychology (Cambridge: Univ. Press, 1987), 256–86. An insightful discussion of various allocations of moral responsibility along lines similar to those suggested here can be found in Jeanette Kennett's *Commonsense Moral Psychology* (Oxford: Univ. Press, forthcoming).

[32] But see Smith, *The Moral Problem*, 187–9; 'Internalism's Wheel', 299–302.

[33] An earlier version of this chapter was read under the title, 'Freedom, Reason and the Analysis of Value', at a conference on Ethics and Practical Reason held at the University, St Andrews, in 1995. I would like to thank Garrett Cullity, my commentator on that occasion, for his helpful response. It was also read to audiences at the Australian National University and Monash University. Robert Audi, David Braddon-Mitchell, Richard Holton, Brad Hooker, Lloyd Humberstone, Frank Jackson, Jeanette Kennett, Christine Korsgaard, Rae Langton, John O'Leary-Hawthorne, Philip Pettit, Peter Railton, John Skorupski, David Velleman, Jay Wallace, and Susan Wolf all gave me very useful comments. Finally, thanks to Garrett Cullity and Berys Gaut for a separate set of comments which they made as editors of this volume.

Reason and Responsibility

R. JAY WALLACE

Can people ever be to blame for doing the rational thing? More broadly, what are the connections between the responsibility of moral agents and the rationality of the moral demands to which they are held accountable?

As I see matters, these questions turn on the relations between two different practical points of view. Questions about the rationality of moral conduct are in the first instance deliberative questions, arising within the first-personal perspective of an agent trying to reach a decision about how to act. The task of practical deliberation, after all, is the task of determining what one has reason to do. The claim that it is rational for a given agent to comply with moral demands can accordingly be understood as the claim that, if the agent deliberated correctly, he or she would acknowledge reason to act morally and would choose to act accordingly. To make out this claim would be to vindicate what is sometimes referred to as the authority of moral demands. As I shall understand the notion of authority, moral demands are authoritative for a given agent, in the relevant sense, if they appropriately regulate the deliberations of that agent. When this is the case, then an agent's deliberations will only count as fully rational when the agent succeeds in complying with the demands of morality.

Questions about responsibility, on the other hand, are essentially third-personal in form.[1] When we ask whether a given person is morally account-able for a given action, we are asking whether it would be fair to hold the person responsible for the action. Holding responsible is in turn an attitudinal stance that we adopt toward a person, involving a susceptibility to reactive emotions on account of what the person has done, and a disposition to respond to the person in ways that express the reaction emotions. Thus a person is blameworthy for having done something morally wrong when it would be fair to feel resentment or indignation in response to the person's conduct, and to engage in sanctioning behaviour that expresses such react-ive sentiments. That this is essentially a third-personal stance is not at odds

---

[1] The ideas sketched in this paragraph are developed and defended in my book *Responsibility and the Moral Sentiments* (Cambridge, Mass.: Harvard Univ. Press, 1994)—henceforth *RMS*. The present essay explores an issue touched on inconclusively on p. 165 of *RMS*.

with the fact that there is such a thing as holding oneself to blame. When we feel guilty for having done something morally impermissible, we are in effect standing in judgement over ourselves, viewing ourselves reflexively as appropriate targets of a certain kind of response. This stance is to be contrasted with the first-personal, deliberative standpoint we adopt when deciding what to do.

The third-personal stance of holding someone accountable defines a certain form of moral relationship. We enter into this kind of relationship to people when we hold them to moral demands, treating them as appropriate targets of reactive sentiment and sanctioning response in case they should flout those demands. The practice of holding people responsible is thus connected with the idea that moral demands can form the basis of a distinctive kind of moral community, one whose members expect each other to comply with those demands, and who hold each other to account when such compliance is not forthcoming. Furthermore, the members of such a community attain a special status when they actually succeed in fulfilling the demands of morality. Doing so equips them to enter into relationships of full accountability with people, relationships in which they are not merely held morally to account for their behaviour, but in which they could actually succeed in providing such an account if asked, justifying themselves by appeal to common moral standards.

My aim in the present essay is to explore some connections between these forms of moral relationship and the question of the rationality of moral conduct—between, as it were, the accountability of moral agents and the deliberative authority of moral demands. To this end, I distinguish two different aspects of the phenomenon of deliberative authority: there is, first, the question whether a given agent has reason to comply with moral demands, or whether those demands provide the agent with reasons for action; and there is, second, the question whether the agent has *most* reason to comply with moral demands, or whether such compliance is *optimal* from the standpoint of deliberative reason. I take up the first issue, concerning reasons for action, in Section 1, and then turn to the second issue, about the optimality of moral conduct, in Sections 2 to 4. A primary theme of my discussion will be that the most serious and consequential issues concerning the authority of moral requirements are raised by the question of optimality, rather than by the question of reasons for action (see Section 1). I shall sketch a framework for thinking about the optimality of moral conduct, which turns on the idea of congruence between the two constitutive perspectives of practical reason, the moral and the eudaemonistic (Section 2). I shall then argue that the ideal of full accountability may contribute to understanding how this kind of congruence is possible (Section 3). Finally, I shall explore the implications of the breakdown of convergence for relationships of minimal accountability, showing how the failure of optimality may lead to forms of diminished responsibility, and tracing the consequences of this result for our understanding of the content of moral requirements (Section 4).

1. Reason and Moral Capacity

There are a number of things that I shall simply take for granted, for purposes of discussion. First among these is the idea there is a form of general competence or capacity that is a basic condition of moral accountability. This is the complex condition I have elsewhere referred to under the heading of the powers of reflective self-control.[2] It includes the capacity to grasp and apply the justifications that support moral demands, as well as the general capacity to comply with moral demands, because one grasps the justifications that support them.

The idea that these moral powers are conditions of accountability reflects the following basic assumption: Given the connection between moral demands and the justifications expressed in moral principles, it would be unfair to hold accountable those who lack the capacity to grasp such justifications and to control their behaviour accordingly.[3] About these moral powers, I shall make the further assumption that they are not to be understood as all-or-nothing capacities that one either has or lacks. Rather, like other forms of general competence or capacity the powers of reflective self-control admit of degrees; they can be more or less developed, so that someone to whom these powers are ascribed may find that they are substantially impaired, either temporarily (due perhaps to local circumstances, such as unusual stress) or persistently and constitutionally (as for instance in certain cases of addiction or neurosis). Acknowledging the range of cases in which the powers of reflective self-control are impaired, I believe we should be prepared to adjust our judgements of moral responsibility accordingly. This follows from the basic idea that the moral powers to which I have referred are conditions of accountability. Granting this idea, we see that cases in which the powers of reflective self-control are substantially impaired, or in which it is extremely difficult for an agent to exercise those powers, should be treated as cases in which the agent's moral accountability is diminished. At any rate, this will be a further background assumption in the discussion that follows.

With these assumptions on the table, we are now in a position to consider the question whether accountability requires that one have reason to comply with moral demands. We may assume, to start with, that any

---

[2] *RMS*, sect. 6.1.   [3] For further discussion, see *RMS*, ch. 6.

plausible theory of reasons for action would endorse the following claim: If a certain consideration counts for a given class of agents as a reason for action, then those agents would take the consideration into account, were they to deliberate correctly.[4] This reflects the truistic idea that reasons for action just are considerations that have deliberative significance.[5] A further point concerns the idea of taking a normative consideration into account, for purposes of practical deliberation. I shall suppose that one who takes account of a given justification in this way is prepared to choose or decide in accordance with the justification, should other considerations not weigh more heavily, and to act on the basis of the choice or decision so arrived at. At least, one will do this in so far as one is practically rational.[6] This may be thought of as the motivational dimension of reasons for action.

Consider now a representative person who is morally accountable. Regarding the deliberative standpoint of such a person, we may say, I believe, that they must have reason to comply with the moral demands to which they are held accountable. Underlying this idea is the conception of moral accountability as a form of general capacity. We think that agents who possess the powers of reflective self-control are morally accountable, because they are competent to grasp and comply with the justifications supporting moral demands. Thus, one familiar set of conditions that deprives an agent of the powers of reflective self-control involves the impairment of the agent's capacities for practical deliberation: either these capacities are generally undeveloped (as is the case with young children), or the capacity for moral deliberation in particular is somehow undermined (as may be the case with some forms of psychopathy). When such impairments are not present, however, we often take even immoral agents to be competent to grasp and comply with moral demands, just because of their general competence as practical reasoners.[7] In order for this assumption to be warranted, however, it must be the case that there is a course of sound deliberation open to the

---

[4] I mean the idea of 'taking account' of a reason in a fairly weak sense here. In particular, it is not to be supposed that one can only take account of a reason if the reason overtly figures in the content of one's deliberation. I take account of the reasons against harming people, for instance, by structuring my deliberations in such a way that the question of harming others does not even arise, for ordinary purposes. For a subtle taxonomy of the variety of ways in which moral considerations might impinge on one's deliberation, see Samuel Scheffler, *Human Morality* (New York: Oxford Univ. Press, 1992), 30–4.

[5] One might contrast the claim that there is reason to act in a certain way with the claim that a given agent *has* reason to act in that way. Perhaps 'there are' reasons that a particular agent might fail to take account of, without thereby failing to deliberate correctly. But to say that the agent *has* reasons of this kind is, it seems, to make a point about what it would be for the agent to deliberate correctly.

[6] Cf. Christine Korsgaard, 'Skepticism about Practical Reason', *Journal of Philosophy*, 83 (1986), 5–25, and Michael Smith, *The Moral Problem* (Oxford: Blackwell, 1994), ch. 5.

[7] As I go on to explain later in this section, Humeans and Kantians may both agree that this presumption is warranted—though they will have different things to say about the cases in which the presumption is defeated.

agent in which moral justifications are acknowledged and taken into account. Only if this condition is satisfied will the general presumption of deliberative competence license the more specific conclusion that the agent is capable of grasping and complying with moral justifications. In a phrase, 'can'—the 'can', that is, of moral accountability—implies 'ought'.

But what needs to be true of people in order for it to be the case that moral justifications provide them with reasons for action in this way? Opinions notoriously divide on this point. Humeans conventionally hold that our reasons must somehow be based in our given desires and projects and interests.[8] A little more precisely, they hold that the normative ideal of correct deliberation must be relativized to particular agents, in that what counts as correct deliberation for a given agent will be constrained by the items in that agent's 'subjective motivational set'.[9] On the other side are (for instance) Kantians, who suppose that the notion of correct deliberation need not be constrained by the antecedent items in a given agent's subjective motivational set. They typically suppose that the norms that define correct deliberation are such that anyone who reasoned in accordance with them would take moral considerations into account. If this is correct, then competence at practical deliberation carries with it the ability to appreciate the force of moral justifications, and we may accordingly say that those justifications apply to, or are reasons for, all persons, just in virtue of their status as competent practical reasoners. By contrast, Humeans such as Bernard Williams seem to think that the capacity to appreciate the force of moral justifications—and hence to take such justifications into account in one's own deliberation—is not an intrinsically rational competence. To appreciate the force of a justification is a kind of evaluative stance, and the adoption of this stance presupposes a prior orientation of the sentiments.

Construed in this way, the dispute between Humeans and Kantians about the rational basis of morality may appear to have great significance for our understanding of moral accountability. Indeed, it is natural to assume that the theory of responsibility is the domain within which this dispute will have its real substantive pay-off.[10] If, as I have suggested, accountability requires that moral justifications count for one as reasons for action, then the divergent theories of such reasons seem to determine different views about the extension of the community of morally accountable

---

[8] In what follows I try to present the Humean idea that deliberation must begin from an agent's desires, without taking a stand on the merits of the idea. For the record I am struck by the difficulty of providing anything like an argument for this idea; compare my 'How to Argue about Practical Reason', *Mind*, 99 (1990), 355–85.

[9] See Bernard Williams's 'Internal and External Reasons', as repr. in his *Moral Luck: Philosophical Papers 1973–1980* (Cambridge: Univ. Press, 1981), 101–13.

[10] Cf. Bernard Williams, 'Internal Reasons and the Obscurity of Blame', as repr. in his *Making Sense of Humanity* (Cambridge: Univ. Press, 1995), 35–45.

persons. Kantians may take us to be warranted in presuming that all practical reasoners may be held morally accountable, since the capacity to appreciate and act on moral justifications is somehow intrinsic to the standpoint of competent practical deliberation. Humeans, by contrast, may reject such a presumption—especially if, as in the case of Bernard Williams, they depart from the naturalism and proto-utilitarianism that Hume himself espoused, in favour of the view that the sentimental bases of ethical concern are plural, contingent, and socially and historically conditioned.[11] On this view (which we might refer to as 'neo-Humeanism'), whether a given agent is morally accountable will very much depend on the particular educational influences to which the agent has been subject, and on the kind of residue that those influences have left on the agent's continuing character.

I think it doubtful, however, that these differences are really as significant for the theory of responsibility as they initially appear to be. The main reason for scepticism on this score has to do with a phenomenon that even the Kantian will have to acknowledge, a phenomenon that we might refer to as inherent irrationality. By this I do not mean the garden variety forms of rational lapse that all of us are subject to, to one degree or another—that is, the *de facto* failure to deliberate correctly, or the different motivational failure to choose and to act in accordance with correct deliberation even when it is actually carried out. In these cases we may continue to suppose that irrational agents are capable of deliberating and choosing correctly, despite their actual failure to do so. In cases of inherent irrationality, by contrast, the assumption of continued capacity to deliberate correctly is suspended. Consider a kind of case that I have already mentioned in passing, that of psychopathy. As ordinarily understood this involves a kind of incapacity to engage in and respond to moral reasoning. Psychopaths may be incompetent to grasp and consistently apply basic moral concepts, or to see any point to those concepts when they obtain; they may thus be unable to occupy a perspective from which moral concepts appear to have genuine deliberative significance. Since Kantians maintain that the norms of correct deliberation require anyone to take moral justifications into account, they must say that psychopaths are unable or incompetent to deliberate correctly. Hence the verdict of inherent irrationality about these cases.

In cases of this sort, the connection is severed between the claim that moral justifications provide a given agent with reasons for action,[12] and the different claim that the agent is competent to appreciate the deliberative

---

[11] This is a leitmotiv of Williams's *Ethics and the Limits of Philosophy* (Cambridge, Mass.: Harvard Univ. Press, 1985); see esp. chs. 2 and 9. It should be remarked that Williams himself is notably alive to the hazards of holding people responsible (cf. ibid. 36–8); he himself might not wish to endorse even a restricted presumption that people are to be treated in this way. See also 'Internal Reasons and the Obscurity of Blame'.

[12] I assume that the Kantian will continue to say about this case that the psychopath has reason to act morally; otherwise the contrast with the neo-Humean view will threaten to collapse.

significance of the justifications. It follows that there may be practical reasoners about whom we cannot say that they are able to appreciate moral justifications, even if the Kantian is correct about the rational status of such justifications.[13] But as I mentioned above, it is the competence or capacity claim that is important for purposes of determining whether an agent can fairly be treated as a morally accountable person. This is shown by the fact that psychopathy is paradigmatically a condition that exempts an agent from accountability, just in virtue of the fact that it deprives the agent of the competence to grasp and comply with moral justifications. Thus we see that a Kantian interpretation of the norms of correct deliberation would not license the conclusion that all practical reasoners are to be included within the community of morally accountable persons. It licenses, at most, a defeasible presumption that those who are capable of practical reasoning may be treated as morally accountable—a presumption that is defeated in some cases of inherent irrationality.

Now it might be thought that this still leaves room for a significant contrast between Humean and Kantian theories on the question of moral responsibility. For it seems that the neo-Humean position would not even license a defeasible presumption that agents have the capacity for reflective self-control.[14] Whether a given agent has these powers will depend on the contingent, socially conditioned dispositions to which the agent is in fact subject, and one cannot simply presume that the right kind of dispositions will generally be present. But this point of contrast seems unlikely to have any real significance in practice. Partly this is because the forms of socialization necessary to instil in people the dispositions that (on the neo-Humean view) enable them to appreciate moral justifications remain fairly widespread in our culture. We have not yet sunk to the point where it cannot generally be taken for granted that the people we interact with are competent to grasp the deliberative significance of moral justifications. So a defeasible presumption of basic moral accountability may be warranted in practice even on the neo-Humean account of practical reasons.[15]

---

[13] This kind of situation will be even more common on an Aristotelian conception of practical reason, according to which an elaborate course of habituation is a condition for being able to deliberate correctly. I believe this reflects important differences between the Aristotelian and Kantian conceptions of practical reason, concerning both its nature (in particular, the role of general principles in moral deliberation) and its social role. For Kant, our status as practical reasoners should provide access to a common framework of moral requirements in a way that is independent of our more particular conception of the good. Hence the idea that there should at least be a presumption that practical reasoners are capable of grasping and responding to moral principles is important for him, as it does not seem to be for Aristotle.

[14] Here in particular the neo-Humean view would seem to diverge in its commitments from Hume's own position, which would ground our moral powers in the sympathetic sentiments endemic to human nature.

[15] At least, the assumption is likely to be as warranted as on the Kantian view. (As I explain below, that moral considerations provide one with reasons for action is only a necessary, not a sufficient condition for accountability.)

Indeed, I am attracted to the following, stronger hypothesis: Those cases in which the neo-Humean will say that an agent is not in a position to appreciate moral justifications are very likely to be cases in which the Kantian will opt for the verdict of inherent irrationality. The plausibility of this hypothesis is connected to the fact that rational competence admits of degrees, and that its development is subject to social and educational influences. Thus the capacity to reason morally is one of the things that children acquire in the course of normal development. The cases in which this developmental process goes awry—resulting in inherent irrationality, by the Kantian's lights—are apt to be the very cases in which the neo-Humean will claim that the agent's socialization has left no psychological niche for moral deliberation to get a foothold. Of course, proponents of the two approaches will continue to say different things about such cases. But at this point the dispute between them threatens to become merely verbal, without any connection to substantive issues in moral psychology or the theory of responsibility that seemed to give the dispute its point. Perhaps it is time to put this issue aside, and focus on more consequential questions concerning the deliberative authority of moral requirements.

2. *Rational Optimality and the Question of Congruence*

At the start of this essay I distinguished between two different aspects of the phenomenon of deliberative authority: There is the question whether a given agent has reason to comply with moral norms, and there is the different question whether the agent has most reason to comply with such norms.[16] I turn to the second question, concerning the rational optimality of moral conduct, in this section and the ones to follow, sketching a framework for thinking about this issue, and tracing its connections with the theory of responsibility.

There is an important initial difficulty saying clearly what it means to hold that someone has most reason to comply with moral demands (the optimality thesis, as I shall henceforth refer to it). I shall start by laying out some basic assumptions that will structure my discussion. First, optimality assertions about what we have most reason to do are not to be confused with psychological assertions about what we are in fact most strongly motivated to do. This follows directly from the basic idea that practical reason is normative, together with the truism that human beings are only imperfectly rational. Second, I shall take for granted that the optimality thesis cannot be interpreted as a claim about what would best advance one's

---

[16] The idea that compliance with moral requirements is always rationally optimal in this sense is often expressed as the claim that such requirements are 'overriding'.

non-moral interests or maximize one's expected non-moral utility. Moral demands function as constraints on the pursuit of individual non-moral utility; in this sense, doing what we are morally obligated to do sometimes requires sacrifices of us. Of course, ingenious attempts have been made, in the spirit of Thomas Hobbes, to show that a strategy of constrained maximization of individual utility is actually optimal, from the standpoint of individual non-moral avantage.[17] For purposes of discussion in this essay, however, I shall assume that compliance with moral norms cannot fully be reconciled with the effective pursuit of non-moral advantage. Morality appears to be a source of autonomous norms, which place constraints on the pursuit of non-moral advantage, and which are not answerable to the different norms that govern the point of view of individual well-being.

If we adopt this assumption, however, it may seem that there is no way to unpack the assertion that moral conduct is optimal from the standpoint of reason. Practical reason appears divided within itself, between a standpoint of morality and a eudaemonistic standpoint concerned with the goodness of the agent's own life, each defined by independent norms of correct deliberation.[18] We can perhaps say what it is rational to do with an eye to morality, and what it is rational to do with an eye to an individual's good, but there seems to be no common currency in terms of which to cash out claims about what it is most rational to do overall. Moreover, this will remain the case so long as we resist efforts either to reduce morality to individual well-being, construed in non-moral terms, or to define the good life in moral terms.[19] In what follows I shall simply assume that these efforts should be resisted, that there is no single common currency of practical reason.

It does not in fact follow from this assumption, however, that we can make no sense of the optimality thesis. Though there are a number of ways one might approach this unusually difficult issue, I shall restrict myself to discussing a general strategy that has been recurrent in the tradition of philosophical ethics.[20] Any defence of the optimality thesis must try to

---

[17] See David Gauthier, *Morals by Agreement* (Oxford: Clarendon Press, 1986).

[18] This contrast should not be assimilated to the different contrast between impersonal altruism on the one hand, and egoism on the other hand. The standpoint of moral deliberation may well acknowledge requirements that are essentially connected with the agent's particular situation (that grow out of personal relationships, for instance). And the standpoint of the individual good will only be egoistic if the agent's interests and projects happen to be exclusively self-regarding. For a general discussion of the possible relations between these points of view, with helpful references to further literature, see Thomas Nagel, *The View from Nowhere* (New York: Oxford Univ. Press, 1986), ch. 10.

[19] Cf. ibid. 195–7.

[20] For a magisterial and sophisticated presentation of this strategy—to which I am heavily indebted —see the 'congruence argument' developed by John Rawls in pt. 3 of *A Theory of Justice* (Cambridge, Mass.: Harvard Univ. Press, 1971). Different versions of the strategy can be found in the work of Aristotle, Butler, Hume, and Kant (among others).

make out the idea that moral demands, though independent from considerations of self-interest, have a kind of normative priority, so that one only
deliberates correctly when one makes one's pursuit of one's non-moral
interests conditional on one's prior compliance with moral demands. The
problem, of course, is to understand the appeal to correct deliberation in
this assertion. This looks like a normative claim, but it cannot itself be
understood either as a moral claim or as a claim about what it is in our non-
moral interest to do. The moral interpretation would amount to the trivial
assertion that moral demands have deliberative priority, from the moral
point of view; while the alternative interpretation of the optimality thesis,
as an appeal to non-moral interest, appears to be false.

The initial difficulty concerning the optimality thesis was that practical
reason seemed divided internally, leaving no single standpoint from which
to formulate and assess the idea that we have most reason to act morally. If
this is the problem, however, then perhaps the solution is to look for a
substantive convergence between the different points of view. I do not
mean by this that we should try to construct a new, overarching standpoint
that is to supersede the original perspectives of morality and the individual
good. The idea, rather, is to reconsider the verdicts reached from within
the original perspectives, to see how far they can be brought into alignment
with each other. If the conclusion that moral demands have priority over
non-moral demands could somehow be endorsed from both deliberative
points of view, it will have been vindicated without prejudice to the idea
that the points of view are independent from each other. The hope is that
practical reason can be unified functionally, despite the plurality of its
constituent perspectives, by showing that those perspectives are congruent
with each other. Though we would have different standards available by
which to assess the correctness of an agent's deliberations and decisions,
these would converge substantively on the conclusion that one should
pursue one's individual ends only in ways that meet the demands and
constraints of morality.

This result cannot possibly be achieved, however, without modifying
our understanding of the eudaemonistic point of view.[21] To this point I
have spoken as if eudaemonistic rationality attends exclusively to an agent's
own well-being, where this in turn is defined in terms of the agent's non-
moral interests. Interpreted in this way, however, eudaemonistic rationality
does not seem to converge on the conclusion that moral demands have

---

[21] As Sidney Morgenbesser has reminded me, this term has potentially misleading connotations. As
I shall understand it, eudaemonistic reflection must often content itself with negative conclusions,
identifying activities that are parts of one's good primarily in the sense that one's own life would be
impoverished if one did not engage in them. It does not follow that to engage in activities of this kind
will necessarily yield 'happiness' or 'flourishing'.

priority over our non-moral interests. If congruence between the stand-points of moral and eudaemonistic rationality is to be so much as possible, we need to question the idea that the eudaemonistic standpoint is to be understood exclusively by reference to an agent's non-moral interests.

But this idea is in fact questionable. The eudaemonistic perspective is one from which we are concerned, in the first instance, with the goodness of our own lives. In deliberating from this point of view, our aim is to answer the practical question, 'What is it for us to live well?', where living well is in turn a matter of having a variety of ends that are worth caring about, and effectively and appropriately pursuing those ends. There is nothing in the formulation of this question, however, that requires that moral ends be excluded from the set of concerns by reference to which the goodness of our lives is understood. On the contrary, for any agent subject to serious moral motivations it would only seem natural that these should have some impact on that agent's conception of living well. Of course, the concern to act rightly would play a different role in moral and eudaemonistic reasoning. From the moral point of view, our question is simply, 'What is the right thing to do?'; the deliberative field is constituted, as it were, from the perspective of our moral concern. From the eudaemonistic perspective, by contrast, we reflect on the fact that morality is one of our concerns, and ask ourselves, in light of this and other facts about our interests, what it would be for us to live well.

When the eudaemonistic perspective is interpreted in this way, however, it is no longer clear that it cannot converge on the substantive conclusion that moral demands ought to be complied with. To reach this conclusion from the eudaemonistic perspective would be to hold that our own life goes best as a whole when the pursuit of our non-moral ends is made conditional on our compliance with the demands of morality. Indeed, for purposes of achieving convergence with the moral point of view it may be sufficient if eudaemonistic reflection yields the weaker conclusion that there is no other life that is better for us as a whole than the life in which the demands of morality are complied with. This would be sufficient to establish the con-clusion that one is reasoning correctly, from the eudaemonistic standpoint, in choosing to comply with one's moral obligations; and that conclusion in turn would bring the standards of eudaemonistic reflection into substantive alignment with the standards of correct deliberation that define the moral point of view.

What I would like to do now is to look at this general strategy of argument—what I shall refer to as the congruence strategy—in light of the remarks made earlier about the role of moral principles in structuring relationships of moral accountability. In introducing this topic at the start of the essay I contrasted two different points of view: the third-person

standpoint of moral accountability and the first-person standpoint of practical reason. It is an assumption of the congruence strategy that the latter
standpoint is subject to a further internal division, reflecting the distinction
between moral and eudaemonistic deliberation, where the truth of the
optimality thesis turns on the question of how far deliberation from these
two constitutive standpoints of practical reason can be brought into substantive alignment. Confronted with this potential proliferation of practical
standpoints, there are two salient questions that need to be addressed: first,
to what extent can the standpoint of moral accountability contribute to
securing congruence between the moral and eudaemonistic points of view?
and what would the breakdown of congruence between these deliberative
standpoints entail for relationships of moral accountability? I take up these
issues in the sections to follow.

3. Full Accountability and the Value of Moral Action

An initial question concerning eudaemonistic reflection about morality is
this: how are moral considerations to be registered when we reflect about
what it would be for us to live well? Should we think of moral motivations
in this context as simple preferences, whose potential satisfaction is to be
weighed in the balance along with the potential satisfaction of our other,
non-moral preferences, in determining which courses of action would be
best for us to perform?

This way of thinking about matters seems to me potentially misleading,
threatening to distort our conception of moral interests by ascribing to
them the wrong kind of role in eudaemonistic reflection. As I see matters,
moral principles define a framework for human social life, specifying *obliga-*
tions that individuals must comply with in their interactions with each
other; they rule out certain forms of behaviour, as impermissible from the
moral point of view, and specify other things that we are positively required to do. If cruelty and manipulation are morally wrong, for instance,
then one simply must not deal with people in these ways. By specifying
obligations of this kind, moral principles carve out a range of potential
actions that are open to us to perform in any given situation, defining other
alternatives as morally out of bounds.

Now this seems to me to have an important bearing on the question of
how moral interests are to be understood within the context of eudaemonistic
reflection. With respect to their content, our central moral interests are not
plausibly thought of by analogy with a standard kind of positive preference
regarding options and outcomes, where the satisfaction of the preference
does not necessarily dictate any particular form of behaviour at the time
when the preference is held. My desire to see the latest Martin Scorsese

movie could be satisfied by going to see the film at the next available opportunity, but it could equally be satisfied by forming and acting on a plan to see the film next week, or when it eventually appears on television. My interest in morality, by contrast, is an interest in complying with the moral principles that govern our interactions with each other, and when these principles specify strict or perfect duties, they can only be complied with successfully by continuously doing what the principles specify (avoiding cruelty and manipulation, for example): to humiliate somebody today, with the thought that one will strive to be kind tomorrow, would not really count as a way of satisfying our interest in morality.[22]

A second and more important point concerns the status of moral interests within the context of eudaemonistic reflection. It seems to me that the connection of morality with obligation has implications for the way in which moral interests are to be reflected in thinking about what it is for us to live well. If we have such interests, and if we take them seriously, then we will not be inclined to view them merely as defeasible preferences—that is, as considerations that are to be taken into account in reflecting about how it would be good to live, but that may be overridden if compliance with moral demands would render inexpedient the pursuit of our personal goals. Rather, an agent who has a serious interest in morality ought to regard compliance with moral principles as a fixed constraint on what may be counted as a good life. The task of eudaemonistic deliberation for such an agent is not merely to enter moral considerations into the balance, as factors to be weighed off against the attractions of ordinary personal projects and interests, but to discover ways of pursuing those projects and interests that also fulfil the requirements of moral principles. The appropriate metaphor for this kind of practical deliberation is not weighing things in a balance, but rather *integration*: one tries to find ways of pursuing and organizing one's activities that advance one's personal projects and interests while also fully satisfying one's moral obligations.

If this is right, then the main philosophical task for the proponent of the congruence strategy will be to show that moral interests ought to be taken into account, from the eudaemonistic point of view. That is, if it can be established that correct reflection about what makes our lives worth while must acknowledge the importance of our basic interest in morality, then we will already have gone a considerable distance toward securing the optimality thesis. For it seems that the only sensible way to register the importance of moral considerations within eudaemonistic reflection is to take moral principles to define fixed constraints within which our personal projects and

---

[22] Kantian imperfect duties are more like ordinary preferences in this respect; in so far as they are genuine obligations, however, they should have the indefeasible status within eudaemonistic reflection that I go on to discuss.

activities are to proceed. This in turn would amount to acceptance of the claim that our lives go better on the whole when the pursuit of our personal ends is made conditional on, and thereby integrated with, our compliance with moral demands. Anything short of reflection with this kind of integrative structure—such as the 'weighing in a balance' model to which I adverted above—would appear to distort our understanding of moral considerations and the interests they generate. It would represent, not an admissible way of representing the contribution of moral interests to the goodness of our lives, but rather the denial that such interests have any independent contribution to make.

The task, then, is to get moral interests on the map, for purposes of eudaemonistic reflection, showing that they are among the concerns that need to be taken seriously if we are to reason correctly about the worth while life. One kind of person for whom this claim might seem problematic would be the complete amoralist, someone utterly lacking in any non-derivative motivations to comply with moral principles. People of this kind would not have any interest in acting morally, and so the question might seem moot whether an interest in morality would be taken into account by them if they were to deliberate correctly about their own well-being.[23]

A different and more interesting challenge is presented by the person who is subject to moral motivations, but who does not see compliance with moral principles as an intrinsic good, from the standpoint of eudaemonistic deliberation. About persons in this position, we might well agree that they have reason to comply with moral principles, in that they are capable of applying and acting on those principles in deliberation from a distinctively moral point of view. But when they reflect on what it is to live well, they will have trouble taking their moral motivations seriously, as important independent determinants of a good life. Perhaps they view moral principles on a loose analogy with traffic regulations: as rules that generally must be complied with in order to facilitate and enable social life, without its being the case that such compliance contributes intrinsically to making one's own life worth while. This sort of person need not regret having developed a motivational responsiveness to moral considerations, and a correspondingly habitual facility at adopting the moral point of view. Nor will they necessarily fail to see anything of value in acting morally, when they engage in eudaemonistic reflection. Just as compliance with traffic regulations is instrumentally valuable in all kinds of ways when one is out on the road (for instance, as enhancing one's own safety), so too can compliance with moral principles contribute instrumentally to one's own good—among other things, it helps to keep one out of trouble with the law.

---

[23] On the figure of the amoralist, see Joseph Raz's contribution to the present volume.

But the persons I am imagining will balk at admitting that acting morally is an intrinsically important ingredient of the good life. In their eyes, this supposition would be akin to the rather absurd view that there is something intrinsically valuable about obeying the speed limit, even when one is on an empty road in the middle of the desert under excellent driving conditions, and the police are nowhere in sight.

If this 'traffic regulation' view of morality is correct, then it seems to me that the congruence strategy is unlikely to meet with much success. That strategy requires that compliance with moral principles should contribute directly to making the agent's own life worth while. But on the traffic regulation view it would simply be a mistake to suppose that compliance with moral principles should have this kind of importance, for purposes of eudaemonistic reflection. If the congruence strategy is to go forward, then, it will be necessary to challenge the traffic regulation model, by showing that there is something of intrinsic value to be attained by acting morally, something moreover that is of sufficient importance within eudaemonistic reflection to be treated as a condition of the good life.

It is here, I believe, that attention to relationships of accountability may be of some assistance. At the start of this essay I drew a distinction between two levels of status that persons may attain within morality. There is, first, the status of being an accountable agent, someone to whom moral principles are appropriately addressed, and who may fairly be held morally responsible with reference to such principles. Someone who achieves this status is eligible for membership in a certain kind of relationship, one defined by the reciprocal stance of holding people to moral demands. But agents who are accountable in this way can attain a different and higher kind of moral status by actually exercising their powers of reflective self-determination in accordance with moral principles. To act in this way is not merely to be a person who can be held morally to account by others. It is, more strongly, to be in a position actually to give a successful account of one's doings to others, a position from which one can justify one's actions by reference to common moral principles. People who achieve this status are thereby able to enter into qualitatively superior relationships with other people. They have no need to fear or shun the gaze of their fellows, since they are capable of justifying their actions in moral terms, terms that all accountable agents should equally be able to understand and to accept.

Now, whether or not we succeed in achieving this kind of status is not a matter of indifference to most of us. On the contrary, it seems to me to be the sort of thing that is intelligible as an intrinsic contribution to our own good, something that is worth caring about for its own sake, when we think clearly about what it is to live well. The fact is that humans are deeply social creatures, and this is reflected in the urge that most people feel to be able to give an account of themselves to others—an urge that manifests itself, somewhat perversely, in the imaginative compulsion we have to rationalize when confronted with evidence of apparent wrongdoing. To put the point slightly differently, it is not a matter of indifference to most of us whether we are the objects of resentment or indignation on the part of our fellow human beings. There is a primitive desire to be thought well of by others, which is refined through socialization into a second-order interest in *justified* regard: the desire not to act in ways that could incur the well-grounded resentment or indignation of others. By enabling us to give an account of ourselves, compliance with moral principles answers to this interest, and thereby contributes to making our own lives worth while.

Of course, nothing I have said can be construed as a proof that attainment of the status of full accountability is an ingredient of the agent's own good. Indeed, I myself am suspicious of the very idea that philosophy could establish a thesis in the theory of value of this kind. What philosophical reflection can do is to help us to how living morally can be a way of living well, by connecting moral behaviour to something that is recognizable to us within eudaemonistic reflection, as an important part of a good human life. This requires not merely that moral behaviour be connected to something that human beings generally find intelligible, as an object of interest or concern, but that such behaviour be shown to make a direct contribution to the goodness of the agent's own life. It seems to me that the status of full accountability—being in a position to give a successful justification of oneself to other persons—is among the things that are familiar and intelligible to us in this context, as direct objects of reflexive concern about our own lives, and that by relating this status to compliance with moral principles, philosophy can help us to understand why such compliance should figure as a central constraint on eudaemonistic deliberation.

Does the argument I have sketched establish that moral behaviour is an objective good, something without which no human being—including even the amoralist—could be said to have flourished or lived well? I doubt it. But for present purposes I would be content with the following, more modest conclusion: that no person who is equipped with moral motivations need regard the satisfaction of those preferences by analogy with the traffic regulation model. There is something recognizable as an appropriate object of reflexive concern about our own lives that is only attainable by complying with moral obligations, namely the achievement of a certain kind of relationship to other people. This in turn lends credence to the assumption that those persons who ascribe importance to their interest in morality, for purposes of eudaemonistic reflection, are in fact reasoning correctly about what it is for them to live well.

4. Accountability and the Stringency of Moral Requirements

To say that our moral interests are important, within the standpoint of eudaemonistic reflection, is of course not to say that they are the only interests that are important in that context. Any individual with a reasonably fulfilling and balanced life is going to have all sorts of personal projects and goals and relationships that are matters of great importance, and that will need to be taken centrally into account in reflecting about how to live well. We are not merely moral agents, but also friends and lovers, philosophers and teachers, train-spotters and Mets fans, and these personal commitments provide much of the raw material for deliberation about our own good. Indeed I suspect that for most people, personal commitments of this sort are apt to be important in a way that the interest in morality almost never is. They are what Bernard Williams has referred to as 'ground projects', the sorts of things that give our lives point and meaning, and without which we would not see much reason to go on. The interest in morality, by contrast, does not seem to have this kind of significance. Even granting the intrinsic goods of moral community to which I earlier referred, these do not appear to be the kinds of goods to organize a life around: one does not live for morality the way one might be said to live for baseball or philosophy or one's children.

The fact that morality does not generally have this kind of importance can make it tempting to suppose that it could have at best a secondary contribution to make in contexts of eudaemonistic deliberation. If morality does not itself have the status of a kind of ground project, then it might seem reasonable to subordinate our interest in it whenever that interest comes into conflict with the things that fill our lives with purpose and zest. But this would be a mistake. To say that morality is not important in the way our typical ground projects are important is not to say that it is not important at all. If compliance with moral principles is an essential part of the good life, and if those principles prescribe obligations, then the person who is deliberating correctly about what it is to live well will take those obligations to define constraints or conditions on a good life. As I said earlier, the deliberative task will be one of integration: finding ways of pursuing one's projects and goals while also satisfying the requirements of morality.

The one sort of case in which this task will tend to break down is the case in which an agent's ground projects are themselves sources of obligation, and those obligations come into conflict with the obligations of morality. A schematic example is provided by any situation in which morality demands of an agent the ultimate sacrifice: if morality requires one to put one's life on the line (for instance, when the officers of a military unit have threatened to execute those soldiers who refuse to carry out their criminal order to massacre a group of innocent civilians),[24] this would naturally appear to conflict with the obligation to preserve one's own life that is grounded in one's personal and familial relationships. Here it would appear that one cannot satisfy the demands of morality while also living up to one's personal commitments, and so the integrative task of eudaemonistic deliberation would have no single solution. A different and perhaps less schematic case would be Susan Wolf's example of the parent, whose personal obligation of protection and support for her child might conflict with the moral obligation to inform the police that she has reason to suspect the child of serious criminal wrongdoing.[25] Here again, there seems to be no course of action available that would integrate the agent's moral obligations with the demands that are grounded in her personal projects.

Cases of this kind, in which integrative eudaemonistic reflection cannot go forward, theaten to undermine the deliberative authority of morality. Presented with a situation of this sort, it seems implausible to maintain that the agent has most reason to comply with the demands of duty. The far more natural response would be that there is no clear answer to the question what the agent has most reason to do; she is confronted with the need to decide on a course of action in a way that exceeds the capacity of practical reason to guide her toward a determinate solution. Furthermore, the forces that are arrayed against morality in this kind of situation are forces that it would be unusually difficult to resist. They represent the demands of one's identity-defining projects, requirements that one must comply with if one is to remain true to the commitments that give meaning and point to one's life. To violate these requirements, for the sake of morality, would be to betray values that are important in a way that morality generally cannot hope to be.

Now it may well be doubted how often genuine conflicts of this kind are apt to arise in life. Did Gauguin really have to leave his family in the lurch in order to remain true to his calling as a painter? Was there absolutely no deliberative solution available that would have enabled him to integrate the demands of his personal projects with his moral obligations to his wife and children? There is much room for rationalization and self-deception in cases of this kind. Nevertheless I see no reason to deny that situations of the form I have described can sometimes come up, in which moral obligations are irreconcilably in conflict with the demands of one's important ground projects. Moreover, when such conflicts occur, and when in the face of such a conflict an agent chooses to violate her moral obligations,

---

[24] Cf. Michael Walzer, *Just and Unjust Wars* (New York: Basic Books, 1977), 313–14.

[25] Susan Wolf, 'Morality and Partiality', in J. Tomberlin (ed.), *Philosophical Perspectives*, vi. *Ethics* (Atascadero, Calif.: Ridgeview, 1992), 243–59, at 253–4.

there is room to question whether it is reasonable to hold the agent fully to blame for this lapse. Let me explain.

At the start of this essay I observed that the powers of reflective self-control are conditions for the reasonableness of holding people morally accountable, and also that these powers can temporarily be impaired, due to local circumstances such as extreme stress or emotional turmoil. Furthermore, when such impairments or difficulties obtain, the appropriate response would be to ascribe to an agent only a diminished level of moral accountability, and to mitigate the reactions of blame and moral sentiment that would ordinarily be called for by a moral wrong. For if the powers of reflective self-control are conditions for the fairness of these kinds of response, and we agree that those powers are severely impaired in the agent's circumstances, then we ought to adjust our reactions accordingly in recognition of this fact.

These reflections suggest a rationale for suspending ordinary relationships of moral accountability in situations in which the requirements of morality conflict irreconcilably with the demands of one's personal projects. Conflicts of this kind can plausibly be viewed as locally impairing an agent's capacity to comply with moral requirements, in so far as they render unusually difficult the exercise of those capacities. This is perhaps clearest in cases in which morality requires us to sacrifice our own life, since requirements of this kind would meet with powerful resistance not only from rational sources (the demands of our personal projects), but also from our primal feelings about death.[26] But the difficulty or impairment of moral power may equally be present in cases involving no primal emotions of this kind, where moral demands conflict with the requirements of one's personal relationships and commitments. To do the right thing in such a situation would mean the certain loss of one's heart's desire, the abandonment of that which invests one's life and one's activities with meaning and point. Even acknowledging the importance of morality, it would be unusually difficult to bring oneself to make a sacrifice of this kind; doing so would be powerfully opposed to forces within the structure of practical reason itself. And when reason itself is an impairment of our moral capacities, we ought to take account of that fact by moderating or mitigating our responses of blame and reactive sentiment. This is the grain of truth in the idea that it would be unfair to blame a person fully if acting morally was not the rational thing to do.

I would like in conclusion to consider briefly an issue that has received much attention in recent moral philosophy, concerning the stringency or

---

[26] Walzer treats the case of the soldiers mentioned earlier in the text as one of diminished responsibility through duress; see *Just and Unjust Wars*, 313–14.

demandingness of moral requirements. It is sometimes thought that extremely demanding theories of the content of moral requirements, such as direct utilitarianism, are inadequate because they render the deliberative authority of those requirements problematic.[27] I am inclined to agree with this verdict.[28] But I think the objection is difficult to articulate if we confine our attention to the first-person perspective of practical reason, and believe that it may be helpful to consider in this connection the role of moral principles in structuring relationships of accountability.

Suppose that moral norms gave us the first-order goal of maximizing the good, impersonally construed, so that deliberation from the moral point of view is answerable exclusively to this maximizing norm. It is a familiar thought that compliance with moral norms, construed in this way, would require a great deal of us in the way of personal sacrifice. But the more interesting point concerns the way in which sacrifice would be imposed by this kind of morality. To say that we are always required to maximize the good, impersonally conceived, means that morality is not only demanding but peculiarly intrusive. There is a standing requirement that we contribute to the realization of a demanding positive goal, and this combination of stringency and pervasiveness—the combination Bernard Williams has pointed to under the heading of 'negative responsibility'[29]—seems likely to generate constant conflicts between the obligations of morality and the demands of our more personal projects and goals. In a world of tremendous inequality and suffering it is very doubtful that the things we are required to do, in the service of our relationships and commitments, would also happen to be the things that maximize expected overall utility, impersonally conceived—working on one's paper for the next conference or watching the Mets' home opener hardly seem to cut it when there are basic human needs and interests to be attended to. The upshot is that the requirements of morality would be in constant conflict with the demands of living an individual human life, and the integrative project of eudaemonistic reflection would be thwarted across the board. There would rarely turn out to be a solution to the problem of complying with moral obligations while also meeting the demands that stem from one's own ground projects. Moreover, given the kind of importance that attaches to such personal projects,

[27] This idea is suggested, for instance, by Nagel's argument for relaxing moral requirements in *The View from Nowhere*, 200–3, and by Scheffler's defence of 'moderation' in ch. 7 of *Human Morality*.

[28] I also think there are other, independent grounds for rejecting particular interpretations of morality as especially stringent. For instance, there is a false conception of the standpoint of moral deliberation as detached and 'impersonal' that exerts pressure in the direction of extreme stringency. Indeed, both Nagel and Scheffler betray a weakness for this conception, which makes their own defences of more moderate interpretations seem somewhat *ad hoc*. But of course these are issues for a different occasion.

[29] Bernard Williams, 'A Critique of Utilitarianism', in J. J. C. Smart and Bernard Williams, *Utilitarianism: For and Against* (Cambridge: Univ. Press, 1973), 75–150, sect. 3.

the breakdown of eudaemonistic reflection would threaten to permanently impair our moral capacities, creating a standing impediment within practical reason to the regulation of conduct by the light of moral principles. As a result, it would never be reasonable to hold people fully accountable by the standards of a moral theory of this kind.

This, I believe, is a sufficient reason for rejecting direct utilitarianism. It is not just that this theory would be extremely demanding, but that it is demanding in a way that would systematically thwart the project of integrative eudaemonistic reflection, and thereby undermine the practice of moral accountability. The concern that we have on this score is a reflection of our conception of morality as defining a common set of standards for a moral community, by appeal to which the conduct of each person can be justified and criticized in terms that all are able to understand and to abide by. This conception commits us to the view that moral demands must be capable of serving as the basis for reciprocal relations of moral accountability, and that constraint would be violated by an interpretation of moral requirements which necessarily resulted, under the familiar circumstances of human life, in a fundamental breakdown of the integrative project of eudaemonistic reflection.

Of course, not everyone accepts the conception of morality to which I have just adverted. Proponents of some religious conceptions of ethics, for instance, tend to see moral standards not as bases of reciprocal relations between persons, but in the context of non-reciprocal relations between the individual believer and god. Someone attracted to this approach will not find the objection to highly demanding interpretations of morality that I have tried to articulate persuasive.[30] Direct utilitarians, who often resemble the proponents of religious interpretations of morality in their view of the stringency of moral requirements, are also notoriously sceptical of our existing practice of moral responsibility.[31] They tend to view this as a residue of primitive retributivist systems of thought, which ought to be replaced, so far as possible, by more therapeutic and constructive forms of moral relationship. If this helps to explain the failure of utilitarians to grasp the force of the objection I have tried to articulate, however, it does not necessarily undermine that objection. The inability of utilitarians to make

---

[30] It seems to me that the ideal of morality as a form of self-transcendence (discussed for instance by Scheffler in *Human Morality*, 120–1) is naturally at home in this kind of context. Note too that one might subscribe to this kind of ideal in the guise of a 'personal morality', without thinking that it should also structure one's relations with other agents. In my view, this is the right way to interpret the form of 'moral perfectionism' discussed by Stanley Cavell, in *Conditions Handsome and Unhandsome: The Constitution of Emersonian Perfectionism* (Chicago: Univ. Press, 1990).

[31] This shows itself, for instance, in the familiar utilitarian distinction between the question of the wrongness of an action, and the question whether the consequences of blaming the agent for it would be optimific; see e.g. J. J. C. Smart, 'An Outline of a System of Utilitarian Ethics', in Smart and Williams, *Utilitarianism: For and Against*, 3–74, at sect. 7.

sense of the practice of holding people responsible as anything other than a relict of primitive retributivism is itself one of the things many of us find problematic about the utilitarian conception of the moral life.[32]

A different line of response would call attention to the fact that the authority of morality, on the account of it I have sketched, is a contingent matter. It has become a commonplace in discussions of the relation between morality and the individual good to observe that this relation is liable to be affected by the social conditions in which an individual lives.[33] The authority of morality can thus be seen as a political achievement. In a more egalitarian social world, for instance, the demands that generalized bene-ficence would make on the currently affluent would presumably be far less stringent than they are at present. Direct utilitarians might insist that moral requirements, on their account of them, can indeed serve as the basis of reciprocal relations of moral accountability—not in the actual world of extreme inequality, perhaps, but in a social world in which such inequalit-ies had been substantially reduced.

There are two difficulties with this response. The first is that it is unclear whether the reduced stringency of direct utilitarianism in a differ-ent social world would alone be enough to remove completely the kind of problem I have identified. That problem stems not just from the fact that utilitarian morality imposes stringent demands, but rather from the way those demands are articulated, namely in the form of a standing first-order goal, by reference to which one is to justify each of one's choices and activities. The achievement of more egalitarian social conditions might bring about a formal reduction in the conflicts between moral and personal obligations, making it more frequently the case that the things one is required to do in the name of one's projects and commitments are also things that satisfy the moral demand that one always seek to maximize the impersonal good. But the intrusiveness of morality remains, on this con-ception of it, imposing a demand that one justify each of one's actions as a direct contribution to a standing and positive moral objective, and this requirement seems likely to distort one's eudaemonistic reflection in other disturbing ways. One of the things that follows from the special kind of importance we ascribe to our ground projects and relationships is that we take them to make demands on us that are independent of our other moral and non-moral commitments, and this way of thinking about them would be threatened by a requirement that we act on our personal projects and

---

[32] Cf. RMS, sect. 3.1.

[33] See e.g. Nagel, The View from Nowhere, 204–7; Shelly Kagan, The Limits of Morality (Oxford: Clarendon Press, 1989), 393–9; Scheffler, Human Morality, ch. 8; and Peter Railton, 'Alienation, Consequentialism, and the Demands of Morality', as repr. in Samuel Scheffler (ed.), Consequentialism and its Critics (Oxford: Univ. Press, 1988), 93–133, at 122–5.

commitments only when doing so coincides contingently with the first-order moral goal of maximizing the impersonal good. A kind of alienation would set in.

The second difficulty is simply that we need moral standards to structure our relations with other persons in the imperfect world in which we actually live. Even if direct utilitarianism could provide a reasonable basis for responsibility relations in a substantially egalitarian social world, it does not follow that it provides a reasonable basis for responsibility relations in the actual circumstances of modern social life. We need to know what is permissible and obligatory under these circumstances, where such judgements can serve in justification and moral criticism of our own conduct and the conduct of others. Theories that violate this desideratum, in virtue of their overly stringent interpretations of the demands of morality, are difficult for us to take seriously as theories of anything we could recognize as morality—even if they could be taken seriously in a social world utterly unlike our own.[34]

---

[34] Different (and variously half-baked) versions of this essay were presented at the St Andrews Conference, at the University of Pittsburgh, and at Columbia University. I am grateful to the audiences on those occasions for stimulating and helpful discussion. I owe a special debt to the members of the Mid-Atlantic Moral Theory Discussion Group, who provided an especially constructive mix of scepticism and sympathy in response to one of the earlier versions; and to the editors of the present volume, whose detailed comments on the original draft were exemplary.

12

Reasons and Reason

JOHN SKORUPSKI

1. We have reasons to believe, to act, to feel. We deal in reasons at every turn—for example, I have reason to believe you covered for me in an emergency, reason to feel grateful, and so reason to thank you in some more or less substantial way. What we make of a person turns on how that person responds or fails to respond to reasons in one or other of these three domains—belief, feeling, and action. Personality is the manner of one's responsiveness to reasons. A testy person is more easily annoyed than he has reason to be. A credulous person believes when there is insufficient reason to believe. A precipitate person acts when there is insufficient reason to act.

How are these various kinds of reason connected with Reason? And where does morality fit in?

2. Let us call a proposition which is about reasons, or from which a proposition about reasons is analytically deducible, a normative proposition. (Some normative propositions will include a factual content.) Such propositions are about *reason* relations, as one may say: relations which hold between facts on the one hand and beliefs, actions, or desires on the other. In the case of belief we have *epistemic* normative propositions, which are or analytically imply propositions about reasons to believe. Example: the fact that the freezer has been left open is a reason for thinking, gives one reason to think, that its contents will melt. I take it to be the fact that rationalizes the belief; if the freezer has not been left open, but you think it has, then you have no reason to believe that the food will melt—unless some other fact, as that the fuse is blown, gives you a reason to believe it. You are indeed right to infer that you have reason to believe the food will melt from your belief that the freezer is open; but your premiss is false and thus your belief that you have reason to believe the food will melt may also be false.[1]

---

[1] Of course it may be reasonable. For you may have good reason to believe that the door is open even though it is not. If you have reason to believe that *p* and the fact that *p* gives reason to believe that *q* (and you have reason in turn to believe *that*) then it's *pro tanto* reasonable for you to believe that *q*. The point implies a distinction between *there being reason* and *your having reason*, but it will not be necessary to pursue it in what follows.

So the reason relation holds in the epistemic case between facts, persons, and beliefs. We should also leave a place for time as a term of the relation,[2] and the relation comes in degrees. Its general form in the epistemic case is therefore something like: *the fact that* p *gives* x *reason of degree* d *at time* t *to believe that* q.

What about reasons for feelings and actions? *Practical* normative propositions are about reasons to act: *the fact that* p *gives* x *reason of degree* d *at time* t *to* ψ, where ψ ranges over action-types as q ranges over belief-types. For example, the fact that the building is about to explode gives you very good reason to get out right now. *Evaluative* normative propositions are about reasons to feel: *the fact that* p *gives* x *reason of degree* d *at time* t *to feel* φ, where φ ranges over types of feeling (i.e. emotions, moods, and desires). The fact that Katie broke the record gives her reason to feel proud. In general reason relations relate facts, persons, times, a degree of magnitude, and a belief, action, or feeling type. *All* thought involves the reason relation: sometimes in the form of explicit normative beliefs but at minimum in the form of primitive normative responses as to what is in context legitimate, justified, reasonable, correct.

3. The view I want to consider is that moral propositions are evaluative normative propositions; propositions about what there is reason to *feel*— specifically, to disapprove, to respond to with blame or guilt.[3] Let us call evaluative normative judgements 'evaluations' for short; so the view is that moral judgements are evaluations in this specific sense.

It should be distinguished from 'expressivist' or 'non-cognitivist' meta-ethical views, such as were advanced earlier this century by emotivists and conventionalists and more recently, with great subtlety, by Simon Blackburn and Allan Gibbard. An expressivist could well adopt it; however, one can adopt it and still hold that moral propositions are genuine contents of judgement. In what follows I shall take it that that is what they are. To judge of evaluative reasons—of what there is reason to blame, admire, despise, be frightened, bored, amused, or irritated by—is still to judge. That view seems to me right in general, of all normative claims in all domains of belief, action, and feeling: they are genuine assertions which convey propositional contents assessable as correct or incorrect, rather than being, as an expressivist about any subclass of them holds, expressions of a feeling or a choice or an act of will. On the other hand, it does not (I believe) follow from this general view that there must be, as well as facts which

---

[2] The fact that Paula has a meeting at noon gives her at noon a reason to believe that she has a meeting then.

[3] I have defended this view (which is not of course new) in 'The Definition of Morality', in A. Phillips Griffiths (ed.), *Ethics*, Philosophy suppl. 35 (Cambridge: Univ. Press, 1993), 121–44.

rationalize, *further* facts about what those facts rationalize—facts in some special domain of reality to which we have non-empirical access. It seems to me that the governing insight from which one must start is that cognition involves a fundamental *dualism* of factual and normative judgements.[4]

Obviously this philosophical account of normative propositions—cognitivist but irrealist—calls for elucidation and extensive defence. It encounters, for example, the deep-laid doctrine that all content is factual content—together with related doctrines tying semantics to ontology. These doctrines will not be touched on here, though some connected issues about the epistemology of the normative will be spelt out a little further in Section 8. I mention them at this point to give an idea of the framework which I assume.

Our main topic, however, is the relation between reasons and Reason and the place of morality within the sphere of reasons. Many of us accept some degree or other of rationalism about the epistemic and the practical. We think that there are pure principles of theoretical reason—some of us, probably a smaller number, think there are pure principles of practical reason. 'Pure principles of reason' in these two cases means something like normative propositions about what there is reason to believe or to do, our knowledge of which does not depend upon empirical knowledge but is attainable by rational insight and accessible to any rational being. Rationalism is the view that there are such propositions, knowable, to put it in an old-fashioned way, by the faculty of Reason.

But are there pure principles of evaluative reason? Does anything stand to evaluative reasons as (many think) pure theoretical reason stands to epistemic reasons and pure practical reason stands to practical reasons? That seems far less clear. My mother comes across an old photograph of her childhood home—she has every reason to be moved. Is it Reason that tells me that? Some sort of rational insight accessible to any rational being? Is it derivable from facts about the actual world and some fundamental evaluation known to Reason? On the contrary. 'Le cœur a ses raisons, que la raison ne connaît point.' *That* seems unchallengeable. Pascal's famous remark was made in another context but it is entirely applicable to this one.

It lends plausibility to emotivism about evaluations, and hence about morality if morality consists of evaluations. But, as already noted, it does not entail emotivism. The plausibility it lends to emotivism comes from certain background assumptions which we alluded to earlier in this section.

---

[4] Thus I agree with Allan Gibbard that factual and normative claims are to be sharply distinguished but do not follow him in his expressivist conception of the normative (Gibbard, *Wise Choices, Apt Feelings* (Oxford: Clarendon Press, 1990)). Another basic point on which we agree is that moral claims are evaluations. Our difference here is about what sort of evaluations moral claims are: i.e. what feelings one is judging reasonable in making a moral judgement. See the next section (Sect. 4).

But just as one can be a cognitivist about evaluations without being a realist so, I think, one can be a cognitivist about evaluations without being a rationalist. The latter claim will become clearer, I hope, in what follows.

If it is right, and if morality does consist of evaluations, the connection between morality and reason cannot be quite as simple as a pure rationalism about morality would suggest. This is not to say that there is no truth in rationalism about morality at all. How much truth there is remains to be seen. We shall also be concerned with another question: if moral judgements are evaluations what is their relation to *practical* reason? It is a question about the relation between reasons to act and reasons to feel.

One might put the two questions as follows. If moral propositions consist of propositions about what there is reason to feel, specifically, about what there is reason to blame or feel guilty about, then

(1) How does reason bear on moral propositions?
(2) How do moral propositions bear on practical reasons? What status does the following inference have: If X is morally wrong then there is reason not to do X?

4. But first let me say a little more about blame and guilt. We have many ways of disapproving actions—holding an action *morally* wrong is only one. An action may be bizarre or tasteless, but not morally wrong. To call it morally wrong is a more serious matter: it amounts to blaming the agent. Blaming is an act or attitude whose notional core is a feeling in the way that feeling sorry is the notional core of apology. That is, these feelings are invoked as appropriate by people who blame or apologize even when they do not actually feel them.[5]

Let us call this emotional core of blame 'the blame-feeling'. We shall be more concerned with the idea that blame has an emotional core than with any particular characterization of the emotion or emotions involved. Still, some currently influential suggestions on this score seems to me very misleading. I do not believe for example that the blame-feeling is a species of anger or resentment. Certainly it is natural for anger, 'righteous indignation', to follow on wrongdoing—and for those (if any) who are injured, to resent and seek revenge. Resentment requires a real or imagined slight or injury to oneself—the Nietzschean story about morality trades on that. Righteous indignation is what is felt by a person of spirit who experiences the need personally to right a wrong whether to himself or to another. But one can blame—and *feel* the sentiment which is at the core of blaming—without

---

[5] There is a wider sense of the word 'blame', in which we may for example blame the car's faulty brakes for the accident, in other words, identify them as its relevant cause. But blame in this wider sense involves no reference, even notional, to a core of feeling. If I blame the faulty brakes I am not saying that it is reasonable or appropriate to have that feeling towards the brakes.

feeling either anger or resentment. The blame-feeling does not require that intentional content. On the other hand, it can resemble, in extreme cases, a kind of horror akin to the reaction to pollution, a horror free of any element of anger or resentment. These dispose to attack; and it may appear that the blame-feeling does too, but that is only appearance. In itself, rather, it disposes to *withdrawal of recognition*, expulsion from the community. Further: to punishment (as feeling sorry disposes to the making of amends). And punishment is not aggression, the expression of anger. When it is not a simple deterrent discipline it is the road to expiation, that is, to return, to the regaining of recognition—the right of the wrongdoer. So guilt, one's withdrawal of recognition from oneself, involves a need of self-punishment —in no way a pathological or pointless, but a fundamentally human need for expiation and redemption.[6]

Hence the affinity of blame to horror or straightforward fear. What they have in common is separation—the creation of distance. However fear disposes to flight, leaving the feared object in place, whereas blame disposes to ostracism, expulsion, cutting off. Here too lies the difference between blame or guilt (self-blame) and disdain or shame (self-disdain). This is a subtler difference than the difference between blame and anger or resentment. Disdain involves demotion, a loss of status and influence within the community of peers, rather than expulsion from it. Obviously there can be subtle and unspoken interactions between these two.[7]

5. These remarks about the blame-feeling are meant mainly to register its salience and occasional gravity in our lives and consequent importance for ethics. Important as it is to get its character right, however, the pertinent thesis for present purposes is that blame has an emotional core. To say that something is blameworthy is to make an evaluation—it is to say that it is reasonable to feel the sentiment of blame towards it. If we now characterize the morally wrong as that which is blameworthy, that towards which it is reasonable to have the blame-feeling, we can go on to characterize the other moral concepts. The morally right is that which it would be morally wrong not to do. Similarly, we can say that 'X is morally obligatory', or 'X morally

---

[6] I discuss the nature of blame and its connection with punishment more extensively in 'The Definition of Morality'. These issues are of course discussed by Hegel. See *The Philosophy of Right*, sects. 102–4, where punishment is presented as the transition from 'abstract right' to 'morality'.

[7] Cf. Bernard Williams, 'Mechanisms of Shame and Guilt', in *Shame and Necessity* (Berkeley: Univ. of California Press, 1993), 119–23 n. 1. Williams seems to me much more accurate in his account of shame than of guilt. I do not find it plausible that the 'primitive basis' of guilt is fear on the part of the blamed at the anger of the blamer. In certain cases, though by no means all (cases of fully free choice of evil one might say), it can seem closer to the truth to say the blame-feeling itself is primitively akin to fear—though for the reasons given above it still remains distinct from it. Williams's distortion of guilt seems to me to connect with his suspicion of 'modern conceptions of morality' and a general tendency to treat these conceptions as more distinctive of modernity than they really are.

ought to be done' will hold just if non-performance of X is blameworthy. Of course we admire people for going beyond the morally obligatory—'beyond the call of duty'—even though we do not blame them for not doing so. We can say that admiration of such actions is moral admiration, because we admire them for the reasons that impelled them, and those reasons are moral reasons. For example, lack of consideration for others' feelings, when it reaches a certain point, becomes blameworthy thoughtlessness. On the other hand, there are degrees of care for others' feelings which go well beyond what we would expect, on pain of blame, from people in general—but which we still admire when we meet with them. (There are also excesses of solicitude of course.) The outstandingly and the ordinarily thoughtful person are both impelled by the same reasons—consideration for others' feelings. And we can say that those reasons are moral reasons—as against, say, prudential or aesthetic reasons, since their absence from a person's mind beyond a certain point becomes blameworthy. Finally the virtues fit into this framework. They respectively involve sensitivity to various types of reason for acting which we recognize as *moral* reasons. And they are traits of character which we could be *blamed* for not attempting to attain or lose, when it is possible for us to do something to attain or lose them.

6. So morality can be 'characterized', as I have put it, in terms of the blameworthy. Does this mean that 'morally wrong' can be *defined* in terms of the blameworthy? That would be a stronger claim. The stronger claim may give an immediate impression of definitional circularity. 'Blameworthy' means 'ought to be blamed'—is this 'ought' itself not a moral 'ought'? If it is, then we won't be able to define 'X is morally wrong' as 'The doer of X ought to be blamed'—even if their equivalence (or some refinement of it) is a priori.

However, we should not accept that the 'ought' in this case is indeed a moral ought. It is rather the 'ought' of evaluative reasons—that is to say, it is definable in terms of reasons to adopt a feeling, or feeling-based attitude. To say that an action is blameworthy is to say that there is adequate reason, taking everything into account, to blame the agent for doing it—it is to say that blame is a fully reasonable response. That is an evaluative claim. It may *also* be true that one has a moral obligation to blame people for their moral wrongdoing—that when it is *reasonable* to feel the sentiment of blame toward someone it is also *morally obligatory* to blame them. But that would be a separate claim.[8] On the characterization of 'morally obligatory'

---

[8] A false one I should think. What is morally obligatory is an action not a feeling. And it might be morally wrong to blame someone who is in an emotionally distressed state even if they are blameworthy. Or it might be expedient to refrain from self-blame when time is short and things need to be done, even though the feeling is reasonable. Or perhaps bygones must be bygones—as sometimes in negotiation with violent activists—so that blame is inopportune even though the blame-feeling is justified.

which we are considering, it would be the claim that it is fully reasonable to blame a person who does not blame people for their moral wrongdoing.

So far then, we have found no circularity in the suggestion that morality can be defined by means of the notion of blameworthiness. None the less, I don't think that 'morally wrong' can strictly speaking be *defined* in terms of blameworthiness. At the semantic level, it seems to me that there is a distinct and indefinable moral sense of 'wrong'. The reasons for this have to do not with the circularity already discussed but with a circularity which arises from the fact that the concept of moral wrongness enters into the intentional content of the blame-feeling.

The blame-feeling requires a belief—that its object is something that has been done or omitted but *morally* ought not to have been done or omitted.[9] It requires it, one might suggest, in the way that fear requires that the object be dangerous. Certainly one can feel guilt about doing something one does not really believe to be morally wrong, just as one can fear something which one does not really believe dangerous. But in that case one's response is open to criticism, indeed self-criticism, as irrational.[10] The blameworthy and the morally wrong are indeed equivalent but the semantically prior term is 'morally wrong'. 'Blameworthy' means something like 'meriting that evaluative response which is appropriate to the morally wrong', and so it is circular to define 'morally wrong' in terms of 'blameworthy'.

7. There is a defence against this point which I am going to consider in some detail (though I will finally reject it). It defends the definition of 'morally wrong' as 'blameworthy', as follows. There is a *disanalogy*, it says, between the dangerous and the morally wrong. The dangerous can be characterized independently, as that which is liable to harm or damage. But, this defence says, in the case of moral wrongness no independent characterization can be given. To say that the object must be morally wrong for blame to be justified is correct. But it does not give an independent characterization of the object, any more than to say that the object must be amusing for amusement to be justified, or boring for boredom to be justified, gives an independent characterization. To say that something is boring is to say no more than that the proper and informed response to it is boredom—that it is boredom-worthy, one might say. Likewise, saying that something is morally wrong is saying that the proper or just response

---

[9] Of course the belief may be false—and the morality invoked may be the morality of thieves.

[10] Fear of fictions is not irrational. But there is supposed to be a philosophical problem about that case. One response to it, for example, is to argue that one does not really fear a fiction but imagines or makes believe that one is fearing it (see Kendall Walton, *Mimesis as Make-Believe* (Cambridge, Mass.: Harvard Univ. Press, 1990).

to it is blame: it is blame-feeling-worthy. In neither case do we appeal to an external standard but only to an internal standard—the standard of what people of competent sensibility would feel. Thus the semantically prior term is 'blameworthy', not 'morally wrong'.

On this view holding that something is morally wrong remains a perfectly objective judgement and forms the intentional content of feeling the blame-sentiment towards it. But then holding that something is boring is a perfectly objective judgement, and forms the intentional content of feeling the sentiment of boredom in relation to it. Evaluations in general are genuine judgements because they are accountable to standards of correctness—but the standards can be entirely internal. We distinguish between having an emotional response and judging it justified, even when there is no external criterion of justification such as danger in the case of fear. For example in the case of boredom and amusement there is no external criterion, but there is a difference between saying 'I am bored/amused' and saying 'This is boring/amusing'. Similarly with other terms of evaluation —'irritating', 'despicable', 'frightening', 'moving', 'boring', 'tasteless', 'contemptible', 'admirable', 'desirable', 'hateful', 'frightful', 'horrific', and so on. In each of these cases having the feeling goes, when certain other resources of concept-possession are in place, with a normative disposition—a disposition to make the corresponding evaluation. For example, when these resources are in place, to feel bored is to experience the feeling as reasonable —to experience the object as boring. Where defeating considerations are absent, it is to judge that it *is* boring.

The element of defeasibility underpins a distinction between the object seeming boring to me and its being boring—generally, between the object seeming to be φ-worthy and its being φ-worthy. Without that general distinction the force of normativity that comes with raw feeling would encounter no resistance and generate no objective evaluative thought. What puts in place the distinction? An evaluator is justified in judging that an object is φ-worthy if

(i) the object makes him feel φ (or, if he is imagining a case, he can see that it would);

(ii) his total state of relevant evidence gives him no warrant to think that other competent evaluators will not or would not feel φ in these circumstances, and thus would not be inclined to judge the object φ-worthy.[11]

The evaluator does not just feel the emotion; feeling it as he feels it, without defeating information about himself or others, he judges it to be *appropriate*, and is committed to holding that other evaluators of competent

---

[11] 'Total state of relevant evidence' is explained in Sect. 8 below.

sensibility would also feel it. If he feels the object of evaluation is not one of which he is a good judge, or that his own state is wrong, he will disqualify himself. 'I must say I was rather bored—but I was feeling tired/distracted/probably didn't understand what the point of it was/don't know much about Dutch flower painting' etc. Similarly, he may disqualify others—as incompetent judges of the subject, or as being in the wrong state. And the content of their judgements, in cases in which he himself feels confident, will for him be an important test of their competence.

I will call (i) and (ii) taken together the internal or 'hermeneutic' criterion of an evaluation. It provides, via (ii), what is needed to make the distinction between an object seeming to be ϕ and its being ϕ. I call it internal or hermeneutic because the only materials it calls on are experience of ϕ, imagining of circumstances in which one would experience it, reflection on it, and inter-subjective comparison. That discipline is in play when we judge that what bored or amused us, or what aroused in us the blame-feeling, is not after all boring, amusing, or blame-feeling-worthy. It is a hermeneutic discipline since its ground is what can intelligibly, understandably, produce a given emotional response. Evaluative judgements, then, are accountable to spontaneous feeling—but the spontaneity in question is that which survives experience, reflection, and intersubjective comparison and agreement. The standard it puts in place is an ideal of competent emotional response. No external criterion is required—and in particular, according to the line of thought we are considering, none is required in the case of the blameworthy.

Let us say that hermeneutically disciplined normative judgements about appropriate feeling are 'purely affectively grounded', and that the concepts which they predicate are 'purely affectively grounded' normative concepts. The defence which we considering says that 'That is morally wrong' is nothing but an affectively grounded judgement, like 'That is boring/amusing/irritating'. It says that the concept of wrongdoing is a purely affectively grounded concept.

8. Before examining this defence further it will be useful to consider the epistemology of the normative, and in particular the connection between judgement and convergence, a little more broadly.

The commitment one incurs in making an evaluation, to the claim that other judges who suffer from no disqualifying defect or limitation would confirm one's judgement, arises because evaluation is judgement. It is not a feature of *evaluative* judgement alone; it is a feature of judgement as such. When I judge, I enter a commitment that inquirers who scrutinized the relevant evidence and argument available to them would converge on my judgement—unless I could fault their judgement or their evidence. Faulting an inquirer's *judgement* would involve identifying some relevant internal weakness or inadequacy in his judging propensity on the subject in question, sufficient to justify me in discounting the judgement. That can include weaknesses of taste or sensibility, and distortions produced by special pleading or wishful thinking etc.—not just faults of logic. Faulting the inquirer's *evidence* would involve showing that the information input into his judging process is faulty or restricted in such a way as to vitiate his assertion on the subject in question—that is, in such a way as to justify me in discounting it, even if I can find no fault in his judgement. The critical standards for fault-finding are those which normally apply. Thus the commitment is that if relevant data (where data are relevant at all) went on being collected, and reasoning rescrutinized, inquirers who did not fall out of consideration through demonstrable faults of evidence or judgement would stably converge on agreement with the judgement.

When I speak of 'entering a commitment' I mean that we are not called upon to give grounds for expecting this convergence, over and above our grounds for the judgement itself. Rather, the existence of the commitment shows itself negatively. If I come, in one way or another, to have reason to doubt that my judgement would attract convergence, I thereby come to have reason to withdraw it. When those grounds for doubt become strong enough, they force withdrawal.

What case can be made for this claim? The first relevant point is:

(1) It is irrational to judge that: *p* but there is insufficient reason to judge that *p*.

There is of course no self-contradiction in a proposition of the form '*p* but there is insufficient reason to judge that *p*'. Indeed it can be true. But to judge such a proposition true would be irrational. I cannot rationally judge that *p* while also judging that there is insufficient reason to judge that *p*.

Now this only shows that if I judge that *p*, *I* am rationally committed to holding that there is sufficient reason to judge that *p*. It does not on its own show that if I judge that *p* I must hold that *anyone* who holds that there is insufficient reason to judge that *p* is faulty either in judgement or in evidence. But consider next the following principles.

(2) Given a total state of relevant evidence [E] *x* is justified in holding that there is sufficient reason for *x* to think that *p* ↔ (*y*)(*y* is in [E] → *y* is justified in holding that there is sufficient reason for *y* to think that *p*).

(3) If *p* then any evidence that justifies *x* in judging that there is insufficient reason for *x* to think that *p* is either
    (i) also insufficient to decide whether or not it is the case that *p*, or
    (ii) is misleading inasmuch as it justifies *x* in denying that *p*.

Since x's judgement that he has such-and-such evidence may be rational but wrong 'evidence' in (2) and (3) refers to the total set of factual propositions, relevant to the question whether p, which x can rationally *take* to specify x's evidence on that question. And where the question can be settled without evidence [E] will be null.

Now suppose I judge that p and that another thinker, y, does not hold that there is sufficient reason to judge that p. By (1) I am committed to judging that I have sufficient reason, and thus (in cases where evidence is required) sufficient evidence, to judge that p. Adding (2) and (3) I am committed to one of three conclusions. The first possibility is that y's evidence is faulty for reason (3)(i) or (3)(ii). That is, it is either insufficient or misleading—partial or distorted in some way. The second possibility is that y has not considered the question whether p—or else is faulty in judgement. That is, he doesn't just fail to consider the question whether p; he refuses to accept that p although the total relevant evidence available to him justifies him in holding that there is sufficient reason to believe that p. (If his total relevant evidence is the same as mine the conclusion that he has not considered the question or is faulty in judgement follows by (2).) The third possibility is that it is my own evidence or judgement which is faulty. In that case, by (1), I must withdraw my judgement that p. So given (1), (2), and (3) if I judge that p I am committed to judging that any thinker who refuses to judge that p is faulty in evidence or judgement.

It is the *judgement* that incurs the commitment—not the judgement's *content* that entails it. I am not defining truth in terms of convergence. There are —of course—factual judgements which would be true if made, but on which convergence could not occur because sufficient relevant evidence could not be collected. But just because evidence for them is not available, they could not be *justified*, even though they would be true. Equally, whenever we accept a judgement—however good our evidence and reasoning for it—the possibility always remains open that we are wrong in doing so and hence wrong also in thinking that impeccable inquirers would converge to stable agreement on it. The convergence commitment is compatible with as radical a form of defeasibility as one likes.

None the less there is here a fundamental asymmetry between normative and factual judgements.[12] In the case of a factual proposition there is the

---

[12] At this point I should explain my use of the terms 'fact', 'factual judgement', and 'factual proposition'. There is a broad or nominal and a narrow or ontologically substantial use of the word 'fact'. In the broad nominal sense 'the fact that' is simply a device of nominalization, equivalent to 'its being the case that'. In the narrow sense to talk about facts is to engage in an ontology which carries with it a corresponding epistemology. It is the narrow sense of 'fact' that I use in contrasting factual and normative propositions.

The correspondence theory of truth holds that truth is correspondence with the facts in this narrow, ontologically committed sense. It may be that a narrow notion of truth is current in ordinary discourse, simple possibility that there may not be enough evidence to pass a verdict, however long and expensive the inquiry. The point arises from the very idea of a world within which we are situated and in which we interact epistemically with other objects. Such a world cannot be fully transparent to us. There are limitations on our possible epistemic interactions in it.

In the case of normative propositions no such point applies. The metaphysics of the normative domain provides no basis for the idea of fundamental normative propositions which we could never be justified in recognizing as true or false.[13] Corresponding to this distinction between normative and factual propositions there corresponds a distinction in their epistemology. It is the distinction between a dialogical epistemology, which can operate with a purely hermeneutic criterion as discussed in Section 7 and the epistemology of correspondence. The hermeneutic criterion and the dialogical epistemology which describes it applies to all fundamental normative propositions, not just fundamental evaluations. My grounds for asserting a normative proposition turn in the first instance on what I'm spontaneously inclined to think, do, or feel. They are corrigible by further reflection and discussion. One route by which they are corrigible goes via the convergence commitment. Corrigibility underwrites the distinction between what seems to me to be true and what is true: it allows one to treat normative claims as genuine judgements. It also underwrites the same distinction in the case of factual propositions; but whether I am justified in asserting a factual proposition turns on whether I am appropriately linked to what it asserts to be the case. Grounds for holding that I am not so linked are grounds for holding that I am not justified in asserting the proposition. Such a notion of breakdown of evidential linkage simply does not apply in the case of fundamental normative propositions.

This view of normative propositions is what I described earlier as cognitivism without realism.[14] It does not hold that there is something which *makes* normative statements true or false, or correct or incorrect— in the realist's correspondence sense. In particular, a normative proposition

of which the correspondence theory is true. That would be a narrow, ontologically substantial notion, and one would not be able to predicate it of normative propositions—a different term would be needed, such as 'correct' or 'valid'. On the other hand, the minimalist view is that truth is a broad, nominal notion: a device of disquotation (see Paul Horwich, *Truth* (Oxford: Blackwell, 1990)). The minimalist can endorse 'p is true if and only if the fact that p obtains', if he uses 'fact' as well as 'true' in the broad nominal sense. But however one opts to use the word 'true', the important point is the difference in the epistemology and ontology of normative and factual propositions, which I refer to below as the difference between a dialogical epistemology and an epistemology of correspondence.

[13] By 'fundamental normative proposition' I mean 'normative proposition knowable independently of deduction from any factual proposition'. A normative proposition deduced from decidable normative premisses together with some undecidable factual proposition would of course also be undecidable.

[14] It has affinities with views developed by Crispin Wright in his *Truth and Objectivity* (Cambridge, Mass.: Harvard Univ. Press, 1992) but differs in an important respect. Whereas my claim is that the convergence commitment is incurred by the act of judgement itself, Wright argues that it is a certain

is not *made true* by some fact to the effect that verdicts on it would ideally converge. That is not its truth condition: it has no non-trivial one. A comprehensive truth-conditional semantics can include normative sentences within its remit, but it should be understood minimalistically. It employs minimalist or nominal notions of truth, reference, and predication, even though stronger notions are applicable to some of the terms and sentences with which it deals.

We can now return to the thread dropped in Section 7.

9. There can be normative judgements about what there is reason to feel which are purely affectively grounded, because such judgements are still subject to an internal or hermeneutic standard. They are grounded on an affective response but subject to the convergence commitment which arises from (1)–(3), that is, from principles which connect the concept of a judgement to that of a reason for judgement. But not only evaluations are disciplined hermeneutically—all normative judgements, be they epistemic, practical, or evaluative, are so. Epistemic normative judgements are grounded on a normative disposition to acknowledge reasons to *believe* which plays the role in their hermeneutic epistemology which a disposition to acknowledge reasons to feel plays in that of evaluations. Practical normative judgements are similarly grounded on a disposition to acknowledge reasons to act. In each of the three cases there are fundamental normative propositions— propositions not derivable from others in combination with factual premises.

In what sense then are fundamental practical and epistemic propositions given by Reason and evaluative ones not? Why do we want to say that evaluative reasons are not given to Reason? One may respond that our notion of Reason is the notion of something that thinkers and choosers can respond to whatever their capacities for feeling may be. Reason yields

---

concept of *truth* as representation or 'fit' that carries with it a convergence commitment (see ibid. and 'Truth in Ethics', *Ratio*, 9 (1996), 209–26). To judge true in that sense is to incur the commitment. But he holds that the concept of truth applicable to ethical judgements does not involve the notion of representation. The concept of truth which is applicable there, he suggests, allows that a person may, without irrationality, judge that an ethical proposition *p* is true while *also* judging that convergence of fault-free thinkers (thinkers who suffer from no 'cognitive shortcoming') cannot be expected to occur on that judgement. I agree with Wright that ethical truth involves no notion of 'fit' to a domain of reality. But if what has been said here is correct that is irrelevant. *No* notion of *truth* allows a person to judge a proposition true without incurring the convergence commitment, because the convergence commitment arises quite generally from the *rationality* of judgement rather than any particular notion of *truth*.

Note, however, that the convergence commitment provides no quick route to eliminating relativism —where that is understood as the view that truth is relative to some framework or whatever. If relativism is true about a class of propositions then in judging some proposition in that class I am judging it to be true relative to a framework or whatever. In that case the commitment is that other competent judgers would judge it true relative to *that* framework. They and I might still judge it false relative to some other framework.

reasons which all thinkers and choosers have in common, whatever their capacities and reasons to feel.

On closer inspection things get more complicated. Consider this general principle (the 'Feeling/Disposition Principle'), which links evaluative and practical judgements:

(F/D) if there is reason to feel ϕ then there's reason to do that which ϕ disposes to.

Thus:

> If there's reason to be frightened of x then there's reason to avoid x.
> If there's reason to be bored by x then there's reason not to attend to x.
> If there's reason to admire x then there's reason to praise, reward x.
> If there's reason to blame x there's reason to withdraw recognition from x or impose a penalty on which continued recognition depends. Etc.

Should we say that F/D is a pure principle of practical reason? It is a fundamental principle about what there is reason to do. Is it then given to Reason? Reason is that which yields reasons which all thinkers and choosers have in common, whatever their capacities to feel. But instances of F/D are intelligible only to those capable of experiencing the relevant feeling. At the limit a pure practical reasoner with no capacity to feel would find no instance of F/D intelligible—an impossible limit no doubt, but illustrative of the point. So let us give the following content to the denial that there is such a thing as *pure* practical reason. It is the denial that there are any fundamental practical propositions *other* than those derived from affectively grounded evaluations via F/D. One might call this a strict sentimentalism about evaluative and practical propositions, without any degree of rationalism.[15]

10. The desire for X disposes to actions which one believes will result in one's attaining X. So, by F/D, if there's reason to desire G then there's reason to do that which one believes will result in one's attaining G. This has a superficial resemblance to two popular theses about practical reason: the desire-satisfaction model of practical rationality, according to which one has reason to act just if the action promotes the satisfaction of one's desires, and the instrumentalist or relativist conception, according to which a reason for action is always relativized to an objective. But it differs in at least two ways. In the first place it does not assert the biconditional: that there's reason to do that which one believes will result in one's attaining G if *and only if* there is reason to desire G. Secondly, it is cast not in terms

---

[15] It is not emotivism in the expressivist sense because it is consistent with taking evaluative and practical normative propositions to be genuine contents of judgement.

of what one desires but in terms of what one has reason to desire. In contrast both the desire-satisfaction and the instrumentalist model of rationality share a defect—they short-circuit the normative connection between feelings on the one hand and action on the other, by dropping out the intervening role played by evaluations. It is not raw unprocessed emotions and desires that come to the court of practical judgement. It is evaluative judgements, about what there is reason to feel and to desire, that come to it.

Thus it simply does not follow deductively from the fact that I desire X and ϕ-ing is a way of achieving X that there's reason for me to ϕ. The question is, whether there is *reason* for me to desire X. It is true (as we acknowledged earlier) that what I desire is a defeasible criterion of what there is reason for me to desire, just as what I am bored by is a defeasible criterion of what there is reason to find boring. But it would be a fallacy to treat that criterial relation as though it sustained a deduction. And only if there's reason for me to desire X and ϕ-ing is a way of achieving X can we go on to argue via F/D that there is reason for me to ϕ.

The problem with instrumentalism is similar but sharper. It adds a further term to the reason to act relation, namely, a set of objectives, *O*: *the fact that* p *gives* x *reason of degree* d *at time* t *to* ϕ *relative to* O. And it says that I ought do that (an) action which there is strongest reason to do relative to *my* objectives. But this is likely to be false. It's false if there is no reason to pursue my objectives, or reason not to. Of course it will be true if my objectives coincide with those which there is reason for me to pursue. But to think that this must be true is a pretty heroic assumption. The trouble again is that we are being served up objectives in raw, unevaluated form.

However, the sentimentalist need endorse neither the desire-satisfaction nor the instrumentalist models of practical reason. He has a route from evaluative to practical judgements, via F/D, which brings in neither of these. But is it sufficiently broad? How does it make sense of the connection between judging that something is morally wrong and judging that there is reason not to do it? Or of the connection between ideals—of excellence in activity and character—and reasons for action? Just as morality stands to the blame-feeling so ideals of excellence stand to the feeling of admiration. Judgements about what is morally wrong and about what is excellent are evaluative judgements about what one has reason to blame and what one has reason to admire. But whence comes the principle that there is reason not to do what is wrong, and not just to blame it, or that there is reason to pursue excellence and not just to admire it?

These two principles, like F/D, are *bridge principles* which take us from a species of evaluative judgement, grounded in its characteristic affect, to a practical judgement, about what there is reason for someone or everyone to do. Indeed all fundamental practical propositions are bridge principles;

they must all, to be intelligible, invoke an evaluation. So long as we restrict attention to F/D the purely sentimentalist position has some plausibility. But what kind of grounding do these other bridge principles have?

Suppose we identify a person's well-being with that which the person has reason to desire. Then formal egoism, the principle that every person has reason to promote his or her own well-being, comes to be a special case of F/D. On the other hand another bridge principle, crossing the same gap, is the 'principle of universal concern', to the effect that any agent has reason to promote any subject's well-being. This principle is no more derivable from F/D than the perfectionist principle of excellence is.

We can characterize the argument between sentimentalist and rationalist as being about whether there are true bridge-principles other than F/D. Rationalism about practical reason is the view that there are true bridge-principles other than F/D, principles which are known by pure rational insight. Perfectionism and the principle of universal concern are possible examples. To take the rationalist view of either of them is to hold that is knowable by any rational being—whatever the *evaluations* proper to that being's community of sentiment might be. In other words: whatever that rational being's affective nature might be, and whatever it might thus have reason to desire or admire, and whatever would therefore constitute its well-being or excellence—it would be able to see, by its Reason alone, the truth or otherwise of the perfectionist principle or the principle of universal concern. But the admirable, like well-being (the desirable) would still be evaluative notions. Pure practical reason would still deal in bridge principles from evaluations to reasons for action, just as pure theoretical reason deals in bridge principles from facts to reasons to believe.

11. The judgement that a particular piano performance is not merely technically accurate, but beautiful, insightful, profound, has its own internal discipline, grounded in what we spontaneously admire. By F/D it sustains the practical conclusion that there is reason to praise, reward. But that judgement in itself does not tell me, for example, whether I should learn to play like that, or whether I ought to put any proportion of the resources I control to the promotion of piano-playing like that. To get a conclusion about reasons for action we need a bridge principle—which a perfectionist ethic seeks to specify.

What of the *moral* source of reasons for acting? Here too, by F/D, we get the conclusion, where there is reason to respond with the blame-feeling, that there is reason to blame—to exclude and offer renewed recognition by punishment. The sentimentalist could add that there is reason to avoid wrongdoing if being blamed by oneself or others is bad for one, that is, one has reason to desire to avoid it. In that case it will be an open question whether avoiding the morally wrong thing is something one has reason to do—it will turn on whether being blamed is bad for one. Similarly it will be an open question whether achieving the admirable is good for one—something one has reason to desire.

In the case of the admirable I find that quite plausible. That an achievement is admirable gives me reason to desire to achieve it, as against applauding it in others, only if it will be good for me, conducive to my well-being, to achieve it. In this sense, I am not a perfectionist.[16] In contrast, the principle of morality, as against the principle of perfectionism, strikes me as correct:

(M) if φ-ing is morally wrong then there is reason not to φ.

(M) states the principle partially[17] but not elliptically—there is no hidden condition. To agree to it is to agree that morality is, in one familiar sense at least, categorical.[18] But is that consistent with the purely affective concept of wrongdoing? Well, the defender of that concept is not necessarily a sentimentalist overall. He can hold that (M) is a bridge principle evident to pure Reason, even though the concept of the morally wrong is purely affective. To refute his view of the concept of moral wrongdoing we must argue that (M) is a conceptual truth, a principle 'constitutive of the concept' of moral wrongdoing. Only then can we conclude that that concept is not a pure affectively determined concept, like the concept of the admirable, or the desirable.

Is (M) correct at all? Of course it is a controversial claim. Some philosophers would deny that (M) is unconditionally true. They would argue that to transform (M) into something true we need at least to add some further condition to the antecedent, for example about what the agent desires, or has reason to desire, or what is in his interests—or what promotes the general good, perfection, etc. So the correct principle would have the form

if φ-ing is morally wrong and C(φ) then there is reason not to φ.

More specifically, if the condition is agent-relative, concerning say the agent's desires or interests, it would have the form

if φ-ing is morally wrong and C(φ, *x*) then there is reason for *x* not to φ.

However, given that the morally wrong is the blameworthy, that which there is reason to blame, (M) becomes

---

[16] i.e. in Tom Hurka's sense (see *Perfectionism* (Oxford: Univ. Press, 1993)).

[17] Partially because it says nothing about the comparative strength of reasons generated from the moral source. Note that given (M) and the definition of 'morally right' above it will follow that if X is morally right then there is reason to do X.

[18] In David Brink's sense it is authoritative, whether or not supreme. See Essay 9 in this volume, p. 255.

if there is reason to blame a person who φs then there is reason not to φ.

And this is just the contraposition of

(M′) if there is no reason not to φ then there is no reason to blame a person who φs.

I submit that (M′) is an obvious truth as it stands. One simply doesn't count as giving reasons for blaming a person *unless* one is giving reasons why that person should not have done what he did. If I can establish that there was no reason not to φ I *have*, unconditionally, established that a person who did φ was blameless. I do not have to establish that any further condition obtains, as I would have to if (M) needed to be expanded by a further condition in the antecedent as suggested above.

Moreover, the unconditional truth of (M′) is a constitutive feature of the concept of blame. Compare the following principle:

If X is not dangerous—has no power to cause injury or harm—then there is no reason to be frightened of X (X is not fear-worthy).

Just as one can argue that there is no reason to fear a thing (a spider, say) because it has no power to cause injury or harm, so one can argue that a person deserves no blame, because there was no reason not to do what he did. The principle about the dangerous can be seen to be true just by reflection on fear and what there is reason to fear. Someone who hasn't grasped that if a thing is not dangerous then there's no reason to fear it hasn't grasped the constitutive relation between the concept of danger and the concept of fear. But this shows that the concept of what there is reason to fear, the 'fear-worthy', is not a purely affectively determined concept. It has a conceptually constitutive external criterion which is external in the sense that, when it comes to determining whether a thing is fear-worthy, our common evaluative responses can be defeated by evidence that it has no capacity to harm. The hermeneutically grounded judgement that spiders are frightening/fear-worthy can be defeated by showing that they are not dangerous—there is nothing to fear. Similarly, the blameworthy is not a purely affectively determined concept. It too has a conceptually constitutive external criterion, which is not a matter of reflecting on our common evaluative responses, and which can defeat them. But in this case the criterion is applied not solely by appeal to evidence but also by appeal to practical reason.

12. The standard of moral right and wrong is thus not fixed solely by the hermeneutics of the blame-feeling. The proposed definition of moral wrongness in terms of blame-feeling-worthiness which we have been considering does express an important insight: our spontaneous sentiments of blame,

shaped by reflection and discussion, shape our judgements of moral right and wrong from the inside. But our concept of moral wrongness allows—via (M) —for an external shaping influence as well, from practical reason as such.

It leaves a place for practical reason to plug in an external criterion, but it makes no determination as to whether there *is* anything with substantive content to plug in, or if there is, what it is. However, we need to have a view before us as to what if anything plugs in, if we are to study the relation between morality and practical reason. So suppose our view is that there is just one principle of practical reason—the principle of universal concern.

What does it mean to say that this is the only principle? We recognized F/D as a bridge principle, but gave a reason in Section 9 for denying that it was a *pure* principle of practical reason. A very strong formulation of the reason would be this: a principle which requires an affective capacity for direct or first-personal knowledge of its truth (as against knowledge by testimony, say) is not a pure principle of practical reason. F/D can only be known through its instances; and each of those instances can be known directly only by someone with the appropriate capacity. By the same argument, (M) is not a pure principle of practical reason. It can be known directly only by someone with the capacity to experience the blame-feeling —just as the principle about fear, that if there is reason to fear something then it is dangerous, can be known directly only by someone with the capacity to experience fear.

But can this same reasoning not be applied to the principle of universal concern itself? That says that every agent has reason to promote every subject's well-being. Is not the concept of well-being affectively determined, being the concept of what the subject has reason to desire?[19] And does this not mean that an agent without the capacity to desire cannot know its truth directly?

One can imagine a number of responses to this, some of them unflinchingly Kantian. My own inclination is to accept that the concept of well-being, or the desirable, is affectively determined—so on the very strong criterion of pure practical reason the principle of universal concern is not a principle of pure practical reason. But on that very strong criterion nothing is—if I am right in arguing that all practical principles are bridge principles with one of their piers grounded on some evaluation or other. If we want a viable concept of practical reason this criterion is too strong. What is relevant, rather, is that rational insight, as well as the affective

---

[19] To identify the notion of a subject's well-being with what the subject has reason to desire is a substantial claim, of course. For example there are sentient subjects whose well-being has an authoritative claim on our concern—can they be said to have reasons to desire? I believe they can—see my 'Quality of Well-Being, Quality of Being', in Roger Crisp and Brad Hooker (eds.), *Well-Being and Morality: Essays in Honour of James Griffin* (Oxford: Univ. Press, forthcoming).

capacity presupposed in grasping the concept of the desirable, is required for direct knowledge of the principle of universal concern, and that the principle is not derived from any other more fundamental practical proposition. In that sense it is a pure principle of practical reason.

To say that it's the only such principle is then to say that it *arbitrates* on what we have reason to do as no other principle does. What I mean by this is that it alone can defeat all affectively grounded reasons for acting. That of course makes the claim that it is the only principle of practical reason a very large one. Here I will only illustrate what it would imply for one particular set of affectively grounded responses—moral ones. In this case the arbitration works via (M): an activity which there is no reason not to do cannot be morally wrong—and the principle of universal concern, as the sole principle of practical reason, arbitrates on whether there is reason to do something.

But this does not mean that all practical reasons must be *derived* from it. If there is a principle of practical reason, a substantive external criterion of moral wrongness, its bearing on our moral judgements can and should be thought of in a conservative-holist, rather than a linear-foundationalist, way. The guidance given for action and evaluation by our internally determined judgements of blameworthiness has default status—neither more, nor less. It is legitimate guidance, in the absence of a well-made case against it; but it is corrigible by practical reason. Our ethical tradition emerges largely from human feelings of admiration and blame. It may nevertheless be shaped in its evolution by Reason. Even where those feelings strongly cluster, for example feelings of blame around homosexuality, we can detach from them, stand back, and ask what is wrong with homosexuality. At this point we ask, for example, what harm a consenting homosexual relationship does, either to those involved or to others.

Structurally, the external standard of practical reason functions in much the way that standards of scientific method do. In each case they operate on an *existing* ethical or cosmological tradition, whose sources lie in the one case in substantive emotional responses, and in the other, in dispositions to substantive beliefs about the world.

With this in mind, let us return to the concept of moral wrongness. It is not *definable* in terms of the blame-feeling because it is not a purely affectively determined concept—it keeps a space open for criteria of practical reason. It is true that a thing is morally wrong just if is blameworthy but that is because a thing is worthy of blame only if it is morally wrong, just as a thing merits fear only if it is dangerous. To acknowledge a reason for blaming or fearing a thing one must judge it to be morally wrong or dangerous; and this is a non-vacuous condition, unlike 'to acknowledge a reason for admiring something one must judge it to be admirable'.

'Wrong', in the moral sense of the word, is a semantically simple predicate. It is semantically simple in the way that 'yellow' is.[20] Moreover the explanation strikes me as similar in each case. Just as 'wrong' signifies a concept which is not determined purely affectively, so 'yellow' signifies a concept which is not determined purely sensationally. In the one case the concept *wrong* leaves a space for correction by criteria of practical reason, in the other, the concept *yellow* leaves a space for correction by criteria of theoretical reason.

Compare the following two principles:

(I) If X arouses in me the blame-feeling then, *ceteris paribus*, I am justified in judging that X is wrong;

(II) If X produces in me a visual experience as of X's being yellow then, *ceteris paribus*, I am justified in judging that X is yellow.

They seem to me to be roughly right, and partially constitutive, respectively, of the concepts *wrong* and *yellow*. They are epistemic norms[21] which partially constitute those particular concepts.

Each of them is a defeasible entry norm for the concept, containing provision for defeat in the *ceteris paribus* clause. In each case, the warrant provided by the norm may be defeated in two ways. It is defeated in the first way if something in my total state of relevant evidence warrants the view that I am not currently a competent judge of the matter in question. That possibility is already provided, as we emphasized earlier, by the internal or hermeneutic discipline which regulates pure affectively determined judgements involving such concepts as 'amusing', 'boring', and 'irritating'. Because these are pure affectively determined concepts the corresponding predicates are not semantically simple. '*x* is amusing/boring/irritating' is analysable as meaning something like 'There is reason to be amused/bored/irritated by *x*'. There *could* be judgements which were similarly determined, wholly internally, by visual experiences of colour. Then '*x* is yellow' would mean something along the lines of '*x* would produce an experience of yellow in a normal person in normal conditions', where the normality of oneself and the conditions is the default assumption. But colour judgements are not like that, any more than moral judgements are. The concept *wrong* has an exit norm, as well an entry norm, provided by

---

[20] 'Yellow' was Moore's example in *Principia Ethica* (Cambridge: Cambridge Univ. Press, 1903) but the comparison he drew (sects. 6 and 7) was between 'yellow' and 'good'. It was the ethical term, 'good', rather than the moral term 'wrong', that he took to be semantically simple. I think he was mistaken in taking that view, and also mistaken in attempting to *define* 'right' or 'duty' in terms of 'good' (e.g. sect. 89). This is not to deny that the good is prior to the right; however the view proposed here is closer on these points to Mill than Moore, even though it does not follow Mill so far as to hold that the moral can be defined, as against characterized, in terms of the penal sentiment of blame. (For more on Mill's view see my 'The Definition of Morality'.)

[21] 'Norm' here is short for 'true normative proposition'.

principle (M). Analogously, the concept *yellow* is the concept of a colour, and the concept of a colour is the concept of a categorical property of perceived and unperceived, even unperceivable, objects.

These exit norms put moral and colour judgements within the remit of general considerations of practical and theoretical reason. Thus if general considerations of practical reason, together with empirical data, show that there is no reason not to do X then it will follow that X is not morally wrong. Similarly, general considerations of theoretical reason, together with empirical data, may issue in a theory of the properties of objects which comes into tension at one point or another with the pattern of our colour judgements, in so far as these are regulated solely by their internal, perception-driven, standard. At the limit they might issue in a theory of the categorical properties of nature onto which our judgements of colour cannot be satisfactorily mapped, but which *can* explain our experiences of colour. That would amount to a case for an error theory of colour judgements. Could there be a similar extreme in the ethical case—one in which general considerations of practical reason lead us to conclude that we should withdraw from making moral judgements entirely? A utilitarian might conclude, in some possible worlds at least, that blaming people never promotes the general good to any degree, and hence that there is never reason to blame. He or she might secondly argue, contrapositively via F/D, that the blame-feeling is never reasonable and that nothing is morally wrong. (Some people seem to think this argument holds in the actual world.) However, the second step in this argument would be unsound. You cannot use a principle of practical reason in that way. What was said earlier in this section was that practical reason *arbitrates* on what we have reason to do, in the sense that its reasons can defeat reasons generated by F/D. But to defeat them is not to strike them down as wholly null: they are defeated but they remain reasons. So there is no contrapositive move to the irrationality of the blame-*feeling*, even if the conclusion that *acts* of blame are never justified is right. Where that latter conclusion, that acts of blame are never justified, would leave the institution of morality is something that requires extended consideration. On the face of it, however, something much stronger is needed to get the genuinely error-theoretical conclusion that nothing is ever morally right or wrong—perhaps a nihilist account of practical reason which then worked through M or a strengthened version of M.

I have tried to indicate, in this last section, why it is that 'yellow' and 'wrong' are semantically simple predicates. The explanation, I have suggested, rests on certain points about the epistemic norms which constitute the concepts *yellow* and *wrong*. How do the points about the concepts connect with the point about the words? This question could only be answered fully within the framework of an account of concepts and a semantic theory. I have in fact been assuming such a framework.[22] The framework takes it that the semantics of a language is given truth-conditionally; within that theory the semantic clauses for 'yellow' and 'morally wrong' will state:

> x satisfies the predicate of English 'yellow' just if x is yellow;
> x satisfies the predicate of English 'morally wrong' just if x is morally wrong.

A person can grasp those clauses, and thus the meaning of 'yellow' and 'morally wrong' in English, only if he possesses the concepts *yellow* and *morally wrong*. The framework further takes it that grasping a concept is acknowledging a pattern of defeasible entry and exit norms which constitute that concept. These constitutive norms come at the level of an account of concepts, or cognitive roles, not at the level of semantic theory. They are not analytic on the *predicates* 'yellow' or 'morally wrong', in the way that 'A father is a male parent' or 'Tomorrow is the day after today' are analytic on 'father' and 'tomorrow'. One can consistently hold that the predicates are semantically simple while holding that the concepts they express are constituted by a complex pattern of entry and exit norms. Thus the relevant interconnections between reasons to blame and reasons to act constitute the concept of the morally wrong, even though 'morally wrong' is a semantically primitive, indefinable predicate.[23]

---

[22] I touch on some but by no means all of the issues it raises in my 'Meaning, Verification, Use', in R. Hale and C. J. G. Wright (eds.), *A Companion to the Philosophy of Language* (Oxford: Blackwell, 1997), 29–59.

[23] I am grateful to the editors for their detailed comments on an earlier draft. I also benefited from discussing that draft in a meeting of the Philosophy Club at the University of Sheffield.

13

The Amoralist

JOSEPH RAZ

1. Who is He?

Sometimes the amoralist is thought to present a problem for moral philo-sophy. If one can be an amoralist then the validity of morality is undermined unless one can be amoral only because of ignorance or irrationality. Moral-ity, the underlying thought is, is rationally defensible only if it can marshal arguments in its support which an amoralist must rationally accept. My contention will be that the confrontation between the moralist and the amoralist is misconceived. Sections 5, 6, and 7 will explain my view by challenging the amoralist and the moralist in turn. I will argue that their confrontation is bogus for neither protagonist has a separate existence. But before coming to that I will, in Section 2, challenge the way that Nagel has recently discussed the problem,[1] and will prepare, in Sections 3 and 4, the ground for the main arguments. First of all (in the current section) I explain who the amoralist is.

I want to discuss one of the stock characters in moral philosophy's wax gallery. But as often more than one can claim the title. The amoralist is not, of course, the immoralist. He does not deliberately defy morality, that is he is not a Miltonian Lucifer knowing the truth and rejecting it in his life. It is best to think of him as someone innocent of all knowledge of morality. Alternatively, if he was told about it he disbelieves it. He does not believe that it has any validity. He would accept it were he convinced of its validity but he is not convinced.

Nor is it essential that the amoralist be immoral. It is likely, perhaps inevitable, that during his life he will act morally wrongly as well as morally unwisely. But if this follows from his nature it does so only in combination with assumptions about common facts of human life. If he is lucky in his life (lucky not from his, but from the moral point of view) he may not act very immorally. He may not be guilty of more gross immoralities than many of us are.

---

[1] Nagel's article 'The Value of Inviolability', *Revue de Métaphysique et de Morale*, 99 (1994), 149–66, not only led me to write this essay, but—in spite of my disagreement with it—greatly affected my own understanding of the problem.

The amoralist does not believe in morality, either because he doubts its validity, or because he is not aware of it, or does not comprehend it. This does not mean, of course, that he does not believe in any values, in anything being valuable. That would reduce the amoralist to the level of an animal able to pursue its bodily imperatives only, a creature driven by hunger for food or sex, by the need to discharge bodily functions, and to protect itself from extremes of heat or cold. Such creatures pose no challenge to moral philosophy.[2]

Elsewhere[3] I have cast doubt on the common assumption (among philosophers) that morality forms a distinct body of considerations which differs from that involved in other areas of practical thought. In a way the purpose of this essay is to reinforce that doubt. To let the argument commence, however, we should suspend the doubt. I will return to it in the concluding section. An amoralist—I will say—is a person who denies that persons[4] are valuable in themselves.

This characterization of the amoralist is not without its problems. It implies an understanding of morality which may be challenged even by some people who believe themselves to uphold morality. True moral views, in their opinion, do not include endorsing that persons are valuable in themselves. As the persevering reader will discover at the end of this essay, it is possible that I myself belong with those people. Yet my view is not that the divide between the moralist and the amoralist is to be drawn elsewhere, but that it is illusory. My argument to that effect applies directly only when the divide is defined by reference to the belief that people are valuable in themselves. Its lessons bear—I hope — on a wider family of ways of identifying the divide.

There is another difficulty with this way of characterizing the amoralist. The thought that people are valuable in themselves is a widely shared belief among moral philosophers, and though it is not often expressed by non-philosophers, moral philosophers usually think that it encapsulates the meaning of common beliefs. It is not, however, a belief which is easy to articulate or comprehend. That people have value in themselves means, one may say, that they are ends in themselves, though this piece of philosophical terminology is not much more perspicuous. Philosophers will generally agree that whatever else people having value in themselves, or

---

[2] You may say that there is a problem if the creature who does not accept the existence of any values can do so—that is, if he has the mental capacity, the cognitive abilities, and the power of agency which enable one to recognize value—but the difficulties which this possibility gives rise to arise also in the case of the amoralist and will be examined below.

[3] In *The Morality of Freedom* (Oxford: Univ. Press, 1986) and in 'On the Moral Point of View', in J. B. Schneewind (ed.), *Reason, Ethics, and Society* (Chicago: Open Court, 1996), 84–116.

[4] Or other people or some other category deemed definitive of the class of those who are of value in themselves.

being ends in themselves, means it means that, other things being equal, their interests should count. That is that, other things being equal, an action is (morally) justified only if it can be justified taking proper account of the interests of all those whose interests it affects. Again—the actual meaning and implication of this principle is much in dispute.

Many will say that an essential element of the idea that people have value in themselves is that they must be respected. This is certainly another philosophical platitude.[5] But it is an open question how much more this notion of respect involves beyond the requirement to take due notice of other people's interests in all actions which affect them, or at any rate not to act in ways which cannot be justified by an account which gives their interests their due recognition.

Notice that the amoralist is not to be equated with the egoist, or if he is an egoist he is only one of several distinct breeds of that character. He is not necessarily self-obsessed. He is not necessarily egocentric, that is, he need not be exclusively or predominantly concerned with himself, his own life or character. Nor need his activities and pursuits be self-regarding. He can take up causes. His life may revolve round a selfless dedication to restoring decaying or otherwise threatened works of art, or to solving the mystery of the basic laws of the universe, or to other (impersonal) ideals. At least if these avenues are not open to him it is not obvious on the surface of things why this is so. Such a conclusion requires a deeper argument.

Another respect in which the amoralist differs from some egoists is that at the basic level he is not partial to himself. He is not a person who believes that he or his life is valuable, but other people or their lives are not. He accepts that he and his life are—just like other people and their lives—devoid of all value. In this regard the amoralist resembles the moral egoist who believes that all life is of value but that only its possessor has any reason to do something about it.[6] Both are impartial at the most fundamental level in that neither claims to himself a value that is denied to others. Both are impartial in a way which leads to the conclusion that they have no reason to respect other people. The difference is that the amoralist, but not the moral egoist, denies that people are bearers of moral value.[7]

I hope that these remarks help in sketching the profile of the amoralist, and in distinguishing between him and other characters familiar from the

---

[5] A 'philosophical platitude' since 'respect' does not mean here what one means when talking of respecting the elderly, etc. For example, I may lose all my respect for a person upon discovering that he is mean and treacherous, without losing my 'philosophical respect' for him as a person.

[6] There are other versions of the moral egoist. Most importantly some maintain that while each person is valuable he is valuable to himself only. This view itself can bear several different interpretations. Nagel identifies his egoist with those who hold this view.

[7] Though I will not elaborate the point the argument of this essay undermines the moral egoist as well.

ethical Madam Tussaud's. Of course, much remains obscure. Some of the remaining unclarities will be dealt with in the sequel. But some will remain, and I will return to this point in the final section. It is time to go back to the argument with which the essay opened.

2. Choosing against the Amoralist: Nagel's Argument

If one can be an amoralist then the validity of morality is undermined unless one can be amoral only through ignorance or irrationality. Why should one think so? The simple argument runs somewhat as follows. If morality is valid, that is, if people are valuable in themselves, then it is possible for people to come to know that. Moreover, it is possible for people who are amoral to realize that there are rationally compelling reasons to accept that people are valuable in themselves. The amoralist who denies the validity of morality must, therefore, be blind to a valid argument available to him. Such blindness can be the result of ignorance of the factors relevant to the soundness of the argument, or sheer irrationality.

True, this argument is too simple. It disguises many ambiguities, and it begs many questions. I will not, however, try to challenge it directly. Rather I will undermine its most fundamental presupposition. It sees morality as a separate domain. The amoralist stands outside it and refuses to go in. The question is: is there anything outside morality which could rationally convince him to take the step of adopting the moral point of view.[8] This is the way Thomas Nagel understands the amoralist, and the way he confronts him. Nagel offers a consideration which purports to show that the amoralist has reason to become a moralist. 'Morality', he explains, 'is possible only for beings capable of seeing themselves as one individual among others more or less similar in general respects.'[9] Once people realize that fact they are said by Nagel to occupy not only their own individual point of view, but also an impersonal point of view which everyone can occupy. We need not be concerned here with the meaning of this statement. The important point is that people who grasp this fact face a choice:

This choice has to do with the relation between the value we naturally accord to ourselves and our fates from our own point of view, and the attitude we take toward these same things when viewed from the impersonal standpoint. . . . One

---

[8] There are no metaphysical implications to my use of 'the moral point of view'. It means: accept the basic beliefs which mark one as a person with moral concerns and sensitivities, however mistaken one may be about various moral issues. The amoralist is not someone who makes moral mistakes (e.g. believing that abortion is wrong, or that it is not wrong, whichever happens to be the mistaken view). He is someone who declines to accept the basic moral beliefs, or who lacks basic comprehension of the nature of the moral. He stands outside morality altogether.

[9] T. Nagel, 'The Value of Inviolability', 160.

alternative would be not to 'transfer' to the impersonal standpoint in any form those values which concern us from the personal standpoint. That would mean that the impersonal standpoint would remain purely descriptive, and our lives and what matters to us as we live them (including the lives of other people we care about) would not be regarded as mattering at all if considered apart from the fact that they are ours, or personally related to us. Each of us, then, would have a system of values centering on his own perspective, and would recognise that others were in exactly the same situation.

The other alternative would be to assign to one's life and what goes on in it some form of impersonal as well as purely perspectival value, not dependent on its being one's own. This would imply that everyone else was also the subject of impersonal value. . . . I believe, as did Kant, that what drives us in the direction of universalizability is the difficulty each person has in regarding himself as having value only *for himself*, but not *in himself*. If people are not ends in themselves—i.e. impersonally valuable—they have a much lower order of worth. Egoism amounts to a devaluation of oneself, along with everyone else.[10]

I will disregard certain aspects of Nagel's argument, including his controversial invocation of Kant, and his equally controversial use of 'universalizability', as well as the fact that he calls our amoralist 'the egoist'. My concern is with the fact that he thinks that people have a choice between amoralism and morality (i.e. holding that people do not have or that they do have 'impersonal' value), and that people's difficulty in not holding themselves to be impersonally valuable exerts a strong pressure for choosing morality.

It is not clear how Nagel means the choice to be understood. Cannot an amoralist accept Nagel's description as a description of the motives which lead people to escape the unflattering but true amoral view ('you do not have value in yourself, nor does anyone else') and find comfort in the delusion of morality's reassurance about our value and worth? Presumably it is not Nagel's view that moralists are deluding themselves. Therefore he must think that 'what drives us in the direction of' the moralist is a rational consideration capable of justifying our acceptance of the moralist's position. What is the rational reason Nagel is pointing to? The proposition that I (along with everyone else) have no value in myself is not self-refuting (or if it is then Nagel has not shown that it is), and the desire to be of value in myself is not a (valid) reason to believe that I have such value. It is difficult to read Nagel as pointing to the presence of any reason to believe the moralist. It seems that we have to take seriously the fact that the point is made in terms of a choice: We are driven—says Nagel—to choose to reject the amoralist, and to join the moralist.[11]

---

[10] Ibid. 160–1.

[11] Indirectly, and as a consequence of this choice we may acquire a reason to believe the moralist. I will examine this possibility below.

What are we choosing, according to Nagel? We could of course choose to act as if the moralist is right. But why should we? There is no reason to do so if he is wrong, and doing so would not satisfy whatever it is that 'drives us' to choose as Nagel suggests, for it will not allay the fear that in ourselves we are of no value. Nagel cannot mean that we choose to believe that the moralist is right, that we are of value in ourselves, for we cannot choose to believe.[12] Besides, to avoid the charge that this is no more than an explanation of our self-deception the drive to embrace morality must make it justified for us to believe that people are of value in themselves, that is, it must bear on the credibility of that belief, on the likelihood that it is true. Wanting it to be true because otherwise we are of no value in ourselves cannot fulfil that role.

The most promising interpretation of Nagel's argument seems to be that the choice we have is neither a choice to believe or disbelieve the moralist nor a choice of acting as if we believe him. It is a choice of accepting the moralist's principle. I will also assume that the argument is that rationally choosing to accept the moralist's principle validates it, that is, renders it true[13] or makes it rational to believe that it is true.

The difference between believing a proposition and accepting it is meant to be fairly intuitive.[14] I accept a proposition if I use it as a premiss in my deliberations, for any purpose other than in order to convince someone that I do believe it,[15] even though I do not believe it. I may indeed disbelieve it. Usually one accepts a proposition for a particular limited purpose. In all other matters one refrains from relying on the proposition, as one does not believe it. In principle, however, one can accept a proposition in all one's deliberations for which it is relevant. One difference between believing a proposition and accepting it which this characterization brings out is that accepted propositions feature only in one's deliberations. Beliefs affect one's imaginative life, one's subconscious thoughts, one's unarticulated reasons, and more.

Assuming that Nagel's argument is meant to show how it is rational to choose to accept the moralist's view how are we to understand it? Two possibilities suggest themselves: According to the first, each one of us has a choice between accepting the amoralist's position and accepting some form of universal morality (as Nagel calls the alternative). Alternatively, it

---

[12] See my explanation of this fact in 'When We are Ourselves: The Active and the Passive', *Proceedings of the Aristotelian Society*, suppl. 71 (1997).

[13] Since moral principles and moral propositions can be either true or false, and since Nagel takes them to be so I will not discuss variants of his arguments which reject that assumption.

[14] Cf. L. J. Cohen's description of the difference on pp. 4 ff. of *An Essay on Belief and Acceptance* (Oxford: Univ. Press, 1992), though my views are not identical with his.

[15] This exception is necessary to distinguish accepting a belief from trying to deceive someone into believing that one believes it.

is not us but some idealized counterpart of us—for example, a rational and well-informed person, unencumbered by our beliefs and commitments—who has the choice.

At first blush we may find the second interpretation unattractive. Given that we are not in that situation doubts must arise as to why it matters what we would have chosen had we been in it. Of course the fact that under some hypothetical conditions I would have chosen not to enter into commitments which I have entered into does not in itself release me from those commitments, unless it can demonstrate one thing—unless it is a way of showing that those commitments were never binding as they rest on a false presupposition. The second reading, therefore, understands Nagel as providing a constructivist argument against the amoralist. It establishes that people are ends in themselves, by showing that our 'unencumbered selves' (if I may be allowed to borrow this jargon) would choose to accept that view rather than join the amoralist in its rejection.[16] Let me consider this second reading first.

Why should our 'unencumbered selves' be interested in the case for accepting the amoralist's position without believing it? Why should they not raise the question whether the amoralist is right, rather than whether his position should be accepted?

One type of case in which people accept propositions, when they do not believe in them, is temporary acceptance for some special purpose, paradigmatically in order to see what would follow from propositions or from their acceptance (as when a proposition is accepted 'for the sake of argument', or as a hypothesis in a *reductio ad absurdum* argument). Alternatively, propositions are accepted where action relying on the proposition or on its negation is required in circumstances in which no sufficient evidence to warrant belief in either is available, nor can it be obtained within the time constraints, and where there are some reasons to prefer the action based on the proposition to the action based on its negation, reasons which depend on the fact that the action is based on that proposition. (They may be that the one is more likely to be true. But they can be other, e.g. ethical, reasons, as when the presumption of innocence may lead one to accept that Janet did not murder John.)

The second type of case in which people accept propositions that they do not believe in is irrelevant here. Given that our 'unencumbered selves' have all the time, rational capacity, and information that they need to find

---

[16] This would have been the natural way to understand Nagel's argument but for the fact that he does not claim that the choosers would be irrational to choose the amoralist's position. This fact makes one incline towards the first reading. However, the fact that on the first reading the argument is incapable of establishing the validity of the amoralist's claim, and can only establish a personal estoppel, suggests that the second reading should be considered in its own right.

out whether to believe in the amoralist's view there seems no reason for them to accept it without believing in it.[17]

Could it be that our 'unencumbered selves' find themselves in the first type of situation? If so this is not part of Nagel's argument. He does not suggest accepting that the amoralist is wrong *arguendo* or as part of a *reductio*. Rather, according to this interpretation of his argument, he puts forward a reason for our unencumbered selves to accept that the amoralist is wrong as their conclusion. But that could never be justified except in the second type of situation, for a practical purpose when time, our resources, or our understanding are deficient. Since the reason given (that if the amoralist is wrong the chooser has greater value than if the amoralist is right) cannot possibly be a reason for believing that he is wrong, nor can it be a reason for accepting that he is wrong.

I have argued that the hypothetical choosers do not have reason to accept that the amoralist is wrong. By the same token Nagel does not provide us with a reason to believe that a hypothetical chooser has reason to accept morality as a principle of self-interest or in some other appropriately re-stricted way. This would not show the amoralist to be wrong, and there is little reason to think that Nagel understands his argument in this way.

So how does he understand it? Perhaps he has in mind choice not by our unencumbered selves, but by each of us as we are, as the first reading suggested. There is an initial difficulty with understanding Nagel in this way. On this reading he takes each one of us to be facing a choice. Though we are all under pressure to choose against the amoralist Nagel does not claim that we will be irrational to choose to join the amoralist. It follows that neither option is irrational, and therefore that choosing either of them cannot establish the truth of the option chosen.[18] If it could we might end with a contradiction if different people chose different options. One way of overcoming this difficulty is to understand the argument as giving rise to a personal estoppel: since we would choose against the amoralist we cannot, in our practical thought, rely on the hypothesis that he may be right. He may be right, but we are estopped from relying on that possibility for we choose against him.

The estoppel interpretation is, however, unacceptable. Obviously those who choose against the amoralist, or who accept that he is wrong, should act in a way consistent with their choice. But there is nothing in the way

---

[17] In *The Morality of Freedom*, 8–11, I argued for similar reasons that no presumptions of burden of proof have a place in philosophical arguments. It is possible that, these remarks notwithstanding, this is precisely the way in which Nagel understands his argument. He may be offering us a provisional morality—as Descartes once did—to serve us until our ability to understand ethics improves.

[18] This remark should not be taken to suggest that we cannot rationally believe what is false, only that if we can rationally believe (or accept) a proposition then our so accepting it cannot be used to show that it is false.

they come to reject the amoralist to stop them from changing their mind, nor anything to stop them from raising doubts about the case, nothing which could constitute an estoppel.

Is there any other way of making good the argument on the assumption that it is addressed to us as we are? Perhaps Nagel does not mean to offer us an argument. I have already drawn attention to the fact that he does not say that those who choose the amoralist are irrational. His comments appear designed to show us that those who choose the moralist are rational in doing so, rather than to refute the amoralist. Perhaps he should be understood as follows: We—that is just about everyone reading him—do in fact believe that the amoralist is wrong, and the moralist right. While there is no compelling argument supporting these beliefs they can be rendered intelligible. They are intelligible as a response to the devaluation of people embedded in the amoralist position, a devaluation which drives us to embrace morality.

It may well be true that thus understood the consideration that Nagel relies on does render the choice of those who choose[19] against the amoralist intelligible. But that does not mean that it shows it to be a rationally defensible choice. If that is all we have to say about the amoralist Nagel's comments are liable to be understood as an explanation of how we come to have a wish-fulfilling false belief in morality.

To avoid the charge of self-deluding wish fulfilment Nagel has to mean his argument to show not only that the choice is intelligible in the sense of being understandable, but that it is intelligible in being a self-validating choice. He must mean either that the fact that people generally accept morality is evidence that they are right or that the fact that it seems to you, and to so many of us, obvious that we, each one thinking of him or herself, have value in ourselves is such evidence. But that form of presumptive intuitionism must be backed by an epistemic theory which explains when the obviousness of a belief can be evidence for its truth and when not. And that theory must then be applied to show why the amoralist's explanation of the belief as a result of wish fulfilment is not the right one.

3. Expanding the Amoralist's Sympathies

Having explained why I find Nagel's argument against the amoralist wanting, I will consider the amoralist from a different perspective. In some ways Nagel's argument is attractively modest. But in one respect his modesty may be excessive. He allows for the intelligibility of the amoralist's view,

---

[19] For this final reading of Nagel's argument, 'choose that so and so' is to be taken to mean 'come to believe that so and so'.

and he allows that people can adopt his perspective. By implication he is suggesting that apart from being amoralist nothing much in their lives will be affected by such a stance. More specifically, and more accurately, he implies that their pursuit of their own self-interest need not be affected by being amoralists, at least that it need not be much affected. Is this true?

A familiar line of attack on the amoralist denies this assumption. If it can be shown that the value of people is presupposed by many goods that many people pursue, and the successful pursuit of which promotes the self-interest of those who pursue them, then an effective argument can be mustered against the amoralist. Some may try to show that since amoralists have to give up many goods which it is in their own interest to pursue, they can be true to their beliefs only at the cost of harming their self-interest. Perhaps it can even be shown that because of this anyone has a self-interested reason to believe in the value of people, though this step falls foul of my objection to Nagel. It does not prove the amoralist wrong. The argument I shall explore is different. It aims to show that there is no greater difficulty in persuading the amoralist of the value of other people than in persuading him of the value of many options whose pursuit is, or could be, in his own interest. It is not more difficult than recognizing the value of good wine. As will emerge I am far from sure, however, how far this argument can take us.

This line of reasoning once seemed sufficient, or almost so, to Bernard Williams. If the amoralist occasionally cares about other people, he pointed out, then

He is still recognisably amoral, in the sense that no general considerations weigh with him, and he is extremely short on fairness and similar considerations. Although he acts for other people from time to time, it all depends on how he happens to feel. With this man, of course, in actual fact arguments of moral philosophy are not going to work . . . This is not the point. . . . The point is rather that he provides a model in terms of which we may glimpse what morality needs in order to get off the ground, even though it is unlikely in practice to get off the ground in a conversation with him. He gives us, I think, almost enough for he has the notion of doing something for somebody, because that person needs something. He operates with this notion only when he is so inclined; but it is not itself a notion of his being so inclined.[20]

Williams follows this passage with a description of how, given this base, one can try to extend the sympathies of the amoralist and motivate him to care about people's needs even when he does not feel like doing so at the time:

---

[20] B. Williams, *Morality* (Harmondsworth: Penguin, 1973), 24–5.

There are people who need help who are not people who at the moment he happens to want to help, or like; and there are other people who like and want to help other particular people in need. To get him to consider their situation seems rather an extension of his imagination and his understanding than a discontinuous step onto something quite different, the 'moral plane'. And if we could get him to consider their situation, in the sense of thinking about it and imagining it, he might conceivably start to show some consideration for it: we extend his sympathies.[21]

We must agree with Williams's central point: anyone who has any concern for other people, who has family attachments or friends, or just likes, is fond of, or loves some people is on the same plane as all people who accept moral considerations. There is no 'bottomless gulf' between them. But in elaborating the point I want to follow a line of thought somewhat different from Williams's.

With Williams we can leave on one side the amoralist who has no concern for people, no friendships,[22] no people he likes or is fond of, and who has no desire for such feelings, attitudes, and relationships. Such a person's well-being is drastically affected by these limitations. Not only relationships, but also all the activities which depend on them or which presuppose the appreciation of their value are denied him. This means, for example, that his ability to appreciate and benefit from literature and the arts, and from many social activities is severely limited. There are things he can enjoy. But his life is so severely limited that—for reasons similar to those explained above concerning the person who denies any values—he poses no challenge to morality. The challenge is posed by an amoralist who can have a rich and rewarding life, while denying the value of people. Such an amoralist is like us in valuing friendship and companionship. He cares, however spasmodically, for some people.[23] Is it possible to be a consistent amoralist of this kind?

It would be a mistake, however, to focus on his limited motivation, as Williams does. The amoralist's refusal of morality is indeed accompanied

---

[21] Ibid. 25. In *Ethics and the Limits of Philosophy* (London: Collins, 1985) Williams seems more doubtful of this point. 'A limited benevolence or altruistic sentiment may move almost anyone to think that he should act in a certain way on a given occasion, but that fact does not present him with the ethical, as Moore's hand presented the sceptic with something material. The ethical involves more, a whole network of considerations, and the ethical sceptic could have a life that ignored such considerations altogether' (p. 25). But it is not clear whether Williams is here discussing the amoralist or someone who rejects all values.

[22] In talking of friendship I have in mind what one may call personal friendships. This excludes purely functional relationships, such as the distanced, though cordial relations which are bred by the need to co-operate to mutual advantage. I will, however, treat close relations between family relatives as a case of friendship.

[23] Notice that I am less of a minimalist than Williams in the sort of concern for others my amoralist is assumed to have. The key is that he should be able to have a successful and rewarding personal life, and someone with very limited concern for others cannot have such a life. That said, it is entirely possible that the argument explored here would succeed equally well given more minimalist assumptions.

by limited sympathies, and limited motivation. However, our sympathies and motivations are not brute facts about us. They are rational (in the sense of being responsive to reasons) attitudes and inclinations. A motivation can be acquired by rhetoric, but this would be rhetoric presenting or pretending to present the agent with reasons. The amoralist's motivation is limited because he does not believe that other people are valuable in themselves. Had he believed that they are ends in themselves we can expect that he would have been motivated to treat them as such. He would not be exceptionally consistent in giving due weight to this belief in his life. He would be just like many of us who are often unsure of the implications of the moralist's belief, and of whether we live up to them, and who are aware that at least some of the time we do not.

If, on the other hand, the amoralist does not come to believe in the value of people his sympathies could not possibly be extended to an adequate degree. He may come to care more often for more people. But so long as his sympathies are not guided by reasons it would be nothing short of miraculous for them to happen to coincide with the attitudes required by morality, assuming that it involves the proposition that all people are valuable in themselves. By examining the amoralist who has at his disposal the full range of goods by which his life can be enriched, and investigating the evaluative presuppositions of these goods we can—I will argue—demonstrate that there is no gulf between the moralist and the amoralist, and we can do so more securely and in a more far-reaching way than if we disregard these value-presuppositions in trying to extend the amoralist's sympathies and motivations.

This comment should not be read as an endorsement of some rationalistic view of how we form our views. When we are properly guided by reason we are not divorced from our emotions and feelings. Not only do they lead us to ideas which we can rationally examine in the light of reason, but reason itself involves an understanding which is informed by a sympathetic imagination. There are two ways in which we can readily imagine people whose reasoning leaves a lot to be desired extending their sympathies in line with moral concerns. First, if they live in a moral society and are merely aping their neighbours for one reason or another. Second, if there is a biological correlation between what we are innately disposed to care about and what we morally should care about. I suspect that the second possibility is misconceived, but will not discuss it here. The aping hypothesis, while explaining why in particularly fortunate circumstances one individual or another may uncomprehendingly come to have appropriate sympathies, makes this explanation dependent on others being guided by reason.

4. Undermining the Amoralist: From Relational to Non-Relational Values

Is the amoralist committed to acknowledging the value of people just because he cares about some of them? Does his friendship with some of them commit him to admitting the value of all people?

He cannot say[24] that his reason for pleasing his friends, helping them in their need, and generally treating them decently is that he wants to do that. No doubt he does want to act as he does. But, as Williams has pointed out, that is not *his* reason, and in any case it is not the sort of thing that *can* be a reason.[25] But the amoralist can say that his reason is that they are his friends, or his colleagues at work, or his children or nephews, or that there is some other special relationship between him and them which makes them people whom he values, and that is his reason for treating them the way he does—not their intrinsic value as people.

This answer, however, will not do. We can start with the point made by Williams that the amoralist 'has the notion of doing something for somebody, because that person needs something'. Not only does he have the notion, he relies on it in his reasoning. That in itself shows no more than that the amoralist's reason for helping his friend may be a compound of (*a*) the fact that there is a person in need, and (*b*) the fact that that person is his friend. It does not show that he is committed to recognizing the value of people who are not friends, nor to recognizing a reason to help people just because they are in need. And I assume that Williams, with his sights firmly set on the restricted sympathies of the amoralist, did not mean to deny that.

We make some progress by introducing, for the purpose of this argument only, a distinction between behaviour which is specific to friendship, or more narrowly, specific to the type of friendship the amoralist has with the person in question, and behaviour which is not specific in that way. No

---

[24] For presentational reasons I am using the amoralist not only as the topic of discussion, but also as his own advocate. This should not mislead. No assumption is made that the amoralist need be a sophisticated exponent and defender of his own position. The amoralist can be as inarticulate and as lacking in self-knowledge and in philosophical understanding as is consistent with his having friends. For ease of exposition I present his *amicus curiae*, who has all the arguments, as if he is an amoralist himself. He need not be, and as I said not every amoralist need be so well armed.

It follows that my argument is not *ad hominem*. I am not out to catch the amoralist admitting to views from which morality follows. I am trying to see how much of morality can be derived from the presuppositions of his life and of the options available to him, regardless of how he himself understands (or misunderstands) them.

[25] See generally on this point G. E. M. Anscombe, *Intention* (Oxford: Blackwell, 1957). For my attempt to explain why this is so see 'Incommensurability and Agency', in R. Chang (ed.), *Incommensurability, Incomparability and Practical Reason* (Cambridge, Mass.: Harvard Univ. Press, 1997).

claim is made that the distinction is either exhaustive or exclusive. The distinction is drawn from the point of view of the amoralist's friend. Behaviour[26] is specific to that type of friendship if it benefits the friend, or is agreeable to him, only because he is a friend, and it would not be beneficial or agreeable otherwise. Various displays of friendship are of this kind, for example, the marking of dates meaningful to the relationship, the display of various forms of familiarity and intimacy.

Of course much that goes on between friends is not specific in that sense. If one saves the friend's life this is, other things being equal, welcome to the friend whoever saved him. What matters to him most is being alive; whether he was saved by a friend, a stranger, or a natural event may matter, but comes a distant second. Many cases (e.g. being offered a loan to purchase a badly needed washing machine) include both specific and non-specific aspects. One may well be reluctant or unwilling to accept from a stranger what one accepts from a friend—to that extent offering or performing such services expresses the friendship. At the same time the act is beneficial or agreeable beyond the fact that it expresses the friendship. It also enables one to have a washing machine, etc., and that aspect of it is not specific in the sense explained.

To know how to conduct oneself with a friend one needs an understanding (inevitably mostly implicit) of what friendship is like.[27] The crucial point for my argument is that that will enable one not only to judge what friendship-specific conduct is appropriate and when. It will also enable one to know that one ought generally to behave in ways attuned to the interest of one's friends. That too is an aspect of friendship. It requires general concern for the friend as a person, not merely concern for his ability to act towards one as one's friend. That is, if I and my friend Jane spend our time together, discussing philosophy, going for walks in the hills, and confiding our marital difficulties to each other, then to continue to be Jane's friend I must not only be concerned with her willingness and ability to carry on with the activities which have come to give our

---

[26] I am using 'behaviour' to include aspects of actions. That is, one action may exemplify two types of behaviour. For example, shaking someone's hand may be both greeting him, and being polite to him. It can be regarded as exemplifying both kinds of behaviour.

[27] If the point is in need of explanation see my discussion of it in *The Morality of Freedom*. I explained there how our ability to have friends depends on knowledge of friendship (or of the relevant kind of friendship we have) and its normative implications. We must know—as must our friends—what is proper between friends, what duties they have to each other and what liberties they can take, etc. I then argued that to acquire this knowledge one has to be socialized into a society whose practices sustain such friendships. I am not, however, relying on this further point in the current argument. All that is assumed is that friendship is a recognized form of relationship, or rather a range of such forms, knowledge of the nature of which is required in order to have friends. This depends on nothing more than the need to act properly towards one's friends, and the need—in some cases—to act from appropriate motives, which sometimes include recognition that some forms of conduct are appropriate whereas others are inappropriate between friends, depending on the circumstances.

friendship its special character. I must also be concerned with her well-being generally. (Other things being equal, I must be willing to help in other matters in her life, when help is needed, and so on.) This general concern with the well-being of one's friends means that one is treating them as people who have value in themselves, and not merely as people who are valuable to one in one's own life.

All that may not worry the amoralist all that much. He may cheerfully admit that he has to treat his friends as friends are to be treated, that is as people who have intrinsic value, or he would not be their friend. He will remember that to have friends you must value them for what they are, value them in themselves, and not merely value them for what they mean to you, and for the benefit that you derive from their friendship. He will readily acknowledge that when he behaves towards them as a friend would, inevitably he is doing so because he values them in themselves. However, he values them in themselves not because they are people but because they are his friends. This is consistent—he will maintain—with his refusal to admit that people *qua* people have intrinsic value.

Think of the following case, the amoralist may say.[28] It shows that he does not value his friend as a person, but as a person who is his friend, a person from whom he derives the benefits of friendship. Suppose that what the amoralist values in the friendship is the wit of his friend, and that his friend's wit depends on the fact that he smokes. If so the amoralist would not want his friend to stop smoking, regardless of the damage smoking causes his health. This shows that he does not really care about the friend as a person, but only for what he gets out of him.

There is no denying that such people exist. They may differ on one point. Some may say that other things being equal they would care about their friend, regardless of whether caring for him benefits them. In the imagined case, however, causing him to stop smoking would kill the friendship. That is why they would not get him to stop smoking. Such people recognize a conflict that any friend would recognize in the imagined situation, and solve it in the wrong way. They are friends—one may say—though not very good ones. They do not present a special problem for my argument, which turns on an other-things-being-equal recognition of the value of people as people. The more extreme amoralist may take a different tack. He may say that he cares about his friend, treats him as a person of value, only when doing so serves his own interest in the friendship. This amoralist simply is not a friend to this other person (though the other person may be a friend to him: their attitudes may diverge; this is common in practice, and need not delay us here).

---

[28] I owe this case and the argument for the amoralist which it yields to Penelope Bulloch.

Several people who heard earlier versions of my argument balked at points like this. Suppose, they said, that the amoralist has no friends in 'my' sense of friendship. Suppose he is simply someone who comes as close to friendship as is possible for a person who has the attitude described in the example. If my argument undermines the amoralist who has friends it would fail to undermine amoralists who have only this kind of limited friendships as we may call them. Indeed amoralists may well tend to have limited rather than full friendships, and would, therefore, be immune to my argument.

Remember, however, that I am not arguing that no amoralist can live without engaging in activities or relationships which commit him to views inconsistent with his amoralism. My argument is that there are activities, pursuits, relationships which though non-moral themselves commit anyone who regards them as valuable to the moralist's principle. Or at least this is the argument I am testing to see how far it will take us. Its aim is to show that those who accept *all* that life offers them, all that can enrich their own life, also accept the moralist principle. This, if successful, would show that there is no gulf between so-called prudence and morality, that the same arguments which would lead one to realize what is of value for his or her life, would also lead to the acceptance of morality.

So the objection must be understood to rely on the claim that limited friendships give one all that full friendships do. Naturally, that may be thought true of cases where attitudes are not reciprocal. Imagine a friendship in which John is a full friend of Jane, but she has only limited friendship for him.[29] She is his friend only in the limited sense. This may be the case openly, and without deceit. John may wish that Jane reciprocated his attitude, but he may be willing to put up with what she is willing to give. Does not Jane, who has—let us assume—only limited friendships, and several of whose friends give her full friendship, does not she enjoy the best of both worlds? She both has the benefits of full friendship, she receives the care and respect that full friends give each other, but she does not give full friendship to her friends.

I take this to be the strongest form of the objection, for I assume that it will be generally recognized that most people crave, and for good reason, to have full friends. Being cared for and respected for one's own sake by a friend is one of the most valuable aspects of friendship. Jane would not pose a challenge to my argument should she need to accept the moralist's principle in order to have it. But, the objection runs, she has the benefit of full friendship, without being a full friend. Obviously the objection points

---

[29] Since asymmetrical friendships are important to the objection I will refer to 'giving' and 'receiving' friendship, to indicate the presence of the difference in attitude between the friends.

to the possibility of another argument against the amoralist, slightly different from mine. It suggests that for the amoralist to have some of the benefits of a good life he must interact with moralists, and benefit from the fact that they are moralists. I think, however, that the objection fails for a separate reason, namely that to give full friendship is in itself a good of great importance in human life. Caring and respecting others—not necessarily all others—is important to people's well-being, and it is doubly rewarding and valuable when it happens within a reciprocated relationship, that is, within a (full) friendship.

Having rejected the objection, I have to admit that whether my argument works still remains to be seen. The amoralist may while accepting the value of full friendship insist that his friends should be treated by him as people with value in themselves only because they are his friends. He should value them in themselves, and not just in friendship-specific ways. But other people may have no reason to value them at all. He may draw an analogy with trees. There is—let us imagine—an apple tree growing outside his window, providing fruit, shade, and improving the view from his window. He is very fond of the tree, and cares a great deal about it. He values the tree and treats it accordingly. To do that he must have a notion of the difference between a tree which is doing well and one which is ailing, or otherwise failing. Only thus can he effectively look after his tree. But it does not follow that he must treat all apple trees in the same way. He understands what it is for a tree to be respected and valued, what it is for a tree to be valuable. It does not follow from that that all trees are valuable. His tree has value for him. Some other trees may have value for other people. Some may have value to no one.

But possibly people are not like trees. I put it like that not because I doubt that people are ends in themselves, but because I want to leave open the possibility that trees are like people—that is, that they are intrinsically valuable, though not necessarily in the same way or to the same degree. It is important not to be diverted into an argument about the value of trees. So let us assume, for the sake of the argument, that trees are not intrinsically valuable. The amoralist is right to say that his apple tree may nevertheless have value for him. One way in which this is true is irrelevant to the argument. His apple tree is of value to him because it provides welcome shade and produces good apples. It is instrumentally good for him, for it has consequences which are themselves good for him. It is uncontroversial, but also irrelevant that instrumental goods can be good for one person and not for another. It is irrelevant because the case against the amoralist is that he is wrong about the intrinsic value of people, not about their instrumental value. Nor does the amoralist claim that his friends are merely of instrumental value to him. He values them in themselves and therefore in drawing the analogy with the tree he does not have in mind the instrumental value of the tree. Rather, his point is that the tree has more than mere instrumental value for him because he is attached to it, and that he can be attached to one tree, without being attached to all trees.

I agree that being attached to an object, person, activity, or project can endow them with a value which they would not otherwise have. They will have that value for the people who are attached to them and not for others.[30] But one can only be attached to something if one believes it to be valuable, and the attachment endows the object with extra value only if that object is indeed valuable. I have discussed these matters at somewhat greater length elsewhere,[31] and will only gesture towards the three main points involved.

First, there is a reciprocal relationship between good (or valuable) and good (or valuable) for one. On the one hand, nothing can be good unless it is possible for it to be good for someone.[32] We can imagine goods which are not actually good for anyone at the moment, or even goods which are unlikely to be good for anyone in the foreseeable future. But it is unintelligible to say of something that it is good or valuable if it is impossible that it be of value to anyone. On the other hand, if anything is good and one can relate to it in 'the appropriate way' then other things being equal it is good for one. So if a novel is a good novel and I can read it with understanding then it is good for me to read it, other things being equal. There is no more to something being good for me than that it is a good which is within my reach (though of course other things may be better, or the cost of reaching it may be more than it is worth, etc.).

Second, all intentional action is undertaken for a reason. This implies that it is undertaken in the belief that it or some of its consequences are good. Some of our attachments were acquired by choice, and therefore in the belief that it is good to be so attached. Many, perhaps most, of people's attachments are not formed by choice. But they are sustained by our continuous engagement and involvement in them. Therefore, they too are accompanied by a belief in their value. The people who have those attachments would lose their will to be involved in them and would try to give them up were they to lose that belief.

Third, what is sometimes called the reality principle means that as our intentional actions (including those which manifest our attachments) are

---

[30] We can here disregard the complications arising because some people may be attached to the person who is attached to the tree and because of that the tree may acquire enhanced value for them as well.

[31] See *The Morality of Freedom*, 288–94; 'On the Moral Point of View', and 'Incommensurability and Agency'.

[32] I am assuming that sometimes being a good x is, or can be, good for that x (being a good person is or can be good for the person who is good).

undertaken for what we believe to be good reasons,[33] they are worth while—unless accidentally—only if those reasons are sound. That implies that only if the objects of our attachments are of value is there any value in our attachments, or in the actions which manifest them. There may be exceptions to this rule, but they are, from the point of view of the current discussion, of minor importance.

In all but exceptional cases the value of an attachment depends on the value of what one is attached to. One's love of Beethoven's music can be valuable—exceptional circumstances excepted—only because Beethoven's music is valuable. In general the attachment will be manifested in a variety of ways, depending on its object, and it can be of value only if the way it manifests itself is suitable to the object towards which it is manifested. One's affection, admiration, respect, etc. are of value only if they are bestowed on objects which merit them.

The upshot of this discussion is that whatever is intrinsically good for a person is so only if it is good in a non-relativized way, only if it is valuable *tout court*. A person may become attached to something which is instrumentally valuable and which thereby acquires non-instrumental value for him. Alternatively people become attached to what they take to be intrinsically valuable. Believing that these valuable goods, relationships, or activities are within their reach they may make their enjoyment or pursuit one of their goals, and by thus becoming attached to them they endow them with greater value for themselves. But these activities and the like have value for them only if they are good and worth while independently of being embraced by them.

It is easy to misunderstand this point, and to think that I am presenting some sort of desert account of attachment and relationships. As if I am saying that it is appropriate to admire only music which deserves admiration, or to love only people who deserve to be loved. My claim was different, though related. For our attachment to something to be of value, and for it to make its object of value to us, its object must have a value independently of it. Moreover it must have value of a kind which is appropriate for that attachment, which makes the attachment appropriate. So that if it involves admiring something or someone it should be admirable, if we love someone he or she must be worthy of love, if we are devoted to someone he or she must be worthy of devotion, and so on. This does not mean that the person or object must deserve the attachment. The notion of desert is more specific. When speaking of people deserving something the idea of desert imports, for example, the thought that the deserving people

---

[33] Though when we display weakness of will we believe that other things make them insufficient to justify the action we are taking.

have accomplished something of value through their well-motivated endeavours. That accomplishment is the basis of their desert. Some forms of caring about things or people or of being attached to them may require that their objects deserve the attitude for the attitude to be valuable. But that is not generally the case. The tree in my example need not deserve the fond devotion its owner has for it. Attachment to trees does not demand that. It is appropriate if the tree is a good specimen of its kind, or if it played a significant role in the life of the person attached to it (even, for example, by bringing him useful income). Similarly in the case of friendship the argument is not that only some people are good enough to be my friends, that only some deserve to be my friends. On the contrary. After all, its purpose is to show that all people, some exceptions aside, are appropriate friends, for its purpose is to show that all people have the value which qualifies them as possible friends, and which is the value the moralist asserts in his basic principle.

5. *The Amoralist's Mistake*

This then is where the amoralist goes wrong. He claims that his friends are valuable to him, but not valuable in themselves, independently of the value with which the friendship endows them. Their value depends on the fact that he is attached to them, that they are his friends. But that cannot be. Admittedly having become a friend of theirs means that in a sense they are valuable to him more than to other people: they mean to him more than they need mean to other people. But their value to him depends on the fact that the friendship is a valuable attachment or relationship. In its turn the value of the friendship depends on it being with people who are worthy of being his friends.

The amoralist is still unimpressed. He will acknowledge—let us assume —that he was too hasty in claiming that it was just his attachment to his friends which endows them with value, and makes them worthy of his respect and concern. He will allow that they had to be independently valuable for his attachment to them to enhance their value for him. But, he will point out, by my own argument the same is true of his attachment to his tree. For as long as the argument does not distinguish people from trees there is nothing for him to worry about. His amorality remains intact.

In one respect the amoralist attitude to the tree of our example is like people's attitude to their friends: the reasons we come to be attached to them are biographical. I can cherish an object which saved my life, or a piece of music which I got to know when depressed, and which played a role in sustaining my spirits, a tree which I admired through the seasons, and I can acquire a friend because he saved my life, or because I got to know him when depressed and he used to cheer me up; and so on. But turn your attention not to why Hilary is Robin's friend, but to what is involved in that state of affairs, to the reasons which guide Robin's conduct towards Hilary, while he is his friend.

The reasons people have for being friends with each other can be—and often are—asymmetrical. Robin's reasons for being Hilary's friend need not be Hilary's reasons for being Robin's friend. Friendship is, however, a reciprocal relationship, in a way in which one's attachment to a tree is not. Within the relationship Robin and Hilary have to treat each other as in some sense equal. That does not mean that they are equal in strength, physical or emotional, or in wisdom or in any other way. It means that to be friends each must care for the other for the sake of the other, and not only for what he gets out of him. And they must recognize that the other merits such an attitude, and that they merit it in themselves, and not merely for their role in each other's biography.

This is where friendships differ from attachments to trees: friends are not merely people who care for each other, who care about the interest of the other as one cares about the well-being of one's tree. Friends are people who share intimacy, who treat each other as people, as persons with emotions, thoughts, and so on and so forth. Friends not only recognize that their friends are such people, and therefore have interests which trees do not have. They recognize that the fact that people can reciprocate each other's attachment, that they are capable of understanding and empathizing with each other is essential to making people appropriate partners in friendships. And these features of people are drawn upon in the friendship, and valued by the friends in each other. This point is briefly summarized when we say that friendship requires that friends should treat each other with respect, that they should treat each other as ends in themselves, and not merely as people whose friendship is valuable.

Friendship requires respecting the friends in themselves, and not only for any instrumental value they may have, nor merely for their role in one's biography. As I explained, this does not mean that Robin need deny that he needs Hilary, that Hilary's support, his interest in Robin, and so on, are valued by Robin, that but for them Robin would not continue with the friendship. Nor need he deny that circumstances may change and he will lose his interest in the friendship and—quite legitimately—let it lapse. It does mean, however, that Robin must acknowledge that while he is Hilary's friend, he cares about Hilary for what he is, and not merely for what he is to Robin. But then Hilary must merit that treatment. There must be a reason which makes him an appropriate object of such an attitude, and that reason cannot be that he is useful to Robin, nor that he features in a certain way in his life (e.g. reminds him of his much missed dead mother). To do that is to deny his independent value, to deny that the relationship is reciprocal between two people each recognizing that the other matters in himself, independently of the relationship.

For Robin to say that Hilary is not of value in his own right, that his value derives entirely from Robin's attachment to him, or from his role in Robin's life, is to reveal the friendship as a sham, as self-serving and egotistical. To care for someone for their own sake requires recognizing merit in them independently of their role in our life. Hence friendships are of value only if they are with people who are worthy of friendship, and of being the object of care and concern. Being worthy of such attitudes means having value in themselves.

Some would object to this argument. They would say that while some friendships are like that others are not. Moreover, they would insist, people may have quite a decent life without enjoying or seeking friendships of this kind. They take a mild interest in people from time to time, seek their company for what they can get out of it, and no more. I acknowledge both points, but they do not affect my case.

First, I should point out that I am using 'friend' in its primary sense, meaning 'one joined to another in mutual benevolence and intimacy' (*Oxford English Dictionary*). Most other uses of 'friend' derive from and retain elements of this meaning. The description of the reciprocal aspect of friendship sketched above, and the way it involves the recognition of the independent worth of the other are meant to be no more than an elaboration on the notion of joining together in mutual intimacy. So while it is true that 'lesser' friendships are common the friendship I described is not some remote and demanding ideal. It is a common experience.

Second, having such friendships is of value to those who have them. Friendships enrich the life of the friends. Indeed it is a common experience that friendship can play a central role in the life of people, that it is among the most significant factors which make many people's lives good and fulfilling. Moreover, and that is crucial for my case, it is not good for them because it is morally good. Volunteering to work for Oxfam in one's spare time may be good for one because it is a morally good thing to do. But there is nothing specifically morally good about having friends. People bereft of friends may have a lonely and impoverished life, but they are not morally at fault. Therefore one need not be a moralist to recognize the value of friendship, not even of full friendship as I described it.

Third, it may be that one's life can be fulfilling and rich enough without having friends of that kind. My amoralist may say: I do not actually want to have such friends, and I do not believe in them. They are based on the falsehood that people are of value in themselves. And living up to that view my amoralist may yet have a decent and successful life without friends of this kind. But you will remember my warning earlier that my argument is not *ad hominem*. Nor is it an argument that one has a so-called prudential reason to be moral for without morality one cannot have a good and fulfilling life. My argument is theoretical in aim: its goal is to deny that there is a divide—epistemological or metaphysical—between moral considerations and values and non-moral ones. That argument is unaffected by the stance I imagine here that the amoralist may adopt: his refusal to have friends does not matter. What matters is that he refuses to acknowledge that friendships are of value to the friends, for he realizes that that would lead to the endorsement of the value of people independently of one's attachment to them. In that refusal he concedes that he cannot sustain the argument that only his attachment to people endows them with value.

6. *The Moralist's Disappointment*

The preceding argument exposes a mistake the amoralist is guilty of. But it is unlikely to give much comfort to the moralist. It seems to leave us in some sort of no man's land. The amoralist has been shown to be wrong in claiming that the people who are his friends are of value only because of his attachment to them. But the argument has not established that they are of value as people. The amoralist can therefore modify the position we ascribed to him. He can say that his friends are people who are valuable in themselves because they are funny, or loving, or wise, or whatever other property he values in them. He is still an amoralist because he denies that all people are of value.

A second feature of the preceding argument may worry the moralist. Allowing that the argument shows that some people are of value, what sort of value is it? I have argued that if they are of value to a person who is their friend, a person who is attached to them, then they must be of value also independently of that attachment. The same can be said about anything which is of value in a person's life. If collecting medieval musical instruments is an activity which contributes to the life of keen collectors, making their life better, then collecting medieval musical instruments must be a valuable activity in itself, regardless of whether or not one is keen on it. If this is all the argument established does it not equate people with medieval musical instruments, or with tennis, paintings, etc.? Surely the moralist's claim is that people are of value in a different way from the value, even the intrinsic value, of the objects, activities, relationships, and the rest which can make people's life better.

I am uncertain in what way the value of people, as understood by moralists, is special. But the following may at least be part of what is meant:

Playing tennis is intrinsically good. It can also be good instrumentally, as a way of keeping fit, making friends or money, or gaining prestige. But apart from any beneficial consequences playing tennis may or may not have it is a valuable activity; it is an activity with intrinsic value. People too have intrinsic value. But that does not mean that they are equal in value to tennis. Think of a person, let us call her Julia, playing tennis. Other things being equal, playing tennis is good for Julia. It is a good thing for her to do. But is the fact that Julia plays tennis good for tennis? Under special circumstances this may be the case. It may be good for the game that Julia plays it if it is in danger of being forgotten, and her playing it helps keep it alive, or if she is such an outstanding and famous player that her example raises the level of the game generally. Even so the asymmetry I am pointing to is intact. In the ordinary case, that a person plays tennis is, other things being equal, good for him, and a good thing for him to do, but it is neither good nor bad for tennis.

We can terminologically mark this asymmetry by saying that whereas playing tennis is an intrinsically good or valuable activity, people are of value in themselves (and not merely intrinsically). Above[34] I referred to a condition for anything being good *tout court*, that is that it be possible for it to be good for someone. The terminological distinction just introduced is meant to chime with that condition: whatever is intrinsically good is capable of being good for something or someone which is good in itself. Being of value in oneself, or an end in oneself, marks one as one who counts, whose good matters because one counts, apart from any other reason why the good may count.

The pursuit of what is intrinsically valuable makes sense only to the extent that it is of value to those who are valuable in themselves. This condition is usually satisfied by the fact that the pursuit of what is intrinsically valuable is good for the person engaged in it (dancing, painting, etc. are good for those who dance or paint). Sometimes the activity is good for the actor (a good thing for him to do) only if it is good for someone else, or at least only if it could be good for someone else. Teaching and practising medicine are obvious examples. Painting and composing music are less obvious examples. They conform to this precept because the standards of excellence in these activities are essentially such that other people can have the benefit of successful creations as spectators, performers, or listeners.

The asymmetry between things which are intrinsically valuable and those which are of value in themselves is central to evaluative thought. The moralist claims not (or not merely) that people are intrinsically valuable but

---

[34] And remember that in Sect. 4 the term 'intrinsically valuable' is used indiscriminately to cover both what I call intrinsically valuable and what has just been dubbed valuable in itself. In common and philosophical usage 'intrinsic value' is often used inclusively to cover both categories.

that they are valuable in themselves. That is—as we saw—one reason why the moralist is disappointed in the conclusion of the argument so far. It has not, he feels, shown that people are of value in themselves, only that they are intrinsically valuable, as tennis is.

If that is the source of the moralist's disappointment then it is unjustified. It overlooks the fact—just alluded to—that many intrinsically valuable activities presuppose that other people besides the agent are of value in themselves. To repeat, to teach is or can be intrinsically good to the teacher but only if he treats his students as of value in themselves; to compose good music can also be intrinsically valuable to the composer but only if it is music which can be and deserves to be meaningful and rewarding to other people. In brief, the value (to the agent) of many intrinsic goods depends on the fact that they are or can be good for people, and that means that it depends on the fact that people are of value in themselves. In friendship—which we assume that even the amoralist seeks—the treating of friends as of value in themselves is central to the relationship. Hence in being committed to the value of his friends, in being committed to their value as creatures worthy of being friends and of being treated as friends should be—the amoralist is committed to their value in themselves.

But—to return to the first objection—is he committed to holding that just being people makes them valuable? Perhaps it is being witty, warm, or generous people, for example, which endows them with value in themselves? If all we have to go on is that a would-be amoralist has John as his friend we will not be able to rebut his claim, should he be disposed to explain himself in this way, that it is John's generous nature which endows him with value in himself. Even so the amoralist's concession is not to be belittled. It reaches beyond the actual friends he has to all those who possess the value-endowing qualities he recognizes.

Yet without doubt one would want to go beyond the amoralist's friendship with John to look at other friendships that he has, or wishes to have, or about which he recognizes that they would be of value if he had them. We would want to explore his relations with his parents, or with his children. In these cases too it may be claimed that his well-being is greatly diminished if he has such relatives, or had them, but is not a friend of theirs, nor wishes to be, nor recognizes the value to his life had he been a friend of his parents or of his children. In these cases it is more difficult for the amoralist to say that his parents are people of value in themselves only because they are witty or generous, or have similar qualities.

Two further important steps in the argument should be noted: To simplify their presentation let us call relationships in which people are duty bound to treat each other as ends in themselves (or as having value in themselves) 'personal relationships'. First, the amoralist has, of course, to acknowledge that all people who possess the qualities which his friends have, and which make his friendships with them reasonable, are also of value in themselves. He has, however, to go one step further. He has to admit that all the people with whom it would be reasonable for him to have a personal relationship are also of value in themselves. This is the case even though at present he has no desire to become their friend, nor does he think he is ever likely to be their friend. None of this matters. As we saw, should he be their friend they would be of value in themselves, and that would not be a result of the fact that he cares for them or is attached to them: his friendship is of value only if they are of value in themselves independently of it. Hence the conclusion that all those with whom it would be OK to have a personal relationship are of value in themselves regardless of how unlikely it is that one would want to have such a relationship with them.

Second, by parity of reasoning the same goes for those with whom it is reasonable for others to have a personal relationship. If the amoralist believes that it is reasonable that Rachel and Robert are friends then he must concede that both of them are of value in themselves.

7. *Doubts about the Moralist*

I will not pursue these reflections in detail. It is not my claim that there is a single knock-down argument which shows that the amoralist in recognizing values which can enrich his own life is committed to recognizing the value of all people. My suggestion was that there is enough in what he is committed to to advance the argument and narrow the gap between the amoralist and the moralist. How has it been narrowed? It is true that they are still separated by the moralist endorsing and the amoralist rejecting the proposition that all people are of value in and of themselves, or that just in virtue of being people they are ends in themselves. But now the amoralist no longer denies that people can be of value in themselves, and that some have such value. He merely insists that those who are of value in themselves are so in virtue of the possession of properties such as being witty, or wise, or good-looking. Moreover, there is no closed list of such properties that the amoralist who has been persuaded by my argument so far is limited to. Anything which could justify a personal relationship between any two or more people shows that they are ends in themselves. The amoralist has to concede that anyone with whom it is reasonable for anyone to have a personal relationship is of value in him- or herself.

The same is true of my response to the second objection—to the effect that the amoralist does not recognize the special value of people which the moralist has in mind. Here too the moralist may feel that the argument I relied on does not go all the way. It may show that people are of value in themselves rather than (just) intrinsically valuable, in terms of the stipulated distinction I introduced. But that does not show that one may never torture an innocent person, nor that the right action is the one which contributes most to the greatest happiness of the greatest number, nor even that all people are in themselves of equal value. The moralist may feel that that shows that I understand 'being of value in oneself' in a thin sense which differs from what he had in mind. For him it follows from the fact that people are of value in themselves that they should not be tortured, or that the right action is the one which contributes most to the greatest happiness of the greatest number, or which treats all people as equal. At this point I am reminded of the fact that I never did understand what the moralist's belief (that all people are of value in themselves) meant.

It is reasonable to understand the difference between those who, say, believe that it is never justified to torture the innocent and those who reject this, those who believe that the right action is the one which more than any other option open to the agent contributes to the greatest good of the greatest number and those who deny that, it is reasonable to understand such debates as disagreements within morality, disagreements about its content and implications among those who in principle recognize its binding force. We regard neither side to such disputes as an amoralist, but rather both as having different views of morality. So the fact that the amoralist rejects such views is not what makes him into an amoralist. What does? We can repeat the principle we assumed to unite them: that people are in and of themselves of value in themselves. I have just acknowledged that the amoralist is still refusing to acknowledge this principle and that we found no argument why he should.

The amoralist who followed us so far will agree that it is possible for all people to possess the qualities which make people valuable in themselves (being witty, wise, good-looking, etc.), when that is understood to mean that they belong to a species of animal which can, consistently with their nature as members of that species, possess these qualities. But that is not the same as holding them actually to be valuable in themselves. Though the two are sufficiently close that it is worth wondering whether the moralist actually means more, that is, whether all moralists must just in virtue of being moralists be committed to more than to the potentiality principle, as we may call it. It is clear that some of them do have more in mind, but is it of the essence of morality that one should?

In fact it is not even clear that it makes sense to say that believing that people are of value in themselves is the mark of the moral position (unless that is an inaccurate way of saying that people have the potential to possess

the qualities which endow them with value in themselves). Try it whichever way you want: does it mean that no other quality (other than being
human, or a person) is of moral relevance? This is hardly possible. Surely
people's actual actions and intentions, virtues and vices are also of moral
consequence.

Does it mean that no other quality is of moral consequence unless it is
a quality of a human being? Some people believe that. They believe that
even if there are non-human creatures who are witty, affectionate, wise,
attractive, and so on and so forth, they have no value in themselves. Therefore, personal relationships with them are of no value, etc. But this is an
implausible position, and not one shared by all moralists.

Does it mean that there are minimum requirements of conduct towards
and entitlements of people just in virtue of being people, though a richer
morality applies to those who possess other qualities beside mere humanity? Again many people believe that to be the case, and even more people
think that they do. But not all moralists do. It is disputable whether
membership in a species *Homo sapiens* endows a creature with value in
itself. People who are born in irreversible coma, or without a brain apart
from the brain stem are considered by many as having no value in themselves. This does not mean that we do not have any obligations regarding
the way they are treated. But we may have such obligations regarding
works of art, or features of the natural environment, even though they are
not of value in themselves.

This is one reason why many prefer to talk of the value of persons,
rather than people, understood as members of the species *Homo sapiens*.
We may suspect, however, that unless persons are defined as being those
creatures who are of value in themselves the same problems will arise.
Neither I nor the amoralist who modified his position as a result of the
previous arguments is denying that possession of some quality or other
endows its possessors with value in themselves. Since the moralist is now
supposed to agree that not all people possess such qualities, and therefore
that not all people are of value in themselves, what is distinctive about his
position? Perhaps that whatever the qualities are they endow all those who
have them with the same value, with value to the same degree. The kingdom
of ends in themselves is, he might say, a kingdom of the morally equal.

This, however, is yet another controversial claim, and it is controverted
within morality. Utilitarians, for example, do not normally accept it. The
question is whether there is only one quality which endows its possessors
with value in themselves, and whether if there is more than one possession
of several of them can endow some with greater value than others who
possess one but not the others. Similarly, even if there is only one property
which endows its possessors with value in themselves it may be that it can

be exhibited by various creatures to various degrees in a way that will justify regarding some of them as having greater value than others. We need
not express any view on these matters here. For our purpose the relevant
conclusion is that the argument about these possibilities is an argument
between different views of morality rather than an argument between the
moralist and the amoralist.

The failure to identify a position which marks the moralist off from the
(reformed) amoralist was a failure to find a way of reading 'people have
value in themselves' which renders it both true and appropriate to be the
mark of morality. But while the arguments that lead to that failure bear on
some other ways of identifying morality, they do not apply to all of the
ways by which philosophers have tried to mark the moral. For example,
they do not apply to the view that there is an argument or a method of
argument which can establish the truth of moral principles, whatever they
are, and which is specific to moral issues. Such argument or method of
argument will be different from the way we argue about the value of wine,
or tennis, or the arts. It is a specifically moral form of argument. According
to this view, the amoralist's mistake is that he denies the validity of that
form of argument.

This is a very different way of identifying morality from the one I have
been pursuing so far. It does not claim that morality is distinctive by its
content. Rather it is distinctive by its employment of a special argument or
by its method of argumentation. If such a form of argument exists then it
is very different from the type of argument which, following Williams, I
have explored in the previous section, for my arguments looked for the
presupposition of ordinary beliefs about familiar values. This is but one
reason to suspect the thesis that there is a distinctive form of moral reasoning: so much moral reasoning seems to be nothing but ordinary reasoning
about what it is reasonable or unreasonable to do. I believe, though the
matter cannot be gone into here, that no attempt to produce such a specifically 'moral' form of argument has been successful. I believe that evaluative
arguments, moral and otherwise, are like all arguments, a matter of tracing
the implications of the structures of our beliefs, in all the ways we know.

What is common to the view that the mark of morality is acceptance of
the principle that people are of value in themselves and to the suggestion
that it is marked by the deployment of a special method of argument is a
conception of morality as an autonomous area, distinct from other practical
concerns. This assumption, seen in operation in Nagel's argument, and
essential to all contractarian approaches to morality, though not only to
them, explains how the amoralist is possible: he is someone standing
outside morality and denying that there is a route, a rationally compelling
route, which could lead him in.

The direction of the arguments of this section and of the previous one was not to adjudicate between the moralist and the amoralist, but to deny the existence of the two characters by undermining that assumption. This does not mean rejecting the moralist's belief that people are valuable in themselves as false. It means, however, demoting it from its status as a foundational moral principle, or as the mark of morality. Principles like the moralist's principle are no more than a convenient—though inaccurate—summary or reminder of the conclusions of arguments like the arguments about the value of people explored in the course of this discussion. They are ordinary arguments employing no special method, and they arise out of and are part of our general understanding of value, reason, and norms, and of the meaning of human life. Neither the arguments nor their conclusions form a distinct realm, the moral realm, in any interesting sense. Moreover, the precise conclusions of the arguments are complex and nuanced. The moralist's principle while an approximation that has its uses, is of little relevance in a discussion of the nature of morality.[35]

[35] I am grateful to Gerry Cohen, John Cottingham, Peter Hacker, Oswald Hanfling, Susan Hurley, John Hyman, Anthony Kenny, Derek Parfit, and Bede Rundle, for many helpful comments on an earlier draft of this essay. I am particularly grateful to Tom Nagel for trying patiently to explain his argument to me. I am also indebted to comments and suggestions by the participants of the St Andrews Conference on Practical Reason in March 1995, and especially to the editors of this volume, Garrett Cullity and Berys Gaut.

CONTRIBUTORS

ROBERT AUDI is Professor Philosophy at the University of Nebraska, Lincoln.

DAVID O. BRINK is Professor of Philosophy at the University of California, San Diego.

GARRETT CULLITY is Lecturer in the Moral Philosophy department of the University of St Andrews.

JAMES DREIER is Associate Professor of Philosophy at Brown University.

BERYS GAUT is Lecturer in the Moral Philosophy department of the University of St Andrews.

T. H. IRWIN is Susan Linn Sage Professor of Philosophy at Cornell University.

CHRISTINE M. KORSGAARD is Professor of Philosophy at Harvard University.

PETER RAILTON is Professor of Philosophy at the University of Michigan, Ann Arbor.

JOSEPH RAZ is Professor of the Philosophy of Law at the University of Oxford, Fellow of Balliol College, Oxford, and Visiting Professor at Columbia Law School, New York.

JOHN SKORUPSKI is Professor of Moral Philosophy in the University of St Andrews.

MICHAEL SMITH is Senior Fellow in the Philosophy Program, Research School of Social Sciences, Australian National University.

J. DAVID VELLEMAN is Professor of Philosophy at the University of Michigan, Ann Arbor.

R. JAY WALLACE is Professor of Philosophy at the Humboldt-Universität zu Berlin.

BIBLIOGRAPHY

In addition to works cited in the volume, this Bibliography lists available editions, in English translation, of those historical works referred to.

ALLISON, HENRY E., *Idealism and Freedom: Essays on Kant's Theoretical and Practical Philosophy* (Cambridge: Cambridge University Press, 1996).

—— *Kant's Theory of Freedom* (Cambridge: Cambridge University Press, 1990).

—— 'On the Presumed Gap in the Derivation of the Categorical Imperative', repr. in his *Idealism and Freedom*, 143–54.

ALTHAM, J. E. J., and HARRISON, Ross (eds.), *World, Mind and Ethics: Essays on the Ethical Philosophy of Bernard Williams* (Cambridge: Cambridge University Press, 1995).

AMERIKS, KARL, *Kant's Theory of Mind: An Analysis of the Paralogisms of Pure Reason* (Oxford: Clarendon Press, 1982).

ANDERSON, ELIZABETH, 'Reasons, Attitudes, and Values: Replies to Sturgeon and Piper', *Ethics*, 106 (1996), 538–54.

ANSCOMBE, G. E. M., *Intention* (Oxford: Blackwell, 1957).

AQUINAS, ST THOMAS, *In decem libros Ethicorum Aristotelis ad Nicomachum Expositio*, ed. R. Spiazzi, 3rd edn. (Turin: Marietti, 1964).

—— trans. as *Commentary on Aristotle's Nicomachean Ethics* by C. L. Litzinger (Notre Dame, Ind.: Dumb Ox Books, 1993).

—— *Quaestiones Disputate*, trans. as *Disputed Questions* by R. W. Mulligan, J. V. McGlynn, and R. W. Schmidt (Indianapolis: Hackett, 1994).

—— *Summa Theologiae*, trans. Fathers of the English Dominican Province (London: Burns and Oates, 1920; repr. Westminster, Md.: Christian Classics, 1981).

—— 1–2, qq 90–7 trans. as *The Treatise on Law* by R. J. Henle (Notre Dame, Ind.: Notre Dame University Press, 1993).

ARISTOTLE, *The Complete Works of Aristotle: The Revised Oxford Translation*, ed. Jonathan Barnes (Oxford: Oxford University Press, 1984).

—— *de Anima*, trans. as *On the Soul* by J. A. Smith, in Barnes (ed.), *The Complete Works of Aristotle*.

—— *Magna Moralia*, trans. St G. Stock, in Barnes (ed.), *The Complete Works of Aristotle*.

—— *Metaphysics*, trans. W. D. Ross, in Barnes (ed.), *The Complete Works of Aristotle*.

—— *de Motu Animalium*, trans. as *Movement of Animals* by A. S. L. Farquharson, in Barnes (ed.), *The Complete Works of Aristotle*.

—— *Nicomachean Ethics*, trans. Terence Irwin (Indianapolis: Hackett, 1985).

—— trans. W. D. Ross and rev. J. O. Urmson in Barnes (ed.), *The Complete Works of Aristotle*.

AUDI, ROBERT, 'Acting for Reasons', repr. in his *Action, Intention, and Reason*, 145–78.

—— *Action, Intention, and Reason* (Ithaca, NY: Cornell University Press, 1993).

—— 'The Architecture of Reason', repr. in his *The Structure of Justification*, 227–56.

—— 'Autonomy, Reason, and Desire', *Pacific Philosophical Quarterly*, 72 (1992), 247–71.

—— 'The Concept of Wanting', *Philosophical Studies*, repr. in his *Action, Intention, and Reason*, 35–55.

—— 'Dispositional Beliefs and Dispositions to Believe', *Noûs*, 28 (1994), 419–34.

—— 'Intending', repr. in his *Action, Intention, and Reason*, 56–73.

—— 'Intrinsic Value and the Dignity of Persons', in his *Moral Knowledge and Ethical Character*.

—— *Moral Knowledge and Ethical Character* (Oxford and New York: Oxford University Press, 1997).

—— *Practical Reasoning* (London: Routledge, 1989).

—— 'Structural Justification', repr. in his *The Structure of Justification*, 274–96.

—— *The Structure of Justification* (Cambridge: Cambridge University Press, 1993).

—— 'Weakness of Will and Rational Action', repr. in his *Action, Intention, and Reason*, 319–33.

AUGUSTINE, *Epistulae*, trans. as *Correspondence* by Sister Wilfrid Parsons (Washington: Catholic University of America Press, 1964–1989).

AUNE, BRUCE, 'Hypotheticals and "Can", Another Look', repr. in Gary Watson (ed.), *Free Will*, 36–41.

—— *Kant's Theory of Morals* (Princeton: Princeton University Press, 1979).

AYER, A. J., 'Freedom and Necessity', repr. in Gary Watson (ed.), *Free Will*, 15–23.

BAIER, ANNETTE, *Postures of the Mind: Essays on Mind and Morals* (Minneapolis: University of Minnesota Press, 1985).

BAIER, KURT, *The Rational and the Moral Order: The Social Roots of Reason and Morality* (Chicago: Open Court, 1995).

BECK, LEWIS WHITE, *A Commentary on Kant's Critique of Practical Reason* (Chicago: University of Chicago Press, 1960).

BLACKBURN, SIMON, 'Practical Tortoise Raising', *Mind*, 104 (1995), 695–711.

BOND, E. J., *Reason and Value* (Cambridge: Cambridge University Press, 1983).

BRATMAN, MICHAEL E., 'Toxin, Temptation, and the Stability of Intention', in Jules Coleman and Christopher Morris (eds.), *Rational Commitment and Social Justice*.

BRINK, DAVID, *Moral Realism and the Foundations of Ethics* (Cambridge: Cambridge University Press, 1989).

—— 'A Puzzle about the Rational Authority of Morality', *Philosophical Perspectives*, 6 (1992), 1–26.

—— 'Self-Love and Altruism', *Social Philosophy and Policy*, 14 (1997), 122–57.

—— 'The Separateness of Persons, Distributive Norms, and Moral Theory', in R. G. Frey and Christopher W. Morris (eds.), *Value, Welfare, and Morality*, 254–89.

BROAD, C. D., *Broad's Critical Essays in Moral Psychology*, ed. David R. Cheney (London: George Allen & Unwin, 1971).

—— *Five Types of Ethical Theory* (London: Routledge & Kegan Paul, 1930).

BROADIE, SARAH WATERLOW, *Ethics with Aristotle* (Oxford: Oxford University Press, 1991).

BROWN, CHARLOTTE, 'From Spectator to Agent: Hume's Theory of Obligation', *Hume Studies*, 20 (1994), 19–35.

—— 'Is Hume an Internalist?', *Journal of the History of Philosophy*, 25 (1988), 69–87.

BUCHANAN, ALLEN, 'Categorical Imperatives and Moral Principles', *Philosophical Studies*, 31 (1977), 249–60.

BUTLER, JOSEPH, *Fifteen Sermons Preached at the Rolls Chapel*, abridged in *Five Sermons Preached at the Rolls Chapel and A Dissertation upon the Nature of Virtue*, ed. Stephen Darwall (Indianapolis: Hackett, 1983).

CAMPBELL, RICHMOND, 'Gauthier's Theory of Morals by Agreement', *Philosophical Quarterly*, 38 (1988), 243–64.

—— 'Moral Justification and Freedom', *Journal of Philosophy*, 85 (1988), 192–213.

CARROLL, LEWIS, 'What the Tortoise said to Achilles', *Mind*, 4 (1895), 278–80.

CAVELL, STANLEY, *Conditions Handsome and Unhandsome: The Constitution of Emersonian Perfectionism* (Chicago: University of Chicago Press, 1990).

CHANG, RUTH (ed.), *Incommensurability, Incomparability and Practical Reason* (Cambridge, Mass.: Harvard University Press, 1997).

CHARLES, DAVID, 'Aristotle and Modern Realism', in Robert Heinaman (ed.), *Aristotle and Moral Realism*, 135–72.

—— and LENNON, KATHLEEN (eds.), *Reduction, Explanation, and Realism* (Oxford: Oxford University Press, 1992).

CHISHOLM, RODERICK, 'Human Freedom and the Self', repr. in Gary Watson (ed.), *Free Will*, 24–35.

CICERO, MARCUS TULLIUS, *de Officiis*, trans. as *On Duties* by M. T. Griffin and E. M. Atkins (Cambridge: Cambridge University Press, 1991).

CLARKE, STANLEY G., 'Anti-Theory in Ethics', *American Philosophical Quarterly*, 24 (1987), 237–44.

COHEN, L. JONATHAN, *An Essay on Belief and Acceptance* (Oxford: Oxford University Press, 1992).

COHON, RACHEL, 'Internalism about Reasons for Action', *Pacific Philosophical Quarterly*, 74 (1993), 265–88.

COLEMAN, JULES, and MORRIS, CHRISTOPHER (eds.), *Rational Commitment and Social Justice* (Cambridge: Cambridge University Press, forthcoming).

COPP, DAVID, 'Moral Skepticism', *Philosophical Studies*, 62 (1991), 203–33.

CRISP, ROGER, and HOOKER, BRAD (eds.), *Well-Being and Morality: Essays in Honour of James Griffin* (Oxford: Oxford University Press, forthcoming).

CROWE, M. B., *The Changing Profile of the Natural Law* (The Hague: Nijhoff, 1977).

CULLITY, GARRETT, 'Aretaic Cognitivism', *American Philosophical Quarterly*, 32 (1995), 395–406.

—— 'International Aid and the Scope of Kindness', *Ethics*, 105 (1994), 99–127.

DANCY, JONATHAN, *Moral Reasons* (Oxford: Blackwell, 1993).

DANIELSON, PETER, 'Closing the Compliance Dilemma: How it's Rational to be Moral in a Lamarckian World', in Peter Vallentyne (ed.), *Contractarianism and Rational Choice*, 307–15.

DARWALL, STEPHEN L., *Impartial Reason* (Ithaca, NY: Cornell University Press, 1983).
—— 'Nagel's Argument for Altruism', *Philosophical Studies*, 25 (1974), 125–30.
DAVIDSON, DONALD, *Essays on Actions and Events* (Oxford: Clarendon Press, 1980).
—— 'How is Weakness of the Will Possible?', repr. in his *Essays on Actions and Events*, 21–42.
—— 'Intending', repr. in his *Essays on Actions and Events*, 83–102.
DEIGH, JOHN, 'Empathy and Universalizability', *Ethics*, 105 (1995), 743–63.
DEPAUL, MICHAEL, *Balance and Refinement: Beyond Coherentism in Moral Inquiry* (London: Routledge, 1993).
DREIER, JAMES, 'Internalism and Speaker Relativism', *Ethics*, 101 (1990), 6–26.
—— 'Perspectives on the Normativity of Ethics', *Noûs*, 28 (1994), 514–25.
ENGSTROM, STEPHEN, 'Happiness and the Highest Good in Aristotle and Kant', in Stephen Engstrom and Jennifer Whiting (eds.), *Aristotle, Kant, and the Stoics*, 102–38.
—— and WHITING, JENNIFER (eds.), *Aristotle, Kant, and the Stoics: Rethinking Happiness and Duty* (Cambridge: Cambridge University Press, 1996).
EPICURUS, *Kuriai Doxai*, in Diogenes Laertius, *Lives of Eminent Philosophers*, ii. trans. R. D. Hicks (Cambridge, Mass.: Harvard University Press, 1925).
FALK, W. D., ' "Ought" and Motivation', *Proceedings of the Aristotelian Society*, 48 (1947–8), 111–38.
FARRELL, DANIEL M., 'Intention, Reason, and Action', *American Philosophical Quarterly*, 26 (1989), 283–95.
FLANAGAN, OWEN, *Varieties of Moral Personality: Ethics and Psychological Realism* (Cambridge, Mass.: Harvard University Press, 1991).
FOOT, PHILIPPA, 'Does Moral Subjectivism Rest on a Mistake?', *Oxford Journal of Legal Studies*, 15 (1995), 1–14.
—— 'Goodness and Choice', repr. in her *Virtues and Vices*, 132–47.
—— 'Moral Dilemmas and Moral Realism', *Journal of Philosophy*, 80 (1983), 379–98.
—— 'Morality as a System of Hypothetical Imperatives', repr. in her *Virtues and Vices*, 157–73.
—— *Virtues and Vices and Other Essays in Moral Philosophy* (Oxford: Blackwell, 1978).
FÖRSTER, ECKART (ed.), *Kant's Transcendental Deductions: The Three Critiques and the Opus Postumum* (Stanford: Stanford University Press, 1989).
FRANKENA, WILLIAM K., 'Obligation and Motivation in Recent Moral Philosophy', in A. I. Melden (ed.), *Essays in Moral Philosophy*, 40–81.
FRANKFURT, HARRY, 'Alternate Possibilities and Moral Responsibility', repr. in his *The Importance of What We Care About*, 1–10.
—— 'Freedom of the Will and the Concept of a Person', *Journal of Philosophy*, 68 (1971), 5–20; repr. in Gary Watson (ed.), *Free Will*, 81–95; and in his *The Importance of What We Care About*, 11–25.
—— 'Identification and Wholeheartedness', repr. in his *The Importance of What We Care About*, 159–76.
—— *The Importance of What We Care About: Philosophical Essays* (Cambridge: Cambridge University Press, 1988).

FREY, R. G., and MORRIS, CHRISTOPHER W. (eds.), *Value, Welfare, and Morality* (Cambridge: Cambridge University Press, 1993).

FUMERTON, RICHARD, *Reason and Morality* (Ithaca, NY: Cornell University Press, 1990).

GAUT, BERYS, 'Moral Pluralism', *Philosophical Papers*, 22 (1993), 17–40.

—— 'Rawls and the Claims of Liberal Legitimacy', *Philosophical Papers*, 24 (1995), 1–22.

GAUTHIER, DAVID, 'Assure and Threaten', *Ethics*, 104 (1994), 690–721.

—— 'In the Neighborhood of the Newcomb-Predictor (Reflections on Rationality)', *Proceedings of the Aristotelian Society*, 89 (1988–9), 179–94.

—— *Moral Dealing; Contract, Ethics, and Reason* (Ithaca, NY: Cornell University Press, 1990).

—— *Morals by Agreement* (Oxford: Clarendon Press, 1986).

—— 'Reason and Maximization', repr. in his *Moral Dealing*, 209–33.

GHENT, HENRY of, *Opera* (Leuven: Leuven University Press, 1987).

GIBBARD, ALLAN, 'Why Theorize How to Live with Each Other?', *Philosophy and Phenomenological Research*, 55 (1995), 323–42.

—— *Wise Choices, Apt Feelings: A Theory of Normative Judgement* (Cambridge, Mass.: Harvard University Press, 1990).

GREEN, T. H., *Prolegomena to Ethics*, ed. A. C. Bradley (New York: Thomas Crowell, 1969).

GUYER, PAUL (ed.), *The Cambridge Companion to Kant* (Cambridge: Cambridge University Press, 1992).

HALDANE, JOHN, and WRIGHT, CRISPIN (eds.), *Reality, Representation and Projection* (Oxford: Oxford University Press, 1994).

HALE, BOB, and WRIGHT, CRISPIN (eds.), *A Companion to the Philosophy of Language* (Oxford: Blackwell, 1997).

HAMPSHIRE, STUART, *Morality and Conflict* (Oxford: Blackwell, 1983).

HAMPTON, JEAN, 'Hobbes and Ethical Naturalism', in James E. Tomberlin (ed.), *Philosophical Perspectives*, vi. *Ethics* (Atascadero, Calif.: Ridgeview, 1992), 333–53.

—— 'On Instrumental Rationality', in J. B. Schneewind (ed.), *Reason, Ethics, and Society*, 84–116.

HARE, R. M., *Freedom and Reason* (Oxford: Oxford University Press, 1963).

—— *The Language of Morals* (Oxford: Oxford University Press, 1961).

HARMAN, GILBERT, 'Moral Relativism Defended', *Philosophical Review*, 85 (1975), 3–22.

—— *The Nature of Morality: An Introduction to Ethics* (New York: Oxford University Press, 1977).

—— 'Practical Reasoning', *Review of Metaphysics*, 29 (1975–6), 431–63.

HART, H. L. A., *The Concept of Law* (Oxford: Clarendon Press, 1961).

HEGEL, G. W. F., *The Philosophy of Right*, trans. T. M. Knox (Oxford: Clarendon Press, 1952).

HEINAMAN, ROBERT (ed.), *Aristotle and Moral Realism* (London: UCL Press, 1995).

HERMAN, BARBARA, 'Integrity and Impartiality', *Monist*, 66 (1983), 233–50.

—— 'On the Value of Acting from the Motive of Duty', *Philosophical Review*, 90 (1981), 359–82.

HILL, THOMAS E., Jr., *Dignity and Practical Reason in Kant's Moral Theory* (Ithaca, NY: Cornell University Press, 1992).

—— 'Humanity as an End in Itself', repr. in his *Dignity and Practical Reason in Kant's Moral Theory*, 38–57.

—— 'The Hypothetical Imperative', repr. in his *Dignity and Practical Reason in Kant's Moral Theory*, 17–37.

—— 'Kant's Argument for the Rationality of Moral Conduct', repr. in his *Dignity and Practical Reason in Kant's Moral Theory*, 97–122.

HOBBES, THOMAS, *Leviathan*, ed. E. M. Curley (Indianapolis: Hackett, 1994).

HONDERICH, TED (ed.), *Morality and Objectivity: A Tribute to J. L. Mackie* (London: Routledge & Kegan Paul, 1985).

HOOKER, BRAD (ed.), *Rationality, Rules and Utility: New Essays on the Moral Philosophy of Richard B. Brandt* (Boulder, Colo.: Westview Press, 1993).

HORWICH, PAUL, *Truth* (Oxford: Blackwell, 1990).

HOWARD, J. V., 'Co-operation in the Prisoner's Dilemma', *Theory and Decision*, 24 (1988), 203–13.

HUBIN, DONALD C., 'Hypothetical Motivation', *Noûs*, 30 (1966), 31–54.

—— 'Irrational Desires', *Philosophical Studies*, 62 (1991), 23–44.

HUME, DAVID, *An Enquiry Concerning the Principles of Morals*, ed. L. A. Selby-Bigge and rev. P. H. Nidditch, 3rd edn. (Oxford: Clarendon Press, 1975).

—— *A Treatise of Human Nature*, ed. L. A. Selby-Bigge and rev. P. H. Nidditch, 2nd edn. (Oxford: Clarendon Press, 1978).

HURKA, THOMAS, *Perfectionism* (Oxford: Oxford University Press, 1993).

IRWIN, T. H., 'Kant's Criticisms of Eudaimonism', in Stephen Engstrom and Jennifer Whiting (eds.), *Aristotle, Kant, and the Stoics*, 63–101.

—— 'Morality and Personality: Kant and Green', in Allen Wood (ed.), *Self and Nature in Kant's Philosophy*, 31–56.

—— 'The Scope of Deliberation: A Conflict in Aquinas', *Review of Metaphysics*, 44 (1990), 21–42.

—— 'Some Rational Aspects of Incontinence', *Southern Journal of Philosophy*, suppl. 27 (1988), 49–88.

JOHNSTON, MARK, 'Objectivity Refigured, Pragmatism Without Verificationism', in John Haldane and Crispin Wright (eds.), *Reality, Representation and Projection*, 85–130.

KAGAN, SHELLY, *The Limits of Morality* (Oxford: Clarendon Press, 1989).

KAHNEMAN, DANIEL, and TVERSKY, AMOS, 'Prospect Theory: An Analysis of Decision under Risk', *Econometrica*, 47 (1979), 263–91.

KAHNEMAN, DANIEL, SLOVIC, PAUL, and TVERSKY, AMOS (eds.), *Judgment Under Uncertainty: Heuristics and Biases* (New York: Cambridge University Press, 1982).

KANT, IMMANUEL, *Kants gesammelte Schriften: herausgegeben von der Deutschen Akademie der Wissenschaften* (Berlin: de Gruyter, 1902–).

—— *Grundlegung der Metaphysik der Sitten*, trans. as *Foundations of the Metaphysics of Morals* by Lewis White Beck (New York: Liberal Arts Press, 1959).

KANT, IMMANUEL, trans. as *Grounding for the Metaphysics of Morals* by James W. Ellington, 2nd edn. (Indianapolis: Hackett, 1981); 3rd edn. (1993).

—— trans. as *Groundwork of the Metaphysic of Morals* by H. J. Paton (New York: Harper & Row, 1956).

—— trans. as *The Moral Law* by H. J. Paton (London: Hutchinson, 1948).

—— *Kritik der praktischen Vernunft*, trans. as *Critique of Practical Reason* by Lewis White Beck (New York: Macmillan, 1956).

—— *Kritik der reinen Vernunft*, trans. as *Immanuel Kant's Critique of Pure Reason* by Norman Kemp Smith (New York: St Martin's Press, 1963).

—— *Kritik der Urteilskraft*, trans. as *Critique of Judgment* by Werner S. Pluhar (Indianapolis: Hackett, 1987).

—— *Metaphysik der Sitten*, trans. and abridged as *The Metaphysics of Morals*, in *Kant's Ethical Philosophy* by James W. Ellington (Indianapolis: Hackett, 1983).

—— trans. as *The Metaphysics of Morals* by Mary Gregor (Cambridge: Cambridge University Press, 1991).

—— *Die Religion innerhalb der Grenzen der blossen Vernunft*, trans. as *Religion Within the Limits of Reason Alone*, by Theodore M. Greene and Hoyt H. Hudson (New York: Harper Torchbooks, 1960).

KAVKA, GREGORY, 'The Toxin Puzzle', *Analysis*, 43 (1983), 33–6.

KENNETT, JEANETTE, *Commonsense Moral Psychology* (Oxford: Oxford University Press, forthcoming).

—— and SMITH, MICHAEL, 'Frog and Toad Lose Control', *Analysis*, 56 (1996), 63–73.

KORSGAARD, CHRISTINE M., *Creating the Kingdom of Ends* (Cambridge: Cambridge University Press, 1996).

—— 'Creating the Kingdom of Ends: Reciprocity and Responsibility in Personal Relations', repr. in her *Creating the Kingdom of Ends*, 188–221.

—— 'From Duty and for the Sake of the Noble: Kant and Aristotle on Morally Good Action', in Stephen Engstrom and Jennifer Whiting (eds.), *Aristotle, Kant, and the Stoics*, 203–36.

—— 'Kant's Analysis of Obligation: The Argument of *Groundwork* I', repr. in her *Creating the Kingdom of Ends*, 43–76.

—— 'Kant's Formula of Humanity', *Kant-Studien*, 77 (1986), 183–202; repr. in her *Creating the Kingdom of Ends*, 106–32.

—— 'Kant's Formula of Universal Law', *Pacific Philosophical Quarterly*, 66 (1985), 24–47; repr. in her *Creating the Kingdom of Ends*, 77–105.

—— 'Morality as Freedom', in Y. Yovel (ed.), *Kant's Practical Philosophy Reconsidered*, 23–48; repr. in her *Creating the Kingdom of Ends*, 159–87.

—— 'The Reasons We Can Share: An Attack on the Distinction between Agent-Relative and Agent-Neutral Values', repr. in her *Creating the Kingdom of Ends*, 275–310.

—— 'Skepticism about Practical Reason', *Journal of Philosophy*, 83 (1986), 5–25; repr. in her *Creating the Kingdom of Ends*, 311–34.

—— *The Sources of Normativity* (Cambridge: Cambridge University Press, 1996).

—— 'Two Distinctions in Goodness', *Philosophical Review*, 92 (1983), 169–95; repr. in her *Creating the Kingdom of Ends*, 249–74.

KYMLICKA, WILL, 'Rawls on Teleology and Deontology', *Philosophy and Public Affairs*, 17 (1988), 173–90.

LAMPE, G. W. H., *Patristic Greek Lexicon* (Oxford: Oxford University Press, 1961).

LEAKE, DAVID B., and RAM, ASHWIN (eds.), *Goal-Driven Learning* (Cambridge, Mass.: MIT Press, 1996).

LEHRER, KEITH, 'Cans Without Ifs', repr. in G. Watson (ed.), *Free Will*, 41–5.

LEWIS, DAVID, 'Are We Free to Break the Laws?', repr. in his *Philosophical Papers*, ii. 291–8.

—— 'Counterfactual Dependence and Time's Arrow', repr. in his *Philosophical Papers*, ii. 32–52.

—— *Philosophical Papers* (Oxford: Oxford University Press, 1986).

LOTTIN, ODON, *Psychologie et Morale aux XIIe et XIIIe siècles* (Louvain: Gembloux, 1948).

LOUDEN, ROBERT B., *Morality and Moral Theory: A Reappraisal and Reaffirmation* (New York: Oxford University Press, 1992).

MACINTYRE, ALASDAIR, *After Virtue: A Study in Moral Theory* (London: Duckworth, 1981).

MACKIE, J. L., *Ethics: Inventing Right and Wrong* (Harmondsworth: Penguin, 1977).

MAHONEY, JOHN, *The Making of Moral Theology: A Study of the Roman Catholic Tradition* (Oxford: Clarendon Press, 1987).

McCLENNAN, EDWARD F., *Rationality and Dynamic Choice: Foundational Explorations* (Cambridge: Cambridge University Press, 1990).

McDOWELL, JOHN, 'Are Moral Requirements Hypothetical Imperatives?', *Proceedings of the Aristotelian Society*, suppl. 52 (1978), 13–29.

—— 'Eudaimonism and Realism in Aristotle's Ethics', in Robert Heinaman (ed.), *Aristotle and Moral Realism*, 201–18.

—— 'Might there be External Reasons?', in J. E. J. Altham and Ross Harrison (eds.), *World, Mind and Ethics*, 68–85.

—— 'The Role of *Eudaimonia* in Aristotle's Ethics', repr. in A. O. Rorty (ed.), *Essays on Aristotle's Ethics*, 359–76.

—— 'Values and Secondary Qualities', in Ted Honderich (ed.), *Morality and Objectivity*, 110–29.

MELDEN, A. I. (ed.), *Essays in Moral Philosophy* (Seattle: University of Washington Press, 1958).

MELE, ALFRED R., *Autonomous Agents: From Self-Control to Autonomy* (Oxford: Oxford University Press, 1995).

—— 'Internalist Moral Cognitivism and Listlessness', *Ethics*, 106 (1966), pp. 727–53.

—— 'Motivational Internalism: The Powers and Limits of Practical Reasoning', *Philosophia*, 19 (1989), 427–36.

—— 'Motivation: Essentially Motivation-Constituting Attitudes', *Philosophical Review*, 104 (1995), 387–423.

MILL, J. S., *On Liberty and Other Essays*, ed. John Gray (Oxford: Oxford University Press, 1991).

—— *Utilitarianism* (Indianapolis: Hackett, 1979).

MILLGRAM, ELIJAH, 'Was Hume a Humean?', *Hume Studies*, 21 (1995), 75–93.
—— and THAGARD, PAUL, 'Inference to the Best Plan: A Coherence Theory of Decision', in D. Leake and A. Ram (eds.), *Goal-Driven Learning*, 439–54.
MOORE, G. E., *Ethics* (Oxford: Oxford University Press, 1966).
—— *Principia Ethica* (Cambridge: Cambridge University Press, 1903).
NAGEL, THOMAS, *The Possibility of Altruism* (Princeton: Princeton University Press, 1970).
—— 'The Value of Inviolability', *Revue de Métaphysique et de Morale*, 99 (1994), 149–66.
—— *The View from Nowhere* (Oxford: Oxford University Press, 1986).
NELL, ONORA, (now O'Neill), *Acting on Principle: An Essay in Kantian Ethics* (New York: Columbia University Press, 1975).
NIETZSCHE, FRIEDRICH, *On the Genealogy of Morals and Ecce Homo*, trans. Walter Kaufmann and R. J. Hollingdale (New York: Random House, 1967).
OCKHAM, WILLIAM of, *Opera Theologica* (St Bonaventure: Franciscan Institute, 1967–86).
O'NEILL, ONORA, 'Consistency in Action', repr. in her *Constructions of Reason*, 81–104.
—— *Constructions of Reason: Explorations of Kant's Practical Philosophy* (Cambridge: Cambridge University Press, 1989).
—— 'Reason and Politics in the Kantian Enterprise', in her *Constructions of Reason*, 3–27.
—— 'Universal Laws and Ends-in-Themselves', repr. in her *Constructions of Reason*, 126–44.
—— 'Vindicating Reason', in Paul Guyer (ed.), *The Cambridge Companion to Kant*, 280–308.
PARFIT, DEREK, *Reasons and Persons* (Oxford: Clarendon Press, 1984).
PATON, H. J., *The Categorical Imperative: A Study in Kant's Moral Philosophy* (London: Hutchinson, 1947).
PETTIT, PHILIP, *The Common Mind: An Essay on Psychology, Society, and Politics* (Oxford: Oxford University Press, 1993).
—— and SMITH, MICHAEL, 'Backgrounding Desire', *Philosophical Review*, 99 (1990), 565–92.
—— and —— 'Brandt on Self-Control', in Brad Hooker (ed.), *Rationality, Rules and Utility*, 33–50.
—— and —— 'Freedom in Belief and Desire', *Journal of Philosophy*, 93 (1996), 429–49.
—— and —— 'Practical Unreason', *Mind*, 102 (1993), 53–79.
PLATO, *Gorgias*, trans. Terence Irwin (Oxford: Clarendon Press, 1979).
—— *Protagoras*, trans. Stanley Lembardo and Karen Bell (Indianapolis: Hackett, 1992).
—— *Republic*, trans. G. M. A. Grube and C. D. C. Reeve (Indianapolis: Hackett, 1992).
POTTS, TIMOTHY C., *Conscience in Mediaeval Philosophy* (Cambridge: Cambridge University Press, 1980).

RADCLIFFE, ELIZABETH, 'Disentangling Hume's Instrumentalism from Kant's Categorical Imperative', *Canadian Journal of Philosophy* (forthcoming).

—— 'How Does the Humean Sense of Duty Motivate?', *Journal of the History of Philosophy*, 34 (1996), 47–70.

—— 'Hume on Passion, Pleasure, and the Reasonableness of Ends', *Southwest Philosophy Review*, 10 (1994), 1–11.

RAILTON, PETER, 'Alienation, Consequentialism, and the Demands of Morality', in Samuel Scheffler (ed.), *Consequentialism and its Critics*, 93–133.

—— 'In Search of Non-Subjective Reason', in J. B. Schneewind (ed.), *Reason, Ethics, and Society*, 117–43.

—— 'Moral Realism', *Philosophical Review*, 95 (1986), 163–207.

—— 'Some Questions about the Justification of Morality', in James E. Tomberlin (ed.), *Philosophical Perspectives*, vi. *Ethics* (Atascadero, Calif.: Ridgeview, 1992), 27–53.

—— 'Truth, Reason, and the Regulation of Belief', *Philosophical Issues*, 5 (1994), 71–94.

—— 'What the Non-Cognitivist Helps us to See the Naturalist Must Help us to Explain', in John Haldane and Crispin Wright (eds.), *Reality, Representation, and Projection*, 292–4.

RAPHAEL, D. D. (ed.), *British Moralists 1650–1800* (Indianapolis: Hackett, 1991).

RAWLS, JOHN, 'Kantian Constructivism in Moral Theory', *Journal of Philosophy*, 77 (1980), 515–72.

—— 'Themes in Kant's Moral Philosophy', in Eckart Förster (ed.), *Kant's Transcendental Deductions*, 81–113.

—— *A Theory of Justice* (Cambridge, Mass.: Harvard University Press, 1971).

RAZ, JOSEPH, 'Incommensurability and Agency', in Ruth Chang (ed.), *Incommensurability, Incomparability and Practical Reason*.

—— *The Morality of Freedom* (Oxford: Oxford University Press, 1986).

—— 'On the Moral Point of View', in J. B. Schneewind (ed.), *Reason, Ethics, and Society*, 84–116.

—— 'When We are Ourselves: The Active and the Passive', *Proceedings of the Aristotelian Society*, suppl. 71 (1997).

REID, THOMAS, *Essays on the Active Powers of the Human Mind*, ed. B. Brody (Cambridge, Mass.: MIT Press, 1969).

ROBERTSON, JOHN, 'Hume on Practical Reason', *Proceedings of the Aristotelian Society*, 24 (1989), 267–82.

RORTY, A. O. (ed.), *Essays on Aristotle's Ethics* (Berkeley: University of California Press, 1980).

ROSATI, CONNIE S., 'Internalism and the Good for a Person', *Ethics*, 106 (1966), 247–73.

ROUSSEAU, JEAN-JACQUES, *The Social Contract*, trans. Maurice Cranston (Harmondsworth: Penguin, 1968).

SANDEL, MICHAEL J., *Liberalism and the Limits of Justice* (Cambridge: Cambridge University Press, 1982).

SAYRE-MCCORD, GEOFFREY, 'Deception and Reasons to be Moral', in Peter Vallentyne (ed.), *Contractarianism and Rational Choice*, 181–95.

SCANLON, T. M., 'The Aims and Authority of Moral Theory', *Oxford Journal of Legal Studies*, 12 (1992), 1–23.

—— 'Contractualism and Utilitarianism', in Amartya Sen and Bernard Williams (eds.), *Utilitarianism and Beyond*, 103–28.

—— 'Moral Theory: Understanding and Disagreement', *Philosophy and Phenomenological Research*, 55 (1995), 343–56.

—— 'Promises and Practices', *Philosophy and Public Affairs*, 19 (1990), 199–226.

SCHEFFLER, SAMUEL (ed.), *Consequentialism and its Critics* (Oxford: Oxford University Press, 1988).

—— *Human Morality* (New York: Oxford University Press, 1992).

SCHNEEWIND, J. B. (ed.), *Reason, Ethics, and Society: Themes from Kurt Baier, with his Responses* (Chicago: Open Court, 1996).

SCHOEMAN, FERDINAND (ed.), *Responsibility, Character and the Emotions: New Essays in Moral Psychology* (Cambridge: Cambridge University Press, 1987).

SCHUELER, G. F., *Desire: Its Role in Practical Reason and the Explanation of Action* (Cambridge, Mass.: MIT Press, 1995).

—— 'Desires, Pro-Attitudes and Directions of Fit', *Mind*, 100 (1991), 277–81.

SCOTUS, JOHN DUNS, *John Duns Scotus on the Will and Morality*, trans. Allan B. Wolter (Washington: Catholic University of America Press, 1986).

SEN, AMARTYA, and WILLIAMS, BERNARD (eds.), *Utilitarianism and Beyond* (Cambridge: Cambridge University Press, 1982).

SIDGWICK, HENRY, *The Methods of Ethics*, 7th edn. (Indianapolis: Hackett, 1981).

SINGER, PETER (ed.), *A Companion to Ethics* (Oxford: Blackwell 1991).

SKORUPSKI, JOHN, 'The Definition of Morality', in A. Phillips Griffiths (ed.), *Ethics, Philosophy*, suppl. 35 (Cambridge: Cambridge University Press, 1993), 121–44.

—— 'Meaning, Verification, Use', in Bob Hale and Crispin Wright (eds.), *A Companion to the Philosophy of Language*, 29–59.

—— 'Quality of Well-Being, Quality of Being', in Roger Crisp and Brad Hooker (eds.), *Well-Being and Morality*.

SMART, J. J. C., and WILLIAMS, BERNARD, *Utilitarianism: For and Against* (Cambridge: Cambridge University Press, 1973).

SMITH, HOLLY, 'Deriving Morality from Rationality', in Peter Vallentyne (ed.), *Contractarianism and Rational Choice*, 229–53.

SMITH, MICHAEL, 'Dispositional Theories of Value', *Proceedings of the Aristotelian Society*, suppl. 63 (1989), 89–111.

—— 'The Humean Theory of Motivation', *Mind*, 96 (1987), 36–61.

—— 'Internalism's Wheel', *Ratio*, 8 (1995), 277–302.

—— 'Internal Reasons', *Philosophy and Phenomenological Research*, 55 (1995), 109–31.

—— *The Moral Problem* (Oxford: Blackwell, 1994).

—— 'Normative Reasons and Full Rationality: Reply to Swanton', *Analysis*, 56 (1996), 160–8.

—— 'Realism', in Peter Singer (ed.), *A Companion to Ethics*, 399–410.

—— 'Valuing, Desiring or Believing?', in David Charles and Kathleen Lennon (eds.), *Reduction, Explanation, Realism*, 323–60.

STOCKER, MICHAEL, 'Desiring the Bad', *Journal of Philosophy*, 79 (1979), 738–53.

—— *Plural and Conflicting Values* (Oxford: Clarendon Press, 1990).

—— 'The Schizophrenia of Modern Ethical Theories', *Journal of Philosophy*, 73 (1976), 453–66.

STRAWSON, P. F., *Freedom and Resentment and Other Essays* (London: Methuen, 1974).

—— 'Social Morality and Individual Ideal', repr. in his *Freedom and Resentment*, 26–44.

STURGEON, NICHOLAS, 'Altruism, Solipsism and the Objectivity of Reasons', *Philosophical Review*, 83 (1974), 374–402.

TIMMONS, MARK C., 'Kant and the Possibility of Moral Motivation', *Southern Journal of Philosophy*, 23 (1985), 377–98.

TOLHURST, MICHAEL WILLIAM, 'On the Epistemic Value of Moral Experience', *Southern Journal of Philosophy*, suppl. 29 (1990), 67–87.

VALLENTYNE, PETER (ed.), *Contractarianism and Rational Choice: Essays on David Gauthier's Morals by Agreement* (Cambridge: Cambridge University Press, 1991).

VAN FRAASSEN, BAS, *The Scientific Image* (Oxford: Clarendon Press, 1980).

VAN INWAGEN, PETER, 'The Incompatibility of Free Will and Determinism', repr. in Gary Watson (ed.), *Free Will*, 46–58.

VELLEMAN, J. DAVID, 'The Guise of the Good', *Noûs*, 26 (1992), 3–26.

—— 'How to Share an Intention', *Philosophy and Phenomenological Research*, 57 (1997), 29–50.

—— 'The Possibility of Practical Reason', *Ethics*, 106 (1996), 694–726.

—— *Practical Reflection* (Princeton: Princeton University Press, 1989).

—— 'The Story of Rational Action', *Philosophical Topics*, 21 (1993), 229–53.

—— 'What Happens When Someone Acts?', *Mind*, 101 (1992), 461–81.

WALLACE, J. D., *Virtues and Vices* (Ithaca, NY: Cornell University Press, 1978).

WALLACE, R. JAY, 'How to Argue about Practical Reason', *Mind*, 99 (1990), 355–85.

—— *Responsibility and the Moral Sentiments* (Cambridge, Mass.: Harvard University Press, 1994).

WALSH, JAMES J., 'Buridan on the Connexion of the Virtues', *Journal of the History of Philosophy*, 24 (1986), 453–82.

WALTON, KENDALL, *Mimesis as Make-Believe: On the Foundations of the Representational Arts* (Cambridge, Mass.: Harvard University Press, 1990).

WALZER, MICHAEL, *Just and Unjust Wars: A Moral Argument with Historical Illustrations* (New York: Basic Books, 1977).

—— *Spheres of Justice: A Defence of Pluralism and Equality* (New York: Basic Books, 1983).

WARNOCK, G. J., *The Object of Morality* (London: Methuen, 1971).

WATSON, GARY, 'Free Agency', repr. in his *Free Will*, 96–110.

—— (ed.), *Free Will* (Oxford: Oxford University Press, 1982).

WATSON, GARY, 'Responsibility and the Limits of Evil', in Ferdinand Schoeman (ed.), *Responsibility, Character and the Emotions*, 256–86.
WIGGINS, DAVID, 'Claims of Need', repr. in his *Needs, Values, Truth*, 1–57.
—— 'Deliberation and Practical Reason', in A. O. Rorty (ed.), *Essays on Aristotle's Ethics*, 221–40, repr. in his *Needs, Values, Truth*, 215–37.
—— *Needs, Values, Truth: Essays in the Philosophy of Value* (Oxford: Blackwell, 1987).
—— 'Truth, and Truth as Predicated of Moral Judgements', in his *Needs, Values, Truth*, 139–84.
WILLIAMS, BERNARD, 'Deciding to Believe', repr. in his *Problems of the Self*, 136–51.
—— *Ethics and the Limits of Philosophy* (London: Collins, 1985).
—— 'Internal and External Reasons', repr. in his *Moral Luck*, 101–13.
—— 'Internal Reasons and the Obscurity of Blame', repr. in his *Making Sense of Humanity*, 35–45.
—— *Making Sense of Humanity and other Philosophical Papers 1982–1993* (Cambridge: Cambridge University Press, 1995).
—— *Morality: An Introduction to Ethics* (Harmondsworth: Penguin, 1973).
—— 'Morality and the Emotions', repr. in his *Problems of the Self*, 207–29.
—— *Moral Luck: Philosophical Papers 1973–1980* (Cambridge: Cambridge University Press, 1981).
—— 'Persons, Character and Morality', repr. in his *Moral Luck*, 1–19.
—— *Problems of the Self: Philosophical Papers 1956–1972* (Cambridge: Cambridge University Press, 1973).
—— *Shame and Necessity* (Berkeley: University of California Press, 1993).
WINCH, PETER, *Ethics and Action* (Oxford: Blackwell, 1972).
—— 'The Universalizability of Moral Judgements', repr. in his *Ethics and Action*, 151–70.
WOLF, SUSAN, *Freedom Within Reason* (Oxford: Oxford University Press, 1990).
—— 'Morality and Partiality', in James E. Tomberlin (ed.), *Philosophical Perspectives*, vi. *Ethics* (Atascadero, Calif.: Ridgeview, 1992), 243–59.
WOLFF, ROBERT PAUL, *The Autonomy of Reason: A Commentary on Kant's Groundwork of the Metaphysic of Morals* (New York: Harper & Row, 1973).
WOOD, ALLEN (ed.), *Self and Nature in Kant's Philosophy* (Ithaca, NY: Cornell University Press, 1984).
WRIGHT, CRISPIN, 'Truth in Ethics', *Ratio*, 9 (1996), 209–26.
—— *Truth and Objectivity* (Cambridge, Mass.: Harvard University Press, 1992).
YOVEL, YIRMIYAHU (ed.), *Kant's Practical Philosophy Reconsidered* (Dordrecht: Kluwer, 1989).

INDEX